The World
of the
Early Sienese Painter

The World
of the
Early Sienese Painter

HAYDEN B. J. MAGINNIS

(With a Translation of the
Sienese *Breve dell'Arte dei Pittori*
by Gabriele Erasmi)

THE PENNSYLVANIA STATE UNIVERSITY PRESS
University Park, Pennsylvania

Library of Congress Cataloging-in-Publication Data

Maginnis, Hayden B. J.
The world of the Early Sienese painter / Hayden B. J. Maginnis ; with a translation of the Sienese Breve dell'Arte del pittori by Gabriele Erasmi.
    p.   cm.
Includes bibliographical references (p.   ), and index.
ISBN 0-271-02004-0 (cloth : alk. paper)
1. Arte del pittori (Siena)   2. Painters—Italy—Siena—
—Historiography.   3. Siena (Italy)—History—Rule of the Nine,
1287–1355.   I. Erasmi, Gabriele.   II. Arte dei pittori (Siena).
Breve.   English.   III. Title.
ND621.S6M34   2001
759.5′58—dc21   99-35892
CIP

Copyright © 2001 The Pennsylvania State University
All rights reserved
Printed in the United States of America
Published by The Pennsylvania State University Press,
University Park, PA 16802–1003

It is the policy of The Pennsylvania State University Press to use acid-free paper for the first printing of all clothbound books. Publications on uncoated stock satisfy the minimum requirements of American National Standard for Information Sciences—Permanence of Paper for Printed Library Materials, ANSI Z39.48–1992.

CONTENTS

List of Illustrations   vii

Acknowledgments   xv

Prefatory Notes   xvii

Preface   xix

A Prologue   1

Introduction   9

I   The Painter's City   16

The Background—Siena Under the Nine (1287–1355)—Civic Christianity—Other Aspects of the Faith—Charitable Foundations—The Guilds of Siena—In Retrospect

II   The Painter's Place   45

Family Matters—Where Did Painters Live?—Numbers—Matters Financial: Property and Dowries—Matters Financial: Income and Comparative Costs—Matters Financial: The Price of Altarpieces—Guido Cinatti—A Question of Status

III   The Painter's Craft: Conditions and Constraints   83

The Painters' Guild and Working Arrangements—Techniques—Forms and Formats—The Imponderables of Circumstance—The Question of Drawings

IV   Painters and Projects, Major and Minor   119

The Other Economy of Art—Patronage of the Commune—The Cathedral—The Ospedale di Santa Maria della Scala—Private Patronage—Parish Churches, Convents, Confraternities, and Charitable Institutions—The Sienese Abroad—Some General Observations

V   The Painter's World   161

Foreign Powers—A Sense of Beauty/A Sense of Order—An Age of Vision—Artistic Progress?—Painters and Texts

An Epilogue   191

Statute of the Sienese Painters' Guild of Siena, Translated by Gabriele Erasmi   199

Appendix I: Placing Painters   225

Appendix II: New Documents on Painters' Property   231

Appendix III: The Minor Masters: Notes on Some Sources   241

Appendix IV: A Sampling of Payments for Decorating Book Covers Under the Nine   275

Selected Bibliography   287

Index: General   299

Index: Siena   307

Color Plates   311

Figures   327

LIST OF ILLUSTRATIONS

Color Plates

1. Duccio di Buoninsegna, *Temptation on the Mountain*. New York, Frick Collection (photo: Frick Collection).

2. Duccio di Buoninsegna, *Temptation on the Mountain,* detail. New York, Frick Collection (photo: Frick Collection).

3. Simone Martini, *Maestà*. Siena, Palazzo Pubblico (photo: Quattrone).

4. Simone Martini, *Maestà,* detail. Siena, Palazzo Pubblico (photo: Quattrone).

5. Ambrogio Lorenzetti, *The Effects of Good Government,* detail: the city. Siena, Palazzo Pubblico (photo: Scala/Art Resource, New York).

6. Ambrogio Lorenzetti, *The Effects of Good Government,* detail: the countryside. Siena, Palazzo Pubblico (photo: Scala/Art Resource, New York).

7. Simone Martini, *Beato Agostino Novello*. Siena, Pinacoteca Nazionale (photo: Scala/Art Resource, New York).

8. Simone Martini, *Beato Agostino Novello,* detail. Siena, Pinacoteca Nazionale (photo: Scala/Art Resource, New York).

9. Simone Martini and Lippo Memmi, *Annunciation,* detail: the archangel Gabriel. Florence, Galleria degli Uffizi (photo: Scala/Art Resource, New York).

10. Duccio di Buoninsegna, *Maestà,* front. Siena, Museo dell'Opera del Duomo (photo: Scala/Art Resource, New York).

11. Duccio di Buoninsegna, *Maestà,* front, detail: Saint Catherine of Alexandria. Siena, Museo dell'Opera del Duomo (photo: Scala/Art Resource, New York).

12. Simone Martini, the Pisa altarpiece. Pisa, Museo Nazionale di San Matteo (photo: Scala/Art Resource, New York).

13. Pietro Lorenzetti, the Arezzo polyptych. Arezzo, Santa Maria della Pieve (photo: Scala/Art Resource, New York).

14. Pietro Lorenzetti, the Arezzo polyptych, detail. Arezzo, Santa Maria della Pieve (photo: Scala/Art Resource, New York).

15. Ambrogio Lorenzetti, *Maestà*. Siena, Pinacoteca Nazionale (photo: Scala/Art Resource, New York).

16. Simone Martini, *Saint Louis of Toulouse*. Naples, Museo di Capodimonte (photo: Scala/Art Resource, New York).

Figures

1. Map of Siena's parishes.

2. The Palazzo Pubblico, Siena (photo: Alinari/Art Resource, New York).

3. Siena cathedral, facade (photo: Alinari).

4. Siena cathedral, interior (photo: Alinari).

5. Plan of Talamone (1306). Siena, Archivio di Stato di Siena (photo: Fot. Soprintendenza B.A.S., Siena).

6. Dossal no. 6. Siena, Pinacoteca Nazionale (photo: Alinari/Art Resource, New York).

7. Dossal no. 7. Siena, Pinacoteca Nazionale (photo: Alinari/Art Resource, New York).

8. San Bernardino Master, San Bernardino *Madonna*. Siena, Pinacoteca Nazionale (photo: Alinari/Art Resource, New York).

9. Replica of the San Bernardino *Madonna*. Arezzo, Museo Statale di Arte Medievale e Moderna (photo: Fot. Soprintendenza per i Beni Ambientali, Architettonici, Artistici e Storici di Arezzo).

10. Duccio di Buoninsegna, Rucellai *Madonna*. Florence, Galleria degli Uffizi (photo: Quattrone).

11. Duccio di Buoninsegna, Rucellai *Madonna*, detail. Florence, Galleria degli Uffizi (photo: Quattrone).

12. Segna di Bonaventura, *Madonna*. Castiglion Fiorentino, Collegiata di San Giuliano (photo: Gabinetto Fotografico, Sopr. Gallerie, Florence).

13. Ugolino di Nerio, Saints Paul and John the Baptist (from the Santa Croce altarpiece). Berlin, Staatliche Museen Preußischer Kulturbesitz, Gemäldegalerie (photo: Gemäldegalerie).

14. Simone Martini, *Beato Agostino Novello*, detail. Siena, Pinacoteca Nazionale (photo: Fot. Soprintendenza B.A.S., Siena).

15. Duccio di Buoninsegna, *Healing of a Man Born Blind* (detail from the

Maestà). London, National Gallery (photo: National Gallery).

16. Duccio di Buoninsegna, back of the *Maestà*. Siena, Museo dell'Opera del Duomo (photo: Fot. Soprintendenza B.A.S., Siena).

17. Simone Martini and Lippo Memmi, *Annunciation* (1333). Florence, Galleria degli Uffizi (photo: Gabinetto Fotografico, Sopr. Gallerie, Firenze).

18. Simone Martini and Lippo Memmi, *Annunciation,* detail: San Ansano. Florence, Galleria degli Uffizi (photo: Gabinetto Fotografico, Sopr. Gallerie, Firenze).

19. Simone Martini and Lippo Memmi, *Annunciation,* detail: Santa Massima. Florence, Galleria degli Uffizi (photo: Gabinetto Fotografico, Sopr. Gallerie, Firenze).

20. Simone Martini and Lippo Memmi, *Annunciation,* detail: head of the Virgin. Florence, Galleria degli Uffizi (photo: Gabinetto Fotografico, Sopr. Gallerie, Firenze).

21. Ambrogio Lorenzetti, *Presentation in the Temple*. Florence, Galleria degli Uffizi (photo: Gabinetto Fotografico, Sopr. Gallerie, Firenze).

22. Ambrogio Lorenzetti, *Presentation in the Temple,* back of the panel. Florence, Galleria degli Uffizi (photo: Muller).

23. Guido Cinatti, Biccherna cover. Siena, Archivio di Stato di Siena (photo: Fot. Soprintendenza B.A.S., Siena).

24. Bartolommeo Bulgarini, *Madonna and Child Enthroned*. Siena, Pinacoteca Nazionale (photo: Fot. Soprintendenza B.A.S., Siena).

25. Bartolommeo Bulgarini, *Madonna and Child Enthroned*. Siena, Pinacoteca Nazionale (photo: Fot. Soprintendenza B.A.S., Siena).

26. Bartolommeo Bulgarini, *Assumption of the Virgin*. Siena, Pinacoteca Nazionale (photo: Fot. Soprintendenza B.A.S., Siena).

27. Bartolommeo Bulgarini, *Nativity*. Cambridge, Mass., Fogg Art Museum (photo: Fogg Art Museum).

28. Master of Palazzo Venezia, *San Vittorio*. Copenhagen, Statens Museum for Kunst (photo: Statens Museum for Kunst).

29. Master of Palazzo Venezia, *Santa Corona*. Copenhagen, Statens Museum for Kunst (photo: Statens Museum for Kunst).

30. Pietro Lorenzetti, *Birth of the Virgin*. Siena, Museo dell'Opera del Duomo (photo: Fot. Soprintendenza B.A.S., Siena).

31. Painted bed (1337). Pistoia, Ospedale del Ceppo (photo: Alinari).

32. Guido da Siena, San Domenico *Madonna*. Siena, San Domenico (photo: Fot. Soprintendenza B.A.S., Siena).

33. Guido da Siena (?), *Annunciation*. Princeton, Art Museum (photo: Art Museum).

34. Saint Peter Master, *Annunciation*, detail of the Saint Peter altarpiece. Siena, Pinacoteca Nazionale (photo: Fot. Soprintendenza B.A.S., Siena).

35. Luca di Tommè and Niccolò di Ser Sozzo, polyptych (1362). Siena, Pinacoteca Nazionale (photo: Fot. Soprintendenza B.A.S., Siena).

36. Simone Martini, the Pisa altarpiece, detail: Saint Mary Magdalen. Pisa, Museo di San Matteo (photo: Artini).

37. Simone Martini, the Pisa altarpiece, detail: Saint Catherine of Alexandria. Pisa, Museo di San Matteo.

38. Simone Martini, the Pisa altarpiece, detail: head of Saint Catherine. Pisa, Museo di San Matteo.

39. Pietro Lorenzetti, diagram of the *giornate* for the *Entry into Jerusalem*. Assisi, San Francesco, Lower Church (photo: De Giovanni).

40. Pietro Lorenzetti, diagram of the *giornate* for the *Crucifixion*. Assisi, San Francesco, Lower Church (photo: De Giovanni).

41. Pietro Lorenzetti, *Crucifixion*. Assisi, San Francesco, Lower Church (photo: De Giovanni).

42. Pietro Lorenzetti, diagram of the *giornate* for the *Deposition*. Assisi, San Francesco, Lower Church (photo: De Giovanni).

43. Pietro Lorenzetti, *Deposition*. Assisi, San Francesco, Lower Church (photo: De Giovanni).

44. Pietro Lorenzetti, fictive altarpiece. Assisi, San Francesco, Lower Church (photo: De Giovanni).

45. Pietro Lorenzetti, *Crucifixion*. Siena, San Francesco (photo: Fot. Soprintendenza B.A.S., Siena).

46. Pietro Lorenzetti, *Crucifixion*, detail: Saint John the Evangelist. Siena, San Francesco (photo: Fot. Soprintendenza B.A.S., Siena).

47. Simone Martini, *Death of Saint Martin*. Assisi, San Francesco, Lower Church (photo: Artini).

48. Simone Martini, saint in the window embrasure. Assisi, San Francesco, Lower Church.

49. Simone Martini, *Saints Louis IX of France and Louis of Toulouse*. Assisi, San Francesco, Lower Church.

50. Simone Martini, *Saints Mary Magdalen and Catherine of Alexandria*. Assisi, San Francesco, Lower Church.

51. Saint, from the roof of Siena cathedral. Siena, Museo dell'Opera del Duomo (photo: Fot. Soprintendenza B.A.S., Siena).

52. Duccio di Buoninsegna, Polyptych no. 28. Siena, Pinacoteca Nazionale (photo: Fot. Soprintendenza B.A.S., Siena).

53. Duccio di Buoninsegna, Polyptych no. 28, detail: head of the Virgin. Siena, Pinacoteca Nazionale (photo: Fot. Soprintendenza B.A.S., Siena).

54. Pietro Lorenzetti, *Enthroned Madonna and Child* (1340). Florence, Galleria degli Uffizi (photo: Gabinetto Fotografico, Sopr. Gallerie, Firenze).

55. Pietro Lorenzetti, *Saint Catherine of Alexandria*. Florence, Museo Horne (photo: Gabinetto Fotografico, Sopr. Gallerie, Firenze).

56. Duccio di Buoninsegna, Polyptych no. 47. Siena, Pinacoteca Nazionale (photo: Fot. Soprintendenza B.A.S., Siena).

57. Ugolino di Nerio, polyptych. Cleveland, Cleveland Museum of Art (photo: Cleveland Museum of Art).

58. Saint Nicholas Master, the Badia polyptych. Florence, Galleria degli Uffizi (photo: Gabinetto Fotografico, Sopr. Gallerie, Firenze).

59. Pietro Lorenzetti, the Carmelite polyptych, detail: central panel. Siena, Pinacoteca Nazionale (photo: Fot. Soprintendenza B.A.S., Siena).

60. Pietro Lorenzetti, the Carmelite polyptych, detail: *Saints Agnes and Catherine of Alexandria*. Siena, Pinacoteca Nazionale (photo: Fot. Soprintendenza B.A.S., Siena).

61. Related to Niccolò di Segna, *Resurrection* polyptych. Borgo San Sepolcro, Cathedral (photo: Gabinetto Fotografico, Sopr. Gallerie, Firenze).

62. Ambrogio Lorenzetti, *Franciscan Martyrdom*. Siena, San Francesco (photo: Grassi).

63. Simone Martini, *Beato Agostino Novello*, detail. Siena, Pinacoteca Nazionale (photo: Fot. Soprintendenza B.A.S., Siena).

64. Duccio di Buoninsegna, *Madonna of the Franciscans*. Siena, Pinacoteca Nazionale (photo: Fot. Soprintendenza B.A.S., Siena).

65. The Sienese Straus Master (?), *Madonna and Child*. Oxford, Ashmolean Museum (photo: Ashmolean Museum).

66. Master of Tabernacle 35, Tabernacle 35. Siena, Pinacoteca Nazionale (photo: Fot. Soprintendenza B.A.S., Siena).

67. Orbit of Ugolino di Nerio, triptych. New York, Metropolitan Museum (photo: Metropolitan Museum).

68. Simone Martini, *Crucified Christ*. Cambridge, Mass., Fogg Art Museum (photo: Fogg Art Museum).

69. Simone Martini, *Holy Family* (1342). Liverpool, Walker Art Gallery (photo: Walker Art Gallery).

70. Simone Martini, *Saint John the Evangelist*. Birmingham, Barber Institute of Fine Art (photo: Barber Institute of Fine Art).

71. The Sienese Straus Master, *Annunciation*. Berlin, Staatliche Museen Preußischer Kulturbesitz, Gemäldegalerie (photo: Gemäldegalerie).

72. The Sienese Straus Master, *Lamentation*. Oxford, Ashmolean Museum (photo: Ashmolean Museum).

73. Andrea Pisano, *Painting*. Florence, cathedral, campanile (photo: Gabinetto Fotografico, Sopr. Gallerie, Firenze).

74. Drawing for the facade of Orvieto cathedral. Orvieto, Opera del Duomo (photo: Worwood).

75. Drawing for the facade of the Siena baptistery. Siena, Museo dell'Opera del Duomo (photo: Fot. Soprintendenza B.A.S., Siena).

76. Drawing for a new campanile. Siena, Museo dell'Opera del Duomo (photo: Fot. Soprintendenza B.A.S., Siena).

77. Drawing for the facade of the Palazzo Sansedoni, Siena. Monte dei Paschi, Siena (photo: Fot. Soprintendenza B.A.S., Siena).

78. Simone Martini, *Obsequies for Saint Martin*. Assisi, San Francesco, Lower Church.

79. Circle of the San Bernardino Master, *Madonna and Child Enthroned*. Florence, Accademia (photo: Gabinetto Fotografico, Sopr. Gallerie, Firenze).

80. Orbit of Duccio, *Maestà*. Massa Marittima, cathedral (photo: Fot. Soprintendenza B.A.S., Siena).

81. Ambrogio Lorenzetti, *Ordination of Saint Louis of Toulouse*. Siena, San Francesco (photo: Grassi).

82. Pietro Lorenzetti, predella scene from the Carmelite altarpiece. Siena, Pinacoteca Nazionale (photo: Fot. Soprintendenza B.A.S., Siena).

83. Shop of Ugolino di Nerio, polyptych, detail: Madonna. Williamstown, Mass., Sterling and Francine Clark Art Institute (photo: Sterling and Francine Clark Art Institute).

84. Follower of Duccio, *Madonna and Child*. Montecchio, Chiesa della Compagnia della Madonna della Grotta (photo: Fot. Soprintendenza B.A.S., Siena).

85. Shop of Ugolino di Nerio, *Madonna and Child*. Princeton, Art Museum (photo: Art Museum).

86. Duccio di Buoninsegna, Polyptych no. 47, detail: Madonna. Siena, Pinacoteca Nazionale (photo: Fot. Soprintendenza B.A.S., Siena).

87. Northeast wall. Sala del Mappamondo, Palazzo Pubblico, Siena (photo: Fot. Soprintendenza B.A.S., Siena).

88. *A Subject Town*. Sala del Mappamondo, Palazzo Pubblico, Siena (photo: Fot. Soprintendenza B.A.S., Siena).

89. Ambrogio Lorenzetti, *Annunciation* (1344). Siena, Pinacoteca Nazionale (photo: Fot. Soprintendenza B.A.S., Siena).

90. Ambrogio Lorenzetti, *Madonna and Child Enthroned*. Siena, Palazzo Pubblico (photo: Fot. Soprintendenza B.A.S., Siena).

91. Biccherna cover for the January–June 1340. Archivio di Stato di Siena, Siena (photo: Fot. Soprintendenza B.A.S., Siena).

92. Biccherna cover for January–June 1353. Archivio di Stato di Siena, Siena (photo: Fot. Soprintendenza B.A.S., Siena).

93. Master of Palazzo Venezia, *Mystic Marriage of Saint Catherine*. Siena, Pinacoteca Nazionale (photo: Fot. Soprintendenza B.A.S., Siena).

94. Ugolino di Nerio, *Saint Anne and the Virgin*. Ottawa, National Gallery of Canada (photo: National Gallery).

95. Lippo Memmi, *Maestà*. San Gimignano, Palazzo Comunale (photo: Fot. Soprintendenza B.A.S., Siena).

96. Master of the Loeser Madonna, *Virgin and Child with Saint John the Baptist and Donor*. Siena, San Domenico (photo: Fot. Soprintendenza B.A.S., Siena).

97. Segna di Bonaventura, *Madonna and Child*. Siena, Santa Maria dei Servi (photo: Fot. Soprintendenza B.A.S., Siena).

98. Lippo Memmi, *Madonna and Child*. Siena, Santa Maria dei Servi (photo: Fot. Soprintendenza B.A.S., Siena).

99. Jacopo di Mino, *Coronation of Saint Catherine*. Siena, Pinacoteca Nazionale (photo: Fot. Soprintendenza B.A.S., Siena).

100. Lippo Memmi, *Madonna and Child Enthroned with Saints Peter and Paul*. Siena, San Domenico (photo: Fot. Soprintendenza B.A.S., Siena).

101. Lippo Vanni, reliquary. Siena, Museum of the Società di Esecutori di Pie Disposizioni (photo: Fot. Soprintendenza B.A.S., Siena).

102. Pietro Lorenzetti, *Crucifix*. Cortona, Museo Diocesana (photo: Gabinetto Fotografico, Sopr. Gallerie, Firenze).

103. Ambrogio Lorenzetti, the Vico l'Abate *Madonna*. Florence, Museo Arcivescovile di Cestello (photo: Gabinetto Fotografico, Sopr. Gallerie, Firenze).

104. Ambrogio Lorenzetti, *Madonna*. Florence, Galleria degli Uffizi (photo: Gabinetto Fotografico, Sopr. Gallerie, Firenze).

105. Ambrogio Lorenzetti, *Stories of Saint Nicholas of Bari*, detail: Saint Nicholas gives gold to a destitute family. Florence, Galleria degli Uffizi (photo: Gabinetto Fotografico, Sopr. Gallerie, Firenze).

106. Ambrogio Lorenzetti, *Stories of Saint Nicholas of Bari*, detail: consecration of Saint Nicholas. Florence, Galleria degli Uffizi (photo: Gabinetto Fotografico, Sopr. Gallerie, Firenze).

107. Ambrogio Lorenzetti, *Stories of Saint Nicholas of Bari*, detail: Saint Nicholas and the miraculous provision of grain. Florence, Galleria degli Uffizi (photo: Gabinetto Fotografico, Sopr. Gallerie, Firenze).

108. Ambrogio Lorenzetti, *Stories of Saint Nicholas of Bari*, detail: Saint Nicholas raises the son of a merchant. Florence, Galleria degli Uffizi (photo: Gabinetto Fotografico, Sopr. Gallerie, Firenze).

For K.V.W.

ACKNOWLEDGMENTS

My greatest debt is to the Social Sciences and Humanities Research Council of Canada, which has generously supported my research over a number of years. That support made it possible to spend long periods in Siena, working in the Archivio di Stato di Siena and in the archives of the Opera del Duomo. Without such stays, this work would have been impossible. The council has also provided me with assistance in preparing this book for publication.

As will quickly become apparent in my footnotes, I am deeply indebted to the recent work of several historians: in particular, William Bowsky, Samuel K. Cohn Jr., Giovanni Cherubini, Duccio Balestracci, Gabriella Piccinni, and Daniel Waley. I happily, and gratefully, acknowledge the very significant contributions they have made to this study.

Many other individuals deserve thanks. Let me give first place to the late Dottoressa S. Fineschi and the staff at the Archivio di Stato di Siena and to the staff of Siena's Biblioteca Comunale. Over many years I have benefited from their kindness and assistance. It is always a great pleasure to work in Siena; these individuals have helped to make it so. Special thanks are also due the staff of Villa I Tatti, Harvard's Center for Renaissance Studies, where I have spent not just many a month but many a year. They too have facilitated my work and have bravely faced my recurrent appearances with problems to be solved. The members of McMaster University's Interlibrary Loan office have coped willingly and cheerfully with my requests for what they must consider arcane items. My thanks, as well, to Edward Sernie.

Very special thanks I owe to Gabriele Erasmi, who kindly undertook the translation of the Sienese *Breve dell'Arte dei Pittori* from the fourteenth century, and to Sabine Eiche, who has provided inestimable assistance in the preparation of this volume.

PREFATORY NOTES

Dating

Although the Treasury of Siena, the office of the Biccherna, kept records according to two semesters, January to June and July to December, the Sienese year began on 25 March rather than on 1 January. Thus, documents dated between 1 January and 24 March generally carry the date of the preceding year. For example, 15 February 1310 is, in modern reckoning, 15 February 1311. Throughout this volume dates are given in the common, modern style. In some cases, however, dates cited in early secondary sources, it has not been possible to determine whether the author was using the original dating or converted the dates to modern usage.

Money

Sienese currency was organized in the fashion of English pounds, shillings, and pence. Twelve denari (pennies) equaled 1 soldo (a shilling), and 20 soldi equaled 1 lira (a pound). The lira, however, was not a coin but rather a money of account. Through the period of this study, the relation between the Sienese lira and the gold florin of Florence changed significantly. In Siena, the Merchants' Guild, the Mercanzia, daily set the rate of exchange.

Measurement

The Sienese *braccio,* the basic unit of measurement, measured 60.1 cm, divided into twenty-four *oncie* of 2.5 cm each.

Land Measurement

The main unit of surface measurement in Siena was the *staio,* or *starius,* probably slightly less than a third of an acre.

Abbreviations

In the footnotes of this volume, authors and titles have been abbreviated after their first appearance. I have, however, used the following abbreviations to reduce repetitions:

ASS   Archivio di Stato di Siena
Spedale   Ospedale di Santa Maria della Scala
BC   Biblioteca Comunale, Siena
BSSP   *Bullettino senese di storia patria*

Documentary Quotations

In quoting documents, I have retained the original spellings, and the reader will note a number of disparities with modern usage. One frequent occurrence is the use of "ng" for words that now contain "gn": for example, "lengo" rather than "legno." Where the wording of a specific document seems open to various interpretations, I quote the original rather than offer a translation, which would itself be an interpretation.

PREFACE

This study is the second volume of an intended trilogy that I began with *Painting in the Age of Giotto* and will complete with *Early Sienese Painting: A History*. The former sought to trace the historiographical tradition of trecento studies from Vasari until the beginning of the twentieth century, and thereby to clarify the origins of ideas that have become conventions of art-historical scholarship. In reexamining specific works and problems of interpretation, I then sought, among other things, to demonstrate that both the preeminence assigned to Florentine painting in the rebirth of the arts and the near-exclusive discussions centered on regional schools have masked a historical situation of greater complexity and greater interest.

As I understand the character and the history of the trecento revolution, of the dramatic developments that between roughly 1260 and 1360 reshaped and then reshaped again the nature and place of painting in Italian civilization, the art of Siena played a role that was by no means inferior to that of Florence. The new art arose as much in the hills of the Chianti as in the valley of the Arno, and the heritage that great masters of the early Quattrocento found meaningful was one in which the Florentine and the Sienese traditions mingled. Much remains to be said concerning the history of early Sienese painting, its dynamic, its response to other traditions, and its influence well beyond Siena itself. These are matters that will be discussed in *Early Sienese Painting*. Here, however, I turn to related, yet different, material, to the historical and cultural circumstances of early Sienese painters. No other city-state of the fourteenth century left us so much original documentation regarding painters and painting. Siena therefore provides us with materials for a case study, a study that may well be the closest we shall ever come to understanding the historical context of early Italian artists.

For the general reader, the Trecento must seem as remote as the world of ancient myth. Seven centuries divide us from the moment when, in 1300, Boniface VIII declared the first jubilee of the Church, and those seven centuries have taken us far from a world characterized by values and beliefs that seem at times familiar and on other occasions very strange. The period here examined did much to structure the modern world; many aspects of thirteenth- and fourteenth-century urban life parallel our own experiences in cities, and many instances of that period's governmental regulation accord with our notions of the appropriate role of the state. In the thirteenth-century recovery of Aristotle, we find the roots of modern intellectual life, and in political philosophy of the period, we discover new, secular conceptions of the state. But on matters as basic as notions of causality or issues as pressing as appropriate earthly justice, the citizens of trecento Siena held beliefs that are now foreign to most of us. Theirs was a world where demons, angels, and saints could intervene in human affairs and stay the course of nature, a world of magic and astrology as well as of Christian faith, and a world wherein an apprehended thief was as likely as not to lose his hand in punishment. Even the greatest intellectuals of the period acknowledged the complex universe I have described: in discussions such as those on vision, so prominent in the period, John Duns Scotus could appeal to the nature of angels as part of his argument, and William Ockham could hypothesize a circumstance in which demons moved mirrors about to deceive human sight.

The discussions that follow arise from a series of questions about early Sienese painters and painting that I have posed for myself over the last two decades. In the beginning, those questions were rather narrowly defined. I wondered about the obvious: What did painters earn? Where did they live? How did they organize themselves in their profession? But slowly, over the years, I have come to see that such questions can be answered in a meaningful way only by placing the relevant evidence within a larger framework. The intimate relation between the development of painting and its urban context then led on to exploration of broader social and religious issues.

This volume is, then, as much about cultural history as about the history of art, and that fact has determined the inclusion of discussions that reach beyond matters directly relating to pictures. For example, I have tried to evoke the character of the Christian faith in Siena of the late thirteenth and early fourteenth centuries. My concern is with the culture in which painters lived and created their art. To define that culture, I have also included a few discussions of contemporary issues that, in the end, we find inapplicable to the Sienese situation; for I believe that negative findings are sometimes as enlightening as simple equations.

I have not been able to answer all my questions in the detail and with the certainty that might be desired. Painters of the thirteenth and fourteenth centuries had no chronicler, no biographer; documents survive in fragmentary series; often one encounters silence at the very points where most might have been learned. And since our notions of historiography prohibit the charming biographical fictions of Vasari, I can offer neither anecdote nor psychological analysis to assuage the curiosity of readers or to enliven the narrative. But if we cannot conjure the motivations or outlook of individual painters, we can watch the emergence of something approaching the modern notion of the artist; we can catch glimpses of how painters were regarded by their contemporaries. If we cannot know the precise material success, or failure, of each painter, we can nonetheless speak of patterns and probabilities. If we cannot follow painters in the routine of their daily lives, we can point to constituents of their world, to elements that informed the society around them and of which they were keenly aware.

The story that follows is tightly focused. I begin with a wide-ranging sketch of the history of the Sienese painter's city, of the society in which he lived and worked. Chapters II through IV deal with the place of the painter in his society, the conditions and constraints of his craft, and issues of patronage. In those chapters, the reader will find a high degree of specificity relating to matters such a property values, painters' incomes, and comparative costs. Such specificity makes, I fear, rather heavy going, but that material takes us to the heart of my enterprise. Chapter V then rapidly broadens our view, to consider issues that require more than Sienese evidence for their evaluation, and an epilogue draws together the previous findings. The book ends with a translation, by Gabriele Erasmi, of the trecento statute of the Painters' Guild in Siena and with a series of appendixes devoted to documentary material.

The reader will soon discover that the majority of this work is dependent upon the documents that survive to us. If the Sienese archives contain less than we might wish for the later thirteenth and early fourteenth centuries, there is still an extraordinary amount of material. Thus, I have constantly been haunted by the question when to stop research for this project. Although there are, undoubtedly, still discoveries to be made, I now have the sense that enough has been done (in the areas where that is possible) to offer a fairly complete picture of the relations between Siena and its painters.

As this volume goes into production, there comes news of a major exhibition to be held in Siena in the summer of 2001, an important exhibition centered on Duccio di Buoninsegna. Undoubtedly, the catalogue of that exhibition will include material relevant to the discussions that here follow.

Readers unfamiliar with the artistic achievements of Sienese painters in the late Dugento and first half of the Trecento, and who thus feel the need of an overview, should consult my *Painting in the Age of Giotto* and the brief overview found here in the Introduction.

H. B. J. M.
Hamilton, Ontario
January 2000

The World
of the
Early Sienese Painter

A PROLOGUE

When, in the *Très Riches Heures* (1413–16), the Limbourg brothers illustrated Christ's temptation on the mountain, all the riches of this world that man or god might covet were embodied in a vision of Jean de Berry's chateau at Mehun-sur-Yèvre; when Duccio di Buoninsegna depicted the same subject in his *Maestà* (1308–11; Color Plates 1 and 2) for Siena cathedral, he made the greatest temptations of our earthly realm its shining cities; and in that difference lies a fundamental distinction between two cultures and a telling comment on the respective sources of great art. The wealth of France in the early fifteenth century still lay in vast estates; a century earlier the wealth of central Italy was that of commerce and banking. In the North, at the time of the Limbourgs, an art that largely served princes and great prelates was only beginning to find patrons elsewhere; in early fourteenth-century Italy, art generally served the communes and their inhabitants. And the latter was the result of changes already old. The century before Duccio's *Maestà* had dramatically altered Italian civilization. It was a century that saw the revival of international trade, the rise of cities, and fundamental alterations in the character of Christianity, as a new vision of the faith brought down from the hills of Umbria, from the town of Assisi, by Saint Francis and his followers swept first across Italy and then throughout Europe. While all this occurred, and largely as its consequence, there arose a new art, an art born amidst city streets: the child, on one side, of that changing faith and, on the other, of banking and commerce.

Duccio's world was that of a civilization in transition. The century that preceded his *Maestà* had been a time of profound change, a time destined to be so very consequential for the West because it gradually altered so many facets of life and thought that the fabric of Western culture was rewoven. And because contemporaries, in the midst of things, could not see the patterns we perceive, no individual, no single generation, realized the full force of change that was upon them.

As the thirteenth century began, the medieval papacy, under the leadership of Innocent III, reached the apogee of its power and prestige; as the century ended, Boniface VIII was dragging the Church into conflict with Philip the Fair, king of France, and into a crisis that would undermine papal authority and lead to that period of Church history—and scandal—known as the Babylonian Captivity, when pope and curia abandoned Rome and, under the watchful eye of the French monarch, settled in Avignon. When the thirteenth century opened, Francis of Assisi had yet to experience the conversion that would lead him to sainthood; as the century closed, the vision of Francis and the Franciscans had redefined much of Christianity. By 1200, most of Aristotle's works had been translated into Latin, but the impact of The Philosopher was slight; by 1300, Aristotle's ideas had permeated the West, given rise to a new class of intellectuals in the new universities, and provided a model of intellectual life radically at variance with the aims and self-definition of many theologians. New thought would move toward novel, secular political theory, providing justification for monarchies and communes independent of the Church. The thirteenth century provided Europeans their first contact with China, witnessed the de facto failure of the crusading spirit, saw Westerners for a time (1204–61) ruling Constantinople, and watched the rise of the fiercely independent Italian communes. And it saw those city-states become the places where all the new ideas of the age were shared.

All these developments had consequences, of greater or lesser measure, for Duccio's city; as this study progresses, we shall have occasion to assess the impact of many of them on Siena. But there are two matters of such fundamental importance for the story told in these pages, so much part of the cultural background for Siena and its painters, that they must be sketched before I turn to the history of the painter's city. I refer to the recovery of Aristotle and to the changing character of Christianity, the condition of the faith. Together, they created an intellectual and religious climate that infused that late thirteenth- and fourteenth-century civilization of which Siena was a part.

It was, in fact, during the twelfth century that Aristotle's works were brought to Westerners through translation into Latin. By 1220 the bulk of his work and a number of pseudo-Aristotelian treatises had been translated not, as we once thought, from the Arabic, but from the Greek. The twelfth century, however, made little use of the material; it stood—as it were—on intellectual shelves, to be pondered occasionally but rarely taken up with a sense of its applicability to contemporary problems or as a guide to problem solving. The thirteenth century changed all that in a decisive and dramatic way. Indeed, so great was the interest in The Philosopher, as he was dubbed, that between c.1260 and c.1280 the Dominican William of Moerbeke revised or retranslated all of his works. During the 1220s and 1230s, Michael Scotus translated the brilliant Arabic commentaries on Aristotle by Averroës, works of such intelligence and thoroughness that the Moslem philosopher became known as The Commentator.

The recovery of an entire, coherent philosophical system from antiquity and the availability of Averroës' commentaries created massive disruptions in the West's intellectual tradition. While Aristotelian thought was largely welcomed and embraced, many things in Aristotle were contrary to the faith, particularly his notion of the eternity of the world: an idea that stood in total opposition to Christian belief in the creation and the coming end of the world. Still more important, Aristotle offered a method for investigation and a purpose for argument that differed entirely from the established Christian approach to problem solving and from its conception of the intellectual's task. Theologians' work was to hand down the Christian tradition as embodied in scripture, in the work of the early church fathers, and in the decisions of the Church councils. When it came to confronting seeming contradictions in different sources, the theologian set out to demonstrate that those contradictions were apparent rather than real, and to show how all ideas could be reconciled. His purpose was not to reveal new truths but to unveil long-known truths masked by accidents of expression. Aristotle, by contrast, taught his followers that their goals were discovery, the acquisition of new knowledge, invention. He also taught them that he was but one seeker after wisdom; his own judgments and theories could be questioned, debated, and rejected if found wanting. Thus two diametrically opposed sets of ambitions and ideals faced each other, often in the close quarters of the new universities.

Aristotelianism soon permeated thirteenth-century and fourteenth-century thought. It was incorporated in political theory and thus became the foundation for Marsilius of Padua's radical *Defensor pacis* (1324). Through Saint Thomas Aquinas (d. 1274) it entered deeply into Scholasticism and particularly deeply into the thought of his order, the Dominicans. In the universities, it produced a class of intellectuals who saw themselves as philosophers and who came to ignore the contradictions between Aristotelianism and Christianity. Happy to admit their conclusions were often contrary to the faith, and to acknowledge that truths of the faith were truths indeed, they nonetheless maintained that philosophers' conclusions were also true. In effect, their position came frighteningly close to suggesting a system of double truths.

The Aristotelians brought a new investigatory approach to things of this world, and that fact points us toward the principal benefit of Aristotelianism in the West. The Middle Ages before the thirteenth century had achieved almost nothing in science; indeed, the earlier centuries clung to ideas about the world and the heavens found in late antique sources and encyclopedias written between the fourth and eighth centuries. Almost without exception, these were handbooks, rehearsals of facts and ideas derived from ancient authors. Most of them reveal their authors' lack of direct knowledge of the sources they are citing, and so, as such information was handed down, distortions and inaccuracies crept into them. But their greatest flaw lay in the encyclopedists' focus on information from ancient sciences rather than on the theoretical bases from which conclusions arose; thus, to read their work was not to begin further exploration. Recovery of Aristotle's works on natural philosophy, his *Libri naturales* as they were known, brought not just information but also the principles of scientific investigation.

Now Aristotle's notion of the intellectual's purpose and task entered deeply into Western thought, making novelty and invention highly prized. In that way, Aristotelians partially created the climate in which painters of the late Dugento and early Trecento worked. We have evidence both written and painted that artistic invention and originality came to be highly prized in the first half of the Trecento. That development was not entirely the legacy of Aristotelianism; a great many other ideas of the time, ideas that originated in very different circumstances and traditions, came to combine with the influence of Aristotle in producing the new attitudes. In a similar way, Aristotelian nominalism perhaps invited more attention to the specific, the individual, the "thing-in-itself"; but prompting for the same was also found in Franciscan thought and was stimulated by encounters with previously unknown cultures. Here, as in so many cases, the dynamism of the age came from the confluence of ideas that together offered a new perspective. Siena was one of the places where that confluence occurred, and Sienese painting one of the demonstrations of that occurrence.

The half century before Duccio's birth (c.1250?) had been a time of momentous changes in the faith. At the beginning of the thirteenth century, Innocent III (1198–1216) had filled his eighteen-year reign with astonishing accomplishments that his reforming predecessors, especially Gregory VII (1075–85) and Alexander III (1159–81), would have commended. From ancient rights and privileges that at the time of his election were little more than fictions, he had fashioned the Papal States as a protective barrier between the pope and the Holy Roman Empire. He had made—and unmade—emperors; he had seen a Latin patriarch established in Constantinople; he had presided over the Fourth Lateran Council (1215), known to history as the Great Council. In short, Innocent had invested the papacy with an authority long desired but rarely realized. The dream of papal hegemony over Europe seemed at hand; for a time, at least, the papacy assumed the mantle of power over matters secular as well as spiritual. These triumphs, however, came at a very high price. Innocent had mired the Church in things of this world, and he left his successors aspirations that grew increasingly out of temper with the times.

For the first half of the thirteenth century, after Innocent's death, the papacy was locked in battle with Frederick II of Hohenstaufen. By inheritance on his mother's side, Frederick was king of Sicily; in a very late and ultimately disastrous change of policy, Innocent had championed Frederick's claim to the imperial title, and so, like his father Henry VI, Frederick became Holy Roman Emperor. He was a man of little moral or religious conviction, and he had no use for the papacy's mighty claims. Imperial and papal ambitions could not be reconciled; church and state were locked in battle. The struggle lasted even beyond Frederick's death in 1250, as the Church pursued his heirs. In the late 1260s, while Duccio was still young, it must have seemed as if the long battles of the first half of the century had brought the Church a final success. Conradin, the last of the Hohenstaufen, was captured and executed in 1268. The defeat had large ramifications for Duccio's city. By tradition, Siena had been Ghibelline (that is, pro-imperial); with defeat of the Hohenstaufen, the city could no longer maintain that allegiance and became Guelf (that is, pro-papal). The change was to create links with other pro-papal communes in central Italy and bring Siena into close relation with the Kingdom of Naples.

In order to avoid any repetition of the circumstances that had united the king of Sicily and the Holy Roman Emperor in one person, Urban IV (1260–64) bestowed the Kingdom of Sicily on Charles of Anjou, brother of Louis IX of France. Through the 1260s and 1270s, the papacy devoted energies and very significant funds to securing Charles's kingdom. Short was the respite that came with success. In 1282, Sicily itself revolted against its new ruler and passed into the hands of the royal house of Aragon. The Angevins and their sponsor, the papacy, would spend two decades (1282–1302) and vast resources in the War of the Sicilian Vespers, but the attempt to reunite the island with the mainland portion of Charles I's kingdom proved futile. What had begun as the Kingdom of Sicily became the Angevin monarchy of Naples.

As Innocent III's aspirations to papal hegemony in Europe drove his successors, so too did his preoccupation with papal security, and thus with domination of the Papal States. Innocent had managed, for a time, to exert control over those territories, but there was no real tradition of papal rule and little desire, on the part of the population, to see it become a reality. The popes who came after Innocent found themselves immersed in an ever-changing world of revolts, pacifications, and shifting allegiances that played themselves out time and time again, well into the fourteenth century. The Papal States, intended to strengthen the papacy, became another enormous drain on papal finances and a still greater drain on the energies and attention of the popes.

Finally, at the beginning of the Trecento, a new physical distance structured the relation of Italians and the papacy. In the aftermath of the struggle between Philip the Fair and Boniface VIII, Clement V (1305–14), the French Bertrand de Got, fell under Philip's influence and, just as Duccio was creating the *Maestà*, settled the papal household in Avignon. Pope and curia were gone from Rome, gone from Italy, and so it would remain until 1377.

If the reader suspects (quite rightly) that the political and territorial ambitions of the papacy did little for the care of souls, there was yet another factor that placed distance between the papacy and the faithful. The Church of the thirteenth and fourteenth centuries was obsessed with law. As secular jurists were deep in consideration of Justinian's *Corpus juris civilis,* popes and jurists of the Church were devoted to the codification of canon law, begun by Gratian in his *Decretum* of the mid–twelfth century. By the middle of the fourteenth century, the Church had more or less defined canon law as it would exist until the early twentieth century. That development was hardly surprising. Between 1198 and 1362, fully eight of the historically most important popes came to their office having been trained as lawyers: Innocent III (1198–1216), Gregory IX (1227–41), Innocent IV (1243–54), Clement IV (1265–68), Boniface VIII (1294–1303), Clement V (1305–14), John XXII (1316–36), and Innocent V (1353–62). In Rome, later in Avignon, it was the lawyer's mind that shaped the faith, convinced that the fate of Christendom might lie in an appeal to law.

Into a faith structured by the papal ambitions sketched above came Francis of Assisi, son of a prosperous merchant and, in time, the embodiment of a new Christian vision. Passionately attached to things of this world as expressions of God's goodness, focused on the story of the Gospels (particularly the stories of Christ's passion and the sermon on the mount), and determined to live in imitation of Christ, Francis espoused a life of poverty, humility, mendicity, and good works. Here was a man who preached to the birds, who tended lepers, who wandered throughout Italy and beyond (even to North Africa), preaching the Gospels and God's love, who had neither church nor convent, who lived without possessions and was sustained by the charity of others. The success of Francis and of those who gathered about him was enormous. His ambitions spoke to the times, and his vision addressed the spiritual needs of those who were party to the urbanization of Italy. The Franciscans were at home in towns and cities; they brought good news to those experiencing a sense of dislocation engendered by the move from the countryside to rapidly growing and rapidly changing cities. They preached a new emphasis on the Gospels. Most important of all, they brought word of a personal savior who had himself lived among us and whose love was boundless, and in the story of Francis they offered a model, an ideal, a pattern, to those who would seek a holy life within the urban setting.

As the thirteenth century passed, there were other responses to the faith in an urban environment, responses that testify to the layman's desire for a participatory religious life, for more immediate involvement than the traditional church structures allowed. One expression of that desire is found in the rise of confraternities, associations of laymen who gathered regularly for devotions and sometimes for rites such as penitential scourging. In cities, the emerging guilds invariably obliged their members to participate in the celebration of designated feasts and guild observances. Finally, Italy saw the rise of what we term "civic Christianity," a phenomenon in which cities created innumerable bonds between the state and the religious life of their citizens, further enhancing the place of the lay individual. Civic Christianity and confraternities were of great importance in structuring Sienese society, and because of the nature of the former in the Sienese context, it was a central and determining factor in the history of Sienese painting.

When we think of the distant world that is the subject of this book, most of us are likely to recall the historical developments treated above, or the grand tradition of vernacular literature initiated by Dante and so splendidly continued in the work of Boccaccio and Petrarch, or the rebirth of the visual arts. We are far less likely to think of the moment as one that saw inventions and innovations of a practical nature. But the enormous vitality of Western civilization did produce developments that, though seemingly minor, were as important and consequential as the larger cultural shifts. When, in 1252, the Florentines introduced the gold florin and guaranteed its continuing value, they laid the foundation for the gold standard and provided a fixed measure for international exchange. It was during Duccio's lifetime that paper became widely available in central Italy, a new material, far less expensive than parchment, that allowed for new kinds of record keeping and, I believe, made drawings a new element in the artistic process. In the last third of the century, cartography took on new life with the introduction of portolan charts, navigational maps of the Mediterranean that found their way to libraries as well as ships. At the same time came the invention of the mechanical clock, although it would be only after Duccio's death that clocks became a major feature of Italian life. By the beginning of the fourteenth century (perhaps even earlier), eyeglasses were being produced in Pisa and Venice, offering promise of a longer productive life to scholars, merchants, and artisans.

We know that in the decade after Duccio's death, the 1320s, the Florentines were buying cannon balls, signaling the advent of that most pernicious of inventions, gunpowder. So great was the success of man's novel means of self-destruction that in the 1350s Petrarch would observe: "[T]hese instruments which discharge balls of metal with the most tremendous noise and flashes of fire . . . were a few years ago very rare and were viewed with the greatest astonishment and admiration, but now they are become as common and familiar as any other kind of arms."

All of these inventions, all of the period's new ideas, index the cultural dynamism of the age here considered. And their number should be enlarged to include painting. Sometimes we overlook the simple but highly significant fact that it was the thirteenth and fourteenth centuries that made painting a major and widespread art in Italy and beyond, and that the period thus laid the foundation of the West's preoccupation with painting, lasting down to our own era.

Influenced by scholarship of earlier generations, perhaps prompted by the historical situation in the Quattrocento, we today still often think of Siena as one of the provincial "hill towns," charming to tourists who shun the noise and crowds of the greater Italian cities. And, thanks to earlier scholarship, we often speak of mysticism as the defining characteristic of Sienese Christianity. Neither idea has anything to do with the city that is the subject of this book. Siena of the late thirteenth and early fourteenth centuries was one of the great cities of Europe, situated such that almost every traveler going to or coming from Rome passed through its streets. Siena was, as it were, in the midst of things. The historical developments and the ideas sketched above came to Siena not as faint and distant rumor but directly, immediately. And when I come to consider the evidence regarding the character of Sienese Christianity, the reader will find that mysticism hardly enters.

As Duccio and his shop worked on the *Maestà,* as the painter devised his scene of Christ's temptation on the mountain, his thoughts may not have been with the grand events and developments sketched above, although they were parts of his heritage and entered deeply into his environment. Rather, his thoughts were likely with his native city. His early career had not enjoyed the Sienese patronage it deserved, but now, less than a decade before his death, the elderly artist had been awarded the commission for the city's most important altarpiece. He had worked for the governing regime before, in executing minor commissions and in creating a now lost *Maestà* (1302) for the chapel of the city's governors; he soon would be given the commission for a new high altarpiece in the chapel of the Ospedale di Santa Maria della Scala. And his last years, it seems, were spent between half a house he owned in Siena and country land at Pian del Lago, rented from the commune.

Around him, Duccio could see younger artists shaped by his example; he could see those who would have dazzling careers, those who, in a time he would not see, would carry the Sienese achievement throughout Tuscany and Umbria, to Naples, and to far off Avignon. He could watch those destined to perpetuate his style long after his own death, and he must have been aware of the numerous minor "minor masters" who were painters fated to obscurity. As he worked on the *Maestà,* he watched completion of Siena's Palazzo Pubblico (Fig. 2), the new center of civic government that would provide work for many painters of a younger generation. Work on the cathedral (Figs. 3–4) was continuing (it was already a project of many decades), and there would be many altars that eventually required altarpieces. Indeed, the expanding urban fabric was filled with promise of work to come.

Into the panel of Christ's temptation (Color Plates 1–2), Duccio put his vision of an ideal city. Jerusalem, at the lower left, is a place of sturdy walls that enclose a rectangle and determine the pattern of parallel streets, so handsomely paved in brick. The city is composed of fine buildings of brick and stone, roofed with tiles. Around the city flows an abundance of water, available to all. This vision, as we shall see, was not merely Duccio's dream; it was an expression of ideals he shared with his fellow citizens. This work, produced for a particular city-state, was the embodiment of the very ambitions that, in large measure, had summoned it into life. But those ambitions, like the general culture of Siena, had been forged in significant part by the larger historical circumstances discussed above.

INTRODUCTION

The story of the Italian rebirth of painting, sketched by Lorenzo Ghiberti, told by Giorgio Vasari, and retold by countless writers to follow, has now the familiarity of a commonplace. To thirteenth-century Florence was born, in 1240, Giovanni Cimabue, who, as a boy, discovered an inclination toward, and a natural genius for, painting. Instructed by Greek masters who had been brought to the city to revive an art long dead, Cimabue soon surpassed his mentors and, bringing "the first lights" to painting, moved away from the Greek manner and began to approach the good manner of the moderns. Cimabue, however, was but a precursor; the true recovery of art's purpose came only when he discovered the ten-year-old Giotto, a child of the countryside born with the ability to draw sheep from nature, and brought him to Florence for instruction. From Giotto, his works, his followers, and most assuredly from Florence came the true rebirth of painting, as the "first age" of the Renaissance restored naturalism and monumental narrative painting to a central place in art, thus opening the way for the great achievements of the Quattrocento and the still greater accomplishments of the sixteenth century.

This fine and simple tale has its virtues, but they are both limited and limiting; its very simplicity makes it incommensurate with the complexity of phenomena it seeks to explain. It replaces the awkward course of history with the engaging simplicity of myth—at a high price. But Vasari's tale also contains an important truth: if nature, as Leonardo da Vinci said, is "mistress of the masters," the new art of the thirteenth and fourteenth centuries arose not among fields and forests but from instruction and careers in an urban context.

We are so accustomed to the association of painting and the urban setting that it may be hard to appreciate what a dramatic change was embodied in the moment when that connection first came to be. I think it almost impossible to exaggerate the symbiotic relationship between the new cities and the new art. Surplus wealth, which first raised towers and walls, palaces and churches, eventually found its way into painters' pockets, as society came to feel the need of images and imaging in a wide variety of contexts. The pictorial art was, in time, deemed necessary to the furnishing of altars; churches old and new acquired frescoed stories, visions of the faith. Civic secular architecture, which in the late Dugento became essential to civic identity, was decorated with pictorial imagery that acknowledged the divine and embodied political aspirations. The urban citizenry eventually would seek to possess the small, private devotional pictures, which in the Trecento became ever more popular. There also arose, as we shall see, a thousand minor tasks that required the painter's art, such as the coloring of statuary, the painting of banners and lanterns and furniture, the decoration of book covers, and the adornment of chests. It was the congregation of people and the number and variety of tasks, typical only of cities, that could support comparatively large numbers of painters living together in comparatively small spaces.

Italian cities lent the history of art an entirely novel dynamic. They offered a living to painters numerous enough to create competition; they created artists who quickly recognized and often appropriated innovation, for painting was all about them. The proximity of painters, sculptors, and architects meant that ideas were rapidly shared and the pace of change thus accelerated. A great number of painters in any one center led to the introduction of guild structures to regulate the craft and ensure the quality of production. And cities became vast source books by gathering the accomplishments of many within their walls. When artists traveled, when they visited cities not their own, other artistic traditions were laid before them almost immediately and almost in entirety, within the compass of not so many square kilometers.

The urban setting also created a new relation between the painter and his audience. Living in the same space, the painter's patrons were his neighbors, and his works were always before both, to be assessed not once but over time. Within the urban fabric, painters eventually attracted the attention of poets. Dante's famous juxtaposition of Cimabue and Giotto was followed by the comments of Boccaccio and Petrarch, the stories of Franco Sacchetti, and the remarks of chroniclers such as Giovanni and Filippo Villani in Florence or Agnolo di Tura in Siena. And those remarks were woven into other developments that slowly changed the status of the artist. Finally, Italian cities introduced distinctions among painters, beginning a process of discrimination that, much earlier than we might have imagined, sought to differentiate the better from the best and clearly recognized that there were those of lesser talent alongside major masters.

In the traditional, Vasarian account of the rebirth of painting, the art of Siena plays a minor role. For Vasari, there was no Sienese school, merely some painters from Siena, Simone Martini and Pietro Lorenzetti among them, who were Giotto's followers. When subsequent scholarship made it impossible to maintain Vasari's vision, when scholars of the eighteenth and nineteenth centuries came to acknowledge the existence of local schools of art, a series of new characterizations of Sienese painting arose to relegate it to a secondary place. There is great irony in that development. While such characterizations preserved Vasari's notions of the primacy and preeminence of Florence, they ignored the reality that one of the features of fourteenth-century art Vasari judged most important, naturalism, was far more at home in Siena than in the city on the Arno.

The view that Sienese trecento art was secondary to that of Florence was clearly not shared by contemporaries. Between approximately 1260 and 1360, prominent Sienese painters (and even some minor ones) were called to work in Pisa, Lucca, Pistoia, Arezzo,

Cortona, Perugia, Assisi, and Orvieto, to say nothing of distant cities such as Naples and Avignon or of the numerous small communities in Tuscany and Umbria that acquired Sienese works. Sienese painters were, in fact, even summoned to Florence comparatively often, to create panel pictures and sometimes frescoes for some of that city's most important institutions. What, we may ask, elicited such widespread response? For some patrons, it may have been the consistently high craftsmanship of Sienese artists that attracted attention; for others, it may have been the fact that Sienese painters, in a variety of works and ways, found means to embody something of the new Christian vision espoused by the mendicant orders, especially the Franciscans, with great eloquence. Some may have been engaged by a history of remarkable innovations. Still others may have prized that exquisite splendor of surface common to the Sienese tradition; in other words, some may have been entranced by the sheer beauty of Sienese images.

Twentieth-century scholarship has done something toward reestablishing the reputation and historical place of early Sienese painting, and a series of comparatively recent monographs have contributed to our knowledge of specific painters; but were one to look for an analysis of the Sienese artist's place within his society or for an account of circumstances that shaped his art, one would look in vain. Perhaps we have taken it for granted that little can be said about such matters, given the seven centuries that separate us from the Sienese achievement? Perhaps other discussions have left the impression that we are now too distant from that world? Certainly, anyone who has taken up Frederick Antal's *Florentine Painting and Its Social Background* in hope of following the lives of trecento Florentine painters will know precisely what I mean. It is not, however, entirely Antal's fault that the reader comes away from his book with a sense of disappointment. Florence, it seems, could not provide him with the necessary documentary materials for such an account; too much is lost. In fact, many nonspecialists would be shocked by a discussion that detailed the paucity of documentary evidence for Florentine trecento painting. Contracts, records of payment, documentation on painters' financial position, material regarding their private lives: all are almost nonexistent or untraced.

A move south to Siena, however, brings us into a very different situation. From late thirteenth- and fourteenth-century Siena, we have a comparative abundance of documentary evidence about painters and their world (although any historian working with the copious sources of later periods would find that description bizarre). In part, the difference between the Sienese situation and that of other cities relates to simple accidents of history. More documentation was preserved. But it also relates to one of the primary themes of this book. If there was ever an Italian commune in which the ties between painters and the state were closer, I know it not. The extensive patronage of the commune lies at the heart of the history of Sienese painting.

Now, it must be said that the surviving documentation introduces a bias in the discussions to follow. We have, for example, almost no indication of private patronage in Siena. But while historical reasons and evidence suggest that private individuals did not play an important role in Sienese patronage, they certainly commissioned more than extant pictures or documents record. The same is true of Siena's guilds and confraternities. Similarly, we have very little record of works for the city's parish churches, yet many of them must have received, at minimum, new altarpieces during the period here examined. As I proceed, these lacunae should be kept in mind.

Even if we must dismiss Vasari's contention that in mid-dugento Tuscany painting was an art long dead, it is true that c. 1250 no citizen of Siena could foresee the glorious future of painting in his native city or the way in which painting would become ubiquitous in the following century, would begin its ascent to claim first place among the arts. A small group of painters, active in the early decades of the century, had furnished Siena's cathedral with the so-called *Madonna degli occhi grossi* (Siena, Museo dell'Opera del Duomo) and had provided an altar frontal of the apocalyptic Redeemer for the *badia* at Castelnuovo Berardenga (Siena, Pinacoteca Nazionale, no. 1). A painter from the same group created the *Madonna* now in the Chigi-Saraceni Collection (Siena); another *Madonna* comes from Tressa, on the outskirts of Siena. There survive, in addition, a few painted crosses. But in spite of the fine qualities in the best of these works, Sienese painting of the early thirteenth century seems to have been modest in the number of its adherents and in the quality of its production. By comparison, Pisa and Lucca had far greater claim to possessing a vital and accomplished school of painters. During the years when Giunta Pisano was creating his marvelous painted crosses, which so beautifully capture the new, more emotive approach to the Gospels, very little, it seems, was happening in Sienese painting.

Beginning in the 1260s, the situation in Siena changed dramatically. Rather suddenly, there appeared a new group of artists usually, though erroneously, identified as the circle of Guido da Siena. Great was their success. From surviving works (and much is lost), we know that they worked for the Dominicans, the Franciscans, and the Poor Clares. They provided the cathedral with the so-called *Madonna del Voto* and, perhaps, an altar frontal on cloth; they were responsible for frescoes in the cathedral crypt. Siena's parish and conventual churches contained their work, and their panels were also sent abroad: to San Gimignano, to Grosseto, to Arezzo, perhaps even to Florence. Such success attended their art that for three decades they held Siena in thrall, shaping the expectations of patrons, determining their taste, and exerting what now appears as almost a stranglehold on Sienese commissions.[1] Thus it was that Duccio, often styled the father of Sienese painting, began his career at a moment and in a place initially unresponsive to his revolutionary new vision. For the first—but certainly not the last—time, a younger painter of genius confronted a situation that seemed to offer limited opportunities in his own city.

And so Duccio's most important thirteenth-century work, and perhaps the greatest single work of his career, the magnificent Rucellai *Madonna* (Figs. 10–11), was commissioned in 1285 by the Confraternity of the Laudesi in Florence's Santa Maria Novella. In

1. For a fuller discussion of these works, see my "Everything in a Name? The Classification of Sienese Dugento Painting," *Studies in the History of Art,* forthcoming.

that work, Duccio radically redefined the meaning of the image and the purposes and devices of art. In an image that makes the production of the "Guidesque" painters seem primitive by comparison, he foreshadowed the course painting would take in the first half of the century that lay ahead.[2] Yet his new vision was so startling that another decade passed before it was welcomed in Siena. When that happened, however, Duccio at once became the city's premier painter and gathered into his orbit painters who would spread his idiom such that it came to occupy the place of prestige previously held by the "Guidesque" style. Almost until the master's death, in 1317/18, he and his followers flooded Sienese churches and institutions with their art. Nor was the Ducciesque style entirely abandoned after Duccio's death. It lingered on for another quarter century, an undercurrent of conservatism in Sienese painting.

Most of the artists in Duccio's circle remain anonymous, identified by eponymous works, but two painters we know by name: Segna di Bonaventura and Ugolino di Nerio. The former seems to have enjoyed a modest success, although his principal surviving work was created for Castiglion Fiorentino (Fig. 12) rather than for Siena. He left two sons, Niccolò and Francesco, who carried a modified Ducciesque idiom into the 1340s. Ugolino's career was considerably more distinguished, but his greatest works were produced for Florence. Vasari says that he authored an altarpiece for the Bardi Chapel in Santa Croce, the high altarpiece for that church, and the high altarpiece for Santa Maria Novella. Portions of the polyptych from the high altar of Santa Croce, painted c.1325, survive (Fig. 13). Ugolino undoubtedly worked also in Siena, but there opportunities were limited, since civic patronage, from the middle of the second decade of the Trecento, had shifted to Simone Martini, an artist who was born c.1280 and survived until 1344.

From the moment, in 1315, when Simone frescoed his *Maestà* for the Sala del Mappamondo of the recently completed Palazzo Pubblico (Color Plates 3–4) until he moved from Siena to the papal court in Avignon (c.1335–36), the artist was the quasi-official painter of the commune. But he was and did much more. The head of a workshop of considerable size, he was able to produce works for Pisa, Orvieto, Naples, Assisi, and Florence, and to forge a remarkably coherent stylistic idiom among his disciples, associates, and then followers. While he remained in Siena, Simone and his shop made his style common currency; after his removal to Avignon, the shop continued for a decade or so to provide Siena and other central Italian cities with images. Among early Sienese painters, Simone was the most famed and the most international—if we take that term to refer to places outside Sienese territory. Ghiberti, in *I commentarii,* tells us that a century after his death, the painters of Siena still regarded him as their most glorious predecessor. With justice, Ghiberti did not share that view.

As had happened in the time of Duccio, so Simone came to dominate civic commis-

---

2. See chapter III in my *Painting in the Age of Giotto* (University Park, Pa., 1997) for a full discussion of this work.

sions, making it difficult for others to compete, even the most talented: Pietro and Ambrogio Lorenzetti. Pietro would seem to have been, more or less, Simone's contemporary; Ambrogio may have been slightly younger. Both were independent masters by the 1310s; indeed, one of Pietro's greatest works, the Passion Cycle in the Lower Church of San Francesco in Assisi, belongs to that decade. But it was only in the second half of the 1320s that Ambrogio and Pietro received major commissions in Siena. With Simone's departure for Avignon, a major impediment to both careers was removed. Each was given a major commission for Siena cathedral, and Ambrogio inherited Simone's status as quasi-official painter to the commune. Ambrogio was the more brilliant painter. His was a career of daring innovations, almost as if he viewed each work as a challenge to push painting in new directions. He was a painter of images of the Madonna and of saints, of narrative and allegorical art, but he was also the painter of a world map. His genius was entirely unique and of a very high order: something Ghiberti understood when he praised the artist as Siena's greatest master. Ambrogio had a group of assistants smaller, it would seem, than Simone's, but none of its members was capable of sustaining Ambrogio's invention, and after his death in 1348, there was no one to carry his vision forward.

During the 1330s, and in the shadow of Simone, Pietro, and Ambrogio, a younger generation made its first appearance, artists such as Lippo Vanni, Niccolò di Ser Sozzo, and Bartolommeo Bulgarini. With the deaths of Simone, Pietro, and Ambrogio during the 1340s, these artists, augmented by anonymous masters and still younger painters, became successors to the Sienese tradition. They were not destined, however, to further the pattern of radical innovation of the previous period, not even to perpetuate its most impressive aspects. Instead, they moved toward a tempered version of what I have described elsewhere as the Mannered Style, borrowing compositions and figural motifs from their predecessors, employing many a device deprived of its original purpose and effect, and generally raising the decorative quality of their images. They and their successors never lost the high craftsmanship and splendor of surface that were meaningful constituents of early-trecento painting in Siena, but rarely were they capable of welding new form and new content in the creation of works of the first order.

The painters named above all belong to the foreground of Sienese painting; as we, seven centuries later, recognize Duccio, the Lorenzetti brothers, and Simone as the great masters of the period, so too did contemporaries. Indeed, during the first half of the Trecento, the Sienese welcomed and seized upon the new, the original, with enthusiasm. But there were in Siena many other painters, who belonged to the artistic background. They were artists whose careers passed in executing minor decorative tasks and/or the occasional modest panel picture. They too deserve our attention, for if we are to understand the dynamic of early Sienese art and the status of the great masters, we must understand the context within which the latter worked. But these "minor masters" were truly secondary, living lives and following careers remote from the circumstances of the great.

The discussions to follow are intended to evoke the Sienese painter's world and his place therein. I am only indirectly concerned with works of art per se; they are used to illustrate currents of thought or aspects of technique, to provide referents for discussions of painters' incomes, to document the patronage of the commune and the fame of Sienese painters abroad. As the task demands, I examine that world as if through a telescope, at other points as if with a microscope, hoping that the combined results leave us with something approaching normal vision.

There are a number of themes that have shaped what follows and of which the reader should be aware at the outset: theses that arose first from study of the material here discussed, but now determine the character of this book. Everything indicates that the lives of Sienese painters were firmly woven into the fabric of Sienese society. By that I do not merely mean the obvious: that painters were cohabitants with their patrons and a part of civic life, but rather that their values and social ambitions were those of their fellow citizens. In their lives, the successful sought to imitate the choices of other prosperous craftsmen and even those of successful merchants. But to understand these developments, one must understand the extraordinary homogeneity of Sienese culture, the ways in which related ambitions informed political philosophy, the state's approach to pious charity, religious life, and commercial enterprises, and the ways in which the lives of the Sienese were woven into a variegated yet continuous fabric.

The chronological parameters here are approximately those of my *Painting in the Age of Giotto*. With a few minor exceptions, I focus upon the period between 1260 and 1363, the latter date marking the second outbreak of the bubonic plague in Italy, an occurrence that we now know had far greater consequence for the survivors than the plague of 1348. But it is also true that these dates correspond with the finest moments in early Sienese art, and thus this volume corresponds with the framework I shall employ in my next project, a history of early Sienese painting.

I The Painter's City

Some thirty or so miles south of Florence, Siena rises on the edge of the Chianti. As a site for a city, the location is as splendid as it is impractical. Coming and going is a matter of ascent and descent; to the north and south travel was once made arduous by the swiftly rolling landscape; and Siena's city walls had to rise and fall with the terrain. Within the city, topography is everything: streets follow hilltops, cling like so many terraces to hillsides, or rapidly rush downward to valleys among those hills and thus to the fountains that provided medieval Siena with water, never in sufficient quantity to support a cloth industry of the size that made Florence thrive.[1] Yet, in spite of disadvantages, Siena of the thirteenth and early fourteenth centuries became wealthy, and became one of the great cities of Europe.

---

1. On the entire matter of water and the history of Siena's remarkable fountains and their aqueducts, see F. Bargagli-Petrucci, *Le fonti di Siena e i loro aquedotti,* 2 vols., Florence, Siena, and Rome, 1903–6.

Three circumstances laid the foundations of Siena's prosperity. First, the city straddled one of Europe's major thoroughfares, the Via Francigena. South of Siena, that road was the most important route to Rome. North of Siena, the Via Francigena led to Lucca, Pavia, and Vercelli, then on into France and to the Champagne, the site of Europe's greatest fairs. At Vercelli, the route joined other roads, which led through Switzerland and up the Rhine and traversed the South of France, ultimately reaching Santiago di Compostella. In addition, the Via Francigena was intersected, north of Siena, by yet another major road, which led to Florence, Bologna, the Veneto, Austria, and Germany; another route led to San Gimignano and Pisa. These roads linked Siena with the rest of Europe.[2] Second, the city had access to silver mines in the nearby communities of Montieri, Roccastrada, and Montecirota. As, in the later Middle Ages, towns and trade expanded and the old barter system was replaced with a monetary economy, Europe faced a serious shortage of coinage. Siena began to mint its own silver coin c.1180, providing its citizens with the means to conduct business at home and abroad.[3] But neither the site of Siena nor its mineral resources would have mattered had it not been for a third factor in the city's history: the rise of an entrepreneurial spirit that created a class of merchant bankers who would found the city's wealth, a wealth that continued, for a time, even after the Sienese had largely withdrawn from international trade and banking.

The city that greets the modern visitor still echoes that long-ago prosperity; few other Tuscan cities are so evocative of those early times. Many of the streets follow courses set seven centuries ago, and often their widths reflect fourteenth-century legislation. One may still discover the remains of fortified towers, now embedded in later architecture, that once rose above the city's silhouette in proud statement of their owners' wealth and prestige. Around the city, in a semicircle that sweeps from west to south to east, one finds the sites of convents and churches that once belonged to the new mendicant orders that came to Siena in the thirteenth century. But it is perhaps at the city's center that we feel most in touch with the distant world that is here my subject.

On the southeast side of the Campo, one of the most beautiful squares in all Italy, rises the Palazzo Pubblico (Fig. 2), the heart of civic government, built between c.1297 and 1310. From the Campo, the land rises quickly to the highest hilltop of the city and the district known as Castelvecchio, the place of the city's origin. There stands the cathedral (Figs. 3–4), banded by white and dark green marble, with a facade adorned in the late Dugento by the sculpture of Giovanni Pisano and his shop. Next to the duomo's south flank, and partially attached to it, are the remains of an unfinished dream, the Duomo Nuovo, that would have made the nave and choir of the original cathedral merely transepts to one of the largest churches in Christendom. Facing Giovanni's facade is the Ospedale di

2. O. Muzzi, R. Stopani, and T. Szabo, *La Valdelsa, la Via Francigena e gli itinerari per Roma e Compostella,* Poggibonsi and San Gimignano, 1988; R. Stopani, *La Via Francigena in Toscana,* Florence, 1984. Both works have extensive bibliographies.

3. C. M. Cipolla, "Per un profilo di storia economica senese," in F. Cardini et al., *Banchieri e mercanti di Siena,* Rome, 1987, 11.

Santa Maria della Scala, the city's grandest charitable institution, devoted to tending the sick, providing accommodation for pilgrims, and caring for foundlings. And if the modern visitor should climb the impressive, incomplete facade of the Duomo Nuovo, he might gaze far to the south and west, across those rolling lands that were once the center of the Sienese state.

The world these structures and circumstances evoke was home to the greater and lesser painters that are the subjects of this study. We shall encounter a few instances of painters native to Siena who moved elsewhere; we shall encounter many occasions when Sienese painters worked in "foreign" places, away from the city; but in large measure Sienese painters remained quite decidedly Sienese, living, working, and dying in the city of their birth. And to a quite remarkable degree, they shaped and were shaped by the Sienese artistic tradition, a tradition that in the first half of the fourteenth century ranked as one of the finest in Europe. If we are to understand the circumstances that made that tradition possible, the conditions under which painters worked and thrived, and the public institutions that so often provided patronage for painters, we must know something of the city, its history, and its citizenry.[4]

The Background

When the thirteenth century began, the Sienese commune was young. It had first declared its independence from the long-standing rule of the local bishop in 1167; by 1179, it had its own constitution; and its right of self-government was confirmed by Frederick Barbarossa, Holy Roman Emperor, in 1186. The twelfth century had also seen significant expansions of the urban fabric. Toward the middle of that century, the city walls were extended from the confines of Castelvecchio to the east, to encompass those areas now occupied by the Campo and the Palazzo Pubblico, and to the north, taking in a long stretch of the Via Francigena that reached to the hamlet of Camollia. Between 1150 and 1220, the latter area was widened on the east to create the Terzo di Camollia; the walls at the southeast were extended to include Castel Montone, which became the center of the Terzo di San Martino;

4. For general discussions of the city and its history: A. Lisini and F. Iacometti, eds., *Chronache Senesi*, in *Rerum Italicarum Scriptores*, n.s., XV, pt. VI, Bologna, 1931–37; O. Malavolti, *Dell'historia di Siena*, 3 vols. in 1, Venice, 1599 (reprint: Bologna, 1968); Giugurta Tommasi, *Dell'historie di Siena*, 2 vols. in 1, Venice, 1625–26 (reprint: Bologna, 1973); L. Douglas, *Storia della Repubblica di Siena*, Siena, 1926 (reprint: Rome, 1969); G. Martini, "Siena da Montaperti alla caduta dei Nove (1260–1355)," *BSSP*, LXVIII, 1961, 75–128; William M. Bowsky, *The Finance of the Commune of Siena, 1287–1355*, Oxford, 1970; Duccio Balestracci and Gabriella Piccinni, *Siena nel trecento: Assetto urbano e strutture edilizie*, Florence, 1977; J. Hook, *Siena: A City and Its History*, London, 1979; William M. Bowsky, *A Medieval Italian Commune: Siena Under the Nine, 1287–1355*, Berkeley and Los Angeles, 1981; L. Bortolotti, *La città nella storia d'Italia: Siena*, Rome, 1982; Daniel Waley, *Siena and the Sienese in the Thirteenth Century*, Cambridge, 1991.

and on the southwest, the walls of Castelvecchio were pushed further south as an enlargement of the Terzo di Città. These "thirds"—the Terzo di Camollia, the Terzo di San Martino, and the Terzo di Città—were to remain the basic units of the city, each subdivided into parishes (*popoli*) and tax districts (*lire*).[5]

The twelfth- and early-thirteenth-century expansions were enormously ambitious and embodied a confidence in, and optimism about, the city's future—even more so the expansion of the mid–thirteenth century. When, at that time, the areas of the Vallepiatta and the Church of San Domenico were brought within the city walls to the northwest and suburbs were added on the southeast, Siena reached the size it would remain until 1326—although the population would more than double in the intervening years. Or, to view the situation from the opposite direction, the Sienese by c.1250 had created a city more than twice the size needed at that time.

By the early thirteenth century, a number of Sienese companies had entered the arena of international trade, buying in Venice spices and other luxury goods from the East and taking them north for sale at the fairs of Champagne. There, Sienese merchants acquired cloth for finishing and wool, which was sent to Siena, turned into cloth, and then exported to other regions of the Mediterranean. So extensive was Sienese business at the fairs of Champagne that the local count took the Sienese under his protection in 1222 and authorized their banking operations. For, early on, Sienese merchants realized that international banking promised to be among the most profitable ventures. Throughout the thirteenth century, they would establish offices across Europe and in England, making loans to kings, nobles, ecclesiastics, and trading ventures, and transferring funds by means of the equivalent of the modern bank draft, thereby avoiding the dangers attendant upon the physical transport of coin. It was, however, when Sienese firms became bankers to the pope that they rose to preeminence.[6]

The papacy of the thirteenth century was plagued with demands upon its resources. It had the Papal States, made a reality by Innocent III, to govern, the battle with Frederick II to win, subsequently the campaigns of Charles I of Anjou to finance, and the cost of Europe's largest and most sophisticated bureaucracy to bear. All this meant that the popes needed to enhance revenues, by imposing general taxes on the clergy and by enforcing the elaborate system of tithes, dues, and fees owing to Rome. And in furthering its ambition of European hegemony, the papacy needed means of transferring funds across Europe. In short, the popes needed a banker, and a banker not subject to the potential turbulence of the Roman citizenry. The Sienese, for reasons of location and experience, were perfectly suited. By 1233, the Piccolomini were part of a firm headed by Angeliero Solafico, who, under

---

5. On the construction of the city walls and for maps of the various stages of development, see Balestracci and Piccinni, *Siena nel trecento,* 17–37, map 2, and Bortolotti, *Siena,* 27–31, figs. 14–16.

6. For the history of Sienese trade and banking, see L. Zdekauer, *Il mercante senese nel dugento,* Siena, 1925; Cardini et al., *Banchieri;* Edward English, *Enterprise and Liability in Sienese Banking, 1230–1350,* Cambridge, Mass., 1988. English provides a good bibliography.

Gregory IX (1227–41), became one of the first designated papal bankers.[7] Under Innocent IV (1243–54), the Bonsignori assumed that role; between 1250 and 1270 they were the chief bankers to the papacy. Indeed, during the reign of Urban IV (1261–64), all pontifical taxes were deposited with the Bonsignori.[8] Although the prominence of the Bonsignori and other Sienese firms declined after the 1260s, Nicholas III (1277–80), Honorius IV (1285–87), and Nicholas IV (1288–92) employed Sienese firms for at least some transactions.[9]

If Rome and Champagne were two focal points for Sienese banking and commerce, that is not to say that Sienese firms were absent elsewhere.[10] The Salimbeni and the Bonsignori were active in England as early as 1228–29 and had permanent establishments in London by 1250. By the end of the century, the Gallerani had a share of English business, which they retained into the early years of the Trecento. By the mid–thirteenth century, the Bonsignori had agencies or affiliations in Pisa, Bologna, Genoa, Marseilles, and Paris. The Piccolomini were also established in Marseilles, in the Veneto, and in Germany. Records of an unidentified Sienese company during the period 1277 to 1282 indicate that firm had offices in Florence, Pisa, Massa, Perugia, Ancona, Orvieto, Viterbo, Rome, and Naples. We have very little evidence concerning the companies associated with the Tolomei, but the family was active in commerce and banking by the mid-century and, given later records of the early Trecento, must have been one of the major firms.[11] There are some, albeit limited, indications that the Sienese were active in the Levant. Sienese bankers in Acre made loans to Louis IX during his first crusade; we know that Sienese bankers were established in the port of Glarentsa in southwestern Greece.[12] Some individuals from Siena are recorded as having been in the East. In May of 1264, the Franciscan Ranierio da Siena was sent on a mission to the emperor Michael VIII in Constantinople, and in January of 1279 Nicholas III dispatched a mission to Constantinople that included Fra Bartolommeo da Siena, the Franciscan provincial minister of Syria.[13]

Remarkably enough, the story of Sienese thirteenth-century banking and trade is only indirectly the story of a rising middle class. The entrepreneurial spirit was first most

7. M. Cassandro, "La banca senese nei secoli XIII e XIV," in Cardini et al., *Banchieri*, 131.

8. Cassandro, "La banca senese," 124.

9. English (*Enterprise and Liability*, 103) points out that after the failure of the Bonsignori firm the papacy claimed that it had never received 80,000 florins deposited with the Bonsignori during the reign of Nicholas IV (1288–92).

10. For the following, see Cassandro, "La banca senese," 113–14, 124, 131, and M. Tangheroni, "Siena e il commercio internazionale bel duecento a nel trecento," in Cardini et al., *Banchieri*, 76–78, 85, 89.

11. See G. Pinto, *I Tolomei, banchieri di Siena: La parabola di un casato nel xiii e xvi secolo*, Siena, 1995.

12. K. Setton, ed., *A History of the Crusades*, II, London, 1969, 273.

13. K. Setton, *The Papacy and the Levant, 1204–1571*, I, Philadelphia, 1976, 100, 129–32. We also have record of an early-trecento case of a Sienese merchant, Vieri del fu Cola di Oliviero Barote, who had acquired various items, including sugar and spices, in the Levant but was robbed by Genoese pirates. (The cargo was worth a great deal, some 7,424 florins.) See L. Catoni, "La brutta avventura di un mercante senese nel 1309 e una questione di rappresaglia," *Archivio storico italiano*, CXXXII, 1976, 65–78.

lively not among the new urban families but rather among the old noble families whose members adapted to a changing world with great perspicacity and success. The Piccolomini, the Bonsignori, the Tolomei, the Malavolti, the Salimbeni, the Saracini, the Squarcilupi, the Gallerani: these were the magnate houses that dominated Sienese commercial and financial life through the Dugento. But the nature of Sienese firms also provided opportunity for others. Most firms were joint-venture companies, established for a fixed period (often three years); although the principal partners were from the magnate class, there was room for other investors. Thus, through the course of the thirteenth century, there arose a prosperous upper middle class, self-identified in the rather misleading terms of *popolo* or *popolani*. This group had nothing to do with the general population; it was a citizen elite that often did business with the nobility and married into noble families. This was the group that came to be known as the Noveschi, after the founding of the regime administered by the Council of the Nine, the Nove, in 1287.

International banking and business were, of course, subject to international politics and, in Siena's case, the favor of the reigning pope. A gradual withdrawal of papal patronage in the last third of the Dugento, papal policies in Italy, disputes between the papacy and the French monarchy, and war between England and France imposed great strains on Sienese firms.[14] The story of the late-thirteenth-century financial crisis and of the concatenation of factors that created it has been well told by Edward English and need not concern us here.[15] The results of the crisis, however, are pertinent to the history of Siena during the first half of the Trecento. By 1298, the Bonsignori faced severe difficulties, which led, eleven years later, to bankruptcy. Four years after that the Tolomei failed, quickly followed by the Malavolti.[16] Although some firms continued foreign business well into the Trecento, essentially the great days of Sienese banking were over.[17] Ironically enough, for both the city and its painters, the result was positive. Throughout the Dugento, the major firms had made loans to the commune; now a much larger percentage of capital once put at risk far beyond Siena's walls found its way into more secure local investments, into loans to the commune.

What of the city that was home to the thirteenth-century merchant bankers? It must have been a study in dramatic contrasts. The areas close to the cathedral and those near the center of the city, around the Church of San Cristoforo, were distinguished by the houses and warehouses of the magnate families. Usually constructed of stone and attached to tall towers of the kind we today still see in San Gimignano, these impressive establishments were surrounded by dwellings of much humbler character. The latter might be construc-

14. For the involvement of Sienese bankers in papal policy 1254–1343, see N. Housley, *The Italian Crusades: The Papal Angevin Alliance and the Crusades Against Christian Lay Powers, 1254–1343*, Oxford, 1982, 161, 208, 224, 226, 229, 232, 239, 240.

15. English, *Enterprise and Liability*.

16. These bankruptcies were part of a larger economic crisis, in the early years of the Trecento, that saw the failure of banks in Lucca, Pistoia, and Florence, as well as in Siena.

17. The financial crises of the early Trecento did not spell financial ruin for all of the families involved. The Tolomei and the Bonsignori remained exceedingly wealthy after the collapse of their firms. Indeed, most of the great magnate families remained prosperous.

tions in which wood predominated; there was perhaps some use of brick; there were houses of *terra murata* (loam); and around the exterior of the city's walls were shanties of the very poor.[18] The width of streets was established by law. The *strade,* such as the section of the Via Francigena that ran through the city, were to be ten or twelve braccia wide (about twenty-four feet); the *vie,* secondary streets, were to be six braccia in width. But civic regulations allowed proprietors to build loggias and balconies out over the street to a maximum of one-third the width of the thoroughfare (Color Plate 7 and Fig. 14). Thus it was possible that in some cases balconies from opposite buildings could cover two-thirds of the street. A passage in the 1290 statutes of the General Road Commissioners describes the street leading to the Church of San Francesco as so overbuilt that at funeral processions the friars had to lower the cross at an angle to get it through.[19] It also seems that the history of the city left it with small, dark alleyways. The same statutes describe the street leading to the Abbey of San Donato as very narrow and dark. In a number of cases where such alleys posed danger during the night, the Nove were to install iron gates at either end so they could be sealed off after dark. Originally, major arteries were paved with stone, but by the late Dugento work was under way to provide the *strade* and the *vie* that fed into the *strade* with paving of brick.

During the thirteenth century, the architecture of government consisted only of the mint and the customs house, structures later incorporated in the foundations of the Palazzo Pubblico (Fig. 2). Government officials lived in rented accommodations and there exercised their office. General meetings of council, wherein large numbers were gathered, occurred in churches. During the Dugento, the most favored church for such meetings was that of San Cristoforo, although San Pellegrino and even, on occasion, the cathedral were also used for General Council meetings. The podestà often conducted business from San Pellegrino, while the Curia del Placito, the council charged with all matters pertaining to orphaned minors, met at San Cristoforo. The city's first efforts to create a *studium generale* were located in the Church of San Vigilio, later in that of San Pietro a Ovile.[20] It was only after the advent of the regime of the Noveschi that secular, civic architecture beyond the city's walls and fountains became a concern.

One further aspect of life in thirteenth-century Siena deserves note: for just slightly more than two-thirds of the century, Siena's allegiance was Ghibelline. Thus, while the banking houses were in service of the pope, the city's policies were pro-imperial. Indeed, Siena's most famous military triumph over the Florentines, the battle of Montaperti (1260), was a victory for the supporters of the Hohenstaufen. When that cause was lost, after the defeat of Sienese forces at the battle of Colle Val d'Elsa (1269), it was only a matter of time

---

18. Waley, *Siena,* 6–10.
19. D. Ciampoli and T. Szabó, *Viabilità e legislazione di uno stato cittadino del dugento: Lo Statuto dei Viari di Siena,* Siena, 1992, 49.
20. L. Zdekauer, *La vita pubblica dei senesi nel dugento,* Siena, 1897 (reprint: Bologna, 1967), 73; G. Prunai, "Lo studio senese dalle origini alla migratio bolognese sec. XIII—1321," *BSSP,* 3d ser., VIII, 1949, 53–79; IX, 1950, 3–54; M. Ascheri et al., *L'Università di Siena: 720 anni di storia,* Milan, 1991.

before Siena became Guelf. The change eventually led to the regime of the Nine (1287–1355), the regime during whose governance the finest of early Sienese painting was created.

Siena Under the Nine (1287–1355)

While international business established Siena's prosperity, the city's population grew and its institutions changed. Around 1250, Siena had a population of roughly 15,000; by c.1260 the inhabitants numbered approximately 20,000, making Siena one of the largest cities in Europe at that time. Forty years later the population had more than doubled to reach approximately 47,000. By 1328, it reached a number just over 52,000, excluding the poor, transients, and the religious population attached to convents and nunneries, and remained more or less constant until the Black Death of 1348.[21] In 1302 the number of poor was assessed at 15,000, and a document of 1307 tells us the number of friars, monks, nuns, and hermits in the city was 900.[22] The urban population constituted but a portion of the city-state. There were approximately forty-one to fifty-one communities in what was known as the Masse, the area immediately surrounding the city;[23] then, to the south and west, lay the *contado*, the communities and rural lands under Sienese rule. By the 1340s the *contado* may have had 100,000 residents.

As the city expanded, so too did the *popolo*, into whose hands government eventually passed. In 1233 half of the offices in the newly created magistracy of the Twenty-Four were reserved for the *popolo*; the same held true for the magistracy of the Thirty-Six, established in 1270. In 1277, fifty-three magnate families, known as the Casati, were entirely excluded from participation in the city's magistracy, and in 1287 arose the regime of the Nine, controlled by the oligarchy of the Noveschi. This group ruled Siena with remarkable care and competence, and it ran the city as a class. The executive Council of the Nine was elected every two months, and no individual could serve another term without a hiatus of twenty months. Moreover, measures were taken to ensure that members of the same family did not occupy civic posts concurrently.[24] At least in theory, then, the system assured a fairly wide distribution of power among Noveschi families.

William Bowsky has drawn a vivid picture of the ability of the Noveschi, their

---

21. Hook, *Siena*, 17; William M. Bowsky, "The Impact of the Black Death upon Sienese Government and Society," *Speculum*, XXXIX, 1964, 5–8. Growth of population during the regime of the Nine was in part the result of immigration. See William M. Bowsky, "Medieval Citizenship: The Individual and the State in the Commune of Siena, 1287–1355," *Studies in Medieval and Renaissance History*, IV, 1967, 193–243.

22. Waley, *Siena*, 25–26, 135–36. There was also a small number of slaves in the city-state. Bowsky, "Medieval Citizenship," 234–35.

23. The population of the Masse is uncertain. See Bowsky, *Medieval Italian Commune*, 11.

24. For a discussion of the organization of government under the Nine, the various offices, officials, and their duties, see Bowsky, *Medieval Italian Commune*, 23–116.

concern for civic institutions, their civic pride, their willingness to tax themselves for the benefit of the commune, and their uncommon financial skills. Undoubtedly because they were merchant bankers, they generally provided Siena with what has been until recently the elusive ambition of all modern governments, a balanced budget; and that accomplishment was truly extraordinary, for civic expenditure could fluctuate wildly. War meant sudden, vast expense.[25] Often the regime extended hold over its territories by buying the rights to castles, even towns, when opportunity arose. At various moments judged propitious, the commune poured exceedingly large sums into the hope of providing Siena with a major university. Even after the plague of 1348, when the city had been devastated by the loss of nearly half its population, the Nove managed to restore civic finances and again approached a perfect balance of revenues and expenditures.

The Noveschi were almost continually active in public works. Their concern with the urban fabric was such that by 1300 there were three hundred statutes dealing with the development of the city, and by 1309 it was forbidden to erect any building in the city without official approval.[26] The Opera del Duomo fell under communal jurisdiction and was funded by the state, so that alterations to the fabric of the cathedral and its interior embellishment were generally civic expenses. Between roughly 1297 and 1310, the Noveschi built the Palazzo Pubblico, to which, following 1325, they added new prisons, a new meeting hall, and the Torre del Mangia. After 1348, they funded the building on the Campo of a chapel attached to the facade of the Palazzo Pubblico as an offering of thanks to the Virgin for driving the plague from their midst. After 1326, there was a continuing project to expand the city walls; in 1346 it became necessary to extend the walls in all three major districts; and throughout the regime there was an extensive endeavor to pave streets and other public places. The Campo received paving in stages between 1333 and 1349.[27] Areas for markets were established. Water supply, that eternal Sienese problem, was a civic responsibility; the Nine were in charge of the fountains and the elaborate system of underground aqueducts that brought water to the various fountains. In 1347, water was finally brought to the Campo for what later became the Fonte Gaia: an astonishing accomplishment given the height of the Campo from valleys and water sources below. The commune also controlled the baths at Macerato and Petriolo as well as smaller spas south of the city, resorts that were a source of communal revenues as well as a pleasure for Siena's citizens and foreign visitors.

The regime was keenly interested in what we would call urban planning. As work began on the Palazzo Pubblico, the Nove passed (May 1297) an ordinance that required all new houses and palaces facing the Campo to have windows with columns and to have no balconies, presumably with the intention of making windows resemble those planned for

25. Bowsky (*Finance,* 45) points out that the campaign that ended in the taking of Montemassi, in 1328, lasted seven months and eleven days and cost the commune 100,000 florins (£335,000). This kind of extraordinary expense was not infrequent.

26. Hook, *Siena,* 27–28.

27. See E. Guidoni, *Il Campo di Siena,* Rome, 1971, and L. Franchina, ed., *Piazza del Campo: Evoluzione di una immagine, documenti, vicende ricostruzioni,* Siena, 1983.

the Palazzo Pubblico. In the vernacular version of the constitution, prepared in 1309–10, they imposed limitations on how far steps or benches or sales tables could extend into the Campo and along city streets. Streets were to be paved in brick, and citizens having houses of *terra murata* facing on the streets were required to face those houses with brick.[28]

One of the most important ambitions that the Nove inherited and were to pursue was the creation of a university, or *studium generale* in Siena.[29] As early as the 1240s, the city was home to a provincial *studium* with schools of jurisprudence, Latin grammar, and medicine. It seems this institution soon went into decline, for c.1264 an unsuccessful attempt was made to revive it. Then, in 1275, the General Council of Siena discussed and approved a petition to found a *studium generale*. Officials were appointed for the purpose, but the necessary sanction from the pope or from the emperor for the creation of a university was not forthcoming. During the early years of the Noveschi regime, the city was again home to schools of grammar, medicine, and law. The Nine's most important intervention in this matter came in 1321, when a crisis arose at the University of Bologna. In hope of attracting both masters and students from Bologna, the commune approved the expenditure of 6,000 florins to cover the cost of bringing those students and masters to Siena. For most, their stay in Siena was short; they largely returned to Bologna when the crisis there ended; but Gherardo da Parma remained, occupying the chair of philosophy and logic. Another attempt to create a *studium generale* was made in 1338–39, but that long-sought institution came only later to the city.

The fabric of Siena today bears eloquent witness to the efforts and management of the Noveschi, but if we want a still more vivid image of the city in the Trecento, we need only look to the works of painters who in their depictions of architecture seem to have been remarkably accurate, reflecting the buildings of their city. The most famous representation of contemporary architecture is, of course, Ambrogio Lorenzetti's ideal city as depicted in the fresco *The Effects of Good Government* in the Palazzo Pubblico (Color Plates 5–6). We see there a scholar lecturing to students, shoemakers with their wares on display, goldsmiths at work, and a panorama of urban architecture wherein potted plants bloom on window sills and the occasional bird cage hangs in an open window. The buildings reflect a wide variety of architectural forms: stone towers of the magnates, projecting balconies and oriels, an upper-storey loggia with an interior wall painted in geometrical design, a palace(?) wherein the second and third storeys are cantilevered beyond the facades at ground level, crenellated buildings, projecting roofs attached to the sides of structures, and extensive use of rose to indicate that specific buildings, like the city walls and gate, are made of brick.[30]

There are other images that provide us with reflections of Sienese architecture, in particular Simone Martini's record of posthumous miracles by the Beato Agostino Novello

---

28. For further discussion of city planning and its relation to contemporary notions of beauty, see "A Sense of Beauty/A Sense of Order" in Chapter v.

29. See note 20 above.

30. A fine set of color illustrations, with many details, of these frescoes may be found in E. Castelnuovo, ed., *Ambrogio Lorenzetti: Il buon governo*, Milan, 1995.

(Color Plates 7, 8, and Fig. 14) and, from the cathedral *Maestà*, Duccio's image of Christ's healing of the man born blind (Fig. 15). In Simone's image (Fig. 14), we behold an entire series of oriels projecting from houses on either side of the street. Duccio's panel (Fig. 15) provides us with glimpses of the wooden shutters used to close windows and of an enclosed but exterior cantilevered staircase.[31] One of the most unusual features of the building behind Christ is the second-storey court open to the sky, a form also depicted by Simone in his frescoes for the Saint Martin's Chapel in San Francesco, Assisi. We might be inclined to dismiss the structure as a flight of fancy by the painter, but a later document describing an expensive house in the parish of San Desiderio in Siena suggests that such arrangements existed.[32]

The city was, of course, only the heart of the Sienese state; the Noveschi also devoted close attention and vast resources to expansion of the *contado*. Sometimes by battle, sometimes by purchase, they pushed the state south and west, into the lands of the great feudatories of the region, the Aldobrandeschi counts of Santa Fiore and the Pannocchieschi. In some cases, as at Paganico, the Sienese established new communities. And in September of 1303, Siena purchased Talamone from the monastery of San Salvatore of Montamiata, hoping thereby to create a major seaport within its territories. Although very large sums were spent on the project, and although the Noveschi repeatedly launched new projects for the town (Fig. 5), Talamone never became what Siena wanted; it remained an unfulfilled aspiration.

To read many accounts of Siena in the Trecento is to discover a world that seems quite modern, a city we would easily recognize and understand should we be transported to that time and place. It is true that management of the city had all the efficiency of that in twentieth-century towns, and there were many aspects of life in Siena that we would commend. In addition to the public works mentioned above, the city had its equivalents of a police force and of fire brigades; it even had an equivalent of fire insurance, since the commune assumed the cost of replacing structures destroyed by fire. But life in fourteenth-century Tuscany was prey to vicissitudes that would alarm us. Famine and disease were all too familiar. Siena suffered from food shortages and disease in 1295–97, 1303, 1306–7, 1308–10, 1318–19, 1323–24, 1328–30, 1339–40, 1346–47, and 1352, not to mention the Black Death of 1348.[33] There was also much to urban life that we would find objectionable. Although Sienese justice was biased in favor of those who could pay fines in lieu of corporal punishment, its underlying principle was "an eye for an eye, a tooth for a tooth." A thief was likely to lose his hand, a false witness his tongue, and a man convicted of sodomy to be hung by his member in the marketplace.[34] In spite of the best efforts to control the city's

31. During the fourteenth century, exterior staircases were not permitted. Since this staircase does not extend to ground level, perhaps it was a way of getting around the prohibition.

32. Balestracci and Piccinni, *Siena nel trecento*, 84. Balestracci and Piccinni provide a very good discussion of private dwellings in the city (pages 77–101).

33. Bowsky, *Finance*, 31–32.

34. William M. Bowsky, "The Medieval Commune and Internal Violence: Police Power and Public Safety in Siena, 1287–1355," *American Historical Review*, LXXIII, no. 1, 1967, 1–17.

sanitation, we would be unhappy with pigs that were originally used to clear the Campo after market days and with the lack of any system to deal with human waste. Many of us would have great difficulty daily facing the poor. Nor would we be happy with the plight of unwanted children. The fine for exposing an unwanted infant was only £10; an inscription still in Siena tells us that in 1298 the Hospital of the Scala took in over three hundred foundlings. Conflicts and vendettas among the magnate families too often brought disturbance to the city; and we would be appalled by the frequency of wars and other armed conflicts in which the Sienese were involved. Most of us today would also find trecento Siena oppressively overregulated; the long arm of Sienese government touched almost every facet of urban life. There were sumptuary laws, building codes, set tariffs on import and export, a night curfew, standardized measures, forced loans to the commune. The list could go on. As early as 1257 there were 860 public offices in the city: watchmen, customs and toll agents, tax assessors, officials to supervise inns, grain, salt, the use of fountains, and the use and size of streets. Under the Nine these offices grew significantly in number.

The endless legislation that the Noveschi passed in hope of managing the city surely reflects the concerns and suspicions raised by the novel experience of having so many people gathered in such a small area. The expansion of the urban population was largely the result of immigration from the countryside, and the change must have left many with a sense of dislocation and with at least initial fear of their neighbors. But much of that legislation is also a tacit acknowledgment that violence and criminality permeated Siena during the regime of the Nine. There were, as we shall see, institutions within the city that were critical to providing a sense of shared place in urban society, but regulation must have seemed to the Noveschi the best assurance of order. That said, the Nine's concept of all-encompassing legislation was an ambition inherited from earlier regimes in Siena. In 1262, the original constitution of Siena was replaced by a weighty document of 1,095 rubrics, and that document was enlarged twice by the Nove, once in 1309–10 and again in 1337–39.[35] For most of us, conditioned by the modern conception of a constitution as the foundation for law and a statement of principles, the Sienese constitution may seem odd. It is at once a much more fluid and a much more detailed document, containing what we view as normal legislation; indeed, it is essentially a compilation of legislation that touches on both major and minor affairs, including things as specific as the number of bricks to be given to various religious orders for construction of their churches and convents.

The history of government necessarily focuses on the Noveschi, and there is more to be said regarding that group, but too exclusive attention to the upper middle class would distort the character of Sienese society at large. Although the magnate families, the Casati, were legally excluded from membership on the Council of the Nine, their role in Sienese life was by no means minor. Members of several magnate families did indeed sit among

---

35. L. Zdekauer, ed., *Il constituto del comune di Siena dell'anno 1262,* Milan, 1897; A. Lisini, ed., *Il costituto del comune di Siena volgarizzato nel* MCCCIX–MCCCX, 2 vols., Siena, 1903. The 1337–39 redaction has not been published. It is ASS, *Statuti, Siena,* 26.

the Nine, and the Casati were related to the Noveschi through marriage and commercial transactions.[36] Moreover, the Casati were not excluded from the Merchants' Guild, the Mercanzia, which played an important and powerful role in Sienese government.[37] The magnates often numbered among the provisors (*provveditori*) of the state treasury or served in other official posts. They sometimes acted as ambassadors for the commune and were frequently entrusted with military operations.[38] The Casati had great interest in the safety and prosperity of the city. In spite of the failures of the great banking companies, a modern survey of property assessments in some twenty-seven tax districts of Siena, compiled in 1316–20, shows that the Bonsignori, the Salimbeni, and the Gallerani owned approximately 20 percent of all real estate in the city.[39]

Several Sienese institutions provided place for the magnates. With the exception of a single decade, the bishopric of Siena was in the hands of the Malavolti from 1282 to 1371, and the canonry of the cathedral was dominated by members of the old families. Between 1314 and 1339 the rector of the prestigious Ospedale di Santa Maria della Scala was Giovanni di Tese Tolomei. His predecessor, Ristoro di Giunta Menghi (1294–1313) had married into the Tolomei, and Giovanni was followed by Mino di Cino Ughi (1340–51), who came from a family no less noble than the Tolomei.[40] A member of the Casati, Bulgarino di Simone Bulgarini, father to the painter Bartolommeo Bulgarini, was rector of the hospital of the Misericordia between 1330 and 1332.

Emphasis on civic institutions and civic accomplishment may lead us to think of the Noveschi and the Casati as essentially urban. Nothing could be further from the truth. During the thirteenth century, the magnate families had acquired castles and lands south of Siena, initially as a means of establishing bases of power beyond the city's walls and thus beyond the impact of civic politics.[41] At the time when the magnates were bankers to the pope but Siena's allegiance Ghibelline, there were many good reasons to assure independence from the vagaries of communal sentiment. But the vast estates also gave the magnates power over foodstuffs, particularly grain, an essential commodity in a society that often suffered from shortages produced by bad weather or excessive demand. Rural holdings also assured self-sufficiency. With the decline of international business, investment in property became even more important. Thus, in spite of the large percentage of urban real estate owned by the Casati, for most of the magnates their rural holdings were far larger and far more valuable. The same, remarkably enough, was true for the Noveschi. The Noveschi had greater real estate investments outside the city than within. The *Table of Possessions*, fifty

36. See, for example, A. Carniani, *I Salimbeni, quasi una signoria,* Siena, 1995, 197–202.

37. See the discussion of the Mercanzia below, in "The Guilds of Siena."

38. See Waley, *Siena,* 75–86.

39. Giovanni Cherubini, *Signori, contadini, borghesi: Ricerche sulla società italiana del basso medioevo,* Florence, 1974, 249–51.

40. See the list of rectors of the Ospedale della Scala at the conclusion of the hospital's statutes (1318–79) in L. Banchi and F.-L. Polidori, eds., *Statuti senesi scritti in volgare ne' secoli xiii e xiv,* III, Bologna, 1877.

41. G. Pino, "I mercanti e la terra," in Cardini et al., *Banchieri,* 236; Cherubini, *Signori, contadini, borghesi.*

volumes of assessments for tax purposes compiled between 1316 and 1320, shows that of the one hundred and twenty Noveschi and their relations who were assessed, all but three held land outside the city. Of seventy-seven Noveschi and their relatives who served in the Concistoro, all but one had rural investments worth two to twenty times their urban holdings, which were in fact minimal. Fourteen members of this sample group had real estate only outside Siena.[42] It is no wonder that half of Ambrogio's *Effects of Good Government* (Color Plate 6) was given over to depicting the countryside; Siena was ruled by what was in fact a rural gentry, and its life and institutions were often influenced by a rural nobility. The city's situation might thus be likened to that of London or Dublin in the eighteenth century. It is a circumstance that makes the care and attention devoted to the city proper all the more impressive.

Civic Christianity

Siena was the city of the Virgin. It was the Virgin who had guarded the city and, through miraculous intervention, assured its victory over the Florentines at the battle of Montaperti (1260). Thus the city was dedicated to her; she was its liege lady. The cathedral and the Ospedale della Scala were named in her honor, as were a number of other churches, charitable institutions, and confraternities. Imagery related to the Virgin was to abound in the Palazzo Pubblico as well as in the cathedral and in the Ospedale di Santa Maria della Scala. The city held great festivities to mark her feast days, the most important of which was the feast of the Assumption (15 August). On that day, all subject territories acknowledged their dependence on Siena by presenting wax for candles and banners to the cathedral.[43] The constitution of 1309–10 required every citizen from age eighteen to seventy to come to the duomo on the vigil of that feast.

It is this mingling of church and state, this "civic Christianity," that, at the end of the twentieth century, we may find among the most peculiar aspects of Sienese life. The constitutions of 1262 and 1309–10 open with dozens of rubrics that touch on a wide variety of religious matters, and their diversity indicates the complex and extensive interrelations between the civic government and the faith. In the 1262 redaction, at least fifteen rubrics deal directly with the affairs of the cathedral, touching matters as various as the structure of the Opera del Duomo (the cathedral works), the provisioning of building materials and of candles for the high altar, and the procedures to be followed in the event of an episcopal vacancy. Nineteen rubrics deal with the Ospedale della Scala, although the hospital had been founded by the cathedral canons and jurisdiction was a matter of intense debate. Here

---

42. William M. Bowsky, "The *Buon Governo* of Siena (1287–1355): A Medieval Italian Oligarchy," *Speculum*, XXXVII, 1962, 375–76.

43. Sometimes large wax candles to be presented to the duomo were decorated. Sometimes the wax from dependent communities was presented in boxes that had been decorated by painters.

again, the matters discussed were wide-ranging, dealing with everything from the alienation of hospital property, and the administration of legacies to that institution, to the annual provision of lime and fifteen thousand bricks for construction. Grants to parish churches and the religious orders were numerous: £50 for the Dominicans, twenty-five thousand bricks for the sisters of Santa Petronilla, fifty thousand bricks for the Servites, and ten thousand for the Carmelites. The commune also signaled its protection of these and other religious and charitable foundations. Four rubrics deal with heresy and the punishment of heretics.

By 1309–10, the number and content of such rubrics had been greatly enlarged. The annual cost of alms and building materials in these provisions exceeded £2,500. The provisions of the 1337–39 redaction of the constitution have been succinctly summarized. They

> listed by name twenty-four monasteries that were to receive a total of £630 a year, nineteen convents to receive £550, and sixteen separate hospitals located throughout the city and state that would receive £375. In addition each holy person living in and within three miles of the city was to be given three lire a year. Other rubrics included the annual allocation of £600 for certain churches, and £300 a year for the assistance of poor prisoners. These rubrics do not include the extraordinary alms granted on special occasions and at times of unusual need.[44]

These items evidence the manner in which the state intervened in religious affairs, distributed charity, and thus co-opted the intercession, the power, of the saints. Members of the governing regime might style themselves the "Governors and Defenders of the Commune and People of Siena," but they knew that on a higher plane the Virgin and the saints were the real guarantors of Siena's peace and prosperity. As a petition of 1329 to the Nove said: "[I]t is firmly believed and hoped that the veneration of the saints that was formerly undertaken in the city of Siena by the said commune and its officials conferred many advantages upon the aforesaid commune, and brought to an end and protected the city from many evils and perils."[45] Also, in the lives of individuals, what most needed to be evoked and invoked was the power of the saints, of the "very special dead." The saints bridged the gap between now and then, between earthly sorrows and the beatitude of paradise, assuring continuity and promising that, in death, one did not but pass into "that dark night." And they did more. They acted as protectors against the evils of this life and promised the potential of miraculous intervention in sickness and in pain, in times of trouble and of despair. Each, along with the Virgin, was an ever-ready help and a vigilant defender.

The Nine often contributed to local cults and, in time, participated in the relevant feasts. They financially assisted in the burial of the Blessed Ambrogio Sansedoni (1287) and to the cost of his chapel in San Domenico.[46] In 1289, they provided an altar over the tomb

---

44. Bowsky, *Finance*, 31.

45. ASS, Consiglio Generale, 107, fol. 33v (16 February 1329), as quoted by Bowsky, *Medieval Italian Commune*, 263.

46. G. D. Urso, *Beato Ambrogio Sansedoni, 1220–1287,* Siena, 1986.

of the Blessed Pier Pettinaio in San Francesco. They sponsored the annual celebration for both these *beati*.[47] During the 1320s, the Nine made efforts to strengthen their connection to those venerated in the city. On 24 October 1326, the Consiglio Generale discussed and passed a measure whereby the commune, in perpetuity, would provide £25 worth of lights for the feast of San Ansano.[48] Then, in the winter and spring of 1329, came a series of decisions that went further. The Consiglio Generale, on 16 February, decreed that the government should participate in the feasts of the Beato Ambrogio and Blessed Pier Pettinaio.[49] This legislation was followed, on 20 February, by a decree that the government should participate in the feast of the Beato Agostino Novello and, on 19 April, a measure for government participation in the feast of Saint Nicholas, at the church of the Carmelites, and the feast of the Beato Giovacchino Senese, at the church of the Servites.[50]

Although the Nine seem to have distributed funds and materials to the religious orders with an even hand, there is evidence that suggests the regime had a special relation with the Dominicans. During the building of the Palazzo Pubblico, and during various phases of expansion, communal funds for these projects were kept in the sacristy of San Domenico. In 1324, 1330, and 1351, Dominicans acted as ambassadors for the Nine.[51] In 1317 and 1330, Dominicans acted as "sacristans" in connection with communal tax collection.[52] Dominicans were summoned to preach before the Nove in 1339, 1343, 1345, and 1348.[53] Finally, we note that the commune provided 103 pounds of wax, at a cost of 32 lire and 5 soldi, for the feast of Saint Thomas Aquinas in 1323, the year of his canonization.[54] The connection between the Dominicans and the government of Siena in fact antedated the regime of the Nove. As early as the late 1240s the commune's archive and seal were kept in the sacristy of the Dominican church.

From our vantage point, it seems clear that civic Christianity was a means of self-

47. Bowsky, *Medieval Italian Commune*, 263–64.

48. ASS, Consiglio Generale 103, fols. 94v–96v.

49. ASS, Consiglio Generale 107, fols. 33r–34v. Since members of the Council of the Nine were ordinarily prohibited from leaving the Palazzo Pubblico during the period of their tenure, I assume these measures constitute permission to leave the palace and participate in the feasts of these *beati*.

50. ASS, Consiglio Generale 107, fols. 39v–40v, 70v–73r. Earlier, in 1320, the council agreed to provide £30 worth of candles for the celebration of the feast of the Beato Giovacchino. The legislation concerning the Beato Agostino Novello is somewhat puzzling, since in June of 1324 the commune spent 44 lire and 18 soldi for candles for the officials attending the feast of the *beato*. ASS, Biccherna 149, fol. 156r.

See also A. Vauchez, "La commune de Sienne, les ordres mendiants et le culte des saints: Histoire et enseignements d'une crise, novembre 1328–avril 1329," *Mélanges de l'école française de Rome: Moyen Âge—temps modernes*, LXXXIX, 1977, 757–67.

51. In 1324 a "frate agustino" acted as ambassador to Florence (ASS, Biccherna 149, fol. 157r). In 1330 two Dominicans were sent on business concerning the new podestà (ASS, Biccherna 167, fol. 35v). On 23 August 1351, Fra Bartolomeo di Mino was paid for service in Pisa on "affari segreti" of the commune (Siena, BC, Spogli: MS A.VII.16, fol. 208v).

52. ASS, Biccherna 133, fol. 111r (28 February 1317); ASS, Biccherna 167, fol. 6v (20 July 1330).

53. Respectively: Siena, BC, Benvoglienti: MS C.v.5, fol. 208v; Benvoglienti: MS C.v.5, fol. 211v; Spogli: MS A.VII.16, fol. 127v; Spogli: MS A.VII.16, fol. 186v.

54. ASS, Biccherna 148, fol. 123v (17 November 1323).

validation for the commune, that the association of the state and the faith gave the former legitimacy. It gave a comparatively new institution, the commune, a place within the time-honored structure of European civilization. By making the association as direct, as immediate, as possible, it bound the state and the citizenry to the holy in a manner that partially bypassed the institutions of the Church. And while no one of the time would have seen this association as much more than appropriate, the linking of the state and the divine would, eventually, make it easier to arrive at a secular definition of the former.

Other Aspects of the Faith

If the state and the city's religious life were closely bound, if church and state mingled in a "civic Christianity," a large proportion of the population was united in the devotions of Sienese confraternities. Siena was one of the most important sites for lay brotherhoods. The oldest confraternity in Siena would seem to have been the "Fraternità della Beata Vergine e San Domenico," connected with the Dominican church of the city. Although it is highly unlikely that it originated in 1221, as it claimed and as Sigismondo Tizio (d. 1528) reported, its origins may well antedate 1260. Later it became a society of flagellants.[55] It seems that the Confraternity of the Virgin and Saint Francis was in existence by 1262. By 1274, there existed the "Compagnia di Sancta Croce," later styled "de Sancto Nicola da Tollentino sotto le volte di Sancto Augustino."[56] A "Compagnia delle laude di Maria Vergine" was associated with the Carmelite Church of San Niccolò by 1289, and by 1295 two confraternities were associated with the Ospedale di Santa Maria della Scala: the company "dei Rachomandati a Jesu Christo Crocefisso" and that "de la Vergine Maria."[57] According to G. Macchi, the archivist of the Ospedale in the late seventeenth and early eighteenth centuries, the former confraternity was created to bring together "gentiluomini, o cavalieri, o titolati."[58] Although Macchi may have aggrandized the membership of the confraternity, specific requirements of members indicate that it was not an organization for the less prosperous.

Other notices give indication of other confraternities in other locations: the "Compagnia minore dela Vergine Maria," founded in 1298 and later (1338) called "della Santissima Trinita"; the "Fraternitas fratrum minorum que vocatur Societas fratres Gualterotti" (1300); the "Fraternitas maior dictj Ovili" (1300); the "Fraternitas di S. Agostino" (1305); the "Compagnia della disciplina del beato messer Sancto Andrea Apostolo" (1320) at the church of the Umiliati; the "Compagnia di S. Maria della Misericordia" (1332); the "Fra-

---

55. G. M. Monti, *Le confraternite medievali dell'alta e media Italia*, I, Venice, 1927, 228–29. The confraternity was in existence by 1257, when the bishop of Siena granted it an indulgence.

56. Monti, *Le contraternite*, I, 231.

57. Monti, *Le confraternite*, I, 233–34.

58. G. Macchi, *Origine dello Spedale di Santa Maria della Scala di Siena*, ASS, MS D-113, fol. 22v.

ternitas del glorioso martire Sancto Ansano" (1336), which met at the hospital of Santa Croce, outside the walls but by the Camollia gate; and a confraternity of the Blessed Andrea Gallerani (1344).[59] We have some indications of the number of members in these associations. The 1316–22 account books of the Fraternity of the Virgin Mary and of Messer Saint Francis contain an entry that suggests the company had roughly forty-five members.[60] An inventory of 1325, listing the possessions of the Confraternity of the Racommandati a Jesu Cristo Crocefisso, includes 186 "cloaks of the brothers."[61] In 1271 the *oblati* of the Misericordia numbered thirty-nine; by 1324 that number had grown to seventy.[62]

The lay organizations offered a forum for individual piety and provided for an active part in religious expression that was generally lacking in traditional structures and rites of the Church. Surely, too, they somewhat cut across class divisions and thus assisted social cohesion. For example: From the statutes of the Confraternity of the Virgin, connected with the Ospedale di Santa Maria della Scala, we know that members met once a month for a chapter meeting. They were compelled to attend the confraternity's mass on Sundays, held in their own chapel, but the obligation to hear mass daily apparently could be fulfilled elsewhere. Every Friday, members met in the chapel for *disciplina,* self-flagellation. There were also occasions for public processions, when they were to carry the confraternity's banner through the streets. The *laudesi* of the Confraternity of the Blessed Virgin and Saint Dominic went in procession twelve times a year and met daily at San Domenico to sing lauds. Such regular contacts surely created and strengthened personal ties among members who may have come from varying social backgrounds.[63]

The statute of the Fraternità della Beata Vergine e San Domenico exists in a version from the 1340s and tells us that it was somewhat different from the Confraternity of the Virgin at the Ospedale.[64] It contains the usual conditions and requirements: members must hear mass daily, observe the Church's feast days and those listed in the statute, attend the funerals of other members and pray for the deceased, practice flagellation as required, and make offerings of candles as prescribed.[65] But two features distinguish the statute: there is, in chapter 21, the assumption that members will belong to a guild, and there are clear

---

59. Monti, *Le confraternite,* I, 128–30, 236, 247. Most of the dates in this list refer to the first documentary notice concerning the relevant confraternity.

60. Bowsky, *Medieval Italian Commune,* 265–66. I advance the number of members with some hesitation. The possessions of the confraternity, listed in 1316–22, include forty-five mitres. Since we do not know what these items were for, we cannot be sure that there was a mitre for each member.

61. L. Banchi, *Capitoli della Compagnia dei Disciplinati di Siena de' secoli XIII, XIV, e XV,* Siena, 1866, 75, and R. Manetti and G. Savino, "I libri dei Disciplinati di Santa Maria della Scala di Siena," *BSSP,* xcvii, 1990, 146.

62. Giuliano Catoni, "Gli oblati della Misericordia: Poveri e benefattori a Siena nella prima metà del trecento," in *La società del bisogno,* by G. Pinto, Florence, 1989, 1–17.

63. Waley, *Siena,* 150–53.

64. G. Prunai, "I capitoli della Compagnia di S. Domenico in Campo Regio," *BSSP,* XLVII, 1940, 117–56.

65. In common with the regulations of other confraternities, members were not allowed to belong to any other confraternity.

prescriptions about caring for sick members and supplying money if a sick brother is in need. Membership in the confraternity was thus a form of health insurance.

Admittedly, we know far less about membership in the confraternities than we would wish; we do know that among the rectors of the Confraternity of the Virgin and Saint Francis, the Noveschi or men of comparable station predominated, but there were also a physician, a knife maker, a tailor, a locksmith, and two men from the Casati.[66] This variety was in marked contrast to the character of the traditional ecclesiastical foundations. The bishopric and the canonry were dominated by the magnates, who also had patronage of many churches both within and outside the city. The Malavolti, for example, rebuilt their parish church, Sant'Egidio, and provided the Dominicans with land for their church and convent. The Tolomei had patronage of the Church of San Cristoforo next to the family palace and apparently provided the land for the church and convent of the Servites.

It is difficult to peer beyond institutional structures and into the character and quality of Sienese religious life, but I would note that the lives of local candidates for sainthood did not conform to the general pattern of fourteenth-century spirituality until the time of Saint Catherine of Siena.[67] The seeming excesses of fourteenth-century spirituality elsewhere in Europe, the tales of introspection, and the tendency to emphasize the darker side of earthly life stand in marked contrast to the biographies of the blessed of Siena. Those individuals were very much a part of "civic Christianity"; their activities (like their fame) were largely confined to the city and its surrounds; none of them achieved the greater glory of sainthood. We have tales of withdrawal (sometimes sporadic); we have tales of asceticism and self-mortification; but it seems that the most prominent of the Sienese blessed were venerated for the active portions of their lives. "The widow Aldobranesca of Siena (1245–1309) was known for her penitential life of solitude and service to the pilgrims, the poor, and the sick."[68] Nearly always we discover a similar combination of penitence and good works. The Blessed Andrea Gallerani (d.1251) spent his life tending the sick and the poor and was credited with founding the Misericordia in Siena. The Blessed Ambrogio Sansedoni (1220–87) also cared for the poor, but he was as much a hero for having negotiated, in 1271, the end of a papal interdict on the city. The Blessed Pier Pettinaio (Peter the Combseller), who died in 1289, was famed for tending the sick in the Ospedale della Scala but also, rather strangely, for refusing to sell damaged combs to his clientele. The Blessed Agostino Novello (d. 1309), although an Augustinian hermit at San Leonardo a Lago, revised the statutes of the Ospedale della Scala. The Blessed Bernardo Tolomei, founder of the Benedictine monastery of Monte Oliveto, gave his life in serving the afflicted in the plague of 1348.

A great many Sienese *beati* and *beate* and a great many individuals involved in establishing religious institutions and/or hospitals came from magnate and Noveschi families. In

---

66. Bowsky, *Medieval Italian Commune*, 266.

67. R. Kieckhefer, *Unquiet Souls: Fourteenth-Century Saints and Their Religious Milieu*, Chicago and London, 1984.

68. Samuel K. Cohn Jr., *Death and Property in Siena, 1205–1800: Strategies for the Afterlife*, Baltimore and London, 1988, 81. See pages 80–82 for descriptions of the lives of Sienese *beati*.

founding (1313) the community at Monte Oliveto, the Blessed Bernardo Tolomei was accompanied by Ambrogio di Nino Piccolomini and the Noveschi Patrizio di Francesco Patrizi.[69] (They had all belonged to the Confraternity of the Virgin located in the Ospedale della Scala.) Andrea Gallerani and Ambrogio Sansedoni came from magnate families. In 1355, the Blessed Giovanni Colombini, from a Noveschi family, turned to the religious life. He had been prior of the Company of the Virgin Mary at the Ospedale della Scala from June to August 1349 and was founder of the lay congregation of the Gesuati.[70] The "Compagnia minore dela Vergine Maria," located at Santa Maria dei Servi, was founded in 1298 by the Blessed Francesco Patrizi.[71] There were other, trecento instances where Sienese from the Noveschi and Casati were numbered among the holy.[72] In short, the upper classes were as prominent in the religious life of Siena as in trade, banking, and government.

The veneration of these individuals singled them out as spiritual heroes, and in bestowing that honor upon them Sienese society was projecting an ideal self-image. A society that was rich saw abstinence as high virtue; a society closely tied to things of this world through commerce, government, and families saw the solitude of withdrawal as offering a closer relation to God. But a society that assured itself of the spiritual and practical benefit of widely distributed alms clearly believed in the efficacy of good works. There was, obviously, a circularity in the situation. The Sienese prized their *beati* for their values and their actions; those *beati* were undoubtedly shaped by their society's ideals. But in the definition of the ideal and holy life, there was a pervasive and compelling model, a figure who combined care for this world with a vision of life beyond. That model was Saint Francis, who was the product of, and lived within, an urban structure. His life was thus a guide, an exemplar of sanctity within the urban environment. In part, then, Sienese society might have argued that its blessed were situated in the larger context of the faith.

In addition to Siena's dedication to the Virgin, the city laid claim to four patron saints: San Ansano, San Savino, San Crescenzio, and San Vittorio. They formed, to put it mildly, a strange group. Ansano was, according to legend, an early Christian martyr from Rome who converted and baptized many in Siena before he was decapitated, at the age of nineteen or twenty, near the place that became San Ansano a Dofana, at the western edge of the diocese of Arezzo. His remains were a subject of dispute between the bishop of Arezzo and the bishop of Siena, but it seems they were transferred to Siena cathedral early in the twelfth century.[73] Savino was an early Christian bishop martyred at Spoleto. His cult spread widely throughout central Italy and to Faenza and Ravenna; it was particularly

---

69. P. Lugano, "Origine e primordi dell'Ordine di Monteoliveto," *BSSP*, IX, 1902, 279–335; X, 1903, 24–36, 206–57, 411–66.

70. Bowsky, *Medieval Italian Commune*, 262; Monti, *Le confraternite*, I, 244.

71. G. Gigli, *Diario senese,* 2d ed., I, Siena, 1854, 533, 568.

72. Religious figures from the Noveschi families are discussed by Gigli, *Diario,* II, 716, 720, 723, 725, 727f., 731f. For two of Siena's greatest magnate families, see R. Mucciarelli, *I Tolomei: Banchieri di Siena,* Siena, 1995, especially 246–57, and Carniani, *I Salimbeni,* especially 187–91.

73. F. S. Barcellona, "Un martire locale: Ansano," *BSSP*, XCVII, 1990, 10–33.

developed in Spoleto and Arezzo. By the late twelfth century there was an altar dedicated to San Savino in Siena cathedral, and somehow the cathedral had come into possession of his body.[74] Crescenzio was a Roman child martyred under Diocletian and Maximian. It is not entirely clear how his remains reached Siena.[75] Finally, Vittorio was a Milanese saint whose cult was early and widely diffused in northern Italy and who was honored in Ravenna; he appears in the mosaics of Sant'Apollinare Nuovo. In 1215, when the *Ordo officiorum ecclesiae Senensis* was compiled, no special event marked his feast day, although there were special celebrations for Ansano, Crescenzio, Savino, and Bartolomeo.[76] Vittorio's cult in Siena, which possessed the relic of his head, seems to have developed over the thirteenth century, although it was the Trecento that gave him new prominence.[77]

Now, the legends of all these saints are filled with the usual topoi of hagiography: curing the blind, destroying idols, healing the sick, and so forth. There is nothing unusual or particularly remarkable in their stories and, in the case of Crescenzio, very little of drama. The Sienese thus had among their protectors a child saint (although he was never depicted as such), two saints whose veneration was widespread and therefore not particular to Siena, and a Roman martyr who, according to which story one believed, belonged to Arezzo or Siena. Perhaps this is partial explanation why, when the Sienese fastened their attention on the Virgin, the four patron saints came to play a decidedly secondary role in the city's life. I take it as highly significant that, with the exception of a notice relating to Pietro Lorenzetti's predella to the San Savino altarpiece (begun 1335) for the cathedral, we have no indication that the lives of these saints were illustrated at any point during the years covered by this study; nor was there a pictorial tradition for episodes from those lives. Even Pietro's project suggests that the cults of the patron saints were not major features in Sienese devotion, for Savino's legend had to be translated into the vernacular for Pietro's use. In other words, it seems that the Sienese did not feel the need of a vernacular version of the legend before Pietro's task.[78] We also have evidence that of the four patron saints only Ansano was

---

74. E. Giannarelli, "Savino, Bartolomeo e l'alternanza dei patroni," *BSSP*, XCVII, 1990, 64–83.

75. F. E. Consilino, "Un martire 'romano': Crescenzio," *BSSP*, XCVII, 1990, 34–48.

76. M. F. Patrucco, "Un Santo 'Milanese': S. Vittore," *BSSP*, XCVII, 1990, 49–63.

77. In the fourteenth century, Bartolomeo was entirely replaced by Vittorio. The change seems to have begun by the mid–thirteenth century, when a papal letter (1257) concerning reform of the cathedral canons makes mention in particular of Crescenzio, Ansano, Savino, and Vittorio. G. A. Pecci, *Storia del vescovado della città di Siena,* Lucca, 1748, 221.

78. My argument regarding the comparatively minor role of the patron saints in the life of the commune is strengthened, I believe, by the lists of feasts observed by the city's guilds. The 1342–43 statute of the powerful Merchants' Guild lists the feasts of Ansano and Savino but not those of Crescenzio and Vittorio. (Q. Senigaglia, "Lo Statuto dell'Arte della Mercanzia senese," *BSSP*, XIV, 1907, 83–85, page numbering separate from that of the rest of this volume.) The statute (1329–35) of the Arte de' Cuoiai e Calzolai, like the 1356 statute of the Painters' Guild and the 1323–1402 statute of the Arte de' Chiarvai, lists only the feast of San Ansano. The statute (1289–1309) of the Arte della Lana is unusual in listing the feasts of Vittorio, Savino, and Ansano (but not that of Crescenzio). See Banchi and Polidori, *Statuti senesi,* I, 311–13; II, 249–53; II, 308–9, 329–31; and the translation of the statute of the Painters' Guild at the end of this volume.

accorded special devotion. In the statutes of most Sienese guilds, the feast of San Ansano, alone among the feasts for the four patron saints, is mandated a holiday.

In addition to communal support for the religious, the prevalence of confraternities, and the character of local *beati,* we have another important indication of the religious outlook of Siena's citizens: their wills. During the period of this study, up until the second outbreak of the plague in 1363, the Sienese generally fragmented their estates through a wide variety of bequests, beyond those to family, to different institutions and different causes—and there was plenty of choice.[79] Wills of the late Dugento and early Trecento refer to some twenty-seven different monastic houses and to at least twenty different nunneries.[80] The 1337–39 constitution mentions twenty-four monasteries and nineteen nunneries. Nor should we forget the sixteen hospitals in and around the city, also mentioned in the 1337–39 constitution, for they were all semireligious foundations and thus sites of devotion and prayer.

Between 1251 and 1362, there were periods in which the average testator in Siena divided his or her pious bequests between a minimum of six and a maximum of twelve separate institutions or causes, although in exceptional cases wills divided estates into twenty-eight, thirty-eight, fifty-eight, or over sixty separate bequests. Throughout the entire period, parish churches and monasteries or convents consistently received the largest percentage of bequests, ranging from 55 percent to 66 percent, and of these the monasteries were the greater beneficiaries in the ratio of roughly three to one. Between 1251 and 1347, hospitals received between 11 percent and 16 percent of pious bequests. In what is the very opposite of that we might expect, that percentage actually shrank to just over 9 percent during the year of the Black Death (1348) and then averaged only 8.33 percent in the years before the outbreak of the second wave of plague in 1363. In spite of the tribulations and the horrors of a plague death, the Sienese continued to look to the monasteries and convents as the best insurance of the soul's future rest.

---

79. On the entire matter of wills and pious bequests, discussed below, see Cohn, *Death and Property in Siena,* and also Cohn's *Cult of Remembrance and the Black Death: Six Renaissance Cities in Central Italy,* London and Baltimore, 1992. My account is based on those works and on work by William Bowsky.

80. Cohn, *Death and Property,* 33–35. Cohn's list includes San Martino, the Abbadia de Arco, the Abbadia de Nove, San Donato, and San Vigilio (all five of which also acted as parish churches); Santo Spirito, Santa Croce, the Humiliati, the hermits of Sant'Agata (who became part of Sant'Agostino), the Templars, the fratres de' Sacco, the fratres sue bachucchii, the fratres de Arminio, the Mantellini, the Fraticelli near the Porta Ulivieri; and monasteries beyond the city walls: Sant'Eugenio, the charterhouse of Pontignano, the charterhouse of Maggiano, the order of Saint John the Baptist, Santa Maria della Rosa beyond the Porta Laterina, the hermitage of San Leonardo al Lago, the Augustinian house at Lecceto, and the charterhouse of Monte Oliveto. To this list must be added the convents of the five mendicant orders.

The nunneries included: Santa Chiara, Santa Barnaba, San Prospero, the sisters of Sperandino, Santa Petronilla, Sant'Abundi, Santa Caterina, Santa Marta, the sisters of Vico Alto, San Lorenzo, San Benedetto, the sisters of Melianda near the Porta Ulivieri, the house of San Gregorio in the village of Lapi, Santa Mamilliana, Omnisanti, Santa Luca, Santa Maria Novella near the Porta Camollia, Santa Margherita in the Masse village of San Maffeo, and the sisters of Santa Maria Maddalena.

Within the categories of bequest, there are some other surprises, especially for the historian of art. During the period 1276 to 1347, the Dominicans and the Franciscans received almost the same percentage of bequests as the monasteries at large. But the Servites received double that percentage. Here we have indication of a popular devotion not reflected elsewhere, certainly not in known commissions for art. By contrast, the confraternities received very little testamentary support, although the statutes of many of them required new members to make a will shortly after their admission.[81]

Individual wills reveal the Sienese tendency, on the part of the rich, to endow or assist charitable and religious foundations. Pestaglio di Tavena Tolomei, in 1298, left the bulk of his large fortune to the Confraternity of the Virgin in the Ospedale della Scala and to the hospital of the Misericordia.[82] The largest pious bequest of the period was that of Blasius quondam domini Tolomei, who directed (1299) that his entire estate be used in founding four hospitals. A notary named Taurello founded (1294) the hospital of Santa Croce; Niccolò Malavolti, brother to Bishop Rinaldo, gave his palace to be turned into a hospital for the poor.[83] Cardinal Riccardo Petroni (d. 1314) created and endowed the Certosa of Maggiano, the monastery of Santa Chiara, and the monastery of San Niccolò.[84] His cousin, Bindo Petroni, papal notary, founded the Certosa of Pontignano in 1343, and another member of the family, Catelino, founded the hospital of Santa Caterina in 1355. In 1337, Emilia, from the noble family of the Conti d'Elci, built the church and monastery of Santa Marta.[85]

Generally, however, it seems that Sienese piety was diffuse, that whatever emphases the state might make or the rich proclaim in endowments, most citizens expressed a more catholic notion of their relation to the holy. Perhaps most telling of all is the fact that the evidence of bequests provides few tales of "enthusiasms," of exclusive devotion to single institutions. Just as the *beati* of Siena were moderate in the character of their faith, the citizenry, at death, relied on a moderate and corporate plan as the "strategy for the afterlife," investing in multiple institutions and various charitable deeds and hoping that one, if not the other, would prove acceptable in the eyes of God.

In the discussion thus far, two factors are missing: the bishop of Siena and the cathedral canons, and that does not represent simple accident. Siena of the late thirteenth and early fourteenth centuries gave the Church few great and consequential figures. For a year, 1298–99, Bishop Rinaldo Malavolti was Boniface VIII's provincial rector for the patrimony in Tuscany, and Boniface charged the Sienese cardinal Riccardo Petroni with preparing the

---

81. Undoubtedly, this provision reflected the hope that members would leave funds to the confraternity involved.

82. Gigli, *Diario*, II, 50. Important as this case is, the legacy to the Confraternity of the Virgin is the exception that proves the rule.

83. Waley, *Siena*, 133.

84. J. Bignani Odier, "Le testament du Cardinal Richard Petroni, 13 janvier 1314," *Papers of the British School at Rome*, XXIV, 1956, 142–57.

85. Gigli, *Diario*, II, 3. The will of Donodeus Malavolti, bishop of Siena from 1316 to 1350, is discussed below.

Liber Sextus of the decretals, but generally the secular clergy seem to have been content with daily life in their native city. There were, I suggest, parallels between the situation of the Sienese church and that of the papal court. As Rome, and then Avignon, were remote from the spiritual life of the faithful, so the bishop and canons of the cathedral seem shadowy, peripheral figures in the spiritual life of Siena. As the thirteenth-century papacy and curia were dominated by the great Roman families, the bishopric of Siena was held by the Malavolti; members of the Malavolti and other magnate families seem to have dominated the cathedral canonry.[86]

During the careers of Pietro and Ambrogio Lorenzetti and Simone Martini, the bishop was Donodeus Malavolti; elected in 1316 and confirmed in his post by John XXII in 1317, Donodeus lived until 1350. Like so many of the popes of the period, he was a lawyer by training, having studied both civil and canon law, and was a cathedral canon at the time of his elevation. Although he excommunicated the podestà and other officials of Siena in 1322 (in a quarrel over money owed the Church), negotiated an alliance (1328) of Siena, Florence, Bologna, and Perugia, and rebuilt his family's parish church of Sant'Egidio, he enters rarely into the history of Siena in his time. Perhaps the most interesting document relating to him is his will, together with various notices connected with its execution.[87] The bishop's principal benefactions were the founding of the Hospital of Santa Marta and founding of a convent dedicated to Saint Agnes, followed by the endowment of four chaplaincies in the cathedral and a fifth in Sant'Egidio. As inventories of his possessions make clear, he was a wealthy man. In making specific provisions for the execution of the will, the bishop involved the rector of Santa Maria della Scala and the rector of the Misericordia, two posts usually held by members of the Casati and thus by men of his own class. But alongside the larger provisions of the will are numerous other bequests, designed to assure the bishop the prayers of clerics in a great many of the city's religious and charitable institutions. Sometimes the sums involved are significant, sometimes modest. In the latter category are bequests ranging between 10 soldi and £3 to approximately twenty-two parish churches, thirty-three monasteries and convents, and thirteen hospitals. In short, the bishop's "strategy for the afterlife" was that of his fellow citizens.

86. In the late thirteenth century and first half of the Trecento, some members of the Malavolti family were cathedral canons. Three of them became bishops. There were some Noveschi among the canons, but more came from the Malavolti, Paparoni, and Tolomei. See Bowsky, *Medieval Italian Commune,* 268–69, and Waley, *Siena,* 128. It may well be that the cathedral canons, as well as other secular clergy, saw their appointments as little more than sinecures. One of the criminal statutes of the *vescovado,* issued in 1297, deprived lay clergy of the privilege of ecclesiastical law if they wore the clothes of a layman. The Church was trying to enforce a decretal of 1232, issued by the bishop of Siena of that time, that said clergy must wear clerical garb not only in performing the office but also in conducting their normal affairs. Apparently that earlier rule had not been effective. L. Zdekauer, "Statuti criminali del foro ecclesiastico di Siena (sec. XIII–XIV), *BSSP,* VII, 1900, 236.

87. C. Mazzi, "Il vescovo Donodeus dei Malavolti e l'Ospizio di S. Marta in Siena," *BSSP,* XIX, 1912, 200–248; XX, 1913, 65–114.

Charitable Foundations

Siena possessed a great many charitable foundations, some of which were destined to short lives because the funds connected with their endowment proved inadequate and/or because they were absorbed by larger institutions. We know very little about many of the smaller foundations that provided care for the sick or accommodations for pilgrims; fortunately, we know more about two of the city's more important institutions: the Casa della Misericordia and the Ospedale di Santa Maria della Scala, the latter unquestionably the most prestigious charitable foundation of Siena.

Creation of the Misericordia was credited to the Blessed Andrea Gallerani (d. 13 April 1251), from one of the great merchant banking families of the Dugento; its purpose was to care for the poor, orphans, the sick, and pilgrims. In addition to providing for the daily requirements of those dependent on the Misericordia, it made gifts, usually in kind, to the poor on Mondays and Thursdays; on Fridays, it sent bread to prisoners of the state. At the death of a poor man or woman, the rector had to send someone to dig a grave and bury him or her. Like other charitable institutions, the Misericordia received many gifts and many legacies that either included land or, if in cash, were used to buy rural property. It was with produce, or through the sale of produce, from that land that the Misericordia sustained its good works. In the tax assessments of 1318–20, the immovable property of the Misericordia was valued at 72,891 lire, 6 soldi, and 10 denari: a veritable fortune.

The Casa della Misericordia and its church, the latter built c. 1280, lay in the parish of San Donato, and reflecting, in part, the character of that parish, members of the Misericordia seem to have come generally from the artisan class. In 1271, a list of members was compiled; including the rector, the oblates numbered 39, only 16 of whom are identified by profession: 3 shoemakers, 1 *tondatore,* 2 saddlers, 2 blacksmiths, 1 woolworker, 1 notary, 1 maker of pans, 1 stone quarrier, 1 worker, 1 tinker, 1 leatherworker, and 1 butcher. A later list (1282) contains the names of 1 baker, 1 smith, 1 shoemaker, 1 barber, 1 saddler, and 2 "magistri."

The Ospedale di Santa Maria della Scala was not only the grandest charitable foundation in Siena, it also became the wealthiest.[88] Like the Misericordia, the hospital served pilgrims and the sick and succored the poor, but where the former cared for orphans, the Ospedale assumed responsibilities for foundlings, whom it raised and who were numerous. It also provided small dowries for its female charges. Over the course of its history, the Ospedale accumulated great wealth from various gifts and legacies and, particularly the during the rectorship (1314–39) of Giovanni di Tese Tolomei, amassed vast land holdings, which provided the income necessary to its distribution of grain to the poor and its other

---

88. For the history of the hospital and works of art connected with it, see D. Gallavotti Cavallero, *Lo Spedale di Santa Maria della Scala in Siena: Vicenda di una committenza artistica,* Pisa, 1985.

activities.[89] And it also became the center of a large system of smaller hospitals, widely scattered, that were its dependencies.

The Guilds of Siena

In Chapter III, I discuss in some detail the statute of the Painters' Guild in Siena, but here a few general remarks about Siena's guilds are necessary, particularly with reference to the two preceding sections of this chapter. The guilds of Siena did not occupy a place in Sienese history and government similar to that of their Florentine counterparts. Most seem to have been entirely commercial societies, regulating and setting standards for their members and thus for trades and crafts, and they existed at the pleasure of the Nove. When, in 1318, the Butchers' Guild was suspected of having conspired in insurrection, the Nine simply abolished it. During the disturbances that led up to the rebellion of 1318, the guild of the powerful judges and notaries tried to exploit the situation by bringing pressure to bear on the Nove, probably in connection with governmental regulation of their fees. After the Nine had regained complete control, in May of 1319, they outlawed the guild; it was restored only in 1341.[90] There was, however, one important exception to the attitude toward and the place of the guilds in Sienese society: the Merchants' Guild, the Mercanzia. Throughout the regime of the Noveschi, the Mercanzia enjoyed great power and often a deciding impact on government. It controlled every aspect of commercial life in the city, supervised the activities of the other Sienese guilds, and selected three consuls who participated in the signory. Those consuls had a dominant role in the administration of the Sienese mint, and thus control of Sienese coinage. In addition, it was the Mercanzia that daily set the exchange rate between the Florentine gold florin and Sienese coinage, with wide ramifications for the life of the city's citizens.[91]

As the wealthiest and most powerful guild in Siena, the Mercanzia unsurprisingly imitated the commune's program in distributing charity in order to guarantee the "preservation and growth" of the guild and its members. Upon installation each July, the new treasurer was to make gifts of 60 soldi to the Dominicans, Franciscans, and Servites; 40 soldi to the Carmelites; 20 soldi to the convent of the Umiliati; 10 soldi to the convent of Santa Croce; and 10 soldi to the brothers of Santo Giovanni Battista. The Opera del Duomo received £3, as did the Ospedale della Scala and the Spedale di Monna Agnese. There were

---

89. See S. R. Epstein, *Alle origini della fattoria toscana: L'ospedale della Scala e le sue terre (metà '200–metà '400)*, Florence, 1986.

90. Bowsky, *Medieval Italian Commune*, 130–34.

See also pages 209–15 for further discussions of the Nine and the city's guilds.

91. Bowsky, *Medieval Italian Commune*, 222–28.

gifts to another eleven monasteries, two convents of nuns, the "frati di Ravaccino," and to the Hospital of Santo Lazzaro.[92]

The guilds fulfilled social functions that, among other things, tied members to the religious life of the city. The 1288 statute of the Butchers' Guild, like the statutes of other guilds, includes a list of feasts to be observed by guild members, although exceptions could be licensed by the guild for the period May to September.[93] And it notes that each year, on the feast of "san Chimento," the treasurer of the guild must present a candle of wax weighing eight pounds at Santa Maria dei Servi, while the consuls of the guild must offer candles of one pound on the same occasion.[94] An addition to the statute, made in 1317, required the treasurer and the consuls to offer, on the feast of the Pentecost, one *doppiero* of wax weighing eight pounds and four candles of one pound each to the brothers of Santo Spirito.[95] The statute (1289–1309) of the Arte della Lana contains a list of feasts to be observed by members and specific requirements scattered elsewhere in the text.[96] Members were to observe the feasts of "messer santo Ambrogio," probably Ambrogio Sansedoni, and of Saint Anthony. Annual gifts of wax for candles included six pounds of wax on the feast of Saint Dominic to the Dominicans, a candle of three pounds of wax on the feast of "sancto Ambrogio" for his altar in San Domenico; a candle of four pounds to the Church of Sant' Agostino on the feast of Saint Augustine; a candle of eight pounds to the cathedral on the feast of the Assumption.[97] The *Statuto dell'Arte de' Chiavari* includes several rubrics dealing with feast days and notes, in 1323, that many guild members have been beginning work on Mondays before going to church and hearing the mass.[98] This disgrace is prohibited. The statutes of the guild of leatherworkers and shoemakers also list the feasts to be observed by members.[99]

Another important aspect to guild membership that fostered a sense of community was the obligations of the guild at the death of a member or of his relations. In this regard, the statute of the Chiavari provides the most extensive regulations. Upon the death of a master of the guild, all other masters and the rector were obliged to go to the house of the

92. Senigaglia, "Lo Statuto dell'Arte della Mercanzia senese," 85–86.

93. Banchi and Polidori, *Statuti senesi*, I, 74–75.

94. Banchi and Polidori, *Statuti senesi*, I, 118. The reference is to Saint Clement. The church of the Servites was raised, beginning c. 1260, on the site of an earlier church dedicated to that saint. See V. Lusini, *La Basilica di S. Maria dei Servi*, Siena, 1908, 2–3.

95. Banchi and Polidori, *Statuti senesi*, I, 123–24. Regarding *doppiero*: the term originally referred to a two-branched candelabra, but in the documents relevant to this study, the term had come to refer to a very large candle—a double candle, as it were. As we see in this and other documents, a *doppiero* was not, literally, a double weight.

96. Banchi and Polidori, *Statuti senesi*, I, 145–380.

97. Banchi and Polidori, *Statuti senesi*, I, 191–92. The list appears on 311–15. The connections between the wool workers' guild and the Dominicans were strong. Water used by the guild came from the Fonte Branda in the valley below San Domenico and in the western part of the city. The main drying shed for cloth was also in this area. The statute requires (I, 180) a meeting, each January, of three members and the Dominicans to draw up a list of all the principal feasts of the year.

98. The various rubrics are found in Banchi and Polidori, *Statuti senesi*, II, 248–54.

99. Banchi and Polidori, *Statuti senesi*, II, 308–9, 329–31.

deceased and then to the church, remaining until the office had been said and the deceased buried. Similarly, every master had to go to and stay at the burial of the father, mother, wife, son, daughter, or brother of a guild member. The statute further required one member from each workshop to attend the burial of any member of the Arte del Fuoco. These provisions date to 1323; an addition of 1330 permitted the rector to ask one master per workshop to attend the burial of any *discepolo* or *lavorente* of the guild who was twenty or older at the time of his death.[100] In the Painters' Guild, the rector was required to summon one or two members per workshop to attend the death of a father, mother, wife, son, blood brother, cousin, or blood nephew of a guild member.[101]

We may therefore say that, with the exception of the Mercanzia and, to a lesser extent, the Arte della Lana, Siena's guilds structured private life much more than public affairs. Like the confraternities, they served to draw members into a community and then, in religious observances, to draw that community into the life of the commune.

In Retrospect

Siena of the early Trecento was a thoroughly modern community. Its economy, its governance, and its institutions captured and embodied much of what was novel in the period. Siena's aspirations were large, confident, and directed to the future. That confidence, that optimism, is reflected in the various redactions of the city's constitution, where particular pieces of legislation are included with the seeming presumption that their validity would persist. It is found in the repeated extensions of the city walls, which enclosed areas far larger than needed in their time. It is manifest in the vast building campaigns of the duomo and the Palazzo Pubblico and the embellishment of the city. In the repeated attempts to found a full-fledged university, the Sienese sought to become part of the intellectual fervor that was characteristic of those relatively new institutions.

The Sienese constitution, in its abundance of particulars, also reflected the conviction, so common to the period, that law was the foundation of communal well-being. That attitude, as I have noted, was surely encouraged by the desire to find means of addressing the sense of dislocation created by urbanization, but it was equally shaped by the work of civilian jurists during the twelfth and thirteenth centuries and their study of Justinian's *Corpus juris civilis*.[102] De facto, the Sienese participated in the process of defining the state as an institution separate from the Church.

Now, many of these observations could be made of other Italian communes, and

---

100. Banchi and Polidori, *Statuti senesi*, II, 256–57, 263. The Arte del Fuoco was Siena's fire department.

101. See the translation of the guild statute below, on pages 201–24. The list is revealing of societal values inasmuch as wives and mothers are the only female relations named.

102. For an important specific instance, see "Artistic Progress?" in Chapter v.

inasmuch as that is true, we deal with the larger movements of the age. But there are two important and distinguishing features of Sienese life that have emerged in the preceding discussions. One is the character of the faith in Siena; the other concerns a still more fundamental notion of the relationship between the individual and the collective.

In the story of Sienese Christianity, I see no compelling evidence of the mysticism that scholars long invoked as explanation of the character of Sienese painting. Indeed, most of the evidence points in the opposite direction. Sienese candidates for sainthood before Saint Catherine of Siena were valued for their good works, not for rapt visions or mysterious apperceptions of the world beyond. The history of civic gifts to religious institutions and holy individuals, like the history of pious bequests by individual citizens, shows no penchant toward religious enthusiasms. The widespread and evenhanded distribution of communal alms and subsidies, the annual charity of the Mercanzia, and the pronounced tendency of individuals to fragment their pious bequests embody shared strategies. The first assured the city's well-being by co-opting the prayers and goodwill of all the city's monasteries, convents, hospitals, and hermits; the second was a means of preserving and strengthening the guild; and the third was a way to garner the prayers of many and the merit of good works. At the last hour, as the individual faced the prospect of God either merciful or vengeful, the Sienese chose to echo the strategy of their government and their guilds, in evident hope that among the resulting powerful chorus of intervention, their plight would find an advocate acceptable to God.

Such attitudes belong to what I see as the most significant characteristic and defining aspect of Sienese life: its corporate nature. And by that I do not merely refer to the fact that civic life was crossed and crisscrossed by interconnections, was bound by a web of associations created by the guilds and the confraternities and the city's charitable institutions. I speak, rather, to an underlying mentality that shaped those institutions, that structured government, that influenced testamentary bequests, and that was integral to commerce and banking. I speak to what might be described as the Sienese predilection for joint ventures. As the wealth of Siena had arisen from joint-venture companies, so the Noveschi sought to assure the well-being of the city by distributing power throughout their own class. In many cases, the regulations regarding the administration of guilds and confraternities and charitable institutions embodied a similar conviction that sharing power among their members was the desirable basis of governance. And in the structure of civic alms and of individuals' bequests, there was a notion that the collective is always more powerful than the solitary. I cannot stress this point enough, for the "corporate" mentality of the Sienese was to have several important consequences for the history of early Sienese painting.

II The Painter's Place

In the city that commerce and banking wrought and that merchants and bankers ran, painters had an important place; but the age was not yet ready to make artists the heroic visionaries they became in the full-blown Renaissance, or to dwell on the circumstances of their lives. Poets and chroniclers occasionally acknowledged the genius of painters, but painters had no biographers. A few artists, primarily Florentine, appear in the pages of Dante, Boccaccio, Petrarch, and Sacchetti, but whether in their true form or in literary conceit, we know not. The bureaucracy of trecento Siena has left us scattered documentation regarding painters and works of art, dowries, marriages, wills, and the acquisition or sale of property. Sometimes we feel that in those sources we catch momentary glimpses of painters' personalities. The Duccio documents, for example, indicate that the painter was often in debt, and it would seem that by his death he had gone through most of what he had earned. Ambrogio Lorenzetti likely belonged to the Confraternity of the Virgin Mary of the cathedral, which was actually resident in the Ospedale di Santa Maria della Scala. Membership in that confraternity meant serving the hospital and the poor, the latter with food and alms. Membership also meant that Ambrogio was participating in one of the most important forms of Sienese devotion. We know but one personal fact concerning one artist: Petrarch tells us that Simone Martini was not handsome.[1] But in no instance does the documentation suffice to make of us the biographers that the Trecento lacked.

We, like generations before us, are disappointed in that circumstance. Since Vasari, we have preferred our painters served up biographically; and until recently, we have lent a willing, and often credulous, ear to Vasari's tales. But if we hope to discover facts about painters' personalities in the Aretine's pages, the project fails from the start, for Vasari's personalities are construed as metaphors for painting itself. In related fashion, we shall never verify or disprove hypotheses based on the passing comments and stories of fourteenth-century poets. The admixture of legend and fact—if facts there be—is usually not to be separated into its constituents.

All that said, there is, nonetheless, a good deal we can learn about early Sienese painters as members of a society and as members of a guild that proclaimed its participants, "by the grace of God . . . able to reveal to the uneducated and illiterate the miraculous things achieved by virtue and in virtue of our Holy Faith." Thanks to the comparative richness of surviving documentation in Siena, we know some things about painters' families. The references, in documents of various sorts, to painters' places of residence are sufficient for us to define the environs where they lived and worked. Similarly, it is possible to say enough about painters' incomes and worth to set those artists in the larger context of their society.[2]

Family Matters

Considerable evidence suggests that painting, like other trades in Siena, was often a family profession. Duccio di Buoninsegna had six sons, at least three of whom (Ambrogio, Gal-

---

1. Francesco Petrarca, *Rerum familiarium libri i–viii,* trans. A. S. Bernardo, New York, 1975, 273.

2. In this and following chapters, there are a good many documents cited from the Archivio di Stato di Siena (ASS). The generous support of the Social Sciences and Humanities Research Council of Canada has permitted me long stays in Siena to survey the documentary material. While the enormity of the task has prevented me from reading through all the documentary material cited by other scholars, I have seen a very large number of volumes and papers, including nearly all the Biccherna vol-

umes for the period of this study. My searches and reviews of documents should prove useful to readers in a very practical way. Since the nineteenth-century publication of documents by Gaetano Milanesi (*Documenti per la storia dell'arte senese,* 3 vols., Siena, 1854, and *Nuovi documenti per la storia dell'arte toscana,* Florence, 1901) and S. Borghesi and L. Banchi (*Nuovi documenti per la storia dell'arte senese,* Siena, 1898), even since the publications of Pèleo Bacci (*Dipinti inediti e sconosciuti di Pietro Lorenzetti, Bernardo Daddi, ecc.,* Siena, 1939, and *Fonti e commenti per la storia dell'arte senese,* Siena 1944), the foliation

gano, and Giorgio) were painters.³ Ugolino di Nerio's father, his two brothers, a son, and two nephews: all were painters. Segna di Bonaventura had two sons, Niccolò and Francesco, who took up their father's profession. Simone Martini had a brother, Donato, and two brothers-in-law, Lippo and Federigo Memmi, who were painters; the latter two artists and their sister Giovanna, Simone's wife, were the children of the painter Memmo di Filippuccio, whose brother Mino was also an artist. As is well known, the brothers Lorenzetti were both painters. Given these instances, I believe we are justified in postulating father/son relations for some of the lesser-known painters documented in Appendix III of this study. Thus Dietisalvi would be father to Petuccio Dietisalvi and Fazio di Dietisalvi; Gilio father to Masarello di Gilio; Masarello father to Niccholuccio di Masarello, Biagio di Masarello, and Sandro di Masarello; and Domenico Orlandi father to Orlando di Domenico.⁴ When, later in this chapter, I come to deal with matters financial, we shall encounter several instances of brothers, both painters, jointly owning property. That phenomenon was by no means something restricted to artists. Quite the reverse. Painters were simply participating in arrangements that were characteristic of their society; but for the art historian such circumstances are highly suggestive. Daily contact between brothers, even if they did not share a workshop, surely meant that ideas, techniques, and perhaps even styles were interwoven.

We also have some evidence that, in addition to the family connections created by Simone's marrying Giovanna Memmi, marriages bound other artists' families. Caterina, daughter of Simone's brother Donato, married the painter Giovanni di Sera.⁵ In 1336, a painter named Romano di Mino married Andrea di Cecco di Martino. The profession of the bride's father is not specified in the relevant document, but we do have record of a painter by that name. In what might be described as a marriage of the arts, the painter Pietro di Ser Dota married Margherita, daughter of the sculptor Tino di Camaino, on 14 February 1348.⁶ This connection is particularly intriguing because, in 1350, Pietro di Ser Dota bought "una possessione" from Ambrogio Lorenzetti's estate; earlier, in 1342, Pietro Lorenzetti had bought land for Tino's sons, Cola and Martino; and in 1344 Pietro and his wife, Giovanna, sold land to the brothers.⁷ Was there perhaps a now unknown connection be-

---

of archival volumes has changed. In all my documentary citations I use the most recent numbering. There are also many instances where the inventory numbers have been changed. I use the current inventory numbers. The most important instance of change occurs in reference to the Archives of the Opera del Duomo in Siena. A new, badly needed inventory has been prepared by Stefano Moscadelli, who has given each item in that collection new numberings (*L'Archivio dell'Opera della Metropolitana di Siena, Inventario,* Munich, 1995). The notes should therefore serve others wishing to locate the notices cited.

3. Pèleo Bacci, "Commentarii dell'arte senese III: Notizia su Duccio, i figli, il nipote e i bisnipoti, pittori," *BSSP,* n.s., III, 1932, 233–48.

4. The number of painters having the first name Mino makes it impossible to be certain of family connections with artists whose names end in "di Mino."

5. See Appendix III for this artist and for Romano di Mino and Pietro di Ser Dota.

6. Milanesi, *Documenti,* I, 30.

7. Borghesi and Banchi, *Nuovi documenti,* 11, and Bacci, *Dipinti inediti,* 97–103.

tween Tino and the Lorenzetti? Such notices provide us with glimpses of connections that were surely more numerous than we can now demonstrate, but I am not convinced that marriages reflect anything more than circumstances of physical proximity. There is nothing to suggest that painters constituted a separate group within Sienese society.

Other family circumstances regarding three of Siena's most important painters are worthy of note for their possible impact on the history of Sienese painting. When, in 1348, Ambrogio Lorenzetti wrote his will, his immediate family included only his wife and his daughters.[8] The 1344 summary of Simone Martini's will suggests he and his wife had no children of their own; generous bequests were made to Simone's nieces, daughters of Donato, and to the latter's sons.[9] We have no indication that Pietro Lorenzetti had children. Although the question is moot, one cannot help wondering if the course of Sienese painting would have been different had these painters had heirs to take up the profession and perhaps to maintain their workshops.

Where Did Painters Live?

Accustomed as we are to the conditions of the modern metropolis, anyone who has never visited Siena may find it initially difficult to envisage the form of the city in the Trecento. It is true that Siena was one of the greatest cities in Europe, but its inhabitants were distributed over an area that seems to us quite small (Fig. 1). From the Porta di Camollia at the extreme north of the city to the Porta Romana on the south, the distance is roughly four kilometers, and at its greatest width, in the south of the city, the distance between the Porta Pispini and the Porta Laterina is approximately three kilometers. But during the Trecento much of the area enclosed by the city walls (and gates) was unoccupied, and the heart of the city, including the duomo, the Campo, and the areas where most painters lived, could be encompassed by a square of 1.2 kilometers to each side. The community was thus highly compact, distances were minimal, and the citizens lived in immediate, daily contact with one another.[10]

It seems the proximity of many painters, one to another, was yet more immediate. In Appendix 1, I have gathered notices from primary and secondary sources that provide

8. V. Wainwright, "The Will of Ambrogio Lorenzetti," *Burlington Magazine,* CXVII, 1975, 543–44.

9. Bacci, *Fonti e commenti,* 185–87.

10. During the late thirteenth century and the first two decades of the Trecento, the city walls enclosed an area of roughly 123.5 acres. Circa 1330, Opicino de Canistris, in his *Liber de Laudibus civitatis Ticinensis,* said that the fifty thousand people of Pavia "know each other so well that if anybody enquires after an address he will be told it at once, even if the person he asks lives in a quite distant part of the city; this is because they all gather twice a day, either in the 'court' of the commune or in the [adjoining] cathedral piazza." Cited by Daniel Waley, *The Italian City-Republics,* 3d ed., Harlow, Essex, 1988, 29. In Siena, the cathedral, the fountains, and especially the Campo provided for close and regular contacts among the citizenry.

information on the districts where painters lived. The lists are confined roughly to the dates of the Noveschi regime (1287–1355). Eighty-one painters appear in the lists, organized according to parishes. The survey reveals that the largest number of painters, forty, appear in the parish of San Donato and the second largest number, nineteen, in the immediately adjacent parish of Sant'Egidio. Four painters appear in both parishes at one moment or another; therefore the real number of painters in the larger unit of the adjoining parishes of San Donato/Sant'Egidio is fifty-four. Both parishes flanked the Via Francigena, and the district was less than six hundred meters north of the Campo.[11] Thus 68 percent of painters lived and/or worked in this area of the Terzo di Camollia. But if we add to this central core artists documented in *popoli* immediately adjacent to San Donato/Sant'Egidio, *popoli* such as Sant'Antonio, San Cristoforo, and San Pietro a Ovile, our earlier percentage rises to roughly 84 percent.

In the south of the city, in the Terzo di Città, some seven painters resided in the adjoining parishes of San Pietro in Castelvecchio and San Quirico in Castelvecchio; the number is proportionally insignificant, but the painters were not. Duccio, Pietro Lorenzetti, and Ambrogio Lorenzetti were among them.[12] Pietro lived in San Quirico, while his brother Ambrogio, at the time of his death, resided in San Pietro in Castelvecchio, immediately adjoining San Quirico to the east. Earlier (1324) Ambrogio had property in Sant'Egidio.[13]

As in other notices regarding the painter, the history of Duccio di Buoninsegna's properties is confused and confusing.[14] In 1286, he paid a total of £7 as taxes in the Terzo di Città, but on property in the parish of Sant'Egidio, in the *lira* of Sant'Egidio a lato dei Malavolti, in the Terzo di Camollia.[15] In 1289, he was resident in San Donato, immediately adjacent to Sant'Egidio.[16] Subsequently, a document of 9 November 1292 may refer to property in the parish of Sant'Antonio,[17] but in 1293 and 1294 he is again recorded in San Donato, while a notice of 16 August 1304 refers to property held just outside the city walls,

11. For the historical background on the *popolo* of San Donato, see P. Nardi, "I borghi di San Donato e di S. Pietro a Ovile: 'Populi,' contrade e compagnie d'armi nella società senesi dei secoli XI–XIII," *BSSP*, LXXIII–LXXV, 1966–68, 7–59.

12. If the "Bindo" of item 4 under San Quirico is the same individual as the miniaturist of item 3, the number would be reduced by one.

13. If the "Ser Bindo Dietavive" of no. 66 is the same individual as the "Bindo" of no. 85, then the number of painters in this area would be five.

We do not know precisely when Ambrogio moved to the Terzo di Città. A document from the Ospedale di Santa Maria della Scala that refers to the "Ambrogio dipentore in champoreggi" (referring to the area near San Domenico in the Terza di Camollia) is dated 9 June 1344 (ASS, Ospedale 851, fol. 47v). This is, however, likely a reference to Ambrogio di Duccio.

14. Documentary appendixes are found in John White, *Duccio: Tuscan Art and the Medieval Workshop*, London, 1979, and James Stubblebine, *Duccio di Buoninsegna and His School*, 2 vols., Princeton, 1979. Unfortunately, each author has documents not included by the other; there are also discrepancies in folio numbers. For a new, complete publication of all the Duccio documents, see J. Satkowski, *Duccio di Buoninsegna: The Documents and Early Sources*, ed. Hayden B. J. Maginnis, Athens, Ga., 2000.

15. ASS, Biccherna 92, fols. 8r and 32r.

16. ASS, Biccherna 725 (Condanne), fol. 647v.

17. Florence, Archivio di Stato, Notarile antecosimiano D53a (Protocollo di Ser Diedi di Goffredo da Monte), fol. 21v.

in the "contrata de Castagneto" on the Tressa.[18] On 7 April 1309, he was definitely living in San Donato.[19] In 1310 Duccio moved to San Quirico in Castelvecchio, Terzo di Città, in the tax district of Stalloreggi di dentro, while executing the *Maestà* for the high altar of Siena cathedral (Color Plates 1–2, 10–11, Figs. 15, 16).[20] In 1311, he also had property in the immediately adjacent *popolo* of Laterino, also known as Stalloreggi di fuore, just outside the city walls; according to the Sienese chronicles of Andrea Dei and Agnolo di Tura, it was Duccio's workshop that was in the *popolo* of Laterino/Stalloreggi di fuore.[21]

Today, the visitor to Siena can easily identify the parishes where painters lived (Fig. 1), although there are some post-trecento changes to streets and piazze. Sant'Egidio is now bounded by the Via della Sapienza on the south, the Via dei Montanini on the east, and the Via del Paradiso to the north. At the extreme north, where today we find the Piazza G. Matteotti, was the area known as the Poggio Malavolti, where that family had its principal palace. San Donato wraps around Sant'Egidio on the east and south, east of the Via dei Montanini (which becomes the Banchi di Sopra in the direction of the city center), south to the Via dei Rossi. West of the Banchi di Sopra, the southern edge of San Donato is marked by streets now called the Via dei Pittori and the Via del Camporegio.

San Pietro di Castelvecchio and most of San Quirico in Castelvecchio lie to the south of the Via di Stalloreggi and, for a very short distance, south of the Via di Città until reaching the Costa Larga. San Pietro includes what is now the Pinacoteca Nazionale. On the east and south that parish is bounded by the Casato di Sopra; San Quirico is bounded on the south by Via Tommaso Pendola and, for a very short distance just east of the Piazza delle Due Porte, includes a narrow area just north of the Via Stalloreggi.

The topography of these two areas of the city is noteworthy. Painters who lived in the sections of Sant'Egidio and San Donato flanking the Via dei Montanini lived on a rather sharp ridge; on both east and west the land falls away rapidly. West of that street, the two parishes, beginning at the Poggio Malavolti and ending at the Via dei Pittori, quickly fall away to the west and south in the direction of the Fontebranda in the valley below. This area, then, is one of southern exposure. San Pietro and San Quirico also fall away, from the center of the city toward the south, although the descent is more gradual.

The district of Sant'Egidio and San Donato was one of very marked contrasts and

---

18. ASS, Archivio Generale, Parchment 468.
19. ASS, Biccherna 727 (Condanne), fols. 164r and 169r.
20. ASS, Biccherna 728 (Condanne), fols. 151r and 154r. This volume is for 1310. Duccio was fined £24.
21. The document regarding Duccio's property in Laterino was published by Bacci, *Fonti e commenti*, 101. For reasons I fail to understand, it does not appear in either of the monographs on Duccio by James Stubblebine and John White. These two areas, San Quirico and Laterino, are also called "Stalloreggi dentro" and "Stalloreggi di fuore" in contemporary documents. Agnolo di Tura ("Cronaca senese attribuita ad Agnolo di Tura del Grasso detta Cronaca maggiore," in *Rerum Italicarum Scriptores*, ed. A. Lisini and F. Iacometti, vol. XV, pt. VI, Bologna, 1931–39, 313) says that Duccio painted the work in a shop in Laterino. Another, anonymous Sienese chronicler also says the *Maestà* was painted outside the Stalloreggi gate (*Rerum Italicarum Scriptores*, vol. XV, pt. VI, 90).

variety.²² It was there that many of Siena's great families had palaces and warehouses: the Malavolti, the Montanini, the Rustichetti, and the Salimbeni. Sant'Egidio was very much the *popolo* of the Malavolti; in addition to their own residences, they owned, c. 1318, 90 percent of the workshops (*bottege*) in the *popolo*.²³ At the same date, roughly 59 percent of the dwellings in the parish were worth less than £100. San Donato was home not only to the magnates, but also to the Hospital of Sant'Andrea and the Casa della Misericordia. The latter had other property, including workshops, which it rented, often to painters.²⁴ Around 1318, approximately 40 percent of houses in San Donato were valued at less than £100, and 7 percent estimated at something between £700 and £2,000.²⁵ Painters of the two parishes, especially those living in the south and west of San Donato, shared their spaces with woolworkers, who had access to the water supply from Fontebranda and, immediately northwest of the fountain, had their tenters. On the east of Via dei Montanini, painters seem to have backed upon tenters of woolworkers in San Pietro a Ovile or in the Abbazia di San Donato.²⁶ Just south of San Donato, in the *popolo* of San Cristoforo, the Tolomei and the Bonsignori families faced each other across the Banchi di Sopra. This district was also home to the Gallerani and the Albizzeschi.²⁷

Sant'Egidio and San Donato lay, as it were, in the shadow of San Domenico, Siena's Dominican convent, which is just slightly west of the two parishes; and it is clear that a number of painters had close relations with the Dominicans. San Domenico commemorated the death of Simone Martini in far off Avignon, and the necrology of the convent marked the deaths of other artists and/or members of their families.²⁸ It might thus seem

22. For the following discussions, see Balestracci and Piccinni, *Siena nel trecento,* and chapter VIII of Cherubini, *Signori, contadini, borghesi.*

23. The Malavolti holdings in Sant'Egidio are recorded in ASS, Estimo 136 (1318–c.1320). The first assessment is for Volto dei Malavolti and comes to a total of 17,322 lire, 16 soldi, and 6 denari (fol. 63v), but the volume also contains many other Malavolti, assessed at £4,000, £5,000, or £6,000. In the Trecento, the greatest Sienese magnate families were the Tolomei, the Malavolti, the Salimbeni, the Piccolomini, and the Saracini.

24. Bacci, *Dipinti inediti,* 44. See also Appendix III at the end of this volume.

25. Balestracci and Piccinni, *Siena nel trecento,* 124–25. Property values near the Church of San Donato varied considerably, as reflected by the information on the various *lire* of the *Table of Possessions*. San Donato di sotto, for example, was a comparatively poor neighborhood, but San Donato a lato dei Montanini, along the Via Francigena, was quite properous. Cherubini (*Signori, contadini, borghesi,* 243) indicates that the median value of private property in the former was 117 lire and 4 soldi, in the latter 1,159 lire and 2 soldi.

26. See the documents for Ugolino di Nerio in Appendix II.

27. San Cristoforo had a very large number of the rich. The median value of property in San Cristoforo a lato dei Tolomei was 6,779 lire and 8 soldi, in San Cristoforo a lato della Chiesa, 5,381 lire and 6 soldi. Modest patrimonies, those assessed at £200 or less, were almost nonexistent. Cherubini, *Signori, contadini, borghesi,* 241.

28. M. H. Laurent, ed., *I necrologi di San Domenico in Camporegio,* Florence, 1937. For example, the wife of Federigo Memmi died in August of 1342 and was buried at San Domenico. His daughter was also buried there, on 15 January 1371 (Laurent, *I necrologi,* 64, 107). Simone Martini's death in 1344 was recorded in the necrology, as was the death of his brother Donato on 16 August 1347 (Laurent, *I necrologi,* 67, 72).

likely that some painters belonged to the Confraternity of the Blessed Virgin and Saint Dominic; by the same token, we might assume that some artists were members of the Compagnia di Santa Maria della Misericordia or simply affiliated with the Misericordia, located at the heart of this district. Unfortunately, there is no documentary evidence to confirm those speculations.

In the southwest of the city, in the Terzo di Città, the *popolo* of San Quirico had approximately 60 percent of structures of very low value and a very few worth more than £400. (Today, one can still see that this district has always been a modest one.) San Pietro in Castelvecchio was a better address. There, only about 22 percent of buildings were valued at less than £100, while roughly 61 percent fell in the range £100 to £400.²⁹

The concentration of Sienese painters in two areas (mainly in one) can be compared to, and contrasted with, circumstances in Florence. In a survey of published and unpublished sources, Erling Skaug summarizes notices indicating Florentine painters' places of residence for the period of approximately 1310 to 1410. Some sixteen painters are included, five (Giotto, Orcagna, Jacopo di Cione, Giovanni del Biondo, and Puccio di Simone) appearing in two different parishes during their lifetimes. Nardo di Cione appears as resident in a total of five different parishes during the period 1343 to 1365. Andrea di Bonaiuto appears briefly absent from the parish of Santa Maria Novella (and in the *gonfalone* of Drago di San Giovanni), which is otherwise recorded as his place of residence. In four cases the parish is not named but the *gonfalone* is, giving us an approximate place.³⁰

Four major painters—Giotto, Nardo di Cione, Jacopo di Cione, and Andrea di Bonaiuto—resided in the parish of Santa Maria Novella at one point in their careers. Bernardo Daddi, Maso di Banco, Orcagna, and Puccio di Simone are documented in the parish of San Lorenzo in the *gonfalone* of Lion d'oro. Since that *gonfalone* contained only one other parish, that of Santa Maria del Fiore, it may well be that Jacopo di Cione and Giovanni Bonsi, documented in that *gonfalone,* were also residents of San Lorenzo. At one moment in the careers of Giotto, Orcagna, and Nardo di Cione, these painters lived in the parish of San Michele Visdomini. Giovanni del Biondo is documented in the *gonfalone* of Vaio, which contained the parish of San Michele Visdomini. Taddeo Gaddi, Agnolo Gaddi, Giovanni da Milano, Puccio di Simone, and Pietro Nelli are recorded in the parish of San Pier Maggiore. Niccolò di Tomasso and Andrea di Bonaiuto appear as resident in the *gonfalone* of Drago di San Giovanni; Tommaso del Mazza resided in the parish of Sant'Ambrogio in the *gonfalone* of Chiavi, and Giovanni del Biondo can be placed in the parish of Bue in the *quartiere* of Santa Croce.

The majority of notices thus places painters in the parishes of Santa Maria Novella, San Lorenzo, and San Michele Visdomini, all at the north of the city and today linked by

---

29. Balestracci and Piccini, *Siena nel trecento,* 116.

30. Erling S. Skaug, *Punch Marks from Giotto to Fra Angelico: Attribution, Chronology, and Workshop Relationships in Tuscan Panel Painting, with Particular Consideration to Florence, c. 1330–1430,* II, Oslo, 1994, 527–35. Florence was divided into four *quartieri,* which were further divided into parishes. Skaug (II, 529) provides a list of the parishes in each *quartiere.*

reinforcing. And that being the case, there is no reason to exclude painters from sharing such widespread interests.[101]

In a recent, important work, Marvin Trachtenberg has argued that trecento Florence saw a highly sophisticated system of urban planning in which architects and builders took great care about the siting of major projects and/or developed carefully planned spaces around major structures such as the cathedral and the Palazzo Vecchio.[102] And all developments, Trachtenberg argues, were based on the geometry of viewing angles. In other words, significant time, care, and cost were devoted to such planning, planning in which the viewer and the viewer's place were the determining factors. We also have clear evidence that sculptors of the late thirteenth and early fourteenth centuries gave new attention to the relationship between the viewer and the viewed. For the upper sections of the facade of Siena cathedral, Giovanni Pisano created figures whose heads are thrust forward so that they will not be obscured by the bodies for the viewer at ground level. In a figure of Boniface VIII for the facade of Florence cathedral (now Museo dell'Opera del Duomo, Florence), Arnolfo di Cambio elongated the torso, presumably to compensate for the foreshortening created by a view from below; the figure was originally on an upper level of the facade. In sum, it is clear that architects and sculptors of the period, like painters, were involved in mapping new relations between the beholder and the beheld.

Artistic Progress?

To what extent did painters and public have a notion that there was progress, improvement, in the arts? The question is difficult to answer, but we have some evidence to guide us. First, I should note that many modern authors quite rightly warn us against naively taking comments on "the arts" as comments on the fine arts; in many, perhaps most, instances, references in medieval and early-Renaissance texts are to the mechanical arts, to shipbuilding, farming, and so forth, and therefore must not be confused with attitudes concerning painting or sculpture. But we do have a case where painting is explicitly included in "the

---

101. Beyond the evidence relating to Siena's attempts to create a university, discussed in Chapter II above, we know only a little about education and literacy in the city and thus about ways in which ideas of the perpsectivists might have reached artists. Two pieces of evidence are, however, noteworthy. In 1316, the Casa della Misericordia assigned a room and revenues to Scabello del fu Chiavellino, master of grammar. Giuliano Catoni suggests that this may have initiated the Misericordia's practice of having an instructor in Latin to teach the orphans in its care ("Gli oblati," 9–10). May we therefore assume that if Latin was deemed necessary to orphans, the general level of education was high?

In 1344 the Ospedale della Scala engaged a certain "maestro Bartolomeo" to teach reading to the foundlings of the hospital ("Ls," "Un contratto per insegnare a leggere," *Miscellanea storica senese*, VI, 1903, 82–83). This may reflect an established practice.

102. Marvin Trachtenberg, *Dominion of the Eye: Urbanism, Art, and Power in Early Modern Florence*, Cambridge, 1997.

noted that there are variations in the clarity of our perceptions, and he distinguished between our first glance at an object, which provides only a superficial impression, and what he considered a "certified" impression. He explained the difference by pointing out that, with one exception, all the rays of the visual pyramid are refracted as they pass through the interface of what he knew as the "glacial" and "vitreous humors," so that they do not converge, but reach the eye nerve in a shape that resembles that of the object perceived. Only one ray, the central ray, passes into the eye without refraction and is thus stronger than any other. Thus, Alhazen anticipates the modern notion of visual scanning. "The certification of a perception (i.e., the verification of the visible qualities of a body) occurs, then, through a rapid motion of the eye, which carries the axis of the visual pyramid over the visible body so that each of its points is perceived through this central ray."[97] We find this idea clearly restated in Pecham's *Perspectiva communis*.[98] It may well be one of the larger ironies of art history that the fourteenth-century absence of a unitary mathematical perspective stems from a more accurate understanding of optical theory than that involved in Brunelleschi's system.[99]

One further commission should be singled out as evidence of the Sienese concern with the imaged. In 1345, Ambrogio Lorenzetti created a world map, the *mappamondo* that gave its name to the room in Siena's Palazzo Pubblico where it was.[100] Of very large dimensions (roughly 4.83 m in diameter) and round in its form, it was mounted on a single, central pivot and rotated to bring, successively, various portions nearer to the viewer. The Sienese desire to have such an image relates to the popularity of written "geographies" and the appearance of portolan maps in the late thirteenth century. In a way, the *mappamondo* might be styled the epitome of the Sienese interest in images and imaging. If Ambrogio's decorations in the Sala della Pace laid before viewers Siena idealized, Ambrogio's map brought the world under their gaze.

We shall never have hard evidence that Sienese painters were aware of the work of the perspectivists, but it seems to me hardly fortuitous that the application of geometry to images, the invention of eyeglasses, and a preoccupation with optics should coincide chronologically with more general evidence of the primacy of sight. I speak not of a *Zeitgeist*, but of a combination and confluence of cultural developments that were mutually

---

97. Lindberg, *Theories*, 85.

98. Pecham provides us with the most straightforward account of the matter. "For although the whole pyramid is perpendicular to the centre of the eye, i.e., the anterior glacial humor, it is not perpendicular to the whole eye. Therefore only that perpendicular called the axis, which is not refracted, manifests the object efficaciously, and the other rays are correspondingly stronger and better able to manifest [the object] as they are closer to the axis. Therefore the eye is turned about so that the object, which is perceived under the pyramid all at once, is discerned efficaciously by appearing along this perpendicular successively." Pecham, *Perspectiva*, 121–23. See also pages 125 and 147.

99. No revolution in optical/perspectival theory occurred between the thirteenth century and the development of mathematical perspective in the fifteenth century. Brunelleschi and his contemporaries worked against the background provided by Bacon, Witelo, and Pecham.

100. See, most recently, Kupfer, "The Lost Wheel Map of Ambrogio Lorenzetti," from which the following summary is drawn.

ing and original spatial experiments. In his *Birth of the Virgin* (1342; Fig. 30) Pietro Lorenzetti employed a complex set of spatial devices that mingle an entirely empirical approach with an interest in the geometrical. The left third of the picture, showing Joachim and a companion receiving news of the Virgin's birth, is governed only by empirical perspective; the tiles of the floor are but a series of parallelograms, and the space of the corridor is not firmly related to the space of the adjoining bed chamber. The latter derives from the circumstance that Pietro shifted the theoretical viewpoint to the left of the panel's center, so that we see more of the passageway than we would have had the image been organized around a single, central viewpoint. From the vaulting above Saint Anne, we see that even the central unit is to be viewed from slightly right of center, thereby explaining the larger view of the right third of the image. But within the chamber we find that the orthogonals of the floor, the bed covering, the foot and head of the bed, and the upper moldings of the walls converge in a vanishing area.[94]

It is, however, in two late pictures by Ambrogio Lorenzetti that we find the clearest attempts to impose geometrical order on pictorial space. In both his *Presentation in the Temple* (Fig. 21) and his *Annunciation* (Fig. 89) of 1344, the orthogonals of the central sections of the floors converge toward a vanishing point. In the *Presentation,* this innovation is part of a larger vanishing-axis construction; in the *Annunciation,* the absence of architecture other than the floor means that the space is generated entirely by the pavement. While there are important features of linear perspective absent in this image, we behold the combination of a specified viewpoint with a geometrical ordering of pictorial content.[95]

Reading the works of the thirteenth-century perspectivists, one often feels that the materials for mathematical perspective are almost there. The notions of the rectilinear propagation of light, the visual pyramid, and the decrease in size with distance: all are central to the system invented by Brunelleschi. And inasmuch as the visual pyramid has both its apex and its central axis in the eye of the beholder, the idea of a stationary viewpoint is also central to the thirteenth-century conception of vision. In fact, the understanding of vision in Brunelleschi's time was still that which I have sketched above; Brunelleschi, Masaccio, and Alberti: none of them was responding to changes in the theory of vision.[96] There are, however, features of the thirteenth-century conception that may have discouraged any attempt to turn those ideas into a mathematical system; and one of them anticipates our twentieth-century understanding of vision. Alhazen himself had identified the problem. He

---

grill. In other words, most viewers could advance only as far as the entrance of those chapels. That fact surely played a large part in painters' decisions to organize perspective according to a viewpoint at the entrance.

94. White, *Birth and Rebirth,* 99–100.

95. As I have pointed out in *Painting in the Age of Giotto,* Florentine artists practically never used tiled pavements in their works. It was surely the popularity of the device among Sienese painters that led the latter to give attention to the geometrical ordering of those forms.

96. That circumstance suggests that the invention of mathematical perspective was tied to something other than optics. Edgerton (*Renaissance Rediscovery*) has suggested that cartography may have played a decisive role.

understood by depictions, the latter must accurately portray "lines, angles, and figures of both solids and surfaces":

> Since, therefore, artificial works, like the ark of Noah, and the temple of Solomon and of Ezechial and of Esdras and other things of this kind almost without number are placed in Scripture, it is not possible for the literal sense to be known, unless a man have these works depicted in his sense, but more so when they are pictured in their physical forms. . . . But no one would be able to plan and arrange a representation of bodies of this kind, unless he were well acquainted with the books of the *Elements* of Euclid and Theodosius of Milleius and other geometricians. . . . For without doubt the whole truth of things in the world lies in the literal sense, as has been said, and especially of things relating to geometry, because we can understand nothing fully unless its form is presented before our eyes, and therefore in the Scripture of God the whole knowledge of things to be defined by geometrical forms is contained and far better than mere philosophy could express it.[91]

Among Sienese painters, concern with order in the depiction of architecture arose early. With great sensitivity to all the ambitions expressed in Sienese legislation regarding the fabric of the city and embodied in the plan for Talamone (Fig. 5), Duccio created his image of Jerusalem (Color Plate 1) with streets paved in brick and its buildings seemingly set in straight lines along those streets. Similar order is found in one of the scenes of the legend of Saint Nicholas by Ambrogio Lorenzetti (Fig. 105). In Duccio's *Healing of a Man Born Blind* (Fig. 15), also from the *Maestà,* the painter placed us within an urban setting. Neither image, however, is evolved from a geometrical system, nor is the view from the left, in both cases, an attempt to situate the viewer at a single viewpoint.[92] The latter first appears in the predella of Simone Martini's *Saint Louis of Toulouse* (Color Plate 16), where the depicted architecture indicates the viewer is to stand opposite the center of the altarpiece.

Simone, a painter so often and so erroneously associated only with gothic lyricism, was in fact quite sensitive to the relation of the imaged and the viewer. In the Saint Martin Chapel, not only the scenes but also the half-length saints and their aedicules (Fig. 48) in the window embrasures are depicted as for a viewer standing just within the entrance of the chapel.[93] But it is in the work of the Lorenzetti brothers that we discover the most interest-

---

91. Burke, *Opus majus,* I, 232–34.

92. The narratives of the *Maestà* are in fact organized in a way that suggests a moving beholder. Like the lighting from the left, the views of architecture seen from the left assist in moving the beholder from left to right. These are, however, mingled with scenes conceived according to a central, frontal view.

93. As Julian Gardner has pointed out ("The Cappellone di San Nicola at Tolentino: Some Functions of a Fourteenth-Century Fresco Cycle," in *Italian Church Decoration of the Middle Ages and Early Renaissance,* ed. W. Tronzo, Bologna, 1989, 107, and "The Decoration of the Baroncelli Chapel in Santa Croce," *Zeitschrift für Kunstgeschichte,* XXXIV, 1971, 89–114), most chapels were closed by an iron

we can see on a plain of the earth's surface and on a mountain the author of Twilights shows, saying that we see on a terrestrial plain about three miles; and on a very high mountain, the greatest height of which is eight miles, we shall see even on a plain of the earth's surface only about 250 miles; and the gibbosity of the earth restricting vision causes this."[85]

But the largest contribution that the perspectivists made to painting lay in the very conception of their subject. "The essential characteristic of medieval optics, distinguishing it from modern optics, is that there is no optical problem without an observer. Medieval optics is a theory of vision."[86] And, as a corollary of that conception, every visual "act" was tied to viewpoint. At the end of the Dugento and through the first half of the fourteenth century, one of the most novel developments in painting, which foreshadows art of the Quattrocento, was painters' desire to situate the beholder. In both altarpieces and fresco cycles, spatial articulation often embodied painters' conviction that their work was to stand in fixed relation to a stationary viewer.[87]

Thus we come to the larger and more complex matter of pictorial space in works where the settings or painted surrounds are architectural. At the very beginning of trecento naturalism, in the *Saint Francis Legend* of Assisi, we find evidence that painters of the new art attempted more than empirical perspective. While there is no geometric scheme embodied in the narratives, the elements of the corbel table above the scenes and the dentil course below them are ordered such that their orthogonals converge on a vanishing axis.[88] The corbels and dentils are thus means of informing the beholder that the scenes of each architectural bay in the nave of San Francesco are to be viewed as a group seen from a central position. It does still more. As John White has pointed out, the perspective of these elements tells the viewer how far back from the scenes he is to stand.[89] This is the first critical step in creating a fixed relation between the imaged and the beholder.

With Giotto of the Peruzzi Chapel in Florence's Santa Croce, the vanishing axis construction is moved from the surrounds to the pictorial content of the scenes; and since the narratives are conceived as seen by a viewer standing directly before them, the orthogonals of architecture are seen from both above and below. The arrangement, however, does not (because it cannot) involve the convergence of orthogonals at the horizon.[90]

It is a noteworthy coincidence that these developments occurred in a Franciscan context, for Roger Bacon believed that the study of optics and geometry would serve artists in serving the faith. He argued that if the literal content of scripture was to be accurately

---

85. Burke, *Opus majus,* II, 464.
86. Pecham, *Perspectiva,* 34.
87. A truly remarkable comment about the relation of viewer and painted image comes from northern Europe at the beginning of the thirteenth century. In his *Poetria nova,* a treatise on rhetoric and poetics composed c.1200–c.1215, Geoffrey of Vinsauf, speaking of ornaments of written style, remarks: "If internal ornament is not in harmony with external, a sense of propriety is lacking. Adorning the face of a word is painting a worthless picture: it is a false thing, its beauty fictitious. . . . It is a picture that charms one who stands at a distance, but displeases the viewer at close range." M.F. Nims, trans., *Poetria Nova of Geofffrey of Vinsauf,* Toronto, 1967.
88. Edgerton, *Renaissance Rediscovery,* 14–15.
89. John White, *The Birth and Rebirth of Pictorial Space,* 3d ed., Cambridge, Mass., 1987, 40.
90. White, *Birth and Rebirth,* 74–75.

notion that the medium through which species travel progressively weakens their intensity by creating resistance to their multiplication.[78] Dante makes reference to this idea in his discussion, in the *Convivio,* of the reason why stars may not appear as bright as they are: "[T]he medium changes the images of the star which pass through it: its density has a darkening effect."[79] And John Pecham remarked: "If the distance is immoderate, sight does not achieve full differentiation of the more remote intervening bodies because the visible species are weak on account of the distance."[80] In the background of Ambrogio's *Good Government,* it is not only that the hills are darkened; they are described as uniform, that is, without internal distinctions to indicate trees, or buildings, or whatever. Pecham speaks to this phenomenon: "[M]any small colors appear from a distance to be one color."[81]

When, in his *Presentation in the Temple* (Fig. 21), Ambrogio Lorenzetti created the deepest interior of the Tuscan Trecento, he tried to enhance the viewer's sense of distance by using a device related to that used for exterior scenes. Although we can see that the sanctuary behind the high priest has windows along its two sides, they provide no light. All the elements are darkened, and Ambrogio even changed the color of the engaged columns from rose to green in order to strengthen the recession.[82]

Pecham addresses a related matter that anticipates what early-trecento painters discovered: that the perception of distance is enhanced by the succession of forms in a series. He says: "[P]erception of the magnitude of a distance derives from the magnitude of the intervening bodies."[83] And he illustrates this fact by contrasting our perceptions of the horizon and the sky: "[I]f distance is gathered from the size of [the intervening] bodies, then the distance must appear greater where greater magnitude is seen to intervene. But between the horizon and the observer, the whole breadth of the earth is seen to intervene; between the observer and the zenith, nothing. Therefore the horizon appears incomparably farther way than any other part of the sky."[84]

One of Ambrogio Lorenzetti's Saint Nicholas narratives (Fig. 107) points to still another reflection of contemporary notions of vision and of the world. In the far distance, we see a number of sails on the horizon, three of them decidedly darkened to indicate distance, but we do not see the hulls of those vessels. Roger Bacon says: "To what distance

78. The thirteenth-century perspectivists were indebted for this idea to Ptolemy, whose *Optica,* written in the second century A.D., was translated into Latin from Arabic in the mid–twelfth century. Significantly enough, Ptolemy makes this point in relation to painters, noting that they paint nearby objects or figures in bright colors and darken those in the distance. See S. Edgerton, *The Renaissance Rediscovery of Linear Perspective,* New York, 1975, 69.

79. Dante, *The Banquet,* 102. Compare Roger Bacon: "And again because it [vision] receives a weaker species from the fixed stars than from the planets, since species is weakened by distance, vision puts forth more effort." *Opus majus,* II, 539. See also the comments in Bacon's *De multipicatione specierum:* Lindberg, *Roger Bacon's Philosophy of Nature,* 205–7.

80. Pecham, *Perspectiva,* 141.

81. Pecham, *Perspectiva,* 153.

82. There is something of a precedent for this feature of Ambrogio's work. In Duccio's scene of *Christ's Temptation on the Temple* from the *Maestà,* we look through an open doorway into the dark interior of the temple.

83. Pecham, *Perspectiva,* 141.

84. Pecham, *Perspectiva,* 143.

Viterbo and Rome.[72] Furthermore, we have clear evidence, in *Il convivio* and in the *Divine Comedy,* that the new thought regarding optics was known to and used by Dante, a circumstance that indicates the availability of the new optical theories to a general educated audience.[73]

Now, it might seem that the lofty matters of optics and epistemology were far removed from painters, and that the general concern with vision, the Franciscan emphasis on all creation as a manifestation of God's love, and the demands that narrative painting placed on artists suffice to account for what we find in images. And I think that in large part true. The Sienese depiction of textiles and the ways in which those depictions accommodate viewing conditions provide a clear instance of acute observation.[74] At San Francesco, Assisi, Pietro Lorenzetti's experiments with depicting cast shadows and night skies surely arose from the painter's own visual experience.[75] But occasionally we encounter developments that are not so easily explained. When, for example, Simone Martini, in his 1333 *Annunciation,* surrounded Gabriel's and the Virgin's haloes (Fig. 20) with incisions to suggest rays of light diffusing from that halo, he embodied the notion of the rectilinear propagation of light.[76] And when he showed those rays partially masking the drape behind the Virgin, he was commenting on the ability of strong light to interfere with perception. Ambrogio Lorenzetti, in his small *Maestà* (Color Plate 15), described light emanating from the principal figures in straight lines and partially masking the surrounding angels.[77]

A still more vivid indication of optical theory's influence on painters is found in the depiction of distance. Two of the scenes of Simone Martini's *Beato Agostino Novello* offer expansive views: one of an urban setting (Color Plate 8), the other of a landscape (Fig. 63). In the former, the ground surface darkens as it moves back from the picture plane; in the latter, we behold in the far distance mountains and architecture darker than the landscape elements of foreground and middle distance. Similar effects are found in one of Ambrogio Lorenzetti's narratives of Saint Nicholas (Fig. 107) and, most dramatically, in the distant landscape of his *Effects of Good Government* (Color Plate 6). And Ambrogio's and Simone's use of this device is in fact preceded by Duccio's *Temptation on the Mountain* (Color Plate 2). We accept this darkening of distant forms as a period convention—it is described by Cennino Cennini—and may ignore the fact that it is not a phenomenon to be seen in nature and thus to originate in observation. It is, however, entirely in accord with the perpectivists'

---

72. Lindberg, "Lines of Influence," 67–68, 72–73, 81–82.

73. See A. Parronchi, "La perspectiva dantesca," in *Studi su la dolce prospettiva,* Milan, 1964, 3–90. This essay originally appeared in *Studi danteschi,* XXXVI, 1960.

74. Hills, *The Light of Early Italian Painting,* 95–114.

75. Hayden B. J. Maginnis, "Cast Shadow in the Passion Cycle at San Francesco, Assisi: A Note," *Gazette des beaux-arts,* LXXVII, 1971, 63–64.

76. The arrangement of the projecting rays around the entire halo accords with the perspectivists' notion that a point of light diffuses itself spherically. See Pecham, *Perspectiva,* 83.

77. The archetypal discussion of this phenomenon, among the perspectivists, dealt with the way the light of the sun obliterates the light of the stars during the day. John Pecham also points out that a fire at night prevents vision of things beyond it. *Perspectiva,* 85.

Alhazen, and he did so as part of his ambition to create a synthesis of all human knowledge. In the work of Robert Grosseteste (c. 1168–1253), Bacon found two ideas that he would meld with the theories of Alhazen. Grosseteste held that God had made the universe by creating a primordial point of light that instantly diffused itself in every direction to create the firmament, which, in turn, diffused its own light back toward the center of the universe to produce celestial spheres and the terrestrial world. The universe, then, was structured by the geometry of light, and understanding the universe was impossible without an understanding of the "lines, angles, and figures" produced by light. That understanding is inextricably linked to an understanding of optics. Grosseteste had also laid the foundation for the theory of the "multiplication of species," the notion that every natural agent sends forth a power "sometimes called species, sometimes a likeness . . . into sense and into matter." This idea Bacon used to explain the particulars of Alhazen's intromission theory of vision. He argued that every object "produces its likeness or species in the adjacent transparent medium [the air], which in turn produces a further likeness in the next part of the medium, and so forth," until a likeness reaches the eye and is carried to the brain.[66]

Bacon wrote his optical works in the early 1260s: *Perspectiva*, which was part 5 of his *Opus majus*; *De multiplicatione specierum*; and *De speculis comburentibus*.[67] These were quickly followed by the optical treatises of John Pecham and Witelo, both of whom saw themselves as followers of Alhazen but were influenced by Bacon as well.[68] Witelo's *Perspectiva* was written between c. 1270 and c. 1273; Pecham's *Perspectiva communis* was probably written between 1269 and 1279.[69] For my purpose, Pecham's work is the most interesting, since it was written as an elementary textbook on optics. So important and influential were these men and their works that "by the end of the thirteenth century and throughout the fourteenth, people devoted themselves to optics simply because it was one of the established disciplines."[70]

There is an Italian connection in this story; the works of Bacon, Pecham, and Witelo intersected at the papal court in Viterbo and around the most important thirteenth-century translator of Aristotle, William of Moerbeke, papal chaplain.[71] It seems Bacon sent Clement IV, resident in Viterbo, his *Opus majus, Opus minus,* and *Tractatus de radis* late in 1267 or early in 1268. Witelo arrived in Viterbo late in 1268 and remained until sometime in the 1270s. John Pecham, who had met Bacon in Paris, arrived at the papal court in Viterbo early in 1277 and spent the following two years lecturing at the papal university in

66. Lindberg, *Theories*, 113. What is involved here is a continuous replication of the species, or likeness, from the object to the eye. We shall see some of the implications of this idea below.

67. Burke, *The Opus Majus*; D. C. Lindberg, *Roger Bacon's Philosophy of Nature: A Critical Edition, with English Translation, Introduction, and Notes, of De Multiplicatione Specierum and De Speculis Comburentibus*, Oxford, 1983.

68. D. C. Lindberg, "Lines of Influence in Thirteenth-Century Optics," *Speculum*, XLVI, 1971, 66–83.

69. John Pecham, *John Pecham and the Science of Optics: Perspectiva Communis*, ed. and trans. D. C. Lindberg, Madison, Wis., 1970.

70. Lindberg, *Theories*, 100.

71. Witelo's *Perspectiva* is dedicated to William of Moerbeke. I would also note that William was a friend of Thomas Aquinas.

This cultural concern with vision is, of course, best demonstrated in the proliferation of images themselves and in the increasingly varied uses found for them. In an important recent study, Anne Derbes has demonstrated how quickly and how early the Franciscans not only employed images but also selected visual sources to convey specific ideas.[61] During the thirteenth century, the tombs of popes and cardinals came to include large-scale effigies of the deceased. Julian Gardner argues that those effigies may not be portraits in the true sense of the word, but sculptors did give them seeming characterization of physiognomy.[62] Likewise, Simone Martini, in the Saint Martin Chapel at Assisi, gave the long-deceased Cardinal Gentile da Montefiore a physiognomy distinct from those in the narratives. In Siena and Florence, the state commissioned depictions of subject territories in a context where, at other times, personifications or coats of arms would have sufficed. And although it is doubtful that anything approaching real portraiture was involved in *pitture infamante,* the use of figures was apparently considered a meaningful component in the intended vilification.

Evidence of the type cited above might easily be multiplied, but my epithet, "the age of vision," is based on more than indications of concern with the visible; it stems also from the thirteenth- and fourteenth-century preoccupation with optics. The recovery of Aristotle and the study of Justinian's *Corpus juris civilis* were not the only manifestations of the period's interest in the thought of antiquity; nor was the study of Averroës the period's only concern with the work of Arabic scholars. By the middle of the thirteenth century, the entire body of Greek and Arabic works on optics was available in the West in Latin translation.[63] The most important work, as it proved, was Alhazen's *De aspectibus,* also known as the *Perspectiva,* a treatise in which its author integrated the anatomical, physical, and mathematical approaches to vision found in ancient thought.[64] Three features of his work were to be of immense importance in the West. First, Alhazen refuted the extramission theory of sight, an idea that had its origins in Plato and Galen and argued that we see through rays sent forth from the eye. Second, he maintained that each point on any object sends forth rays that travel in straight lines in all directions. And third, he argued that the eye sees only via those rays that are perpendicular to the curved surface of the eye; this means that sight occurs through a visual pyramid that has its base on the object seen and its apex in the eye.[65]

It was the Franciscan Roger Bacon (c. 1214–c. 1292) who first made much of

---

it is a happy fact that this item makes such concern explicit. And its context is such that it contains none of the problems of interpretation that attend Petrarch's account of the view from Mont Ventoux.

61. Anne Derbes, *Picturing the Passion in Late Medieval Italy: Narrative Painting, Franciscan Ideologies, and the Levant,* Cambridge and New York, 1996.

62. Julian Gardner, *The Tomb and the Tiara: Curial Tomb Sculpture in Rome and Avignon in the Later Middle Ages,* Oxford, 1992.

63. D. C. Lindberg (*Theories of Vision from Al-Kindi to Kepler,* Chicago, 1976, 209–23) provides a guide to translations from Greek and Arabic.

64. Alhazen (c.965–c.1039) also wrote a treatise on "burning mirrors," *De speculis comburentibus.*

65. The notion of a visual pyramid had been central to the optics of Euclid and Ptolemy.

hears. Similarly, although to a greater extent, the legend of the Beata Umiliana de' Cerchi repeatedly assures us that Umiliana witnessed miraculous events with open eyes, that is, when she was awake. Her servant saw for herself that Umiliana's chamber, at night, was often illuminated with a great light, and as visual witness she provides testimony to the truth of the legend. There was also a witness, a fellow Dominican, to the fact that Thomas Aquinas levitated while in prayer. Dante, rather scornfully, tells us that "many people have become so obstinate that they are doubtful about those miracles [of Christ and his saints] because their minds are somewhat clouded, and they are unable to believe in any miracle unless they have visible evidence of it."[54] This emphasis on seeing informs various types of devotional literature as well.

One the most important and influential texts of the entire period is the *Meditations on the Life of Christ,* written by a Franciscan who may have been from San Gimignano, near Siena. The lengthy work, which retells the Gospel stories in much greater detail, is conceived as a series of "imagined representations," as the author tells us, in which the reader is repeatedly admonished to "see," "observe," "watch," or "behold" the scenes that are conjured.[55] Indeed, when we come to the story of Christ's Passion, the author announces: "Now we shall see each event individually."[56] The entire purpose of these meditations is tied to visualization, so that the reader should feel himself "present in those places as if the things were done in [his] presence."[57]

It is not at all difficult to find other types of literature that reflect the period's preoccupation with sight and seeing. Throughout the *Divine Comedy* Dante is frequently concerned with vision, telling us what he saw or beheld. His concern is also with the reliability of vision. The poems of Guido Cavalcanti are peppered with references to eyes, to seeing, to looking.[58] The central conceit of Boccaccio's *Amorosa visione,* and thus the means of the poet's early instruction, is the author's seeing a series of frescoes in two rooms of a castle.[59] And perhaps it is worth noting that when Fra Giordano told his Florentine audience about the new art of eyeglasses, he said: "I have *seen* the man who first invented and created it" (emphasis mine).

Sight and appearances are, of course, fundamental to all Sienese attempts, discussed above, to order the visual experience of the urban environment. Order was to be seen. We also have indication of a more subtle concern with the visible. The Sienese constitution of 1309–10 asked the Dominicans to remove a wall, or actually an extension of a wall, that obstructed the piazza around their church, because it interfered with those who had come to the piazza to hear sermons, and "obstructs the view of the church toward the city."[60]

54. Dante, *The Banquet,* 96 (III.vii.20–23).
55. I. Ragusa and R. B. Green, trans. and eds., *Meditations on the Life of Christ: An Illustrated Manuscript of the Fourteenth Century,* Princeton, 1961, 49.
56. Ragusa and Green, *Meditations,* 320.
57. Ragusa and Green, *Meditations,* 387.
58. M. Cirigliano, trans., *Guido Cavalcanti: The Complete Poems,* New York, 1992.
59. Hayden B. J. Maginnis, "Boccaccio: A Poet Making Pictures," *Source,* xv, no. 2, 1996, 1–7.
60. Lisini, *Costituto volgarizzato,* I, 336–37: the wall that "impedisca l'aspetto de la chiesa verso la città." Although we might have anticipated this concern with view from the legislation on beauty,

If carpenters, painters, and patrons were familiar with design procedures, and if all displayed preferences for symmetry and the uniformity of regularly repeated elements, that is not to say that these notions conditioned, or even were relevant to, judgments about "beautiful figures" or what was "a very beautiful picture." But there are various sources that can assist us here as well. For example, Thomas Aquinas remarked: "There are three requirements for beauty. Firstly, integrity or perfection—for if something is impaired it is ugly. Then there is due proportion or consonance. And also clarity: when things that are brightly coloured are called beautiful."[50] And Saint Bonaventure said: "The relation of beauty (of an image) to its model is such that beauty is in the image as well as in what it is an image of. From this one may conclude that beauty is two-fold. . . . an image is said to be beautiful when it is well painted, and also it gives a good representation of the object."[51] Bonaventure was, then, an advocate of craftsmanship, but also of mimesis. Naturalism is, however, a relative thing, and there were many secondary figures who were as skilled in their art as the great masters of the Trecento, as Giotto and Simone. There were many painters who created images as "brightly coloured" as pictures by the greater talents. Something more must have entered into judgments than the factors we have thus far considered. That something was originality and invention.[52]

An Age of Vision

> For Aristotle says in the first book of the Metaphysics that vision alone reveals the differences of things; since by means of it we search out experimental knowledge of all things that are in the heavens and in the earth. . . . But concerning vision alone is a separate science formed among philosophers, namely optics, and not concerning any other sense. Wherefore there must be a special utility in our knowledge through vision which is not found in the other senses. . . . Therefore it [optics] is the flower of the whole of philosophy and through it, and not without it, can the other sciences be known.
> —Roger Bacon, *Opus majus* (c. 1260)[53]

The tales of miraculous painted images told above are, I believe, primarily the extension of stories earlier told of sculpture and the echoes of the legends of Byzantium. But they are also related to another development that here requires our attention. In the story of Saint Francis and the crucifix of San Damiano, the moving lips of the Crucified assure Francis and the reader of his legend that the crucifix is indeed the source of the words that Francis

---

50. Eco, *Art and Beauty*, 71.
51. See W. Tatarkiewicz, *History of Aesthetics*, II, The Hague, 1970, 239.
52. See "The Invention of Art" in Maginnis, *Age of Giotto*, 193–97.
53. Roger Bacon, *The Opus Majus of Roger Bacon*, trans. R.B. Burke, II, New York, 1962, 419–20.

assume. There was no possibility that Siena's major streets could be straightened in the sense of being made rectilinear. The Via Francigena snaked its way through the city; some streets paralleled its curving course; others were determined by the rising and falling terrain of Siena's hills. Thus, the dugento legislation must have been intended to promote a regularity of facades, an intention made explicit in 1346. What I shall call continuity of line was, then, one ambition, while the brick paving of the *strate* gave them continuity of surface. There were also prohibitions on balconies, on exterior staircases, and on cantilevering second storeys into the streets.[46] These were certainly intended to keep the streets light, to ensure ease of passage, and to restrict the damage of fires, but they too led toward uniformity. Finally, the 1309 statute regarding brick facing for houses urged a uniformity of design, texture, and color along the streets: an aspect that would have been further enhanced by the fact that the commune had established a standard size for bricks. When we bring all these factors together, we realize that the underlying conception for Siena's streets is quite sophisticated.

These laws and remarks suggest that the Sienese of the period might have been quite articulate about their use of "beauty" in such contexts. The provision for the Costa Larga associates beauty, size, and brightness, and we know that light was symbolic as well as utilitarian for medieval man. The concern for uniformity and continuity, displayed in architecture of the period as well as in this legislation, echoes long-standing preoccupations, ultimately derived from the *Book of Wisdom,* with number, order, and proportion.[47] In these matters, the Sienese would have been instructed by the learned, especially the secular clergy and the friars, but closely related ideas they also would have encountered among artists, particularly builders. Medieval architectural design was founded in geometry and on a system of proportional relations. Indeed, the geometric system of design was so widespread that it influenced the design procedure for altarpieces.[48] And since the designs for altarpieces were provided to carpenters for execution, carpenters as much as stone masons must have been familiar with such systems.

The aspirations behind the Sienese ordinances regarding streets and buildings are clarified further for us by the phenomenon of new towns, communities founded where there had been no settlement before and thus planned from the ground up. Florence, in the late Dugento and in the Trecento, was particularly active in this regard, but Siena established at least two new towns: at what the Sienese hoped would be their port of Talamone (Fig. 5) and at Castelfranco di Paganico. Regarding the latter, the Sienese constitution of 1309–10 required everyone living on the principal thoroughfare to construct a portico four *braccia* (roughly 2.4 meters) wide before their houses.[49] The plan of Talamone, found in a document of 1306, shows us an urban fabric determined by rectilinear streets crossing each other at right angles and by a space, inside the walls, almost entirely filled with buildings.

46. Lisini, *Costituto volgarizzato,* 1309–10, II, 89.

47. For an introduction to these matters, see U. Eco, *Art and Beauty in the Middle Ages,* trans. H. Bredin, Hew Haven and London, 1986.

48. See the discussion of altarpiece formats in Chapter III.

49. Lisini, *Costituto volgarizzato,* I, 120. This item is dated May 1309.

to be taken in regard to the Duomo Nuovo for its "greater beauty."[36] It was for the beauty of the city that, in September of 1324, the Consiglio Generale ordered the demolition of balconies along a stretch of the Via Francigena in the *popoli* of San Vincenzo and Magione del Tempio.[37] In September and October of 1334 the commune paid two "officials in charge of the beauty of the city."[38] In November of the same year, it was decided that the street now known as the Costa Larga should be at least ten *braccia* wide (5.9 meters) and "beautiful and luminous."[39] And in 1346 the commune revived the office of praetor, to supervise and regulate new construction in the city, because "it redounds to the beauty of the city of Siena and to the satisfaction of almost all the people of the same city that any edifices that are to be made anew anywhere along the public thoroughfares of the Sienese commune in the city of Siena and its boroughs proceed in line with existent buildings, and one building not stand out beyond another, but they shall be disposed and arranged so as to be of the greatest beauty for the city."[40]

This last document helps point us toward what was meant by "beauty" in such legislation. In terms of the urban fabric, beauty is clearly related to order and uniformity; the city is more beautiful when the line of buildings along its streets is continuous. Indeed, this idea determined much of the legislation regarding what we would call urban planning throughout the late Dugento and early Trecento. Late-thirteenth-century regulations had tried to regularize the streets, urging that they be straightened and fixing their widths. The constitution of 1309–10 ordered that all houses constructed of *terra murata* have their facades covered in brick in order to "lend beauty to the city."[41] A statute that appears in the same redaction of the constitution but that was originally approved in May of 1296 declares that the ruined condition of the baptistery, San Giovanni, is such that it should be removed "per belleza del vescovado."[42] Another statute of May 1297, also included in the 1309–10 constitution, orders that all newly built houses surrounding the Campo must have double windows with colonnettes and be without balconies.[43] Undoubtedly this provision was intended to bring newly constructed facades into harmony with the planned Palazzo Pubblico.[44] When legislation reaches such specificity, the desire for order and uniformity is indeed great.[45]

As cursory as these references to beauty are, they reveal more than we might first

36. Milanesi, *Documenti*, I, 226.
37. ASS, Consiglio Generale 101, fols. 98r–99v.
38. Bowsky, *Finance*, 273.
39. ASS, Consiglio Generale, Deliberazione 116, fol. 42v (24 November 1334).
40. Bowsky, *Medieval Italian Commune*, 295.
41. Lisini, *Costituto volgarizzato*, II, 406–7.
42. Lisini, *Costituto volgarizzato*, II, 130–31.
43. Lisini, *Costituto volgarizzato*, II, 29. The fine for violation was a significant but not outrageous £25.
44. Restrictions on windows and specifications about size go back to the constitution of 1262. See Zdekauer, *Il constituto*, 306–7. If my reading of the situation is correct, it means that the plan for the Palazzo Pubblico was fully realized by 1297.
45. We have evidence of similar concerns in Florence. Giovanni Villani, in his chronicle, tells us that in 1293, in connection with work on the Florentine baptistery, "all the monuments and tomb stones and marble arches that were around San Giovanni [were removed], for the greater beauty of the church." Villani, *Nuova cronica*, II, 14.

were possible candidates for the commission. The list included, among others, Taddeo Gaddi, Orcagna, and Nardo di Cione from Florence, and Jacopo del Pelliciaio and Bartolommeo Bulgarini from Siena. Our concern, however, is with the preamble to the list—"These are the best masters of painting that are in Florence"—and, at its midst, the remark "These are the masters of Siena who are held to be the best."[29] When Petrarch, in his will, specified that his *Madonna* by Giotto was to go to Francesco da Carrara, he noted that it astonished masters of the art, although its beauty was not intelligible to the ignorant.[30] The Laudesi of Santa Maria Novella, when they commissioned the Rucellai *Madonna* (Figs. 10–11), required Duccio "to do each and every thing which will contribute to the beauty of said panel," and made a condition of acceptance that the panel, upon completion, be judged "a most beautiful picture." Guido Tarlati required of Pietro Lorenzetti "most beautiful figures." The Carmelites of Siena, when petitioning the commune for a grant-in-aid for their new altarpiece (1329) by Pietro, described it as "indeed beautiful." The document of 1316, regarding the preservation of murals in the hall of the palace of the podestà, states that the interior "should please the eye, bring joy to the heart, and satisfy everyone's senses; [it is] to the glory of the whole community that the leaders and rulers of the commune should enjoy surroundings which are fine, beautiful, and honorable."[31]

Undoubtedly, craftsmanship entered greatly into such judgments, as did a concern for materials. Guido Tarlati, in his agreement with Pietro Lorenzetti for the Arezzo polyptych (Color Plates 13–14), stipulated that Pietro should use "the best gold of a hundred sheets to the florin," "the best silver," and the "best colors," including ultramarine blue. As we well know, the combination of such materials with high craftsmanship produced exquisite surfaces and paintings that more than rivaled works in enamel or mosaic. But Tarlati's requirement of beauty, considered in light of similar concerns elsewhere, seems to point to something more than materials and technique.

Beauty was much on the minds of the Sienese. A civic statute of 1309 regarding the park to be created between the Camollia gates says that the project was "for the beauty of the city and . . . for the delight and joy of citizens and foreigners."[32] The constitution of 1309–10 provided for money to be set aside for building and repairing the palace and houses of the commune for the "beauty of the city."[33] Even before these notices, in 1292, a certain Porrino, when petitioning the commune for citizenship, sought favor with the Nine by promising to acquire "most beautiful and agreeable possessions" in the city.[34] On 17 February 1322, Lorenzo Maitani, Niccola Nuti, Ciono di Franco, Tone di Giovanni, and Vanni di Cione of Florence recommended that the commune begin construction on a new cathedral "beautiful, large, and magnificent,"[35] and a document of 23 August 1339 speaks of measures

29. Ladis, *Taddeo Gaddi*, 257.
30. See R. Salvini, *Giotto (bibliografia)*, Rome, 1938, 5. Vasari, II, 117, also gives the relevant text.
31. Milanesi, *Documenti*, I, 180–81; translation from Borsook, *Mural Painters*, xix. See the discussion of the patronage of the commune in Chapter IV.
32. Bowsky, *Finance*, 20.
33. Lisini, *Costituto volgarizzato*, 98.
34. Waley, *Siena*, 74.
35. Milanesi, *Documenti*, I, 188.

ignoring the fact that the cumulative effect was to generate a set of expectations and anticipations, a growing belief that all images were potentially miraculous. That lack of general policy had two consequences. In the first place, it created a gulf between the attitude documented in the epigraphs to this section and that we discover in legends, in sermons, in the history of Italian spirituality. Second, it left Italians free to play "fast and loose" with their Byzantine borrowings. The whole Eastern notion of venerated archetypes, for example, was briefly felt in the Dugento but rapidly disappeared as other forces made innovation and originality the things to which Western painters and patrons aspired. To put it metaphorically, a great many lacunae were left in the Western transcription of the Eastern conception of images.

Now, I have devoted attention to this matter for two reasons. First, I believe my explanation accounts for many (but not all) tales of miraculous images that arise in Italy during the thirteenth and fourteenth centuries. Second, this history and explanation have very little to do with Siena during the period here examined. And I see that as profoundly revealing. Siena was little blessed with miraculous images and/or generally paid them little heed. The cathedral *Madonna,* which received the commune's prayers before the battle of Montaperti and the keys to the city, was the nearest thing Siena had to a major wonder-working image. An image of the Crucified spoke to the Blessed Andrea Gallerani, and an image of the Madonna foretold his death. Deliberations of the Consiglio Generale, in 1348, speak of an image of the Madonna, apparently in a street tabernacle, that had begun to perform miracles.[28] But there is no contemporary evidence that major cults arose around any of these pictures.

Once again, we have evidence of a distinctive Sienese culture. Although Florence reveled in wonder-working images, the Sienese apparently felt no great need to possess such images of their own. And although Florence, as well as other centers, possessed a vital tradition of wax votives—sometimes associated with images, sometimes with relics—there is, to my knowledge, no evidence of their use in early-trecento Siena. The city might have been closely linked with others through trade and banking, might have been a mere thirty miles from Florence, but that does not mean that Siena's culture was recast to conform to patterns elsewhere. Perhaps, then, this material serves as a healthy caution, reminding us to avoid generalizations that, based on the evidence of one center, purport to apply generally to an Italian or even a Tuscan outlook.

A Sense of Beauty/A Sense of Order

As the Opera of San Giovanni Fuorcivitas in Pistoia planned, at the mid-Trecento, a new altarpiece for the high altar, someone produced a list of Florentine and Sienese painters who

---

28. ASS, Consiglio Generale 143, fol. 6.

confraternities as those explained by the theory. But most relics did not behave in the way of our images. They were not inclined to bleed, to speak, or to be objects from which the Christ Child stepped forth. Relics were, quite obviously, physically unique. God had left to the remains of his saints, and sometimes the objects they had worn or touched, the miraculous powers that had been the saints' in life, so that these things should witness to God's power and the sanctity of the saints. Relics were the identifying traces of "the very special dead." But the power of images was not similarly founded in unique substance. The angelic portrait of the Virgin in Florence's Annunziata was replaced by a fourteenth-century fresco, but the power of the image was undiminished. The miracle-working image of Orsanmichele was replaced, perhaps twice, and is now Bernardo Daddi's panel of 1346. Moreover, our examples include images that we might expect to be classified, and therefore to function, in different ways. They include images miraculously created, images that were the means of special communion between God and his saints, interventionist images that acted on behalf of ordinary men and women, and, finally, the random, "chanced-upon" images that bled or punished sacrilege in other ways.

It seems to me that the greatest refutation of the image/relic thesis lies in the stories of Saint Francis and Saint Thomas Aquinas discussed above. Those who repeated such stories, stories whose accuracy was acknowledged by the Church, were hardly writers to mistake images for relics. We need a broader and more convincing explanation.

The answer to our questions and the explanation of the circumstances recorded in our examples lie in the West's increasing absorption of Eastern thought. Just as the Western presence in Crete, Cyprus, and Constantinople itself was gradually to bring a reformation in style and compositions in Italian dugento art, so that contact was to influence Westerners' expectations of how images might behave. After the long struggle of the Iconoclastic Controversy, the Eastern Church had a well-defined position on images: they were doorways to and from heaven. No better illustration of the Eastern attitude and conception can be found than the *Letter of the Three Patriarchs,* produced in the mid–ninth century, although purporting to be earlier.[27] The miracles connected with images in this text are highly reminiscent of those stories told by Fra Filippo degli Agarazzi. The *Veronica* and, later, the Shroud of Turin were surely the Western responses to the Mandylion of Edessa, while the story of Master Bartholomew in Santissima Annunziata recalls a much earlier legend of Eastern origin according to which God, during the night, finished a picture of the Madonna that Saint Luke had begun.

The great problem, as I have indicated, was that the Western Church could not accommodate such stories. Indeed, the long-standing fear of idolatry meant that the Church took no official, general position regarding such ideas or such wonder-working images. Only in allowing image cults to continue, or in recognizing particular cases of miraculous images in relation to canonization, did the Church make place for these tales—all the while

---

27. See the text of the letter in R. Cormack, *Writing in Gold: Byzantine Society and Its Icons,* new ed., New York, 1996.

and twelve years after his canonization. The story was, I might add, clearly acceptable to Bonaventure, who included it in the *Legenda maior*.

Later in the century the Dominicans acquired their own legend of a speaking image, in no less illustrious a context than the life of Saint Thomas Aquinas. Toward the end of Aquinas's life, the saint was praying before a *Crucifixion* panel in Naples, and as he did so, he heard the Crucified speak to him: "You have written well of me."[23] In contrast to the legend of Francis, where the spoken words are a summons, the story of Aquinas, although also marking him as the recipient of special grace, is one of final approval for all the saint had written. It is a conclusion, rather than a beginning, and, quite transparently, a divine confirmation of the orthodoxy of Thomas's work.[24] The two miracles, the two stories, are deeply revealing of the differences in outlook in the two orders.

We cannot leave this issue without noting that it was the Franciscan model that won out. In 1370, a crucifix was the means whereby the Lord spoke to Saint Bridget of Sweden, and in 1372 Saint Catherine of Siena received the stigmata while praying before a crucifix in Pisa.

Now, these tales are not to be reconciled with the Church's official position on images as embodied in the quotations that begin this section. At the same time, they cannot be regarded as constituting a subculture or a popular and subversive counterculture; the Church's acknowledgment and acceptance of such miracles is too clear. Why, then, the constant declarations of the view first espoused by Gregory the Great? The fundamental problem was that the Western Church had no articulated framework within which to understand or discuss miracle-working pictures; it had no theology of images. Miracles great and small involving images could only be treated as acts of divine intervention specific to individuals and to discrete objects. But why did such miracles become so widespread in the thirteenth and fourteenth centuries? How did they become so central to the lives of contemporary saints?

Many years ago, Joseph Braun argued that pictures came to stand for absent relics and in that capacity acquired the miraculous properties of the latter.[25] More recently, this argument has been espoused by Hans Belting and many who follow him.[26] It is, however, a position that I find less than convincing. The Church required that every consecrated altar contain a relic, and that in itself must eliminate all altarpieces from the Braun/Belting hypothesis, leaving only private devotional works and perhaps some images belonging to

---

23. For discussion of the image, which still exists, see Maginnis, "The Thyssen-Bornemisza Ugolino."

24. The import of the miracle is very clear. In 1277, the bishop of Paris condemned as heretical a series of Aristotelian propositions and conclusions then being taught by the Arts Faculty at the University of Paris. Among these were ideas that were part of Thomism, and thus doubt was cast on the orthodoxy of some of Saint Thomas's views. In the miracle, Thomas is vindicated.

25. Joseph Braun, *Der christliche Altar in seiner geschichtlichen Entwicklung*, 2 vols., Munich, 1924–28.

26. Hans Belting, *Das Bild und sein Publikum im Mittelaltar,* Berlin, 1981, and Belting, *Likeness and Presence.*

stigmata out of a picture, likely a fresco, of the saint in the refectory of his convent.[21] The next day, the stigmata had reappeared. The assault and reappearance were repeated until the Dominican took a knife and "dug the marks of the Stigmata out of the picture, cutting out the color and the stone," but just as he finished, blood began to gush violently from the openings, staining the friar's face, hands, and habit. Terrified, the perpetrator of this sacrilege fell to the ground as if dead. The flow of blood stopped, the friar revived, the stigmata reappeared, but only when the entire community of the convent submitted to discipline and prayed for Francis's forgiveness.

If we move on almost a century, we can find vivid reflections of a similar mentality in stories that echo earlier models. Between 1397 and c. 1420, Fra Filippo degli Agarazzi collected a set of "ensamples," or *assempri,* to be used in sermons.[22] Born c. 1340, Fra Filippo came from a good and prosperous Sienese family, and from 1398 until his death in 1422, he was prior of the Augustinian monastery at Lecceto, just beyond the walls of Siena itself. In other words, he was no provincial and superstitious cleric. Most of Fra Filippo's tales are illustrative and moralizing; a number of them relate to the vice of gambling and the passions it provokes. For example, he tells the story of a Neapolitan gambler who, having lost great sums, takes out his anger by wounding the face in a frescoed image of the Virgin; the image immediately bleeds. In another instance, a gambler who has lost heavily after invoking the aid of his patron, Saint Anthony, comes upon an image of the saint and stabs it above the hip bone. The gambler himself experiences the pain and dies three days later, infected with Saint Anthony's fire, which began just above his hip bone. Yet another gambler stabs the figure of the Virgin on a Pisan coin, and the coin is bathed in blood. A rope-maker of Siena who hurls a gambling piece at an image of the Madonna is struck down paralyzed until he repents.

We have, then, much evidence that stories such as those summarized above were both current among and acceptable to the educated and the religious orders, but the miraculous power of images is most dramatically emphasized in the approved legends of major thirteenth-century saints. Most famous of all is the story of Saint Francis and the speaking crucifix of San Damiano. It is the miraculous event that initiated his calling; it is the story of divine intervention that marked Francis as the recipient of special grace, foreshadowed the stigmatization, and ultimately made him an *alter-Christus.* The words of the Crucified first summoned Francis to his future; the wounds of the Crucified marked him as one who had achieved perfect identity with his Savior. But this tale of an event that purportedly occurred in 1205, this tale so central to the characterization of Saint Francis as we know it, first appears only c. 1240, after Celano's first *Life,* fourteen years after the saint's death

---

21. M. Habig, ed., *St. Francis of Assisi, Writings and Early Biographies: English Omnibus of Sources for the Life of St. Francis,* 4th ed., Chicago, 1983, 1481–82.

22. W. Heywood, *The "Ensamples" of Fra Filippo: A Study of Medieval Siena,* Siena, 1901. That these stories reflect earlier models has been pointed out by N. Sapengo, *Storia letteraria d'Italia: Il trecento,* Milan, 1942, 548.

of sorrow and loss, prayed before an image of the Madonna that she earlier had had painted on parchment.[19] In consequence, she was filled with grace, courage, and resolve. Umiliana also had a panel picture of the Madonna. Later, one of Umiliana's daughters fell down dying before her, but as Umiliana prayed before the panel of the Virgin, a beautiful boy emerged from it to make the sign of the cross, and the daughter was restored to health. Still later, during the night, the cloth that covered the image of the Madonna in Umiliana's room was surrounded by fire, without damage to the panel, indicating the presence of the Holy Spirit. Finally, at the time of her death, Umiliana was tormented by the devil, who was banished only when lighted candles in the form of a cross and the panel picture of the Madonna were placed on her chest.

The legend of the Beata Umiliana is also important for references to another type of image, the wax ex-voto. In a trecento vernacular version, we read the story of Ricco da Camerino of Florence, whose seven-year-old son contracted leprosy on his legs, feet, and hands. Ricco promised the *beata* that if she would cure the boy, he would present a wax image of his son at her tomb. In the longer version of the legend, the original Latin text now found in the *Acta Sanctorum,* there are many stories of ex-votos offered at Umiliana's sepulchre. In some instances, the nature of those votives is not specified; in other cases, it is said they were candles. But in fully eight other instances, in addition to the story of Ricco da Camerino, the ex-votos are described as "images in wax."

Offerings of wax votives, in the form of figures or of parts of figures, were widespread in Florentine religious life. Giovanni Villani tells us that pilgrims came to the miraculous image of the Virgin in Orsanmichele, on her feast days, "bringing various images of wax for the miracles effected, so that a great part of the loggia before and around the figure was filled up." We know that there were a great many wax ex-votos offered to the image of the Annunciate in Santissima Annunziata. Franco Sacchetti tells two stories that involve wax images presented at the Annunziata, and complains that "[d]i questi boti e di simili ogni dí si fanno, le quali son piú tosto una idolatria che fede cristiana."[20]

Now, the stories of Beata Umiliana, of the image in Impruneta, of the fresco in Santissima Annunziata, or of the image in Orsanmichele might be taken as reflections of popular enthusiasms, a ground swell, as it were, of devotions among the masses that made its way upward in the culture to reach the literate and the clergy. Obviously that explanation cannot be applied to the *Veronica,* or to situations in which such tales required sanction. On 9 November 1304, Fra Giordano of Pisa, preaching in Florence's Santa Maria Novella, told his audience a story, "of more than a thousand years in the past," of an image of the Crucified painted by Nicodemus that miraculously bled. We must assume that in that great center of Dominican learning, such a story was entirely acceptable and to be taken at face value. In the *Fioretti* we read of a Dominican who, in hatred of Saint Francis, cut the

---

19. This passage provides us with rare testimony of this type of inexpensive image, on parchment, clearly a forerunner of the prints of religious subject matter that later became common.

20. Sacchetti, *Il trecentonovelle,* 329–31, 621–25.

more ordinary men and women. It is also clear that in Italy, after 1200, legends increasingly focus on painted images, as opposed to sculpture. One of the most famous cases of this change is reflected in the story of the *Veronica,* a relic long venerated and long in Rome, although the tale of its origins, even of its nature, is full of contradictions. The legend of Veronica identified her as the woman with issue of blood who was healed by Christ and, in gratitude, had painted an image of him. But Petrus Mallus, c. 1160, identified the Roman relic as "the cloth into which he [Christ] pressed his most holy face before his Passion, when his sweat ran in drops of blood to the earth."[14] About 1210, Gervase of Tilbury indicated that the *Veronica* was on panel, and Gerard of Wales, c. 1215, described it as an image miraculously created when Veronica pressed her robe to Christ's face. Matthew Paris, sometime after 1245, also referred to an image on cloth. Hans Belting has argued that the Roman relic originally bore no image; then, roughly six years after the Latin conquest (1204) of Constantinople, it acquired one, and in 1216 Innocent III granted ten days' indulgence for anyone who recited a prayer, of his composition, to that image.[15]

Florence seems to have been particularly blessed with many powerful and wondrous images. In 1252, a certain Master Bartholomew was executing a fresco of the Virgin in the Church of Santissima Annunziata. One night, when the painter was away from his work, an angel came and finished the face of the Virgin. As the origin of the work was partly miraculous, so too were the picture's powers; it became one of the most important of Florence's wonder-working images. By the mid-Trecento, the Florentines had also created a cult around the panel of the Virgin in the suburban village of Impruneta. Although "residing" outside the city, the image's principal miracles were performed when the panel was brought to Florence itself. The *Virgin of Impruneta* then functioned as a rain goddess, bringing water in times of draught.[16] Toward the end of the thirteenth century, on 3 July 1292, a painted figure of the Virgin on a pilaster of the loggia of Orsanmichele began to perform "great and open miracles." Giovanni Villani, who recounts the story, says that the fame of the miracles and merits of the image spread abroad, so that people came in pilgrimage from all across Tuscany, often presenting votive wax for the miracles received.[17]

Other stories relate to more personal experiences of the power of images. In 1246, the year of the death of the Beata Umiliana de' Cerchi, Vita da Cortona, a Franciscan, set down her legend, a legend that contains four significant passages involving images.[18] After the death of her husband, Umiliana returned to the house of her father and, in that moment

---

14. See Hans Belting, *Likeness and Presence: A History of Images Before the Era of Art,* trans. E. Jephcott, Chicago, 1994, 541–44, for this text and others related to the Veronica.

15. Belting, *Likeness and Presence,* 215–24.

16. One of the earliest descriptions of the image's power is found in Matteo Villani's chronicle, under the year 1354. See R. Trexler, "Florentine Religious Experience: The Sacred Image," *Studies in the Renaissance,* XIX, 1973, 7–40.

17. Giovanni Villani, *Nuova cronica,* ed. G. Porta, I, Parma, 1991, 628.

18. G. De Luca, ed., *Prosatori minori del trecento,* I, *Scrittore di religione,* Milan and Naples, 1954, 723–68. The full original text is found in the *Acta Sanctorum,* XVI, *Maius,* 386–400. On 400–407 is a collection of posthumous miracles, collected in 1249, by another Franciscan, Brother Hippolytus.

And in a remarkable passage, he purports to explain why one picture painted by Giotto might enjoy greater fame than another: it all depended on the position of the stars when each was created.⁷

There is plentiful evidence of belief in the power of images. William of Auvergne, bishop of Paris (1228–49), was convinced that wax images of lambs blessed by the pope could ward off thunderbolts.⁸ That belief must have been widespread, for Matthew Paris (who did not share Bishop William's conviction) recorded a fire at Saint Albans caused by lightning and remarked: "And, just as it is no use relying on privileges and indulgences of the saints, so the impression of the papal seal, in which the Lamb of God is figured, which is placed at the top of our tower, did not prevent the lightning although it is said to have the power and virtue to ward off such commotions."⁹ In 1318, the archbishop of Aix, Robert Mauvoison, had a Jew carve seals on his pastoral rings to avert disease and bring good fortune.¹⁰ In a case brought before the Inquisition during the reign of John XXII, the prior and brothers of a monastery were said to have made a lead image that would speak to them once a month with instructions on how to succeed at alchemy.¹¹ In 1317, the bishop of Cahors was accused of an attempt on John XXII's life by sorcery with wax images.

As Julian Gardner has pointed out, one of the distinguishing characteristics of the early fourteenth century was a new concern with idolatry. It was one of the charges that Philip the Fair laid against Boniface VIII; he also used it as part of a propaganda campaign that led to his destruction of the Order of the Temple. But we have other evidence that demonstrates it was not only the French monarch who was concerned with such matters.¹² Stories, beliefs, and concerns such as those just described were part of the culture of images, and it would be as foolish to dismiss them as having no relation to religious images as it would be to claim that they completely account for reactions to Christian pictures. They are part of the background to the perception of holy images. But in the thirteenth century there were more important influences that shaped contemporary reactions.

It is often said that the masses, through the Middle Ages, preserved all the superstitions of antiquity connected with images, with idols; and indeed, there is plentiful evidence that images of Christ, the Virgin, and the saints inherited the powers of representations of the pagan gods. From the Middle Ages there are many legends dealing with stories of images that move, speak, and perform miracles.¹³ Yet one has the impression that after 1200 such stories not only multiply, they achieve a new prominence as they are increasingly recognized by the Church and begin to touch the lives of the great saints as well as the lives of

---

7. C. E. Gilbert, "Cecco d'Ascoli e la pittura di Giotto," in *Poets Seeing Artists' Work,* Florence, 1991, 33–48.

8. Thorndike, *A History of Magic,* II, 352.

9. R. Vaughan, trans. and ed., *Chronicles of Matthew Paris: Monastic Life in the Thirteenth Century,* Gloucester and New York, 1984, 73.

10. Thorndike, *A History of Magic,* III, 9.

11. Thorndike, *A History of Magic,* III, 28.

12. Julian Gardner, "Boniface VIII as a Patron of Sculpture," in *Roma anno 1300,* ed. A. M. Romanini, Rome, 1983, 513–27, especially 519–20. See also M. Barber, *The Trial of the Templars,* Cambridge, 1978.

13. See Camille, *The Gothic Idol.*

images in his diocese. As the citations indicate, Gregory's position was echoed through the centuries. In Siena, it found expression in the statute of the Painters' Guild and in a Dominican antiphonary of the late thirteenth century. The only miniature in the manuscript, a *Crucifixion,* is accompanied by the following:

> This image you look at is neither God nor man.
> But this image signifies God and man.
> Do not hesitate to pay honour to the portrait of Christ.
> However, do not adore the portrait, but whom it depicts.
> Do not believe this is Christ, but believe in Christ through this.
> The Lord Jesus has been mutilated on the cross for us.
> Through this sign of the cross may all evil flee far away.
> And through the same sign may anything good be saved.[2]

I have chosen for the beginning of this chapter merely a few passages from a multitude of works that essentially make the same argument. Images are means of instruction, particularly for the illiterate, and means to incite devotion. Yet were we left only with these texts, we would have a highly distorted understanding of the various roles religious pictures played in dugento and trecento society.

Before I continue the discussion of Christian art, however, I would remind the reader that images played a major part in contemporary notions of magic and astrology. Many individuals, for example, believed in the power and differing effect of images created under the influence of specific constellations. Michael Scotus, who was astrologer to Frederick II of Hohenstaufen but also enjoyed the patronage of Honorius III and Gregory IX, devoted portions of his *Liber introductorius* to describing images appropriate to every hour of the day and night, images capable of everything from promoting love to assisting in the capture of birds or fish.[3] Arnold of Villanova (d. 1311), physician to kings and popes, wrote of the efficacy of stones engraved with images in accordance with the constellations and, for Boniface VIII, prepared a seal in the form of a lion to aid the pope when he was suffering from stone.[4] Other prominent scholars of the period, such as Robert Grosseteste, Albert the Great, and Roger Bacon, recorded their belief in the power of images influenced by the stars.[5] Cecco d'Ascoli, in his *Commentary on the Sphere,* offered instructions for creating astrological images that would enable their possessor to receive responses from demons.[6]

2. Siena, BC, MS F.VI.11. Cited from van der Ploeg's translation in *Art, Architecture, and Liturgy,* 22. A lengthy, though sometimes questionable, account of the fear of idolatry inherent in the use of images, is found in M. Camille, *The Gothic Idol: Ideology and Image-Making in Medieval Art,* Cambridge, 1989. For the fifteenth century, see Baxandall, *Painting and Experience in Fifteenth Century Italy,* 40–45. More generally: D. Freedberg, *The Power of Images,* London and Chicago, 1989, especially chapter 8.

3. L. Thorndike, *A History of Magic and Experimental Science,* III, New York, 1934, 327.

4. L. Thorndike, *A History of Magic and Experimental Science,* II, New York, 1929, 857–58.

5. Thorndike, *A History of Magic,* II, 440, 556–58, 673.

6. Thorndike, *A History of Magic,* II, 959.

Foreign Powers

> For it is one thing to venerate a picture, and another to learn the story it depicts, which is to be venerated. The picture is for the simple man what writing is for those who can read, because those who cannot read see and learn from the picture the model which they should follow. Thus pictures are above all instruction of the people. And if anyone should want to make pictures, do not forbid him, but avoid the veneration of them at all costs.
>
> —Gregory the Great (590–604)

> Illiterate men can contemplate in the lines of a picture what they cannot by means of the written word.
>
> —Synod of Arras (1025)

> Pictures and ornaments are the lessons and the Scriptures of the laity. Whence Gregory: It is one thing to adore a picture and another by means of the picture historically to learn what should be adored. For what writing supplieth to him which can read, that doth a picture supply to him which is unlearned, and can only look.
>
> —William Durandus (c. 1290)

> Know that there are three reasons for the institution of images in churches. First, for the instruction of the simple people, because they are instructed by them as by books. Second, so that the mystery of the incarnation and examples of the saints may be the more active in our memory through being presented daily to our eyes. Third, to excite feelings of devotion, these being aroused more effectively by things seen than by things heard.
>
> —John of Genoa, *Catholicon* (late thirteenth century)[1]

> As by the grace of God we are able to reveal to the uneducated and illiterate the miraculous things achieved by virtue and in virtue of our Holy Faith, . . .
>
> —"Statute of the Painters' Guild of Siena" (1356)

The problem of images haunted the West—and with good reason. As heir to classical civilization, the Church inherited a world in which images abounded and a culture long accustomed to visible manifestations of the divine. Thus, in spite of the clear and explicit prohibition of images found in the Old Testament, especially in the Second Commandment, an accommodation with reality was inevitable. Indeed, Gregory the Great's letter to Serenus, bishop of Marseilles, cited above, was a reproach for the latter's having destroyed

---

1. This text is here quoted from M. Baxandall, *Painting and Experience in Fifteenth Century Italy*, Oxford, 1972, 41.

V The Painter's World

In the last three chapters, I have been much concerned with specifics, not only because they help us understand the working life and social position of early Sienese painters, but also because it is impossible to compose a similarly detailed picture of the painter's life for any other central Italian city at the beginning of the Renaissance. I am not suggesting that we may take the Sienese situation as the perfect model for what occurred elsewhere; for example, I have already noted several contrasts with the situation in Florence. But there are threads and themes in our story that tie the history of Sienese painters to the history of painters throughout central Italy. Here, however, I turn to larger cultural issues, to a discussion of some of the ways in which the painter and his audience were bound together by the history of ideas and the faith. To accomplish that task, I must combine evidence from Siena with evidence from elsewhere. The more expansive view is warranted because the views and ideas I discuss were undoubtedly known to the Sienese.

corded in the payment to Ambrogio Lorenzetti, "pro ornamento facto" in the palace, a notice often taken to refer to Ambrogio's *Mappamondo*.[230] In June of 1347, Bonfigli was *operaio* for the Fontebranda, and in October of 1349 was *operaio* of the commune.[231] He was reimbursed 51 florins, 1 lira, and 6 soldi by the Biccherna in 1352, for money spent on the Torre del Mangia.[232]

I suspect that these few instances speak to a broader phenomenon of which surviving documentation leaves only partial record.[233] Thus painters dealt frequently with the same members of the upper classes in a variety of situations and in connection with various Sienese institutions. And those officials may well have called on the services of those artists familiar from other tasks.

---

230. ASS, Biccherna 217, fol. 125r (31 October 1345).

231. ASS, Biccherna 225, fol. 96v (29 October 1349).

232. ASS, Biccherna 412, fol. 92v. The payment is "per li oriuogli dela torre."

233. Other individuals had long been in service of the Nove in other capacities. For example, the Biccherna volumes from the first half of the Trecento contain many notices of payment to a Giotto di Buondone, who seems to have been a career diplomat for Siena. These notices have yet to be systematically assembled, but Giugurta Tommasi makes reference to one of these embassies, to Pisa in 1314. Tommasi, *Dell'historie di Siena*, II, 186. According to the *Table of Possessions*, Giotto di Buondone had considerable property, valued at £800, in the district of L'Abbazia di S. Donato di sotto. ASS, Estimo 134, fols. 1–1v.

We encounter some of these figures in quite another context. There exists a comparatively short document that records the festivities organized by Sozzo di Bandinello for the knighting of his son Francesco, celebrations held between 18 and 25 December 1326. The document lists the guests invited to banquets on each of those days. On Christmas day, the guests included Biagio Chiavelli, "Segna lini," and "Giotto buondoni." (Another guest was "Ser Sozzo buondoni.") The Buondone were either close to the Bandinelli family or of particular importance, for both had also attended the first day of festivities, Thursday, 18 December. See C. Mazzi, "Descrizione della festa in Siena per la cavalleria di Francesco Bandinelli nel 1326," *BSSP*, XVIII, 1911, 342, 350, 353, 356, 358.

Another figure, Biagio Chiavelli, comes first to our attention in June of 1330, when his name appears among thirty-six individuals petitioning the Nine for a three-year exemption from serving on the commissions that set the total annual *gabelle* for the *contado*.[217] From July to December 1334, he was one of the *esecutori* of the Gabella.[218] In January/February of 1339, Chiavelli was one of the Nove;[219] in July of the same year he is described as the "oparaio vechio" of the cathedral and is named in connection with Ambrogio Lorenzetti's work on the angel for the high altar of the duomo.[220] In January of 1338, he is named as *operaio* of the cathedral and for the new aqueducts of the Fontebranda.[221] He still held those offices in January of 1339.[222] Between August and November of 1341, he was the "operaio del nuovo palazo del Comune" and was involved in payments to Lippo and Federigo Memmi for a project, ultimately abandoned, for the Torre del Mangia.[223] In 1344–45 and 1350–51, Biagio was again *operaio* of the cathedral. On 2 November 1347 he was removed from a commission supervising a change in the riverbed of the Arbia because his brother was serving as one of the Nine.[224]

Mino di Cino d'Ughi, who came from a Casati family and in 1340 became rector of the Ospedale di Santa Maria della Scala, sat on the Council of the Nine in November/December 1316 and in May/June 1323.[225] On 31 December 1321, he is named in a payment to Simone Martini for a crucifix for the chapel of the Nove in the Palazzo Pubblico.[226] It was during Mino's rectorship of the hospital that Ambrogio Lorenzetti worked in the hospital's cemetery and that Lippo and Federigo Memmi produced the three panels for the rector to send to "misser don Bruno."[227]

Finally, a certain Coltino Bonfigli appears several times in documents of the 1340s: as *operaio* of the commune in both semesters of 1343, as *operaio* of the "fonte Vallis Montonis" in August of 1345, as *operaio* of the commune in both semesters of 1345, as *operaio* for the task of bringing water (for a fountain) to the Campo in January of 1347, September of 1348, and July of 1349.[228] As the communal *operaio* in February 1345, he received £100 to spend "in picturis et ornamentis novi palatii,"[229] and in October of that year, he is re-

217. Bowsky, *Finance*, 229–30.
218. Borgia et al., *Le Biccherne*, 88.
219. Bowsky, *Medieval Italian Commune*, 197 n. 19.
220. Bowsky, *Medieval Italian Commune*, 196; Siena, Opera del Duomo 178, fol. 51v.
221. Bargagli-Petrucci, *Le fonti*, II, 200.
222. Bargagli-Petrucci, *Le fonti*, II, 200.
223. ASS, Biccherna 407, fol. 120v. The "nuovo palazzo" is a reference to the extension on the southeast side of the Palazzo Pubblico that was to contain the new prisons and the new council chamber.
224. Bowsky, *Medieval Italian Commune*, 196.
225. Bowsky, *Finance*, 40 n. 85; Bowsky, "Buon Governo," 373 n. 22.
226. See note 31 above.

227. Bargagli-Petrucci, *Le fonti*, II, 221. Mino appears in another context that sheds light on the mentality of the period. After the death of his father, Cino di Ugone, a process was initiated to restore funds earned through usury by Cino from the people of Auxerre. In 1351, Mino di Cinto, anxious to have the matter resolved, sent a brother from the Ospedale to Auxerre to search out those to whom funds were due. Tangheroni, "Siena e il commercio internazionale," 56.
228. ASS, Biccherna 216, fol. 103r; Biccherna 217, fol. 125r; Bargagli-Petrucci, *Le fonti*, II, 215, 220, 224.
229. ASS, Biccherna 216, fol. 103r (16 February 1345). The reference would seem to be to the extension of the palace, cited above.

was involved in payments to Simone Martini for his *Maestà* (1315) and in acquiring (1319) an angel to stand before the *Maestà* in the "casa de' Nove." In the *Table of Possessions* (1316–20), Chele is listed as owning a *domus*, in the *lira* of San Donato al lato dei Montanini, valued at 383 lire, 6 soldi, and 6 denari.[203]

In 1319, the Biccherna registered a credit of £8 to Segna di Lino, who had paid Segna di Bonaventura for the restoration of a figure of the Virgin "dinanzi al Concistoro" in the Palazzo Pubblico. The transaction suggests that Segna was *operaio* of the commune.[204] Segna di Lino was the *operaio* of the cathedral in 1329, 1330, 1331, 1335, 1337, and 1339 and is mentioned in the summary of expenses for Simone's *Annunciation*. In 1337, the *operaio* of the cathedral became the *operaio* for the Fontebranda, indeed, for all fountains except that being built for the Campo, and Segna is mentioned in connection with repairs on the waterways for the Fontebranda.[205] He is listed among the councillors for the Fontebranda in 1338,[206] and is numbered among the Nine in July/August 1308, October 1308, March/April 1330, January/February 1332, and March/April 1339.[207]

Bono Campuglia first appears to us as *operaio* of the cathedral in 1330, and then in a notice of 1332, where he is described as the "camarlengho dela chamara del chomune."[208] He was *operaio* of the commune in May of 1333. In 1334, as the official for "la camera del comune," he received £160 for a missal and other furnishings for the altar of the Nine.[209] He was *operaio* of the commune in May of 1333 and October of 1335.[210] In December of 1336, Bono is recorded as *operaio* of the fountain at Tressa and of the "fonte a piè le Sperandie."[211] He was the *operaio* for a new dormitory for the Nine in the Palazzo Pubblico in July/August 1337,[212] and in the same year he is described as *operaio* for the new well for the state prisons.[213] In February of 1338, he was likely the *operaio* for the commune, and in April of 1338 he definitely was, and is described as, the one in charge of painting the new dormitory in the Palazzo Pubblico;[214] in January, February, and May of 1339 he was *operaio* of the commune and, as such, involved in the payments to Ambrogio Lorenzetti for the Sala della Pace.[215] In April of 1340, he is again mentioned as *operaio* of the commune, and in November of 1341 he was in charge of work on the Fonte Nuova.[216]

203. ASS, Estimo 131, fol. 299r. It is instructive to compare the value of this holding with those of properties owned by painters. See Chapter II.
204. ASS, Biccherna 381, fol. 75v.
205. Bargagli-Petrucci, *Le fonti*, II, 196.
206. Bargagli-Petrucci, *Le fonti*, II, 199.
207. Bowsky, *Finance*, 174 n. 22.
208. ASS, Biccherna 398, fol. 72r.
209. ASS, Biccherna 400, fols. 95v (£100 on 20 April 1344), 115v (£60 on 28 June 1334).
210. ASS, Biccherna 183, fol. 44r (30 October 1335).
211. Bargagli-Petrucci, *Le fonti*, II, 194.
212. ASS, Biccherna 190, fol. 4v (15 July 1337).
213. Bargagli-Petrucci, *Le fonti*, II, 194.
214. ASS, Biccherna 191, fol. 109r (18 April 1338); Biccherna 194, fol. 26r (18 April 1338); Biccherna 404, fol. 109r (18 April 1338).
215. ASS, Biccherna 201, fols. 8r (29 January 1339), 22r (28 February 1339), and 66r (29 May 1339); Biccherna 190, fols. 4r, 15v; Bargagli-Petrucci, *Le fonti*, II, 194; ASS, Biccherna 404, fol. 109r. The February notice concerns the treasury's reimbursement of Bono for £13 he had spent in acquiring a painted panel for the loggia of the baths at Petriolo.
216. Bargagli-Petrucci, *Le fonti*, II, 203, 205.

Some General Observations

I have earlier remarked that the history of communal patronage in Siena reveals a pattern in which the commune gave sufficient commissions to single painters, in succession, that we are justified in speaking of quasi-official painters. I have also noted that the major institutions of Siena patronized the very artists that history has judged the finest and the most original. And the evidence considered above shows that all three major institutions in Siena—the commune, the cathedral, and the Scala hospital—largely employed the same painters. Duccio created his 1302 *Maestà* for the Nove, his great *Maestà* for the cathedral, and no. 47 for the high altar of the main chapel in the hospital. Simone painted the Uffizi *Annunciation* for the cathedral, executed a fresco for the facade of the Opera del Duomo, painted two frescoes on the facade of Santa Maria della Scala, and often worked at the Palazzo Pubblico. Ambrogio, who created the most magnificent of the side altarpieces for the duomo, worked with his brother on the facade frescoes for the hospital, painted in the chapel of the hospital's cemetery, and also often worked in the Palazzo Pubblico. Pietro, although not known to have worked in the communal palace, was employed by the cathedral for the altarpiece of Saint Savino and for other works now lost, and painted on the facade of Santa Maria della Scala.

We have very little indication of how, or by whom, specific artists were chosen for specific commissions. In the case of the Ospedale della Scala, the rector may have had overriding influence. Since communal funds were used for the Opera del Duomo, the commune must have had control over the selection of projects to be financed. The records of deliberations by the Consiglio Generale make it clear that that body made decisions about projects for the Palazzo Pubblico and other undertakings that fell directly under the purview of the state treasury. But, to my knowledge, there is no surviving documentation regarding the selection of individual artists. (The process may have been informal.) We have, however, evidence that among Sienese officials there existed something like a management level, career administrators who were often called upon to fulfill various posts. Remarkably enough, these men were not artisans, but members of the Noveschi and the Casati classes, some of whom were qualified to sit on the Council of the Nine. I suspect that these individuals may have had an important role in selecting painters, sculptors, and architects for state-funded projects; it is therefore worth surveying the evidence in some detail.

An addition to the guild statute of the Arte della Lana, dated 6 May 1308, indicates that the relevant material was assembled and the rubrics composed by a group of members, including Chele Moccolelli.[200] On 30 March 1307, Chele had been one of the officials in charge of the aqueducts of Fontebranda.[201] During the first and second semesters of 1315 and the second semester of 1316 Chele Moccolelli was the *operaio* of the commune.[202] He

---

200. Banchi and Polidori, *Statuti senesi*, I, 334–35.
201. Bargagli-Petrucci, *Le fonti*, II, 175.
202. ASS, Biccherna 376, fol. 13r (7 June 1315); Biccherna 377, fol. 139v; Biccherna 132, fol. 142r (31 December 1316); Bacci, *Fonti e commenti*, 134–35. Maginnis, "Chiarimenti documentari," 12.

We have, to my knowledge, only four pieces of evidence that might be interpreted as pointing in another direction. In a 1332 list of expenses connected with San Giovanni Fuorcivitas, Pistoia, there is reference to a panel of the *Madonna,* by Guido di Cino, that "fare facta in Siena," and another reference in an inventory of that date to the panel "che vene da Siena."[194] On 4 March 1344, the Memmi were paid by the rector of the Hospital of Santa Maria della Scala for three panels and their framing that were to be sent to "don Bruno." Berto Lotti, on 11 May, received the significant sum of 4 florins (13 lire, 4 soldi, and 4 denari) for the transport of those items to "don Bruno." The amount suggests the task was complicated and the distance far.[195] The third piece of evidence is very different. Norman Muller has pointed out that Ugolino di Nerio devised a novel system of stabilizing his altarpiece for the high altar of Santa Croce, replacing the customary horizontal battens of the back (usually single planks of wood) with a series of separate elements that interlocked when the work was installed on the altar.[196] In other words, it seems Ugolino created a system that would have allowed the main panels to be painted elsewhere, sent to Santa Croce, and there assembled. Finally, at the top of the back of Ambrogio Lorenzetti's *Presentation in the Temple,* there are two slots cut into the panel (Fig. 22), suggesting that the altarpiece was crowned by a separate gable that was attached by rods inserted into those slots at a moment of final assembly.[197]

We have some, albeit limited, evidence that a few Sienese painters actually changed their place of residence, leaving their native city. The most famous instance involves Simone Martini's move to Avignon, but in 1319, Meo di Guido da Siena is documented as living in Perugia, where he had obtained citizenship. Guido, Ugolino di Nerio's brother, is documented as in Florence in 1327; we have no evidence that he returned to Siena. Pasquino di Cenne, documented in Florence in 1330 and 1341, does not appear among notices of painters in Siena. On 2 January 1305, "Piastra pictor condam Bindi de Senis," described as living in Pisa, contracted to provide an altarpiece for the Hospital of Santa Chiara in that city; he is not found in Sienese documents.[198] In the early Trecento, Andrea and Fino da Siena were documented in Volterra.[199]

---

194. Zdekauer, "Opere d'arte senese nella chiesa di San Giovanni Fuorcivitas di Pistoia," 177–78.

195. See note 137 above. The sum involved should be compared with the 1 lira, 8 soldi, and 6 denari paid to sixteen porters who brought Simone's San Ansano altarpiece to the cathedral, presumably from Simone's shop (Bacci, *Fonti e commenti,* 170). Milanesi claimed that a now untraced document recorded payment of 12 lire and 10 soldi to porters for transporting Duccio's *Maestà* to the cathedral (White, *Duccio,* 197).

196. Muller, "Reflections on Ugolino di Nerio's Santa Croce Polyptych."

197. Here, of course, there was no question of a device to facilitate transportation of the panel over long distances, but rather a device that made the work more easily moved from the painter's shop and, perhaps, a device that made the actual painting easier for having separate elements to deal with. I suspect that the predella for this work was also a separate feature, as I have argued above.

198. C. Lupi, "L'arte senese a Pisa," *BSSP,* XI, 1904, 379–80.

199. M. Battistini, "Andrea e Fino da Siena, pittori del sec. XIV dipingono a Volterra," *BSSP,* XXVII, 1920, 107. There are documents, but none of them relates to paintings.

individuals. Simone's selection for the *Saint Louis of Toulouse* (Color Plate 16; c. 1317) may have arisen from the presence in Siena, during 1314–15, of Prince Pietro of Anjou and Filippo of Anjou, Prince of Taranto. In fact, Filippo was in Siena between 27 July and 4 August 1315, just as Simone was creating the Palazzo Pubblico *Maestà*.[190] I have proposed that the magnificent triptych, no. 35 in the Siena Pinacoteca (Fig. 66), may have been created for the ill-fated Prince Pietro, who arrived in Siena for the feast of the Assumption in 1314 and died at the battle of Montecatini on 29 August 1315.[191] But it may be that the idea of acquiring such a work was not entirely Pietro's own; his brother, King Robert, had been in Siena in 1310, while Duccio was working on the *Maestà*. When the Palazzo Comunale of San Gimignano acquired Lippo Memmi's version (Fig. 95) of Simone's *Maestà*, the podestà was the Sienese Nello di Mino de' Tolomei, and his very prominent place in the fresco suggests that he may have paid for the work.[192] Sigismondo Tizio said that Simone moved to Avignon as the result of an unnamed cardinal's visit to Siena. Simone had commissions from the Orsini and from Cardinal Jacopo Stefaneschi; his Virgil frontispiece, created for Petrarch, arose from the circumstance that painter and poet were both in Avignon after 1338, the year when Petrarch recovered his prized Virgil manuscript, earlier lost.[193]

We have far too little evidence to generalize about how "foreign" commissions for panel pictures were handled. As noted earlier, the contract for the Rucellai *Madonna* indicates that the Laudesi gave Duccio the panel that the confraternity had had made; that circumstance and the presence of Florentine features in the finished work suggest the enormous panel was painted in Florence. Several documents indicate Pietro Lorenzetti's presence in Arezzo in the early 1320s; in the contract for the Pieve altarpiece he is, in fact, described as "qui fuit de Senis" (who was of Siena). But in those years he may also have been executing a fresco cycle for the same church, and before that he had worked in Cortona and Assisi. Altarpieces, of course, had their widths determined by the width of the altars on which they were to stand; therefore, we might assume that working at the site of installation made matters easier for the painters. In addition, most polyptychs were constructed before painting, with large horizontal battens on the back used to stabilize the structure. This too might suggest that they were executed more or less *in situ*, for otherwise their large size might make them difficult to transport. On the other hand, working in Orvieto, Perugia, or Pisa would have entailed finding local carpenters to construct the support and, quite clearly in the case of Simone Martini, bringing assistants along for what could be a lengthy process.

190. For this altarpiece, see Julian Gardner, "Saint Louis of Toulouse, Robert of Anjou, and Simone Martini," *Zeitschrift für Kunstgeschichte*, XXXIX, 1976, 12ff.

191. See Maginnis, "Tabernacle 35."

192. If it strikes some readers as doubtful that a "foreign" official should pay for paintings in a public place such as San Gimignano's palace, they should recall the Sienese document of 1316 that says the damaged paintings in the hall of the podestà were paintings that he had had made. See above.

193. Maginnis, *Age of Giotto*, 122–23 and fig. 112.

piece for Santa Croce in Florence. In the same church, according to Vasari, he painted the altarpiece for the Bardi Chapel. Vasari also says he created the high altarpiece for Santa Maria Novella.

The circumstances described above were not, however, the only conditions under which Sienese painters worked abroad. In the first decade of the Trecento, Duccio's shop produced a polyptych for the Dominican church in Perugia. In the decade or so following his *Maestà,* Simone Martini and his shop worked for the Dominicans of Pisa and Orvieto, the Franciscans of Orvieto and Assisi, the Servites of Orvieto, and the Angevins of Naples. Pietro Lorenzetti, in 1340, finished his *Madonna* for San Francesco, Pistoia (Fig. 54; now in the Uffizi Gallery). During the 1330s, Simone's shop or following created the frescoed New Testament Cycle in the Collegiata of San Gimignano. That town had strong links to the Simone circle.[187] In 1319, Lippo Memmi created a version of Simone's *Maestà* for the Palazzo Comunale (Fig. 95). A polyptych from Simone's shop was painted for the Augustinians of San Gimignano. One of Simone's most talented followers created a *Madonna and Child* for the Church of San Francesco in Asciano. Lippo Memmi produced a polyptych for the Church of San Niccolò in Casciana Alta (Pisa); the Siena Pinacoteca contains two panels of saints (nos. 48, 49) by Lippo that came to the gallery from San Francesco in Colle Val d'Elsa. An artist from the Simone/Lippo circle created the *Glorification of Saint Thomas Aquinas* for the Dominicans of Pisa.[188] Bartolommeo Bulgarini painted the altarpiece for the Bardi di Vernio Chapel in Florence's Santa Croce and left works in several other centers.

Now, the foregoing summary is highly revealing. By far the majority of "foreign" commissions came to Sienese painters from the new religious orders that had grown up during the thirteenth century. The new churches built for those orders had altars to be furnished and walls that could be frescoed. That Sienese painters were so often summoned to the new opportunities requires something more by way of explanation, although none of the factors involved was complicated. Undoubtedly, the completion of a project judged successful for one convent of an order led to further commissions as the movement of friars and annual general chapter meetings allowed others to see or hear of new works.[189] Then, more generally, there was the Via Francigena that brought thousands of visitors to Siena on their way to or from Rome. Finally, the Sienese polyptych format, which so tellingly evokes the idea of the heavenly city, may have been prized by the knowing.

Other "foreign" commissions likely depended on chance and on the prompting of

---

187. In part, the presence of Simone, his shop, and Lippo Memmi in San Gimignano may be connected with the fact that Memmo di Filippuccio, father-in-law to Simone and father to Lippo, had previously lived and worked in that town.

188. Maginnis, *Age of Giotto,* color plate 12.

189. It was Innocent III who, at the Fourth Lateran Council, extended the practice of general chapter meetings, a permanent institution of the Cistercians, to all monastic orders. H. Tillmann, *Pope Innocent III,* Amsterdam, New York, and Oxford, 1980, 192. For a very fine account of the way chapter meetings could contribute to patronage of Sienese artists outside Siena, see J. Cannon, "Simone Martini, the Dominicans, and the Early Sienese Polyptych," *Journal of the Warburg and Courtauld Institutes,* XLV, 1982, 69–93.

connection between the Florentine confraternity and its Sienese counterpart.[184] I have also suggested that Duccio's revolutionary new vision was slow to inform the art of Siena because the "market" there was dominated by the "Guidesque" painters, their works, and the expectations both had engendered in Sienese patrons. That circumstance, it seems, was repeated more than once, so that through the first and much of the second decade of the Trecento Duccio and his shop had a near stranglehold on urban commissions. Toward the last years of Duccio's life, Simone Martini emerged as the new, quasi-official painter to the commune, beginning with his Palazzo Pubblico *Maestà* of 1315. Although Simone's career c. 1320 had another side, the Nine began to turn to him regularly, and for a time, his contemporaries found it difficult to claim a market share.

What we know of the early career of Pietro Lorenzetti indicates that between approximately 1315 and 1325 he sought employment outside Siena. In those years, he painted the Passion Cycle in the Lower Church of San Francesco in Assisi, a panel of the *Madonna Enthroned*, a large crucifix (Fig. 102), and another, small, portable crucifix for Cortona (all now Museo Diocesano, Cortona), and both the high altarpiece and a frescoed cycle of the life of the Virgin for the Pieve in Arezzo. His brother Ambrogio likewise looked abroad for work. His *Madonna Enthroned* of 1319 (Fig. 103) was created for Vico l'Abate, near Florence; a document of 30 May 1321 refers to property the painter had left behind in Florence; and in 1327 he matriculated in the Florentine guild of the Medici e Speziali, to which painters of that city belonged. Ghiberti says that, in Florence, Ambrogio painted the chapter house of Sant'Agostino, a panel and a chapel for San Procolo, and an image of the Annunciate for the Hospital of the Scala, a dependency of the Ospedale di Santa Maria della Scala in Siena. The Uffizi Gallery now houses panels of the Virgin (Fig. 104), Saint Nicholas, and Saint Proculus and four scenes from the life of Saint Nicholas of Bari (Figs. 105–108), all of which came from the Church of San Procolo and were executed by Ambrogio and his shop. In the 1330s, Ambrogio created his *Maestà* for Massa Marittima.[185] Ambrogio's shop was responsible for frescoes in the Chapel of San Galgano in Montesiepi.[186]

The tendency for one painter and his shop to dominate Sienese commissions affected not only younger and more original painters. Segna di Bonaventura's most important picture, created while Duccio held sway in Siena, is his *Madonna and Child Enthroned with Saints and Angels* (Fig. 12) from Castiglion Fiorentino. In 1319, Segna is documented in Arezzo, where he executed a large painted crucifix for the Badia. Also in 1319, Meo di Guido da Siena is documented as living in Perugia, where he had acquired citizenship; there he created a polyptych, now in the Galleria Nazionale dell'Umbria (no. 22), for the Church of S. Maria di Montelabate, north of the city. This and other surviving works by the artist indicate that his was a modest, Ducciesque talent. Then there is the case of Ugolino di Nerio. We know of no major Sienese commission awarded the painter, unless it be the Ottawa *Saint Anne and the Virgin* (Fig. 94), but in the mid-1320s he created the high altar-

---

184. See Maginnis, *Age of Giotto*, chapter III.
185. Maginnis, *Age of Giotto*, color plate 9.

186. E. Borsook, *Gli affreschi di Montesiepi*, Florence, 1968.

As our knowledge of trecento pictures created for the confraternities is slight, so too our knowledge of images connected with charitable institutions other than the Ospedale di Santa Maria della Scala. The Siena Pinacoteca contains a pair of reliquary shutters, painted inside and out by a "Guidesque" painter, devoted to the legend of the Blessed Andrea Gallerani, reputed founder of the Misericordia. Stubblebine suggested, on the basis of an unclear secondary source of the sixteenth century, that they came to the gallery from San Domenico. They might just as well have come from the Misericordia itself and may be connected to a bull of 29 March 1274 wherein Bernardo, bishop of Siena and brother or nephew to the Blessed Andrea, granted indulgences to those who visited the *beato*'s relics. From the Misericordia comes a panel of the Beato Andrea Gallerani, now in the Church of San Pellegrino alla Sapienza, attributed to a painter from the Simone shop.[183]

I do not claim this list is exhaustive. Nor is it my intention here to give a detailed account of these works or to discuss lost works recorded in secondary sources. Instead, I provide the lists above to give the reader a sense of how little we can now see—or recognize—of what must have been a far more extensive production for Siena's churches, convents, confraternities, and charitable institutions.

The Sienese Abroad

Although my central concern in this volume is the relationship between Siena and its painters, some words must be given to the matter of commissions for those artists outside Siena, for the careers of all the major, and some minor, painters took them away from the city of the Virgin. From the very early days, Sienese painters found an audience and patrons "abroad."

At some point shortly after the creation of the "Guidesque" San Bernardino *Madonna* (1262), Arezzo acquired a replica of the picture (Fig. 9). Another "Guidesque" *Madonna,* now in the Palazzo Comunale of San Gimignano, comes from the Church of Sant'Agostino in that town. From the same orbit comes the *Saint Francis* altarpiece in the Pinacoteca of Siena (no. 313), which was originally in the Church of San Francesco in Colle Val d'Elsa; a polyptych in the Siena gallery (no. 7; Fig. 7) by Guido himself comes from the same church; and a large panel of the Last Judgment in the Museo Diocesano of Grosseto seems to have come from the cathedral of that city. Although its provenance is unknown, a polyptych (1280) in the Galleria Nazionale dell'Umbria of Perugia, signed by Vigoroso da Siena, likely came from a foundation within that city. It is against this background that we should situate Duccio's 1285 commission for the Rucellai *Madonna* by the Compagnia delle Laude of Florence's Santa Maria Novella.

Elsewhere I have suggested that the Laudesi commission may have stemmed from a

---

183. See Bagnoli and Bellosi, *Simone Martini e "chompagni,"* 78–81.

Various frescoes, often fragmentary, survive to us. In San Domenico, there are the *Madonna and Child Enthroned with St. John the Baptist and a Donor* (Fig. 96) by the Master of the Loeser Madonna, and a partial fresco, the *Madonna and Child Enthroned with Saints Peter and Paul* (Fig. 100) by Lippo Memmi. San Francesco now houses two frescoes by Ambrogio Lorenzetti (Figs. 62, 81) and one by Pietro (Figs. 45–46): both moved from the chapter house into the church itself. In addition, we have recently recovered fragments of Ambrogio's decorations in the cloister of San Francesco, and this project has special interest because the scenes were accompanied by the arms of the Petroni family.[173] Sant'Agostino contains a *Maestà* and other figures by Ambrogio.[174]

Our knowledge of trecento images for Siena's confraternities is all but nonexistent. In 1325, an inventory of the possessions of the Confraternity of Jesu Christo Crocefisso, attached to the Ospedale di Santa Maria della Scala, was prepared. It lists a crucifix, a banner (presumably painted), "tre tovagle brustate e dipente che stanno su l'altare," and "due panni dipenti, nell'uno el crucifixo che sta su l'altare e ne l'altro el san Cristofano."[175] An illuminated manuscript (Siena, Biblioteca Comunale, I.v.8), with miniatures painted c.1290, has been identified as the "libro di Collationi de' santi Padri" mentioned in the 1325 inventory. Another manuscript belonging to the confraternity (Siena, Biblioteca Comunale, I.vi.9) and dated 1333 contains drawings for unfinished miniatures.[176] There survives to us the seal of the Raccomandati, attributed tentatively to the Sienese goldsmith Guccio di Mannaia and dated, by Giovanni Previtali, to post-1295.[177] In addition, the Società degli Esecutori delle Pie Disposizioni, which was heir to the possessions of the Disciplinati, still has a large reliquary of gilded wood and gilded glass (c.1340; Fig. 101) attributed to Lippo Vanni.[178]

We have some further evidence concerning the Confraternity of the Virgin and Saint Francis. In April of 1316, that body purchased oil for the lamp before the panel of the Virgin.[179] In February of 1319, the miniaturist Cola di Fuccio was paid 15 soldi for "lo sequenziale grande."[180] And in September of 1320, Cola was paid for illuminating the confraternity's book of lauds.[181] A rather puzzling document pertains to a panel for the Confraternity of the Beato Andrea Gallerani.[182]

---

173. M. Seidel, "Wiedergefundene Fragmente eines Hauptwerks von Ambrogio Lorenzetti," *Pantheon*, XXVI, 1978, 119–27.

174. Maginnis, *Age of Giotto*, color plate 15.

175. Chapter 23 of the confraternity's statute required the treasurer to "keep a lantern continually burning, day and night, before the crucifix of the chapel."

176. For this and the previous manscript, see G. Previtali et al., *Il gotico a Siena: Miniature pitture oreficerie oggetti d'arte*, Florence, 1982, 86–87, 258–59.

177. Previtali et al., *Il gotico a Siena*, 95. The 1325 inventory of the possessions of the confraternity lists, as item 48, a gilt silver seal, with the image of the Crucified, for sealing letters. It is likely this item refers to the surviving seal, although the latter is gilt bronze.

178. Previtali et al., *Il gotico a Siena*, 246–49.

179. ASS, Patrimonio Resti Ecclesiastici 199, fol. 4r.

180. ASS, Patrimonio Resti Ecclesiastici 119, fol. 24r.

181. ASS, Patrimonio Resti Ecclesiastici 219, fol. 47v.

182. Bonoccorso di Pace was ordered to return to the Biccherna 11 florins "for the painting of a panel" for the "governors," but the carpenter Meo was to have 2 florins as the remainder of funds owing for a panel for the confraternity (Siena, BC, MS P.III.53, fol. 369v: citing "Annali 4, f. 500r").

Christ Enthroned from the same stylistic ambient still in the Sienese convent of the Poor Clares.[167]

From the first half of the Trecento come two panels of the Madonna in Santa Maria dei Servi, one by Segna di Bonaventura (Fig. 97) and another by Lippo Memmi (Fig. 98). Over time, one or the other has been connected with the 1319 petition by the Servites for a subsidy from the commune to help with the expense of their new altarpiece, which had cost £300.[168] Jacopo di Mino produced his *Madonna del Belvedere* for the same church in 1362. Pietro Lorenzetti's Carmelite altarpiece (1329), from San Niccolò, survives to us, now divided between the Norton Simon Museum in Pasadena and the Siena Pinacoteca. The Pinacoteca contains a number of works from the city's convents and churches: a Ducciesque cross (no. 21) from the Church of San Giusto, a cut-down *Madonna and Child Enthroned* (no. 18) by a painter close to the Master of Città di Castello and from the Church of San Pellegrino, four saints (nos. 85, 86, 93, 94) from the Hospital of Santa Marta by an ungifted member of the Simone circle, an inferior Lorenzettian polyptych (no. 50) from San Giusto, a painted crucifix (no. 598) from the church of the Carmelites and from the circle of Ambrogio, and several panels (nos. 77, 77a, 77b, 77c) by Ambrogio and his shop from the convent of Santa Petronilla. That gallery also contains an altarpiece of the *Coronation of Saint Catherine of Alexandria* (no. 145; Fig. 99) from the Church of Sant'Antonio (destroyed) in Fontebranda, dated 1362 and signed by Jacopo di Mino del Pellicciaio.[169] The Pinacoteca now houses Simone Martini's *Beato Agostino Novello* altarpiece (Color Plates 7–8), from the Church of Sant'Agostino. According to Tizio, Pietro Lorenzetti painted a panel for the Sienese church of the Humiliati.[170] There is a polyptych by Ambrogio Lorenzetti and his shop in the Church of San Pietro alle Scale.[171] But the comparatively small number of these works and the inferior quality of some of them leave me convinced that much has been lost. Surely the Dominicans and Franciscans acquired new altarpieces in this period. Are we to believe that Bishop Donodeus Malavolti rebuilt Sant'Egidio without providing an altarpiece? Did the commune build the churches of San Biagio and San Luca without furnishing their altars? Altarpieces were surely included in the new foundations by individuals such as Cardinal Petroni, Emilia d'Elci, and Donodeus Malavolti.[172]

---

167. For all of these works, see Stubblebine, *Guido da Siena*.

168. ASS, Consiglio Generale, Deliberazioni, 92, fols. 122–122v. The commune agreed to a grant of £100, but the final £25 of that grant was paid out only in June of 1321 (ASS, Biccherna 140, fol. 189r [30 June 1321]). The cost of the altarpiece makes it doubtful that either the panel by Segna or the panel by Lippo, both comparatively small, was the center of this altarpiece.

The commune's grant is very large compared, for example, with the £50 it gave the Carmelites in 1329 for their altarpiece, which had cost significantly more. Perhaps the amount reflects the popularity of the Servites, as indicated by pious bequests, discussed in Chapter I.

169. For these works, see P. Torriti, *La Pinacoteca Nazionale di Siena: I dipinti dal XII al XV secolo*, Genoa, 1977, 72, 85, 92–93, 105, 110–11, 146, respectively.

170. Siena, BC, MS B.III.7, 485–86.

171. L. Cateni, "Un polittico 'too remote from Ambrogio' firmato da Ambrogio Lorenzetti," *Prospettiva*, XL, 1985, 62–67.

172. See Chapter I, pages 38–39.

The production of private devotional works during the first half of the Trecento seems not to have been a major feature of Sienese painting; and in that circumstance lies yet another significant difference from the situation in Florence. Surviving works by Bernardo Daddi and his shop—to take one early example—indicate that the creation of small works for private individuals was a major aspect of artistic life in Florence. There are a number of small, presumably private images from the circle of Duccio;[164] there are various smaller works from the orbit of Simone and the Lorenzetti. But altogether, the collective number of surviving triptychs, diptychs, and single panels from Siena is small. Whether small works were always produced under commission or were sometimes produced on speculation of finding a buyer in the future is not entirely clear. We do know that in the later trecento works were created on speculation. We also know of one secular task that offered painters employment. Anyone selling wine in small quantities, that is, anyone having a tavern or wineshop, was required to have a painted sign. The requirement applied to both the city and the *contado*.[165]

Parish Churches, Convents, Confraternities, and Charitable Institutions

I believe that the absence of documentation regarding private patronage does not significantly distort our historical understanding. Lack of documentation regarding parish churches, convents, confraternities, and the churches of the mendicant orders presents us with much more serious problems. All these institutions must have participated in the flowering of the new art during the first half of the Trecento, and yet our evidence is scant. Strangely enough, we know more about the situation in the late Dugento. The eponymous work (1262) of the San Bernardino Master (Fig. 8; Siena, Pinacoteca Nazionale, no. 16) belonged to the Franciscan Confraternity of the Virgin. Guido da Siena's *Madonna* (Fig. 32) was created for San Domenico, either for the high altar or for the Confraternity of the Virgin and Saint Dominic. Two "Guidesque" dossals, nos. 6 and 7 (Figs. 6–7) in the Siena Pinacoteca, have both been reduced by a figure at either end and yet have widths of 208 cm and 186 cm respectively. Their size suggests they were both made for high altars; no. 7 includes Saint Francis and has a Franciscan provenance, but connected to Colle Val d'Elsa rather than Siena.[166] The Saint Peter altarpiece (Siena, Pinacoteca Nazionale, no. 15) was originally in the parish church of San Pietro in Banchi (destroyed), and there is a *Virgin and*

---

164. See Stubblebine, *Duccio,* II.
165. Lisini, *Costituto volgarizzato,* II, 389–90.
166. I am not, however, entirely convinced that the Colle Val d'Elsa provenance is meaningful. A number of works in the Pinacoteca of Siena came from the Franciscan convent in Colle, which may have become the depository for works removed from other sites. (It seems likely that the bishopric of Siena used Santa Cecilia in Crevole, part of the *vescovado,* for similar purposes.)

pictures for these dependencies were made, we have no idea. Similarly, the hospital in Siena developed an extensive network of *grancie* (granges) in the Sienese *contado,* and each of these had a chapel or church.[158] It seems highly likely that the Ospedale della Scala would have had some concern with furnishing the altars of these chapels and churches.[159]

Private Patronage

The hospital documents direct our attention to the matter of patronage for painters by specific individuals. The general patterns of pious bequests in Siena before the second outbreak of the plague in 1363 explain why Siena possesses no equivalent of the splendid private chapels created in Florence during the period.[160] On the one hand, fragmentation of estates meant that large sums were not available for single projects; on the other, there was a societal reluctance to create monuments of self-commemoration. A question of class may also have been involved. By far the greatest number of connections we have traced to the establishment of altars, nonarchitectural chapels, and tombs relate to members of the magnate class and/or prelates. It is in this light that we should recall that a member of the Tolomei, acting as podestà in San Gimignano, likely commissioned Lippo Memmi to create a version (Fig. 95) of Simone's *Maestà* for the Palazzo Comunale of that town and had himself portrayed in full scale, kneeling before the Virgin. In Siena itself, images of donors are rare indeed, and I doubt that represents merely chance loss and survival. A fresco fragment in San Domenico shows a full-size figure presented by Saint John the Baptist as he kneels before the Virgin and Child (Fig. 96). Noteworthy enough: he is a knight in full armor, surely indicating an elevated social rank.

The circumstances I have noted are tied to the corporate nature, the corporate mentality, of Sienese society, in which individual display was, if not discouraged, surely not encouraged. Even among surviving private devotional works, donor images are scarce. The magnificent triptych Siena no. 35 (Fig. 66), containing a prince kneeling at the Virgin's feet, was likely commissioned by or for Prince Pietro of Anjou (the brother of Robert the Wise of Naples), who met an early death at the battle of Montecatini.[161] The even more magnificent London triptych by Duccio has no indication of the commissioner.[162] Similarly, a large triptych in Boston, with a *Crucifixion* at its center and from the Duccio shop, has no donor image. We have documentary record (1340) of two panels Pietro Lorenzetti had promised Paolo Tingo de' Pilestri of the *popolo* of San Giorgio, but we do not know whether the intended destination of those works was private or public.[163]

158. Epstein, *Alle origini della fattoria toscana;* F. C. Franchi and G. Cascarella, "Le Grance dello Spedale di Santa Maria della Scala nel contado senese," *BSSP,* XCII, 1985, 66–92, especially 68–69.

159. Perhaps the triptych sent to "don Bruno" was for one of these locations?

160. See Chapter I.

161. Hayden B. J. Maginnis, "Tabernacle 35," *Source,* XII, no. 4, 1993, 1–4.

162. Maginnis, *Age of Giotto,* fig. 62.

163. Bacci, *Dipinti inediti,* 95.

original series. Even at that, the idea of having three painters collaborate on the same project was highly unusual; no entirely comparable situation in the first half of the Trecento, in Siena, is known.[153] The project may have been unusual in another, important way. There is very little evidence to suggest any major commission of the period reflected the interests and devotions of any single official. But the episodes depicted on the hospital's facade, while normally viewed as expressions of Siena's devotion to the Virgin, are very much about the Virgin's parents, Joachim and Anna; and we know that the rector of the hospital, Giovanni di Tese Tolomei (1314–39), and his wife, Andrea, had a special devotion to the Virgin's parents. Giovanni's will (1325) specified that the hospital was to celebrate the feast of Joachim and Anna in the chapel of the "pellegrinaio nuovo." In 1328, Giovanni and Andrea offered to build in that location a chapel dedicated to Joachim and Anna.[154] Then, in 1333, the Consiglio Generale debated and approved a resolution that the feast of Joachim and Anna should be celebrated every year, on July 26, in the hospital. Finally, Girolamo Macchi tells us that when the protective roof above the frescoes was at last taken down, in 1720, one of the supporting brackets was discovered to bear Giovanni's arms.[155]

The hospital facade frescoes were, to my knowledge, unique in the history of Sienese institutional patronage: the rector may well have determined the content of this major project. But it may also be that we have other instances of Giovanni di Tese Tolomei's concern with painting. It must have been shortly after he became rector, in 1314, that Duccio and his shop provided no. 47 (Fig. 56) for the high altar of the Ospedale's chapel. We can only wonder about the furnishing of the altar in the chapel of the "pellegrinaio nuovo," but I would note that, in the late twenties or early thirties, Ugolino di Nerio and his shop produced a panel, now in the National Gallery of Canada, of Saint Anne and the Virgin (Fig. 94). Since this is the only surviving treatment of this particular subject from early-trecento Siena and the subject would have been appropriate to Giovanni's devotions, we must at least consider the possibility that the panel was painted for Giovanni's chapel.[156]

There are two aspects of the history of the hospital that give us pause and make us wonder about commissions now hidden from us. During the first half of the Trecento, the Ospedale had a great many smaller hospitals, in locations outside Siena, dependent upon it, including the Hospital of the Scala in Florence. Ghiberti indicates that Ambrogio Lorenzetti painted an *Annunziata* for the Florentine hospital.[157] How and by whom decisions regarding

153. For a full discussion of these works and their influence, see Maginnis, "The Lost Facade Frescoes from Siena's Ospedale di S. Maria della Scala" and, for use of the compositions by Sano di Pietro, Eisenberg, "The First Altarpiece for the 'Cappella de' Signori' of the Palazzo Pubblico in Siena: '. . . tales figure sunt adeo pulcre. . . .'"

154. Both ASS, Spedale 119, fol. 260r, and Spedale 256, fol. 369r, tell us that the chapel Giovanni endowed was dedicated to Joachim and Anna.

155. For the relevant documentation, see Maginnis, "The Lost Facade Frescoes from Siena's Ospedale di S. Maria della Scala."

156. The hospital's statute provides a glimpse into hospital life. The sacristan of the hospital was obliged to keep a gessoed panel on which to write the names of the brothers and sisters of the hospital who had died during the year. Every Monday during mass in the chapel, each was to be remembered. Each name was to be erased a year after the individual's death. Banchi and Polidori, *Statuti senesi*, III, 114–15.

157. Schlosser, *Lorenzo Ghibertis Denkwürdigkeiten*, I, 42.

ence to Paolo di Neri's having painted "l'archo che va al pelegrinaio."¹⁴³ Another notice, of 3 January 1361, refers to Monna Becha's endowment of a chapel of Saint Luke at the side of the sacristy in the hospital.¹⁴⁴ The chapel was later used by the Painters' Guild.¹⁴⁵

Other documents or transcriptions of documents are suggestive of other works. The will of Giovanni di Tese Tolomei, dated 14 October 1325, made provision for a candle to be placed "su d'angnoletto che sta dinanzi alla nunziata delo spedale" and refers to both the high altar of the hospital chapel and to an image of the Virgin in the "Peregrinario Infirmor."¹⁴⁶ A document of 1345, in reference to the charity of Jacomo de' Silevena, count palatine of Tuscany, refers to "l'altar posto a capo del' Infermeria di mezzo di detto spedale sotto il titolo di S. Giovanni Battista."¹⁴⁷ According to Faluschi, on 7 July 1349, "Neri detto Bustorcio del quondam Bandini da Sticciano" endowed an altar in the hospital through the bequest of 1,000 Pisan lire.¹⁴⁸ Another notice refers to the chapel that the papal notary Messer Bindo "intended to make"; the commitment seems to have been made on 5 December 1331.¹⁴⁹ Giralomo Macchi, the archivist of the hospital through the late seventeenth and early eighteenth centuries, said that the Cappella del Manto was founded in 1356.¹⁵⁰ We know that when, in 1359, the Hospital of the Scala acquired a goodly number of relics from Constantinople, a new chapel for those relics was planned. It was finished by 11 December 1363, when the Opera del Duomo asked the rector to repay the 600 florins that the hospital had borrowed for its construction.¹⁵¹ In all these projects, painting surely played a role.

One of the major projects in the decoration of the hospital we do know about, though only through secondary sources. In 1335 Pietro and Ambrogio Lorenzetti completed frescoes, on the facade of the hospital, of the *Birth of the Virgin* and the *Presentation of the Virgin in the Temple*. These works were part of five scenes of the life of the Virgin that ran in a horizontal band across the facade and were covered by a projecting roof; the last traces of them were still visible in the early eighteenth century.¹⁵² Following the *Presentation* were scenes of the marriage of the Virgin and the return of the Virgin to the house of her parents, executed by Simone Martini. The fifth scene was an *Assumption of the Virgin*. Its authorship is unknown, and, indeed, we are not entirely certain that it belonged to the

ication of the altar seems to have been to San Biagio.

143. Faluschi, Siena, BC, MS E.v.14, fol. 145v.

144. ASS, Spedale 119, fols. 166v, 293r, 509v. This chapel was near the high altar. The original donation for the chapel, of 80 florins, seems to have been made on 18 January 1353.

145. ASS, Spedale 119, fol. 175r. In 1379 the Painters' Guild decided that the feast of Saint Luke should be celebrated at the Ospedale. According to G. Macchi (ASS, MS D.108, fol. 272r), the chapel, originally founded by Monna Becha, was assigned to the Painters' Guild in that year (1379).

146. ASS, Spedale 64, fol. 3v; Spedale 119, fol. 262r.

147. ASS, Spedale 119, fols. 171r, 272r. See also Spedale 89, Protocolo x, fols. 108r–109r.

148. Faluschi, Siena, BC, MS E.v.14, fol. 145v.

149. ASS, Spedale 119, fol. 172v.

150. ASS, Macchi, MS D.108, fol. 272v.

151. Milanesi, Siena, BC, MS P.III.49, fol. 375r.

152. The longevity of the hospital murals reminds us that Cennino Cennini remarked: "I have told you above that the noblest and strongest tempering which can be done upon a wall consists in working in fresco, that is, on the fresh mortar. And know that no matter how much water ever rained upon the front surface of the wall, it could never do any harm at all." Cennini, *The Craftsman's Handbook*, 120.

to an anonymous artist in the circle of Simone Martini, the Master of Palazzo Venezia.[135] We know that Ambrogio Lorenzetti painted in the chapel of the hospital's cemetery in 1341, but we do not know the subject matter of that project.[136] In 1344 Lippo and Federigo Memmi produced three panels (a triptych?) for the rector of the hospital, who sent them to "don Bruno."[137] And during the same year, Lippo Vanni and Cola Fucci were paid for work on miniatures for a new antiphonary, and Lippo was further paid for work on a lectionary.[138] Between 19 January and 17 August 1355, Jacopo di Mino, "painter of our chapel," was paid 26 florins and 38 soldi, but the nature of his work is unknown.[139]

The fact that there are large gaps in the surviving documentation means that many commissions are undoubtedly hidden from us. Certainly, many locations within the hospital must have received images of which we have no record. In 1252, the bishop of Siena accorded the hospital the privilege of building a chapel.[140] It seems highly unlikely that the altar of the chapel remained without an image until the installation of Duccio's no. 47. On 26 March 1328, the rector of the hospital, Giovanni di Tese Tolomei, received the right to be buried in a new chapel that he would construct in the *pellegrinaio nuovo* and for which, on 27 June 1328, he provided £500.[141] The will of Biagio Montanini, dated 9 November 1346, provided for the construction of a new altar "in un luogo evidente" and for images on the adjoining wall (presumably frescoes) of "la Nunziata ed un' immagine di Gesu Cristo pendente in croce come ancora la passione del b. Biagio."[142] A notice of 1349 makes refer-

135. Like the commune, the hospital employed painters to "mark" their properties. From 1344, we have a series of payments for such work to Antonio, the painter. ASS, Spedale 851, fols. 22v, 51v, and 78v.

136. ASS, Spedale 514, fol. 63v. The notice of payment in this case is particularly interesting, since Ambrogio was paid not in cash but in grain. This type of payment was quite common in Florence, but this is the only Sienese notice we have of payment in goods.

137. ASS, Spedale 514, fol. 52v, and Spedale 851, fol. 18v (3 March 1344). Published by Bacci, *Fonti e commenti*, 181–82: "Maestro Lippo e Tederigho figliuogli che furono di Memmo, dipentori, ebero per iij pezzi di tauole e per la basa e civorii che fecie fare misser Mino [di Cino] nostro Rettore, per mandare a misser don Bruno, xxv fiorini d'oro, j libra, vj soldi, iiij denari." On 11 May 1344, 4 florins were paid to Berto Lotti "per la portatura de le tauole che si mandorono a misser Don Bruno." ASS, Spedale 514, fol. 73r; Spedale 851, fol. 39r.

138. ASS, Spedale 514, fols. 26r (6 florins paid to Cola—date uncertain), 66v (3 florins to Lippo, for miniatures in the antiphonary, paid on 24 November 1344). Another series of payments to Cola and Lippo are found in ASS, Spedale 851: fol. 35r (Cola paid 5 florins, 2 lire, 17 soldi, and 6 denari on 27 April 1344 for the new antiphonary, at a rate of 12 denari for each miniature); fol. 6r (Lippo receives 16 florins, on 27 January 1344, for unspecified work); fol. 6v (Lippo receives, for miniatures, 2 florins on 30 January 1344); fol. 20v (Lippo is paid 4 florins for miniatures on 11 March 1344); fol. 25v (Lippo receives 1 florin, 1 lira, 16 soldi, and 4 denari for thirteen miniatures in the new antiphonary, at the rate of 8 soldi apiece, on 30 March 1344); fol. 26r (Lippo receives 7 florins on 31 March 1344); fol. 29v (Lippo is paid 10 florins and 15 soldi for work on a lectionary, on 9 April 1344); fol. 67r (Lippo receives 2 florins and 8 soldi for work on the lectionary, on 14 August 1344); fol. 92v (on 31 December 1344, Lippo is paid 3 florins for work on the lectionary).

139. ASS, Spedale 515, fol. 80r.

140. See "I rettore dello Spedale di Santa Maria della Scala," in Banchi and Polidori, *Statuti senesi*, III, 11–13.

141. ASS, Spedale 119, fols. 259r–260r; Spedale 122, fol. 369r; Spedale 256, fol. 308r; Spedale 850, fol. 24v.

142. ASS, Spedale 119, fols. 28r, 383r. The ded-

clearly seen in Domenico di Bartolo's fresco *Distribution of Alms* in the *pellegrinaio* of the Ospedale di Santa Maria della Scala. Like any painted object exposed to the elements, its coloring had to be renewed on a regular basis. Ambrogio (Lorenzetti?) renewed the head and hands in 1335.[131] Consumed by time and weather, the *Madonna* was finally removed in 1704 and replaced with the *Name of Jesus*.[132]

The Ospedale di Santa Maria della Scala

In the case of the great hospital of Siena, we have nothing like a comprehensive record of commissions, and what we do know about painting connected with the institution has been pieced together using fragments from a variety of sources.[133] With a few works, we know that their provenance leads back to the hospital: Duccio's polyptych no. 47 (Fig. 56), the Bulgarini *Assumption of the Virgin* (Siena no. 61; Fig. 26), a *Madonna and Child Enthroned* also by Bulgarini (Siena no. 82; Fig. 24), and another panel of the same subject by the same painter (Siena no. 80; Fig. 25).[134] Siena no. 108, the *Mystic Marriage of Saint Catherine* (Fig. 93), also came to the gallery from the Ospedale della Scala. The panel is usually attributed

---

131. Siena, Opera del Duomo 174, fol. 59r (December 1335). Rowley (*Ambrogio Lorenzetti*) associates this notice with Ambrogio Lorenzetti, although the document gives only the first name. There was, however, a "Ambrogio di Duccio," documented in 1339, and in 1344 the Ospedale employed a "Ambrogio dipentore in champoreggi" to paint two candlesticks for the Chapel of San Jacopo Interciso in the duomo (see Appendix III). For later payments regarding this task, see Lusini, *Il duomo*, 242 n. 36, 244 nn. 59–60, 330 n. 143.

The most interesting and full account of this project, written during the period here discussed, comes from 1358. In August of that year the Opera del Duomo bought five hundred sheets of gold leaf, at a rate of 4 lire and 10 soldi per hundred, for restoration of "la madonna dela facciata di duomo sopra a la porta di mezzo." Cristofano, a painter, sold the Opera blue, red lake, and other colors for the project. The same painter and his "compagno" were paid 18 lire and 5 soldi for repairs. In September of 1358, he was paid for a further seventeen sheets of gold; he and "lucha" received 8 lire and 8 soldi for ultramarine and other colors. Cristofano and Luca were paid, in the same month, for fifteen days' work on the project by each, the total cost coming to 24 lire and 3 soldi. A further six hundred sheets of gold leaf were acquired at the same time, at a cost of £27. Then, in December, Cristofano was paid for 225 sheets of gold, and for gold and tin and other colors "per fare istelle intorno a la madonna del la facciata del Duomo e mettare ad oro el ale degl'angoli." This time the Opera spent 11 lire, 19 soldi, and 6 denari. Siena, Opera del Duomo 185, fols. 41v–42r, 45v–46r, 48v. In the previous year, 1357, Domenico Agostini had been paid for "una ala, chi à fatto del detto mese per l'agnolo della facciata" (Lusini, *Il duomo*, I, 237 n. 1). Lusini thought this referred to the *Saint Michael* on the facade; it could just as well have been a replacement for a wing on one of the kneeling angels above the door.

132. Siena, BC, Macchi: MS A.XI.22, fol. 87v.

133. For the hospital, see Banchi and Polidori, *Statuti senesi*, III, *Statuto dello Spedale di Siena*; A. Liberati, "Nuovi documenti artistici dello Spedale di S. Maria della Scala in Siena," *BSSP*, XXIII–XIV, 1926–27, 147–79; D. Gallavotti Cavallero, *Lo Spedale di Santa Maria della Scala in Siena: Vicenda di una committenza artistica*, Pisa, 1985.

134. These three works by Bulgarini date to the period c.1340 to c.1360.

addition of a second angel for the back of the *Maestà,* for at the same moment, the cathedral purchased two *baccini,* presumably drip-trays for the candle wax, and Minuccio the locksmith was paid for two locks for the angels.[122] In August of 1339, the painter Guido (not further identified) was paid 6 soldi "for painting the drip-trays [*baccini*] of the angels that are in the cathedral."[123] Such objects obviously needed the occasional refurbishing, to deal with accumulated wax and any losses that wax might have caused. Romano di Mino was paid for such work in 1355 and 1356, and Paolo di Neri was paid for the same in 1366.[124]

In June of 1360, "Jachomo dipentore" received £1 for painting four shields on a house the Opera had purchased.[125] In August of that year, "jacomo dipintore" was paid for painting three poles to carry banners.[126] Bartolommeo Bulgarini, Luca, and Jacomo, all painters, were given a total of 4 lire and 10 soldi for removing the panel of the Madonna "quando si trasmuto e posesi dal crociefisso."[127] A whole series of minor tasks fulfilled by "gano del maestro minuccio dipentore," including painting poles, brought the artist only 4 lire and 13 soldi in August of 1361.[128] For the decoration of another pole and other tasks for the feast of the Assumption in August of 1362, Bonaccorso was paid 2 lire and 5 soldi,[129] and in December, Francesco received 2 lire and 5 soldi for painting "a panel of marble."[130]

There was a recurrent task that has often confused writers dealing with the cathedral or with individual artistic careers. In the tympanum of the central door of the cathedral's west facade, there was a sculpted, standing Madonna and Child with kneeling angels. It is

---

122. Siena, Opera del Duomo 178, fol. 52r. The cost of the *baccini* was 1 lira and 6 soldi (Opera del Duomo 178, fol. 52v). The locks cost a very modest 10 soldi, and the payment included reimbursement for "other things." Further, illumination of the *Maestà* was a requirement connected with the will of the rector, Giovanni di Tese Tolomei, made in favor of the Ospedale in 1325, which specified that the hospital was to keep a lamp perpetually burning before the high altar of the cathedral. ASS, Spedale 119, fol. 262r.

The Nove were fond of locking things down; in 1346 they paid a locksmith for repairing what I assume to have been locks on the vernacular rendition of the Sienese constitution, kept in the Biccherna. ASS, Biccherna 219, fol. 120r (2 March 1346).

123. Siena, Opera del Duomo 178, fol. 62r. This comparatively small project is of great interest because we seem to have all, or nearly all, the original documentation connected with it, and because of the number of individuals, five, involved. That number suggests a high degree of specialization among Siena's artists and craftsmen, and may well reflect the complexity of other projects where documentation is lacking.

124. In August of 1355, Romano had "restored" two angels in the cathedral and executed other minor tasks. Siena, Opera del Duomo 181, fol. 43v. In April of 1356, he was also paid for repairing and "refreshing" two angels from the high altar. Siena, Opera del Duomo 181, fol. 80v. Thus, it would seem, four angels were involved. See, for later records, Lusini, *Il duomo,* I, 329–30 n. 139, 331 n. 143. Panels also underwent periodic cleaning. In 1360, Pietro di ser Dota received 30 soldi for washing and cleaning the panels of "Santo Sano" and "Santo Bartolomeo." Siena, Opera del Duomo 186, fol. 66v (see Appendix III).

125. Siena, Opera del Duomo 186, fol. 78r.

126. Siena, Opera del Duomo 188, fol. 44r.

127. Siena, Opera del Duomo 190, fol. 4v (July 1362). The reference is likely to Duccio's *Maestà.*

128. Siena, Opera del Duomo 189, fol. 31r. This volume also contains small payments to Meo di Cecco (fol. 31v) and Jacomo di Cino (fol. 31v). In addition to receiving gifts of wax on the feast of the Assumption, the cathedral also received banners, valuable pieces of textiles. We know that later these (or some of them) were hung in the cathedral. Perhaps these painted poles were part of such displays.

129. Siena, Opera del Duomo 190, fol. 7r.

130. Siena, Opera del Duomo 190, fol. 14r.

frescoes neared completion. Perhaps those same notices also tell us something about the priorities of the Nine. We have almost no reliable evidence concerning the time the execution of a major altarpiece, such as Ambrogio's *Presentation,* took. Work could be, and was, broken off for intervals we cannot measure. But I would note that when Orcagna, in 1354, accepted the commission for the Strozzi altarpiece for Florence's Santa Maria Novella, he promised to complete the work in twenty months, apparently judging that time sufficient, although the work is dated 1357.

The Opera del Duomo, like the office of the Biccherna, paid for many minor tasks as well as the larger projects. In June of 1328, it paid the painter "Petro di Lorenzo," presumably Pietro Lorenzetti, £20 for "storie" in the "casa" of the Opera and reimbursed him for the gold and colors he had used.[114] In August of 1333, a "maestro pietro dipentore" was paid £2 for painting the new door to the cathedral.[115] Then, regarding the candle-bearing angels on the high altar of the cathedral, the constitution of 1262 required the commune to keep two candles burning there perpetually. That requirement was repeated in the constitutional redaction of 1309–10.[116] On 19 October 1312, the Consiglio Generale approved a motion that the commune keep a continually burning candle before the altar of the Virgin in the duomo.[117] In spite of the phrasing of the document, this was surely the addition of a third candle to those already required, a candle placed before the back of the *Maestà*.[118] On 12 February 1339, the Consiglio Generale approved the addition of a fourth candle to stand behind the *Maestà*.[119] Work perhaps proceeded slowly, for it was only in July that Ambrogio Lorenzetti was paid 17 lire and 7 soldi for painting the angel and a candlestick.[120] At the same time, the painter Ambrogio di Duccio received 2 lire and 5 soldi for gilding a candlestick held by an angel for the high altar.[121] I assume that this represents the

---

114. Siena, Opera del Duomo 173, fol. 43v. The gold and colors cost a further £6.

115. Siena, Opera del Duomo 174, fol. 26r. This has been taken as a reference to Pietro Lorenzetti, but the small sum, indicative of a modest task, makes me think it more likely that the artist was Petro di Pietro, a painter of small devotional works.

116. Zdekauer, *Il constituto,* 26.

117. ASS, Consiglio Generale 81, fols. 116r–117v.

118. This interpretation is supported by the expenditures of 28 April 1339, when the commune paid for a 150 pounds of candles, each weighing 2 pounds, to burn "before the panel of the Virgin Mary in the cathedral on the angels," and for 80 candles of 1 pound each "to place above the angel that is behind the high altar in the cathedral until the new angel is placed there" (ASS, Biccherna 201, fol. 47v). A similar payment in the same volume (fol. 21v) of 27 February 1339 also refers to the angels before the *Maestà* and to the angel behind the panel.

119. ASS, Consiglio Generale 1339, 4 January–29 June 1339, fols. 13r–13v. It may strike some readers as strange that such a lengthy period should separate the decisions about a third and fourth angel, since symmetry would seem to argue the necessity of a pair. The explanation is, however, straightforward: the comparatively small cost of acquiring such an item committed the city to the perpetual expense of providing candles for it. See the cost of wax, discussed on page 69 above.

120. Siena, Opera del Duomo 178, fol. 51v. The documentary evidence is confusing. The cited document says Ambrogio was paid for completing the angel. A loose sheet found in Opera del Duomo 178 records receipt of 19 lire and 12 soldi by the painter for "the angel and the candlestick he painted." Both amounts are very large for the task; something more than polychromy must have been involved. See Maginnis, "Chiarimenti documentari," 17.

121. Siena, Opera del Duomo 178, fol. 52r.

panel of Saint Savino." Tura Giovanni was given 2 lire and 5 soldi in December for wood "per mettare ne la terza tauola che si farà."[111] During the same month, a "maestro Ciecho de la grammatica" was paid £1 for translating the legend of San Savino into the vernacular "per farla ne la tauola."[112]

The notices for Ambrogio's *Presentation in the Temple* (1342) are also incomplete. In June of 1337, two different masters, both likely carpenters, were paid a total of 13 lire and 8 soldi: Muccio for "sette pezi di tavole" and Feuccio for "due pezi di tavole per la detta tavola per civori e predella." Then, in July of 1339, Paolo Bindi, surely a carpenter, received 49 lire, 12 soldi, and 2 denari for making the predella and for the wood he had used. Bindo Ricci, in January of 1340, was given the small sum of 15 soldi for battens; in May of the same year, Paolo Bindi was paid 42 lire, 9 soldi, and 2 denari for the predella and the "colone dela tavola," while Bindo Ricci received a further 6 lire and 8 soldi for the wood used in both. The cost of wood and carpentry thus amounted to 112 lire, 12 soldi, and 2 denari, even though there is no mention of the construction of the main panel. In July of 1339 and in January of 1340, Ambrogio received two payments of 30 florins each for painting the altarpiece. We have no record of the gilding of the panel or of the gold used in that part of the project.

These notices are informative in other ways. Four different individuals provided wood and carpentry for Ambrogio's altarpiece. The fact that wood for the predella was purchased three times, in 1337, 1339, and 1340, suggests that design of the predella changed during the execution of the altarpiece; and since Ambrogio was paid 30 florins for painting the panel in 1339, it seems likely that the predella was a separate entity. The payment for the "colone" of the altarpiece in 1340 is rather surprising because, generally, the carpentry was finished and gilded before the painting began. Perhaps these were buttresses of the type first discussed by C. Gardner von Teuffel, used for the installation of the work.[113] Slots in the upper portion of the back of the panel (Fig. 22) indicate that the center of the altarpiece was crowned by a detachable gable.

Several observations arise from these documents. First, the translation of the legend of Saint Savino for Pietro's altarpiece suggests the painter did not read Latin. I think we may safely assume that was true for all, or the vast majority of, painters of the period. Second, the notices demonstrate how multiple individuals contributed to the production of an altarpiece. The Ambrogio documents point toward my remarks about tempera painting in Chapter III, specifically my observation that such projects could be interrupted at many points. It seems clear that Ambrogio began his altarpiece, was then called to decorate the Sala della Pace, and therefore set aside the cathedral project, only to return to it as his

111. The reference to "the third panel" is puzzling, and open to several interpretations.

112. One panel of the predella to Pietro's altarpiece, *Saint Sabinus Before the Governor*, survives and is now in the National Gallery, London (no. 1113). It measures 37.5 x 33 cm.

113. Gardner von Teuffel, "The Buttressed Altarpiece."

The surviving documentary notices for the first three altarpieces dedicated to Siena's patron saints afford glimpses of how such major projects were structured, although they do not, in any single case, permit a complete equation with surviving panels. For Simone's *Annunciation,* we have a summary of expenses made at the end of the project, but that means we do not have a chronological progression from its inception to its conclusion.[107] Moreover, the altarpiece was reframed in the late nineteenth century, so we no longer see all the original carpentry. The notices for Pietro's and Ambrogio's altarpieces are incomplete, and elements are missing from both.[108]

The notices for the San Ansano altarpiece begin in July of 1333. In that month, the Opera del Duomo paid the carpenter Duccio, from the parish of San Maurizio, 4 lire and 13 soldi for "panels and other wood"; in November he received another 2 lire and 5 soldi for "panels." It was, however, another carpenter, Paolo from Camporegio, and his apprentices who in December were paid £52 for the decorative elements of the frame, "civori e le cholone e ciercini," and a further 2 lire and 8 soldi for "aghuti cholla bulette chievellini e mele" for the surround of the altarpiece.[109] A "mastro Guidono" received 1 lira and 4 soldi for "due pontelli" used for the "roof" above the altarpiece, and the carpenter Guerzone, from the parish of San Pietro a Ovile, was paid 1 lira and 19 soldi for the panels (i.e., wood) for that roof or canopy. An unnamed master was given 1 lira and 6 soldi for "l'armadura de la detta tavola quando si recò e per lengi e tortizi." For the wood and carpentry we thus have four individuals involved; the wood and work cost 62 lire, 6 soldi, and 6 denari. "Lipo dipintore," presumably Lippo Memmi, received in December 1 lira and 2 soldi for "irons" used in the altarpiece, and 70 florins (212 lire, 6 soldi, and 8 denari) for adorning (gilding) the elements of the frame. For the actual painting, Simone and Lippo received 100 florins (£300). The summary also includes expenditures amounting to 7 lire and 5 soldi for the porters who carried the altarpiece to the duomo and for candles used on that occasion.[110]

All of the notices regarding Pietro's *Birth of the Virgin* (1342) date to 1335. In November, the painter was given 30 florins (£90) as "the first payment for the painting of the

---

four altarpieces might not seem noteworthy in another context, but we have ample evidence of the Sienese concern with regularity and order in the civic fabric. See "A Sense of Beauty/A Sense of Order" in Chapter v.

107. Siena, Opera del Duomo 174, fols. 20v, 44r, 49r, 49v, 54r.

108. For Pietro's altarpiece: Siena, Opera del Duomo 176, fols. 52v and 58v. For Ambrogio's *Presentation:* Siena, Opera del Duomo 177, fols. 49r, 97r, 122r, and a loose folio in that manuscript. See Maginnis, "Ambrogio Lorenzetti's *Presentation in the Temple.*"

109. Contrast this sum with the 34 florins paid the carpenter for similiar elements of the San Vittorio altarpiece. It seems likely that the Bulgarini altarpiece had a much more elaborate frame.

110. Various notices from the second half of the Trecento speak to the accumulation of further ornament and decoration around the altar and altarpiece (see Lusini, *Il duomo,* chapters vi and vii). I would also note that, according to the *Kalendarium Ecclesiae Metropolitanae Senensis* (9), lightning struck the cathedral on Easter Sunday, 1359, splitting the altar stone of the San Ansano altar, causing stones to fall from the campanile, and creating a fire of lightning around figures and things within the cathedral. We have no indication whether the altarpiece by Simone was damaged.

As far as we know, it was another twenty years before attention turned again to the matter of altarpieces. In 1331, Simone Martini and Lippo Memmi began work on the San Ansano altarpiece (Figs. 17–20), now in the Uffizi and dated by inscription and documents to 1333. Like the altarpieces of San Savino, San Crescenzio, and San Vittorio that followed, the saint honored was depicted in one side panel flanking a central narrative scene, in this case the Annunciation, relating to a major feast of the Virgin. Here we have a restatement of Siena's devotion to the Madonna and, I suspect, a decision not unrelated to the character of Siena's four patron saints, whose legends were lackluster and possibly not well known.[103] Two years later, in 1335, Pietro Lorenzetti was given the commission for the San Savino altarpiece, whose center was the *Birth of the Virgin* (Fig. 30), now in the Museo dell'Opera del Duomo, originally flanked by panels of San Savino and Saint Bartholomew. Then, in 1337, work began on Ambrogio Lorenzetti's San Crescenzio altarpiece, the central panel of which was his *Presentation in the Temple* (Fig. 21), now in the Uffizi. As with Pietro's altarpiece, the flanking saints, in this case Crescenzio and Michael Archangel, are now lost. Both altarpieces are dated by inscription to 1342, which seems likely to be the date of installation rather than the date of actual completion, even though we know Ambrogio was still working on his contribution in 1340. After the Lorenzetti panels were installed, another break in furnishing the altars occurred; it was only c.1350 that Bartolommeo Bulgarini and the Master of Palazzo Venezia created the altarpiece of San Vittorio, to which belonged a fragmentary *Nativity* (Fig. 27), now in the Fogg Art Museum, and panels of Saints Catherine of Alexandria and Vittorio (Figs. 28–29), now in Copenhagen.[104]

Whether Simone's commission represented the first step in a plan already worked out for the four altars is open to debate. I have been puzzled that the first commission, Simone's, was followed by Pietro's altarpiece, which shows an antecedent moment in the legend of the Virgin: her birth.[105] Moreover, the Opera del Duomo seems to have taken no trouble to bring the formats of the four works into accord. While it is reasonable to assume that, originally, all were of the same width, determined by the matching widths of the four altars, only the *Annunciation,* the *Birth of the Virgin,* and the fragmentary *Nativity* are of approximately the same height (in the range of 170.5 cm to 187 cm). Ambrogio's *Presentation,* which is missing a secondary element, a pinnacle, at its top, is nonetheless 257 cm high.[106]

103. See "Civic Christianity" in Chapter I.

104. Beatson, Muller, and Steinhoff, "The St. Victor Altarpiece in Siena Cathedral." On 28 May 1351, the carpenter Giovanni di Goro was paid the handsome sum of 34 florins for making the "civori e cercini e colonine" of the altarpiece (Siena, Opera del Duomo 180, fol. 87v).

Although the authors of the *Art Bulletin* article do not so argue, I suspect that the altarpiece may relate to Bishop Donodeus Malavolti, who died in 1350. Tizio (Siena, BC, MS B.III.8, 200) tells us Do-nodeus was buried at the altar of San Vittorio. According to a document of 3 December 1415 (Siena, Opera del Duomo 8, fol. 3r), the will of the bishop stipulated that four chaplains be appointed to the altar of San Vittorio.

105. On the other hand, we have evidence suggesting that San Ansano was more highly regarded than Crescenzio, Savino, and Vittorio. He alone figures among the feasts observed by members of the Painters' Guild.

106. The discrepancies in size and framing of the

cerning Duccio's *Maestà* for the high altar is dated 9 October 1308; it is a contract, but likely not the original agreement, between Duccio and the Opera del Duomo, for it does not mention the original provision of the unpainted support for the altarpiece.[100] Moreover, the *Maestà* was installed in the cathedral in June of 1311; in light of information about the length of time needed for the execution of other, smaller altarpieces, the period of October 1308 to June 1311 seems far too short for a work of the size and complexity of Duccio's panel, even though the master was assisted by a fairly large workshop.

The *Maestà* (Color Plates 1–2, 10–11; Figs. 15–16) is unquestionably one of the most important and influential works of the Trecento. Painted on front and back and combining a vision of the Virgin and her celestial court with many narratives depicting the infancy of Christ, his mission, his passion, his posthumous appearances, and scenes of the last days of the Virgin, the work became both a challenge and a source book for painters who followed. The opulence, refinement, and high craftsmanship of the work established a standard for later works by other painters, and the narratives were filled with settings and compositions that were often reworked by those same later artists. But the *Maestà* is also a key historical document that tells us much about the society in which it was produced, for it is a work that simultaneously points in two directions. The narratives of the back (Fig. 16), with the *Crucifixion* rising through two registers, seem to have been inspired by the New Testament Cycle in Old Saint Peter's in Rome.[101] That connection was surely more than fortuitous; Siena cathedral shared its day of dedication, November 18, with Saint Peter's and Saint Paul's-outside-the-walls.[102] Many writers have noted that the Passion Cycle, occupying the main portion of the back of the altarpiece, is particularly extensive and that the number of trial scenes is very large. While there is no specific literary source that explains this circumstance, it strikes me as not unrelated to the prominence of flagellant confraternities in Siena. It is, however, the front of the *Maestà* (Color Plate 10) that reveals most about Siena and the faith. I have noted above that the subject of the Virgin in majesty was closely connected with the commune and that its depiction in the sites of government was a tradition. An enthroned Madonna and Child had long appeared on Sienese coins and seals. Now that subject was moved from secular contexts and placed at the heart of Sienese devotion. Nothing could speak more eloquently of Siena's "civic Christianity," especially since the imagery was borrowed back, as it were, by Simone for the Palazzo Pubblico.

crowns the cupola was installed in 1264, marking the completion of the dome. All of this makes it unlikely that the *Madonna degli occhi grossi* was on the high altar in 1260. Then, we have the rubric of the 1262 constitution that speaks of constructing a new chapel dedicated to the Virgin. It is at least possible that the *Madonna del Voto* was intended for that chapel.

100. ASS, Diplomatico, Opera della Metropolitana, Parchment 603. Satkowski, *Duccio*, 69–72.

101. W. Tronzo, "Between Icon and Monumental Decoration of a Church: Notes on Duccio's *Maestà* and the Definition of the Altarpiece," in *Icon*, ed. G. Vikan, Washington, D.C., 1988, 41.

102. Tradition dates the dedication of the cathedral to 1179 and claims the dedication rites were performed by Pope Alexander III, born Orlando Bandinelli, from the important Sienese family of that name. Thus the Roman connection was strong.

to other altars in the first half of the fourteenth century are lost, it is perhaps true that the cathedral did not provide painters of the early Trecento with as much work as did the Palazzo Pubblico. There is no need to think that the situation, if it existed, represented anything like the preeminence of the secular or reflected the commune's failure to provide the Opera del Duomo with adequate funds. Rather, it would have to do with the nature and extent of cathedral projects during the late Dugento and the first half of the fourteenth century. Many of these were monumental undertakings, architectural and sculptural projects that were complex and costly. During the 1270s a new episcopal palace was constructed on the south flank of the cathedral. Work on the duomo facade seems to have begun in 1285. Agnolo di Tura says that in 1317 work began on extending the cathedral choir to the east and on constructing the facade of the new baptistery. Then came the extraordinarily ambitious project to enlarge the cathedral in a dramatic way, by turning the old nave and choir into a set of transepts and building a new nave. Work on this project was certainly under way by 1339. As part of the project, a new campanile was also envisaged, as indicated by the drawing (Fig. 76) discussed in the previous chapter. The architectural projects were accompanied by significant sculptural endeavors: decoration of the west facade, figures to stand on the exterior of the nave aisles, sculpture for the facade of the baptistery, and some sixty gargoyles, likely used as drain spouts. From 1310 we have reference to a mosaic or mosaics (*"opus mosaicum"*) likely for the west facade, and from 1358 notice of a mosaic figure of Saint Michael Archangel on a corner of the facade.[97] All things considered, I have the impression that the history of work on Siena cathedral proceeded much as did work on the cathedral of Florence during the Quattrocento: architecture and sculpture were given priority, painting came later.[98]

What we do know concerning major pictures from the first half of the Trecento involves panels for the high altar and for the side altars, located in the transepts, of Siena's four patron saints: Ansano, Savino, Crescenzio, and Vittorio.[99] The earliest document con-

97. Milanesi, *Documenti*, I, 175–76 and 103 n. 5, respectively.

98. See M. Wackernagel, *The World of the Florentine Artist: Projects and Patrons, Workshop and the Art Market*, trans. A. Luchs, Princeton, 1981, 20–37.

99. The history of dugento images and the cathedral's high altar is problematic. Van Os (*Sienese Altarpieces, 1215–1460*, I) has argued that the *Madonna degli occhi grossi* (Siena, Museo dell'Opera del Duomo) was a companion to the Redeemer altarfrontal (Siena, Pinacoteca Nazionale, no. 1) and also originally an antependium, which was elevated to a place on the altar by 1260, thus becoming an altarpiece. It is generally held that sometime after the battle of Montaperti (1260), and in thanks to the Virgin for her miraculous intervention on behalf of the Sienese, the original image was replaced by the "Guidesque" panel, now only a fragment, known as the *Madonna del Voto*, presently in the Chapel of Alexander VII in the cathedral. Stubblebine (*Guido da Siena*, Princeton, 1964, 72–75) dated the latter to the 1280s. The truth is that this account contains a great deal of speculation and, perhaps, makes a complicated historical situation seem clearer than it is.

First, I am not convinced that the *Madonna degli occhi grossi* was originally an antependium (although I leave that argument for consideration elsewhere). Second, the matter is complicated by the building history of the cathedral. In 1259, a new high altar was under construction. (We have no evidence for another rebuilding of the high altar before Duccio's *Maestà*; it may well be that the *Maestà* was installed on the dugento altar.) The duomo roof was covered with lead only in 1262. The gilded globe that

dono at the end of the right transept; but we know nothing of its furnishings at that date.[91] The Sienese constitution of 1262 makes reference to a chapel to be constructed in honor of the Madonna for the victory of Montaperti (1260), and to a chapel of Saint James, presumably that of San Iacobo Interciso.[92] According to Agnolo di Tura, Cardinal Riccardo Petroni (d. 1314) was buried above an altar dedicated to Saint Catherine of Alexandria that was furnished with a picture or pictures.[93] A document of 28 April 1323 makes reference to the altar of Saint Michael Archangel, apparently furnished with a crucifix; another notice, of February 1337, refers to the altar of Saint John.[94] We have a 1363 notice of the commune's intention to build in the cathedral a chapel to Saint Paul and to provide it with an altarpiece.[95]

Just as the 1215 list of altars is both suggestive and frustrating, the earliest surviving trecento inventory of the cathedral (1389) is similarly worrisome. It names a total of twenty altars in the duomo, but does not record altarpieces.[96] Yet if both objects and records relating

91. Milanesi, *Documenti*, I, 143–44. This altar had disappeared by the time of the inventory of 1389 (Siena, Opera del Duomo 864, fols. 12–12v). According to Tizio (Siena, BC MS B.III.8, 28–29), Bishop Rinaldo Malavolti (d. 8 June 1307) was buried above the altar. This is confirmed by the *Kalendarium Ecclesiae Metropolitana Senensis* in *Rerum Italicarum Scriptores*, XV, pt. VI, 20–21. It may have been only after the period of our discussion that it vanished, for Milanesi (Siena, BC, MS P.III.49, fol. 344r) says that the Entrata/Uscita of 1366 states: "A maestro Neri vannucio gli quarante e quatro lire e quatro soldi per due predelle che fecie alatare [*sic*] di santa maria dele grazie e laltra allatare di santo barttolomeio." These may have been steps rather than painted predellas, for, according to Milanesi, the same cathedral volume records payments to Francesco del Tonghio for predellas for the altars of San Savino and San Vittorio.

92. Zdekauer, *Il constituto*, 29. The Chapel of Saint James appears to have been under the patronage of the hospital of Santa Maria della Scala. This altar stood next to the campanile in the place where a door now opens to the south flank of the cathedral. It was here that the miraculous crucifix of Montaperti was placed. See the Biccherna cover of 1483; Tizio, Siena, BC, MS B.III.6, fol. 641r; and G. Aronow, "A Description of the Altars in Siena Cathedral in the 1420s," in H. W. van Os, *Sienese Altarpieces, 1215–1460: Form, Content, Function*, II, Groningen, 1990, 226.

93. Tizio (Siena, BC, MS B.III.8, 75–76) tells us that the altar had a panel of the crucifixion and images of Saint Nicholas, Saint Catherine, and Saint Peter. The Petroni monument and the altar of Saint Catherine stood where the Chapel of the Baptist is today, and both were moved when that chapel was built. The 1389 inventory of the cathedral refers to a cross with a pedestal and two silver figures that had come from the cardinal (Opera del Duomo 1489, fol. 1r). According to the *Repertorio* (Siena, Opera del Duomo 1557, fol. 46v), the rector Giugurta Tommasi removed the altar of Saint Catherine entirely and placed the "panel" from the altar in the rooms of the Opera in 1591.

94. Lusini, *Il duomo*, I, 144 n. 31: A codicil to the will of Guido Ventura leaves money to the Opera on the condition that it keep a lamp perpetually burning before the crucifix. Siena, Opera del Duomo 177, fol. 23r (5 February 1337): two soldi are paid to Nuto Ghezi *chanicciaio* for a *chaniccio* to be placed on the altar to Saint John.

95. Lusini, *Il duomo*, I, 322 n. 77. The project was to commemorate the Sienese victory over the mercenary Compagnia del Cappelletto, but the project was delayed. Only on 26 February 1374 was Luca di Tommè paid the handsome sum of 105 florins (roughly £368) for providing the altarpiece. S. Fehm (*Luca di Tommè*, Carbondale and Edwardsville, Ill., 1986, 198) publishes the relevant Biccherna notices, but does not make the connection with the earlier document.

96. Siena, Opera del Duomo 1489. At this point, one inevitably recalls that Ghiberti said (Schlosser, *Lorenzo Ghibertis Denkwürdigkeiten*, I, 42) Simone Martini executed two *tavole* for the duomo and Ambrogio Lorenzetti executed three.

No discussion of communal patronage is complete without acknowledgment of the funds provided to churches and to the religious orders by the governors of Siena. The commune's largest contributions related to architecture, in providing building materials, especially bricks, for the construction of churches and convents. As noted in Chapter 1, many of these grants appear in redactions of the city-state's constitution; but subsidies were also granted to cover the cost of paintings. On 16 October 1319, the Consiglio Generale debated a petition that it had received from the Servites, asking for help with the cost of an altarpiece for Santa Maria dei Servi that, they said, had cost £300. The council awarded £100.[87] A decade later, on 30 June 1329, the Consiglio Generale gave the Carmelites £50 to help with payment for an altarpiece, painted by Pietro Lorenzetti, that was said to have cost 150 florins (approximately £498).[88] Given the way that the commune was fairly evenhanded in its other gifts to the religious orders, we may assume that these two cases were not unique and that we simply lack surviving documentation in relation to other grants of this kind.

The Cathedral

As noted above, the documentation for the cathedral is much slighter than the surviving records of the commune per se.[89] This paucity of information is particularly frustrating, since the 1215 *Ordo officiorum* for the cathedral indicates that, in addition to the altar of the Virgin, the duomo contained altars to Saint John the Evangelist, Saint Michael Archangel, San Ansano, San Crescenzio, San Savino and San Vittorio (together), Saint Bartholomew, Saint Lucy, Saint Nicholas, Saint Silvestro, and Saints Fabrina and Sebastian.[90] A documentary notice of 31 May 1260 refers to the construction of vaults in the cathedral "ex parte altaris sancti Bartolomei per directum ut tendit ad illam januam que est ex dicte parte sancti Bartolomei," indicating that the altar of Saint Bartholomew stood near the Porta del Per-

---

87. ASS, Consiglio Generale 92, fols. 121v–122v. A final installment of the grant, some £25, was paid out by the Biccherna in 1321, suggesting that the work may not have been finished until that year. ASS, Biccherna 140, fol. 189r (30 June 1321).

88. ASS, Consiglio Generale, Deliberazione, 108, fols. 59v–62r. Bacci, *Dipinti inediti*, 83–86. If the Carmelites were not exaggerating too much—some exaggeration is likely involved—this would make their altarpiece one of the most expensive of the period, among those for which we have indication of total cost.

89. For the cathedral, see G. A. Pecci, *Storia del vescovado della città di Siena*; Lusini, *Il duomo*; E. Carli, *Il Duomo di Siena*, Genoa, 1979; H. Keller, "Die Bauplastik der Sieneser Doms: Studien zu Giovanni Pisano und seiner künstlerischen Nachfolge," *Kunstgeschichtliches Jahrbuch der Biblioteca Hertziana*, 1, 1937, 138–220; A. Middeldorf Kosegarten, *Sienesische Bildhauer am Duomo Vecchio: Studien zur Skulptur in Siena 1250–1330*, Munich, 1984. The feasts for the city's four patron saints, who each eventually had an altar in the cathedral, were as follows: Ansano, 1 December; Savino, 30 October; Crescenzio, 12 September; Vittorio, 15 May.

90. G. C. Trombelli, ed., *Ordo officiorum ecclesiae Senensis*, Bologna, 1766. For a discussion of this work, see K. van der Ploeg, *Art, Architecture, and Liturgy: Siena Cathedral in the Middle Ages*, Groningen, 1993.

had the custom of marking property that belonged to it with coats of arms or insignia. In the grandest cases, these escutcheons or emblems were sculpted, but in most cases they were simply painted. The records of the commune and of the hospital often indicate payments to painters for that task ("segnare le case").[78]

There was also the genre of *pittura infamante,* images painted in a public place to designate crimes and criminals.[79] The practice was well established in Siena by the late Dugento, when, in 1292, the statute of the Woolworkers' Guild called for depictions in the guild's "court" of members who had stolen from the guild or violated guild regulations.[80] In 1298 Minnuccio di Filippuccio was paid for painting false witnesses in or on the communal palace.[81] As noted above, in 1302 a certain Guido received payment for painting twelve false witnesses and counterfeiters of coin "in palazzo."[82] Although documentation on subsequent images of this type is not extensive, the practice certainly continued, for the 1342–43 statute of the powerful Mercanzia required that any member of the guild who gave false witness or produced false papers was to be fined £100 and "ancho sieno dipenti ne la casa del la Mercantia col nome et sopranome suo et colla spetia de la falsità scritto" (and also be painted in the house of the Mercanzia with his name and nickname and the nature of his falsity written).[83] Also, part of a peace agreement with the Pisans in 1333 required that painted images of those condemned or banished during the conflict, in either city, be entirely removed.[84] In fact, even depictions of criminals were not necessarily intended to be permanent. A statute of 1305, incorporated in the constitution of 1309–10, required the podestà to advise the General Council every July whether images of forgers of coin were to be removed.[85]

There were still other small tasks that provided work for painters, especially in service of the Sienese habit of decorating the covers of official volumes, particularly the parchment volumes of the Biccherna, with small images and coats of arms (Figs. 23, 91–92). Since the financial year was divided into two semesters—January to June and July to December—a large number of such covers were acquired, and many of them still exist.[86]

---

78. A rather odd, and therefore puzzling, task seems to be involved in a 1361 payment to the painters Fede di Nalduccio and Bindotto di Cecco for going "per richercare e chaseri," each with a horse (see Appendix III). Professor Erasmi suggests that these may have been visits to dairy farms, presumably owned by the commune.

79. On the entire subject and history of these images, see G. Ortalli, *La pittura infamante,* Rome, 1979. Such images were, in many cases, the trecento equivalent of our "WANTED" posters.

80. Ortalli, *La pittura,* 45. The text of chapter X reads: "E che neuno sottoposto possa nè debbia avere a fare o mercatare di cose che appartengano a la detta Arte, e sia dipinto lo furatore e lo tollitore, lo suo nome, ne la corte dell'Arte, e non si ne possa nè debbia spegnare la detta figura infino tanto che sia ribandito." And in chapter XI, which forbids the selling of anything stolen from the guild: "et sia dipenta la sua figura e la cosa furata ne la corte dell'Arte, e scripto lo suo nome e la sua figura." Banchi and Polidori, *Statuti senese,* I, 266–67; see also 303.

81. ASS, Biccherna 114, fol. 192v (12 November 1298).

82. ASS, Biccherna 117, fol. 312r.

83. Senigaglia, "Lo Statuto dell'Arte della Mercanzia senese," 128.

84. Malavolti, *Dell'historia di Siena,* II, 94.

85. Lisini, *Costituto volgarizatto,* II, 271–72.

86. L. Borgia et al., *Le Biccherne,* Rome, 1984. See Appendix IV to this volume, which contains an extensive record of payments for book covers during the regime of the Nine.

for a panel with "several figures," to be placed in the loggia of the baths of Petriolo.[69] On the same day, Guido and his *compagni* received 19 lire and 1 soldi for painting at the baths of Macereto.[70] In October of the same year, the Nine paid the cost of another panel for the "house of the commune" in the same location,[71] and in February of 1339 the *operaio* of the commune, Bono Campuglia, received £13 for purchase of a panel of the Virgin to be placed in the loggia of the baths of Petriolo.[72] Generally, however, painters were employed at the baths to provide painted inscriptions, as in the 1291 notice. Donato and his companions, in 1331, received £30 for twenty-two days' work at Petriolo "marking the houses with letters," and 41 lire and 8 soldi for further inscriptions at Petriolo and at the baths of Macereto.[73] These inscriptions could have taken any of several forms, but most of them probably indicated that the accommodation belonged to the Commune of Siena or listed, per regulation, on a sign on the door of each space for visitors, the name of the proprietor, the price of rental, and a list of the household effects with which the accommodation was furnished.[74]

The commune paid for other types of projects, sometimes, as in the case of the earliest notice regarding the Camollia gate, involving more than one artist. The 1327 payments for the *palii* presented to the duke and duchess of Calabria included, in addition to the sums given Simone, payments to Lolo Zendadaio, a mercer, for 148 *braccia* of white, black, vermilion, and indigo silk for *"guazaroni,"* for *aslieri* to tie the fabric to the poles of the baldachins, and for the actual assembly of these objects. Then there were the very small projects that painters might be given, many of them temporary, thus impermanent. In 1278 a certain "Guidoni" was paid 3 lire and 5 soldi for painting two banners, one of them apparently for the Terzo di San Martino.[75] On 12 December 1310 the painter Niccola di Mino received £14 for painting twenty-five "penoni de vichariati," and on 20 December 1310 Masarello received 2 lire and 10 soldi for the same type of work.[76] On 27 September 1331 the painter Meuccio received 6 soldi for painting a garland on the banner of the "vichariato di munistero."[77] The commune, like the Hospital of Santa Maria della Scala,

69. ASS, Biccherna 191, fol. 145v; Biccherna 194, fol. 62v. The sum involved was 26 lire, 19 soldi, and 2 denari.

70. ASS, Biccherna 191, fol. 145v; Biccherna 194, fol. 62r; Biccherna 401, fol. 51r.

71. ASS, Biccherna 198, fol. 35v (8 October 1338).

72. ASS, Biccherna 201, fol. 22r (28 February 1339). It is unclear whether this was an image added to that acquired in June of 1338 or a replacement, or whether the original provision had not been realized.

73. ASS, Biccherna 171, fols. 101v, 108r (31 December 1331). Payment records for Petriolo are also found in Biccherna 397, folios 5r and 164v. The first item records payment to Simone of 2 florins on 21 December 1331 for his brother. The second notice records Donato's total payment of £30, from which the 2 florins given to Simone were deducted. It also states that on 1 January 1332 Donato received the remaining 24 lire and 14 soldi.

74. See Pesciolini, "I bagni," 113.

75. ASS, Biccherna 73, fol. 47v (16 November 1278).

76. ASS, Biccherna 124, fols. 263r, 269r. The vicariates were districts in the *contado* that were organized as military units. See Bowsky, *Medieval Italian Commune,* 146–47.

77. ASS, Biccherna 171, fol. 47r.

expenses incurred in connection with the image and "altro aconcime" that he had had done on the Camollia gate.[61] In June of 1346, the Consiglio Generale debated and approved a motion to pay expenses necessary to complete "quia imago Virginis Gloriose jan est satis, designata fuit ex portam Kamollia in ipsa porta."[62] Later, between August and November of 1362, Bonaventure Aiuti, the *operaio,* received a total of 185 lire and 10 soldi for painting on the gate of Camollia.[63] Because the Camollia gate was the entrance to the city from the north for travelers using the Via Francigena, it may well have received special attention. According to Ghiberti, the Porta Romana on the southeast of the city (the entrance for the Via Francigena from the south) carried an incomplete *Coronation of the Virgin* by Simone Martini.[64] The only other surviving records of such decorations are of a payment of June 1331 for a roof over the image of the Virgin on the Porta Salaia and for the purchase, on 13 November 1332, of a panel of the Virgin to be placed on the Porta San Viene.[65]

From the mid–thirteenth century onward, the Sienese commune took great interest in the baths at Petriolo and Macereto, well to the south of the city.[66] Indeed, the constitution of 1262 dealt with the regulation and improvement of the facilities. In the constitution of 1309–10 is found a notice, first passed on 6 May 1293, that records an annual grant by the commune of £10 for the "new hospital" at Petriolo, and the constitution of 1337–39 records an annual gift of £50 to the Church of San Niccolò, also in Petriolo.[67] The Nove's employment of artists in connection with undertakings at the spas was generally for very modest tasks. In February of 1291, the commune paid an unnamed painter some 87 soldi for inscriptions in large letters at Macereto and Petriolo.[68] On 30 June 1338, the Nove paid

61. ASS, Biccherna 167, fol. 72v (15 May 1333).

62. ASS, Consiglio Generale, Deliberazione 138, fol. 41v (14 June 1346). The literature of early Sienese painting has often claimed that Simone Martini was author of an *Assumption of the Virgin* on the Camollia gate. The origin of that idea lies in a record of payment by the Biccherna, in August of 1347, of 10 florins for painting on the gate: "Mastro simone dipentore die dare a di [blank] daghosto diece fior. demo contanti a lui—x fior" (ASS, Biccherna 408, fol. 81v). The payment is, obviously, puzzling, since Simone died in 1344. We may deal here with a simple error, although I should note that one of Donato Martini's sons was called Simone. There is another interesting aspect to the document: one of the officials in charge of the painting of the gate was Simone di Gheri Bulgarino, cousin to the painter Bartolommeo Bulgarini.

63. ASS, Biccherna 242, fols. 99r (9 August 1362), 118v (6 October 1362), 132v (23 November 1362).

64. Schlosser, *Lorenzo Ghibertis Denkwürdigkeiten,* 42: "era cominciato sopra alla porta che va a Roma una grandissima storia d'una incoronatione." Tizio (Siena, BC, MS B.III.7, 485), under 1329, says the Porta Romana was founded in that year and that it was painted with an image of the Virgin.

65. ASS, Biccherna 168, fol. 213r (30 June 1331); Biccherna 174, fol. 54r (23 November 1332). The latter reference is to the very modest sum of 1 lira and 10 soldi, approximately the cost of a Biccherna cover at this date. This would seem to suggest that the image was perhaps for a small shrine within the gate rather than a great image on its exterior; but the payment of June is for repairing the roof over the "Immagine beata Maria vergine ad porta salaria" and amounts to 22 lire and 12 soldi.

66. See G.V. Pesciolini, "I bagni di Petriolo nel medievo," *La Diana,* VI, 1932, 110–35.

67. Lisini, *Costituto volgarizzato,* I, 80; ASS, Statuto 26, fol. 14r.

68. ASS, Biccherna 105, fols. 72, 73v (10–23 February 1291).

mento facto per eum in palatio comunis Senensis, in quo morantur domini Novem."[53] Two important works that may or may not relate to these notices are a *Madonna and Child* (Fig. 90) originally in the third-floor loggia and Ambrogio's extraordinary *Mappamondo,* the world map that gave its name to the first chamber of the Consiglio Generale.[54]

Other pictures—and intended pictures—are documented. On 15 July 1337, Bono Campuglia, *operaio* for the commune, received £300 to spend on the "new dormitory of the Nine," and on 18 April 1338 he received £58 for the "painter who painted the rooms of the new dormitory";[55] Domenico Orlandi was paid 6 lire, 8 soldi, and 9 denari.[56] Between August 1341 and January 1342, Lippo and Federigo Memmi were paid 125 lire, 2 soldi, and 6 denari in connection with a project in the Torre del Mangia, a project that was ultimately aborted.[57] On 22 December 1351, the carpenter Meo di Mino and a painter named Andrea received payment of 23 florins (77 lire and 5 soldi) for the "tabula" of Bernone di Monforte, the constable of the commune.[58] Lippo Vanni, in 1352, frescoed a large *Coronation of the Virgin* in the office of the Biccherna; and in 1361, after the fall of the Nine, Bartolo di Fredi received £70 for pictures of unspecified subject matter in the new Sala del Consiglio.[59]

Commissions of the Nine were by no means restricted to the decoration of the Palazzo Pubblico. Just a month after the Nove decided to create a park between the inner and outer gates of Camollia (May 1309), two painters, Ciecco and Nuccio, and a carpenter named Chello were paid £12 for painting the Virgin and other saints on the gate of Camollia and for repairing the roof, probably a roof projecting over the image to shield it, at least partially, from the weather.[60] As the gate faced northwest and was thus particularly exposed to bad weather, maintenance of the decoration was an ongoing affair. On 15 May 1333, the *operaio* of the commune, Bono Campuglia, was given 8 florins (24 lire and 4 soldi) for

---

53. ASS, Biccherna 206, fol. 59r (20 June 1340); Biccherna 217, fols. 125r (31 October 1345) and 130r (22 November 1345).

54. Rowley, *Ambrogio Lorenzetti,* I, 53–54, 98. For the Mappamondo, see Marcia Kupfer, "The Lost Wheel Map of Ambrogio Lorenzetti," *Art Bulletin,* LXXVIII, 1996, 286–310. The concentric markings seen on the fresco illustrated in Figures 87 and 88 seem to have been made by Ambrogio's rotating map.

55. ASS, Biccherna 190, fol. 4v (15 July 1337); Biccherna 194, fol. 26r (18 April 1338). Was this one of our "painters of walls"? The sum is significant; we are reminded of Fra Giordano's complaint (discussed in the previous chapter) about the rich who were willing to spend £300 to have their houses painted.

56. ASS, Biccherna 404, fol. 190r.

57. ASS, Biccherna 407, fols. 120v, 131r, 168v, 169r, 170v, 176r, 187r, 211r; Biccherna 209, fols. 84r, 125v. The relevant documents are published in Maginnis, "Chiarimenti documentari," 20–22. The nature of this uncompleted project is unclear. The documents speak of a "cupboard of the painting of the tower" and of "the painting of the tower."

58. ASS, Biccherna 228, fol. 130r (22 December 1351). Biccherna 159 (fol. 63v) records a payment in December of 1328 for a "tabula" for the "chonestabile" of that period. The amount is £25. I have been unable to determine the precise nature of these panels.

59. ASS, Biccherna 229, fol. 138r (30 June 1352); Biccherna 241, fol. 66v (28 July 1361). See also Giovanni di Benedetto in Appendix III.

60. ASS, Biccherna 122, fol. 201v.

(1338–39) for the Sala della Pace (Color Plates 5 and 6), the council room for the Nine and thus the meeting place for the executive branch of government.[52] The frescoes undeniably constitute one of the greatest accomplishments in the history of art. With its extraordinary and panoramic landscape, the first since antiquity, and its image of Siena idealized, *The Effects of Good Government* opened new avenues to art so daring, so original, that they would not be heavily traveled by subsequent painters in central Italy for many decades.

Beyond the artistic genius that the frescoes embody, the Sala della Pace marks a major turning point in the history of artistic usage. In the adjoining Sala del Mappamondo, the citizen of trecento Siena could see a loose association of separate images that produced a larger collective meaning. The Virgin of Simone's *Maestà* (Color Plates 3 and 4) admonished the General Council to good government, and the Child's scroll instructed that council to cherish justice. Around the room, depictions of subject territories gave immediacy to the lands that were to be wisely governed. Now, in the Sala della Pace, came a single decorative scheme that would occupy all but the window wall of the room. The change speaks to the elevation of secular decoration, for this kind of homogeneity had earlier been associated with chapels. And that comparison is all the more striking given the content of Ambrogio's murals. With the exception of images of the three theological virtues, the content of the frescoes is entirely secular. There is no image of the Virgin, of Christ, or of the saints; and where, in the fresco borders, angels might have watched over man's governance of the earth, we discover images of the seasons, the planets, the arts, coats of arms, and figures from antiquity. The change is integral to developments in law and political theory during the period; the frescoes announce a growing conviction that governance might be defined outside the Church.

Payments for the decoration of the Sala della Pace vividly demonstrate the regime's very cautious approach to paying for major works of art. In February, May, and June of 1338, the painter received, each time, 10 florins. A smaller payment of 2 florins was made in July, but payment returned to the 10-florin level in September and December. Ambrogio was given 6 florins in February of 1339. But it seems the commune was holding funds back, for when the painter received his final payment in May of 1339, the sum was 55 florins. This system of payment was neither new nor, in its period, unique. In 1295, the Nove had paid Guidoni for his *Maestà* in installments, and, as we shall see, the same arrangement pertained in connection with some of the altarpieces for the cathedral. The system was not exclusively Sienese; the contract (1320) for Pietro Lorenzetti's Arezzo polyptych (Colors Plate 13–14) specified that the bishop of that city was to pay the artist in three installments: at the beginning, in the middle of the project, and at its end.

Ambrogio Lorenzetti was to make various other contributions to the decoration of the palace. He was paid 10 florins, in June of 1340, for numerous, unspecified paintings; and in October and November of 1345, he received £85 and £3, respectively, for "orna-

---

52. All the relevant documents are transcribed in Maginnis, "Chiarimenti documentari," 13–17.

In the mid-1320s, Simone created an image of Saint Christopher in the office of the Biccherna.[45] The Nine had had such an image painted by Bindo Dietisalvi in 1296, and the subject was surely chosen in remembrance of the time when Siena's government, and many of its offices, did business in the Church of San Cristoforo.[46] Simone executed pictures of unspecified subject in the "house of the Lords Nine," noted in a document of 17 June 1322; and on 11 February 1324, £3 were given to Gura Benciarini for expenses in connection with an image of the Virgin painted on the facade, "before where [the Nove] live."[47] Between 1326 and 1327 Lippo Memmi painted an image of San Ansano for the office of the Gabella.[48] Nonetheless, one has the impression that after the mid-twenties commissions for paintings grew sporadic for roughly a decade. Possibly, attention and revenues were occupied by the major architectural projects the Noveschi had launched to enlarge the Palazzo Pubblico. In 1325 work began on the Torre del Mangia, the magnificent tower that is now integral to our vision of the palace; the construction continued until 1344. At the same time, work began on a significant expansion of the palace along the Via di Malcucinato. New prisons and a new chamber for the Consiglio Generale were started. The prisons necessitated a new chapel for prisoners, and in 1331 the prisons themselves received images of the Virgin and of numerous saints.[49]

The decade of the thirties was, however, distinguished by a new, or renewed, interest in secular subject matter. As noted above, Simone painted Montemassi and Sassoforte in 1330, Arcidosso and Castel del Piano in 1331.[50] But in February of 1330, he also painted a figure of the Roman hero Marcus Atilius Regulus in the Concistoro, beginning an association between Siena and Roman heroes that found one of its most elaborate treatments in the Antecappella of the palace when Taddeo di Bartolo frescoed that area in the early Quattrocento.[51] According to Agnolo di Tura, Ambrogio Lorenzetti painted "Roman stories" on the facade of the palace in 1337. But the most extraordinary example of the commune's new interest in secular decoration is embodied in Ambrogio Lorenzetti's frescoes

---

45. ASS, Biccherna 146, fol. 69r (30 June 1323).

46. ASS, Biccherna 113, fol. 236r (28 December 1296). See Appendix III. Among the various civic bodies that met in San Cristoforo was the Curia del Placito, the Court of Wards, responsible for matters concerning orphaned minors. The image of the giant Christopher carrying the Christ Child was particularly suitable for that council.

47. Respectively: ASS, Biccherna 144, fol. 127r (17 June 1322); Biccherna 149, fol. 115v (11 February 1324). The latter must have been a fresco, since the document describes the image of the Virgin as "on the wall and facade."

48. ASS, Biccherna 390, fol. 50r (December 1326–7 February 1327), and fol. 125r (9 March 1327).

49. ASS, Biccherna 168, fol. 213r (30 June 1331). The project for the new prisons seems to have begun in 1327. Beginning in April, the commune bought properties to be cleared for the construction, and at the end of June (the 26th), over £2,000 had been assigned to the *operaio* for the new prisons.

50. Respectively: ASS, Biccherna 165, fol. 31v (2 May 1330); Biccherna 171, fol. 81v (14 December 1331). See also Biccherna 397, fols. 55v, 144v (14 December 1331). On 7 September 1331 "Maestro simone dipegnitore" was paid 8 lire and 25 soldi for seven days service (at the rate of 25 soldi a day) to the commune in Arcidosso, Castel del Piano, and Scanzano. Biccherna 397, fol. 123v.

51. ASS, Biccherna 165, fol. 15v (20 February 1330). Simone was paid 3 lire and 5 soldi.

when we recall the 1302 payment to Duccio for a panel or *Maestà* "for the altar in the house of the Nove." Was Simone's altarpiece really a replacement for a work twenty years old, the creation of a great master but recently dead? It is possible that the form and/or dimensions of Duccio's work were ill suited to the chapel of the new palace; but it is also possible that we deal with a problem created by the terminology of the documents. To my knowledge, all modern discussions of the documents concerning the Palazzo Pubblico equate references to the "palace of the commune" and to the "house of the Nove" and from that equation conclude that all references to the "altar of the Nove" refer to an altar in a single location, the chapel of the palace. I am not entirely certain that is warranted. There were various altars and places for devotion throughout the complex of the Palazzo Pubblico. From 1323, 1329, 1330, and 1339 we have records of the commune's purchasing candles to be burnt before "the image of our Lady in [the] Biccherna."[40] A document of 1327 refers to a triptych (?) of the Virgin with Saints Peter and Andrew as belonging to the commune.[41] In 1339 the commune paid for a triptych with figures of the Virgin and San Ansano and San Galgano.[42] The same year, the painter Cecchino received 8 lire and 17 soldi for painting the Annunciation in the "coram bancho sindici" in the palace of the commune.[43] And in 1344, Ambrogio Lorenzetti produced his splendid panel of the *Annunciation* for the office of the Gabella (Fig. 89; now Siena, Pinacoteca Nazionale). But beyond the questions raised by these works, we face the fact that the Nine lived in the Palazzo Pubblico during their tenure in office and were in nearly all cases prohibited from leaving it during their two-month stay. It therefore seems to me that their living quarters may be the area intended when documents speak of the "house of the Nove," but that is an unverifiable hypothesis.[44]

fol. 148r), says that Simone's altarpiece was removed from the chapel of the Palazzo Pubblico "pochi anni sono," indicating it occurred during his lifetime. K. Christiansen ("Simone Martini's Altar-Piece for the Commune of Siena," *Burlington Magazine,* CXXXVI, 1994, 148–60) has proposed a series of panels by the shop of Simone Martini as components of the Palazzo Pubblico altarpiece, works hardly worthy of the commission. The dimensions, moreover, do not fit the size of the predella panels by Sano di Pietro that, in the Quattrocento, were commissioned to stand below the older polyptych. Nor is Christiansen's argument strengthened by the bizarre framing he proposes for the altarpiece. There is absolutely no evidence that any quattrocento Sienese altarpiece was so framed.

40. ASS, Biccherna 148, fol. 102r; Biccherna 163, fol. 62r; Biccherna 167, fols. 3r, 12r; Biccherna 201, fol. 81r. Whether this image was the painted panel created by Segna in 1306 for the Biccherna is unclear.

41. ASS, Biccherna 391, fol. 16r. On 7 February, the commune lent the "vicario" a painted panel with the Virgin in the center and Peter and Andrew at the sides. The panel was valued at £30. At the time of the notice, the panel had been returned and was in the "casa de Signori nove."

42. ASS, Biccherna 201, fol. 60r (2 May 1339).

43. ASS, Biccherna 202, fol. 144v (31 December 1339).

44. There is also a tendency in modern literature to interpret all references to the "palace of the commune" as references to the Palazzo Pubblico and/or the original building that housed the mint and customs offices. I am not convinced that interpretation is always accurate. We cannot eliminate the possibility that a scribe might have used the phrase simply to indicate the quarters of the Nove at any one moment.

Regarding the Palazzo Pubblico, there are, as we shall see, later references to the dormitory of the Nine.

goldsmith Duccio di Donato had received £30 for a chalice, and on 5 May he was paid 6 lire and 14 soldi for repairing two silver lamps for the altar.[32] This chapel would later acquire, in 1329, two wooden angels, painted by Simone, that acted as candle bearers;[33] in 1333 Simone provided a pedestal for a crucifix and "other things," while on 28 March a chalice was acquired for the sacristy.[34] Bono Campuglia, the official in charge of the "camera del comune," was reimbursed on 20 April 1334 for £100 spent on a missal and "other things for the furnishing of the altar of the Nine," and on 29 June of the same year, he received £60 for a Gospel book for the chapel of the Nove.[35] The commune paid a significant sum (29 lire, 19 soldi, and 3 denari) on 1 April 1343 for a drape of gold to cover the altar in the chapel of the Nine, and on the twelfth Fra Andrea Betti and Coltino Bonfigli received 8 florins, 2 lire, and 18 soldi for various adornments of the altar.[36] Regarding religious observances, I would also note that on 27 August 1321 the Nine paid Segna for a panel, "in the *domo* of the Lords Nine," on which were written the *articuli fedei*, the Credo; and in May of 1322 the goldsmith Tondino di Guerino provided "uno pelvi argenti, quem emerunt domini Novem ab eo pro altari domus dominorum Novem."[37] Other areas of the civic complex were not ignored. On 5 October 1321 the commune paid for a "painted panel with the crucifix [crucified?] with our Lady" for the altar of the palace of the podestà.[38]

We have good reason to believe, if not conclusive proof, that Simone provided a new altarpiece for the Nove c. 1321–22.[39] And that acquisition takes on special interest

32. ASS, Biccherna 120, fols. 320r, 330r.

33. ASS, Biccherna, 163, fol. 14v (11 August 1329). The payment was 1 lira and 5 soldi. On 31 December 1328, the Biccherna had paid 34 lire and 10 soldi (10 florins) to the Augustinian brothers at San Leonardo al Lago for two angels that were to ornament the chapel of the Nove. ASS, Biccherna 159, fol. 71r. This was likely the payment for the carved wooden angels themselves. Agnolo di Tura ("Cronaca senese," 433) says that a major fire broke out in the Palazzo Pubblico in January of 1326 and "arse la sagrestia e fe' gran danno" (burnt the sacristy and did great damage), but we do not know what was destroyed.

34. ASS, Biccherna 176, fol. 72r (14 May 1333). On 10 March 1333, Simone received 5 florins (15 lire and 5 soldi) for unspecified work; the sum was part of a larger payment to Bono Campuglia, who is described as "camarlengo dela camera del comune" (ASS, Biccherna 399, fol. 138r). For the chalice: ASS, Biccherna 176, fol. 40v (18 March 1333). The very next item on the folio is a payment of £10 for a velvet cover for the missal in the sacristy.

35. For the books: ASS, Biccherna 400, fol. 97v, fol. 115v.

36. ASS, Biccherna 212, fols. 159r, 163v.

37. ASS, Biccherna 143, fol. 53v (27 August 1321); Biccherna 144, fol. 119v (17 May 1322). In 1328, Bindo Manucci was compensated £4 for expenditures he had made in "dipentura fatta nel palagio" (ASS, Biccherna 159, fol. 70v). No subject is specified.

38. ASS, Biccherna 142, fol. 128r (5 October 1321), and Biccherna 143, fol. 68r. To my knowledge, the earliest reference to this altar is dated 20 June 1309 (ASS, Biccherna 122, fol. 193r); candles were bought for the altar. In the same year, the painter Guido was paid 12 soldi for work of an unspecified nature "in the house of the Nine" (ASS, Biccherna 382, fol. 6r).

39. The evidence is discussed by M. Eisenberg, "The First Altarpiece for the 'Cappella de' Signori' of the Palazzo Pubblico of Siena: '. . . tales figure sunt adeo pulcre . . . ,'" *Burlington Magazine*, cxxiii, 1981, 134–48. Further supporting evidence for Eisenberg's argument is found in Maginnis, "The Lost Facade Frescoes from Siena's Ospedale di S. Maria della Scala," 180 n. 1. Perhaps the best testimony comes from G. A. Pecci, who, in his manuscript dealing with inscriptions (Siena, BC, C.III.9,

further deterioration of the paintings, the Consiglio Generale prohibited future lighting of fires in that room.²⁵ In 1319 Segna was paid for restoring the figure of the Virgin "before the Concistoro of the Nine,"²⁶ and in the same year, on 11 August, the *operaio* of the commune, Chele Moccolelli, paid 4 lire, 9 soldi, and 8 denari for an angel to be placed before the *Maestà* in the "casa de' Nove," presumably Duccio's panel.²⁷

In 1321, the commune spent 320 lire and 3 soldi on the "palace of the podestà" and the "loggia before the palace."²⁸ Simone Martini, in 1323, was paid 13 lire and 8 soldi (4 florins) for "certain pictures that he made in the loggia of the communal palace."²⁹ E. Southard believes that the reference is to a second-storey loggia now occupied by the Sala dei Pilastri and the small room behind it on the second floor, but the phrasing of the documents suggests the reference is to the side of the palace on the Campo.

We have a number of documentary notices related to religious observances in the palace. In 1317, the Nine acquired a missal and a paten and chalice for their altar, at a cost of 100 lire and 2 soldi;³⁰ Bindo, miniaturist and scribe, received 70 lire and 8 soldi in June of 1321 for an antiphonary for the "altar of the Lords Nine," and on 31 December Simone was paid £66 (20 florins) for a crucifix above the altar of the chapel of the Nove.³¹ There had been earlier expenditures connected with the altar of the Nine. In April of 1307, the

---

fol. 154r).

25. ASS, Consiglio Generale 87, fols. 164r, 166r–67r (28 October 1316). On 31 December 1316 the *operaio* of the commune, Chele Moccholelli, received £430 for the period July to January "for having painted the *camera* of the podestà and for other repairs in the palace of the commune" (ASS, Biccherna 132, fol. 142r). We have no evidence that any of the rooms of the palace had fireplaces, so the fires mentioned must have been made directly on the floor and vented only by the windows.

26. ASS, Biccherna 138, fol. 119v; Biccherna 139, fol. 125r.

27. ASS, Biccherna 381, fol. 10r. Bacci (*Fonti e commenti,* 135) and E. Carli, (*Mani d'Angelo per Simone,* Siena, 1973) associated this payment with the pair of wooden polychrome hands still to be seen attached to one of the rafters of the Sala del Mappamondo, directly before the Simone *Maestà*. (These were originally part of the mechanism of lamps before the fresco.) Although it cannot be proved, I doubt this interpretation is correct. The reference to the "casa de' Nove" reminds us of the Duccio document of 1302 concerning a *Maestà*.

On 12 November 1319, the Biccherna paid the *operaio* of the Opera del Duomo £3 for "an angel of wood he had made at the request of the Nove for the commune." ASS, Biccherna 138, fol. 120r.

28. ASS, Biccherna 140, fol. 165r (28 April 1321). On 30 April 1321, the *operaio* of the commune was given a further £195 to spend "in the loggia made before the palace of the commune" (ASS, Biccherna 140, fol. 166v). The history of this structure is unclear. Already in 1307 (8 April), "the treasurer of the work of the loggia that ought to be made before the palace of the commune" was given £200 for that project (ASS, Biccherna 120, fol. 317r).

29. ASS, Biccherna 146, fol. 44v (28 April 1323).

30. ASS, Biccherna 134, fol. 130r (31 December 1317). According to a summary of deliberations of the Consiglio Generale, the commune had approved the expenditure of 100 lire and 2 soldi on 28 December 1317 for "a missal and a chalice for celebrating mass in the palace of the commune" and for remaking the seal of the commune (ASS, MS C.5, 37).

31. ASS, Biccherna 140, fol. 189r (30 June 1321): 70 lire and 8 soldi paid to "ser Bindo miniaturist and scribe." For Simone: ASS, Biccherna 142, fol. 156v (31 December 1321), and Biccherna 143, fol. 96v (31 December 1321). The sum includes reimbursement for colors, gold, and other necessities for the project, so the project may not have been as significant as the £66 might suggest.

an enthroned Madonna and Child with saints, was already an important civic emblem. On 12 August 1289, the painter Mino (not otherwise identified) had received £19 as salary, as part of £22 owing, for painting the Virgin and other saints in the palace of the commune.[15] On 14 April 1291, a certain Jacobuone was given 50 soldi for the cover of a lamp before the *Maestà,* and on 27 June 1291, the painter Dietisalvi was paid for "letters," presumably an inscription, before the *Maestà*.[16] Then, in 1295 and after a change in quarters, the subject was depicted again.[17] Between August and October, Guidoni was paid a total of £35 for painting the Virgin in the palace of the commune, and on 15 November he received 6 lire and 10 soldi more for figures of Saints Peter and Paul and for 102 gold letters before the image of the Virgin.[18] We shall in time encounter other early uses of this imagery. Perhaps a *Maestà* for the new palace was planned from the beginning, but size and location were matters of debate. Simone's idea of devoting almost all of one wall to the work (Color Plates 3–4) necessitated closing two doors on that wall, and the sum he earned, 81 lire and 4 soldi, was almost twice the cost of the 1295 project. In 1321 Simone and his assistants returned to the *Maestà* to "repair" it.[19] The technical evidence, however, suggests that they actually replaced some of the heads in the fresco.[20]

There had been some other early projects. Guido, on 26 October 1302, had been given £9 for painting twelve figures, "in palazo," of false witnesses and forgers of coin.[21] Duccio, also in 1302, received £48 as his salary for a *Maestà* panel to be placed "nell'altare ne la casa de' Nove là due si dice l'ufficio [of the mass]."[22] In 1306, Segna was paid the sum of £10 for a painted panel for the office of the Bicchierna,[23] and a document of October 1316 informs us that the podestà, who occupied the northeast wing of the Palazzo Pubblico, had had his hall painted but that the smoke of fires had darkened the walls.[24] To avoid

---

Bicchierna 377, fols. 28r, 139v (20 October–12 December 1315).

15. ASS, Bicchierna 101, fol. 74v (12 August 1289).

16. ASS, Bicchierna 104, fol. 80r (14 April 1291), and Bicchierna 105, fol. 84r; Bicchierna 104, fol. 94v, and Bicchierna 105, fol. 97r.

17. On 8 March 1294 the Nove bought the palace of Sugio Iuncte degli Arzocchi, "detto Nigio," to use while the Palazzo Pubblico was built. Waley, *Siena,* 15. On 5 April 1294, the painter Jacopo was paid 5 lire, 8 soldi, and 8 denari for painting in that palace (subject unidentified). ASS, Bicchierna 110, fol. 125v.

18. ASS, Bicchierna 112, fols. 97r (8 August), 101v (27 August), 121v (29 October), 124v.

19. ASS, Bicchierna 142, fol. 154r (30 December 1321), and Bicchierna 143, fol. 94r (30 December 1321).

20. Borsook, *Mural Painters,* 19–23.

21. ASS, Bicchierna 117, fol. 312r. See, below, the discussion of *pittura infamante*. On folio 358v of the same Bicchierna volume, the *operaio* of the commune was given £31 for various tasks he had undertaken, including the painting of false witness "in palazzo del comune" (29 December 1302). Forging of coin was taken very seriously; Agnolo di Tura ("Cronaca senese," 265) tells us that in the very year of these paintings, a certain "Nicoluccio detto Bricha" was burnt at the stake for his crime.

22. ASS, Bicchierna 117, fol. 347 (4 December 1302).

23. ASS, Bicchierna 118, fol. 227v (26 April 1306). The same folio records payment of £6 to Masarello for painting a cross for the altar of the Nine.

24. In 1294, the painter Rinforzato had been paid for painting the "camera" of the podestà in his palace (ASS, Bicchierna 110, fol. 125r). But the sum, a mere 50 soldi, does not indicate a major project. Moreover, in June of 1294, the commune was renting a house for the podestà (ASS, Bicchierna 110,

were in rebellion against the commune and should be painted.⁹ (This is an instance of the public vituperation mentioned above.) From a now lost Biccherna volume for January to June 1312, U. Benvoglienti transcribed a notice of February in which £16 were paid to a painter who had painted one "story of the Count d'Elci" and ought to paint another, the rate of payment being £8 apiece.¹⁰ Then, on 30 March 1314, the Consiglio Generale decided that the castle of Giuncarico should be painted in the palace of the commune, "where the other castles acquired by the Sienese commune are painted" (Figs. 87–88).¹¹ This series of subject territories was later expanded when Simone Martini, in 1330–31, added first depictions of Montemassi and Sassoforte, and then of Arcidosso and Castel del Piano.¹² We also have a somewhat puzzling reference to a depiction of Ansedonia c. 1329.¹³ The idea of depicting subject territories seems to have been borrowed from similar images in the Bargello of Florence. Three aspects of these early projects are noteworthy: that the frescoes were secular in subject matter, that they were painted in the great new chamber for the Consiglio Generale (later called the Sala del Mappamondo), and that even in the case of Simone's later additions the remuneration was quite low. Apparently the regime's first priority was to provide visual testimony to the success of its "foreign" policy and to do so where it would be seen by the largest numbers.

It was only in 1315 that the commune engaged Simone Martini to produce his large frescoed *Maestà* (Color Plates 3 and 4) on one entire end wall of the Sala del Mappamondo.¹⁴ The delay is somewhat surprising in that we know that the theme of the *Maestà*,

9. ASS, Consiglio Generale 80, fols. 70–70v (4 February 1312).

10. Uberto Benvoglienti, *Miscellanee*, Siena, BC, MS C.v.4, fol. 131r. Benvoglienti cites folio 245r of Biccherna 106 and dates the entry to 1311. He was presumably using the Sienese calendar in which the new year began on 25 March. Another collection of archival extracts, *Spogli di notizie dai libri dell'archivio della Biccherna del comune di Siena,* compiled in 1700–1701 at the request of Galgano Bichi, refers to the same folio and same volume, but indicates that the entry is under February 1312 (Siena, BC, MS A.vii.15, fol. 238r).

11. ASS, Consiglio Generale 83, fol. 120r (30 March 1314). Figures 87 and 88 show the recently discovered fresco in the Sala del Mappamondo, opposite Simone's *Maestà,* that depicts the surrender of a town to Siena. There has been endless debate about the town involved and therefore the date of the work. Stylistically, the fresco must date to the second decade of the Trecento.

12. ASS, Biccherna 165, fol. 31v (2 May 1330); Biccherna 171, fol. 81v (14 December 1331); Biccherna 397, fols. 55v (14 December 1331), 144v (14 December 1331). The first pair brought Simone £16, the second pair 22 lire and 8 soldi.

13. Sigismondo Tizio (d. 1528), in his unpublished history of Siena (Siena, BC, MS B.iii.8, fol. 134), says, in relation to 1329: "Senenses vero Ansidoniam appellantes, hoc Anno dextruxere, unde et Columnellae versicoloris lapidus insignes notis etiam aureis, ut notavimus, Senam advectae, ad nobilissimi ambonis, seu peregrigii marmorei pulpiti in Senensi aede substentaculum postea locate. Tabellam autem demolitionis pictam Seneses, super portam, quae est inter primam et secundam palatii aylam suspendere" (as transcribed by Lusini, *Il Duomo di Siena,* I, Siena, 1911, 145 n. 2). The taking of Ansedonia, which was inhabited by brigands, is recorded by Malavolti (*Dell'historia di Siena,* II, 88v–89r) and Tommasi (*Dell'historie di Siena,* II, 241). To my knowledge, Tizio's is the only reference to this panel. Where the panel hung is not entirely clear. Other passages in his text seem to indicate that he identified the Sala della Pace as the "first hall" of the Palazzo Pubblico, and the Sala del Mappamondo as the "second hall." Perhaps, then, it was placed in the Sala del Mappamondo, where there is now an image of San Vittorio (1529) by Il Sodoma (Fig. 87).

14. ASS, Biccherna 376, fol. 13r (7 June 1315);

the natural and supernatural merged. With painting offering all this, no other comparative expenditure was as rewarding, in fact or potential, on such a scale.

Patronage of the Commune

Around 1310, the Nove occupied the first phase, just completed, of the Palazzo Pubblico (Fig. 2).[7] Work on the new communal palace had gone on for at least a decade; the idea of having such permanent quarters for communal government was even older. We know nothing of ceremonies to mark the event, but I think it significant that, for the first time, a vernacular version of the Sienese constitution was produced in 1309–10.[8] Before occupying the Palazzo Pubblico, the Nove had been housed in, and had conducted their business from, rented accommodations, usually palaces of the great families. Large meetings were held in the city's churches, including, sometimes, the cathedral. The changes of c. 1310 were therefore of considerable significance. As the translation of the constitution increased the citizenry's access to the legal foundation of the commune, so the new Palazzo Pubblico presented to the citizenry a permanent manifestation of the governing regime. Both lent a new transparency to government, the palace by now linking the activities of government with identified spaces.

The temporary nature of earlier arrangements had not prevented the Nine from commissioning some works of art, but now the situation had altered dramatically. With permanent living quarters, offices, and meeting halls at their disposal, members of the regime were offered the opportunity to commission works that would be more or less permanent. That opportunity may have seemed rather daunting at first. The personnel of the Council of the Nine changed every two months, and although continuity could be provided in the person of the *operaio,* individual Noveschi must have reflected on the fact that their decisions about works of art were likely to be fully realized only after they had left office.

Unfortunately, the Biccherna records for the second half of 1311 and all of 1312 are lost, but other sources inform us of what seem to have been the earliest commissions. On 4 February 1312 the Consiglio Generale discussed the fact that the Count of Elci and his son

---

7. For the history of the building and matters related to its decoration, see F. Donati, "Il palazzo del comune di Siena: Notizie storiche," *BSSP,* xi, 1904, 311–54; E.C. Southard, *The Frescoes in Siena's Palazzo Pubblico, 1289–1539: A Study in Imagery and Relations to Other Communal Palaces in Tuscany* (Ph.D. dissertation, Indiana University, 1978), New York, 1979; C. Brandi et al., *Palazzo Pubblico di Siena: Vicende costruttive e decorazione,* Milan, 1983. The last contains a summary of documents relating to the palace, but a good deal is missing. Many of the notices discussed here are not found in that summary.

8. The constitution itself contains the following explanation of the vernacular version, which was to be kept in the office of the Biccherna: "acciò che le povare persone et l'altre persone che non sanno gramatica [i.e., Latin], et li altri, e' quali varrano, posano esso vedere et copia inde trare et avere alloro volontà." Lisini, *Costituto volgarizzato,* i, 126–27.

out that the visions of Saint Catherine of Siena owed much to painted images she had seen;[4] a great deal of evidence points up the way in which the seen was being tied to the revealed. When the crucifix of San Damiano spoke to Saint Francis of Assisi, the image opened in the West a new conduit between God and man. When, in 1259, the Lord sent his angel to paint the face of the Virgin in Florence's Santissima Annunziata, he signaled his willingness to communicate truths through the painted form. When Thomas Aquinas, at the end of his life, was assured of the value of his life's work and of his future rest by the voice of the Lord coming from a painted *Crucifixion,* the notion of image as conduit was securely affirmed.[5]

There was, of course, a less private, more public function of images. As Siena sought to co-opt the powers of the Virgin and of the saints as it wove the fabric of civic Christianity, so pictures became visible assurances of the city's well-being. They gave physical form to Siena's protectors; they left simulacra of the city's own *beate* and *beati;* and they generally assured the citizenry and the governing regime of a collective salvation. So important did the idea of divine guidance and protection become that in one instance the Nine did not wait for a miracle; they made the Virgin of Simone Martini's *Maestà* (Color Plates 3 and 4) speak to her audience in inscriptions realized by the painter![6]

In a much more general way, the second importance of painting lay in the provision of signs, signs in the popular use of the term and signs as emblems of ideas and means of propaganda. Images of the Virgin on city gates, in the cathedral, on the Ospedale di Santa Maria della Scala, or in the Palazzo Pubblico told visitors of the city's dedication and its special devotions. Secular imagery was used in many ways, including the advertisements of success in the depictions of subject territories. We have records of criminals depicted in public places for public shame and of "foreign" adversaries depicted in vituperation. Other secular images are discussed below.

Finally, pictures were rungs on a ladder that led to God. That view was rooted in Christianity's neo-Platonism and in the world of Saint Francis, and it was clearly articulated in Saint Bonaventure's *Soul's Journey into God.* Bonaventure demonstrated how Christians, beginning with contemplation of God's creation, could follow the great chain of being back to the Creator. Painters, imaging the faith in terms of a persuasive naturalism that aped creation, also offered departure points for the spiritual journey.

As we turn to the history of patronage, we should thus keep in mind that the trecento cost/benefit assessment of art differed radically from our own. Holy images were central to the faith, and the faith the only assurance of immortality. In other words, holy images were of great utility, in a very practical sense. And secular images were a means of ordering experience. Combined with other ideas of the period, discussed in Chapter v, secular—sometimes holy—images became a mapping of the world, but a world in which

---

4. Millard Meiss, *Painting in Florence and Siena After the Black Death,* Princeton, 1951, 105–25.

5. Hayden B. J. Maginnis, "The Thyssen-Bornemisza Ugolino," *Apollo,* CXVIII, 1983, 16–21.

6. This "speech" by inscription seems to go back to an earlier version of the *Maestà* created for the Nine. See "Patronage of the Commune" below.

The Other Economy of Art

All art signals the availability of wealth deemed surplus and disposable, whether it be on the most primitive level of the expenditure of time and energy or, as in our modern world, the diversion of capital into objects that are unproductive in the normal sense of that word. The story of trecento Siena and its art is very much about surplus wealth; for that reason, I devoted part of Chapter 1 to explaining the sources of Siena's prosperity. But we should not confuse our own motivations with those of the fourteenth century. We acquire modern works of art in the conviction that the unique, individual vision of the artist will be ever more prized, ever more elevated, as a component of our culture—and ever more expensive. We acquire works of art as signs of social elevation; we acquire pictures to embellish our surroundings. And, perhaps, we acquire paintings in a cultural strategy haunted by the fear that individual expressions of the human spirit may one day be no more.

Now, inasmuch as the thirteenth and fourteenth centuries laid the foundation of modernity, the historian will find anticipations of our own views in the period. But those discoveries should not blind us to the fact that the primary aspirations embodied in fourteenth-century commissions represent a very different value structure and reflect choices motivated by cultural circumstances not our own. I suggest that to considerations of patronage we must bring a macroeconomic point of view, seeking not merely to write a history of monetary implications but to explore much larger aspects of societal cost and gain. For behind the diversion of funds to the works of painters, and behind society's willingness to support comparatively large numbers of picture makers, are at least two major aims that, at the end of the twentieth century, are largely foreign to us. Both belong to nonmonetary conceptions of utility and speak to the conviction that images performed useful functions.

The most important function of painters, without question, was to image the divine, and in so doing to provide a type of direct access to God and his saints that no other part of quotidian experience—with the exception of the Mass—could offer. In that imaging, painting witnessed to the fact that something other than mere chance governed the affairs of men. It spoke of another world, but a world that was as much the future of the individual as tomorrow. And when painting told the stories of the saints and the history of salvation, it enfolded the viewer in the promise of, and struggle for, redemption, for the soul's repose. Images could do much more. As thirteenth-century Italy came to know more of Byzantium and its miraculous icons, it borrowed and adapted the idea that pictures could serve as "doorways to heaven," allowing the Virgin, Christ, and his saints to come and go through a painted panel or a frescoed wall.[3] Records of the period are generally silent about these matters, not because the attitude was rare, but rather because it was a commonplace.

In hagiography we glimpse the new prominence of painting. Millard Meiss pointed

---

3. For more extensive discussion of this matter, see "Foreign Powers" in the next chapter.

such discussions of individual careers rarely allow us to maintain a sense of the relative cost of various projects. More can be done, and our understanding of the artistic/social environment of Siena is incomplete until we achieve some sense of what the Sienese wanted of their painters, when they wanted it, and what they were willing to pay. Losses of works themselves and documents relating to patronage undeniably restrict our ability to take the pulse of artistic activity, but the comparatively large quantity of surviving documentation in Siena allows us to understand more of the general situation than in any other center of equal importance. Thus, my principal aim in this chapter is to sketch the history of Sienese patronage connected with the city's three most important institutions: the commune, the cathedral, and the Ospedale di Santa Maria della Scala.[2]

The documentary evidence from these three institutions varies tremendously in quantity and scope. The most extensive collection of notices is found in the records of the Biccherna, the financial office of the commune. In volumes generally separated into Entrata and Uscita, credit and debit, the treasurer of the commune, the *camerlengo,* and his scribes kept itemized accounts for the Nove. Although these accounts represent the most complete set of records we have, volumes are missing. To complicate matters further, payments to artists were not always direct; often the accounts show only transfers to the *operaio,* the master of works for the commune, and without other documentation, we cannot know the projects that such transfers sustained. Some help is provided by the volumes called Memoriale, discussed earlier, but that series is the most fragmentary. While the Opera del Duomo was, in reality, an office of the state, it kept its own financial records; unfortunately those records have major lacunae. Thinnest of all is the documentation regarding the Ospedale.

We know even less about images created for Siena's other charitable institutions, its confraternities, parish churches, and convents. In many cases, only the provenance of a specific work makes a connection for us. These circumstances mean that as we move from commune to cathedral to hospital and on to other institutions, my account must be less and less comprehensive. I want also to make some general observations about Sienese painters active outside their native city, because those commissions both reflected and determined developments in Siena itself.

Before turning to the specifics of patronage, we should pause to consider matters that set the general conditions for painting of the period. For each work embodies a new outlook that we may fail to perceive, simply because we continue to live in a world of images, in the world that the Dugento and the Trecento created. But that beginning was, by definition, a novelty, a refocusing of attention and a redirection of resources. Without a fundamental change in society's ambitions and in its relation to art, the commissions that appear in documents or are recorded by paintings themselves would never have arisen.

---

2. Of necessity, this chapter repeats some of the material of Chapter II, where projects are discussed in terms of painters' remunerations. While some readers may have that earlier discussion firmly in mind, clarity seems best served by repetition rather than by references back to those pages.

IV Painters and Projects, Major and Minor

In a society where painters almost exclusively depended upon commissions, the greatest constraint they faced lay in what patrons wanted.[1] Although discussions of individual painters may give us a sense of how successful they were, especially in receiving communal patronage, they offer a less vivid picture of what the ongoing commissioning of art represented to those responsible for the embellishment of specific institutions in Siena. Similarly,

---

1. One of Franco Sacchetti's tales supposedly tells the story of a Sienese painter who specialized in the production of crucifixes, and given the details of the story, it would seem that he had a collection of those crucifixes in his shop, presumably produced on speculation for future purchasers. In the later Trecento, Marco Datini from Prato seems to have acquired, for resale, private devotional works of this type (I. Origo, *The Merchant of Prato, Marco Datini*, London, 1957). It may be that some small devotional pictures of the early Trecento were produced in Siena without a specific commission, but we have no early-trecento evidence to confirm that circumstance.

published a note that centered on documents, of 1369, connected with Giovanni di Milano's decoration of the ceiling in the Capella Magna of the Vatican Palace.[113] He pointed out the acquisition of paper and wax for *patrones* to be used in the project. Since the quantity of paper was insufficient to produce cartoons for the entire ceiling, Shearman suggested that *patrones* were cartoons for single figures or for parts of a few narratives.[114] A more recent, highly convincing discussion of the term has been provided by Bruno Zanardi.[115] In his impressive and extremely important study of the *Saint Francis Legend* in Assisi, Zanardi argues that *patroni* were drawings on waxed paper that were used for the heads of the figures in the cycle. Having traced every frescoed head on transparent acetate, he found that many of those heads are based on four prototypes, presumably the *patroni*. Waxing the paper would have protected the drawing as it was placed on the wet *intonaco* so that its outlines and major features could be traced and thus impressed on the plaster. But waxing had a second purpose; it meant that the drawing could be turned over and used from the reverse to create the same head type, now shown as looking in the opposite direction.

Nothing comparable to Zanardi's tracings has yet been done for other fresco cycles or for panel pictures. There is thus no present evidence that early Sienese artists employed *patroni*. However, it is hard to imagine that, if Zanardi's position is correct, Sienese painters would not have known about this aspect of production in the Assisi *Legend*. Even for those Sienese artists who, unlike Simone or Pietro Lorenzetti, did not work in San Francesco, the *Legend* must have been among the most important monuments of the period.

---

113. J. Shearman, "A Note on the Early History of Cartoons," *Master Drawings*, xxx, no. 1, 1992, 5–8.

114. It seems that genuine cartoons, pricked so they could be pounced on the surface with charcoal, only became frequent in the fifteenth century.

115. Bruno Zanardi, *Il cantiere di Giotto: Le storie di San Francesco ad Assisi,* Milan, 1996, 32–38.

was drawing an angel on certain tablets. And while I was drawing, I turned my head and saw alongside me some men to whom all consideration was due. . . . When they had left, I returned to my work of drawing figures of angels."[107]

It is often remarked that parchment, used as ground for presentation drawings and for manuscripts, was too expensive for painters to employ for mere sketches. There was no need to do so. Millard Meiss noted that two paper mills existed in Italy by 1283 and that during the Trecento manufacture spread from Fabriano to Colle Val d'Elsa (near Siena), Bologna, Forlì, Parma, Padua, and Treviso.[108] The evidence for the availability of paper in Siena is explicit and of much earlier date than previous discussions of drawing would suggest. From 1248 onward, the deliberations of the Consiglio Generale were recorded on paper; from at least 1302 the vernacular account books of the commune were kept on paper. Those very books naturally record the acquisition of paper, or *carta di bambagia,* for the commune. Waley has pointed to purchases of paper by the commune in 1278, 1281, and 1282, but it seems such purchases go back all the way to 1226.[109] Nor was paper used by the city government alone. Between 1329 and 1335 the Sienese guild of the leather-workers and shoemakers mandated the a "livro di carta di bambagia" be kept to record the names of its officials.[110] Certainly, the import of paper at the very beginning of the Trecento was regular enough that the *Statuto della Gabella e dei Passagi dalle Porte della Città di Siena* of 1301–3 includes paper as one of the taxable commodities.[111] Notices regarding the cost of paper make it clear that successful painters could afford it. In January of 1278, the commune bought six reams of paper (2,880 sheets) at the rate of 3 lire, 7 soldi, and 6 denari a ream. In 1306, a ream (480 sheets) of paper of large format (presumably of the size used for the Memoriale volumes of the Biccherna) cost 4 lire, while paper of small format, in the same quantity, cost 2 lire, 2 soldi, and 6 denari. The commune paid 2 lire and 7 soldi for a ream of paper in December of 1338, and in 1347 it paid 2 lire and 2 soldi for the same quantity of paper.[112]

Altogether, the various factors I have outlined and the logic of the situation suggest preparatory drawings were used by painters of the period. The loss of such drawings is not surprising if we assume that they were kept in workshops as material to be reused and that they were executed on paper. It was only later in the Renaissance that drawings came to be prized as the most immediate expression of the artist's genius and thus as objects to be cherished and preserved.

It seems quite possible that Sienese artists also employed drawings of a type that has only recently been the subject of renewed scholarly consideration. In 1992, John Shearmen

---

107. M. Musa, trans., *Dante: La Vita Nuova,* Bloomington, Ind., 1962, 71. Cennini (*The Craftsman's Handbook,* 4) gives instructions for drawing on little tablets.

108. Tintori and Meiss, *The Painting of "The Life of St. Francis" in Assisi,* 21.

109. Waley, *Siena,* 156; "Ls," "Il prezzo della carta da scrivere nei secoli XIII e XIV," *Miscellanea storica senese,* v, 1898, 57–59.

110. Banchi and Polidori, *Statuti senesi,* II, 288–89.

111. Banchi and Polidori, *Statuti senesi,* II, 11.

112. Waley, *Siena,* 60, 155–56.

Copies after other works undeniably played an important role in the creative process, offering lesser talents a repertoire of forms to adapt and greater talents stimulus for invention. But in trecento painting there were many situations where drawings based on other, earlier works would have been of no assistance—indeed, could not have contained relevant material. When Simone Martini created his altarpiece of the *Beato Agostino Novello* (Color Plate 7), the *beato* having died in 1309, there was no established iconography from which to copy. Similarly, the legend of Saint Martin of Tours was by no means known in visual depictions, and thus Simone, working in the Saint Martin's Chapel at Assisi, must have consulted a written version of the story. When Pietro Lorenzetti devised the propagandistic predella for the Carmelite altarpiece, he was forging new imagery. We know that a similar situation arose when Pietro prepared to paint the San Savino altarpiece for Siena cathedral, for "maestro Ciecho de la gramatica" was paid for translating the legend of San Savino into the vernacular, suggesting there was no earlier imagery from which scenes could be borrowed. Just as it is highly unlikely that Ambrogio worked out his *Effects of Good Government* (Color Plates 5–6; approximately fourteen meters long) by first composing on the wall, it is unlikely that Simone or Pietro worked out their compositions merely with charcoal drawings on the gessoed panels.

The practice of drawing was more common than often supposed. Ghiberti tells us that Ambrogio Lorenzetti executed a drawing of a Lysippan *Venus* that had been discovered in Siena.[103] Petrarch said of his portrait of Laura, which Simone created, that the artist "la ritrasse in carte" with a "stile"; the reference to a stylus suggests a drawing. And, in fact, we have a pen and water-color drawing produced by Simone or his shop, a drawing on the cover of Cardinal Jacopo Stefaneschi's *De Miraculo Mariae* (Bibliothèque Nationale, Paris, MS lat. 5931).[104] In Sienese manuscripts we discover some remarkable pen drawings from the second quarter of the Trecento. Prefacing the text of one of the statutes in a copy of the Sienese constitution is a lively drawing of the governing Nove, and in the margins of a twelfth-century manuscript someone added drawings of the penitent Magdalen and Saint Anthony Abbot.[105] These drawings possess a fluidity and vivacity that indicate the artist was no stranger to drawing, no novice struggling with formulation. We also know that drawing was common beyond the world of the artist. The margins of official Sienese records occasionally have small sketches by the scribes. Petrarch produced drawings in the margins of his manuscripts.[106] And Dante says in the *Vita nuova*, written between 1292 and 1294: "I

---

model book. To my knowledge, no model book from Italy during the period c.1250–c.1350 survives, although there are earlier and later (north Italian) examples. (See R.W. Scheller, *Exemplum: Model-Book Drawings and the Practice of Artistic Transmission in the Middle Ages [ca. 900–ca. 1450]*, Amsterdam, 1995.) Could it be that the situation reflects more than historical accident? Could it be that it reflects a new central Italian practice of keeping portfolios of drawings on separate sheets of paper?

103. J. von Schlosser, ed., *Lorenzo Ghibertis Denkwürdigkeiten (I Commentarii)*, Berlin, 1912, 63.

104. B. Degenhart, "Das Marienwunder von Avignon: Simone Martini's Miniaturen für Kardinal Stefaneschi und Petrarca," *Pantheon*, XXXIII, 1975, 191–203.

105. Respectively Degenhart and Schmitt, *Corpus*, pt. I, vol. 3, plates 63a, 64a, 64b.

106. Degenhart and Schmitt, *Corpus*, pt. I, vol. 3, plates 101c and 101d.

Although fresco, which required the painter to reproduce on the *intonaco* a *sinopia* composition already covered by fresh plaster, involved remarkable powers of visual memory, I, like Meiss, find it impossible to believe that monumental compositions were initially and only worked out on the *arriccio*. Artists often had to cope with curved or otherwise irregular surfaces; the very scaffolding on which painters worked, in the case of sizable frescoes, would have obscured their view of and hindered their access to the entire field. And should we posit the unlikely, because expensive, use of scaffolding with several platforms, the painter's task would become only more complicated.[99] The internal evidence of frescoes is mixed. When Simone Martini, in the Saint Martin's Chapel, adapted an architectural setting from the Upper Church[100] for his *Obsequies of Saint Martin* (Fig. 78), he was close to his model, but if we turn to two figures on the intrados of the chapel, to *Saint Mary Magdalen* and *Saint Louis of France,* we encounter a different situation. The *Magdalen* (Fig. 50) was inspired by one of the exterior nave-pier figures of Siena cathedral (Fig. 51)—although she is not a simple quotation. Surely this extravagant figure suggests a sketch, made in Siena, in which the transformation was achieved. The *Saint Louis* (Fig. 49) was the inspiration for *San Ansano* (Fig. 18), flanking the Uffizi *Annunciation,* and both are related to the Altomonte *Saint Ladislas of Hungary.* Are we to assume that Simone made drawings after his own fresco or, much more likely, retained an original drawing for the figure?

Panel paintings present us with similar problems. As noted elsewhere, *Saint John the Evangelist* in Siena no. 6 (Fig. 6) is essentially the same figure in Siena no. 7 (Fig. 7). The *Annunciation* (Fig. 34) and the *Nativity* in the Saint Peter Master's eponymous work are derived from those same scenes in the Badia Berardenga narratives (Fig. 33). I earlier noted that the "Guidesque" *Madonna* (Fig. 79) in the Accademia of Florence (no. 435) conflates elements from the San Bernardino *Madonna* (Fig. 8) and from Guido's *Madonna* for San Domenico (Fig. 32). The Virgin and Child (Fig. 80) from the face of the Ducciesque *Maestà* in Massa Marittima come from the face of Duccio's cathedral *Maestà* (Color Plate 10).[101] Pietro Lorenzetti used the setting of Ambrogio's *Ordination of Saint Louis of Toulouse* (Fig. 81) in San Francesco, Siena, for two scenes in the predella of his Carmelite altarpiece (Fig. 82). Some may wish to see such connections as only indicating visual memory, but that theory is stretched far beyond credulity when we discover the shop of Ugolino di Nerio, in the Williamstown polyptych (Fig. 83), quoting a composition used by a Ducciesque painter for a *Madonna* in Montecchio (Fig. 84), or when Ugolino's shop, in the Princeton *Madonna* (Fig. 85), borrows the composition from the central panel of Siena no. 47 (Fig. 86). This evidence, however, points only to the likelihood of copy-drawings and model books.[102]

99. Using Meiss's example: Are we to suppose that Giotto jumped about from platform to platform in order to work out the design of the *Last Judgment* in the Arena Chapel?

100. Maginnis, *Age of Giotto,* fig. 30.

101. Another instance of replicas should be noted. There exist two versions of a composition for the Virgin and Child, one in the Seminario Arcivescovile of Siena and the other in the Sienese Church of Santa Maria dei Servi. Both are from the orbit of Segna di Bonaventura (that in the Seminario is the superior work). See Stubblebine, *Duccio,* II, figs. 342–43.

102. Perhaps I should qualify my reference to a

assume that church windows were removed (or not yet installed) when frescoes were painted, in most instances painters must have relied on some artificial and irregular illumination, particularly when chapels were filled with scaffolding. In all cases of fresco and of panel painting, maximum use must have been made of daylight, and thus the working hours must have varied with the season.

Trecento painters, as much or more than most of us, were not immune to the problem that comes to many with age: the failure of vision. Given the character of tempera painting, farsightedness must have created great difficulties. And when we recall the relief on the Florentine campanile illustrating painting (Fig. 73), whose figure bends over a panel on an easel, the problem in relation to the execution of small works becomes even more apparent. Preaching in Florence's Santa Maria Novella, c. 1305, Fra Giordano of Pisa said that just short of twenty years earlier the new art of eyeglasses had been discovered, and he added: "I have seen the man who first invented and created it and I have talked to him." In the *Annals of the Dominican Monastery of St. Catherine in Pisa,* under the year 1313, we read: "At that time, through a beautiful, useful and novel invention, somebody invented the glass lenses which are commonly called 'eyeglasses' and did not want to communicate to anybody the art of making them. Having seen them, this good man [Fra Alessandro Spini], a craftsman, mastered them immediately without anybody teaching him." Fra Alessandro died in 1313; the passage is part of a commemoration of his life and therefore unhelpful regarding specific chronology; however, it serves to corroborate Fra Giordano's statement. This evidence immediately raises the question: Were eyeglasses employed by early trecento painters?[75]

The first surviving depiction of eyeglasses is found in Tomaso da Modena's decorations, of 1352, for the chapter house of the Dominican Church of San Nicolò in Treviso. There, among a gallery of forty images of Dominicans of note, Cardinal Hugues de St. Cher is seen writing at his desk and wearing a pair of spectacles. It is less often noted that Cardinal Nicholas of Rouen, from the same series, reads with a single lens mounted at the end of a handle, essentially what we would call a magnifying glass.[76] Petrarch (1304–74), in his *Letter to Posterity,* remarks that "for a long time I had very keen sight which, contrary to my hopes, left me when I was over sixty years of age, so that to my annoyance I had to seek the help of eyeglasses." And in Sacchetti's eighty-third *novella,* in a story that is dated by its circumstances to 1358, one of the priors of Florence says: "I don't see well without my eyeglasses." These images and notices may lead us to assume spectacles became common only toward the mid-century, but other evidence suggests that is untrue. A notice of 1316 indicates that eyeglasses with a case cost 6 Bolognese soldi. Among the possessions of the recently deceased bishop of Florence, inventoried in 1322, was "one pair of eyeglasses,

---

75. The following discussion and the translations of early sources are derived from David Rosen, "The Invention of Eyeglasses," *Journal of the History of Medicine and Allied Sciences,* xi, 1956, 13–46, 183–218. Rosen discusses depictions of eyeglasses but does not speculate on what they may have meant to painters.

76. See R. Gibbs, *Tomaso da Modena: Painting in Emilia and March of Treviso, 1340–80,* Cambridge, 1989, 83–84, and plates 19, 27.

and the opportunities of fresco. The use of gold grounds in such works created conditions analogous to those of the altarpiece, but Sienese painters produced private works of varied size, subject, and format. Duccio's tiny *Madonna of the Franciscans* (Fig. 64; 24 × 17 cm), with its early form of the Madonna of Mercy, relates to a similarly small panel in Oxford with a half-length *Madonna and Child* (Fig. 65), although the former originally had wings to fold over the central panel. While Duccio's large London triptych[73] (61.5 × 77.5 cm opened) is an image of elegance and intimacy, the center of his shop's Boston triptych (61 × 77 cm opened) is an adaptation from the *Crucifixion* of the *Maestà,* and the splendid Tabernacle 35 (67 × 87 cm opened) combines narrative with the formality of an enthroned Madonna and Child with saints and angels (Fig. 66). From the orbit of Ugolino comes a large triptych (59.5 × 76.8 cm opened) in the Metropolitan Museum (Fig. 67), with narratives on the wings and an iconic Crucifixion at its center, but the work abandons the gabled shape used by Duccio and his shop and uses a rectangular format for wings and center panel. Simone or his shop produced the *Crucified Christ* (Fig. 68), a gabled rectangle (86 × 36 cm), in the Fogg Art Museum; the small *Saint Ladislas of Hungary* (45.5 × 21.5 cm) in Altomonte; and the extraordinary rectangular *Holy Family* in Liverpool (49.6 × 35.1 cm; Fig. 69), which has always been a solitary panel. Simone also produced the Birmingham *Saint John the Evangelist* (42 × 30.2 cm; Fig. 70), likely one wing of a folding rectangular triptych; the folding Orsini polyptych, with narratives of the Passion; and a much less discursive *Annunciation*. The Sienese Straus Master produced a diptych of rectangular panels, now divided between Oxford and Berlin (Figs. 71–72). The size and variety of content, limited or extensive, were undoubtedly determined by the patron's intended expenditure. But the various shapes suggest painters may have sought innovations in such works. All said, however, the production of private devotional works during the first half of the Trecento was a modest feature of Sienese painting.

The Imponderables of Circumstance

Before we leave questions of materials and techniques, I would note three rather obvious factors in artistic production that the conditions of modern life may obscure: weather, illumination, and quite simply the frailties of age. Of panel painting, Cennini writes: "And know that this sizing and gessoing call for dry and windy weather. Size should be stronger in summer than in winter. Gilding calls for damp and rainy weather."[74] Thus we learn that the periods for drying layers of size and gesso must have varied with the weather and thus the season; the Italian summer was clearly not the best moment for gilding. Similarly, the drying of fresco was influenced by temperature and humidity.

Conditions of illumination also must have affected execution of a work. Even if we

73. Maginnis, *Age of Giotto*, fig. 62.

74. Cennini, *The Craftsman's Handbook*, 70.

images. It is true that in chapel decoration some loose conventions developed that linked works such as Simone's Saint Martin's Chapel with other chapels in Assisi, but Ambrogio Lorenzetti's Sala della Pace (Color Plates 5–6) or his lost cloister decoration at San Francesco in Siena help us appreciate the variety of forms frescoes might take. Pietro Lorenzetti faced an extraordinary situation when, in Assisi, he had to continue the framing system inaugurated by the Giottesque painters of the Infancy Cycle and to make several of his frescoes conform to the size of those in the right transept; generally, fresco offered painters larger opportunities for innovations.

When Simone created his *Maestà* for the Palazzo Pubblico of Siena (Color Plates 3–4), use of the entire end wall of the Sala del Mappamondo led him to order the figures in depth and to depict a contemporary object, a baldachin like those presented to visiting dignitaries, as a device to enhance the spatial arrangement. The settings of Pietro's Assisi frescoes allowed the artist to explore both naturalistic devices and the fancifully exotic, while the availability of large secondary areas below the scenes provided place for his unequaled feats of illusionism (Fig. 44).[70] In the Saint Martin's Chapel and in the experience of Assisi, Simone seems to have revised his style—at least for a time—and to have become fascinated with opportunities for illusionism: not only in the window embrasures of the chapel (Fig. 48) but also in the scene of the *Death of Saint Martin* (Fig. 47), where a demon flees from the site and indeed out of the fresco. Ambrogio's *Franciscan Martyrdom* from the chapter house of San Francesco, Siena (Fig. 62), involved novel oriental types among the figures, and his enormous fresco from the cloister, which elicited high praise from Ghiberti, must have been one of the most marvelous murals of the period. Most of all, perhaps, fresco confronted each painter with the problem of pictorial space, and in rationalizing exteriors (as in cityscapes) and interiors, Sienese painters set many of the precedents for developments in the early Quattrocento.

Frequently, the innovations of fresco redounded to panel painting. I take it as significant that Pietro's *Birth of the Virgin* (Fig. 30) was commissioned as he finished a fresco of the same subject on the facade of the Ospedale della Scala.[71] The side scenes of Simone's *Beato Agostino Novello* (Color Plates 7–8, Figs. 14, 63) owe a good deal to the painter's experience at Assisi in the Saint Martin's Chapel. Ambrogio's *Presentation in the Temple* (Fig. 21) surely arises from the painter's experience of creating settings in narrative fresco, and the presumed predella of that work owes much to both Ambrogio's work in the Sala della Pace and, possibly, to his fresco of the Franciscan martyrdom in the cloister of San Francesco, Siena.[72]

Private devotional works fall somewhere between the constraints of the altarpiece

---

70. See also Maginnis, *Age of Giotto*, fig. 70, for an entire fictive bench illuminated as if from natural light entering the left transept from a door into the cloister above.

71. Hayden B. J. Maginnis, "The Lost Facade Frescoes from Siena's Ospedale di S. Maria della Scala," *Zeitschrift für Kunstgeschichte*, LI, 1988, 180–94.

72. For what I have argued is the central predella panel of Ambrogio's altarpiece, see my *Age of Giotto*, fig. 79.

rection polyptych (Fig. 61), wherein the painter combined the form of Pietro's Carmelite altarpiece with a narrative inspired by the cathedral altarpieces and three-quarter-length figures derived from works such as Pietro's altarpiece in Arezzo (Color Plate 13).

The Carmelite altarpiece and the panels for the side altars of the cathedral in Siena represent special cases; in all of them the ideation prompted formal changes. But the increasing popularity of full-length figures was undoubtedly encouraged, once again, by the issue of height. As painters strove to maintain naturalistic proportions in figures while increasingly dwelling on the physical settings depicted in altarpieces, the full-length figure, like the enthroned Madonna, offered a solution (Fig. 35) to both issues.

Now, the rich variety in Sienese altarpieces should not obscure the fact that altarpieces were hedged about by constraints; painters generally had to respect certain imposed conditions. The width of the altarpiece, for example, was determined by the width of the altar on which it was to stand, and with the width predetermined, the question of proportion and thus height that I have outlined came to the fore. Furthermore, convention decreed that the background and the framing of altarpieces be gilded. Pietro Lorenzetti, in his Uffizi *Madonna* (Fig. 54) or *Birth of the Virgin* (Fig. 30), might challenge the convention, but generally gold was what patrons favored, demanded, and got. The consequences were extensive. The convention forced painters to harmonize their palette with the gold background, and it set the problem of generating relief from a contour that had gold, with its varying luminosity according to varying illumination, as its foil. It further created the problem of haloes reading as glories attached to specific figures, when they were articulated gold upon gold; and because draperies might be embellished with gold, an interplay between ornament and ground was often created. Finally, just as the initial construction of an altarpiece involved panels and framing alike, the gilding of frames and backgrounds visually brought the two together and, although there were important exceptions, seems to have urged many painters toward a limitation on the theoretical elasticity of the depicted space. Painters frequently sought to introduce distinctions by tooling or stamping borders along the edges of panels (Color Plate 16), but this device was only modestly successful, since it simply created one frame within another.

The altarpiece, especially as developed in the polyptych, repeatedly focused attention on the single figure, making it an object of close scrutiny and prompting the more gifted to dwell on aspects of organic articulation. But it also allowed less talented painters to avoid the problems of context and interrelations. Painters of the second or third rank, especially those who rarely dealt with narrative art and/or never worked in fresco, were not forced to meditate on the greater complexities of composition and figural movement. Narrative called forth powers of composition and conceptions of the figure in action that most altarpieces did not require, and artists who worked in fresco had the greater opportunities for revising their art. The larger scale of fresco invited painters to explore means of unifying their compositions and of creating a concordance between figural groupings and settings. And the simple fact that in most instances painters had entire walls or chapels at their disposal meant that they had greater latitude in determining the size, shape, and framing of

My last remark directs us to the popularity of this altarpiece form beyond Siena, in Arezzo, Pisa, Perugia, and Florence. Two features explain that phenomenon. The first is simply the design constraints intrinsic to the first four decades of the Trecento. In that period there was a paucity of forms suited to the vast choirs of churches such as Santa Croce or Santa Maria Novella. The principal problem was one of height. Remaining with the Florentine situation: the form of neither the Giottesque Badia polyptych (Fig. 58) nor the Baroncelli *Coronation of the Virgin* was adequate to the large, high choir of Santa Croce. One might assume that the large Madonnas, such as Giotto's Ognissanti panel or the Rucellai *Madonna* (Fig. 9), embodied possible solutions, but the type seems to have been associated with confraternities. Moreover, the issue was further complicated by the dugento and trecento tendency to increase the width of high altars well beyond the horizontal dimensions of the Ognissanti or Rucellai *Madonna*s. But on altars of approximately four or four and a half meters width, any of the low forms we have considered would have created a predominantly horizontal impression, while panels of the type of the Rucellai *Madonna* would have had to rise to an incredible height. The Sienese storeyed polyptych, which could be raised still further by the addition of a predella, offered a scale and a magnificence more suited to large altars and their surrounds, and the combination of several tiers with soaring buttresses, pilasters, and finials manifested an aspiration heavenward that the low, horizontal forms could not provide. In the case of the Santa Croce altarpiece, we have explicit evidence that height was a conscious concern, for between the principal and second tiers Ugolino inserted a band of figured and decorated quatrefoils to make the panels higher (Fig. 13).

The second reason for the form's popularity surely lies in its symbolic meaning. In Christian thought, each church is an image of the heavenly Jerusalem, the material reflection on earth of the city of God. The equation is explicit in the rites of dedication for a new church or cathedral, which quote Revelation, chapter 21, in which the heavenly city is described. When Sienese painters borrowed the architectural vocabulary of churches for ordering altarpieces, they echoed the larger imagery. The assembly of saints, angels, sometimes prophets, and the Madonna and Child, surrounded by the golden light of paradise, became indeed a vision of the heavenly city. The Sienese polyptych of this type was one of the most beautiful marriages of form and content in the entire history of art. It seems therefore strange that the most innovative painters abandoned the form soon after its perfection.

In his Carmelite altarpiece of 1329 (Figs. 59–60), Pietro adapted the form so that full-length standing figures, surmounted by half-length figures in a second tier, flanked a large central panel with an enthroned Madonna and Child accompanied by saints and angels, imagery inspired by Duccio's *Maestà*. By bringing some figures directly into the presence of the Virgin, Pietro suggested that the side saints belonged to a more distant realm; and when the Siena cathedral altarpieces dedicated to the city's four patron saints were composed of standing figures, left and right, beside a central narrative, the inner and outer figures embodied two separate worlds (Fig. 17). The resulting potential for works lacking a fundamental coherence is vividly demonstrated by the Borgo San Sepolcro *Resur-*

trecento polyptych, had an extended life. It suited modest circumstances such as chapels or small churches, and among Ducciesque painters it survived for many years. But within a decade or so, Duccio and his shop elaborated the form in Siena no. 47 (Fig. 56), thereby providing the precedent for Simone's altarpiece for the Dominicans of Pisa (Color Plate 12), Pietro Lorenzetti's polyptych for the Pieve of Arezzo (Color Plates 13–14), Ugolino di Nerio's grand altarpiece for the Franciscans of Santa Croce, and Meo da Siena's polyptych in Perugia (Galleria Nazionale dell'Umbria, 22), although some of these works involved important modifications of the original conceit.

In no. 47 (Fig. 56), as in no. 28, the five main panels were originally separated from each other by pilasters that rose through the entire height of the altarpiece to become soaring finials above the main body of the polyptych. These elements provided vertical emphasis, but only by firmly separating the principal figures and thus diminishing the unity of the imagery. Ugolino's early Cleveland polyptych (Fig. 57) indicates that painters were aware of the problem, for there the arches of the arcade are coterminous, and thus the arcade runs unbroken the entire width of the altarpiece. The main figures are drawn together more firmly but at the cost of isolating the pinnacles and returning to an emphasis on the horizontal. Ugolino's work introduces us to a feature that also appears in no. 47, the box frame that runs across the bottom of the altarpiece and along its two sides. This framing element was both an inheritance from earlier images and a feature that stabilized the entire construction, but such box frames were fundamentally irrelevant to the architectural forms that otherwise articulated the polyptych. Pietro Lorenzetti resolved both problems in his Arezzo polyptych (Color Plates 13–14). He eliminated the box frame and stabilized his work with great decorated buttresses (now lost) to either side of the altarpiece, buttresses that extended downward, flush with the sides of the altar table, to the floor of the choir.[69] The altar was wrapped by the altarpiece, and the architectural vocabulary of the latter maintained throughout. The artist did more. Above the main figures in no. 47, the horizontal molding was repeatedly broken by the pilasters that originally separated the panels. Although those pilasters in the Arezzo altarpiece are lost, we note that the comparable horizontal moldings are beveled at each end, indicating that the moldings came forward, crossed the face of the pilasters, and returned to join the horizontal continuation in the next panel. In no. 47 (Fig. 56), the horizontal molding above the Virgin is unrelated to the moldings above the saints. Pietro, inspired by the lost framing on the face of Duccio's *Maestà* (Color Plate 10), merged these elements by having the molding above the Virgin rise from the level of the molding above the saints, cross horizontally only a portion of the central panel, and then descend to continue above the saint in the next panel. In these innovations, Pietro gave the polyptych greater coherence, both visual and conceptual.

---

posed of vertical planks that constituted the support for the main image and for the pinnacle above. In altarpieces of the new type and having a predella, that predella alone was usually created on a horizontal plank.

69. On the entire matter of side buttresses used to stabilize large altarpieces, including Pietro's, see C. Gardner von Teuffel, "The Buttressed Altarpiece: A Forgotten Aspect of Tuscan Fourteenth-Century Altarpiece Design," *Jahrbuch der Berliner Museen*, XXI, 1979, 22–65.

cause each was linked to different expectations on the part of patrons. Further reflections on patronage are found in the next chapter; here my concern is with the opportunities provided by, and the constraints inherent in, specific forms.

By the 1270s, the low-pitched, gabled dossal containing half-length figures, as in Siena nos. 6 and 7 (Figs. 6–7), entered Sienese art. The conception, ultimately derived from Byzantine iconostasis beams, must have had wide currency, for in 1271 Meliore da Toscana devised an alternate form in which half-length figures, separated by attached colonnettes, stand below trilobed arches.[65] The "Guidesque" circle did not follow Meliore's example; instead, Sienese painters devised a form based on architectural gables, complete with elements highly reminiscent of the repeating corbel tables found below the eaves of Romanesque churches. The form had the advantage of giving prominence to the central Madonna and Child by placing them on the largest surface area, and the unbroken picture field brought the two central figures into immediate relation with the attendant saints. At the same time, however, the sloping upper moldings produced a steady diminution in the height of the picture field as it approached the lateral extremities. Although the progressively decreasing areas could be used to reflect a hierarchy among the saints, I doubt that the distinctions created were always justified or desired; that is one of the reasons, I suspect, that the form had a very short life. But, for reasons that will soon be apparent, the gabled dossal was extremely important, in that it shifted the altarpiece away from forms based, for example, on the altar frontal and into an architectural mode.[66]

Between 1280 and 1290, Vigoroso da Siena created an altarpiece, now in the Galleria Nazionale dell'Umbria, that embodies a transitional design and looks toward the altarpiece forms that were to follow.[67] Therein, the four saints that flank the Madonna and Child stand below semicircular arches, all of the same height; above them, four angels appear in triangular fields, just as a Blessing Redeemer appears above the Virgin. But it was Duccio, in Siena no. 28 (Fig. 52–53), who instituted the critical reform of the "architectural" altarpiece that left a larger central field for the Madonna and Child but more or less restored equality to the saints. Now distinctions were embodied in the proximity to or distance from the central panel: a development that required a rather more subtle reading of the imagery. The angels that in Siena no. 6 (Fig. 6) occupy the spandrels or, as in Vigoroso's altarpiece, are placed directly on the arches of the framing below them, were separated out and placed in their own spaces, in the crowning, separately framed gables, and made attendants to the Blessing Redeemer, also separately framed, over the central panel. This higher degree of rationalization was accomplished by the conflation of interior and exterior architectural elements, by uniting arcades and gables.[68] The format, the simpler version of the Sienese

---

65. Maginnis, *Age of Giotto,* fig. 51.

66. For a thirteenth-century Sienese altarpiece based on the form used earlier for altar-frontals, see Maginnis, *Age of Giotto,* fig. 18.

67. F. Santi, *Galleria Nazionale dell'Umbria: Dipinti, sculture e oggetti d'arte di età romanica e gotica,* Rome, 1989, 41–42 and figs. 16a–16b.

68. The new organization entailed a new carpentry for the support. Works such as the altarpieces derived from the form of frontals, and the low gabled dossals were assembled from large wooden planks ranged horizontally. The new form was com-

modeling in the early works of even great painters. An early panel by Pietro Lorenzetti now in the Museo Horne, Florence (Fig. 55), provides an excellent example of the phenomenon; the plasticity of the head contrasts markedly with the rather flat draperies. The most inventive masters of the early Trecento explored various means to increase the volume of their figures. But most figures nonetheless arise from their contours, and particularly in early works by great masters or in the works of less gifted painters, discrepancies between the modeling of heads and that of draperies remain pronounced.

The techniques I have discussed were not unique to Siena; they were common to painters throughout central Italy. But I have lingered over technical matters relating to textiles and halo design because they set the temper of Sienese panels and thus were parts of a larger system of harmonies. They were also the principal components in that splendor of surface that made Sienese panel pictures so appealing to an audience beyond Siena itself. Although Florentine pictures of the first half of the Trecento have many merits, the elegance of Sienese works is not generally among them. And although Florentine painters certainly saw enough Sienese works to know the means of their magnificence, they rarely sought similar effects and were slow to appropriate Sienese developments.[64] In Siena, all painters participated, to a greater or lesser degree, in Duccio's legacy and that of later, major masters, so that when, in the later Trecento, meaningful invention and innovation were at a premium, the elegance of Sienese painting remained. But I have also included this discussion of techniques so that the reader may form a conception of just how labor-intensive works of the Trecento were. And Sienese works, with their unrivaled refinements in halo design, textile patterns, and articulated grounds, were particularly demanding of time and energy. Although Simone Martini revived, adapted, and pioneered techniques such as halo stamping and *sgraffito,* which made for a more mechanical execution, his panels are often of such extensive embellishment that time saved in one aspect of execution was lost to another. In other words, each fresco project or altarpiece structured its author's life in a way entirely foreign to modern artistic production; each was a major and long-lasting event in a painter's life.

Forms and Formats

If media and techniques conditioned and circumscribed the painter's art, so too did the forms and formats generally required of him. With the exception of decorative tasks and some secular imagery, major painters worked predominantly with religious subject matter and within established forms and formats: the narrative or iconic fresco, the altarpiece, and the small, private devotional work. Each offered the artist differing degrees of latitude be-

64. The first securely documented use of *sgraffito* in Florence occurs in a *Madonna* (Uffizi, Depository) painted by Taddeo Gaddi in 1355. See Maginnis, *Age of Giotto,* fig. 101.

Florence for that project.⁶⁰ Clearly, some type or types of wood were not available locally, and it is tempting to think it was the massive timbers needed for floor beams—and altarpieces.

We lack documentary material concerning the methods of design painters used in planning their works, but John White has demonstrated that Duccio, in planning his *Maestà* and smaller works as well, used a proportional system common to architects throughout the Middle Ages, a system later (1486) published by Matthias Roriczer.⁶¹ In brief, the system was one in which the painter could evolve his entire design from one side and the diagonal of a given square, basing larger and smaller squares on the diagonal of the square immediately below it in the series. In other words, the basis of the design for the support was geometrical. We await further work on other artists that will tell us how widespread this usage was, but it seems highly likely that Duccio's design methods accorded with those of contemporaries.⁶²

Too rarely do we reflect on the relations between artistic techniques and the resulting image, yet methods of execution and means of articulation inform the painter's conception of his work. In both fresco and panel painting, the sinopia drawings in one and the incised lines of the other placed primary emphasis on contour, on figural silhouette. Combined with the practice of modeling up, that emphasis meant that the figure was conceived as a relief. On occasion, Duccio, Ugolino, and Simone provided visual metaphors for the substance of their figures by creating patterns of deep folds that swing across the figures; the figure of Santa Massima in Simone's and Lippo Memmi's 1333 *Annunciation* is an excellent example (Fig. 19).⁶³ But such treatments have little to do with the idea of a hidden, supporting form. The central panel of the same work (Fig. 17) shows us other features stemming from the Sienese stress on contours: the rhythmic harmonization of the silhouettes of the two figures and the extension of the emphasis on line into the treatment of drapery edges. From Duccio's Rucellai *Madonna* (Fig. 10) onward, the Sienese treatment of mantle borders intermittently employed the line of those borders to impart vitality to the figure, in yet another visual metaphor for a reality otherwise undepicted.

The fact that heads were painted last in panel pictures, that they required complex articulation in a relatively small area, and that, as the modern psychology of perception has demonstrated, we naturally devote most attention to faces, often created discrepancies in

60. Siena, BC, Benvoglienti: MS C.v.5, fol. 198v.

61. John White, "Carpentry and Design in Duccio's Workshop," *Journal of the Warburg and Courtauld Institutes,* XXXVI, 1970, 92–105; John White, "Measurement, Design, and Carpentry in Duccio's Maestà," *Art Bulletin,* LV, 1973, 332–66, 547–69; White, *Duccio,* 49–52, 93–95, 201–8.

62. Investigations to discover such geometrical systems are in many cases hampered by the modern state of altarpieces. Frequently, they have lost at least part of their frames. Predellas and buttresses on each side have disappeared. Pinnacles may be missing. It is therefore difficult to define the complete original width, which would have been a key element in such design procedures.

63. A similar, although much less robust, use of this device is found in the central panel of Pietro Lorenzetti's Arezzo polyptych (Color Plate 14), begun in 1320. But there the effect is less plastic because the drapery of the Virgin was articulated by overglazing.

the number of painters who could work on an altarpiece at any one moment was determined by the width of the panel.⁵⁶

If fresco and panel painting involved different working methods, there was another difference we ought to note. For a painter to approach a fresco project was, at worst, for the painter to face a rough masonry wall. It might need its initial plastering, an *arriccio,* but from that point forward the painter and his shop could carry forth their work independently. Altarpieces were different. Painters undoubtedly furnished the designs for the supports, but wherever we have record, it was a carpenter or carpenters who actually produced the panels and all their framing elements. In and of itself, the woodworking aspect of any altarpiece must have been an assignment that rivaled, or more likely surpassed, the complexities of contemporary furniture. Indeed, it seems clear that framing became increasingly more complex, eventually combining the original inspiration provided by architecture with elaborate details derived from the goldsmith's art. The carpenter's task thus became ever more demanding and presented him with particular problems. Altarpieces, constructed of poplar, required thick planks and, to ensure minimum movement, planks of maximum width ideally taken from the very center of a tree.⁵⁷ It is hard to imagine the situation wherein a carpenter would have such material readily available in such a size and sufficiently seasoned for immediate use, unless he were involved in a major architectural project, such as the building of the Palazzo Pubblico, where enormous wooden beams support the floors. There is here a time factor that we cannot estimate. There may also have been a means of communication between painters and carpenters for which we have no concrete, documentary evidence.

We know, for certain, nothing about the sources for wood used in altarpieces. The Sienese commune directly controlled several forests: the Selva del Lago, a forest at Montefalcone, and other forests in the valley of the Merse.⁵⁸ At Selva del Lago, cutting of wood, hunting, and fishing were prohibited to all except the Augustinians of San Leonardo al Lago. For civic commissions, those of the commune or cathedral, wood may have come from these forests. On the other hand, I would note two records that seem, on the face of things, rather puzzling. Apparently on 21 May 1309, the master carpenter "Maestro Guido" was sent to Lucca to buy wood for construction in the Palazzo Pubblico.⁵⁹ Similarly, in 1328, after it was decided to enlarge the Palazzo Pubblico along the side of the Via di Malborghetto, two men were paid for seven days' work for the commune, buying wood in

---

56. This matter (among others) raises severe difficulties when it comes to James Stubblebine's division of authorship for the narratives on the back of Duccio's *Maestà* ("Duccio and His Collaborators on the Cathedral *Maestà*," Art Bulletin, LV, 1973, 185–204). It would make no sense to employ different painters for the upper and lower portions, since they could not work simultaneously.

57. One would choose a wide plank over a narrow plank to minimize "twisting" and "bending," though with the greater width one would risk greater motion across the grain (expansion and contraction) with changes in temperature and humidity. The heartwood is chosen to avoid "cupping," caused by shrinkage along the rings. My thanks to Keith Monley, who has supplied this note.

58. O. Redon, "L'ermo, la città e la foresta," in *Lecceto e gli eremi agostiniani in terra di Siena,* Milan, 1990, 16.

59. Siena, BC, Spogli: MS A.VII.18, fol. 236r.

The altarpieces by Pietro and Ambrogio Lorenzetti for Siena cathedral (Figs. 21, 30) are both inscribed with the date 1342. The documents for Ambrogio's *Presentation* indicate that the work was begun in 1337 and that a change in the predella design occurred during the execution.[50] Moreover, it was between 1337 and 1342 that Ambrogio decorated the Sala della Pace in Siena's Palazzo Pubblico. Pietro's *Birth of the Virgin* was begun in 1335. Yet in 1340 Pietro signed and dated his *Madonna* from Pistoia (Fig. 54, now in the Galleria degli Uffizi) and acknowledged that he was under obligation for two panels for Paolo di Tingo de' Pilestri. The documents related to Pietro's Arezzo altarpiece suggest its execution stretched over a considerable period of time, while, presumably, he worked on the lost frescoes that Vasari mentions, for the apse of Santa Maria della Pieve.[51]

One aspect of panel painting is generally ignored, simply because we know so little; I refer to the actual painting of large works. When Duccio approached the Rucellai *Madonna* or the *Maestà,* or when Ambrogio began his *Presentation,* these painters were faced with completely assembled supports of very significant dimensions for the principal imagery.[52] We can only assume that, while being painted, such supports stood vertically, and that, in turn, suggests they were painted from the top down, a practice almost universal in fresco painting.[53] There is evidence that painters eventually sought to reduce the area that had to be treated as a unit. Ugolino apparently devised a separate predella box for his altarpiece in Santa Croce and employed an original batten system that allowed the altarpiece to be assembled after the carpentry, and presumably painting, for each vertical panel.[54] At the top of Ambrogio's *Presentation in the Temple* (Fig. 22), on the back, are two dovetailed slots that suggest there was once a crowning pinnacle that was inserted after painting, and there may have been a change in the predella design well after the project had begun, suggesting that the predella was a separate component.[55] By and large, however, supports remained generally treated as single units. Needless to say, this question bears heavily on the possibility of collaborative execution of a work when it reached the stage of painting. If panels were upright while being painted, and if the execution proceeded generally from top to bottom,

50. Maginnis, "Chiarimenti documentari."

51. A. Guerrini, "Intorno al politico di Pietro Lorenzetti per la Pieve di Arezzo," *Rivista d'arte,* XXXII, 1988, 3–29.

52. Ambrogio's altarpiece also had some detachable parts. See the discussion below.

53. Cennini (*The Craftsman's Handbook,* 92), after specifying that several steps preparatory to painting are completed with the panel lying flat on trestles, says: "Then set your ancona up in front of you."

54. Norman Muller, "Reflections on Ugolino di Nerio's Santa Croce Polyptych," *Zeitschrift für Kunstgeschichte,* LVII, 1994, 45–74. Polyptychs were usually composed of vertical planks, one for each saint in the main tier and one for the central image (although these planks, especially for the central panel, could be themselves assembled from more than one piece of wood). The planks usually extended upward to act as support for figures on a second or even a third tier. Generally, all the planks were tied together by large horizontal battens, on the back, before the painting began.

55. For an important, recent discussion of Sienese altarpiece construction and design, see Norman Muller, "The Sequential Assembly of Sienese Trecento Altarpieces," in *The Materials, Technology, and Art of Conservation: Studies in Honor of Lawrence J. Majewski on the Occasion of His 80th Birthday, February 10, 1999,* ed. R.A. Rushfield and M.W. Ballard, New York, 1999, 104–33.

The Sienese attention to refinement in textile depictions was matched by a concern with exquisite refinement in the articulation of haloes. Once more, our story begins with Duccio and the Rucellai *Madonna* (Figs. 10–11). It was in that panel that the painter introduced a new complexity and richness of detail in the rendering of haloes. The perimeters of each halo and concentric interior bands were created with a compass or divider, thereby assuring the regular geometry of the basic form. In several cases, the outside edge of the halo was articulated using small punches. Within the larger, internal bands are decorative motifs of floral, leaf, trilobe, and quatrefoil shapes, executed freehand; often the background to those forms was crosshatched. Although the enormous size of the Rucellai *Madonna* somewhat canceled the intended effect, these surfaces were planned to respond to flickering candlelight and to a viewer moving before the image and thus experiencing changing reflections, while the burnished, undifferentiated gold of the background appeared darker.[48] Haloes of this type occur in later works by Duccio and his circle (Fig. 52) and in the early works of both Lorenzetti (Color Plates 13–15); by far the most elaborate and intricate examples are found on the front of Duccio's *Maestà* (Color Plate 10). It was Simone Martini and his shop who brought a major and pervasive change to halo execution, replacing the freehand incisions of decorative motifs with the use of metal punches. The floral, leaf, and geometric designs continued to be used, but they were now realized with a variety of punches that could be combined and recombined in the creation of varying patterns (Figs. 20, 38). The result was a textured surface, one in which the varying angles of the gold created, for the moving viewer, a series of sparkling lights.[49] So prized was the effect—and perhaps the quasi-mechanical nature of the process—that during the 1320s almost every Sienese painter changed to this method of execution.

Although tempera imposed important restrictions on the painter, the fact that panel painting was composed of discrete stages also offered advantages. First of all, it allowed for the division of labor I mentioned above. Gessoing, laying the bole, gilding, burnishing, and the stamping of haloes: all these tasks could be given over to assistants, even when the master wished to retain full control over the actual painting. Where extensive use was made of *sgraffito*, as in the figure of Gabriel from Simone's *Annunciation* (Color Plate 9), an assistant could remove the paint surface to expose the gold and then punch the patterns, following which the master could apply the glazes that gave the drapery form. The division of labor, like the intervals necessary between various stages of a work, meant that more than one project could be undertaken at any given time. The technique of tempera painting also meant that work on a specific project could be suspended at any of several points, and we have evidence that just such breaks occurred.

48. Modern conditions of viewing reverse the intended effect of halo decoration, bright light making the background appear brighter and the articulated haloes darker. In their original settings, where illumination was comparatively slight, the opposite pertained: it was the worked areas of the haloes that read as bright, sparkling surfaces. This is also true of stamped haloes, discussed below.

49. Simone and, eventually, his contemporaries used punches on drapery borders to create the impression of gold-thread brocade. In those forms, the changing lights were an imitation of light playing across such surfaces and, in some cases, meant as an indication of changing planes.

too abrupt nor too subtle to realize shape. Not all painters were converted to the new treatment. Simone Martini, for example, generally remained an advocate of glazing over a uniform middle tone to create receding and advancing forms.

Simone, however, was much influenced by Duccio's enthusiasm for the rendering of luxury textiles. As early as 1315, in his Palazzo Pubblico *Maestà,* he followed Duccio's example, giving the Virgin a costume in which the fine gold pattern is foreshortened and broken at the fold edges (Color Plate 4). In his polyptych for the Dominicans of Pisa (Color Plate 12), the draperies of Saint Catherine of Alexandria (Fig. 36) ring changes on Duccio's example. Simone constantly explored means to give his draperies an appearance of great luxury. In his *Saint Louis of Toulouse* altarpiece (Color Plate 16), the saint's cope was painted a rich crimson, created by laying silver leaf and glazing it with transparent red lake.[44] Then small gold discs, which have largely fallen away, were applied over the surface. The great borders of the cope are richly punched and otherwise adorned. In the Saint Martin's Chapel of San Francesco, Simone conducted complex and successful experiments in the renderings of plaids and in giving garment borders in fresco the gilding and articulation of borders in his *Saint Louis of Toulouse*. But it is in the Uffizi *Annunciation* (1333) that we discover the most eloquent witness to the painter's concern with this aspect of his art.

In the *Annunciation,* Simone transferred his Assisi experiments with plaid to Gabriel's extravagant cloak (Color Plate 9), which, lifted and tossed by the air, demanded consistent and continuous articulation of the rapidly swinging fabric, here achieved through foreshortening and the use of multiple glazes. The archangel's stole and sleeves are decorated with patterns created by punches of gradated size. And in Gabriel's robes and in the throne's drape, Simone made extensive use of *sgraffito*. The technique involves gilding the entire drapery area, overpainting it in a solid color, and then picking away patterns in the paint layer to reveal the gold beneath. The patterns may then be articulated by stippling or punching. Finally, as in this instance, the surface is overglazed to create folds and indicate recession. As we still see, the result could be stunning; but the technique had serious consequences for Sienese painting as it reached the mid-century.[45]

Two related points about fabrics depicted by Sienese painters should be noted. First, the vast majority of representations were based on real textiles or, at minimum, features of real textiles. Second, during the Trecento, the painters of Siena showed a marked preference for textiles with motifs of Chinese or Sino-Persian origin.[46] For example, King Robert's robe, in Simone's *Saint Louis of Toulouse* (Color Plate 16), is decorated with a Chinese leaf-and-lotus pattern.[47] Here, then, is a point at which the thirteenth-century opening of China, like the opening of Mongol Persia, to Western trade touched the life of distant Siena.

44. Hoeniger, "The Painting Technique of Simone Martini," 242–43. The egg-tempera medium has caused the silver to darken. Silver leaf, in spite of its tendency to tarnish and therefore darken, was probably more widely used than we know. The contract (1320) for the Arezzo polyptych requires Pietro Lorenzetti to use the "best silver" as well as gold.
45. Maginnis, *Age of Giotto,* 182–83.
46. Hills, *The Light of Early Italian Painting,* 96.
47. Hoeniger, "The Painting Technique of Simone Martini," 213.

Sienese pictures also tell us that painters considered the very direction of their brush strokes in modeling facial forms (Figs. 20, 35, 53).[41]

Pictures reveal various means of rendering draperies and sometimes a combination of means in the same passage. In the San Bernardino *Madonna* (Fig. 8), the blue of the Virgin's mantle is a solid, undifferentiated color to which chrysography has been added, through mordant gilding, which creates the illusion of drapery folds. But the modeling of Christ's tunic results from the application of a darker glaze over the ground color; the cloth below Christ is articulated by a blue glaze over white; a similar glazing articulates the throne's drape. In the Rucellai *Madonna* (Figs. 10–11), the Virgin's throne is draped with the most intricate textile depicted in the thirteenth century, a fabric that is at once bold in its patterns and refined in its detail. The drapery pattern was rendered flat, without foreshortenings or interruptions, and then overglazed to provide the highly convincing illusion that the drape gathers in folds dependent on the points of attachment to the throne's back. On the other hand, the modeling of the azurite robe of the Virgin is revolutionary, since it is modeled upward.

By the time of the cathedral *Maestà,* Duccio's concern with drapery depiction was such that, on the front of the panel, he devoted great attention and surely considerable time to articulating the throne's drape and the robes of Saint Catherine (Color Plate 11), San Savino, and Saint Agnes. In these draperies Duccio combined overglazing with foreshortening of patterns and interruption of those patterns to indicate a change of plane. The intricacy of design is also heightened. Yet more remarkable is the way in which the textiles are devised for both close reading and illusion at a distance. At close proximity to the panel, the viewer can contemplate the details of the material and see how the foreshortenings and the breaks in pattern assure the three-dimensionality of drapery and thus of figure; at a distance, the indications of recession remain, but the specific patterns disappear and the draperies take on a shimmering luxury.[42]

Eventually, in the works of some painters, such as the Lorenzetti, the painting of draperies on panel was altered as the result of a cross-fertilization from fresco painting. In executing draperies in fresco, the painter kept a series of bowls or dishes of each color in successive gradations and, working in precisely the same direction as in painting faces in tempera, worked up from dark to light.[43] When painters adopted this full-color modeling for panels, the same imperatives that applied to faces were carried over into the drapery areas, with a consequent increase in time and labor to ensure transitions that were neither

41. There are some fine color illustrations of heads and faces in L. Bellosi, ed., *Simone Martini: Atti del convegno,* Florence, 1988, 123, 125, 127–28. The brushwork is visible in many.

42. P. Hills, *The Light of Early Italian Painting,* London and New Haven, 1987, 97–98.

43. Cennini, *The Craftsman's Handbook,* 49–52. Draperies, however, did not begin with an overall ground color as was the method for heads. Instead, Cennini recommends first laying the darkest color in the areas that will represent the valleys of folds and then moving up through increasingly lightened color to the final highlights on the crests of folds.

described by Cennino Cennini in the work we know as *Il libro dell'arte*.[37] Panels and their attached framing elements, produced and assembled by carpenters, were first given several coats of size and then covered with linen. Next, they received a layer of *gesso grosso,* plaster of Paris, and then several coats of *gesso sottile,* each, in succession, scraped down to a perfectly flat surface. Each of these steps had to be separated by at least a few days to let the previous layer dry before the next was applied.[38] A charcoal drawing on the gessoed surface laid in the composition, which was then fixed by scratching outlines of the figures and sometimes fold patterns for drapery into the gessoed ground with a metal stylus.[39] A layer of red bole was then applied to the areas destined for gilding, and the bole was followed by the application of gold leaf itself.[40] This, in turn, needed to be burnished before the haloes were created either by incision or by stamping. Draperies and, when applicable, background elements were painted first, the flesh areas executed as the last step in the painting. Many Sienese painters decorated draperies with gilded motifs created by applying a mordant in the form of the desired pattern, placing gold leaf on that surface, and then brushing away the unattached gold. It is hard for us to imagine the intricacy of this task or the time required. A robe such as that of Saint Catherine in Duccio's *Maestà* (Color Plate 11) was a major project in itself. But each step in panel painting required great care, and each was time-consuming. This was particularly true of the actual painting.

The extremely viscous and comparatively quick-drying nature of egg tempera meant that the pigments had to be applied with very small brushes and in short strokes. Forms were carefully built and carefully considered, for there was little room for alteration. Faces were the most complex of all painted surfaces because they were built up from a ground color (usually *terra verde*), and that meant that the progressively lightening colors had to be placed exactly to create the impression of consistent and convincing relief. Early

37. Many technical studies point toward this conclusion. The reader will want to consult C. Brandi et al., *Il restauro della "Maestà" di Duccio,* Rome, 1959; A. Del Sera, "Il restauro," and O. Casazza, "Analisi, diagnosi e documentazione in un sistema informativo per l'archiviazione di test e immagini," in *La Maestà di Duccio restaurata, li Uffizi: Studi e richerche,* VI, Florence, 1990, 57–89 (the Rucellai *Madonna*); Bomford et al., *Art in the Making*; Cathleen Hoeniger, "The Painting Technique of Simone Martini," Ph.D. dissertation, Princeton University, 1989. Cennino Cennini is here quoted from the translation of D.V. Thompson Jr.: *The Craftsman's Handbook.*

38. Cennini, *The Craftsman's Handbook,* 69–74. I have wondered if Sienese painters did not originally choose the area of Sant'Egidio and San Donato because there the Via Francigena passed along the spiny ridge of a hilltop, at either side of which the terrain rapidly descends. The location must have provided for good strong breezes, and Cennini himself says that the drying of gesso requires dry and windy weather. See below.

39. Cennini, *The Craftsman's Handbook,* 76. Cennini also recommends scratching in ornaments and various special types of drapery.

40. There are a few instances in Sienese painting where silver, rather than gold, was used for the ground. Although silver could be varnished in the hope of preventing tarnish, the practice was risky and the ground, over time, could darken. For an example, see Pietro Lorenzetti's *Madonna* from Castiglione d'Orcia, illustrated in the catalogue of the *Mostra di opere d'arte restaurate nelle province di Siena e Grosseto,* Genoa, 1979, 49–51.

ings (*sinopie*) may be leisurely, once work on the final surface (the *intonaco*) begins, the artist using true fresco is well advised to see the project move steadily toward completion.

A painter can significantly alter the situation, however, by making extensive use of tempera colors, doing much of the work *a secco,* after the *intonaco* is dry. Pietro Lorenzetti largely worked in true fresco in his Assisi Passion Cycle until the last stages of the project, when significant portions of the *Deposition* (Fig. 43) and *Entombment* as well as of the fictive altarpiece (Fig. 44) below the *Crucifixion* were finished after the plaster was dry. In Pietro's *Crucifixion* for San Francesco, Siena (Figs. 45–46), most of the draperies were finished *a secco* with tempera colors that have flaked away, as has the blue of the sky, revealing in the latter case a red underpaint on the *intonaco* that would have given the sky a richer color. By contrast, Simone Martini used gilding and *secco* painting extensively in the Palazzo Pubblico *Maestà* (Color Plates 3–4) but a much greater proportion of true fresco in the Saint Martin's Chapel at Assisi (Figs. 47–50). Frescoes *a secco* have proved far less durable than true fresco; in many cases, the original surface colors of the *intonaco* have flaked away. In both types of fresco, painters worked downward from the highest place on the wall they were decorating; this sequence of execution prevented colors accidentally falling onto completed surfaces.

One of the more unusual features of working *a secco* involves very elaborate drawings on the *intonaco*. In the wonderful figure of Saint John the Evangelist in Pietro Lorenzetti's Siena *Crucifixion* (Fig. 46), extraordinary care was given to articulating the draperies, although their coloring was to be done later. The practice was not restricted to Pietro, not even to Sienese artists. *Intonaco* drawings are found in Simone's *Maestà* for the Palazzo Pubblico, but also for the draperies of the Virgin in Giotto's *Flight into Egypt* and elsewhere in the Arena Chapel, Padua. Perhaps such drawings were guides to assistants who would later do the actual painting, but that purpose is not certain, for the modeling may have been intended to read through the later surface executed *a secco*. Whatever their purpose, they provide us with indication of what a finished figural drawing by these painters must have looked like.

The history of true fresco by Sienese painters presents us with something of a mystery. Simone Martini, Lippo Memmi, and the Lorenzetti brothers all worked in true fresco, in the cases of Simone and Pietro Lorenzetti quite early in their known careers. But although there have been several unconvincing attributions of frescoes to Duccio, we have no real evidence that he ever worked in fresco.[36] The same is true for many of his closest followers. There are some dugento, vaguely "Guidesque" frescoes in the former crypt of Siena cathedral and a fresco fragment from the same orbit on the upper wall of the nave in the Abbazia di San Donato, but none of them suggests their authors were capable of training the great masters of the Trecento. How and where Sienese painters of Simone's generation learned fresco technique is therefore a puzzle.

Sienese painters generally created their panel pictures according to the system later

36. I have always suspected that one of the reasons that the commission for the Palazzo Pubblico *Maestà* was awarded Simone, rather than Duccio, was the fact that the latter did not work in fresco.

held in the church of the Ospedale della Scala (chapter LV), where it seems to have remained.

Techniques

Early Sienese painters worked primarily in two media: tempera on panel and fresco. The two were not entirely unrelated inasmuch as certain pigments, indissoluble in water, had to be applied to frescoes after the plaster was completely dry, using the same egg-yolk binder employed for tempera on panel or animal glue; gilding of plaster surfaces, particularly evident in Simone Martini's *Maestà* (Color Plates 3 and 4), also required the use of a nonaqueous binder. But the two techniques were different in working method and urged different paces of execution. For fresco, the artist had to lay a smooth plaster bed, an *arriccio,* over the wall surface. Generally this was followed by drawings, *sinopie,* of varying detail that laid in figures and architectural features where needed. In true fresco, by far the most durable, the final image was created by the artist's laying successive plaster patches (*giornate*) over the *arriccio* to create the *intonaco* and painting the plaster of each *giornata* while it was still wet. *Giornate* can range from the very large to the very small, depending on the pictorial content and on what the painter feels he can accomplish before the surface begins to dry.[34] In order to ensure a unified surface and satisfactory adhesion of one *giornata* to another, work needs to proceed at a regular pace, the painter laying a new plaster patch before the adjoining one, of the previous day, is entirely dry and overlapping the new plaster upon the old (Figs. 39–43).[35] Thus, while the initial phases of a fresco project may be stretched over time to suit the artist, while preparation of the ground (the *arriccio*) and the execution of underdraw-

cording to a manuscript in the Opera del Duomo (MS 19, fols. 9ff.), the Consiglio Generale, on 7 July 1329, set aside £600 for the construction of a house for the rector of the Church of Saint Luke and for the provision of things necessary for the altar, including a painted panel. On 31 December 1332, the Biccherna paid the *operaio* of the duomo £300 for construction of the Church of Saint Luke (ASS, Biccherna 174, fol. 90v).

Perhaps the painters decided that they would move the celebration elsewhere because the church had been constructed in the suburb known as Borgo di Santa Maria and was thus comparatively far from the district in which most painters lived. But it is also likely that after the Black Death of 1348 this area lost its local population, which would have been the mainstay of the church. By 1402, the church was in a state of collapse. See Balestracci and Piccinni, *Siena nel trecento,* 35–36.

34. See the discussions of fresco technique in L. Tintori and Millard Meiss, *The Painting of "The Life of St. Francis" in Assisi,* New York, 1962, and E. Borsook, *The Mural Painters of Tuscany,* 2d ed., Oxford, 1980.

35. Because painters carried the plaster of a new *giornata* over the edge of a previously completed *giornata* in order to ensure adhesion, one can map not only the boundaries of each *giornata* but also the sequence of execution. The author mapped the *giornate* for Pietro Lorenzetti's Assisi Passion Cycle with the kind and generous assistance of Leonetto Tintori. For diagrams for the complete cycle, see Hayden B. J. Maginnis, "The Passion Cycle in the Lower Church of San Francesco, Assisi: The Technical Evidence," *Zeitschrift für Kunstgeschichte,* XXXIX, 1976, 193–208.

tic outlook of a second-rate artist. The Painters' Guild statute in Florence said apprenticeships should not be less than three years if paid for by the apprentice, and not less than six years if the master was paying. Late-thirteenth-century contracts from Florence specify apprenticeships of three, four, even eight years.[32]

One final observation about the 1356 statute: the 1356 approval of the statute, following chapter XLIII, contains an intriguing remark. The statute is approved by all the necessary officials, who have erased "all those statutes that . . . did not reflect well on the honor and status of the Commune of Siena, and adding the provision that no one should make use of any of the invalidated or abrogated statutes under pain of sanctions contained in the Statutes of the Commune of Siena." The comment speaks to the existence of an earlier draft of the statute or, I would argue, an earlier version.

In 1358 and 1361 a total of six more chapters were added to the *Breve,* a number of which themselves say they are further clarification of earlier chapters in the 1356 version and, perhaps, suggest that the painters were an unruly lot. One chapter, XLV, explicitly commands that the secretary of the guild obey the rector. Chapter XLVI requires that a general assembly of the guild must have at least ten councillors present, and those must represent the various categories in the painting trade. In chapter XLVII, the rector is required to hold an assembly eight days before the feast of the Assumption, apparently for the purpose of considering the matter of candles to be presented on that occasion, and "since it is never the case that everybody is present at the General Assembly," the rector must issue a personal notice to each and every member of the guild. Combined with the earlier regulations about not refusing offices in the guild and the repeated regulations about feasts to be observed and celebrated, this chapter suggests that members were negligent of their obligations.

The single addition of 1361 is noteworthy in that it addresses the matter of a general collection to be made in order to provide £4 to buy candles and *doppieri* to be placed in the Church of Santa Maria della Misericordia on the feast of the Blessed Andrea Gallerani. Also, all painters are required to attend the celebration of the feast. Here, at long last, is official recognition of the proximity of painters to the Misericordia, located in the parish of San Donato. Indeed, chapter L, an addition of 1367, declares that the guild will celebrate the feast of Saint Luke at the church of the Misericordia.[33] By 1379, the celebration was being

---

32. D. Bomford et al., *Art in the Making: Italian Painting Before 1400,* London, 1989, 9–10. The reader will want to consult this very useful work for detailed discussion of artistic techniques. Milanesi (*Nuovi documenti,* 9–15) published the texts of several of these arrangements.

33. The guild was somewhat peripatetic. Chapter 1 of the *Breve* places the celebration of the feast of Saint Luke in the Sienese church of that name. In 1367, as indicated here, painters celebrated the occasion at Santa Maria della Misericordia. Chapter 55, added in 1379, places that celebration in the church of the Ospedale di Santa Maria della Scala.

The original Church of Saint Luke in Siena was demolished during the building of the Palazzo Pubblico, and the commune assumed responsibility for replacing it. Things moved slowly. The constitution of 1337–39 declared that the new church should be built at communal expense, and put aside money for the project (ASS, Statuti 26, fols. 13v, 15r). The new church seems to have been completed in 1339 and would have been the site named in the 1356 *Breve.* I would note, however, that the documents relating to the project are somewhat confusing. Ac-

San Vittorio altarpiece (c. 1350) for Siena cathedral, they must have worked as equals—or nearly so—and we easily identify Bulgarini in the central panel (Fig. 27) and the Master of Palazzo Venezia in the side saints (Figs. 28–29).[26] But the joint signature of Luca di Tommè and Niccolò di Ser Sozzo on a polyptych of 1362 (Siena, Pinacoteca Nazionale, no. 51; Fig. 35) has stirred much discussion because, although we know independent works by both painters, we cannot easily separate one hand from another. The situation parallels that concerning the signatures of Simone Marini and Lippo Memmi on the 1333 *Annunciation* (Figs. 17–20); long-standing debates have ended in tacit agreement that we cannot separate Lippo's contribution from Simone's. We know of three specific collaborations between Lippo and Federigo Memmi: an aborted project related to the tower of Siena's Palazzo Pubblico, three panels for the rector of the Ospedale di Santa Maria della Scala, and a polyptych once in Avignon, signed by both and dated 1347. Unfortunately, none of these works survives. There are, of course, also situations that are best understood in terms of masters, apprentices, and followers. Pietro Lorenzetti seems to have had but one significant follower, the Master of the Loeser Madonna (Fig. 96).[27] Ambrogio Lorenzetti seems to have had a larger shop. Whether it included independent masters as well as assistants is uncertain, although I feel confident that was the case.[28]

Strangely enough, the 1356 statute of the Painters' Guild has almost nothing to say about apprentices beyond a requirement, in chapter XXXII, that no one was to have an apprentice in his shop unless that apprentice was registered with the guild. The statutes of other Sienese guilds provide us with some relevant information. The Goldsmiths' Guild prohibited anyone, "garzone" or "lavorente" or foreigner, from opening a shop without at least six years' apprenticeship.[29] And the guild of the leatherworkers and shoemakers required that every April and November the guild search out all "gignori" who were fourteen years old, and if they had not sworn allegiance to the statute of the guild, they were then forced to do so.[30] I believe that we can take these items as approximate guidelines for conditions in the Painters' Guild.[31]

By comparison, Cennino Cennini, in his *Libro dell'arte,* recommends apprenticeships of thirteen years, but that recommendation was either wishful thinking or the rather pedan-

---

26. Beatson, Muller, and Steinhoff, "The St. Victor Altarpiece in Siena Cathedral," 610–31.

27. Hayden B. J. Maginnis, "The So-called Dijon Master," *Zeitschrift für Kunstgeschichte,* XLII, 1980, 121–38. I would now make some modifications of the text.

28. Several works from the Ambrogio circle are illustrated in volume II of George Rowley's eccentric and rather unreliable *Ambrogio Lorenzetti,* Princeton, 1958.

29. Milanesi, *Documenti,* I, 78.

30. Banchi and Polidori, *Statuti senesi,* II, 292.

31. On the age of majority: Magnate families seem to have emancipated sons at age twenty-five, but it seems that, generally, twenty was the age of majority. The constitution of 1309–10 indicates that the Biccherna could not employ anyone younger than twenty (Lisini, *Costituto volgarizzato,* I, 109). At the midcentury, marriages by those younger than twenty were prohibited (F. Donati, "Provvisioni della repubblica sopra i matrimoni," *Miscellanea storica senese,* I, 1893, 167–68). On the other hand, the 1309–10 constitution required all foreign judges, notaries, and other officials to be at least twenty-five (Lisini, *Costituto volgarizzato,* I, 137–38).

Pinacoteca Nazionale, no. 15). It should be emphasized that the Sienese situation is unique. We have no evidence for comparable developments elsewhere in the central Italy of the Dugento.[24]

For a time, at least, a similar organization must have formed around Duccio, although his economic circumstances, toward and at the end of his life, suggest it is unlikely he sustained the arrangement for long. It is, instead, with the circle of Simone Martini that the dugento precedent found its trecento equivalent. Quite early in the painter's known career, several different painters appear in his works, executing not merely secondary elements but also entire figures. A cluster of works produced for churches in Orvieto in the 1320s speak of different authors, although all are tied to the Simone shop; even in Simone's Pisa polyptych of 1319 (Color Plate 12, Figs. 36–38), different painters were responsible for the Magdalen and Saint Catherine in the main tier of the altarpiece. And after Simone's departure for Avignon, a group of painters of or from that shop produced the New Testament cycle in the Collegiata of San Gimignano, as well as numerous panel pictures.

I suggest that we may have documentary evidence, although indirect, of a collaborative shop in the orbit of Simone. In the last chapter, I noted large-scale property acquisitions by the brothers Memmi in 1343/44, property acquired for the very significant sum of £1,255. We know that the Memmi continued to work after these purchases, but one explanation for the sudden availability of such sums could well be the dissolution of an artistic consortium in anticipation of retirement.

It is hardly surprising that Siena should produce such arrangements: painters were responding to the corporate mentality that, as we have seen, infused Sienese society. As the wealth of Siena had been created by joint ventures, and as the organization of everything from government to confraternities to pious bequests expressed the conviction that collective effort was of greatest efficacy, so painters understood the benefits of alliance.[25] Here is an aspect of Sienese artistic production that must figure prominently in any history of Sienese images.

Other arrangements among painters come closer to our long-held ideas about collaborations. When Bartolommeo Bulgarini and the Master of Palazzo Venezia created the

---

24. For a fuller discussion of this problem, see my "Everything in a Name? The Classification of Sienese Dugento Painting," *Studies in the History of Art,* forthcoming.

From the turn of the thirteenth/fourteenth centuries we have, of course, the collaboration of several painters in the *Saint Francis Legend* in the basilica of San Francesco, Assisi. This would seem, however, to be an instance of painters coming together for a single project, not for continued work on multiple projects.

25. I suspect that within the framework I am proposing, specifics varied in individual "joint ventures." For example: In May of 1384, Fede di Nalduccio and Lando di Stefano formed a yearlong partnership in which Fede provided the equipment, the workshop itself, and some cash, valued together at 110 florins. Lando was responsible for all the work (i.e., the actual painting) and for selling the work. In a year's time, the cost of materials was to be deducted from the gross income and returned to Fede, while the remaining profits were to be divided equally between the two painters. In other cases, partnerships were, I suspect, more on the line of collaboration. See Milanesi, *Documenti,* I, 307–9, and Larner, *Culture and Society,* 289–90.

of categories of members of the guild found in the rubric on the celebration of the feast of Saint Luke. We may therefore presume that "compagni" are included among "maestri." Yet there may be a nuance to the term. The guild's prohibition, in chapter XXXI, on a painter's taking a shop in his own name when "compagno uno overo più" will work there indicates that the fine of £10 is to be imposed only on the painter who rents the premises; and a related chapter, from the statute of the Goldsmiths' Guild, on the head of the shop who takes a "compagno" without prior deliberation of the guild, specifies that the head is to be fined £25, while the "compagno" is to pay £10.[23] The painters' statute makes another reference to a "compagno." Chapter XVI, which deals with the election of officials of the guild, prohibits those charged with electing new officials from electing a family relative or their "compagno in buttiga" (close collaborator in the shop).

Given the comparative rarity of notices (about painters) that refer to a "compagno" or "compagni," one might assume that instances of such collaboration were equally infrequent. That would be to err. The visual evidence urges us toward the conclusion that associations of equal or near equal painters, what I shall call artistic consortia, were major factors in Siena from the 1260s onward. The pictures normally associated with Guido da Siena and his following and dated to the 1270s and 1280s are not to be explained by our traditional notions of workshop organization and master/pupil relations. Among surviving pictures (and much is lost) are works of equal importance executed by different painters. The San Bernardino Master, an artist often confused with Guido, created his eponymous work (Fig. 8; Siena, Pinacoteca Nazionale, no. 16) for a Franciscan confraternity, likely the Company of the Virgin and Saint Francis, discussed in Chapter I; Guido painted a large *Madonna* (Fig. 32) for the Dominicans or for a confraternity attached to their church; but neither painter created the so-called *Madonna del Voto* believed to have once stood on the high altar of Siena cathedral. Guido produced the dossal no. 7 in the Siena Pinacoteca (Fig. 7); another artist was responsible for the dossal no. 6 (Fig. 6). These two works, which have both been reduced in size by one figure at either extremity, were surely created for high altars in major churches. Within the group of panels normally attributed to Guido and his followers, there is a complex web of interconnections. For example, a *Madonna* now in the Accademia of Florence (Fig. 79) combines compositional elements from the San Bernardino and San Domenico *Madonna*s. The painters of the Siena dossals nos. 6 and 7 used the same figure for Saint John the Evangelist. Clearly, there are connections between the panel of the *Annunciation* now in the Art Museum of Princeton University (Fig. 33) and the treatment of the same subject in the eponymous work of the Saint Peter Master (Fig. 34; Siena,

23. Since the 1985 exhibition, *Simone Martini e "chompagni,"* the word has been increasingly used in connection with Simone. While this is, I believe, justified, we should note that the term is not found in any document relating directly to Simone himself. A. Bagnoli and L. Bellosi, *Simone Martini e "chompagni,"* Florence, 1985.

For the Goldsmiths' Guild, see Milanesi, *Documenti*, I, 97: "Et neuono orafo sel possa fare compagno, se prima non è diliberato per la detta università: pena a colui che facesse buttiga, lire vinticinque, e a colui che sel facesse compagno, diece lire."

December 1310 the *sindaco* of the hospital of the Misericordia in Siena brought the painters Sabatino di Ramo, Mino Prete, and Mino di Graziano before a judge of the Terzo di Camollia to enforce payment of rent owed by the painters to the Misericordia.[15] The document refers to the rental property as a *domo,* or house, but since the painters are identified as belonging to different parishes, we may assume the property rented was for the exercise of their art.[16] Pasquino di Cenne, a Sienese painter living in Florence, formed a society with five other painters on 25 September 1330 in order jointly to pursue their work.[17] While this is a Florentine arrangement, Pasquino obviously found the idea acceptable. On 13 December 1353 Bartoli di Fredi and Andrea Vanni jointly rented a workshop from the Misericordia of Siena.[18] It would be unwise, however, to draw conclusions from the paucity of documentary evidence regarding such associations. Such documents were generated largely by rental agreements, and the renting of workspace was most common among the less successful, those who did not own real estate that could accommodate their trade. A case in point is that of Niccolò di Segna, who on 4 November 1331 rented a workshop for two years from the Sienese Misericordia, at the rate of 4 florins a year.[19] By contrast, one would not expect to find such rentals on the part of the more prosperous painters, the major figures, among whom the whole issue of collaboration is most pressing. Moreover, it is hard to believe that the guild would be intent on regulating a phenomenon as rare as these few notices suggest.

Four documentary notices provide us with evidence of another sort. One deals with a payment of 1 lira, 2 soldi, and 6 denari, on 30 December 1316, to a minor master, Vitaluccio di Rosso, and "suo compagno dipentore" for painting the covers of fifty-four books belonging to the podestà.[20] Two are related to Donato (Martini) and "tre compagni," who, on 31 December 1331, were paid for inscriptions painted at the baths of Petriolo and Macereto.[21] Remarkably enough, it was as partial payment for "dipentura del bangno di maciereto" that a certain "Guido dipentore e compagni" were paid 19 lire and 1 soldo on 30 June 1338.[22] The word "compagno" suggests a relation of equality, not only because of its literal meaning, but also because the statute does not include "compagni" among the list

---

15. Borghesi and Banchi, *Nuovi documenti,* 8–10.

16. Sabatino di Ramo and Mino Prete resided in the *popolo* of Sant'Egidio, Mino di Graziano in San Donato. The word *domo* is also used in the document recording Niccolò di Segna's rental (1331) of a workshop from the Misericordia. Borghesi and Banchi, *Nuovi documenti,* 16–17.

17. Borghesi and Banchi, *Nuovi documenti,* 14–16. On 17 December 1344, Pasquino and Vanni Cinuzzi provided the Mercanzia of Florence an estimate of the merchandise and equipment on the workshop shared by Tommè di Vanni "da Siena" and Francesco di Cialli "da Firenze, pittori." See Milanesi, *Nuovi documenti,* 37.

18. Borghesi and Banchi, *Nuovi documenti,* 27.

19. Borghesi and Banchi, *Nuovi documenti,* 16–17. This agreement was made while Simone Bulgarini, father to the painter Bartolommeo Bulgarini, was rector of the Misericordia, as the document itself testifies. The contract also specifies that Niccolò had declared "that he exercises the profession of painting by himself."

20. ASS, Biccherna 132, fol. 140v. Vitaluccio, in 1311, decorated book covers along with a painter identified only as Nichuluccio, and in 1314 he was collaborating with Guido di Cino in decorating book covers. See Appendix IV of this volume.

21. ASS, Biccherna 171, fols. 101v., 108r.

22. ASS, Biccherna 191, fol. 145r; Biccherna 194, fol. 62r.

Chapters I and XVII raise important and vexing questions about working arrangements among painters. In detailing the observances for the feast of Saint Luke, the guild's patron saint, the first chapter specifies that "each and every painter, whether he be a master or a laborer engaged for the year, or the month, or the day, or just for a specific job," must carry a candle to the celebration. Chapter XVII, we recall, forbids painters to lure away "laborers [on contract] . . . on an annual or a monthly basis" from another painter.[12] The significance of these brief passages cannot be over emphasized. They point to circumstances otherwise unrecorded in contemporary documents, and acknowledge arrangements that fall well beyond our usual conception of workshop structure. In spite of the fact that this text has been available to scholars in printed form since 1782, most discussions of workshops suggest a situation wherein the master was surrounded by apprentices at various stages in their training.[13] But the passage quoted above suggests that the reality could be more complex. Of course, it makes perfect sense that for projects such as Duccio's cathedral *Maestà* (Color Plates 1–2, 10–11) or Pietro Lorenzetti's frescoes in the Lower Church of San Francesco, in Assisi (Figs. 39–44), the master would require a far larger équipe than he ordinarily maintained, but the passage allows for far more. The availability of workers for a month or a day suggests painters may have engaged others on a short-term basis as the workload varied, and that suggests the existence of painters capable of adapting their own style—insomuch as they had one—to that of their temporary masters, at least to the degree that ensured general uniformity in any one work.[14]

Chapter XXXI deals with the prohibition on a painter's renting a workshop in his own name when the space was to be shared by an associate or associates ("compagno uno overo più"), and was a means by which the guild had record of all painters working in the city and assurance that no one, unbeknownst to the guild, was violating the guild statute. But the need for a provision on this subject directs us again to questions of workshop structure and collaborations. Documentary evidence on this matter is scant indeed. On 4

Further to the matter of working days: R. Goldthwaite (*The Building of Renaissance Florence: An Economic and Social History,* London and Baltimore, 1980, 289) estimates about 270 working days a year. M. Haines (*The Sacrestia delle Messe of the Florentine Cathedral,* Florence, 1983, 53) estimates the working year at 248 days. See also D. Degrassi, *L'economia artigiana nell'Italia medievale,* Rome, 1996, 73. I thank Margaret Haines for advising me on this comparative material.

12. The statute of the Goldsmiths' Guild also speaks of "lavorenti o gignori che fussero obligati a' loro maestri, o ad anno o a mese." Milanesi, *Documenti,* I, 71.

13. The *Breve* of the painters was first published by Guglielmo della Valle, *Lettere sanesi sopra le belle arti,* I, Venice, 1782, 143–61.

14. The text thus challenges some of our most basic assumptions and our conviction that all works can be ordered according to artistic personalities. On the other hand, it may explain why, in many instances, we have "identified" minor artists in one or two works but can map no larger oeuvre for those painters.

Perhaps the best case for study of such possibilities is Duccio's cathedral *Maestà,* wherein a number of the narrative scenes suggest different hands were involved. James Stubblebine argued that Duccio gathered his most distinguished followers to assist in the enormous task of executing the altarpiece, but his claims to have identified painters such as Simone and the Lorenzetti in the work are entirely unconvincing. I believe that we are better served by hypotheses arising from the situation here discussed.

The guild's statute tempts us to speculate on the shape of a painter's work-year. Chapter x prohibits working on holidays decreed by the Church and the Mercanzia. Still later, in chapters xxxv and xxxvi, there are further clarifications and a noteworthy qualification of the previous regulations. Chapter xxxvi lists fifty-seven feasts on which work was prohibited, and describes them as feasts declared by the Church "as well as *some* other holidays established by order of the Consuls of the Mercanzia" (emphasis mine).[9] In addition, painters had to observe the vigils for the major feasts of the Virgin, Easter day, and Saturdays. But several uncertainties enter the matter. Chapter x makes a noteworthy exception to required holidays: "[T]he Rector will be able to grant permission to work to those who will request it discreetly and for a good reason, keeping always in mind the necessities of the time and work and *being it understood that no dispensation will be required for work commissioned by the Commune*" (emphasis mine). Whether the prohibition in chapter xxxv regarding work on Saturdays meant all day is unclear, but it is unlikely that it did; the Goldsmiths' Guild specifies all Saturdays beginning at Vespers, and that is probably the intention here.[10] There is no mention of Sundays in the *Breve dei pittori*, but in the statutes of the Goldsmiths' Guild, the Butchers' Guild, the Leatherworkers' and Shoemakers' Guild, and the statute of the powerful Mercanzia, which oversaw the other guilds, every Sunday is specified as a time when work must stop. The statute also requires guild members to attend the funerals of their colleagues and of close relatives of fellow painters, thus introducing absences from work that we cannot estimate.

Undoubtedly there were exceptions made, as in the case of work for the commune, and violations unrecorded in connection with all these prohibitions. There were, of course, also occasions when the named feasts fell on Sundays, but those days could be counterbalanced by part-day holidays on Saturdays and obligations such as those to attend funerals. I would therefore suggest that painters had something like 242 working days a year and, in reality, perhaps something less, perhaps something more.[11]

---

9. Note that the list of chapter xxxvi included the feast of San Ansano but not the feasts of Crescenzio, Savino, or Vittorio. See my remarks about these figures in Chapter II.

10. The *Breve dell'Arte degli Orafi senesi* similarly provides us with what was likely the intention of the painters in declaring the observance of the vigils of various feasts: work was to halt at Vespers on vigils. Milanesi, *Documenti*, I, 74.

11. Those painters who belonged to confraternities would have had other obligations to fulfill that took them away from work. See the discussion of confraternities in Chapter II.

Some comparative numbers are in order. The Arte della Lana specifies (1289–1309) some seventy-eight feasts and, presumably, all Sundays. The Arte de' Cuoiai e Calzolai (1329–35) lists all Sundays and sixty-two feast days. The statute of the Mercanzia (1342–43) lists all Sundays and sixty-four other feasts to be observed, but the opening chapter provides for a large number of exceptions. The Arte de' Chiarvari's statute (1323–1402) lists, as holidays, Maundy Thursday (at the discretion of the rector), all Saturdays after Vespers, Christmas, Easter Sunday, Good Friday, Pentecost, Corpus Domini, All Saints, and the four feasts of the Virgin after Vespers and the feasts themselves, and twenty-nine other feasts as nonworking days. Although not mentioned, all Sundays were presumably included. The statute of the Butchers' Guild (1288–1361) declares as holidays all Sundays and thirty-two other feast days. See Milanesi, *Documenti*, I; Banchi and Polidori, *Statuti senesi*, I and II; Senigaglia, "Lo Statuto dell'Arte della Mercanzia senese," 81–85.

period of 1295 to 1363 that relate to "foreign" painters either trained or active in Florence; in 1327 the Sienese Guido di Nerio and Ambrogio Lorenzetti matriculated in the Florentine Guild of the Medici e Speziali; in 1330 the Sienese Pasquino di Cenne formed a consortium with other painters in Florence.[5]

Two chapters of the 1356 statute are fascinating for indicating variety within the guild's membership. The chapter that deals with foreign painters speaks of "all shop and wall master painters" and chapter VIII, which prohibits one painter's taking work away from another, speaks of "painters of figures, coats of arms, and walls." The latter suggests that there were distinctions—we might say specializations—within the profession that guild members recognized. The former also indicates differences, but is still more interesting for seeming to indicate that "wall master painters" might not (or did not) have a workshop. In combination with the categories of chapter VIII, which separate painters of figures and painters of walls, this passage may refer to painters of what we would describe as interior decoration.[6] One of the additions of 1358, chapter XLVII, provides further evidence; it speaks of "figure painters, sign and wall painters," and describes these as "all the different categories of the painting trade."[7]

The *Breve dell'Arte dei Pittori senesi* provides us with evidence that painters themselves acknowledged differences in status within the profession. When, in chapter III, the statute lays down the requirement of attendance at the funerals of painters or their relatives, it says that the rector shall request the presence of one or two men from every shop "according to the importance of the deceased." In chapter XXIV, which speaks of appointing two or three members to assist the rector in emending the statute, it says those chosen should be "the best and wisest" of the guild. And in chapter XLVIII, which concerns the appointment of the rector, the statute specifies that the three chosen electors are to be from "the best and most capable." It was, then, not only patrons who distinguished between major and minor talents.[8]

---

of the fourteenth century or the beginning of the fifteenth. The repetition of Antonio di Giovanni may signal that these names have been inserted from another list.

Arti 59 is a highly confusing document that needs more study. The manuscript contains many insertions. Many of the sections on approvals of the statutes are insertions later than the principal text.

For some of the painters in this list, see the appendixes that conclude this volume.

5. Milanesi, *Nuovi documenti,* 11–58. See also Appendix III of this volume.

6. My interpretation is supported, I believe, by the fact that "figure painters" worked both in tempera and fresco. No one would expect otherwise. Therefore the distinction made here is not a separation between those who worked on panel and those who worked in fresco, but rather a separation of those producing "fine art" and those concerned with decoration.

7. Franco Sacchetti, in his *Trecentonovelle,* tells a story regarding Buonamico Bartolo Gioggi, "dipintore de camere," who is painting a room for Pino Brunelleschi di Firenze and has been told to paint many birds above and in the trees. Here, then, we deal with what we would describe as interior decoration. See Franco Sacchetti, *Il trecentonovelle,* ed. V. Marucucci, Rome, 1996, 568–70.

8. Perhaps something similar is found in chapters XLII and XLIII, where, in fining members for violating guild regulations, the rector is left to determine the amount after considering "the quality of the person" to be fined. But this passage is less clear in its intent.

of the guild and for refusing to assume guild offices, the latter suggesting that members were perhaps reluctant to take on such appointments. At the still higher level of £10 were fines for a painter who took work away from another, who rented a workshop in his own name when he intended to share the space with others, and who substituted one metal for another or one pigment for that promised, such as "false gold for fine gold, tin for silver, azurite for ultramarine blue, ceruse or indigo for blue, terra rossa or minium for cinnabar." Chapter XVII indicates that the highest fine, some £25, was reserved for those who try to "entice, flatter, and suborn laborers to leave employment with another painter, to whom they are contractually bound on an annual or monthly basis." This list of more-major fines indicates the offences the guild regarded as most serious—and most likely.

Chapter XI deals with the matter of non-Sienese painters working in the city and requires "foreign" artists to pay the guild 1 florin and to provide a surety of up to £25 before beginning work. The sums were not inordinate for a painter with a major commission; the regulation was, however, academic. After Coppo di Marcovaldo's *Madonna del Bordone* (1261) for the Servites of Siena, no major work in the city was created by a "foreign" artist. But the same fees applied to a "foreign" assistant hired by a Sienese painter, a circumstance that must have discouraged artists from looking abroad for assistants. Indeed, with the notable exception of Giovanni da Pisa, named as "discepolo" of Lippo Memmi in 1327, Sienese documents do not indicate the presence of non-Sienese assistants in the city during the period here studied.[3]

The situation in Siena differed markedly from circumstances in Florence. When, in 1356, a list of members was included with the Sienese statute, not a single artist was specified as having come from another town or city, unless it were "Franciescho di Vanni deto *Chiancianese*."[4] By contrast, Gaetano Milanesi published some nineteen notices from the

3. Bacci, *Fonti e commenti*, 149–50.

4. The list includes Lippo di Vanni, Iacomo di frate Mino, Lucha di Thomè, Christofano di Chosona, Fede di Nalduccio, Giovanni di Sera, Pietro di Ser Dota, Paolo del maestro Neri, Angnolo di Nalduccio, Bartalo del maestro Fredi, Iacomo di Cino Arrighi, Andrea di Vanni, Nicholò di Buonachorso, Galgano del maestro Minuccio, Biago di Ghoro, Christofano del maestro Bondoccio, Francesco di Piero, Nello Betti, Iacomo di Bindo, Franciescho di Neri, Nicchollò del maestro Vannuccio, Francio di Vannuccio, Andrea di Franciescho, Paolo di Viva, Andrea di Turino, Tomassso di Niccholuccio, Chele di Vanni, Franciescho di Vanni, Ghabriello di Saracino, Lorenzo di Vanni, Piero di Bacharello, Giusaffà di Filippo, Nuccio di Neruccio, Meo di Piero, Nanni di Franciescho, Angnolino di Gintile, Lando di Stefano, Paolo di Giovanni Fei, Franciescho di Vanni deto *Chiancianese*, Neri di Franciescho di Neri, Jacomo di Piero, Paulo di Giovanni, Nerino di Jacomo, Simone di Giovanni, Piero di Donato, Domenicho di Buonachorso, Andrea di Ghuido, Franciescho di Mano, Giovanni del maestro Lippo, Brandino di Ser Cieio, Antonio di Giovanni, Antonio di Giovanni, Ghuido di Domenico, Tadeo di Bartolo, Jahomo di Lippo, Franciescho d' Antonio, Nicolò d'Ambruogio, Maestro Jachomo del Vetro, Mochata di Chontro, Nicholo di Magino, Bartolomeo di Nutino, Nanni di Giovanni, Tadeio di Franciescho, and Gianino. (I preserve the original spellings.) This is the list given by Milanesi; however, there is a problem. Starting with Lippo Vanni, on fol. 20v of Arti 59, and continuing through Antonio di Giovanni on fol. 21r, the names of artists are in good lettering and have ornamented initial capital letters. After that point the names do not have ornamented capitals. Moreover, the thirteen painters that supposedly conclude the 1356 list include Taddeo di Bartolo and several artists for whom Milanesi published notices only from the end

The Painters' Guild and Working Arrangements

The earliest surviving version of the statute of the Sienese Arte dei Pittori is dated 19 February 1356 (1355 Sienese style), and that comparatively late date might seem to make it tangential to this study. But the document itself suggests it is a combination of regulations new and old, the latter derived from an earlier redaction.[1] Chapter XXIV, for example, empowers the rector of the guild to appoint two or more councillors to emend the statute: a provision one might expect to find at the end of such a document, although another twenty-four chapters follow. Moreover, there are indications that specific, subsequent chapters are additions to earlier regulations. Thus, chapter XXVII, dealing with the celebration of the feast of Saint Luke, itself says it is an elaboration of chapter I.[2] Chapter XXVIII expands upon the responsibilities of the rector, dealt with earlier, and the list of feasts to be observed by guild members, found in chapter XXVI, is an expansion of chapters II and X. Even the initial twenty-four chapters were accumulated over time. Chapter X, for example, is an elaboration of chapter II. Internal evidence therefore points to the conclusion that in 1356 the guild was by no means a new creation, nor was its statute compiled of novelties designed to address the specific historical circumstance of the previous year, the collapse of the regime of the Nine.

As we might expect of a guild statute, the majority of regulations deal with matters of the corporation: the appointment of officials, the responsibilities of the rector and the treasurer, and the members' responsibilities to the guild and its officers. We also learn that the rector was paid 20 soldi (£1) for a six-month period, that the treasurer of the guild received 15 soldi for the same period, and that the guild's messenger, or envoy, had a salary of 5 soldi for a half year's service. The statute thus tells us more about the organization of the institution, less about the individual practice of guild members. There are, however, passages that are suggestive, particularly those that include specific fines for violations of the regulations. Most offences resulted in a fine of £1, but seven chapters provide for significantly higher penalties. Three lire was the fine for perjury, £5 the fine for revealing secrets

---

1. The statute has been published by Milanesi, *Documenti*, I, 1–56, and by L. Manzoni, *Statuti e matricole dell'Arte dei Pittori delle città di Firenze, Perugia, Siena*, Rome, 1904, 81–105. A translation of the statute appears on pages 199–224 below. Professor Erasmi has translated not only the sections belonging to the 1356 redaction but also the additions made up to 1402. Among the most interesting later additions are a chapter (XLIX) that deals with celebrating the feast of the Blessed Andrea Gallerani at the church of the Misericordia, another (L) that decrees that the feast of Saint Luke should also be celebrated at Santa Maria della Misericordia, and a third (LV), of 1379, that declares the feast of Saint Luke is to be celebrated at the Ospedale di Santa Maria della Scala. Another added chapter (LIV) decrees that no painter can make signs for taverns unless he be the guild treasurer. Half the fixed price, 8 denari, must go to the guild. The Sienese constitution of 1309–10 says that no one may sell wine in small quantities (i.e., for immediate consumption) unless he has a painted sign. Lisini, *Costituto volgarizzato*, II, 389–90.

2. Apparently, some guild members were cheating on their obligation to present a candle on the feast of Saint Luke by bringing shortened (and therefore less expensive) candles to the celebration.

III   The Painter's Craft: Conditions and Constraints

In the preceding chapter I have tried to place painters physically, economically, and socially within Siena and to sketch some of the larger circumstances that bore upon their art. Although major, and some minor, painters created works away from Siena, most remained attached to their native town, living, working, and dying in the city of the Virgin. Thus, painters' careers developed from an artistic tradition constantly before their eyes and in light of the achievements of the entire school; they also developed in a situation where one painter was another's neighbor. And their careers unfolded in a society financially capable of supporting many artists and in a society shaped by shared values and shared conceptions of the faith. Now it is time to turn to other factors directly related to artistic production. Working arrangements, media, and forms and formats of the period defined the opportunities for, and set limitations upon, artistic practice.

This linking of painters and poets, in a recollection of Horace's famous *ut pictura poësis,* lays the foundation for the changing conception of the painter that develops over the course of the fourteenth century.

The new praise and reputation of painters were part of a larger cultural strategy. As writers looked back to antiquity for the rhetoric of praise for literary works, they discovered the ancient praise of painters. From the earlier preoccupation with Aristotle, with antique philosophy and science, and with ancient law as embodied in Justinian's *Corpus juris civilis,* writers sought to appropriate the distant past, and that past linked painter and poet.[206] Thus, to what may have been an independent change in the painter's social status was added an enabling discourse that created expectations among patrons as much as it contributed to the painter's self-definition. We should note that Petrarch did not scorn to call Simone Martini a friend, nor King Robert the Wise of Naples to describe Giotto as "our faithful and familiar [friend]." When the great poet and scholar and the great monarch were willing so to do, we cannot doubt that painters had risen above the station of cobblers or tailors.

206. See Norman Land, *The Viewer as Poet,* University Park, Pa., 1994. See also Norman Land, "Giotto as an Ugly Genius: A Study in Self-Portrayal," *Explorations in Renaissance Culture,* XXIII, 1997, 23–26, with astute and related observations.

other words, the Florentines here introduce a distinction that sets the artist apart from the other craftsmen with whom he had earlier been associated.[202]

There are even adumbrations of this change in Dante. In his *De monarchia* (II.2), he writes: "Art is found on three levels: in the mind of the artist, in the tool, and in the material that receives its form from art." In the *Convivio*, he is still more explicit: "[W]e know that a painter who cannot first possess an image in the very texture of his own being is incapable of giving form to this in paint. . . . For no painter can depict externally any image that he has not first created in his own mind exactly as it is to appear."[203]

Petrarch also provides us with evidence of changing attitudes toward painters. In one of the sonnets devoted to Simone Martini's portrait of Laura, he writes:

> Quando giunse a Simon l'alto concetto
> Ch'a mio nome pose in man lo stile
>
> (When there came to Simone the elevated conceit
> That in my name placed the stylus in his hand)

Here, his "alto concetto" speaks to an intellectual capacity on the part of the artist. And, in another place, Petrarch provides us with a precious glimpse into painters' converse, one that points to their handling of ideas. Explaining that good poetry ought not merely to copy the style of venerated masters but should have only a family resemblance, he likens the desirable relation to that of father and son: "In these, even though very diverse of aspect, something indefinite and what painters call an air, seen above all in the face and eyes, produces a similarity which immediately upon seeing the son reminds us of the father, although, if one descends to an examination of particulars, all appears diverse."[204]

As far as I can determine, the earliest source that points toward the attitudes discussed above is found in the work of William Durandus. In his *Rationale divinorum officiorum*, written c. 1290, Durandus writes:

> But the diverse histories of the Old and New Testaments may be represented after the fancy of the painter. For
>
> Pictoribus atque poetis
> Quod libet addendi semper fuit aeque potestas.[205]

---

202. P. L. Rubin, *Giorgio Vasari: Art and History,* London, 1995, 292–93.

203. Dante, *The Banquet,* trans. C. Ryan, Saratoga, Calif., 1989, 120, 148.

204. Petrarca, Francesco, *Prose,* ed. G. Martellotti et al., Milan and Naples, 1955, 1018–19.

205. Durandus, G. *The Symbolism of Churches and Church Ornaments: A Translation of the First Book of the Rationale Divinorum Officiorum Written by William Durandus,* trans. J. M. Neale and B. Webb, 3d ed., London, 1906, 52.

ebbe, le quagli vinti e tre libre et iiij soldi demo per lui a maestro Lippo Memmi, in mano di Gabriello di misser Mino, suo garzone."[197] Pèleo Bacci believed that "Gabriello di misser Mino" was the son of Mino di Cino, rector of the hospital, and that "suo garzone" referred back to Lippo Memmi; in other words, the son of the rector was apprenticed to Lippo. For obvious reasons, I would like that to be so, but the phrasing of the document is far from clear. Documents generally refer to the "worker" or "disciple" of a painter, not the "boy," and we have no subsequent record of a Gabriello di Mino as a painter, although that might be blamed on the plague of 1348. So perhaps the "boy" was only Mino's son and not a painter, or simply the son of another Mino who really was an apprentice to Lippo Memmi. For the time being, at least, the question remains open.[198]

There are other, non-Sienese sources that reflect the changing status of the painter in the minds of his contemporaries. Around 1400, Cennino Cennini proclaimed painting's equality with poetry and sought to equate the painter and the theorist: "And it [painting] justly deserves to be enthroned next to theory, and to be crowned with poetry. The justice lies in this: that the poet, with his theory, though he have but one, it makes him worthy, is free to compose and bind together, or not, as he pleases, according to his inclination. In the same way, the painter is given freedom to compose a figure, standing, seated, half-man, half-horse, as he pleases, according to his imagination."[199] When Filippo Villani composed his *De origine civitatis Florentiae et eiusdem famosis civibus* (c. 1380–81), he concluded brief remarks on painters with the following observation: "According to the view of many intelligent people, indeed, painters are not inferior in mind to those made masters by the liberal arts, since the latter obtain by study and learning in books what is required by their arts, while painters depend only on the high mind and tenacious memory which is manifest in their art."[200] Other Florentine sources provide yet more evidence of change.

In 1334, Giotto was appointed *capomaestro* of Florence cathedral. Within the document of appointment, the priors of the commune offered an explanation of their choice: "It is said that in the whole world no one can be found who is more capable in these and other things than master Giotto di Bondone, painter of Florence. He should have cause for agreeing to a continued domicile. Within this many will profit from his knowledge and learning [*scientia et doctrina*] so that no little beauty will come to this city."[201] As Pat Rubin has pointed out, the document speaks clearly to the changing status of the artist, for *scientia* and *doctrina* are the very terms used to distinguish the liberal from the mechanical arts. In

---

197. ASS, Spedale 851, fol. 65r (7 August 1344). Bacci, *Fonti e commenti*, 189.

198. If all the notices, in Appendix III, referring to Bonaccorso di Pace are really references to the painter, then we have an artist old enough to marry in 1348 who rose to hold places in Siena's government.

199. Cennino d'Andrea Cennini, *The Craftsman's Handbook: The Italian "Il Libro dell'Arte,"* trans. D. V. Thompson Jr., New York, 1960 (originally published in 1933), 1–2. It should be noted that no less an author than Boccaccio had argued, in defense of his *Decameron*, the reverse: that the poet should be given the freedom of the painter. See Maginnis, *Age of Giotto*, 194.

200. Larner, *Culture and Society*, 279–80.

201. Larner, *Culture and Society*, 305.

career as a painter, we do not know, but we here have evidence that painting was not regarded as only suitable for those of humble background; and that must have been the case by the 1330s, when Bartolommeo was trained. Bartolommeo Bulgarini may well have been the first gentleman painter of the Renaissance.

I would also note that, as their names indicate, Pietro di Ser Dota, Brandino di Ser Cieio, and Niccolò di Ser Sozzo were sons of men of learning, probably notaries. Here, then, are three further instances of painters whose family backgrounds were not those of artisans.

Another, rather remarkable case that suggests social mobility for painters involves Pietro Lorenzetti. When, in 1344, Pietro sold land to the sons of Tino di Camaino, the painter's wife was identified as "domina Iohanna eius uxor et filia olim Mini Cicerchie" (Lady Giovanna, his wife, and daughter of Mino di Cicerchia). Now, the Cicerchia were a Noveschi family. Niccolò di Mino Cicerchia was treasurer of the General Gabella for the first half of 1355.[195] References to the family are rare in Sienese documents, but it seems highly unlikely that there was more than one Mino di Cicerchia in the city during the early years of the Trecento. Pietro, then, seems to have married into the Noveschi class.[196]

One last and highly problematic document belongs to the discussion. On 7 August 1344, the Ospedale della Scala paid 7 florins and 2 soldi, which it owed to Simone Martini, to Lippo Memmi. The document reads: "Sabato a dì vij d'agosto. Maestro Simone Martini,

---

is recorded as resident in that *popolo* in 1302. For these notices, see Stefano Moscadelli, "Appendice documentaria," in *Ambrogio Lorenzetti cronista nuziale,* by M. Seidel, Turin, 1993, 288–89.

Bartolommeo and his wife retained use of their property for life. A list of the properties involved is found in ASS, Ospedale 170, fol. 244v, published by Millard Meiss, "Bartolommeo Bulgari, altrimenti detto 'Ugolino Lorenzetti,'" *Rivista d'arte,* xviii, 1936, 119 n. 1. The list, which indicates the painter and his wife lived in the parish of San Pietro a Ovile, has seventeen items, and includes three houses and nineteen pieces of land. Unfortunately, there are no estimated values. Another document (ASS, Ospedale 62, fol. 78r), also published by Meiss, that deals with the same donation refers to a farm in Castel Berardenga. In 1374, Bartolommeo is described as "vicar" of the hospital (C. Alessi, "Bartolomeo Bulgarini," in *Il gotico a Siena,* Florence, 1982, 250).

195. Bowsky, *Medieval Italian Commune,* 303. Milanesi (*Documenti,* i, 194) says that Giovanna was Niccolò's sister, but he does not cite a source. To Niccolò di Mino Cicerchia have been attributed two lengthy poems, "La passione" and "La risurrezione," edited by G. Varanini (*Cantari religiosi senesi del trecento,* Bari, 1965, 537–606) and dated to 1364. But, as B. Degenhart and A. Schmitt have pointed out (*Corpus der italienischen Zeichnungen 1300–1450,* Berlin, 1968, pt. i, vol. 1, 84), the Biblioteca Comunale in Siena has a manuscript (I.vi.9) that contains "La passione" and a note (fol. 122v) that dates the manuscript to May of 1333 or 1334 and tells us that the manuscript belonged to the Compagnia dei Disciplinati at the Ospedale di Santa Maria della Scala. (The manuscript also contains lauds by Jacopone da Todi.) There is, however, no author named in connection with "La passione." If, as it would appear, the poem belongs to the first half of the fourth decade of the century, then it is worth noting that it seems to have had little or no influence on contemporary painted imagery.

196. In November of 1337, Pietro paid the commune 1 lira, 11 soldi, and 9 denari, and in November of 1338, 1 lira, 11 soldi, and 6 denari, for the right to carry defensive arms (Bacci, *Dipinti inediti,* 93–94). Perhaps, in light of the social background of Pietro's wife, the painter's desire for these licenses was not so much connected with the threat of real harm and the need for personal defense as with the social status implied in the bearing of arms.

defray the expense of their new high altarpiece, claiming that it had cost £300, or roughly 83.5 florins. When the Carmelites approached the commune, on 30 June 1329, for a similar subsidy, they said that their new high altarpiece, painted by Pietro Lorenzetti, had cost them 150 florins (roughly £498). The Servite altarpiece is lost or unidentified; most of the Carmelite altarpiece survives, and thus we know it was a very large work, with a central *Madonna and Child Enthroned with Saints and Angels* (Figs. 59–60), four panels—two to either side—with full-length saints below and half-length saints above, and a complete painted predella. In November of 1335, Pietro received 30 florins (£90) from the Opera del Duomo as "the first payment for painting the panel of San Savino" for the cathedral. The phrasing suggests that the payment is salary. The next month, December, saw the Opera pay "maestro Ciecho de la grammatica" for translating the story of San Savino into the vernacular, to be used for Pietro's altarpiece, presumably in the predella. Clearly, these payments related to the very beginning of the project, yet they amounted to more than half of Pietro's total income from the Arezzo altarpiece, although in the Aretine commission he had to bear the costs of materials.[156] On 27 October 1340, Pietro promised to paint two panels for Paolo di Tingo de' Pilestri, of the parish of San Giorgio, for which he had already received 40 florins.

As in Pietro's case, we have only partial record of expenditures on Ambrogio Lorenzetti's altarpiece for the cathedral, the central panel of which (Figs. 21–22) is inscribed with the date 1342. Although the Opera acquired wood for the altarpiece in June of 1337, the first surviving payment to Ambrogio "for painting the panel of San Crescenzio" comes from July of 1339. He was then paid 30 florins, or 95 lire and 10 soldi. In January of 1340, Ambrogio received a further 30 florins as partial payment for painting the altarpiece. Further acquisition of wood for the "columns" and predella of the work occurred in May of 1340, indicating that the commission was still unfinished. Thus we have a total of 60 florins paid the painter, although the earliest payment may be lost and the project was incomplete.[157]

In the Entrata/Uscita volume of the Opera del Duomo for the semester July to December 1333 is the summary of expenditures for the San Ansano altarpiece by Simone Martini and Lippo Memmi. The project was begun in 1331; the surviving notices contain separate payments for the wood of the panel and for woodworking. Lippo Memmi received 70 florins (212 lire, 6 soldi, 8 denari) for adorning the "cholone civori e ciercini de la tavola," surely the gilding and the gold acquired for that gilding. But the most remarkable item, now legible only under ultraviolet light, records the payment of 34 florins to Simone and Lippo for "the completion of the painting of the panel" and says explicitly that this is the final installment on 100 florins (£300) that the painters ought to have for painting the panel.[158] We assume this record is complete, but I should note that the entries themselves

156. If the Opera del Duomo was employing a system similar to that used in Arezzo, that is, payment in three installments, Pietro would have received some 90 florins in total.

157. See my "Chiarimenti documentari."

158. When Bacci published his discussion of Simone in his *Fonti e commenti,* he was unable to read all of this item. Martindale published a faulty transcription, which was corrected (with a few small inaccuracies) by Frederick. I owe the follow-

teem. It also suggests that major painters were in a position to negotiate advantageous arrangements. The Noveschi generally tried to set financial arrangements in terms of local currency and, in the case of the lira, local accounting because they were fully aware of the ongoing decrease in its value against the florin. Indeed, a rubric of the 1337–39 version of the Sienese constitution ordered that all contracts with mercenaries were to be made only in Sienese coin, not in florins.[155]

Does this change indicate a new ability of artists to negotiate with greater effectiveness? Does the change signal an alteration in the social status of the painter? This is a matter to which I return below.

The observations above point toward two general conclusions. My estimates regarding the annual incomes of painters and the cost of specific projects might have startled workers and officials lower on the economic ladder. We deal with real prosperity, at least in regard to major masters. But it is difficult for us to grasp the meaning of the sums discussed, because our modern notions of proportional costs are simply inapplicable. Simone's *Annunciation* cost the commune the price of a very good house indeed, but only about two-thirds the cost of acquiring candles for a five-month period or of paving a street.

Finally, I would note that in Siena of the period, as in most preindustrial societies, the cost of living was extremely high. My example above concerning the price of grain is one demonstration of that fact, but we might easily accumulate others. And it is that high cost of living that makes the property values, discussed earlier, so important to my theme. Property acquisitions could only come from disposable wealth, after all the necessities of existence had been paid for.

Matters Financial: The Price of Altarpieces

The reader will have noted considerable variation in the costs of altarpieces given above, and those figures, when set in comparison, reveal something that I, at least, find startling. Duccio, for the Rucellai *Madonna* (Fig. 10), received approximately 91.4 florins, the artist providing the gold and colors for the work. In his native city, in 1302, he was paid £48 (roughly 19 florins) as salary for his lost *Maestà* and a predella for the chapel of the Nove. The contract for the Arezzo altarpiece (Color Plate 13), drawn up in April of 1320, specified that Pietro Lorenzetti had to supply labor, gold, silver, and colors, for which he was to receive approximately 54 florins (160 Pisan lire). In both cases, the patron was to supply the panel. Given the difference in size between the Rucellai *Madonna* and the Arezzo altarpiece, it might seem that the rate of payment for the two was similar. But we need to look again at developments in Siena itself.

On 19 October 1319, the Servites of Siena petitioned the commune for a grant to

---

155. Bowsky, *Medieval Italian Commune*, 229.

tino di Giovanni, also for 6,000 florins.[148] From surviving documentation (notices of unknown number are certainly lost), Bargagli-Petrucci calculated that in the Trecento the commune spent 43,005 lire, 1 soldo, and 1 denaro on this project alone.[149]

One other commodity should briefly occupy our attention, since it was so very important to the fabric of Siena. I refer to bricks.[150] In 1301, while the Palazzo Pubblico was in construction, a thousand bricks cost 2 lire and 15 soldi. This was more than double the cost (1 lira and 6 soldi) of 1250. By 1303, the cost had risen to £3, and in 1309–10 the commune officially lowered the price to 2 lire and 15 soldi for the best quality bricks, while the price of lower-quality brick was set at £2. Balestracci and Piccinni indicate that these sums did not reflect the actual market price. In 1325, when the commune set the price of a thousand bricks at £3, £4 was the real cost. Cost continued to rise throughout the period of this study, reaching 4 lire and 10 soldi in 1336, and 6 lire and 10 soldi in 1362.[151] These increases, which were significantly more than inflation required, obviously influenced the price of real estate.

Two other economic issues demand brief attention at this point. Siena, like many a modern state, was afflicted with inflation. Between 1287 and 1355 the Sienese lira suffered a monetary devaluation of approximately 50 percent in relation to the florin.[152] We have some indications that painters tried to protect themselves from this phenomenon and that patrons were willing to assist. Payments for decorating Biccherna covers rose from approximately £1 in the late thirteenth century to roughly £1.5 or even £2 by the mid-Trecento.[153] But the most important change came in the way payments for large projects were reckoned. With the exception of one document for the *Maestà,* all payments to Duccio were calculated in lire, as was the contract for Pietro Lorenzetti's Arezzo polyptych. One of Simone's payments for the Palazzo Pubblico *Maestà* (1315) was reckoned in lire, the other in florins. From this date on, payments by the commune and the Opera del Duomo to major artists were increasingly noted in florins first and then converted, at the current rate of exchange, into lire.[154] This suggests that the initial agreements were set in terms of florins. With projects stretching over some time, that arrangement could be an important insurance for the painter, a protection of his real income against erosion.

The fact that the commune was willing to conduct business with painters in florins is revealing; it suggests that painters, at least major painters, were held in considerable es-

148. Bargagli-Petrucci, *Le fonti,* II, 214–26.

149. Bargagli-Petrucci, *Le fonti,* II, 132–33. These pages include a breakdown, in table form, of the sums spent on the various fountains. For the entire Trecento, all recorded expenditures come to 87,550 lire, 3 soldi, and 9 denari.

150. See the various civic projects and provisions discussed in Chapter V, in the section "A Sense of Beauty/A Sense of Order."

151. All of these figures are from Balestracci and Piccinni, *Siena nel trecento,* 69–70.

152. Bowsky, *Finance,* 46.

153. See Appendix IV.

154. There might seem to be an exception to my generalization in that the Opera del Duomo's record of expenditure on Simone's San Ansano altarpiece is in lire. But this seems a record of payments already made and likely transferred to the cathedral's general accounts from a volume devoted to the project. The original payments may therefore have been reckoned in florins.

4 denari.¹³⁶ The 1324 celebration of the feast of the Beato Agostino Novello cost the city 44 lire and 19 soldi.¹³⁷ Expenses connected with the feast of San Ansano in 1349 came to 79 lire and 4 soldi.¹³⁸ The 1352 expenses for the funeral of the captain of war, Guidorriccio da Fogliano, came to 497 florins and 32 soldi.¹³⁹

Perhaps even more startling to modern conceptions of reasonable expenditure were the sums involved for candles. On 10 December 1338 the Biccherna paid 110 lire, 2 soldi, and 1 denaro to Andrea Tofano for candles, standards, and their transport on the feasts of San Ansano and the Blessed Pier Pettinaio.¹⁴⁰ On 29 December of the same year the commune bought £163 worth of candles for its own use, and on 31 December paid a total of 329 lire, 10 soldi, and 8 denari for candles used in the Palazzo Pubblico, on the altar of the Nove, and on the high altar of the cathedral.¹⁴¹ These purchases were followed, in February of 1339, by an expenditure of 109 lire and 4 soldi for more candles for the high altar of the cathedral and, in April, by another £133 for candles destined for the same location.¹⁴² In just five months the commune had spent 844 lire, 16 soldi, and 8 denari on these items, and the February and April 1339 expenditures solely for candles for the cathedral came to 242 lire and 4 soldi, almost two-thirds of the entire (salary?) expenditure on Ambrogio's decorations in the Sala della Pace.¹⁴³

What we might consider a simple project of urban development could prove very expensive, at least in comparison with art prices. In 1333, the paving of the Costarella dei Barbieri with brick cost 42 lire and 4 denari.¹⁴⁴ In 1334, the paving of the Via Malcucinato, adjoining the Palazzo Pubblico, lasted approximately thirty-eight days and cost 278 lire, 2 soldi, and 5 denari.¹⁴⁵ During the same year, 206 lire, 7 soldi, and 7 denari were spent on paving the Campo, and this represented only a fraction of the expenditure on that project.¹⁴⁶ Between 1309 and 1311, the commune spent well over £1,200 for the creation of a park/marketplace between the inner and outer gates of Camollia.¹⁴⁷

The city's fountains were enormously expensive. On 16 December 1334 the commune made an agreement with Jacopo di Vanni Ugolini to bring water to the Campo within three years; in return Jacopo was to received 6,000 florins. Work was not completed, and in 1339 a new agreement was made with Jacopo di Vanni, Lando di Pietro, and Agos-

---

136. ASS, Biccherna 373, fol. 28v.
137. ASS, Biccherna 149, fol. 156r.
138. ASS, Biccherna 225, fol. 101r.
139. ASS, Biccherna 411, fol. 25v.
140. ASS, Biccherna 119, fol. 11v.
141. ASS, Biccherna 119, fols. 16r, 118r.
142. ASS, Biccherna 201, fol. 47v.
143. The price of wax and the quantities consumed help us better to understand the obligation Siena placed on subject territories of the state to present gifts of wax each year, on the feast of the Assumption of the Virgin, to the cathedral. (See also the gifts of wax by the guilds, discussed below.)

Rather than largely symbolic gestures, acknowledging Siena's authority, those gifts represented what otherwise would have been serious expenditures by the commune.
144. Balestracci and Piccini, *Siena nel trecento*, 58–59.
145. L. Zdekauer, "Le spese di selciatura e di riparazione della via di Malcucinato (1334)," *BSSP*, III, 1896, 402–5.
146. Balestracci and Piccini, *Siena nel trecento*, 59.
147. Bowsky, *Finance*, 20.

sessed between £1,000 and £5,000; eleven had properties worth less than £1,000, and fourteen had possessions valued from £10,000 to £37,000. By way of extreme contrast, a shoemaker rarely had real estate valued at £100, but the evaluation for a butcher might reach £1,000. Judges and notaries might have holdings of several thousand lire.[126] I would also note that only the most successful painters had worth that began to approach the patrimonies of the city's best goldsmiths. In 1318, the goldsmith Guccio di Mannaia had property valued at roughly £2,490, and Duccio di Donato had a patrimony of approximately £2,132.[127]

But if these figures suggest that major painters were reasonably well off, my observation about the cost of bread directs our attention to the value of art in relation to commodities and other communal expenses. Contemporary sources tell us that in 1317 a horse cost between £60 and £67, but regulations of 1304 and 1305 indicate that the loss of a warhorse could cost the commune up to 60 florins, or roughly £153.[128] In 1310 the commune decreed that £50 be spent on a *palio* for the feast of the Assumption, and indeed that was the sum spent in 1315.[129] But in 1322 total expenditures for marking the Assumption came to 175 lire and 3 soldi, and in 1327 they rose to 263 lire, 12 soldi, and 5 denari.[130] As might be supposed from the figures given above, the baldachins presented to visiting dignitaries were expensive indeed. In March of 1294 two *palii* for the king and queen of Sicily cost the commune 85 lire and 3 soldi.[131] The *palii* given to the prince of Taranto and his son in 1315 came to a total cost of 144 lire, 12 soldi, and 6 denari.[132] Those presented to the duke and duchess of Calabria in 1327 had a total cost of 246 lire, 17 soldi, and 3 denari.[133] But the cost of baldachins was only a fraction of expenses involved in the visits by, for example, members of the Angevin monarchy of Naples. The expenditures for the 1310 visit of Robert the Wise and his queen totaled some 3,070 lire, 13 soldi, and 7 denari.[134] When, in 1326, the duke and duchess of Calabria came to Siena, the visit cost the commune approximately 2,254 florins, 4 soldi, and 6 denari, or £13,599.[135]

Innumerable visits by foreign dignitaries cost the commune much, and other occasions required significant expenditure. In connection with the arrival (1314) in Siena of the body of Cardinal Riccardo Petroni, a native son, the Bicherna spent 211 lire, 7 soldi, and

126. Bowsky, *"Buon Governo,"* 373–78.
127. E. Cioni, *Scultura e smalto nell'oreficeria senese dei secoli xiii e xiv*, Florence, 1998, 151–53, 190–91.
128. Balestracci and Piccini, *Siena nel trecento*, 113 n. 1; Bowsky, *Finance*, 43.
129. Bowsky, *Finance*, 275; ASS, Biccherna 130, fol. 62r.
130. ASS, Biccherna 145, fol. 103v; Biccherna 155, fol. 14r.
131. ASS, Biccherna 100, fol. 121v.
132. ASS, Biccherna 377, fol. 115r.
133. Bacci, *Fonti e commenti*, 153–54.
134. ASS, Biccherna 124, fol. 231v.

135. ASS, Consiglio Generale 103, fols. 13r–13v (21 July 1326). One item in the list of expenses is illegible. The Sienese must have felt that the duke and duchess of Calabria were something of a trial. They came to Siena, for this visit, in 1326, on their way to Florence, which had invited the duke to assume the signory of the city for a ten-year period. As the payments to Simone Martini indicate, the duke and duchess were again in Siena in 1327. The size of the 1326 expenditures may reflect Siena's refusal to follow Florence's example of giving the signory to the duke.

the cost of other goods and services, we find that the sums were by no means insignificant. For example, c. 1333 the *operaio* of the Palazzo Pubblico received a maximum salary of £6 a month, or £72 annually.[118] The treasurers of the Biccherna and the General Gabella were ordinarily paid £50 a semester, or £100 a year, while the notary who acted as scriptor to the Biccherna treasurer earned just £10 a semester. Messengers for the Nove customarily received £2 a month, or £24 a year.[119] The constitution of 1309–10 specified that communal musicians, trumpeters, and players of shawms and tambourines should receive 30 soldi a month and be given new clothes once a year.[120] A cook, working at the Ospedale di Santa Maria della Scala in 1344, received a monthly average wage of 1 lira, 8 soldi, and 6 denari.[121] The *quattrini* who, after 1344, were charged with daytime policing of the city were paid a salary of £5 a month.[122] During work on the aqueduct of Fonte Becci, between 1340 and 1342, the masters of the work were paid an average of 6 lire, 13 soldi, and 4 denari a month, while the laborers received an average of 3 lire, 13 soldi, and 4 denari a month (43 lire and 19 soldi annually). Duccio Balestracci has argued that this last sum was insufficient to provide a laborer with caloric intake sufficient for his work.[123] In 1344, for example, a *moggia* of grain cost £15, meaning that a family of four would spend £30 annually on bread alone.[124]

We also know a good deal about remunerations for military service. Siena in this period did not have a standing army; as need required, citizens were called to arms. The podestà and other captains of that assembled force were reasonably paid: in the late thirteenth century, they received £5 a day. Members of the cavalry unit, well-to-do financially because they were drawn from those able to keep a warhorse, received £1 a day in 1292. From the beginning of the Trecento forward, Siena came to hire *condottieri* and their mounted troopers for military ventures; the latter received £22 a month in 1323 and £20 a month in 1343. But when we turn again to the citizen army and rates of pay for ordinary soldiers, the situation changes dramatically. In 1288, infantrymen received £5 a month; the same rate was used in 1307.[125]

We can do still more by way of situating painters if we return to the *Table of Possessions*. Of some seventy-one members of the Noveschi, the majority had real property as-

---

118. Martindale, *Simone Martini*, 37, 44 n. 3. This sum seems very low, but this particular remuneration may have been more of an honorarium than a salary. The position was often occupied by members of the Noveschi and magnate classes. See, in Chapter IV, "Some General Observations."

119. Bowsky, *Finance*, 7–8, 15.

120. Lisini, *Costituto volgarizzato*, I, 112–13.

121. Duccio Balestracci, "Li 'lavorati non cognosciuti': Il salariato in una città medievale (Siena 1340–1344)," *BSSP*, LXXXII–LXXXIII, 1975–76, 92.

122. Bowsky, *Medieval Italian Commune*, 122.

123. Balestracci, "Li 'lavorati non cognosciuti,' " 143.

124. My estimates regarding food are based on Fumi's calculation that each individual consumed roughly half a *moggia* of grain a year. See E. Fumi, "Fioritua e decadenza dell'economia fiorentina," *Archivio storico italiano*, CXVI, 1958, 464. U. Benvoglienti tells us that in 1329 the Nine had an allowance of 7 soldi a day for their food, or roughly £128 annually (Siena, BC, Benvoglienti: MS C.v.5, fol. 199r: citing B. 143, fol. 24r).

125. All these figures are from Bowsky, *Medieval Italian Commune*, 138–53.

salary plus the cost of materials. We have no evidence concerning the payment of assistants; even in the rare cases where a document makes clear that a painter was assisted, payment was generally made to the master, who was left to do his own internal accounting. Finally, we have limited indication of the time spent on specific projects and, at the same time, indications that painters worked on more than one project at once. Yet, with all these qualifications, there is information that is enlightening.

Two complete contracts of commission survive to us: one for Duccio's Rucellai *Madonna* (Figs. 10–11) and another for Pietro Lorenzetti's Arezzo polyptych (Color Plates 13–14). The Duccio contract, of 1285, indicates that the Laudesi of Santa Maria Novella were to supply the panel, while Duccio was "to paint the said panel and to adorn it with the image of the Blessed Virgin Mary and her omnipotent Son and other figures, in accordance with the wishes and pleasure of the said commissioners, and to gild it, and to do each and every thing which will contribute to the beauty of said panel, all at his own expense."[85] In other words, the artist was to supply labor, pigments, and gold. For this he was to receive £150, or 91.4 florins.[86] Pietro Lorenzetti's contract similarly specified that Guido Tarlati, bishop of Arezzo, would supply the panel, but the painter was to provide his labor, the pigments, silver, and gold required for the work. His remuneration was set at 160 Pisan lire (about 54 florins), to be paid in three installments, at the beginning, the middle, and the end of the project.[87] Neither contract specifies a completion date, although Pietro's contract

---

quite late in a volume. Finally, the scribe seems to cite the items that one encounters in the Entrata or Uscita volumes and therefore differentiates them, by omission, from those that are not. I also know of one case where the scribe cites the page of the relevant Uscita volume for a payment made at the very end of the semester. As indicated, the entries of the Memoriale do not always find equivalents in the volumes of the Entrata and Uscita, making me believe that the Memoriale should not be considered either sources for or derivations from those volumes.

Taken together, these observations suggest that the Memoriale were informal documents compiled on the basis of now lost sources, probably toward the end of each semester. They seem to represent the internal accounting of the Biccherna, containing details not considered necessary for the more formal and public volumes of the Entrata and Uscita. I hasten to add, however, that these conclusions are tentative and that the Memoriale volumes warrant much more attention.

These observations are drawn from Maginnis, "Chiarimenti documentari: Simone Martini, I Memmi e Ambrogio Lorenzetti," *Rivista d'arte*, XLI, 1989, 9 n. 21, an article that contains examples of the various problems discussed above.

85. Satkowski, *Duccio,* 49–53. The contract is printed and translated in both Stubblebine, *Duccio,* I, 192–94, and White, *Duccio,* 185–87. Florence, Archivio di Stato, Diplomatico, S. Maria Novella di Firenze, 1285, 15 April.

86. Here, as in all the following conversions between lire and florins, I have relied on the tables in C. M. Cipolla, "Studi di storia della moneta," *Università di Pavia: Studi nelle scienze guiridiche e sociali pubblicati dall'istituto di esercitazioni presso la facoltà di giurisprudenza,* XXIX, 1948, 31–239, especially "Appendice III: Corso de cambio tra fiorino e moneta piccola a Siena dal 1300 al 1400," 156–238.

87. Bacci, *Dipinti inediti,* 76–79. John White (*Duccio,* 34–36) uses the fact that the measurements of Pietro's altarpiece are specified to argue that the Rucellai *Madonna* is indeed the work commissioned by the Laudesi. The argument assumes that artists were paid by the square *braccia*. Some evidence concerning frescoes suggests such an arrangement (although the matter is not as clear as often thought), but it is difficult to see how artists could make such agreements for panels where, depending on the design, the necessary amounts of gold and expensive pigments, such as ultramarine, might vary consider-

Donato Martini's wife, in 1324, had a dowry of £400; and in 1348 the future bride of Bonaccorso di Pace had a dowry of £450.

Unfortunately, it is impossible to say what, if anything, these figures mean in relation to the wealth of the grooms. It would seem likely that the two were linked, but that is only speculation. Although enough documentation for Siena survives to make a study of pre-1348 dowries possible, no one has yet tackled the matter.[83] For the time being, the sums given above should be compared with the price of real estate and the cost of commodities and salaries discussed below.

Matters Financial: Income and Comparative Costs

In light of property values discussed above, we want to know something of painters' incomes. Several problems complicate any calculation of the sums artists received for their work, and these should be noted at once. In relatively few cases can we feel confident that we have full record of payments for a specific project. Siena's ruling oligarchy was very careful in its expenditures and generally paid painters in installments as the work progressed and they could see the results. Many of the cathedral's account books are missing, and thus we lack complete record of the Opera del Duomo's expenditures. Moreover, we have evidence that indicates accounts for altarpieces were kept in separate volumes devoted to single projects. Although there are lacunae in the Entrata and Uscita volumes of the Biccherna, the civic treasury, the documentation is much fuller; nonetheless problems lurk there too. In some instances, payments to painters do not appear in the regular account books of the commune, but appear in surviving Memoriale volumes; however, that series is incomplete.[84] Payments also rarely specify whether they represent only the artist's salary or

---

83. Communication from Samuel K. Cohn Jr., whom I thank.

84. In these cases it seems that the Entrata and Uscita volumes contain only global payments to the *operaio* of the commune, the official in charge of civic works. The sum was then used for the project in hand.

There is no satisfactory discussion of the role the Memoriale volumes played in the accounting procedures of the Biccherna. While the volumes of the Entrata and Uscita are organized in chronological order, day by day, and items posted line by line, the entries in the Memoriale volumes are grouped in clearly separated blocks, each dedicated to a specific individual or project. Often they refer to various dates, which in some cases extend into the succeeding semester.

It is, therefore, useful to note some of the characteristics of the Memoriale. As in the vernacular versions of the Entrata and Uscita volumes, the Memoriale are paper rather than parchment. Blocks of interrelated payments, separated by lines above and below, appear to be written by one hand at the same time. However, one finds not only references to preceding pages of each volume, but also to following pages, sometimes considerably later in the volume. One therefore assumes that the volumes were bound and the pages numbered before the writer began to use them. One also notes that two entries regarding the same payment are sometimes found under different headings. Moreover, an entry dated to the end of the semester can appear in the first pages of a volume, and, vice versa, an entry dated to the beginning of the semester can appear

on the Tressa. On 16 October 1319, Duccio's children officially renounced their inheritance, presumably to the benefit of their mother.⁷⁷ Surviving documentation indicates that Duccio was often fined by the commune for a variety of offences. In 1281 and again in 1309 he had to pay the very significant sum of £100, the first described only as a fine for "a condemnation," the second as a penalty arising from "the register of civil litigations."⁷⁸ Other items relate to debts. The year 1302 was bad for Duccio; he paid a total of 15 soldi on three unpaid debts (one of them for £42), £5 for obstructing a city street, and 18 lire and 10 soldi for not being present at the mustering of communal forces at Monteano, by Collecchio, and at Roccastrada. Duccio, on 20 December 1308, acknowledged a debt of 50 florins (approximately £133.7) to Ser Jacopo di Giliberti de' Mariscotti, director of the Opera del Duomo.⁷⁹ Still more surprising is acknowledgment of a debt of £40, borrowed for six months from "Ser Tomuccio of the late Dino," made on 9 June 1313, just two years after completing the cathedral *Maestà*.⁸⁰ Other circumstances also suggest Duccio could not manage his financial affairs. In 1315 and again in 1317 he is recorded as renting land from the commune in Pian del Lago, north of Siena, while other successful painters were acquiring rural property.⁸¹

Another economic issue returns us to family matters; I refer to the dowries brought by future brides to their marriages with painters. If, as Simone Martini intended, his niece Caterina used her inheritance (approximately £396) from him as her dowry, then her husband, the painter Giovanni di Sera, received one of the larger dowries documented for the entire period of this study. At the other extreme, Neruccia di Neri brought a mere £54 to her 1304 marriage to Sandro di Masarello, and the bride of Guido di Nerio brought, in 1318, only £50. Romano di Mino did not do well either. In 1336, his future wife brought £80 to the marriage. Generally, however, painters seem to have made reasonably advantageous unions. In June of 1343, Galgano di Duccio received a dowry from his wife of £100. Lando di Vinuccio, in 1344, and Fede di Nalduccio, in 1348, received dowries of £100. Masarello had done rather better than his son Sandro; his bride brought a house in San Donato valued at £140. Paolo di Nerio, in 1343, received a house in the *popolo* of Sant'Andrea worth £80 and cash in the amount of £170. Francesco di Segna's wife had a dowry of £300 (1328); Cristofano di Muccio's wife had a dowry (1348) of 100 florins, or roughly £305, while Bartolo di Fredi's wife brought to her marriage approximately £344 in 1356.⁸²

77. ASS, Consiglio Generale 92, fols. 121v–125. The procedures for refusing an inheritance were laid out in the constitution of 1309–10. Lisini, *Costituto volgarizzato*, 461–62. Satkowski, *Duccio*, 85–88.

78. ASS, Biccherna 79, fol. 11r (March/April 1280); Biccherna 727 (Condanne), fol. 169r. Satkowski, *Duccio*, 49, 76.

79. ASS, Diplomatico, Opera della Metropolitana, Parchment no. 608. Satkowski, *Duccio*, 73–75.

80. ASS, Notarile 25 (Protocollo di Ser Colleto di Chele), fol. 39r. Satkowski, *Duccio*, 81.

81. ASS, Consiglio Generale 86, fols. 121v–125v (15 October 1315); Consiglio Generale 88, fols. 118–19 (25 January and 9 March 1317). Bowsky, *Finance*, 61 and 61 n. 53. Satkowski, *Duccio*, 81–82.

82. With the exception of Bartolo di Fredi, the painters involved and the sums they received are found in Appendix III of this study. For Bartolo, see Borghesi and Banchi, *Nuovi documenti*, 27.

From the *Table of Possessions,* we have other notices of artists with property, notices that take on special interest because they concern painters whose works we do not know. Mino di Voglia and his brothers owned a cultivated piece of land in the district of "Manciani" (Terzo di Città) worth £150, a house in the district of "Mansionis Templi" (Magione, Terzo di Camollia) valued at 138 lire, 6 soldi, and 8 denari, and half a house with a garden or orchard in the district of San Donato estimated at £200, for a total worth of £388.[65] Vannuccio and Niccola di Mino, both painters, had a house in the "Mansionis Templi" valued at £350.[66] Later in the same assessment volume, Vannuccio di Mino is recorded as having a house in San Donato worth 110 lire, 6 soldi, and 8 denari.[67] Another painter of unknown works, "Monaldus Palmerii," owned three-fifths of one piece of land in San Donato valued at £56 and four parts of land with a garden or orchard in the district of Vallepiatta worth 33 lire, 6 soldi, and 8 denari.[68] What I take to be a reference to the painter named Guido Cinatti tells us that his house in San Donato a lato dei Montanini was worth a mere £60.[69] The painter Guido di Ghezzo is recorded as owning a piece of cultivated land, with vines, in the "popolo de Arsiccioli" worth £58 and another property in San Donato valued at 218 lire, 6 soldi, and 8 denari.[70] The widow of the painter Sabatino owned a house in Sant'Egidio valued at 73 lire, 6 soldi, and 8 denari.[71] In the same area, Cecco di Puccio owned a house worth £80, and Masarello di Gilio a house valued at 153 lire, 6 soldi, and 8 denari.[72] As we consider these sums, we should recall that the Nine required immigrants to the city to build a house worth at least £100 in return for naturalization.[73]

A rather atypical case is that of Tavena d'Andrea, a painter about whom we know very little. He owned two houses in the *lira* of San Donato al lato dei Montanini, one valued at 76 lire, 13 soldi, and 4 denari and another worth £100. The artist had a series of smaller holdings in multiple pieces of land, most of them half-shares of the property involved.[74] He also had one major holding in the form of a vineyard, valued at £420. The painter's total worth was roughly £1,000.[75] We know of no major commission awarded this painter.

It would seem that Duccio's financial situation was the exception. After his death, likely early in 1318, his widow, Donna Tavinia, is recorded as owning half a house, in the parish of San Quirico, valued at £110.[76] There is no mention of the property that, in 1311, Duccio had owned in Stalloreggi di fuore, and no reference to property outside the city and

65. ASS, Estimo 131, fol. 242r.
66. ASS, Estimo 131, fol. 286r.
67. ASS, Estimo 131, fol. 311r.
68. ASS, Estimo 131, fol. 304r.
69. See the discussion of this artist below.
70. ASS, Estimo 131, fol. 245r.
71. ASS, Estimo 136, fol. 219r.
72. ASS, Estimo 136, fols. 417r and 87r respectively.
73. Bowsky, *Medieval Italian Commune,* 21.
74. It seems highly likely that Tavena's half-shares are inheritances. It was common for the Sienese to leave, in their wills, shares in property they owned but with the condition that the property be kept together. Such arrangements are usually accompanied by the phrase *pro indiviso,* in reference to the property itself. The matter is discussed by Balestracci and Piccinni, *Siena nel trecento,* 131.

75. See Appendix II of this volume, and especially the introductory comments on problems with the Tavena documents.

76. ASS, Estimo 105, fol. 153r.

Documentation on the worth of Simone Martini is equally revealing, if also incomplete. The painter was very prosperous, and that not so many years after his documented career began. The total outlay connected with his 1324 marriage to Giovanna Memmi came to approximately £1,122.[59] Other notices belong to the period after Simone's death and include a summary of his will made in Siena for taxation purposes (and that therefore did not record any charitable bequests the painter may have made).[60] In his will, Simone left his wife a house and contents valued at £200, or 60.6 florins.[61] To his niece Francesca Salvucci he left a vineyard "in piagiis de Vico" valued at £95, another "in contrata de Vico" estimated at £50, use of part of a house that Simone shared with Donato valued at £30.[62] The total of these bequests comes to £175, or 53 florins. To his married niece Giovanna Salvucci, sister to Francesca, he left 10 florins. When Simone came to his niece Caterina, daughter of his brother Donato, he did things in the grand manner, leaving her a vineyard and cash as a dowry, valued at 120 florins, or roughly £396. (The vineyard was actually a half share; Donato owned the other half.) He also left land, cash, and vines, a total worth of £80, to Donato's other two daughters, Agnola and Diambra. To Donato's sons, Giovanni, Barnaba, and Simone Donati, Simone left £50. The total comes to approximately 283 florins, or £934.[63]

In a transaction between 10 November 1347 and 29 March 1348, Lippo Memmi received, on behalf of his sister Giovanna, land and vineyards with a house "in contrada de Fighillis," purchased for £750.[64] We do not know the source of the funds spent in this purchase, but it seems likely it was from Simone's estate. Martindale suggests that Simone probably had assets in Avignon that would not appear in the Sienese summary of the will for tax purposes. Given the worth of the brothers Memmi, even a total of £1,684, derived from adding the cost of this house to the provisions of the will, seems low for Simone.

the parish of San Giorgio. On 20 June 1350, he bought from the Ospedale della Scala a house and vineyard, apparently near the Porta Busetto, and another piece of land with vines in "sanaciano." The value of the purchase was £175. It seems the painter did not have the sum at hand, for the purchase was concluded only with a last payment, of two, on 5 December 1352 (ASS, Spedale 514, fol. 222r).

59. Bacci, *Fonti e commenti*, 145–47.

60. On 24 January 1347 Simone's widow, Giovanna, presented a missal and a chalice to San Domenico to be kept in the sacristy and used for saying the mass of the dead for the souls of her relatives and of Simone. The gift was valued at 19 florins and seems to have been Simone's bequest (Bacci, *Fonti e commenti*, 177–78). The lengthy period between Simone's death and this notice may suggest Giovanna had returned from Avignon only slightly earlier.

61. The figures for Simone's will are taken from A. Martindale, *Simone Martini: Complete Edition*, Oxford, 1988, 37–38, who corrects some errors made by Pèleo Bacci in his transcription for *Fonti e commenti*, 185–87.

62. I have been unable to ascertain the precise location referred to, since the area contains many places called Vico, usually with a further designation to distinguish each. It is most likely that the site was Vico d'Arbia, a very short distance to the east of Siena.

63. If each of Donato's sons had received £50, then the total would come to £1,034.

64. ASS, Gabella/Contratti 51, fol. 18; Bacci, *Fonti e commenti*, 190. Bacci incorrectly cites this item as Gabella/Contratti 31.

was relatively secure and safe from one of the city's greatest dangers: fire. But Sovignano's distance from Siena makes it hardly a place for short and frequent visits, especially for painters active in their profession. Perhaps this explains the size of their cultivated land in Siena itself; it was necessary to have a more immediate source of food. But that leaves us wondering how the Sovignano property was managed. Did the brothers have sharecroppers on the land? It seems highly likely.

Owning rural property may also have been the trecento equivalent of a retirement fund. Given the chronology of transactions, that would seem to be the case with our next pair of brothers, Lippo and Federigo Memmi. The financial circumstances of the Memmi family are particularly puzzling. In the tax assessments of 1318, Memmo di Filippuccio, the brothers' father, and his brother Mino di Filippuccio are recorded as jointly owning a house in San Donato valued at 333 lire, 6 soldi, and 8 denari.[53] This house was their only holding in Siena.[54] On 2 January 1324, Simone Martini bought a house from Memmo for 120 florins, or roughly £400.[55] The same day, Simone provided his future bride, Giovanna Memmi, with a dowry of 220 florins.[56] It is, in sum, unclear what Lippo and Federigo could have inherited from their father, although the value of the house Simone bought would suggest that Memmo was prosperous.

Our story begins with Lippo and Federigo's purchasing land in Monsindoli, immediately southeast of the city and in the Masse of the Terzo di Città. The Gabella de' Contratti shows that on 1 July 1343, they bought "possessiones" there from the Ospedale della Scala for the very considerable sum of £1,000.[57] They were putting together a larger holding, for on 7 July 1343, Lippo bought land in the same location from the order of the Humiliati for £225. Neither notice of purchase specifies the size of the acquisition. Allowing for inflation, the Memmi holdings were approximately of the value of rural property held by the brothers Neri but, being so close to the city, may have been considerably smaller in size. The only other financial information we have for the Memmi is puzzling. For unspecified reasons, Lippo, during 1344, lent the Ospedale della Scala 73 florins (about £240). The combined worth of the brothers as indicated in these notices was £1,465 (Lippo's share roughly £852), and this amount does not include urban property, although undoubtedly there were properties in the city.[58]

---

53. See Appendix II of this volume.

54. Memmo had previously been active in San Gimignano and may well have owned property there, property that would not appear in Sienese tax assessments.

55. The documentary situation involving this transaction is somewhat confusing. The notice of purchase places Simone in the parish of San Donato, and Memmo (and his house) in Sant'Egidio. But Bacci (*Fonti e commenti*, 146) suggested this was a confusion because other documents place the painters in the opposite parishes. This seems a highly likely interpretation. We have no way of knowing whether the house involved was that owned by Memmo and Mino di Filippuccio c. 1318. The property obviously belonged to Memmo alone, but we do not know Mino's date of death.

56. Bacci, *Fonti e commenti*, 145–47.

57. For this and the other relevant documents, see Bacci, *Fonti e commenti*, 179–80. By this date their father, Memmo, was deceased, as the documentary notices indicate.

58. A more modest case of property acquisition involves Francesco di Nerio, a painter who lived in

initial listings were compiled, Ugolino's father, the painter Nerio, was already deceased. The list contains some eight items, only two of which refer to property in Siena itself and concern a house, with a garden or orchard, in the parish of San Donato, valued at £250, and approximately three acres of land estimated to be worth 83 lire and 10 soldi. (Nerio di Ugolino, between 12 June and 7 July 1311, had bought "land and other things" from the widow Bonaventura di Viva de' Mocali for the sum of £130.)[48] The additional entries concern six parcels of land in Sovignano, about eighteen kilometers south of Siena in the direction of Buonconvento, that together came to roughly eighteen acres. None of this property was solely in Ugolino's possession; it was held jointly by his brother Muccio, also a painter.[49] (Other sources tell us that Ugolino had a second brother, Guido, but he nowhere figures in this matter.)[50] In terms of proportional investment, the rural holdings amounted to £651, or 66 percent of their combined worth as represented by immovable property. Toward the end of the relevant volume, and thus likely dating to 1320 or thereabouts, an addition notes another piece of property of about three and a half acres in Sovignano valued at £110, bringing the total value of Ugolino's and Muccio's rural holdings to £761, or roughly 70 percent of their combined worth. In addition to these items, Muccio bought yet another piece of land, between August and September of 1319, in Sovignano for £46.[51] In the Estimo volume (no. 79) for Sovignano we find an entry, dated 20 April 1323, wherein a local resident, Minnuccio di Mino, sold land valued at 24 lire and 2 soldi to the brothers. If we add these items to the foregoing, the brothers had £831 in rural property and a combined worth of £1,164. Early in 1327 Ugolino sold a piece of property for the small sum of £17, property not listed in the Estimo of 1318–20.[52] Clearly, there is much that we do not know. In due course, we shall discover what the actual sums mean in terms of comparative values; for the moment, there is still a good deal we can draw from these notices.

In having more than two-thirds of their wealth invested in the country, Ugolino and Muccio were following the general pattern of their society. Accustomed to our artists' being urban, we may be surprised by this choice, but in the conditions of the Trecento it made perfect sense. The landholdings were surely sufficient to provide some income from agriculture while providing foodstuffs for the family's use. Moreover, investment of this sort

---

48. Bacci, *Dipinti inediti*, 142. The painter is indicated as resident in the parish of San Donato.

49. In a type of error I have encountered occasionally in documents of the period, the scribe recording the holdings of the brothers Neri has written "Duccius" at the beginning of the document rather than "Muccius." The mistake is corrected as the text goes on.

The joint ownership of property by siblings was not only typical of the period, it was a custom that was carried through the Renaissance and, indeed, into modern times.

A Nerio di Muccio, a painter and likely Muccio's son, was buried in San Domenico on 31 May 1340 (Bacci, *Dipinti inediti*, 149; Laurent, *I necrologi*, 56).

50. In preparation for marriage, Guido received a dowry of £50 from his future wife in 1318. A Guido di Nerio da Siena is listed in the matriculation of the Florentine guild of Medici e Speziali in 1327. Bacci, *Fonti e commenti*, 144–46.

51. Bacci, *Dipinti inediti*, 146–47. No item in the Estimo assessments is valued at this sum. Whether this land is included in the notice of a larger parcel or simply was missed by the assessors is unclear.

52. Bacci, *Dipinti inediti*, 143–44.

During the period of 1316 to approximately 1320, the Nove launched an enormous project to compile registers of all the immovable property of Siena's citizens, the so-called *Table of Possessions,* to be used for tax purposes. Many of these volumes survive; some are lost. Fortunately, a team led by Giovanni Cherubini has conducted a detailed study of the 1316–20 assessments of real property in twenty-seven tax districts of the city.[43] The results of that study allow us to place figures regarding the worth of painters' properties in a larger context. They show that just short of half of all private property owners in Siena had patrimonies (immovable property) that did not exceed £200; in fact, the median value of property in this group was roughly £78. The median value of urban property worth between £200 and £500, belonging to a group comprising some 16.5 percent of all property owners, was approximately £226. At least in terms of urban real estate, Simone and Ambrogio apparently belonged to this group. The same study well illustrates the tendency, discussed in Chapter 1, for the Sienese to invest in rural properties. In every economic group, the value of rural holdings was found to exceed the value of urban property; and as the value of patrimonies rose, so too did the percentage of wealth invested outside the city. Overall, city property, c.1316–20, represented only 21.4 percent of the total assessed wealth in the twenty-seven districts studied. In this matter our evidence regarding painters is limited, but it is suggestive of a larger practice and includes documentation on at least two startlingly surprising situations.

Between September of 1344 and February of 1345, Pietro Lorenzetti and his wife, Giovanna, sold approximately two acres of land in Bibbiano Giulieschi to the sons of the sculptor Tino di Camaino for £150.[44] Bibbiano Giulieschi is roughly four kilometers southwest of Buonconvento, the latter about thirty kilometers south of Siena. In the contract (1320) for Pietro's altarpiece in Arezzo, he is described as having come from Siena; it therefore seems unlikely the rural property was in the place of his birth, but rather was a holding owned by the painter.[45] A note of 1349, attached to the summary of Ambrogio Lorenzetti's will refers to the sale of his house in Siena; another note refers to a "possessione" sold by the Company of the Virgin to the painter Pietro di Ser Dota. Pietro paid 46 florins, or £143, but the notice makes clear that this was only a partial payment of the total cost. In documents from the Ospedale della Scala, "possessione" is used to indicate the house of a worker, often with a vineyard of variable size and cultivated land.[46]

From the tax assessments compiled c. 1318, we have records relating to Ugolino di Nerio.[47] These hitherto unpublished notices provide us with a rare glimpse into the affairs of an artist and, I believe, may be more representative than we might first think. When the

---

43. Cherubini, *Signori, contadini, borghesi,* 231–311, and Giovanni Cherubini et al., "La proprietà fondiaria in alcune zone del territorio senese all'inizio del trecento," *Rivista di storia dell'agricoltura,* XIV, 1974, 2–176.

44. Bacci, *Dipinti inediti,* 97–103. Borghesi and Banchi (*Nuovi documenti,* 11) said that Pietro had bought land in the same location, in 1342, for the brothers. The relevant document is untraced.

45. Bacci, *Dipinti inediti,* 76–79.

46. Wainwright, "The Will of Ambrogio Lorenzetti," 544. Epstein, *Alle origini della fattoria toscana,* 167.

47. See Appendix II of this volume.

ventura. Fourteenth-century painters for whom Lisini cited documents earlier than 1363 number 140.

In Appendix III of this book, the reader will find a digest of documents for secondary minor masters that includes items under 202 names. Because I have been careful not to combine notices having only a first name with others that have the same first name but a fuller designation, it may well be that in a number of instances the same painter is listed more than once. It may also be that the same artist is meant in two or more entries where the spelling differs; orthography of the period allowed of more variation than at present. Conversely, two or more painters of the same name may here appear in a single list.[36] To the names of that appendix, however, we would have to add at least a dozen more to account for the more important masters from the first half of the century. Whatever the exact number of early Sienese painters was, it was certainly far larger than anyone would suspect from reading heretofore published accounts of early Sienese painting.

Matters Financial: Property and Dowries

We have several specific indications of the value of painters' properties. After Duccio's death, his widow owned half a house in San Quirico evaluated for tax purposes at £110.[37] Upon marriage, in 1324, Simone Martini bought his house in Sant'Egidio for 120 florins, or approximately £400.[38] By the time of his death, he owned jointly with his brother Donato another house in Sant'Egidio or San Donato; Simone's share was valued at a modest £30.[39] Ambrogio Lorenzetti's house in San Pietro in Castelvecchio was sold, after his death, for £275, but the amount tells us little in relation to other values discussed here, for the sale occurred after the plague of 1348.[40] Real estate prices must have dropped dramatically because of the many empty dwellings. Earlier, in 1324, Ambrogio had sold property in Sant'Egidio for £200.[41] We deal thus far with the urban property of the most successful and therefore the most prosperous painters; the vast majority of painters were likely (though not always) of much humbler condition. In 1318, Segna di Bonaventura's house in San Pietro a Ovile was valued at a mere £50, and that was the lowest value assigned any dwelling in the tax assessments of that parish in that year.[42]

36. See, for example, the items under "Guido" (a common name in Siena), where the dates make it clear that more than one artist is involved.
37. ASS, Estimo 105, fol. 154r.
38. Bacci, *Fonti e commenti*, 145–46.
39. Bacci, *Fonti e commenti*, 186.
40. Wainwright, "The Will of Ambrogio Lorenzetti."
41. G. Rowley, *Ambrogio Lorenzetti*, Princeton, I, 1958, 129.
42. Bacci, *Fonti e commenti*, 39. Segna's house is described as "retro murus Comunis Senarum." Thus it lay to the extreme east of the parish, against the city walls and near the church of San Francesco. On one side of his house lived a tailor, on the other the heirs of a carpenter. For the amount assessed, see Balestracci and Piccinni, *Siena nel trecento*, 124.

the Via del Giglio from Santa Maria Novella to San Lorenzo, and then from San Lorenzo to San Michele Visdomini by the Via Gori, which becomes the Via de' Pucci.[31] These streets actually mark the old boundaries of the *quartiere* of San Giovanni. Thus the situation in Florence differs slightly from that in Siena, in that all three principal clusters of painters' residences are separated rather than immediately adjoining. On the other hand, the real distance between Santa Maria Novella and San Lorenzo, and between San Lorenzo and San Michele Visdomini, is roughly 350 meters in both cases, distances short enough for us to speak of a district favored by many painters.

Numbers

An exact count of Sienese painters for the period 1260–1363 is impossible; we cannot assume each and every painter is mentioned in surviving documentation. But we can, perhaps, form an approximate estimate of their numbers. When Gaetano Milanesi published the statute of the Painters' Guild in Siena, he included a list of some sixty-four painters that, he claimed, belonged to the guild in 1356.[32] The relevant manuscript, however, is an ambiguous document that is not always ordered chronologically and contains many insertions.[33] It is possible that the last thirteen names of Milanesi's list were not part of the original list, and that the real count for 1356 is fifty-one.[34] Of course, this number is probably unreliable as indication of painters normally working in the city; the original list comes just eight years after the devastating Black Death, which took roughly half of Siena's population. All of the major masters from the first half of the century are missing, since all were deceased.

In 1927, A. Lisini published lists, composed from documentary references, of Sienese painters active in the thirteenth and fourteenth centuries.[35] His list for the Dugento includes some sixty-two names; among them we find ten artists still active in the fourteenth century, including Duccio, Masarello di Gilio, Memmo di Filippuccio, and Segna di Bona-

---

31. There is no evidence of a pattern among those who changed parishes. Giotto was first in Santa Maria Novella and later in San Michele Visdomini; Nardo moved from the latter to the former. Orcagna moved from San Michele Visdomini to San Lorenzo; Jacopo di Cione moved from the area of Santa Maria Novella to San Lorenzo. Andrea di Bonaiuto, as noted above, lived most of his life in Santa Maria Novella.

32. Milanesi, *Documenti*, I, 27–40.

33. ASS, Arti 59.

34. Antonio di Giovanni, fifty-first in the list, seems to reappear as fifty-second, suggesting that what follows may be an addition originally of another date. That suspicion seems to be confirmed by the presence, in the last thirteen names, of Taddeo di Bartolo, who died in 1422. It is impossible to believe he was enrolled in the guild sixty-seven years earlier.

35. A. Lisini, "Elenco dei pittori vissuti nel secolo XIII e XIV," *La Diana*, II, 1927, 295–306. Lisini cites a wide variety of archival sources, including the lists of names in the statutes of the Painters' Guild. I have not been able to verify all his citations.

arts," where a notion of progress is also involved, and where the ultimate source is Aristotle. In his *Defensor pacis* (1324), Marsilius of Padua remarked: "From the imperfect kinds, men have advanced to perfect communities, regimes, and modes of living in them. For from the less to the more perfect is always the path of nature and of its imitator, art."[103] This particular remark has a specific context and is clarified in just a few following pages. Marsilius expands on his argument:

> In order to moderate the actions and the passions of our body caused by the impressions of the elements which externally surround us, there was discovered the general class of mechanics, which Aristotle in the *Politics,* Book VII, Chapter 6, calls the 'arts.' To this class belong spinning, leathermaking, shoemaking, all species of housebuilding, and in general all the other mechanic arts which subserve the other offices of the state directly or in directly, and which moderate not only men's touch or taste but also the other senses. These latter arts are more for pleasure and for living well than for the necessity of life, such as the painter's art and others similar to it.[104]

Painting, then, clearly belongs to Marsilius's definition of the arts and, although here classed as one of the mechanical arts, takes part in the movement "from the less to the more perfect."

There are three works in Siena that bear upon this issue. In the early years of the Trecento, Coppo di Marcovaldo's *Madonna* (1261) for the Servites and Guido's *Madonna* for San Domenico (Fig. 32) were each "modernized" by a painter from Duccio's circle; the heads of the Virgin and Child and parts of the throne in the Guido were repainted.[105] Simone Martini, in 1321, "repaired" his 1315 *Maestà* in the Palazzo Pubblico (Color Plates 3 and 4). Technical and visual evidence demonstrates that the "restoration" was not a reworking of damaged areas; the heads of the Virgin and Child, as well as the heads of six saints, were changed so that they embodied the blonder palette and more differentiated modeling that Simone used in the 1320s. The changes to these works are, I suggest, testimony to a conviction that art moves from the better to the best, and that the newer is regarded as the most desirable.

Fra Giordano of Pisa provides us with a more homely indication of contemporary ideas that nonetheless points toward a sense of development and is surely closely related to the three "modernizations" mentioned above. In the sermon where he discusses the inven-

103. A. Gewirth, trans., *Marsilius of Padua: The Defender of Peace: The Defensor Pacis,* New York, 1957, 10. Note this important definition of art as the imitator of nature.

104. Gewirth, *Marsilius of Padua,* 17.

105. Cathleen Hoeniger (*The Renovation of Paintings in Tuscany, 1250–1500,* Cambridge, 1995, 21–42) does not accept the idea that these renovations were connected with a change in taste, but argues that the changes came as a result of Byzantine influence, particularly influence from the Byzantine practice of repainting icons to renew and increase their efficacy. I cannot see the grounds for this argument, especially since the author herself simultaneously suggests that the involvement of Ducciesque painters indicates a desire to make these images conform to the most important image of the city, the new cathedral *Maestà* by Duccio.

tion of eyeglasses, he prefaces that report with the observation that "[a]ll the arts are found by man. Man doesn't make them, but he finds them; and yet they haven't all been found. The finding of arts will never come to an end."[106] Even more revealing is another of Giordano's remarks: "Familiar things which man knows, he ordinarily cares little about and has little desire for them; but should there be something new and unfamiliar, people usually want very much to know it."[107] Siena's Nine reflected another, related side of the matter. In legislation of January 1335 dealing with the jurisdictions of the Biccherna and Gabella, they ordered that in the following May–June the Nove should review the arrangements in light of experience "because it is fitting that human statutes be changed according to changing times."[108]

Although I shall not argue the connection here, these remarks belong to the idea of historical progress that was spreading in Western civilization and had its origin among the Franciscans. And they belong beside the growing appreciation of artistic innovation that characterized the fourteenth century.[109] Together, all these ideas were laying the foundations for the premium placed on invention in the High Renaissance and Mannerism.

Painters and Texts

It is not my intention here to offer a full and particularized discussion of the relations of individual painters and pictures to specific textual sources; that discussion belongs elsewhere. But the purpose of this volume necessitates some general reflections on the matter: not citations of texts relating to specific works, but rather thoughts about the broader connections between painting and contemporary texts, particularly the literature of the faith.

The period of this study was particularly rich in the literature it produced. Readers will immediately think of Dante, his *Vita nuova* and the *Commedia divina,* of Boccaccio and the *Decameron,* and of the poems and prose of Petrarch; but those authors and their works were part of a much larger phenomenon whose other constituents frequently had wider impact. I think of lauds, of poems and songs of celebration and praise often, though not exclusively, associated with the new confraternities. Today, to speak of lauds is usually to speak of the Franciscan Jacopone da Todi, whose works are easily accessible in modern editions, but there certainly were innumerable lauds now lost to us that were connected

---

106. C. Delcorno, ed., *Giordano da Pisa: Quaresimale fiorentino 1305–1306,* Florence, 1974, 75. Fra Giordano's remark and the distinction he makes between discovery and invention are highly revealing. Clearly, he wants to reserve invention for the Creator and to allow men only discovery of what God has made. We can only wonder if he felt a necessity to make the distinction because others in his society had begun to think otherwise.

107. D. M. Manni and A. M. Biscioni, *Prediche del b. F. Giordano da Rivalto,* Florence, 1739, 26.

108. Bowsky, *Finance,* 259. This idea derives from Justinian's *Corpus juris civilis.*

109. See "A Question of Status" in Chapter II above, and my remarks on artistic invention in *Age of Giotto,* chapter IX.

with specific brotherhoods. Equally important to Christian life were texts by Saint Bonaventure, who essentially defined Franciscan spirituality in the second half of the Dugento. In addition to new lives of Saint Francis, discussed below, Bonaventure authored two works of extraordinary importance and influence: the *Soul's Journey into God* (*Itinerarium mentis in Deum*) and the *Tree of Life* (*Lignum vitae*).

Now, I cite the lauds and the devotional works of Bonaventure to make the point that we have no evidence that Sienese painters ever tried to give visual form to such works in a literal way.[110] Those texts may have engendered a mood or attitude that influenced the treatment of Christian subject matter—I think that to be the case—but they were not themselves subjects of illustration.[111] While we may find this unsurprising given the difficulties attendant upon such attempts, we should also recall that in other times and places artists have given visual form to the poetic and the mystical. Those efforts, however, have often been most successful in styles where naturalism was not a determining impulse. But the absence of illustrations to poetic and mystical texts stemmed from something more than the tendency of artistic ambitions toward artistic naturalism; it was, in significant measure, a result of the fact that other forms of contemporary literature offered impulse in another direction.

The age of vision was also the age of narrative. Here too the Franciscans were of great account. Bonaventure's *Legenda maior* (1263) of Saint Francis, though not strictly chronological in its organization, was the story of a life, and a story that acquired enormous meaning from the Franciscan view of the saint's place in history. In that view, Francis himself had passed into the seventh and final age of New Testament history, and since he had thus participated in that age of beatitude and repose that the rest of mankind still awaited, his life was a model for imitation and a foreshadowing of things to come.[112] In other words, the *Legend* did more, needed to do more, than list miracles. Francis's story had to be told in a way that offered examples of faith and conduct, and that could be achieved only in narrative. It is not by chance that Bonaventure's text formed the basis for the most extensive pictorial rendition of a saint's life during this period: the *Saint Francis Legend* in San Francesco, Assisi. Nor is it by chance that the imagery of that cycle was widely copied in other Franciscan churches.[113] It was not, however, only Bonaventure's text and the Franciscan view of history that made for an emphasis on narrative.

Around 1260, the year in which Bonaventure was assigned the task of producing a

---

110. In Florence, Pacino di Bonaguida and Taddeo Gaddi created depictions of *The Tree of Life,* the former on panel, the latter in fresco. See *Age of Giotto,* figs. 93–95.

111. The miniaturist Cola di Fuccio worked for the Confraternity of the Virgin and Saint Francis and was paid for "the miniature" of their book of lauds. But, as the use of the singular makes clear, Cola did not provide many illuminations, but probably something on the order of a frontispiece. See Appendix III.

112. See Maginnis, "Time, History, and Painting," in *Age of Giotto,* 114–23.

113. See D. Blume, *Wandmalerei als Ordenspropaganda: Bildprogramme in Chorbereich franziskanischer Konvente Italiens bis zur Mitte des 14. Jahrhunderts,* Worms, 1983.

new life of Francis, there appeared Jacobus de Voragine's *Golden Legend,* a work that enjoyed immense popularity for centuries.[114] Composed of 182 chapters and filling two substantial volumes in modern print, the *Golden Legend* told the stories of the Church's "official" saints and of major feast days. The tales of saints are "biographies," and the sequence that of the Church's calendar. Once more, narrative is used to define the exemplary aspects of the lives of the saints and to insert those figures into the lives of the faithful.

It is around this question of narrative that a number of my earlier themes coalesce. In addition to emphasizing the legend of Saint Francis, the Franciscans followed their founder in fastening attention on the Gospels and thus on the literal story of Christ's life. Preaching the imitation of Christ, they made knowledge and study of that story the foundation of the faith; and they did so at a time, the thirteenth century, when the study of the Bible was beginning increasingly to emphasize the literal sense of Scripture. The mystical reading of the Bible, which had so dominated medieval thought, was not so much abandoned as supplemented by a new sense of the importance of the literal meaning of the text.[115] That new importance is evident in the lengthy quote from Roger Bacon in the preceding section on vision.[116]

Both the Franciscans and the Dominicans contributed to this new emphasis; so too did Aristotle, in at least two ways. On the one hand, Aristotle's position that substance can be known only through its sensible manifestations was transferred into a guiding principle for treating the biblical text. In contrast to earlier exegesis of the Bible, "the Aristotelian would perceive the 'spirit' of Scripture as something not hidden behind or added on to, but expressed by the text," and that made a clear understanding of the literal meaning of the text a prerequisite for further considerations.[117] Second, Aristotle's *Libri naturales* brought not only some of the greatest achievements of ancient science to thirteenth-century thinkers, science that might be applied to biblical studies by way of explanations of specifics, but also a new attitude.

> Postillators of Scripture would have studied Aristotle in the arts courses [of the new universities]; they would inevitably compare the *Libri naturales* with biblical science and cosmography. Moreover, a person accustomed to reading a scientific text, to reflecting on the mechanism of the universe and its component parts, will proceed to the study of any other text with new eyes. He will not be content to know that things happened but will ask how they happened. And he will fasten on anything that adds to his stock of scientific knowledge.[118]

114. Jacobus de Voragine, *The Golden Legend: Readings on the Saints,* trans. W.G. Ryan, 2 vols., Princeton, 1993.

115. B. Smalley, *The Study of the Bible in the Middle Ages,* 3d ed., Oxford, 1983, especially chapter VI, "The Friars."

116. Bacon, however, was old-fashioned in his attitude toward Bible studies in general and held a view that "made Scripture a divine encyclopedia, written in cipher." Smalley, *The Study of the Bible,* 294.

117. Smalley, *The Study of the Bible,* 293.

118. Smalley, *The Study of the Bible,* 309.

The demand for narrative painting that arose from the popularity of narrative texts was for painters often the stimulus to new ideas regarding composition and new complexities in figural articulation. The need to combine figures in representation of events drawn from literary narrative and at the same time to give order to those depictions, and the concomitant need to devise figural poses that made figures active participants in such events, were among the most important factors in encouraging the new naturalism. There is here a highly suggestive parallel with Ernst Gombrich's explanation of the "Greek revolution" in the arts.[119]

Now, the role of narrative and many of the specific texts mentioned above can be related to developments in early Italian painting generally. But we have one text that seems to provide a close parallel for the character of much of early Sienese painting, the *Meditations on the Life of Christ,* composed in the 1260s. I have already noted its emphasis on seeing, on envisioning, something that suggests an obvious connection to the painter's art, but the character of the text and character of early Sienese painting are still closer. Although we have evidence that Sienese painters knew and used specific material from the *Meditations,* I am not speaking simply or primarily about textual sources, but rather about a similarity of approach to sacred history. One modern scholar has lamented "the sentimentality and flights of fancy" found in the work, but those are among the very things that made the *Meditations* one of the most popular texts of all time. Telling the story of Christ's earthly life, the text seeks to provide all the circumstantial detail that is lacking in biblical accounts. It also seeks from the reader an emotional response to the various events of Christ's life (and the Virgin's). The text is discursive in the manner of Duccio's narratives of the *Maestà,* of Pietro Lorenzetti's Assisi Passion Cycle, of Ambrogio's Saint Nicholas narratives. It is, in sum, the embodiment of an attitude that parallels that expressed in the Sienese tradition of rich naturalism.

Of necessity, the discussions of this chapter have focused more on painting than on painters. But to understand the early Sienese painter requires an understanding of the circumstances and ideas that shaped his life and works as well as the lives of his patrons. With works of art now the primary sources for knowledge of painters' attitudes and interests, we must relate those images to contemporary thought in order to assess the ideas that did, or did not, influence the painter's outlook, the ideas that were, or were not, part of the larger ambitions he brought to painting and that shaped the expectations of his patrons.

To create an image in Florence was to create a potentially miraculous image; everything suggests that that was not the case in Siena. To produce a work in Siena or elsewhere was, for the painter, to encounter patrons' expectations of order and beauty and, at the same time, to help shape those expectations. In many ways and many instances, the early Sienese painter became an exponent of the period's concern with optics, and his works became

119. E. H. Gombrich, *Art and Illusion: A Study in the Psychology of Pictorial Representation,* Princeton, 1960.

reflections of contemporary ideas concerning vision. To be a painter in Siena may well have been to encounter expectations of novelty and improvement, to work for an audience that had expectations of artistic progress. To be a painter in Siena was often to participate in the new vision of the faith and, specifically, in the vision embodied in the *Meditations on the Life of Christ*. All these elements were part of the painter's life—and they were among the foundation stones of early Sienese painting.

AN EPILOGUE

On 9 June 1348, as the Black Death swept through Siena, Ambrogio Lorenzetti wrote his will. Neither he nor his family survived the epidemic, and his estate passed to the Confraternity of the Virgin, resident in the Ospedale della Scala. Inasmuch as we know, Ambrogio was the last surviving great master of the first half of the Trecento. His brother, Pietro, disappears after a final documentary notice of 1345; in 1344 Simone Martini died in distant Avignon. Several secondary masters were also gone. Lippo Memmi is last mentioned in a document recording his purchase of land on behalf of his sister, Giovanna, Simone's widow, a transaction completed in March of 1348. Donato Martini had died on 16 August 1347. Among Ducciesque painters, Niccolò di Segna is last known in a painted cross, now in the Pinacoteca of Siena, inscribed with his name and with the date 1345. His father, Segna di Bonaventura, was deceased by 1331. Consensus would have it that Ugolino di Nerio died in the late 1330s. Yet it comes as something of a shock to realize that Ambrogio's testament was written only thirty years after Duccio's death. So much had been achieved in so short a time.

There were painters trained in the first half of the fourteenth century who made safe passage across that summer of pestilence, Bartolommeo Bulgarini foremost among them, and they were soon joined by artists of a younger generation. But the latter were, in large part, painters to be ranked with Lippo Memmi rather than Simone, with Ugolino rather than Duccio. They were painters who first homogenized the achievements of their great predecessors and then grew indifferent to maintaining meaningful contact with the past. They were also painters destined to live in a city much changed and constantly changing around them. By 1349, half the population of Siena had died, leaving dwellings and perhaps some churches empty. In 1355 the regime of the Noveschi, which had done so much to shape the city and sustain its painters, came to an end. Then, in 1363, in what was going to become a pattern, the Black Death struck Siena once more, stealing the future and altering both individual and societal attitudes. The plague of 1348 had seemed, in retrospect, a dreadful but isolated catastrophe; the plague of 1363 was far more sinister for being familiar.

In Duccio's *Temptation on the Mountain* (Color Plates 1–2), the regularity of Jerusalem's streets speak of aspirations to order and beauty that Siena, with its irregular topography, could never realize. But that did not discourage the Noveschi from urban planning. In Duccio's ideal city, as in Ambrogio's city of *The Effects of Good Government* (Color Plate 5), no tree, no vineyard, no garden, has place within city walls. Siena through the thirteenth and early fourteenth centuries had been always in a state of becoming; but that does not mean that the Noveschi's ideal differed from Duccio's. In 1363, that ideal became impossible. In the centuries to follow, Siena's walls would shelter not just houses, warehouses, palaces, churches, and charitable institutions, but also vineyards, orchards, and gardens. And painters of that later era would not know a society like that which, for a considerable time, had placed Siena on the international stage.

The relation of painters to their city in the decades that followed 1363, and then on into a new century, has yet to be studied in any depth. Archival material and early secondary sources are abundant, far more so than for the period I have examined. For the moment, however, we must content ourselves with a backward glance to the questions I originally posed, originally set out to answer, and to our findings. What was it to be a painter in Siena during the late Dugento and first half of the fourteenth century?

We can begin, as all good stories should, with the birth of our protagonists. To be born a painter's son was likely, though not necessarily, to be directed toward an artistic career; and if one were born to a painter who had other male children, one was likely to have siblings who also took up the family profession. But that outcome was not universal; Duccio, for example, had three sons who became painters, while other sons did not. We do not know the trade or profession of Simone Martini's father or of the father to the Lorenzetti brothers. But if one's father was a painter, there was a high probability that one would be surrounded by other painters' families, for odds were that one's parents had settled in the adjoining parishes of Sant'Egidio and San Donato, the painters' district. There our young painter-to-be was to make his childhood friends; there he was likely to meet his future wife; there he probably received his training.

Concerning the apprenticeships of young painters, we know almost nothing. I assume that, where possible, children trained with their fathers; in part, economics would urge such arrangements, not only to keep expenses within the family but also to provide the senior painter with assistants. On analogy with the Goldsmiths' Guild, I think it probable that apprenticeships lasted six years, likely between the ages of fourteen and twenty. But these proposals are only informed speculations. We lack hard evidence for these matters.

Having completed his apprenticeship, the young painter was likely to settle himself in the area of Sant'Egidio/San Donato, perhaps eventually inheriting property from his father, although possibly only a share of the patrimony if such property had been left to, and was thus jointly held by, brothers. Whether his workspace was owned or rented depended on the degree of his success and/or the success of his father. For example, in the case of Niccolò di Segna, we know that his father's property, c. 1318, was valued at a mere £50 and that in 1331 Niccolò rented a workshop from the Misericordia. By that time his father, Segna di Bonaventura, was deceased and his property divided among his heirs. I therefore take it that Segna had little to leave his sons and that Niccolò's career had not been stellar. More successful painters undoubtedly owned the premises in which they and their assistants worked.

In the parishes of Sant'Egidio and San Donato, the best properties lay along an urban stretch of the Via Francigena, making workshops easily available to those coming or going along the road to and from Rome. I have noted that the topography of the area may have recommended itself. Situated on a ridge and thus open to strong breezes, the district was suitable for the various stages in the creation of panel pictures. In San Donato, the relation of painter to painter was even closer than my earlier discussion suggested. For taxation purposes the parish was divided into two *lire:* San Donato a lato de' Montanini and San Donato a lato alla chiesa. All the 1316–20 notices concerning painters' properties come from San Donato a lato de' Montanini; in the Estimo volume for San Donato a lato alla chiesa, I have found not a single item belonging to a painter. The majority of early Sienese painters lived primarily not only in one district but also side by side, as the closest of neighbors.

Given the preponderance of painters in Sant'Egidio and San Donato, we are drawn to the exceptions, especially to those artists who lived in the south of the city, in the area of Castelvecchio. Duccio moved to that district during creation of the cathedral *Maestà,* and it seems reasonable to assume that the painter judged working nearer the duomo to be somehow more practical. But we have no evidence that explains why Pietro and Ambrogio Lorenzetti settled in the area. And we cannot know what the majority of painters, living to the north, made of the fact that three of Siena's greatest painters had distanced themselves from Sant'Egidio/San Donato. Whether place bore upon social status we shall never know, but I would note that the Terzo di Città, containing Castelvecchio, seems to have been the district favored by goldsmiths, who were generally prosperous.

Earlier accounts of Sienese painting and painters generally ignore the evidence that artists were gathered together in two small areas of a city small enough to ensure frequent contacts among the citizenry. Scholarly pages generally isolate one painter from another, in a way that is just the reverse of the historical reality. And since I cannot believe that one painter's shop was closed to fellow painters, I must assume that every new technique, every new idiom, developed by one painter was almost immediately known to other artists. In other words, it is no wonder that one painter influenced another; one of the most remarkable things about early Sienese painting is the degree to which various painters maintained the autonomy they did.

Earlier accounts of Sienese painting generally ignore the large number of painters active during the period of this study. Detaching major figures from their historical context, many studies leave the reader with the impression that the history of Sienese art is fundamentally the story of a few. But if we are to understand the dynamics of creation, if our vision of Sienese art is to have depth of field, we must meditate on the secondary and minor painters whose production was background to the high achievements of genius. Indeed, I would suggest that those lesser lights were necessary to an artistic culture substantial enough to raise the few above the many.

As careers unfolded, distinctions among painters became evident, distinctions that were monetary but also something more. Artists became "shop master painters" or "wall master painters" or "figure painters" or painters of signs. Some painters would have surplus income to be invested in property, urban and/or rural; others would maintain only a small patrimony and perhaps need to rent workspace. Within the guild, notions would form of who was among "the best and wisest" and "the best and most capable." Those ratings were surely linked to the kind of commissions one received, for time would differentiate painters according to patronage, and those differentiations had economic consequences.

What can we say about the daily working lives of Siena's painters? Minor masters, such as Guido Cinatti, must have gone from one comparatively small task to another: decorating book covers, signs, furniture, banners, poles for banners, chests, and candles to be presented in the duomo. Whether such figures maintained real workshops or merely working spaces in their dwellings, we do not know. Occasionally, it seems, they formed partnerships for their mutual benefit. We are, as so often, least informed about these figures whose place was at the bottom of the artistic ladder; we glimpse them only in the type of notice found in Appendix III below. We know still less about "wall painters," who may not have maintained workshops and may have specialized in what we would call interior decoration.

The life of a major painter was varied and complex. There were drawings to be prepared for major projects; carpenters to be consulted about the provision and design of panels; pigments, paper, and gold leaf to be acquired. In the workshop there were apprentices and assistants who needed instruction, guidance, and supervision, for multiple commissions could be at various stages of production. The master might be called to participate in civic commissions created to deal with the placement of a fountain, or with work on the cathedral, or with arrangements for visiting dignitaries. He might, in addition, have some role within the government of the city, as had Duccio on the auxiliary membership of the General Council or Ambrogio on the council of peacemakers. All these matters, perhaps responsibilities within the Painters' Guild, and the management of personal property placed significant demands on a major artist, even before he began to do that for which he was employed: to paint.

Periodically, major masters with major commissions, especially frescoes, faced the necessity of expanding their équipe—by year, by month, by day, or by project—with those workers so described in the Guild's Statute. How this was done is unclear. Presumably, there were minor masters who could be trusted to prepare a panel, to lay an *arriccio*, to mix colors, to execute haloes, perhaps even to paint draperies. Where possible, major painters undoubtedly called first on family members or on painters who had been trained in the master's shop; but the Guild's prohibition on one painter's luring away the workers of another seems to point to a larger phenomenon. Here, once more, we come upon a circumstance almost completely ignored in the literature, although the existence of this "floating" population of painters should play a part in our considerations of major artists.

All the major painters here discussed worked away from Siena at one or more points in their careers, but we have very little evidence on how such projects "abroad" were handled. When Duccio created the Rucellai *Madonna,* he worked on a panel that had been made in Florence, and he employed at least one Florentine assistant, who created the halo for the lowest angel on the right and may have been responsible for the overall working of the gold background. When Ambrogio Lorenzetti, in 1327, matriculated in the Florentine Painters' Guild, had he come with Sienese assistants or did he intend to employ Florentine assistants in the event of a major commission? I very much doubt that Simone Martini or Pietro Lorenzetti went to Assisi with the intention of using local artists as helpers. Did Simone, in the late 1310s and early 1320s, move his shop to execute altarpieces in Pisa and Orvieto, or were they dispatched from Siena? Was Simone's *Saint Louis of Toulouse* altarpiece painted in Siena or Naples?

After lengthy careers, when the time seemed appropriate, painters wrote their wills. In 1348 and 1363 the deed was prompted by the catastrophe around them; in "normal" times wills were usually the products of old age. Where we know something of specific contents (our evidence being slight), there are no surprises. Both Simone and Ambrogio Lorenzetti thought first of family. Without children of his own, Simone took care of his nieces and nephews. Ambrogio thought first of his daughters and then, in the case of their demise, of his sisters-in-law. Finally, anticipating that the plague might take them all (as it did), Ambrogio and his wife left their possessions to the Confraternity of the Virgin at the Ospedale della Scala. The passing of other painters and members of their families we note only in the laconic entries of the necrologies of San Domenico.

Altogether, the evidence we have indicates that early Sienese painters lived lives deeply embedded in the values and customs of their society. At the end of a century in which the arts have become increasingly solipsistic and painters have often defined themselves as standing outside societal norms, this aspect of Sienese art needs to be stressed. The Painters' Guild did much not only to structure the professional lives of artists but also, in the requisite observances, to integrate painters' religious devotions with Siena's civic Christianity. The successful painter aped the investment strategies common to his society by acquiring property. Participation in matters related to government points in the same direction. The nonconformity, if such it be, recorded in the various fines Duccio had to pay was the exception, not the rule.

Now, many, if not all, of the matters I have discussed thus far may, in time, be found to apply to early painters in other central Italian cities. One day someone may argue that, by changing the names and places, the circumstances detailed above can be made to fit another group of painters. I suspect that the fit, in such cases, will be forced; for the particular character of Sienese culture had enormous impact on the early Sienese painter's life and career.

The painters of this study were born to a prosperous and growing city. In the thirteenth century that prosperity had been the fruit of international trade and international banking;

in the early fourteenth century it was manifest in increased investment in the city. We, with hindsight, may see the early fourteenth century as marking a change, and a change that presaged a less glorious future for Siena, but contemporaries could not have viewed things in those terms. Indeed, appearances all pointed in the other direction. The paving of streets, the attention devoted to fountains, continuing work on the cathedral, the building of the Palazzo Pubblico, and, shortly after its initial completion, the projects to add a tower and expand the fabric of the palace, like the 1326 expansion of the city's walls—all must have been viewed as signs of promise and indexes of Siena's wealth. And just as all the projects of urbanism flowed from Siena's rulers, so, where painters were concerned, was access to that wealth dependent largely on the Noveschi.

The degree to which the early Sienese painter's fortune was tied to the culture and the decisions of the ruling regime can hardly be overemphasized. One need only imagine away all the works created for the Noveschi to see how that is so; a history of Sienese painting would be impossible to write. It was the Noveschi's vision of the necessity of art and its possible uses that spurred the commissions painters received. The Noveschi understood how the success of their "foreign" policy could be embodied in fresco; they saw how enemies could be imaged in *pittura infamante;* they came to see that Ambrogio Lorenzetti, in the Sala della Pace, could give form to their ideals of governance. But most of all, the Noveschi made images central to Siena's civic Christianity. Religious imagery in the Palazzo Pubblico, in the cathedral, on the city gates, bound the state to the faith in a manner that augmented and paralleled the Nove's distribution of alms and their participation in the feast days for local saints and *beati*. Painting was an important element in defining the relation of church and state, but it was part of a much larger cultural strategy.

The character of Siena's civic Christianity, so firmly centered on the Virgin, had quite specific consequences for painters. Where many a quattrocento painter prospered in providing images of Saint Catherine of Siena or San Bernardino, there was little trecento demand for images of the city's four patron saints. Nor, it seems, was there significant demand for images and narrative scenes of local *beate* and *beati*.

Closely related to the Nove's use of painting is a circumstance we should note again. Patronage in Siena was largely corporate. It was the city's institutions that generally took responsibility for imaging the holy and the secular and for providing Siena with its painted beauties. Apparently, Sienese society harbored strong feelings about the differences between public and private and marked painting as belonging to the former. We can, of course, find exceptions to that generalization, but I take it as revealing that those exceptions relate, almost entirely, to prelates, members of the Casati, and the nobility of the *contado*. Bishop Renaldo Malavolti, Cardinal Riccardo Petroni, and Bishop Donodeus Malavolti were all buried in the duomo, the last two likely responsible for images there as well. The Ospedale della Scala benefited, in ways that likely involved pictures, from the gifts or legacies of Giovanni di Tese Tolomei, Biagio Montanini, Count Jacomo de' Silevena, and the papal notary, Messer Bindo. It seems that the decoration of the cloister of San Francesco, Siena, was funded by the Petroni. These instances may speak to one area where there were differing attitudes in differing classes. Whatever, Siena did not produce anything like the great family chapels of Florence, nor did its guilds provide patronage similar to that of the Florentine guilds.

The Noveschi were responsible for more than the awarding of commissions; their outlook touched painters' lives at any number of points. First, let me emphasize that the regime most often employed the very best painters, making distinctions between major and minor figures. Over time, the magnates and the Noveschi decided that there were painters, such as Guido Cinatti, who would do for decorating a book cover or a chest but would not do for an altarpiece. At times, art historians have been accused of projecting onto the past very modern views, foremost among them judgments of quality. But the evidence from trecento Siena is unequivocal. Those who became quasi-official painters to the commune were Duccio, Simone Martini, and Ambrogio Lorenzetti, not Segna di Bonaventura, Lippo Memmi, or Niccolò di Segna. The very painters we judge the best were so judged by their contemporaries. And if readers should think that such decisions were fortuitous, let me remind them that the regime demonstrated its judgments in the most concrete way: the Noveschi voted, as it were, with their checkbooks. Beyond that, they were willing to assist major painters by making financial arrangements in florins rather than lire, and it seems they were willing to bear a rapid increase in the cost of altarpieces. On the other hand, the distinctions made by the Nove placed large numbers of painters in the second or third class, and if the payments for book covers are reflections of a larger situation, the painters so classed must have been increasingly disadvantaged and financially pressed.

There is no doubt that the Noveschi's tendency to employ the same painter on many occasions, and thus to create quasi-official painters to the commune, was a mixed blessing. For the painter in favor, the practice ensured regular income and afforded a significant advantage. The Painters' Guild Statute tells us that artists working for the commune were freed from observing otherwise-enforced holidays. But for the painter or painters not in favor, the custom was limiting. At various times, major painters worked away from Siena, largely, I suppose, because another artist had firm grasp on commissions of the commune. Particularly in the case of the Lorenzetti brothers, sojourns abroad helped shape the mature style of both painters.

One further aspect of Noveschi patronage must be underscored: the fact that the regime saw no need to look beyond Siena's walls for its painters. Indeed, the commune, like the Painters' Guild itself, may have sought to discourage the presence of "foreign" artists. As I earlier noted, the Sienese situation differed significantly from that in Florence. This insularity, paralleled in other aspects of Sienese culture, was a major factor in defining the course Sienese painting would take.

Let me conclude with two observations about painters themselves. As recently as 1979, one historian of Siena said: "Lacking high status, and rarely providing wealth, the artistic life was in no way an avenue for upward social mobility in Siena before the sixteenth century. Even the most successful Sienese artist could not hope to earn much more than a reasonable competence."[1] I would redirect the reader to my earlier discussion of the social status of painters and to the evidence that the artist's profession allowed of a certain social mobility. Our most important case is, of course, that of Bartolommeo Bulgarini, who came to the painter's trade from a Casati family. But we also know, from their names, of painters who had learned fathers: Pietro di Ser Dota, Niccolò di Ser Sozzo, and Brandino di Ser Cieio. If my interpretation of Pietro Lorenzetti's desire to bear arms is correct, and if his marriage was indeed to the daughter of a Noveschi family, then a shift in status is clearly evident. The various nonartistic functions fulfilled by Ambrogio Lorenzetti in the city's governance, and Simone Martini's dealings with the curia in Avignon, point toward a status above that of the humble craftsman. I would, however, caution the reader. Until we have more evidence about individuals from other trades and professions, it is uncertain whether the developments I have noted were particular to painters.

In the matter of artists' finances we should also take care not to suggest a greater certainty than exists; but I would suggest that the most successful painters enjoyed a prosperity that many of their fellow citizens would have envied.[2] They never became rich in the manner of the Casati or Noveschi, not even wealthy in the degree of goldsmiths, but they certainly belonged to a place well above that of at least half of Siena's population.

And so we come to the conclusion: we may be unable to write biographies of the artists discussed in this volume, but what we do know of them, six and a half centuries after their deaths, is in fact a good deal.

Just more than a century wraps the splendid achievement that was early Sienese painting. It began at the time of the long-remembered Sienese victory at the Battle of Montaperti (1260) and ended, more or less, amidst the plague of 1363. In the fifteenth century Siena would produce painters of invention and great charm, figures such as Sassetta and Giovanni di Paolo and the Osservanza Master; but these were artists who flowered like exotic blooms sprung up on the edges of the Renaissance, painters who cast a loving eye back to the early Trecento. They would, in fact, often produce images inspired by those of their early-fourteenth-century predecessors. They were painters who told Ghiberti that Simone had been their greatest master. The painters discussed in this volume were, by contrast, among the founders of the Renaissance, and it is for that reason that I have been prompted to explore what it meant to be a painter in Siena during years so central to defining artistic ideas and practice that would have long-lasting impact on art in the West. But I recognize that the types of social and cultural history embodied in the pages of this book are only a part of the history of art. The other part is the story of images, for which this material is the necessary background. A history of early Sienese painting is now the task that lies ahead.

1. Hook, *Siena,* 104.
2. I would remind the reader that c.1318 Chele Moccolelli, sometime *operaio* to the commune, owned a house (his only holding) valued at roughly £383, while in 1324 Simone Martini bought a house not so far from Chele's for approximately £400.

Statute
of the
Painters' Guild of Siena

A translation by Gabriele Erasmi of the
Breve dell'Arte dei Pittori senesi
from the text edited by
Gaetano Milanesi in
Documenti per la storia dell'arte senese, I,
Siena, 1854

Statute of the Painters' Guild of Siena

At every stage of our endeavors, be it the beginning, the middle, or the end, let us act and speak in the name of the almighty God, and of his Mother, the Holy Virgin Mary. Amen.

As by the grace of God we are able to reveal to the uneducated and illiterate the miraculous things achieved by virtue and in virtue of our Holy Faith, our faith consisting mainly in worshiping and believing in one Trinitarian God and in his infinite power, knowledge, clemency, and love, let it be said that nothing, no matter how insignificant, can ever be taken up or brought to a conclusion without these three prerequisites: having the means to do it, knowing how to do it, and having the will to do it. And since in God is all perfection, in order that, in this endeavor, however small it be, we may have sufficient assurance of a good beginning and a successful conclusion of whatever we say or do, we shall therefore invoke and wish for the assistance of divine grace, and we shall begin by prefacing everything in the name and with the name of the Most Holy Trinity. And because spiritual things must be, and are indeed, infinitely higher and far more important than temporal ones, we shall begin by stating how the feast of our venerable and glorious patron, Messer Saint Luke, shall be observed, for not only did he depict the physical image of the glorious Virgin Mary, but he described her exceedingly holy life and customs, whereby our Guild is honored.

CHAPTER I

On the observance of Saint Luke's Day and the duty to carry a candle in procession.

We hereby decree that the holy day of Saint Luke, patron and guide of the Guild of Painters, be solemnly observed and celebrated in this fashion: on that feast day, each and every painter, whether he be a master or a laborer engaged for the year, or the month, or the day, or just for a specific job, shall carry to the festivities a candle bought at his own expense; in addition, two *doppieri,* or large candles, will be bought as offerings from the Painters' Guild, their size to be decided in accordance with whatever the times will allow. Eight days before the feast, the Rector shall call a general assembly to decide on all those things that will be needed for the celebrations. Should it happen that some painter, without legitimate justification, will not be seen with the others carrying a candle in the procession, he will be made to pay a 10-soldi fine to the Treasurer, and bring, moreover, as an offering, a candle weighing one pound to the Church of Saint Luke.

CHAPTER II

[Rubric missing in the original.]

Item, we hereby decree that all the holidays established by the Holy Church as well as, in general, all those sanctioned by the Consuls of the Merchants' Guild [the Mercanzia] will be observed by each and every member. Anyone who will disobey will be punished, and a 10-soldi fine will be levied each time.

CHAPTER III

How the rector must enjoin the members of the guild to take part in the funerals of relatives of guild members.

Item, we hereby decree that, whenever a relation of a member of the Painters' Guild passes away, such as one's father, or mother, or wife, or offspring, carnal brother, cousin, carnal nephew, or paternal cousin, the Rector shall request, through his envoy, the presence at the funeral of members of the guild, one or two men out of every shop, according to the importance of the deceased; whoever, without a legitimate excuse, will fail to go to the funeral, will be punished, and a 5-soldi fine will be levied.

CHAPTER IV

There shall be a Rector, a Treasurer, and three Councillors.

Item, we hereby decree that a Rector, a Treasurer, and three Councillors will be elected in the following way: the old Rector shall order a convocation of the members of the Guild, and when these will be gathered in general assembly, six pieces of paper will be prepared, three with some writing on them and three blank ones. Six good men will be presently nominated, and each of them will take one of these pieces of paper, which will be folded so that no one may be able to see which are the ones containing some writing and which are the ones that do not. The three of the six men who will get the written pieces of paper will immediately stand aside without speaking to anyone. The Rector will ask that they take an oath to oversee the election of the above-mentioned new officers and to choose them among the best and most competent people in the Guild. These same electors will also choose two members of the Guild to act as the judges who will hear whatever petitions may be presented against the previous officers, the aforesaid petitions being about perceived wrongs committed against those who feel aggrieved. These judges so elected will have the faculty of hearing, deliberating on, and investigating any and every case of abuse committed by the previous officers, and, according to the outcome of their investigations, they will have the faculty of passing judgment, condemning and absolving according to the gravity of the crime.

CHAPTER V

On calling an assembly within the fifteen days following the election of the Rector.

Item, we hereby decree that the new Rector must call a general assembly within fifteen days of taking office; at the assembly, the rector will ask, in the presence of every one, whether there may be anything that needs to be done for the improvement and the general good of the Guild. Having put this question to the assembly, each and every member will be free to stand up and express whatever he may think pertinent. If someone's proposal will seem worth implementing, it will be voted on in such a way that, when this proposal will be put to a vote, no one will dare say anything until a decision will be reached by means of the ballot box. Moreover, should not the Rector call a general assembly within those fifteen days, he will be fined each time 40 soldi.

CHAPTER VI

On the stipend of the Rector.

Item, we hereby decree that, in order that the officers be assiduous and scrupulous in the exercise of their duties, the Rector will receive a six-month stipend in the amount of 20 soldi, and the Treasurer a six-month stipend of 15 soldi.

CHAPTER VII

On the Guild's having an envoy.

Item, we hereby decree that the Guild shall have an Envoy entrusted with the delivery of communications, requests, and orders. His stipend for a six-month period will be in the amount of 5 soldi. Moreover, the Envoy will receive 2 denari for the delivery of each summons, and should he deliver a summons to someone who is not a member of the Guild, he will receive 4 denari.

CHAPTER VIII

That no one take work away from someone else.

Item, we hereby decree that neither painters of figures, coats of arms, and walls nor laborers attached to any such painters dare or presume to take work away from another painter, if such work was contracted in writing, receipts have been issued, or there are witnesses available, without having express permission to do so from the painter who first undertook or contracted such work. Any legitimate justification produced by persons accused of having taken someone else's work will be accepted, but he who would make false statements about these matters will be punished and fined up to the amount of 10 lire, after due consideration of the circumstances and the gravity of the action.

CHAPTER IX

That he who issues a summons against another man must pay a fee.

Item, we hereby decree that whoever will issue a summons against another person must pay a fee corresponding to the tenth part of the amount requested if this be up to 20 soldi, i.e., 1 denaro for each soldo; for amounts over 20 soldi, he will pay 12 denari per lira. If the summons will be issued without registering it, the fee will be 6 denari; if it is registered, 12 denari; in case witnesses are to be called, for every witness questioned, the fee will be 12 denari.

CHAPTER X

On refraining from work on holy days and on retaining secret watchmen.

Item, we hereby decree that no painter be allowed or forced to work on religious holy days mandated by the Holy Church nor on any holy day decreed by the Consuls of the Mercanzia. We decree, moreover, that the Rector, upon taking office, must deputize one or more secret watchmen, as he may see fit, to bring forth accusations against those who do work on such days. The Rector will order them to take an oath that they will never accuse anyone out of spite or hatred but only as part of the proper exercise of their duties. The names of said watchmen will remain secret. It is understood and stipulated that the Rector will be able to grant permission to work to those who will request it discreetly and for a good reason, keeping always in mind the requirements of the time and work and being it understood that no dispensation will be required for work commissioned by the Commune.

CHAPTER XI

That foreign painters wishing to work in Siena be bound to pay a florin.

Item, we hereby decree that any foreign painter who will wish to practice his art in Siena, before he may begin to work, will have to pay to the Painters' Guild, in the hands of the Treasurer of the Guild, the sum of a gold florin. He must also lay down good and sufficient security up to the sum of 25 lire. No painter will be allowed to hire a foreigner unless the fee owed to the Guild has been paid and the security provided. And should the foreign painter refuse to provide security, every Rector, upon taking office, is duty bound to order all shop and wall master painters not to hire any foreign painters unless they have provided security and paid the fee owed to the Guild. Whoever will contravene the above dispositions will be punished and condemned to pay the sum of 40 soldi.

CHAPTER XII

That security be provided by anyone issuing a summons against a member of the Guild.

Item, we hereby decree that, if any person who does not belong to the Guild obtains a summons against a painter, the said painter will be permitted to request a security from the person presenting the summons, in order that, should that person do something against the painter, the Rector will be empowered to hold on to the security, said security to become property of the Guild of Painters. As soon as the Rector discovers that the painter is requesting a security, that painter must be made to declare under oath whether or not the person presenting a summons against him owes him anything. If he finds that something is owed to the painter, an order must be issued for a security to be requested. But, if he finds that nothing is owed the painter, then the Rector must give open satisfaction to the person presenting a summons against the painter.

CHAPTER XIII

On the levying of duties and their extent.

Item, we hereby decree that, in order that monies be available for the needs of the Guild, every Rector will have the faculty to impose dues, and dues will be levied against all members of the Painters' Guild. Dues may be imposed up to the amount of 2 soldi and no more. Under that amount, the total, in lire and soldi, will be left to the discretion of those imposing the levy. The Guild, moreover, in order that monies, documents, and other properties of the Guild be kept safely, must keep a safe-box where monies paid to the Treasurer will be kept together with the Statute of the Guild and the Accounts Books detailing income, expenses, and summonses.

CHAPTER XIV

On refraining to employ one type of gold for another or a pigment for another.

Item, we hereby decree that no member of the Painters' Guild dare or presume to employ in his work any quality of gold or silver or pigments different from that originally stipulated, such as false gold for fine gold, tin for silver, azurite for ultramarine blue, ceruse or indigo for blue, terra rossa or minium for cinnabar. Whoever will contravene will be punished and fined 10 lire each time.

CHAPTER XV

On not revealing and discussing secrets.

Item, we hereby decree that, in order that no one dare to reveal or make known anything that was discussed in confidence or declared a secret by the Rector of the Painters' Guild, anyone who makes manifest any of the aforementioned things will be stripped of any position of honor in the Guild for a period of two years, in addition to having to pay to the Guild's Treasurer a fine of 5 lire.

CHAPTER XVI

That no officer of the Guild may nominate as Rector someone close or related to him.

Item, we hereby decree, in order that the election of the officers be accomplished in an orderly and rational way, and without special interests being involved, that the individuals overseeing the election of new officers be unable and be actually forbidden to nominate as an officer of the Guild anyone related to them, whether he be a brother or a cousin, a brother-in-law or one spouse's brother-in-law, or even a close collaborator in the shop. Contraveners will be fined each time 20 soldi.

CHAPTER XVII

That no one presume to suborn or entice away someone else's laborers.

Item, we hereby decree that no painter dare or presume, for whatever reason, to entice, flatter, and suborn laborers to leave employment with another painter, to whom they are contractually bound on an annual or a monthly basis, with the clear intention of depriving that employer of a laborer, unless this be also the intention of the employer as well as of the one enticing the laborer away. The same punishment shall apply to whoever is guilty; contraveners will pay a 25-lire fine.

CHAPTER XVIII

That no one should speak of the Rector in an offensive manner.

Item, we hereby decree that, being it right and proper that the Rector and the other officers of the Guild be treated with honor and respect, no one dare speak of them in a villainous and dishonest manner such that it will cause offence and embarrassment to the Rector and his officers, especially if such words are employed in the exercise of their office. Contraveners will be punished and fined, each time, 20 soldi, or more or less, according to the condition of the person and the gravity of the action.

CHAPTER XIX

On the Rector's acting to make peace.

Item, we hereby decree that, should it happen that members of the Guild become hostile to one another because of words spoken and actions taken, as soon as the Rector will learn of any quarrels and conflicts developing among people under his jurisdiction, he shall have the power to force them to make peace. Moreover, at least once during his term of office, the Rector shall have the faculty to summon each and every member of the Guild and examine him in secret in order to find out whether he is aware of any ill feelings being harbored by members of the Guild against each other, and, should the Rector discover that there are, indeed, quarrels and ill feelings among those subject to him, he will endeavor, as much as possible, to bring about peace and harmony.

CHAPTER XX

That the Rector, before the end of his mandate, must collect all bills.

Item, we hereby decree that every Rector, before the end of his mandate, must have collected all the money that was to be paid to the Guild from levies and fines issued to different individuals during his term of office. It is understood as well as stipulated that this does not apply to those enjoined to provide payment within a specific period of time that exceeds the term of office of the Rector issuing the fines. And, if it should happen that, for various and different reasons, the Rector has not been able to collect all these fines by the end of his term of office, we hereby decree that, on the power and authority of the present statute, he shall be allowed to collect those monies, within the fifteen days following his leaving office, with the same power and authority he had in the exercise of his functions as Rector. Contraveners will be fined 20 soldi.

CHAPTER XXI

That no Treasurer may issue fines or condone them except according to the Statute.

Item, we hereby decree that the Treasurer, unless specifically instructed by the Rector and his Council, will not have the power or faculty, because of complaints or questions to which he may be subjected, to deviate in any way from the prescriptions contained in our Statute, and, under all circumstances, he shall collect the fines, levies, and tithes that must be paid, exactly as stipulated in the various chapters. Whoever will contravene will be fined 20 soldi.

CHAPTER XXII

That no one should oppose the actions of the Rector's Envoy.

Item, in order that the Rector be obeyed and feared, we hereby decree that no member of the Guild, if ordered by the Rector to surrender a pledge, dare in any way oppose the Envoy who will come to take the pledge. Whoever, by such an action, shows contempt for the Rector's order will be punished and condemned to pay, in each instance, a fine of 10 soldi.

CHAPTER XXIII

That the Rector be empowered to order levies as needed.

Item, we hereby decree that the Rector will have the power to order levies as he sees fit according to perceived need. Those who contravene and disobey will be fined 10 soldi.

CHAPTER XXIV

That the Rector together with his Council must elect two or more individuals to emend the Statutes.

Item, we hereby decree that the Rector shall be bound, just before his term of office comes to an end, to elect, together with his Council, two or three good members of the Guild, chosen from the best and wisest. These men so elected must look at the Statutes and study them with a view to adding or deleting any items in the text of the Statute, if they feel this is in the interest of the Guild. To this purpose, should they conclude that emendations are useful and needed, they will have the authority to write new statutes. The Rector, by means of his envoy, will remind the members of the Guild in case they wish to present any petition to these officers. Whatever proposals these officers shall bring forth, these will be put in writing and brought to the Rector. The Rector will then call a general assembly (children excluded),[1] and the officers in charge of the Statute will read the ordinances that will have been proposed to them as well as all the petitions presented to them. After they have been read, the proposals will be voted upon, item by item, and the items presented and approved by a majority of two-thirds or more of the assembly will be solemnly written in the Book of Statutes and added to the other ordinances. Should the Rector be negligent in executing any of the above things, he will be fined, in each instance, 10 soldi.

CHAPTER XXV

On the punishment for perjury.

Item, we hereby decree that, if any painter will take an oath that he will be required to take by the Rector or the Treasurer, and it will be satisfactorily proved that, in so doing, he perjured himself, he will be condemned to pay 60 soldi.

CHAPTER XXVI

That no one be allowed to refuse an office.

Item, we hereby decree that no painter, unless he has proper cause for exemption, will be able or allowed to refuse any office to which he will be elected or appointed by the Guild, in order that honors and duties be shared by every one in the Guild. Contraveners will be punished and fined 5 lire.

CHAPTER XXVII

On carrying a candle on the feast of Saint Luke.

Item, we hereby decree, as an addition to the chapter dealing with the feast of Saint Luke and the duty to carry a candle in procession (*see chapter 1*), that no one will be allowed to bring to the feast a candle that has been shortened. This would neither be proper nor would it honor our Saint. Therefore, contraveners to the disposition contained in this chapter will be fined 10 soldi.

---

1. In Italian: "fanculli." Junior laborers and apprentices had to take an oath of fealty to the guild (see chapter XXXII), but it seems this chapter denies voting rights to those under the age of majority. [H.M.]

CHAPTER XXVIII

That it be the Rector's faculty and duty to account for the actions of the members of the Guild.[2]

Item, we hereby decree that the Rector, i.e., the Lord Overseer of this Guild, shall be rightfully allowed to keep detailed records in order that he be able to account, to anyone making inquiries, for those under his jurisdiction. He shall also be generally informed at all times about the paintings and the works being commissioned as well as other facts pertaining to activities going on in the Guild. Moreover, he should be able to account for all the things a painter appearing before the aforementioned Rector might ask of another painter.

CHAPTER XXIX

That each officer must account for the matters entrusted to him.

Item, we hereby decree that the Lord and Rector, the Treasurer, and all other officers of the Guild shall provide the officers especially appointed for this purpose with an account of their administration as far as the area of their competence is concerned, as well as an account of all those other matters for which they are responsible during their term of office. There will be three of such appointed officers, who will be elected at the same time a new Lord and Rector of the Guild is elected. These three officers or comptrollers must syndicate the actions of the incumbent officers and verify the quality of their performance in office, and if the latter have been negligent and lazy, and these three officers find they have sinned or committed infractions against the provisions contained in the Statute and Ordinances of this Guild, or have perjured themselves and betrayed their duties of office, they will exact punishment from those they will find guilty and will fine them a sum of 40 soldi, or a larger or smaller sum, as they will see fit, according to the nature of the infraction. They shall report their findings at a general assembly that will be called at their pleasure and will. All these actions must be undertaken and completed within the fifteen days after the old Rector and Treasurer leave office.

CHAPTER XXX

On the punishment of those summoned who do not show up.

Item, we hereby decree that, if anybody who has been summoned and will not be present at the assembly at the appointed time, or will not present himself before the Lord

---

2. In this chapter a change comes in references to the rector, who, until this point has been referred to merely by that name. Now comes "the Rector, i.e., the Lord Overseer of this Guild." In the next chapter this changes again, to "Lord and Rector." "Rector" reappears in chapters XXXIII, XXXV, XXX- VII, XXXVIII, XXXIX. In chapters XL and XLI the title is again "Lord and Rector," and returns to "Rector" alone in chapters XLII, XLIII, and XLIV. Perhaps these differing references indicate that the relevant chapers first appeared at different times? [H.M.]

and Rector of the Guild, he must immediately pay a 5 soldi fine, unless the Lord and Rector grant him license not to, such license to be obtained only for just cause.

CHAPTER XXXI

On renting a shop in one's own name.

Item, it is hereby decreed that no one who has one or more associates is to rent or let someone else rent a shop in his name only, but must rent the shop together with his associate or associates. Contraveners will be fined 10 lire each time, unless they have all agreed and stipulated to do so in the first place.

CHAPTER XXXII

That no one keep a junior laborer, unless the latter has taken his oath of fealty to the Guild.

Item, it is hereby decreed that no one will keep, in his own or in someone else's shop, any junior laborer or apprentice or anyone else for the purpose of training in or practicing the art of painting, unless this person is bonded, has taken the oath of fealty to the aforementioned Art and Guild, and has paid his dues to the Guild as prescribed in the Statute.

CHAPTER XXXIII

That no one speak or act against the Art and the Guild.[3]

Item, it is hereby decreed that no one shall act, speak, or have others act or speak against the Guild. No one shall be so daring as to authorize or have someone else authorize actions against the Guild, or against the honor, welfare, and status of the aforementioned Art and Guild. Contraveners, once proof of their actions has been made manifest to the Rector, the Treasurer, and the Councillors of the Art and Guild, or to a two-thirds majority of the assembly, will be condemned to pay a fine of 40 soldi in each instance.

CHAPTER XXXIV

That everyone be bound to denounce those who contravene the Statutes.

Item, it is hereby decreed that each member be bound by oath to denounce anyone who will act against and thus contravene the Statute of the Art. He who will bring forth

3. In Italian: "Che neuno debbia fare contro l'arte o contro l'università."

accusations and denunciations will receive half of the fine meted out to the person so denounced and accused, and his name will be kept secret.

CHAPTER XXXV

On observing feast days and the vigils of Saint Mary.

Item, it is hereby decreed that, whenever the Rector or the Envoy dispatched by him will order the observance of Saturdays, the vigils of Saint Mary, or other feasts, no one will work on such days, if so ordered as stated above, and each person will stop working completely, unless he has obtained a special license from the Rector. Contraveners will be fined 5 soldi each time.

CHAPTER XXXVI

Rubric pertaining to the holy days prescribed by the Holy Church.

All the holy days prescribed by the Holy Church of Rome, as well as some other holy days established by order of the Consuls of the Mercanzia, which we are bound to observe according to our Statute and Ordinances, will be herein indicated.

HOLIDAYS

January
The Circumcision of Christ
The Epiphany
St. Agnes Virgin
St. Paul's Conversion

February
St. Mary's Purification
St. Blaise Bishop[4]
St. Peter's Chair
St. Matthias the Apostle

March
St. Gregory Pope
The Annunciation

---

4. Patron saint of the Sienese *vescovado*. [H.M.]

St. Ambrose [Sansedoni] of Siena
Good Friday

April
St. Mark the Evangelist
St. Peter Martyr

May
St. James and St. Philip
The Invention of the Holy Cross†
St. John at Porta Latina
St. Michael Angel
The Ascension of our Lord
St. Justus

June
St. Barnabas
St. John the Baptist
St. Peter and St. Paul

July
St. Margaret Virgin
St. Mary Magdalen
St. James and St. Christopher

August
St. Peter *in vincula*
St. Dominic the Confessor
St. Lawrence Martyr
The Assumption of St. Mary
St. Bartholomew Apostle
St. Augustine
The Decapitation of St. John the Baptist

September
The Nativity of St. Mary
The Exaltation of the Holy Cross†
St. Matthew Apostle
St. Michael Archangel

October
St. Francis the Confessor
St. Luke Evangelist
The Blessed Eleven Thousand Virgins and St. Ursula
St. Simon and St. Judas

November
All Saints
The Holy Savior of the World
St. Martin Bishop
St. Clement Pope
St. Catherine Virgin
St. Andrew Apostle
St. Peter of Alexandria Pope

December
St. Ansano Martyr
St. Nicholas Bishop
St. Lucy Virgin
St. Thomas the Apostle
The Nativity of Our Lord
St. Stephen Martyr
St. John the Apostle and Evangelist
St. Innocent
St. Silvester Pope

CHAPTER XXXVII

On anyone acting against the Statute.

Item, it is hereby decreed that the Rector shall investigate as he may deem best whether anyone has acted, is acting, or will act against the Statute and the Ordinances of the Guild and the oath taken to uphold them. If proof be found of such actions, he that contravenes will pay, in each instance, a fine of ten soldi to be collected by the Treasurer of the Guild. This fine will be increased or reduced at the discretion of the Rector, after consideration of the nature of the action and the person involved.

CHAPTER XXXVIII

That the Rector must proceed against those who act against the Statute.

Item, as an addition to the preceding chapter, it is hereby decreed that the Rector of the Guild must proceed against each and every member of the Guild who contravenes, or acts in any way against the Statute, or does not obey the injunctions of the Lord and Rector of the Guild. The Rector will do so by setting up indictment or inquisition proceedings or any other inquest procedure, be it formal or informal.

CHAPTER XXXIX

On the punishment of those offending against the Guild.

Item, it is hereby decreed that, should anyone offend against the Guild and Commonwealth of Painters in words or deeds and were he then denounced to the Rector, the said Rector must investigate and punish the offender according to the forms prescribed by the Statute, and, in a public general assembly, he must formally denounce, accuse, and interdict such person.

CHAPTER XL

On the punishment of those who do not pay their fines.

Item, it is hereby decreed that, should any painter be punished and fined by the Lord and Rector and were he not to pay his fine within the time prescribed by the aforesaid Rector, or not otherwise to obey the orders of the Rector of this Art and Guild, he shall be interdicted and all the other painters will be enjoined not to deal with him, receive him, or have anything to do with him.

CHAPTER XLI

How each and every one must provide service and assistance to the Rector.

Item, it is hereby stipulated and decreed that each and every member of the Guild will provide and give aid, assistance, and counsel to the Lord and Rector of the Guild in the performance of his task of implementing the statutes and ordinances of the Guild, as well as in his endeavors to increase, advance, and protect the interests and the goals and the dignity of the Art, and, in whatever way he so wishes and requests, in each and every thing that, for whatever reason and in whatever way, pertains or may pertain to his office.

CHAPTER XLII

That each and every one be bound to keep secret every privileged information provided in confidence by the Rector.

Item, it is hereby decreed that each and every member of the Guild will be bound to keep secret all privileged information provided in confidence by the Rector of the Guild either verbally or in writing or through his Envoy and concerning matters and questions pertaining to the Painters' Guild. Such privileged information is not to be made manifest to others in any way or for whatever reason, under pain of a fine of 20 soldi, or more or less, as the Rector will deem appropriate after considering the quality of the person and the nature of the action.

CHAPTER XLIII

About those who commit actions to the detriment and shame of the Guild and their punishment.

Item, it is hereby stipulated and decreed that, should it happen that a member of the Guild does or says something that will be deemed by the Rector and by his Councillors as being to the detriment and shame of the Guild, or to be contrary to the reputation and status of the same Guild, such a person shall be punished and condemned by the Rector to the payment, in each instance, of a 10-soldi fine, or a larger or lesser sum, at the Rector's discretion, in consideration of the quality of the person and the nature of the need.

In the name of the Lord, Amen. On the nineteenth day of February of the year 1355 [1356] A.D., in the ninth indiction, all the above written statutes were corrected and approved by that most eloquent and learned man, Lord Rico de Morrano of Modena, distinguished Doctor of Laws, Appellate Judge and Mayor of the Commune of Siena; by the Consuls of the Mercanzia, and by other learned men chosen for this purpose by the Council of the Twelve, Governors and Defenders of the Republic and Commonwealth of Siena, according to the form of the Statutes of the Commune of Siena, after deleting all those statutes that, in some respect, did not reflect well on the honor and status of the Commune of Siena, and adding the provision that no one should make use of any of the invalidated or abrogated statutes under pain of sanctions contained in the Statutes of the Commune of Siena.

I, Simon, son of the late Ristoro dei Ristori di Modena, notary by imperial authority, and presently notary and officer of the aforesaid Lord Rico, was a witness to the approval and, by order of the Lord Mayor Rico, countersigned and published it.

CHAPTER XLIV

On giving work estimates and the manner of paying fees.

Item, it is hereby stipulated and decreed that, in the Painters' Guild, no one will be authorized to provide a work estimate without permission from the Rector; no one will be allowed to provide an estimate unless he is a member of the Painters' Guild; and, finally, no one will provide an estimate if those who are requesting it have not paid beforehand to the Guild's Rector a fee of 8 soldi per lira for an estimate under 40 lire, or 40 soldi per lira for an estimate over 40 lire. Half of the estimate fee will go the Guild; the other half will be retained by him who makes the estimate. Whoever will contravene this chapter will be fined 5 lire in each instance.

[A leaf is missing. It might have contained the approval of these Statutes as issued by the Council of the Nine, which the Council of the Twelve may have later removed (written in a seventeenth-century hand).][5]

CHAPTER XLV

That the Treasurer will obey the Rector and in what manner.

Item, it is hereby decreed that, being it the duty of the Treasurer to implement the orders and commands of the Rector, something in which he should never be negligent or slow, and for which he should retain a good Envoy capable of delivering every message or request, if the Treasurer will be tardy in this respect, he will incur very stiff fines every time he will be found wanting. The fine will be, each time, 15 soldi.[6]

CHAPTER XLVI

How the Rector must call a General Assembly.

Item, as an addition to the chapter on the Rector's having the faculty of calling an assembly whenever he so wishes (*see chapter XXIII*), the assembly shall be constituted by no less than ten Councillors. It is understood that the number will include the Rector's Councillors; these ten or more Councillors must represent in equal numbers, as far as that is possible, all the different categories of the painting trade, i.e., figure painters, sign and wall

---

5. This is Milanesi's note. [H.M.]

6. In the Italian, the fine is described as "buona et grossa." The description reveals that the sum, 15 soldi, which we might regard as so small as not to matter, was in fact considered by contemporaries significant. It therefore helps us understand that fines of £10 or £25 must have been regarded as enormous. [H.M.]

painters. It is hereby decreed that, should the Rector be found negligent in this respect, he will be fined, in each instance, 25 soldi.

CHAPTER XLVII

On the obligation of carrying a candle for the feast of St. Luke.

Item, it seems necessary to make this addition to the chapter dealing with the feast of St. Luke and specifically with the obligation of carrying a candle (*see chapters I, XXVII*). Although the Rector does call a general assembly eight days before the feast, he should have the order issued personally to each and every one, since it is never the case that everybody is present at the general assembly. Should the Rector fail to do this, he will be fined 20 soldi.

CHAPTER XLVIII

On the election of the Rector and Treasurer.

Item, as an addition to the chapter on the election of the Rector (*see chapter IV*), it is hereby decreed that the three electors, as they proceed in the selection of the Rector, will secure the nomination of three good men, to be chosen among the best and most capable in the whole Guild, who will be elected by secret ballot at the general assembly. The one of the three who will gather the majority of votes will be and must be the Rector of the Guild. Should it ever happen that there be a dead heat between two of the three, the oldest man shall be the Rector. The vote counting will be conducted by the incumbent Rector. He and the incumbent Councillors will cast their ballot in advance in order to avoid their being able to decide the election of the new Rector insofar as, by one or more votes, they could determine the election or the defeat of whomever they wished. Moreover, the three men overseeing the election will proceed to the selection of the Treasurer, the Councillors, and the Comptrollers, as it was previously done. The incumbent Rector and his Councillors must take an oath, which will be administered by the Treasurer, that they will conduct the elections and count ballots scrupulously and honestly without employing any malice in the attribution of the votes. Should the Rector fail to do so, he will be fined 40 soldi.

In the name of the Lord, Amen. On the twentieth day of February of the year 1357 [1358]*, in the eleventh indiction, all the above written statutes and ordinances were approved by the noble and learned Lord Ludovico da Spoleto, Appellate Judge and Lord Mayor of Siena, by the Consuls of the Mercanzia, and by other wise men elected for this purpose by the Council of the Twelve governing and defending the State of the Commune of Siena, in order to delete and invalidate all those statutes and ordinances that might somehow offend the honor, status, and freedom of the Commune of Siena. This approval is not intended to be construed as an exception to decrees and statutes presently enacted or to* *be enacted in the future in the Commune of Siena, nor is it intended as an exception to the jurisdiction and statutes pertaining to specific officers of the Commune of Siena, nor to the jurisdiction and statutes of the Consuls of the Mercanzia, which they might exercise by tradition or by right. The approval implies as well that no one is to make use of whatever statutes have been abolished and invalidated, under pain of sanctions prescribed in the Statutes of the Commune of Siena.*

I, Francesco Angelitti of Treviso, notary by imperial authority, presently notary and officer of the aforesaid Lord Mayor, was a witness to the aforementioned approval, and by mandate of the same Lord Mayor, countersigned and published it.

[There are two more approvals, one from late February 1359 (1360), and one from 21 April 1361.][7]

CHAPTER XLIX

On making contributions for the feast of Saint Andrew Gallerani at the Church of the Misericordia.

Item, it has been stipulated and decreed that, every year from now on, the Painters' Guild will raise and spend 4 lire for the feast of St. Andrew Gallerani. This sum shall be raised in full and shall be apportioned to each and every one in lire or soldi, as is necessary and deemed appropriate by those ordering this contribution, in order that the aforementioned 4 lire be spent for the purchase of candles and the placement in church of two *doppieri,* as specifically decided on that occasion by the Painters' Guild. It is understood, as well as stipulated, that the feast will be celebrated in the Church of Santa Maria della Misericordia in the city of Siena and that each and every painter will be expected, under pain of a 10-soldi fine, to be present at the Feast and carry a candle of the prescribed size.

[This is followed by five approvals dating respectively from 15 February 1361(1362); 21 February 1362 (1363); 27 February 1364 (1365); 24 February 1365 (1366); 16 May 1384.][8]

CHAPTER L

[*No rubric.*]

In the name of the omnipotent God, of his Blessed Mother, the Holy Virgin Mary, and of all the Saints of the heavenly host, especially the Blessed Saint Luke the Evangelist, lord and guide of the Painters' Guild, who depicted and gave us the image of the Virgin Mary, the mother of the Son of God.

We hereby decree that the feast of the venerable Saint Luke be solemnly observed

7. Milanesi's note.   8. Milanesi's note.

by each painter, whether or not he be present in the city, and that, for this feast, each and every painter, whether he be a master or a laborer engaged for the year, the month, or the day, or just for a specific work, will be expected to carry and absolutely must carry a candle bought at his own expense. Should it happen that someone be out of the city, and be in the country around Siena, in that case his partner[9] or master will have to send a candle for the celebrations on behalf of the person who is absent from Siena, always keeping in mind the condition of the person and the nature of the fact. Henceforth the feast will take place and will be always celebrated in the Church of Santa Maria della Misericordia in Siena, as decreed by the general assembly of the Painters' Guild with a more than two-thirds majority, the vote having been cast with black or white ballots. This deliberation took place in the Casa della Misericordia in Siena on 30 August 1367.

CHAPTER LI

That no one complain against the previous deliberation.

Item, we order that no painter dare or presume, in assembly or out of assembly, to criticize, protest, or seek to turn others against the above written deliberation, which was formally approved by the Guild. Should anyone do so, he will be fined and will pay to the Treasurer, who will receive it on behalf of the Guild, the sum of 10 lire. Moreover, the contravener, from that moment on, will forfeit his right to hold office in and receive benefits from the Guild for a period of ten years.[10]

CHAPTER LII

That no foreigner be allowed to cause trouble.

Item, in order that no foreigner be the cause of trouble or trickery, we hereby decree that, should a foreign painter come to the City of Siena and work in the city with a local master on an annual, monthly, or daily basis or be engaged for a specific work, as soon as he is about to begin his labors, his master must give the Guild a surety on his behalf for the amount of 25 lire of Sienese denari, *or pledge to provide the equivalent in labor* [text in italics added at a later date].[11]

---

9. In Italian: "suo compagno." [H.M.]

10. Given the size of the fine and the additional penalties connected with this provision, the matter was serious indeed. Because the provision of a candle for this feast was an old and presumably long-standing requirement, perhaps controversy had arisen over the site of the celebrations? [H.M.]

11. Milanesi's note.

CHAPTER LIII

On a foreign painter's setting up shop.

Item, we order that, if any foreign painters were to set up shop in Siena, alone or in partnership with a local master, they must pay the Treasurer of the Guild 5 lire of denari, *or they must pledge to provide the equivalent in labor* [text in italics added at a later date].[12]

CHAPTER LIV

On the painting of signs for taverns.

Item, we order that no painter, other than the Treasurer of the Guild, will be allowed to paint signs for taverns, provided these conditions will be observed: the sign will be sold for no more than 8 denari, half of which will go to the Guild, the other half to the Treasurer himself. Should the Treasurer not be interested in painting such signs, he will be able to extend this privilege to anybody he may wish to choose, provided the price will stay the same.

In the name of the Lord, Amen. On the 26th day of February of the year 1367 [1368], *in the fifth indiction, the above Statutes were emended and approved by the good and noble Lord Angelo Perilli de Guadagiaris*[?] *from Foligno, Doctor of Laws, Appellate Judge, and Lord Mayor of the Commune of Siena, by the learned Consuls of the Mercanzia of the aforementioned city, and by officers elected by the office of the Council of the Twelve. Having deleted and invalidated, etc. etc.*

I, Giovanni, son of the late Puccio of Camerino, etc.

[Followed by another approval dated 26 March 1370.][13]

CHAPTER LV

Henceforth the feast of Saint Luke will be observed and celebrated by the painters in the Church of the Hospital of Santa Maria della Scala in Siena.

In the name of almighty God, of his mother, Saint Mary, of the Blessed Saint Luke the Evangelist, guide, patron, lord and master of the art of painters, and of all the Saints in the heavenly host. Amen.

Some wise men in the Painters' Guild, elected and called upon with the Rector to

---

12. Milanesi's note.
13. Milanesi's note.

participate in the general assembly of painters, gathered together in order to establish where, in the future, the Guild will celebrate the feast of Saint Luke; by virtue of the power delegated to them by the general assembly, having first invalidated every statute in contradiction with their mandate, as is evident from the Treasurer's records, they agreed to stipulate that, henceforth, in the name of God, the Rector and all the members of the Guild will celebrate the feast of Saint Luke in the Church of the Hospital of Santa Maria della Scala, according the manner, forms, conditions, and punishments that were in force when that same feast, in the past, was celebrated in the Church of Santa Maria della Misericordia. This means that all painters, whether they be masters or laborers, masters or partners, will be expected, on the day of the Blessed Saint Luke, to carry a candle and follow the Rector in procession to the feast that will be held at the Hospital of Santa Maria della Scala, just as, before, they were expected to carry a candle and follow the Rector in procession to the Hospital of Santa Maria della Misericordia. This statute will have validity and precedence over whatever other statute that might contradict it.

In the name of the Lord, Amen. On the last day of November of the year 1379 of the Incarnation of the Lord, in the third indiction, under the rule of the Lord Urban VI, Pope by Divine Providence, the preceding Statutes and Ordinances were emended and approved by the noble and distinguished Doctor of Laws, Ser Giovanni, son of the late Bernardino de Lapis of Bologna, honorable judge, etc.

I, Giovanni di Jacopo from Sacile, public notary by imperial authority, etc.

CHAPTER LVI

That each and every one must carry a candle for the feast of St. Luke.

Item, we hereby decree that, in order that the feast of Saint Luke be celebrated in the most solemn and appropriate way, each painter who happens to be in Siena or within a four-mile distance from it, will carry in procession a one-pound candle and will follow the Rector until the latter returns to the Guild's quarters. As for specifics, this ruling is to be as follows: shop masters and wall-painting masters must carry a one-pound candle; apprentices will carry a half-pound candle. Those who happen to be ill on the day of the feast as well as those who will be away from the city and in the countryside will be obliged to send a candle as indicated above (*see chapter L*). Contraveners will pay the Guild a fine of 5 lire, half of which will be kept the Guild, while the other half will be given to the Consuls of the Mercanzia.

CHAPTER LVII

That, in dealing with cloth dyers, nothing be done that contravenes the Statute.

Item, we hereby decree that no one who is under the jurisdiction of the Painters' Guild will be allowed to lend, sell, or donate to any cloth dyers, or any of their apprentices, any tools or materials of the painters' trade, such as brushes, pigments, or mordants. Moreover, nobody will be allowed to do drawings on paper or cloth unless these belong to him or his dependents. In addition, no one is to do anything for the dyers' benefit that could be deemed detrimental to the Guild's interests or might bring shame to it. Contraveners to these dispositions will be fined in the amount of 10 lire, half of which will go the Guild, the other half to the Consuls of the Mercanzia. The Rector will ensure the payment of fines, and anyone will be free to denounce contraveners to the Rector with the assurance that his name will be kept secret and that he shall have as compensation one-fourth of the value of the collected fine.

CHAPTER LVIII

On addressing the Rector in a villainous and offensive way.

Item, we hereby decree, as an addition to the chapter dealing with those who insult the Rector (*see chapter XVII*), that anyone under the jurisdiction of the Guild who will address the Rector, while the latter is exercising his functions, in a villainous, offensive, or threatening manner will be fined, in each instance, 5 lire to be paid to the Treasurer, who will receive them on behalf of the Guild. Half of the amount will be retained by the Guild; the other half will be paid to the Consuls of the Mercanzia.

CHAPTER LIX

On taking away from another painter work originally contracted to the latter.

Item, we hereby decree, as an addition to the chapter on not taking away work from one another (*see chapter VIII*), that, should anyone take over work originally contracted to another painter, and receipts be kept, or other written documentation be available, or someone bear witness to the fact, that person will be punished. Contraveners will be fined 25 lire to be paid into the hands the Treasurer of the Guild, being it understood that half of the sum will go to the Guild, and the other half will be paid to the Consuls of the Mercanzia. Moreover, the work will be given back to the individual who had it first. This will not apply to the case in which the action was undertaken with the agreement of the person first contracted to do the work. Should the Rector be negligent in imposing the above-mentioned fine, upon leaving office, he shall be forced by his successor to pay the fine himself.

CHAPTER LX

That, after leaving office, the Treasurer must present an accounting of his actions within fifteen days.

Item, we hereby decree that, in the interest of the Guild's assets, each Treasurer, who will eventually be elected, shall, within fifteen days after leaving office, present an accounting of his actions while in office and surrender to the new Treasurer all appurtenances, pledges, and items belonging to the Guild. His report will be read at the first assembly called by the new Rector. If he does not provide an account of his actions and does not surrender what belongs to the Guild within that time, it is understood that he will have to pay to the Guild a fine of 40 soldi. Should the rector be negligent in imposing the payment of this fine, he will be condemned to pay a fine of 5 lire himself, half of this amount going into the Guild's coffers, the other half to be paid to the Consuls of the Mercanzia.

Item, at the meeting of the Council of the Thirty-Six of the Guild of Merchants of the City of Siena, held on 28 April 1402, it was deliberated that the following chapter be added to the present Statute.

CHAPTER LXI

On avoiding the purchase of presumably stolen items and on punishments thereof.

With a view to avoiding commission of crime, and especially theft, it was deliberated and decreed in the aforementioned Council that no person subject to the jurisdiction of this Statute may purchase for himself or for others any item, such as clothes, hardware, cloths, linen, gold, or silver, from any suspicious individual when there is reason to presume that such a person may have illicitly and illegally come into possession of that item, or may not have legitimately bought it; buyers of stolen merchandise will be subjected to losing the item thus bought and being fined for an amount equal to the market value of the item purchased. The Treasurer will be bound to collect such fines, and the Rector will ensure that this regulation be observed, on pain of being themselves fined double the amount involved, should they be negligent in the execution of it. Anyone will have the faculty of bringing forth accusations and denunciations, and his name will be kept secret.

[There is a deed signed by Salerno di Giannino and a note signifying that the Statute was approved on 10 May 1402. On the verso, there are the two names of Lippo di Vanni and Iacomo di frate Mino.][14]

---

14. Milanesi's note.

APPENDIX I: PLACING PAINTERS

The evidence for placing painters in the city of Siena comes from archival records, a good number of which are published and some of which not. In what follows, I have gathered a representative sample from unpublished primary sources, published sources, and unpublished secondary sources, the latter taken from manuscripts in the Biblioteca Comunale of Siena. I have organized the material by parish and ordered it chronologically. For a map of Siena's parishes, see Figure 1.

THE NOTICES

Terzo di Camollia: San Donato

1. Duccio (1289, September 1293, 7 April and 4 May 1302, 4 December 1302, 1309), Satkowski, *Duccio,* 55, 59, 64–66.
2. Vigoroso (1291), Ettore Romagnoli, *Biografia cronologica de' bellartisti senesi* (c. 1832), 13 vols., Florence, 1976, I, 309–10.
3. Guido di Graziano (1291), Romagnoli, *Biografia cronologica,* I, 415–16; (1292), Siena, BC, MS C.IV.17, fol. 236r (Benvoglienti).
4. Guarnieri di Graziano (1292), Romagnoli, *Biografia cronologica,* I, 399.
5. Angolo and Giacommucio sell land in the parish (1289), Romagnoli, *Biografia cronologica,* I, 427.
6. Jacomuccio (8 October 1292), ASS, Biccherna 108, fol. 126r.
7. Masarello di Gilio (30 May 1303), Borghesi and Banchi, *Nuovi documenti,* 6–8.
8. Mino di Graziano (4 December 1310), Borghesi and Banchi, *Nuovi documenti,* 9; (12 June 1312), Siena, BC, C.VII.20, separate sheet following fol.147r (Carli).
9. Gano di Orlando (1310), Romagnoli, *Biografia cronologica,* II, 61.
10. Nerio di Ugolino (12 June–7 July 1311), Bacci, *Dipinti inediti,* 142.
11. Pietro di Pietro (2 January 1317), Romagnoli, *Biografia cronologica,* II, 116; (1340), Romagnoli, *Biografia cronologica,* II, 129.
12. Memmo and Mino di Filippuccio (c. 1318), ASS, Estimo 131, fol. 49r. See also Appendix II.
13. Guido di Ghezzo (c. 1318), ASS, Estimo 131, fol. 245r. See also Appendix II. 27. (1328, 1332, 8 June 1333, 1334) Borghesi and Banchi, *Nuovi documenti,* 12–13, 19, 21.

14. Vannuccio and Niccola di Mino (c. 1318), ASS, Estimo 131, fol. 285r. These brothers also had property in Magione. See also Appendix II.
15. Vannuccio di Mino (c. 1318), ASS, Estimo 131, fol. 311r (property separate from that in the previous notice). See also Appendix II.
16. Ugolino and Muccio di Nerio (c. 1318), ASS, Estimo 131, fols. 154v–155r. See also Appendix II.
17. Guido di Nerio (24 May–8 July 1318), Bacci, *Dipinti inediti,* 144–45, and ASS, Gabella contratti 40, fol. 11r.
18. Monaldo di Palmerio ("Monaldus Palmerii") (c. 1318), ASS, Estimo 131, fol. 304r. See also Appendix II.
19. Tavena d'Andrea (c. 1318), ASS, Estimo 131, fols. 159r–162v. See also Appendix II.
20. Muccio di Nerio (25 August–20 September 1319), Bacci, *Dipinti inediti,* 146.
21. Cosone di Cello (9 May 1318), Siena, BC, MS P.III.49, fol. 526r (Milanesi).
22. Mino di Voglia (c. 1318), ASS, Estimo 131, fol. 242r. See also Appendix II.
23. Simone Martini (2 January–4 February 1324), Bacci, *Fonti e commenti,* 146. (Bacci believed the notice was an error and that the parish should be Sant'Egidio.)
24. Donato Martini (3 October–29 November 1324), Bacci, *Fonti e commenti,* 147.
25. Ugolino di Nerio (26 February–21 May 1325, 24 January–6 February 1327), Bacci, *Dipinti inediti,* 143–44. See also Appendix II.
26. Vanni di Dietisalvi (26 April 1331), Siena, BC, MS C.v.7, fol. 274r (Benvoglienti).
27. Niccolò di Segna rents a workshop in this parish (4 November 1331), Bacci, *Fonti e commenti,* 44.
28. Guccio "chiamato Pietro Tavena" (1332–33), Siena, BC, MS P.III.46, fol. 428r (Milanesi).
29. Romano di Mino (30 November 1336), Siena, BC, MS P.III.51, fol. 224v (Milanesi).
30. Cecco di Martino (24 March 1343), Siena, BC, MS P.III.50, fol. 590r (Milanesi); (1344), Romagnoli, *Biografia cronologica,* II, 499.
31. Galgano di Duccio (15 June 1343), Bacci, "Commentarii," 247.
32. Bonaccorso di Pace (19 November 1348), Siena, BC, MS P.III.50, fol. 589r (Milanesi), and Milanesi, *Documenti,* I, 50.
33. Angelo di Nalduccio (1349), Romagnoli, *Biografia cronologica,* II, 626.
34. Biagio di Goro has workshop in this parish (12 April 1350, 2 April 1353), ASS, MS B. 82, fols. 75r and 87r. See also G. Freuler, *Biagio di Goro Ghezzi a Paganico,* Florence, 1986, 125.
35. Bartolo di Fredi and Andrea Vanni rent a workshop in this parish (13 December 1353), Borghesi and Banchi, *Nuovi documenti,* 27.
36. Jacomo di Bindo in San Donato (no date), Milanesi, *Documenti,* I, 34.

Terzo di Camollia: Sant'Egidio

1. Duccio (January 1286), Stubblebine, *Duccio,* I, 194; Satkowski, *Duccio,* 54.
2. Dietisalvi (1285, 1291), Romagnoli, *Biografia cronologica,* I, 167.
3. Fazio di Dietisalvi (1301), Romagnoli, *Biografia cronologica,* I, 209; (15 May 1302), Bacci, *Fonti e commenti,* 70.
4. Sandro di Masarello (19 July 1304), Siena, BC, MS A.VIII.1, fol. 320v.
5. Sabatino di Ramo (4 December 1310), Borghesi and Banchi, *Nuovi documenti,* 9; (1315, 1321), Romagnoli, *Biografia cronologica,* II, 111.

6. Mino Prete (4 December 1310), Borghesi and Banchi, *Nuovi documenti,* 9.
7. Masarello di Gilio (c. 1318), ASS, Estimo 137, fol. 87r; (19 March 1337), Borghesi and Banchi, *Nuovi documenti,* 8.
8. Cecco di Puccio (c. 1318), ASS, Estimo 136, fol. 417r. Living in Sant'Egidio (1323–25?), Siena, BC, MS P.III.49, fol. 528v (Milanesi).
9. Sabatino's widow has a house (c. 1318), ASS, Estimo 136, fol. 219r.
10. Ambrogio Lorenzetti (2 January 1324), Rowley, *Ambrogio Lorenzetti,* I, 129.
11. Simone Martini (2 January–8 February 1324), Bacci, *Fonti e commenti,* 142; (1329) Bacci, *Fonti e commenti,* 157–58.
12. Memmo di Filippuccio (2 January–4 February 1324), Bacci, *Fonti e commenti,* 145 (who believes this is an error for San Donato).
13. Francesco di Simone (1325–26), Siena, BC, MS P.III.46, fol. 428r (Milanesi).
14. Guido di Cinatto (1326), Romagnoli II, 118–19.
15. Romano di Mino (1348), Romagnoli, *Biografia cronologica,* II, 495.
16. Piero di Bacharello (no date), Milanesi, *Documenti,* I, 36.
17. Nutino Piovani (1347?), Milanesi, *Documenti,* I, 49.
18. Guido di Cino (2 December 1349), Siena, BC, MS P.III.50, fol. 590v (Milanesi).
19. Pietro di Vannuccio (10 April 1355), Siena, BC, MS P.III.50, fol. 209r (Milanesi).
20. Giacomo di Pietro (1363?), Milanesi, *Documenti,* I, 38.

Terzo di Camollia: Sant'Antonio

1. Tuccio di Betto (no date), Romagnoli, *Biografia cronologica,* II, 498; (27 February 1342), Siena, BC, MS P.III.50, fol. 590r (Milanesi).
2. Franciescho di Vanni (no date), Romagnoli, *Biografia cronologica,* II, 35.
3. Guidone di Jacopo (1343), Siena, BC, MS P.III.50, fol. 591r (Milanesi).
4. Viciento di Vanni (1346), Romagnoli, *Biografia cronologica,* II, 615; (1347) ASS, Biccherna 408, fols. 30v, 92r.
5. Jacomo (1351), Romagnoli, *Biografia cronologica,* II, 642.
6. Matteo di Mino (1355), Siena, BC, MS P.III.50, fol. 209r (Milanesi).
7. Nello di Betto (1357), Milanesi, *Documenti,* I, 34.

Terzo di Camollia: San Pietro a Ovile

1. Segna di Bonaventura (13 August–15 September 1316, 1318), Bacci, *Fonti e commenti,* 37, 39.
2. Biagio di Masarello (1320), Romagnoli, *Biografia cronologica,* II, 171.
3. Fede di Nalduccio (27 July 1348), ASS, Gabella contratti 51, fol. 49r.
4. Jacomo di Cino (1352?), Milanesi, *Documenti,* I, 31.

Terzo di Camollia: San Cristoforo

1. Pietro di Ser Dota (1348?), Milanesi, *Documenti,* I, 30.
2. Giovanni di Paolo (18 November 1348), Siena, BC, MS P.III.50, fol. 587v (Milanesi).
3. Fede di Nalduccio (1356), Siena, BC, MS P.III.50, fol. 209r (Milanesi).

Terzo di Camollia: Magione

1. Guido di Ghezzo (1340), Borghesi and Banchi, *Nuovi documenti*, 20.
2. Niccola di Mino and his brother Vannuccio (c. 1318), ASS, Estimo 131, fol. 286r. These brothers also had property in San Donato. See also Appendix II.

Terzo di Città: San Quirico in Castelvecchio

1. Duccio (1310), Satkowski, *Duccio*, 76–77 [Contrada of Stalloreggi]; (1311), Satkowski, *Duccio*, 80. [two notices, one for the Lira of Stalloreggi di dentro, part of San Quirico, and another for Stalloreggi di fuore]; (June 1313), Satkowski, *Duccio*, 81.
2. Pagno di Compagno (1311), Bacci, *Fonti e commenti*, 100. [NOTE: the notice is actually for the *lira* of Porta all'Arco, part of San Quirico.]
3. Ser Bindo Dietavive, miniaturist (1311), Bacci, *Fonti e commenti*, 101.
4. Bindo (30 June 1324), ASS, Biccherna 149, fol. 170v.
5. Ambrogio di Duccio (1326), Bacci, "Commentarii," 247.
6. Pietro Lorenzetti (27 October 1340, 26 February 1341, 18 September 1344), Bacci, *Dipinti inediti*, 95, 98. [NOTE: the notice of 1341 is actually for the *lira* of Porta all'Arco.]
7. Paolo di Neri (5 July 1342), Siena, BC, MS P.III.50, fol. 590v (Milanesi).

Terzo di Città: San Pietro in Castelvecchio

1. Ambrogio Lorenzetti (9 June 1348), Wainwright, "The Will of Ambrogio Lorenzetti."

Terzo di Città: San Salvatore

1. Lando di Vinuccio (1344?), Siena, BC, MS P.III.50, fol. 224r (Milanesi).

Terzo di Città: San Pellegrino

1. Piero di Bacharello (no date), Milanesi, *Documenti*, I, 36.

Terzo di San Martino: San Vigilio di Fuore[1]

1. Meuccio di Bernardino (3 March 1312), Bacci, *Fonti e commenti*, 104.

Terzo di San Martino: San Giorgio

1. Francesco di Nerio (20 June 1350), ASS, Spedale 514, fol. 222r; (1352) Siena, BC, MS P.III.49, fol. 533r (Milanesi).

---

1. Adjoining San Vigilio, but outside the city wall.

Terzo di San Martino: San Martino

1. Bartolo di Fredi and Andrea Vanni (13 December 1353), Borghesi and Banchi, *Nuovi documenti*, 27. [NOTE: The notice indicates this is the parish of residence for the painters, but concerns a workshop rented in San Donato.]

The following notices do not include reference to the specific parish where a painter lives, but to the *lira* and *terzo* or simply to the *terzo*.

Terzo di Città

1. Verio di Ugolino (before 1318?), Bacci, *Dipinti inediti*, 141.
2. Pietro Lorenzetti (before 1318?), Bacci, *Dipinti inediti*, 141.
3. Sons of Petruccio Dietisalvi (1311), Bacci, *Fonti e commenti*, 97.
4. Ghezzo bendaio (Lira de' Manetti, 1311), Bacci, *Fonti e commenti*, 99.
5. Ghezzo Buonfigliuoli detto Bitatto (Lira de' Manetti, 4 April 1312), Bacci, *Fonti e commenti*, 103.
6. Cecco di Vanni (29 June 1355), Siena, BC, MS C.v.5, fol. 10v (Benvoglienti).

Terzo di Camollia

1. Cola di Fuccio, miniaturist (before 1318?), Bacci, *Dipinti inediti*, 141.
2. Donato Martini (before 1318?), Bacci, *Dipinti inediti*, 141.
3. Simone Martini (before 1318?), Bacci, *Dipinti inediti*, 141.

ANALYSIS

These lists of painters in specified parishes contain eighty-one names. Forty names, by far the largest group, appear under San Donato. Under Sant'Egidio, there are nineteen names, but of those four also appear in San Donato. In other words, a total of fifty-five different painters are recorded in these two parishes, some 68 percent of painters listed. But if we add to this central core the painters living in the immediately adjacent parishes of San Cristoforo, San Pietro a Ovile, and Sant'Antonio, some thirteen painters not recorded as resident elsewhere, we find 84 percent of painters lived or worked in this larger unit, which was, in real measurement, quite small.

APPENDIX II: NEW DOCUMENTS ON PAINTERS' PROPERTY

It often seems that documentation concerning individual early Sienese painters survives precisely in a quantity large enough to seize our attention and then to frustrate our attempts to answer the questions it raises. This is particularly true of documentation relating to the real worth of painters. In the discussions of Chapter II, where the evidence for Simone Martini, the Memmi, and Pietro and Ambrogio is examined, we are keenly aware just how partial that evidence is. But there is one case of documentation, partially unpublished, that helps us see further into the painters' world. I refer to documentation related to Ugolino di Nerio and his family, and I suggest that what it reveals we may regard as paradigmatic.

A notice of 1311 records the purchase of land and "other things" by Ugolino's father, Nerio di Ugolino, described as a painter living in the parish of San Donato.[1] By 1318, when Guido di Nerio, also a painter living in San Donato, received a modest dowry of 50 lire from his future bride, Nerio was dead.[2] In 1327 Guido matriculated in the Arte de' Medici e Speziali, the Painters' Guild, in Florence.[3] Obviously he was working or intended to work in that city, but this is the last we hear of him. Ugolino had another brother, Muccio or Minuccio di Nerio, also a painter and a resident of San Donato. He received, in 1333, two very modest payments for painting coats of arms on the books of the captain of the people and of the podestà; by 3 September 1342 he was deceased.[4] A painter named Nerio di Muccio, perhaps Muccio's son, was buried in San Domenico on 31 May 1340.[5] Another painter, Cristofano di Muccio, possibly another son, is perhaps recorded in 1343, and on 17 October 1348 received the large sum of 100 florins as dowry from his future wife.[6] Thus far, we have evidence only that painting was a family profession and that father and two sons lived in the parish of San Donato.

In 1316, Siena began to plan for a new round of taxes and ordered the creation of a complete *Table of Possessions* in the city and in the contado. William Bowsky has pointed out that the *Table* for the city and its immediate surrounds were finished by October of 1319 and the volumes for the

1. Bacci, *Dipinti inediti,* 142.
2. Bacci, *Dipinti inediti,* 144–45.
3. Bacci, *Dipinti inediti,* 145. Perhaps it was the success of his brother Ugolino with Florentine patrons, especially the commission for the high altarpiece of Santa Croce, that led Guido to anticipate success of his own in that city.
4. Bacci, *Dipinti inediti,* 147–49.
5. Bacci, *Dipinti inediti,* 149.
6. Bacci, *Dipinti inediti,* 150. Bacci suggests (149–50) that a Nerio di Ugolino, mentioned in 1325, may have been Ugolino's son, but the document is not clear on this. The document supposedly relating to Cristofano provides only the first name.

contado were nearing completion.⁷ The so-called Estimo volumes contain records of each individual's real property, listed with indication of its location and an evaluation. Estimo 131 contains the records relating to Ugolino.⁸ All the property is listed as the joint possessions of Ugolino and Muccio. The initial entries—there is a later addition—are made up of urban real estate, a house and garden in San Donato valued at £250, and a field of approximately three acres in the same parish and valued at 85 lire and 10 soldi. There are also notices of six pieces of property, amounting to roughly eighteen acres and valued at £874, in Sovignano in the Val d'Arbia, approximately twenty kilometers south of Siena. Between August and September of 1319 Muccio bought a vineyard in Sovignano for £46.⁹ Although the relevant notice names only Muccio, it seems likely he was adding to the land held with his brother. Toward the end of Estimo 131, an additional entry records one more field in Sovignano, valued at £110.

In Estimo 79, which includes the assessments for Sovignano itself, we discover a notice of 20 April 1323 concerning a piece of land sold to the brothers by a local resident, Minnuccio di Mino.¹⁰ The value of the purchase was 24 lire and 2 soldi. Four years later, between 24 January and 6 February 1327, Ugolino sold a piece of rural land at the Villa di San Giovanni a Pompegiano valued at £17.¹¹

Now, even in this instance documentation may be missing, but the notices we have tell us a great deal. The joint ownership of the house in San Donato suggests Ugolino and Muccio lived together and may have worked together as well. The value of the house compares favorably with that of Ambrogio Lorenzetti's holding in Sant'Egidio, sold in 1324 for £200. The garden directly behind the house and the field of roughly three acres, also in San Donato, could well have provided foodstuffs for daily use, possibly a necessity given the distance of the rural holdings from the city. In terms of these documents, Ugolino and Muccio had 34 percent of their wealth in urban holdings, 66 percent in the property at Sovignano.¹² There is no way of knowing how much of this wealth represented inheritance from their father or their own purchase. Certainly, however, the brothers were well situated financially. Excluding Muccio's 1319 purchase, since it may have been part of the added entry in Estimo 131, the brothers' joint wealth c. 1320—and before Ugolino's work in Santa Croce—was approximately £1,319, slightly more than the Memmi brothers' later investment in land at Monsindoli.

The very same Estimo volume affords us some comparative material of interest.¹³ Simone Martini's future father-in-law, Memmo di Filippuccio, is listed as having a house in San Donato, jointly owned with his brother, Mino, and evaluated at 333 lire and 6 soldi. Apparently this was the sum of Memmo's real property in Siena and its *contado*.¹⁴ Guido di Ghezzo owned a piece of cultivated land with a vineyard valued at £58 and "unam superficiem" in San Donato worth 218 lire, 8 soldi, and 8 denari. The painters Vannuccio and Nicchola di Mino had a house in the *popolo* of Magione del Tempio valued at £350; in a later addition to the volume, Vannuccio di Mino also had a house in San Donato valued at 118 lire, 6 soldi, and 8 denari. The painter Mino di Voglia and his

7. Bowsky, *Finance*, 89 n. 72.

8. For the texts of these previously unpublished records, see below.

9. Bacci, *Dipinti inediti*, 146.

10. ASS, Estimo 79, fol. 259r.

11. Bacci, *Fonti e commenti*, 143–44.

12. In this calculation and those to follow, I am not including the land at Pompegiano.

13. Unfortunately, this manuscript is badly damaged, with major losses at the beginning. Before folio 31 (original numbering), almost three-quarters of each folio is lost.

14. Memmo di Filippuccio (and perhaps Mino?) had been very active in San Gimignano before this date. It would seem likely that he also owned property there.

brother owned a piece of cultivated land in "populi Manciani", a house in the *popolo* of "Mansionis Templi," and half share in a house in San Donato, and thus a patrimony estimated at 388 lire, 6 soldi, and 8 denari.

These documents and similar notices allow us certain insights beyond the mere facts. Clearly joint ownership of family property, something still common in Italian families, was frequent. It is also clear that owning something in the way of land that could be cultivated and of vineyards was important. For the less successful, such as Mino di Voglia or Guido di Ghezzo, that land was likely to be within the city. Painters such as the brothers Memmi or Ugolino and Muccio di Nerio might assemble holdings in the *contado*. But even here there were differences. The Memmi lands, much closer to Siena itself than Sovignano, were likely more expensive than land farther off. On the other hand, Ugolino and Muccio were purchasing land much earlier and thus at a moment when the Sienese lira had greater worth. In the case of smaller, jointly held patrimonies, the real worth of each individual's property was only slightly above the value of houses (£100) that the Nove required of those wishing to obtain Sienese citizenship. Thus, as I have noted earlier, there were important differences in economic position among painters.

A rather atypical case of property ownership is found in Estimo 131's notices regarding Tavena d'Andrea, a painter about whom we know very little. In addition to owning two houses of modest worth, one valued at 76 lire, 13 soldi, and 4 denari, the other at £100, and a major vineyard, estimated at £420, the painter had much smaller investments in multiple pieces of land, most to them held as half shares of the property involved. I suppose these represent inheritance that was likely shared with another family member, perhaps a brother. The assessors' evaluations were apparently totaled prematurely (and inaccurately), on folio 162r, to 767 lire, 11 soldi, and 2 denari. Another piece of land, with vines, is recorded on folio 162v. Tavena's total worth in terms of the property he owned came to roughly £962.

THE PREVIOUSLY UNPUBLISHED DOCUMENTS[15]

Memmo and Mino di Filipuccio

ASS, Estimo 131, fol. 49r:

Memmus et Minus] olim Filippuccii, pictores, habent quandam domum cum quandam platea post ipsam domum, positam Senis in populo Sancti Donati et libra predicta [San Donato a lato de Montanini], quibus ex uno latere est Cini Ture, ex alio Feducci Lappetarii, ante via et retro sunt tiratoria, extimatam in trecentis trigintatribus libris, sex soldis, VIII denariis, patet in libro domorum terzerii Camollie, folio CLXXV.

Summa patrimonii dictorum Memmi et Mini librarum trecentarum trigintatrium, soldorum sex, denariorum octo.

---

15. At my request, these notices were transcribed by Gino Corti, to whom I extend my thanks.

Ugolino and Muccio di Nerio

ASS, Estimo 131, fols. 154v–155r:

Duccius[16] et] pictores, filii olim Nerii, habent unam petiam terre laboratorie posite in curia
Ugolinus] Sancti Stefani de Sivignano, in loco dicto Casalino, ex duabus partibus via, ex alio Landi Venture, et ex alio Bindi Baldi, que est stariorum undecim et tabularum octuaginta, extimatam in libris ducentis denariorum Senensium, ut constat in libro cx, folio xliii.

Item habent unam petiam terre laboratorie posite in dicta curia et districtu, in loco dicto Teschio, cui ex uno via et ex alio heredum Bindi Baldi et ex alio fossato et ex alio Bindi Aiuti, que est stariorum sex, tabularum quinquaginta, extimatam in centum quattuor libris, ut constat in libro cx, folio xliiii.

Item habent unam petiam laboratoriam posite in dicta curia, in loco dicto Aiore, cui ex uno latere via et ex alio heredum Guccii Aiuti et ex alio Bene Arrigi et ex alio Guccii Viviani, que est stariorum quattuor et tabularum decem, ut constat in libro cx, folio xlvi, extimatam in settuaginta sex libris et decem soldis, ut constat dictis libro et folio.

Item habent unam domum positam Senis, in populo Sancti Donati et libra Montaninorum, cui ante via, retro est quidam ortus eorum, et post ortum tiratoria, ex alio est Iacobini Benzii, et ex alio heredum Giughonis et ser Cambii, extimatam ducentis quinquaginta libris, ut patet in libro domorum terzerii Camollie, folio clxxxi.

Item habent dicti Meuccius et Ugolinus pictores unam petiam terre campie, positam in dicta curia, in loco dicto Lavatoio, cui ex duobus partibus est via, ex alio fossatus et ex alio Iannis Assai, que est stariorum novem et tabularum vigintiquinque, estimatam octuagintatribus libris et decem soldis, ut patet libro ccxxxii, folio lx. Que petia terre scripta erat ad postam Bindi Aiuti, in libra Salicotti desuper, folio cxiii.

Item habent unam petiam terre campie, positam in loco dicto Trendilati, cui ex duobus via, ex alio Cecchi Venture, que est vigintiduorum stariorum et viginti tabularum, extimatam in octuaginta octo libris, sedecim soldis, ut patet in libro ccxxxii, folio lxxiii, et erat scripta ad postam Bartaluccii Ture, in libro Suvignani, folio clxxxiiii.

Item habent unam petiam terre laboratorie, positam in curia Sancti Stefani de Suvignano, in loco dicto Casalino, cui ex uno latere et ex uno [sic] via, ex alio heredum ser Nini medici, et ex alio Duccii Gratie de Suvignano, que est stariorium novem et tabularum lxxv, extimatam in centumquinquaginta septem libris et decem soldis, ut constat in libro ccxxxii, folio xliiii, que scripta erat ad postam Vive calzolarii, folio ccxl in presens libro.

Item habet unam petiam terre campie, positam in villa de Suvignano, in loco dicto Fralefosse, cui ex uno latere est via, ex alio Cecchi Venture, ex alio Cennis de Murlo, ex alio Giannini Orlandini, que est stariorium ii et tabularum lxxvii, extimatam in xxiiii libris et i soldo, ut patet libro ccxxxiii, folio x.

16. This is clearly an error on the part of the scribe, as is made clear near the end of the documents for Ugolino and Muccio, where the latter is correctly named.

ASS, Estimo 131, fol. 333r:

Item habent predicti Muccius et Ugolinus unam petiam terre campie, positam in curia Suvignani, in loco dicto Ortagli, cui ex uno via, ex alio Vannelli coiarii, ex alio Benis Herrighi, ex alio heredum ser Nini, que est xi stariorum, extimatam in cx libris, ut patet in libro ccxxxii, que scripta erat ad postam Turini Michi, in libro de Quinciano, folio cxli.

Tavena d'Andrea

ASS, Estimo 131, fols. 159r–162v:

Tavena Andree pictor habet medietatem pro indiviso unius petie terre laboratorie in populo Sancti Iohannis ad Collansoli et contrata de Vigniuole, cui extra latere via et extra Ghezzii Venture et extra fossatum et extra Meuccii Bartalini, que est quinque stariorum et viginti tabularum. Extimatam dictam medietatem in undecim libris et quattuordecim soldis, et in totum vigintiquinque libris et otto soldis, ut constata in libro xxiiii, in folio xxxiii.

Item habet unum petium terre laboratorie in medietatem pro indiviso, posite in dicto populo, in loco dicto Macchioni, qui in communem habet cum Vanne Bardi, cui extra latere via comunis et extra heredum Bartoli et extra Marchi Insegne et extra predictorum Vannis et Tavene, que est stariorum settem et tabularum quadraginta trium. Extimatam dictam medietatem in vigintiquinque libris et decim octo soldis, et in totum quinquaginta una libra et sedecim soldis, ut constat in libro xxiiii, folio xxxvii.

Item habet medietatem pro indiviso unius petie terre laboratorie, posite in populo Sancti Iohannis ad Collansi et vocabulo Fosse, cui extra via et extra dicte ecclesie et extra duobus fossis, que est novem stariorum et quinquaginta tabularum. Extimatam Extimatam [*sic*] dictam medietatem in trigintaduabus libris et duodecim soldis, ut constat in libro xxiii, fol. lv.

Item habet medietatem unius petie terre laboratorie, posite in dicto populo et contrata, cui extra via comunis et extra Baduzii et extra fossatum et extra Turchiolini Naconis, quam comunem habet cum heredibus Bardi. Extimatam dictam medietatem v soldos, licet in totum extimatam sit in decem soldis, ut constat in dicto libro, folio lvi.

Item habet dictus Tavena medietatem pro indiviso unius petie terre laboratorie in dicto populo, in contrata Bosthi, cui extra via et extra dicti Turchiolini et extra fossatum, que est quactuor stariorum et quinquaginta tabularum, extimatam dictam medietatem in vigintisettem libris, licet in totum extimata sit quinquaginta quactuor libras, ut constat in libro xxiii, folio lvi.

Item habet medietatem pro indiviso unius petie terre laboratorie, posite in dictis populo et contrata, cui extra latere via et extra heredum Peponis et extra heredum magistri Aczonis et extra heredum Bartali, que est duorum stariorum et settuaginta tabularum. Extimatam dictam medietatem in triginta sex libris et decem soldis, ut constat in libro dicto et folio, licet in totum extimata sit in settuaginta tribus libris.

Item habet medietatem pro indiviso unius petie terre boschate, posite in dicto populo et contrata Boschi, cui extra heredum Bartali et extra heredum Salvi, quam comunem habet ut supra, que est stariorum settem, extimatam dictam medietatem in quattuordecim libris, licet in totum extimatam in vigintiocto libris, ut constat in libro xxiii, folio lviii.

Item habet medietatem pro indiviso unius petie terre sode, posite in dicto populo et contrata Righi, cui extra heredum Pieri et extra ecclesie de Lucano et extra Iohannis Fatii et extra heredum Bartali, que est quattuor stariorum, extimata dictam medietatem in una libra, licet in totum extimata sit duabus libris, ut constat dicto libro, folio LVIIII.

Item habet medietatem pro indiviso unius petie [terre] laboratorie, posite in dicto populo et contrata Righi, cui extra fossatum et extra Rigi et heredum Adote et heredum Bartali et extra Pauli Cinie, quam comunem habet ut supra, que est decem et octo stariora, et vigintisettem libras extimatam dictam medietatem, licet in totum extimatam in quinquaginta quattuor libris, ut constat in libro XXIII, folio LX.

Item habet medietatem pro indiviso unius petie terre laboratorie in dicto populo et contrata Righi, cui undique sunt vie comunis, quam comunem habet ut supra, que est decemsettem stariorum, extimatam dictam medietatem in octuaginta quinque libris et decem soldis, ut constat in libro et folio supradictis, licet extimata in totum in centum settuaginta libris.

Item habet medietatem pro indiviso unius petie terre laboratorie, positam in dicto populo, in loco supradicto, cui extra Ture Martini et extra fossatum Righi et extra heredum Pieri de Solterrano et extra heredum Sozii Buonifacii, comunem ut supra, que est unius starii et quinquaginta tabularum, extimatam dictam medietatem in settem libris et decem soldis, ut constat in libro dictis et folio, in totum extimatam in quindecim libris.

Item habet medietatem pro indiviso unius petie terre laboratorie, posite in dicto populo et contrata Collis Maioris, comunem cum heredibus Bardi ut supra, cui extra via et extra Turchiolini dicti et extra duobus et via, que est sex stariorum et viginti tabularum, extimatam dictam medietatem in novem libris et sex soldis, licet in totum extimatam in decem octo libris et duodecim soldis, ut constat dicto folio LX.

Item habet dictus Tavena medietatem pro indiviso unius petie terre laboratorie, comunem ut supra, positam in dicto populo, in contrata Collis Maioris, que pro parte soda, cui extra duobus [lateribus] via, extra ecclesie de Bacano et extra heredum Bartali, que est decem stariorum et quinquaginta tabularum. Extimatam dictam medietatem in quinque libris et quinque soldis, licet in totum extimatam in decem libris et decem soldis, ut constat in libro XXIII, folio LXI.

Item medietatem pro indiviso unnius [sic] petie terre laboratorie et sode, posite in dicto populo, in loco et contrata Collis Maioris, comunem ut supra, cui extra via et extra Turchiolini Maconis et extra duobus canonica de Falteriano, que est stariorum octo et tabularum nonaginta. Extimatam dictam medietatem in sex libris et tredecim soldis, licet in totum extimata sit in tredecim libris et settem soldis, ut constat dictis libro et folio.

Item habet medietatem unius petie terre laboratorie, posite in dicto populo et contrata supradicta, cui ex duobus via comunis et extra duobus Turcholini predicti, comunem ut supra, que est duorum stariorum et vigintiquinque tabularum. Extimatam dictam medietatem in duabus libris et sedecim soldis, et in totum in quinque libris et duodecim soldis, ut constat in libro [sic] dictis libro et folio.

Item habet medietatem pro individo unius petie terre laboratorie, posite in dictis populo et vocabulo, cui ex duobus Pagni Ugolini lanifex et extra Ture Becchi, et extra fossatum, que est trium stariorum et tabularum octuaginta. Extimatam dictam medietatem in tribus libris et sedecim soldis, et in totum in settem libris et duodecim soldis, ut constat in dictis libro et folio.

Item habet medietatem pro indiviso unius petie terre laboratorie, posite in dicto populo et in contrata Olmorum Vaiani, cui extra in heredum Nutii et heredum Georgii extra et extra fossatum, que est duorum stariorum et vigintiquinque tabularum. Extimatam in duabus libris et quinque soldis dictam medietatem, et in totum in quattuor libris et decem soldis, ut constat in libro xxiii, folio lxii.

Item habet medietatam pro indiviso unius petie terre laboratorie et partim non, posite in dicto populo, in loco dicto Sale, cui extra Mature Adote, et extra heredum Accorsi, et extra fossatum, que est duorum stariorum, comunem ut supra, extimatam dictam medietatem in duobus soldis, in totum extimatam in quattuor soldis, ut constat in libro xxiii, folio lxiii.

Item habet medietatem pro indiviso unius petie terre laboratorie, posite in dicto populo, in contrata Sale, comunem ut supra, cui extra Ghezii Gorii et extra fossatum, que est trium stariorum et quinquaginta tabularum. Extimatam dictam medietatem in duobus libris et duodecim soldis et vi denariis, extimatam in totum in quinque libris et quinque soldis, ut constat in libro xxiii, folio lxiiii.

Item habet medietatem unius petie terre laboratorie et (Kallarie?) comunem ut supra, cui extra via et Pauli Vivoli et extra. [Incomplete item.]

Item habet dictus Tavena unam petiam terre laboratorie, positam in populo Sancte Lucie de Medina, in loco dicto Drago, cui extra fossatum et extra Maian [blank] dicti Pauli, que est stariorum quattuor et tabularum nonaginta quinque. Extimatam in viginti libris, ut patet in libro lv, folio lxviii.

Item habet unam petiam terre laboratorie in dicto populo et loco dicto, cui ex duobus lateribus Pauli Vivoli et extra fossatum et extra Ture Martini, que est trium stariorum et trigintasex tabularum. Extimatam in tredecim libris, ut patet in supradicto libro et folio supradictis [sic].

Item habet unum hedificium positum Senis, in populo Sancti Donati et libra Montaninorum, super plateam domini Benuccii, cui ex uno est Cennis Regrecterii et ex tribus est via. Extimatam septuagintasex libras, trecedim soldos, quattuor denarios, ut patet in libro et folio supradictis.
Item habet unum hedificium positum Senis, in populo predictis [sic] super plateam filiorum Ghaddi, cuius ex uno est Magalocti Duccii, et ex uno et ante est via. Extimatam centum libras, ut patet in libro domorum predicto, folio clxxxvi.

Item unam possessionem vineatum et laboratoriam, positam in populo Sancti Petri de Marciano et in contrata Coste Salti, cui ex uno via, et extra Vannis Chiari, et extra fossatum, et extra Peruzii Saracini, que est trigintaduorum stariorum et tabularum triginta, extimatam in quadringentis viginti libris denariorum, ut constat in libro xvi, folio liiii, que erat ad postam heredum Ghini et Guelfi Saldere.

Summa patrimonii dicti Tavene librarum septingentorum sexagintaseptem, s. undecim, denariorum duorum.[17]

17. This summation is found at the bottom of folio 162r, but is followed on folio 162v by the last entry for the painter. The total here does not correspond to the sum of the items above, which is approximately £966 to that point. Presumably, the total was made earlier, and some of the items above it were actually inserted after it was made. There is a similar case with the Mino di Voglia notices below.

Item habet dictis Tavena medietatem pro indiviso unius petie terre laboratorie et vineate, posite in curia Sancti Iohannis ad Collansi, loco dicto Fosse, cui ex uno via comunis, ex uno Eustadii Pierio, ex uno Barduccii, ex uno Dote. Que est starioram duorum et tabularum quinquaginta. Extimatam medietatem sexagintaseptem libras, decem soldos, ut patet libro XXIII, folio LVI.

Mino di Voglia

ASS, Estimo 131, fol. 242r:

Minus Vollie, pictor, et fratres habent unam petiam terre laboratorie, positam in districtu seu vocabulo Vallochii, populi Manciani, que est pro parte ulivata, cum una domo, cui ex uno latere via, et ex alio Misericordie, et ex alio Andree Tolomei, que est trium stariorum et tabularum duodecim, extimatam in centumquinquaginta libris, ut patet in libro VI, folio XXXII.

Item habent unam domum, positam Senis in populo Mansionis Templi,[18] cui ex uno latere est Landi Mini Baglionis, ex alio Mini Gorii, et ante viam; extimatam centumtrigintaocto libris, sex soldis, VIII denariis, ut patet in libro domorum terzerii Camollie, folio CLXXXXIIII.

Item habent medietatem unius domus posite Senis in populo Sancti Donati et libra ex latere Montaninorum, contrata de Camporegio, cum orto post dictam domum, cui ex uno Iacobini Benci, ex alio Francischi Luccii, ante viam et retro tiratorium, extimatam dictam medietatem in centum libris, licet in totum extimatam sit in ducentis libris. Alia vero medietas est Arcolani eius nepotis, ut patet libro domorum terzerii Camollie, folio XLVIIII, que [est] ad postam domini Carlli, in libro Sancti Petri.

Summa patrimonii dictorum Mini e fratrum: librarum duecentarum octuaginta octo, soldorum sex, denariorum octo.[19]

Guido di Ghezzo

ASS, Estimo 131, fol. 245r:

Guido Ghezzi pictor habet unam petiam terre laboratorie et vineate, de populo Arsiccioli, cui ex uno via, ex alio hospitale Sancte Marie, ex alio Ghezzi Ghallerani, ex alio cuiusdam neptis domine Imiglie, que est III stariorum et LXXV tabularum, extimatam in LVIII libris, ut constat in libro VII, folio VIII.

Item habet unam superficiem positam super solo Salinbenorum, in populo Sancti Donati, in libra predicta. Extimata ducentis decem et otto libris, soldis VI, denarius VIII, ut patet in libro domorum terzerii Camollie, folio CLXXXVIII. Que scripta erat Iacobo Meuccii, in libra predicta, folio CCCI.

---

18. The parish of Magione del Tempio is in the extreme north of the city, close to the Camollia gate.

19. Obviously, this summary was made when Mino owned only the first two items, so, as in the case of Tavena d'Andrea, space was left between the listing of the individual items and the summation, a space large enough to accommodate the later addition of the half house.

Vannuccio and Niccola di Mino

ASS, Estimo 131, fol. 286r:

Vannuccius et ⎤ Mini, pictores, habent unam domum positam Senis, in populo Mansionis
Nicchola ⎦ Templi, cui ante et retro est via, ex alio CornacchiniBindi et ex alio Binduccii de Monteorgiali, extimatam trecentis quinquaginta libris, ut patet in libro domorum terzerii Camollie, folio CLXXXII.

Anno Domini MCCCXXIII, indictione VII, die XX decembris, coram Bertoccio Guidoccii et Petro Baldi testibus presentibus, cassa est dicta posta per Andream Bindi notarium [etc.] et scripta pro medietate ad postam Cerrachini et Binducci Tolli, in libra Mansionis.

Summa dictorum Vannuccii et Nicchole: librarum trecentarum quinquaginta.

ASS, Estimo 131, fol. 311r:

Vannuccius Mini, pictor, de populo Sancti Donati, habet unam hedificium positam Senis, in populo Sancti Donati et libra predicta super platea domini Benuccii, cui ante et retro est via, ex alio est domus Misericordie, ex alio est heredum Niccholo; extimatum in centum decem et otto libris et VI soldii et VIII denariius, ut patet [in] libro domorum terzerii Camollie, folio CLXXXVI, que scripta erat Ceccho Puccii, in libro predicto.

Monaldo di Palmerio

ASS, Estimo 131, fol. 304r:

Monaldus Palmerii, pictor, habet de quinque partibus tres partes unius superficiei super solo Malavoltorum, in populo Sancti Donati et libra Montaninorum, cui ante via, ex uno latere est Tinaccii, ex alio Mini linaiuoli, extimatam quinquagintasex libris, ut patet in libro domorum terzerii Camollie, folio CLXXXX.

Anno Domini millesimo CCCXX, indictione tertia, die XII mensis Iunii [etc.] cassa hic supra, posita fuit in folio CCCXXV ad postam dicti Antonii [Dietisalvi].

Item habet quartam partem unius superficiei et orti, positam Senis, in populo Sancti Iohannis et libra Vallis Piacte de subtus,[20] super plateam Canonichorum Episcopatus, cui ex uno mura Comunis, ex alio via Michelis, et ex alio heredum Iusti, extimatam trigintatribus libris, sex soldis, VIII denariis, ut patet in libro et folio predictis.

Summa dicti Monaldi: librarum octuagintanovem, soldorum sex, denariorum octo.

---

20. Terzo di Città.

APPENDIX III: THE MINOR MASTERS: NOTES ON SOME SOURCES

The financial records of the Commune of Siena contain many notices of painters whose work is either completely unknown or known only in small decorative works such as the covers to the Biccherna volumes. They are figures like Guido Cinatti, discussed in Chapter II above, although none of them seems to have been employed by the commune with the regularity that distinguished Guido's career. The notices are often problematic inasmuch as they frequently give only a single name, rather than the fuller form of "Guido Cinatti" or "Guido di Cinatto." Thus, as references to "Guido" may or may not be to Guido Cinatti, so references simply to a "Pietro" or a "Mino" may or may not be to an artist we also find named in longer forms. In the digest that follows, arranged alphabetically, I have taken the cautious route and kept such notices separate, although in many cases I am convinced that the same painter has been treated under different formulations of his name. I want the reader to be sure that the relevant document contains precisely the name under which it appears. One of the recurring problems, especially of earlier scholarship, was a rush to the conclusion that a reference to a "Pietro" was a reference to Pietro Lorenzetti, or a "Simone" meant Simone Martini. Indeed, a long-standing confusion regarding the latter arose because there was a Sienese carpenter of the very same name. A "magistro Nerio Ugolini" appears in a document of 1 March 1325; we know that Ugolino di Nerio's father, called Nerio di Ugolino, was deceased by 1318. Bacci therefore supposed that this Nerio di Ugolino must be Ugolino's son and Nerio's grandson, but there is no real evidence one way or another.[1] Scholars such as Milanesi and Bacci, when summarizing documents that contained only a first name, generally expanded the name by adding an assumed surname. This was especially the case when earlier scholars tried to create genealogies for painters. Much confusion was the result.

    Still another problem attends the notices from primary sources. In the thirteenth and fourteenth centuries, the spelling of names was not fixed. Where, for example, we refer to "Francesco," contemporaries might refer to the same individual also as "Francescho" or "Franciescho." Similarly, a "Angelo" might be recorded as "Angnolino," or a "Pietro" as "Petro." On the other hand, such differences may reflect common usages in conversation. When a document's formulation of a name differs from that under which it appears, I have included that formulation in square brackets preceding the notice.

    In addition to the original documents cited below, I have taken some material from second-

---

1. Bacci, *Dipinti inediti,* 144–45, 149–50.

ary sources, including unpublished manuscripts of notes taken by various scholars working with archival material, now in the Biblioteca Comunale of Siena.[2]

A good many difficulties attend consideration of the manuscript material in Siena's Biblioteca Comunale. There are, in my opinion, significant differences in reliability. I have selected notices from the sources I consider most trustworthy, and cited less reliable notices in the footnotes. For example, Uberto Benvoglienti was educated as a historian and seems to have been careful in his note taking; Gaetano Milanesi also seems a reliable source, since his career was spent dealing with documents. The reader should be aware that I have excluded, from the following, notices in Ettore Romagnoli's *Biografia cronologica de' bellartisti senesi* (c. 1832) for three reasons. First, this multivolume work is available in a facsimile edition printed in Florence in 1979. Second, since that work is organized by artist, notes on specific painters are easily located (in contrast to the material below, which is scattered). Finally, there are very significant problems created by inaccuracies. Of all sources, perhaps this is the one most to be treated with care—and skepticism. I have, however, indicated those painters discussed by Romagnoli by placing an asterisk (★) after the relevant names and have indicated, in some cases, where the artists treated below are found in Romagnoli under another name.[3]

In citing the unpublished secondary sources, I have included the references that various writers give as the source of their notes. Here arise more problems. The Sienese year began on 25 March rather than 1 January, and it is usually impossible to tell which system any one scholar is using. Not only the numbering of volumes from the Biccherna has changed over the centuries; there have been changes in the folio numbers as well. And then there are the simple mistakes that occur: wrong dates, wrong folio numbers, confusions between lire and soldi, and so forth. Given the quantity of this material, it has proved impossible for me to check many of these notices by searching for the original documents. All these problems urge the utmost caution in using the Biblioteca Comunale material.

Among the painters documented below, there are several who had careers that stretched well into the later Trecento, after 1363, the chronological end of this study, but I have somewhat arbitrarily limited my notices to 1363 or earlier because I feel reasonably certain I have surveyed sources up to that date. That said, it would be a folly inviting hubris to claim that absolutely everything relevant is here. While working in Siena, I chose to concentrate on a systematic reading of the Biccherna volumes and of unpublished secondary sources; other classes of original documents were surveyed in a piecemeal fashion. Even my reading of complete Biccherna volumes began only with 1287, the year the Noveschi came to power.

I want, therefore, to emphasize the fact that the material below does not claim to be complete. It should be viewed simply as a (partial) foundation on which others can build.

In each case below, a summary of the document is followed by the date, in parentheses, and the relevant citation, in square brackets.

2. In this category is a particular case I should explain: the citations to Milanesi's lists of members of the Painters' Guild. For reasons I gave earlier, the last thirteen names that Milanesi dates to 1355 may represent a later addition. Taking again the cautious route, I have not included those names in the following. Milanesi (*Documenti*, I, 49–51) publishes a list taken from the "Libro delle Capitudini delle Arti," which he dates to 1363. The document itself (ASS, Arti 165) carries no internal date, although the names themselves suggest a possible date in the 1360s.

3. Romagnoli had the habit of discussing brief notices about some painters in the entry for another, in his mind, related artist and not giving them separate entries. I have largely used the indexes provided by Romagnoli. We are in serious need of a critical edition of this work.

THE NOTICES

Agnolo di Nalduccio (★ under Angelo di Nalduccio Mazzetti)
1. Buys a house for £100 (23 April 1349) [ASS, Spedale 514, fol. 203r].
2. Registered in the Painters' Guild (1356) [Milanesi, *Documenti*, I, 31].
3. In the "Libro delle Capitudini delle Arti" (1363?) [Milanesi, *Documenti*, I, 50].

Ambrogio di Duccio (★—and under Duccio di Bino della Buoninsegna)[4]
1. Living in San Quirico in Castelvecchio, he is listed in the Libro de' Giuriati of the Mercanzia (1326) [Bacci, "Commentarii," 247].
2. Is paid 2 lire and 5 soldi for a gilded candlestick "held in the hand of the angel of the panel of the cathedral" (July 1339) [Siena, Opera del Duomo 178, fol. 52r][5]

Ambrogio "dipentore in champoreggi"
1. Is paid £1 for painting two candlesticks for the Chapel of San Jacopo Interciso in the duomo (9 June 1344) [ASS, Spedale 851, fol. 46v].[6]

Andelo
1. Paid *dazio* of 7 soldi and 6 denari (8 October 1292) [ASS, Biccherna 108, fol. 126r].[7]

Andrea (★ under Andrea di Vanni)
1. Is paid 14 soldi for forty-two coats of arms in the books of the "vicharo vecchio" (20 January 1328) [ASS, Biccherna 157, fol. 5v].[8]
2. [andree] Andrea and the carpenter Meo Mini received 23 florins (77 lire and 5 soldi) for a "tabula" for Bernone di Monforte, "conestabili del comune" (22 December 1351)[9] [ASS, Biccherna 228, fol. 130r].

Andrea di Franciescho
1. Registered in the Painters' Guild (1356) [Milanesi, *Documenti*, I, 35].[10]

Andrea di Guido
1. Registered in the Painters' Guild (1356) [Milanesi, *Documenti*, I, 39].

Andrea di Turino (★)
1. Registered in the Painters' Guild (1356) [Milanesi, *Documenti*, I, 35].

---

4. Perhaps Duccio's son.

5. The reference is to one of the angels holding candles on the high altar. This is perhaps a repair or an addition. Although a new angel was added to the others in 1339, Ambrogio Lorenzetti was paid for both the angel and its candlestick. See Chapter IV.

6. This may be a reference to Ambrogio di Duccio.

7. For the direct tax called the *dazio*, see Bowsky, *Finance*, 98–113.

8. By 1310, the *contado* of Siena had been divided into nine vicariates for the supply of military forces when needed by Siena. The reference to the "former vicar," however, is so unspecific that it cannot be interpreted. See Bowsky, *Medieval Italian Commune*, 146–47.

9. On fol. 92v (11 July) of the same Biccherna volume, this individual is listed as the "conestabile" of the commune. The designation "constable" was usually given to *condottieri* who, along with their mercenary cavalry, were hired by the commune. See Bowsky, *Medieval Italian Commune*, 151.

10. Here, as elsewhere below, the absence of notices after 1363 does not necessarily mean that none exist.

Andreino
1. Among those who paint items for the funeral of the captain of war, Guidorricio da Fogliano, he receives 8 florins on behalf of several painters (January–June 1352) [ASS, Biccherna 411, fol. 23v].
2. Is paid £6 (January–June 1352) [ASS, Biccherna 412, fol. 175v].
3. Is paid £6 for "uno paio de gofanetti" (21 July–10 August 1352) [ASS, Biccherna 411, fol. 42v].

Andrernus
1. Buried in San Domenico (16 April 1353) [Laurent, *I necrologi*, 80].

Angelo di Conociuto
1. Involved in sale (of property?) (1289) [Milanesi: Siena, BC, MS P.III.51, fol. 509r: citing "Arch. dei Contratti, Perg. 144"].

Angnolino di Gintile
1. Registered in the Painters' Guild (1356) [Milanesi, *Documenti*, I, 36].

Antonio
1. Is paid 3 soldi for two signs marking a house near the Stalloreggi gate (19 March 1344) [ASS, Spedale 851, fol. 22v].
2. Is paid 3 soldi for placing two "segni" on a house belonging to the hospital (24 June 1344) [ASS, Spedale 851, fol. 51v].
3. Is paid 10 soldi for signs at a vineyard belonging to the hospital (12 October 1344) [ASS, Spedale 851, fol. 78v].

Antonio Dietisalvi (★ under Dietisalvi di Guido)
1. He and his wife, Lapia, mentioned in 1331. [Faluschi: Siena, BC, MS E.V.14, fol. 69r].[11]
2. Died in 1343 [Faluschi: Siena, BC, MS E.V.14, fol. 69r].
3. His widow dies in 1348 [Faluschi: Siena, BC, MS E.V.14, fol. 69r].

Antonio di Giovanni
1. Registered in the Painters' Guild (1356) [Milanesi, *Documenti*, I, 39].

Balduccio di Dino
1. Is paid 9 soldi and 6 denari for nineteen coats of arms in the books of the former captain of the people (20 November 1307) [ASS, Biccherna 121, fol. 323r].

Barna Bertini
1. Appears in a list composed by Milanesi from the "Libro de' Giurati" (1339–40) [Milanesi: Siena, BC, MS P.III.46, fol. 428r][12]

Bartolomeo di Vanni (★)
1. [bartalomeo di vani] Among the painters providing decorations for the visit of the duke of Calabria, his wife, and his son (July 1326) [ASS, Biccherna 390, fol. 2v].

---

11. This manuscript by Faluschi deals with documents concerning the Ospedale della Scala.

12. This is the only reference that we have to a painter in Siena called Barna. Generally, Vasari's Barna is now thought to be Vasari's invention.

2. Is paid 8 soldi and 9 denari for twenty-one coats of arms on twenty-one books of the captain of the people (21 April 1327) [ASS, Biccherna 154, fol. 24r].

Bataxe
1. His daughter is buried in San Domenico (21 April 1363) [Laurent, *I necrologi*, 90].

Biagio di Goro (★)
1. Has a workshop in a house, in the *popolo* of San Donato, rented from the Misericordia by Paganello di Biagio Bernarducci. Paganello pays 8 florins a year as well as providing a candle of one pound for the feast of S. Andrea (12 April 1350) [Freuler, *Biagio di Goro Ghezzi a Paganico,* 125].[13]

2. He has the same workshop in San Donato (2 April 1353) [Freuler, *Biagio di Goro Ghezzi a Paganico,* 125].

3. Listed as a member of the Painters' Guild (19 February 1356) [Freuler, *Biagio di Goro Ghezzi a Paganico,* 125, and Milanesi, *Documenti,* I, 32].

4. Biagio di Goro and two other individuals petition the Consiglio Generale to take charge of the prisons for two years, in return for their payment of £300 and a candle of twenty-five pounds to be presented at the feast of the Assumption (23 August 1361)[14] [Falletti-Fossati, *Costumi senesi,* 154–55].

5. Listed, as "Blasius Gori" in the "Libro delle Capitudini delle Arti" (1363) [Freuler, *Biagio Goro Ghezzi a Paganico,* 125].[15]

Bindo[16] (★ under Bindo di Guido)
1. As "miniaturist and scribe" is paid 70 lire and 8 soldi for the antiphonary for the altar of the Nove (30 June 1321) [ASS, Biccherna 140, fol. 189r].
2. Given £40 for fire damages to his house in San Quirico (30 June 1324) [ASS, Biccherna 149, fol. 170v].
3. Is paid 23 soldi and 6 denari for parchments to be used by Lando di Pietro "per fare disegnamenti" for the cathedral (30 March 1339) [Milanesi, *Documenti,* I, 228].
4. Is paid £381 for "Carte Scrittura e miniature" of the three volumes of the new statute of the commune [the constitution] (December 1339) [Spogli: Siena, BC, MS A.III.16, fol. 132v, citing B 187, fol. 56r].
5. Is paid for three "statutes" of thirty-nine gatherings each for officials of the commune (22 December 1341) [ASS, Biccherna 209, fol. 141v].[17]

Bindo di Cecco
1. He and Fede di Nalduccio are sent by the commune "per richercare e chaseri" (29 May 1361); no location given [Borghesi and Banchi, *Nuovi documenti,* 49].

---

13. Freuler, *Biago di Goro Ghezzi a Paganico*. See also Appendix 1, no. 34 under "Terzo di Camollia: San Donato."

14. The painter and his colleagues had to make various other commitments as well. These are detailed by Falletti-Fossati, *Costumi senesi*.

15. Freuler publishes later notices of the painter, running until 1384, 125–29.

16. The commune often bought parchment from individuals described as miniaturists. It seems that on 30 June 1317 a certain Bindo supplied parchment at the value of 52 lire, 10 soldi, and 8 denari. [ASS, Biccherna 133, fol. 143v.]

17. At the same time, Cola di Fuccio receives payment for one "statute" of thirty-nine gatherings.

Bindo di Dietisalvi (★ under Dietisalvi di Guido)
1. Is paid for his expenditures in relation to an image of Saint Christopher painted "in domo comunis sen. in curia dominorum" (28 December 1296) [ASS, Biccherna 113, fol. 236r].

Bindo Dietavive "miniatore"
1. Living in the *lira* of San Quirico in Castelvecchio, Terza di Città (21 May–1 December 1311) [Bacci, *Fonti e commenti,* 101].[18]

Blasio
1. Is paid 18 soldi and 4 denari for twenty-three coats of arms on the books of the malefactors (27 February 1352) [ASS, Biccherna 229, fol. 96r].

Blasius Marinelli
1. In the "Libro delle Capitudini delle Arti" (1363?) [Milanesi, *Documenti,* I, 50].

Blaxius
1. His daughter is buried in San Domenico (8 May 1363) [Laurent, *I necrologi,* 91].

Bonaccorso
1. [buonachorso] Among artists who prepared painted items for the funeral of the captain of war, Guidoriccio da Fogliano (28 June 1352). He himself receives 7 florins and 1 lira; he and his "compagni" receive 8 florins, 2 lire, and 16 soldi [ASS, Biccherna 412, fol. 176v].

Bonaccorso di Pace (★)
1. Living in San Donato, he receives a dowry of £450 from his future wife, Magdalena di Ceccho di Nuccio (29 November 1348) [Milanesi, *Documenti,* I, 50 (as 27 November), and Milanesi: Siena, BC, MS P.III.50, fol. 589r: citing Denunzie dei contratti 1348, fol. 243v (as 29 November)].
2. In government (1354 and 1360) [Milanesi, *Documenti,* I, 50].
3. Between 16 March and 2 April 1356, he is given a total of 13 florins, 3 lire, 8 soldi, and 8 denari (as repayment of a loan?) [ASS, Biccherna 415, fol. 36r].
4. Was captain of the people for six months in 1362 [Milanesi, *Documenti,* I, 50].
5. Listed in the "Libro delle Capitudini delle Arti" (1363?) [Milanesi, *Documenti,* I, 50].
6. Made his will leaving his estate to the Ospedale di Santa Maria della Scala (4 June 1363) [ASS, MS 45, fol. 373r].
7. Buried in San Domenico (7 June 1363) [Laurent, *I necrologi,* 94].
8. A son is buried in San Domenico (13 June 1363) [Laurent, *I necrologi,* 97].[19]
9. His son, Pace, is buried in San Domenico (21 August 1363) [Laurent, *I necrologi,* 98].[20]
10. Ordered to return to the commune 11 florins that he had been paid for the "pittura d'una tavola dei Signori Governatori" (no date) [Milanesi: Siena, BC, MS P.III.53, fol. 369v: citing Annali 40, fol. 500].[21]

18. It is highly likely that this artist is the miniaturist, listed merely as Bindo, who had fire damage to his house in San Quirico.

19. The entry does not, however, specify that he is a painter.

20. That the father and two sons died in the summer of 1363 is surely a result of the recurrence of the bubonic plague in that year.

21. This unusual notice reads: "Bonaccorso del quondam Pace Pittore ordina restituissi al Comune di Siena 11 fiorini d'oro che ebbe da Ventura d'Andrea camarlengo di Biccherna per pittura d'una tavola dei Sig. Governatori. Lascia a M° Meo Legnajolo due fiorini d'oro che doveva avere per residuo del prezzo d'una tavola della compagnia della disciplina di S. Andrea de' Gallerani."

Bonaventura (?)
1. [buonventore?] Is paid £3 for salary May/June 1330 for unspecified work (21 June 1330) [ASS, Biccherna 165, fol. 44v].

Brandino di Ser Cieio
1. Registered in the Painters' Guild (1356) [Milanesi, *Documenti*, I, 39].

Cecchino (★ under Cecco di Martino)
1. Is paid 8 lire and 14 soldi for painting the Annunciate in the Palazzo Pubblico before the "coram bancho sindici" (1339) [ASS, Biccherna 202, fol. 144v].

Cecco (and Nuccio) (★ under Cecco di Duccio, Cecco di Martino Seniore, and Luccio Pontani)
1. [cieccho] Along with the carpenter Chello, is paid £12 for painting the Virgin and other saints on the Camollia gate and for restoring the roof (30 June 1309) [ASS, Biccherna 122, fol. 201v].

Cecco di Goro
1. Alive in 1350 (20 April 1350) [Benvoglienti: Siena, BC, MS C.v.7, fol. 267r: citing "contratti della Sapienza"].

Cecco di Martino (★)
1. Sale (of land?) appears in the Denunzie dei contratti (1343) [Milanesi: Siena, BC, MS P.III.50, fol. 589v].
2. Mentioned in the Denunzie dei contratti, when he buys land from "Sozzo olim bindi mannuccii" (24 March 1343); living in San Donato [Milanesi: Siena, BC, MS P.III.50, fol. 590r].
3. [ceccho martini] Is paid 1 florin by the rector of the hospital for the feast of the Blessed Ambrogio (15 March 1344) [ASS, Spedale 851, fol. 21v].[22]

Cecco di Puccio (★ under Cecco di Duccio)
1. [ciecho puci] Is paid 8 soldi for fourteen coats of arms in the books of the former captain of the people (13 November 1310) [ASS, Biccherna 124, fol. 243r].
2. Is paid £1 for painting the covers of the books of the *camarlengo* and the *provveditori* (31 December 1310) [ASS, Biccherna 124, fol. 301v].
3. His house in Sant'Egidio is valued at £80 (c. 1318) [ASS, Estimo 136, fol. 417r].
4. Mentioned in the Denunzie dei contratti as living in Sant'Egidio (1323–25?) [Milanesi: Siena, BC, MS P.III.49, fol. 528v].

Cecco di Tuccio (?)
1. [Ceccus tuccii] Living in the *popolo* of San Martino (1323/24) [Milanesi: Siena, BC, MS P.III.49, fol. 528r: citing Denunzie dei contratti 1323–34].

Cecco di Vanni
1. In Terza di Città (29 June 1355) [Benvoglienti: Siena, BC, MS C.v.5, fol. 10v: citing the *Caleffo Nero*, fol. 284r].

Cechus de Bozoli
1. Listed in the "Libro delle Capitudini delle Arti" (1363?) [Milanesi, *Documenti*, I, 51].

22. This is likely a reference to the feast of the Beato Ambrogio Sansedoni.

Chele di Vanni (★)
1. Registered in the Painters' Guild (1356) [Milanesi, *Documenti,* I, 35].
2. Listed in the "Libro delle Capitudini delle Arti" (1363?) [Milanesi, *Documenti,* I, 51].

Christofano del Maestro Bindoccio (★)
1. Registered in the Painters' Guild (1356) [Milanesi, *Documenti,* I, 33].
2. He and Francio di Vannuccio paid, by the Biccherna, 48 lire and 4 soldi for painting in several places "ne la terra di Montalcino" (27 September 1361) [Milanesi, *Documenti,* I, 33].
3. Listed in the "Libro delle Capitudini delle Arti" (1363?) [Milanesi, *Documenti,* I, 51].

Cientti di Mino
1. Is paid 19 soldi for fifty coats of arms on the books of the podestà (30 December 1307) [ASS, Biccherna 121, fol. 353v].

Cola di Fuccio
1. Named as one of the approved "fideiussori idonei," the oath helpers for the Terzo di Camollia (before 1318?) [ASS, Concistoro 2468, fol. 20v].
2. Is paid 15 soldi by the Confraternity of the Virgin and Saint Francis for "lo sequenziale grande" (2 February 1319) [ASS, Patrimonio Resti 199, fol. 24r].
3. Is paid 2 florins for the miniature in the book of lauds belonging to the Confraternity of the Virgin and Saint Francis (September 1323) [ASS, Patrimonio Resti 219, fol. 47v].
4. Is paid 6 florins for miniatures in "our book for the sacristy" of the Hospital della Scala (1339/40?) [ASS, Spedale 514, fol. 26r].
5. Is paid 5 florins, 2 lire, 17 soldi, and 6 denari for three hundred miniatures (at the rate of 12 denari apiece) and blue pigment for the new antiphonary (27 April 1344) [ASS, Spedale 851, fol. 35r].

Cosone
1. His widow has rented a workshop, in the *popolo* of San Cristoforo, to Guido di Ghezzo, who lives in the *popolo* of San Donato (3 March 1328) [Borghesi and Banchi, *Nuovi documenti,* 12–13].

Cosone di Cello
1. Mentioned in the Denunzie dei contratti as living in San Donato (May 1318) [Milanesi: Siena, BC, MS P.III.49, fol. 526r].

Cristofano
1. [Christofano] Is paid 6 soldi for two coats of arms of the commune on the "house of the commune" near the Porta Peruzzini (31 December 1343) [ASS, Biccherna 213, fol. 155v].[23]
2. Is paid £63 for work on the "paglio" connected with the visit of "the cardinal" (23 April 1350) [ASS, Biccherna 410, fol. 22r].

Cristofano di Cosa
1. Is paid for painting the angels of four *doppieri* with the arms of the Petroni and Rossi families (1363) [Faluschi: Siena, BC, MS E.v.14, fol. 66r, citing: Conti Correnti, fol. 4r, 1363].

23. Bacci (*Dipinti inediti,* 150) thought this is Cristofano di Muccio, nephew to Ugolino di Nerio, but the document contains only the first name.

Cristofano di Cosone
1. Receives 3 lire and 6 soldi for painting six coats of arms on banners, likely for the feast of the Assumption (August 1357), and £4 for "painting the angels and gilding their wings" (August 1357) [Siena, Opera del Duomo 184, fol. 34r].[24]
2. Listed in the "Libro delle Capitudini delle Arti" (1363?) [Milanesi, *Documenti*, I, 50].

Cristofano di Muccio
1. Receives dowry of 100 florins from his future wife, Lucia di Orsuccio (17 October 1348) [Bacci, *Dipinti inediti,* 150].

Cristofano di Stefano
1. Is paid by the Opera del Duomo 5 lire and 6 soldi for blue (pigment), lake, and other colors to be used in restoration of the *Madonna* on the facade of the cathedral (August 1358) [Siena, Opera del Duomo 185, fol. 41v].
2. He and his "companion painter" receive 18 lire and 5 soldi for restoring the *Madonna* (August 1358) [Siena, Opera del Duomo 185, fol. 42r].
3. Cristofano sells the Opera 117 sheets of gold leaf for this project (September 1358) [Siena, Opera del Duomo 185, fol. 45v].
4. He and the painter "lucha" are paid for ultramarine and other colors bought for the project (September 1358) [Siena, Opera del Duomo 185, fol. 45v].[25]
5. Cristofano and "lucha" are paid a salary of 7 florins (29 lire, 3 soldi) for fifteen days' work on the project (September 1358) [Siena, Opera del Duomo 185, fol. 46r].
6. Cristofano is paid 11 lire, 19 soldi, and 6 denari for blue, tin, colors, and 225 sheets of gold leaf to "fare istelle intorno a la Madonna de la facciata del duomo e mettare ad oro el ale degl' agnoli" (December 1358) [Siena, Opera del Duomo 185, fol. 48v].
7. He is paid £8 for eight days' work on the same project (December 1358) [Siena, Opera del Duomo 185, fol. 48v].[26]

Cristofano di Tura
1. In a list compiled by Milanesi of the artists in the "Libro de' Giuriati alla Mercanzia" (1331) [Milanesi: Siena, BC, MS P.III.46, fol. 428r].

Dietisalvi[27] (★ under Dietisalvi di Guido)
1. Is paid 8 soldi for painting the cover of the Entrata/Uscita (1281) [ASS, Biccherna 80, fol. 61r].
2. Is paid 8 soldi for painting the cover of the Entrata/Uscita (22 January 1282) [ASS, Biccherna 82, fol. 98v].
3. Is paid 8 soldi for painting the cover of the Entrata/Uscita (24 July 1282) [ASS, Biccherna 83, fol. 84v].
4. Is paid 8 soldi for painting the cover of the Entrata/Uscita (January–June 1284) [ASS, Biccherna 85, fol. 26v].

---

24. See item 6 under "Cristofano di Stefano."
25. Fehm (*Luca di Tommè,* 195) assumes that "lucha" in this item and those that follow—all dealing with the restoration project—is Luca di Tommè. See below, under "Lucha."
26. See item 1 under "Cristofano di Cosone."
27. For other, earlier notices of this painter, see A. Lisini, *Le tavolette dipinte di Biccherna e di Gabella del R. Archivio di Stato in Siena,* Florence, 1901.

5. Is paid 9 soldi for painting the cover of the Entrata/Uscita (December[?] 1284) [ASS, Biccherna 86, fol. 106v].
6. Is paid 8 soldi for painting the cover of the Entrata/Uscita (1284) [ASS, Biccherna 87, fol. 108v].
7. Is paid 8 soldi for painting the cover of the Entrata/Uscita (January? 1285) [ASS, Biccherna 88, fol. 182r].
8. Is paid 9 soldi for painting in the book of the *camarlengo* and the *provveditori* (2 October 1288)[28] [ASS, Biccherna 97, fol. 101r].[29]
9. Is paid 4 soldi for decoration of the boxes for wax at the feast of the Assumption (August, 1290) [ASS, Biccherna 103, fol. 67r].
10. Received 20 soldi for painting letters before the *Maestà* in the palace of the commune (27 June 1291) [ASS, Biccherna 104, fol. 94v].[30]

Domenicho di Buonachorso
1. Registered in the Painters' Guild (1356) [Milanesi, *Documenti*, I, 39].

Domenico Maffei
1. Is paid 4 soldi for two coats of arms on a house of the commune at the Fonte Nuova (16 March 1345) [ASS, Biccherna 217, fol. 101r].

Domenico Orlandi (★ under Domenico di Lando)
1. Pays a fine of 7 lire, 12 soldi and 2 denari (8 April–4 May 1338) [ASS, Biccherna 404, fol. 30r].
2. Bono Campuglia, the *operaio* of the commune, is to have £58 for painting "le camere del palazo." Of this, Domenico is given 6 lire, 8 soldi, and 9 denari (18 April 1338) [ASS, Biccherna 404, fol. 109r].[31]

Donato[32] (★ under Donato di Mino)
1. Donato and his three "companions" are paid £30, as salary, for twenty-two days at the baths of Petriolo, marking the houses "with letters" (31 December 1331) [ASS, Biccherna 171, fol. 101v].
2. Donato and "companions" paid 41 lire and 8 soldi for 138 "ischrite" in the rooms of the baths of Macereto and for twenty-one inscriptions at Petriolo (31 December 1331) [ASS, Biccherna 171, fol. 108r].

28. Such payments are undoubtedly for the covers of the Entrata/Uscita, but I reflect the wording of the payment.

29. The notice is repeated in Biccherna 98, fol. 96v.

30. Also recorded in Biccherna 105, fol. 97.

31. I take "le camere del palazo" to refer to the living quarters of the Nove, and that is confirmed in the latin version of the payment to Bono Campuglia, where the painters are described as having painted the "cameras novi dormentorii" (Biccherna 191, fol. 109), and in another vernacular rendition as "le camere del nuovo domentorio" (Biccherna 194, fol. 26r). It is only in the pertinent Memoriale volume and the passage concerning this project (Biccherna 404, fol. 109r) that Domenico Orlandi is mentioned by name.

This seems to have been part of a project to create an entirely new dormitory, for the *operaio*, Bono Campuglia, earlier received significant sums for the new facility. See Biccherna 190, fols. 4v and 15v (July and August 1337).

32. These two notices are references to Donato Martini.

Donato Martini
1. Living in San Donato, he receives from his future wife, Giovanna, a dowry of £400 (3 October–29 November 1324) [Bacci, *Fonti e commenti,* 147–48].
2. Buried in San Domenico (16 August 1347). Bacci, *Fonti e commenti,* 190].[33]

Fazio di Dietisalvi (★ under Dietisalvi di Guido)
1. [fazo Dietisalvi] While living in Sant'Egidio, he pays a fine of £5 for eating in a tavern (15 May 1302) [Bacci, *Fonti e commenti,* 70–71].

Fede di Nalduccio (★)
1. Living in San Pietro a Ovile, he receives £100 as dowry of his future wife, Toma di Jacomuccio di Guido (27 July 1348) [ASS, Gabella Contratti 51, fol. 49r].[34]
2. Registered in the Painters' Guild (1356) [Milanesi, *Documenti,* I, 30].
3. Living in parish of San Cristofano, he rents, for 3 florins, a workshop from the Misericordia for three years (1356)[35] [Milanesi: Siena, BC, MS P.III.50, fol. 209r: citing the "Protoc di S. Mino di Feo, Carte della Misericordia"].
4. He and Bindotto di Ceccho go "per richercare e chaseri, con uno cavallo per uno" (28 May 1361) [Borghesi and Banchi, *Nuovi documenti,* 49].[36]
5. Listed in the "Libro delle Capitudini delle Arti" (1363?) [Milanesi, *Documenti,* I, 50].[37]

Federigo Memmi (★)
1. He and his brother Lippo are involved in a project regarding the tower of the Palazzo Pubblico that was, in the end, abandoned (8 August 1341–2 January 1342) [Maginnis, "Chiarimenti documentari," 19–22].
2. His wife is buried in San Domenico (24 August 1342) [Laurent, *I necrologi,* 64].[38]
3. He and Lippo acquire property in Monsindoli (1 July–7 September 1343) [Bacci, *Fonti e commenti,* 179–80].
4. He and Lippo are paid by the Ospedale della Scala 25 florins, 1 lira, 8 soldi, and 4 denari for a triptych(?) to be sent to "don Bruno" (3 March 1344) [Bacci, *Fonti e commenti,* 181–82].
5. He and Lippo sign an altarpiece in Avignon (1347) [G. de Nicola, "L'affresco di Simone Martini ad Avignone," *L'arte,* IX, 1906, 340 n. 6: citing a letter of 5 June 1663 to Cardinal Barberini from J. M. Saurez, bishop of Vaison].

Filippo Vannis
1. Listed in the "Libro delle Captudini delle Arti" (1363?) [Milanesi, *Documenti,* I, 49].

33. The entry itself indicates Donato is the brother of Simone.

34. This item is published by Borghesi and Banchi (*Nuovi documenti,* 49), but they inaccurately describe the dowry as 100 florins. Fede's wife, Tommasa, died in 1383 and left all her possessions to the Ospedale di Santa Maria della Scala. In the same year, the painter received a dowry of 200 florins for his second wife (21 September 1383). Milanesi: Siena, BC, MS P.III.50, fol. 579r: citing Denunzie/contratti, 1383, fol. 49v.

35. The rent was likely 3 florins a year.

36. For later notices, see Milanesi, *Documenti,* I, 309, and Borghesi and Banchi, *Nuovi documenti,* 49.

37. A painter called simply "Fides" was buried in San Domencio on 13 December 1389. See Laurent, *I necrologi,* 150. For other, later documents regarding this painter, see Borghesi and Banchi, *Nuovi documenti,* 48–49.

38. The document speaks of the "Uxor Tederighi pictoris."

Fina Jacomi
1. [Fina Jacomi] Mentioned in the "Libro della Presta del 1321" (1321) [Milanesi: Siena, BC, MS P.III.50, fol. 527r: citing "Libro della Presta del 1321," fol. 96r].

Francesco
1. [francescho] Is paid 15 soldi and 4 denari for forty-six coats of arms in the books of the "vicharo vecchio" (6 July 1328) [ASS, Biccherna 159, fol. 2v].
2. [franciescho] Is paid 8 soldi for painting the books of the former captain of the people (30 October 1335) [ASS, Biccherna 183, fol. 44r].
3. Duomo pays him 15 soldi (1362) [Milanesi, *Documenti*, I, 35 n. 1].

Francesco di Nerio (★)[39]
1. Living in the *popolo* of San Giorgio, he acquires, for £175, a house and vineyard in "chontrada di busete" and land and a vineyard in "sanaciano" from the Ospedale della Scala (20 June 1350) [Spedale 514, fol. 222r].[40]
2. [Franciescho] Living in San Giorgio, he sells (land?) (1352) [Milanesi: MS P.III.49, fol. 533r: citing Denunzie dei contratti, 1352, fol. 96v].
3. Registered in the Painters' Guild (1356) [Milanesi, *Documenti*, I, 34].
4. Listed in the "Libro delle Capitudini delle Arti" (1363?) [Milanesi, *Documenti*, I, 49].

Francesco di Piero
1. Registered in the Painters' Guild (1356) [Milanesi, *Documenti*, I, 34].
2. Listed in the "Libro delle Capitudini delle Arti" (1363?) [Milanesi, *Documenti*, I, 51].

Francesco di Segna[41]
1. Witness to a document (18 April 1326) [Contratti/Sapienza: Siena, BC, MS A.VII.1, fol. 197r].
2. Receives £300 as dowry of his future wife, Nuta di Palamede (25 August 1328) [Bacci, *Fonti e commenti*, 47].
3. Paints books of the former captain of the people (1335) [Bacci, *Fonti e commenti*, 47].[42]
4. [Franciscum Segnie] Is paid, through Bono Campulia, £13 for a painted panel for the loggia of the palace of the commune at the baths of Petriolo (27 February 1339) [Bacci, *Fonti e commenti*, 46–47].[43]

Francesco di Simone
1. Living in Sant'Egidio, per a list compiled by Milanesi of the artists in the "Libro de' Giurati alla Mercanzia" (1325–26) [Milanesi: Siena, BC, MS P.III.46, fol. 428r].

Francesco di Vannuccio
1. [franchiescho di Vannuccio] Is paid 10 soldi for forty coats of arms of the podestà "vecchio" in books of his officials (23 July 1337) [ASS, Biccherna 190, fol. 6r].

39. There is no documentation connecting this painter to Ugolino di Nerio.
40. Two payments follow this notice, the last dated to 5 December 1352.
41. Son of Segna di Buonaventura and brother of Niccolò di Segna.
42. This is Bacci's interpretation. The document, cited here in the appendix on book covers, simply names the painter "Francesco." See "Francesco" above.
43. On 28 February 1339 the *operaio* of the commune, Bono Campuglia, was reimbursed for the £13 he had spent on acquiring this panel (ASS, Biccherna 201, fol. 22r).

2. [franchescho di vanucio] Involved in a condemnation against "Vicientj di vanni" (January–June 1347) [ASS, Biccherna 408, fol. 30v].
3. [Francio di Vannuccio] Registered in the Painters' Guild (1356) [Milanesi, *Documenti*, I, 35].
4. [Francio di Vannuccio] He and Christofano del Maestro Bindoccio are paid 48 lire and 4 soldi for painting in several places "ne la terra de Montalcino" (27 September 1361) [Milanesi, *Documenti*, I, 33].

Franciescho di Mano
1. Registered in the Painters' Guild (1356) [Milanesi, *Documenti*, I, 39].

Franciescho di Vanni[44]
1. Registered in the Painters' Guild (1356) [Milanesi, *Documenti*, I, 35].
2. As "Franciscus Vannis," listed in the "Libro delle Capitudini delle Arti" (1363?) [Milanesi, *Documenti*, I, 49].

Franciescho di Vanni deto *Chiancianese*
1. Registered in the Painters' Guild (1356) [Milanesi, *Documenti*, I, 38].

Francio
1. Is paid 15 soldi for his work for the Opera del Duomo (1362) [Milanesi, *Documenti*, I, 35].[45]

Galgano di Duccio[46] (★)
1. Living in San Donato, he receives from his wife, "Iohanna magistri Buondi," dowry of £100 and half a house in San Quirico (15 June 1343) [Bacci, "Commentarii," 247].

Galgano di maestro Minuccio (★)
1. Registered in the Painters' Guild (1356) [Milanesi, *Documenti*, I, 32].
2. [Galganus magistri Mini] Listed in the "Libro delle Capitudini delle Arti" (1363?) [Milanesi, *Documenti*, I, 51].[47]

Gano di Orlando (★)
1. Mentioned as citizen of Siena (30 October 1310) [Milanesi: Siena, BC, MS P.III.53, fol. 377r: citing "Carte di S. Agostino"].

Ghabriello di Saracino
1. Registered in the Painters' Guild (1356) [Milanesi, *Documenti*, I, 35].

Ghezzo (★ under Ghezzo di Guido)
1. Listed among members from the Terzo di San Martino for the General Council (30 June 1288) [Spogli: Siena, BC, MS A.VII.9, fol. 173r].
2. Is paid 4 soldi and 3 denari for thirteen coats of arms of the captain of the people in the books of his notaries (27 April 1306) [ASS, Biccherna 119, fol. 237r].

---

44. This is not Francio di Vannuccio, since both are named in the 1356 list of guild members. The painter would also seem distinct from "Franciescho di Vanni deto *Chiancianese*," whose name also appears in that list. Milanesi, *Documenti*, I, 38.

45. Milanesi assumed this was Francio di Vannuccio.

46. Likely Duccio di Buoninsegna's son.

47. A "Ghalghanus magistri Minuccii" was buried in San Domenico on 9 March 1386 (Laurent, *I necrogoli*, 145).

Ghezzo bendaio [Bonfigliuoli?].
1. Living in the *lira* of the Manetti, Terzo di Città (21 May–1 December 1311) [Bacci, *Fonti e commenti,* 99].

Ghezzo Buonfigliuoli detto Bitatto
1. Living in the *lira* of the Manetti, Terzo di Città, he pays 18 soldi and 8 denari as his contribution to a *dazio* (4 April 1312) [Bacci, *Fonti e commenti,* 103].[48]

Giacomuccio di Conociuto
1. Mentioned in sale of land (?) by himself and his brother, Angelo (1289) [Milanesi: Siena, BC, MS P.III.51, fol. 509r: citing "Archivio dei Contratti, Perg. 144"].

Giorgio di Duccio[49]
1. Is paid 5 soldi by rector of the Ospedale di Santa Maria della Scala (13 March 1344) [ASS, Spedale 851, fol. 21r].

Giovanni
1. Is paid 8 soldi for painting the books of the former captain of the people (26 May 1339) [ASS, Biccherna 201, fol. 65v].
2. Is paid 11 soldi for painting the books of the podestà (25 June 1339) [ASS, Biccherna 201, fol. 79v].
3. Is paid 9 soldi for painting the books of the captain of the people (5 November 1339) [ASS, Biccherna 202, fol. 121r].
4. Is paid 14 soldi and 4 denari for forty-three coats of arms on books of the notary in charge of malefactors (30 June 1340) [ASS, Biccherna 206, fol. 64r].
5. Is paid 13 soldi for thirty-nine coats of arms of the captain of the people (26 April 1341) [ASS, Biccherna 207, fol. 123v].
6. Is paid 12 soldi and 4 denari for thirty-seven coats of arms on the books of the podestà (30 June 1341) [ASS, Biccherna 207, fol. 148r].
7. Is paid 14 soldi for painting the books of the captain of the people (23 April 1342) [ASS, Biccherna 210, fol. 151v].
8. Is paid 15 soldi for painting coats of arms on the books of the commune in the Biccherna (1 October 1343) [ASS, Biccherna 213, fol. 111v].
9. Is paid 14 soldi for painting the books of the podestà (25 June 1345) [ASS, Biccherna 216, fol. 159r].
10. Is paid 2 lire and 10 soldi (23 April–11 May 1350) [ASS, Biccherna 410, fol. 8r].

Giovanni di Benedetto
1. Is paid, along with Lippo (Vanni?), for painting in the Sala del Consiglio of the Palazzo Pubblico (1361) [Milanesi, *Sulla storia dell'arte Toscana,* Siena, 1873, 49].

Giovanni di Guido
1. Is paid 28 soldi for miniatures he made (17 December 1288) [ASS, Biccherna 97, fol. 123r].[50]

48. Likely the same artist as that listed immediately above.

49. Perhaps Duccio's son.
50. Also recorded in Biccherna 98, fol. 118v.

Giovanni di Paolo (★)
1. Living in San Cristofano, he and his wife Petra sell land (18 November 1348) [Milanesi: Siena, BC, MS P.III.50, fol. 587v: citing Denunzie dei contratti 1348, fol. 135r].

Giovanni di Sera (★)
1. Is paid 9 soldi for painting twenty-seven coats of arms on the books of the captain of the people (28 April 1340) [ASS, Biccherna 206, fol. 38v].
2. Married Caterina, daughter of Donato Martini (no date given) [Milanesi, *Documenti*, I, 30, and Bacci, *Fonti e commenti*, 191].[51]
3. Is paid 9 soldi for painting twenty-seven coats of arms on the books of the former *capitano del popolo* (3 November 1341) [ASS, Biccherna 209, fol. 130r].
4. Receives 13 soldi for painting thirty-nine coats of arms on the books of the podestà (12 December 1341) [ASS, Biccherna 209, fol. 139v].
5. Is paid 14 soldi for painting thirty-five coats of arms on the books "of the officials" [of the Biccherna?] (27 June 1342) [ASS, Biccherna 210, fol. 185r].
6. Receives 10 soldi for painting twenty-five books of the captain of the people (30 April 1343) [ASS, Biccherna 212, fol. 173r].
7. For thirty-three escutcheons on the books of the podestà, receives 13 soldi and 9 denari (21 June 1343) [ASS, Biccherna 212, fol. 199v].
8. Is paid 15 soldi for painting the "libros casseros" (30 June 1345) [ASS, Biccherna 216, fol. 174r].
9. Receives 13 soldi and 6 denari for a total of thirty-three coats of arms on the books of the *capitano del popolo* and on the books of the captain of war (26 October 1345) [ASS, Biccherna 217, fol. 122v].
10. Receives 15 soldi and 9 denari for forty-two escutcheons on books of the lord Guidoni(?) de Montone (31 December 1345) [ASS, Biccherna 217, fol. 141v].
11. Is paid 7 soldi for nineteen coats of arms on the books of the captain of the people (23 October 1347) [ASS, Biccherna 221, fol. 129v].
12. Named among various painters who painted items for the funeral of the captain of war, Guidoriccio da Fogliano, he receives £2 for painting "una coverta" (January–June 1352) [ASS, Biccherna 412, fol. 176v].
13. Registered in the Painters' Guild (1356) [Milanesi, *Documenti*, I, 30].
14. Is paid 15 soldi for painting the pole of a banner for the feast of the Assumption (August 1356) [Siena, Opera del Duomo 182, fol. 35r; 183, fol. 59r].
15. Receives 8 soldi for painting three chests with the emblem of the Opera del Duomo (March 1361) [Siena, Opera del Duomo 188, fol. 73v].
16. Is paid 2 lire and 8 soldi for four coats of arms (August 1361) [Siena, Opera del Duomo 189, fol. 31v].
17. [Johannes Sere] Listed in the "Libro delle Capitudini delle Arti" (1363?) [Milanesi, *Documenti*, I, 50].
18. His daughter is buried in San Domenico (15 April 1363) [Laurent, *I necrologi*, 90].[52]

51. The marriage occurred between 1344 and 1363. In the latter year, Caterina's daughter was buried in San Domenico, presumably a victim of the second outbreak of the Black Death.

52. This item reads: "filia uxoris Iohannes di Seta pictoris," surely a scribal error for "di Sera." A "Iohannes de Sera" was buried in San Domenico on 10 July 1383, but no profession is given. Laurent, *I necrologi*, 133.

Giovanni di Vitalera
1. In a list of artists, compiled by Milanesi, from the "Libro de' Giurati alla Mercanzia" (1331) [Milanesi: Siena, BC, MS P.III.46, fol. 428r].

Giusaffa di Filippo (★)
1. Registered in the Painters' Guild (1356) [Milanesi, *Documenti*, I, 36].

Guccio
1. [Guccio Boninsegne] Pays 20 soldi for breaking the night curfew (January–June 1285) [ASS, Biccherna 88, fol. 1v].[53]
2. [Ghuccio] Is paid 10 soldi for painting the books of the treasurer and the Four (November[?] 1289) [ASS, Biccherna 101, fol. 132r].
3. In a list of artists, compiled by Milanesi, from the "Libro de' Giurati alla Mercanzia" (1332–33); living in San Donato and described as "Guccio chiamato Pietro di Taverna" [Milanesi: Siena, BC, MS P.III.46, fol. 428r].[54]

Guido (★ under Guido di Graziano)
1. Is paid 18 soldi for painting fifty-four books of the notaries of malefactors, in the time of the present podestà, with his arms (June 1299) [ASS, Biccherna 115, fol. 3v].
2. Is paid £9 for twelve figures of false witnesses and forgers of coin "in palazo" (26 October 1302) [ASS, Biccherna 117, fol. 312r].[55]
3. Is paid 10 soldi for twenty-five coats of arms on books of the former captain of the people (23 October 1319) [ASS, Biccherna 138, fol. 116r].
4. Is paid 10 soldi for fifty-one coats of arms in the "court" of the captain of the people (4 May 1321) [ASS, Biccherna 141, fol. 189v].
5. Is paid 1 lira, 7 soldi, and 8 denari for painting arms of the commune on "ghofani" (22 September 1321) [ASS, Biccherna 142, fol. 124r].
6. Is paid 7 soldi for painting twenty-one coats of arms on books of the captain of the people (12 October 1321) [ASS, Biccherna 142, fol. 128v].[56]
7. Is paid 12 soldi for painting "in the house of the Nove" (15 October 1321) [ASS, Biccherna 382, fol. 6r].
8. [Ghuido] Is paid 2 lire and 8 soldi for coats of arms on various books (31 October 1323) [ASS, Biccherna 148, fol. 118r].
9. Is paid 14 soldi for forty-three arms on the books of the former podestà (9 January 1324) [ASS, Biccherna 149, fol. 109r].
10. Is paid £1 for painting the cover of the Entrata/Uscita (30 June 1328) [ASS, Biccherna 157, fol. 72v].
11. Is paid 7 soldi for twenty-one coats of arms on books of the captain of the people (15 November 1328) [ASS, Biccherna 159, fol. 56r].
12. Is paid 6 soldi and 3 denari for four "bosogli" of the Council of the Bell (23 December 1331) [ASS, Biccherna 171, fol. 86v].[57]

53. This notice is usually interpreted as containing a scribal error for "Duccio."
54. See "Petrus Tavene" below.
55. On 29 December 1302 Giovanni di Guido, *operaio* of the commune, received £31 for various projects, including painting false witnesses in the palazzo of the commune (Biccherna 117, fol. 358v).
56. Also in Biccherna 143, fol. 68v.
57. "Bosogli" were ballot boxes.

13. Is paid £1 for painting the cover the Entrata/Uscita volume (31 December 1331) [ASS, Biccherna 171, fol. 111v].
14. Is paid 10 soldi for painting the coat of arms of the captain of the people on his books (15 November 1334) [ASS, Biccherna 181, fol. 43r].
15. Is paid 4 soldi for painting a book cover (12 July 1337) [ASS, Biccherna 190, fol. 4r].
16. Is paid, with his "companions," 6 florins (19 lire and 1 soldo) for part of the painting at the baths of Macereto (30 June 1338) [ASS, Biccherna 191, fol. 145r, and Biccherna 194, fol. 62r].
17. Is paid 6 soldi for painting the "baccini" of the angels in the cathedral (August 1339) [Siena, Opera del Duomo 178, fol. 62r].
18. Is paid £8 for twelve pictures of false witnesses and forgers of coin in the Palazzo Pubblico (1339) [Benvoglienti: Siena, BC, MS 6.IV.C, fol. 16r: citing B. 186, fol. 322r].

Guido Cinatti (★)
1. See the discussion of, and the documentation for, this painter in Chapter II, pages 73–75.

Guido di Cino
1. He and Vitaluccio are paid 14 soldi for painting twenty-one coats of arms on the books of the captain of the people (28 October 1314) [ASS, Biccherna 128, fol. 82r].
2. In a list of painters, compiled by Milanesi, from the "Libro de' Giurati alla Mercanzia" (1326) [Milanesi: Siena, BC, MS P.III.46, fol. 428r].
3. [Guido di Cenni] Is paid £4 by the commune (1329) [Benvoglienti: Siena, BC, MS C.IV.6, fol. 15r: citing Entrata B. 144, fol. 24r].
4. Mentioned in a notice from the cathedral that is more than half lost (December 1334) [Siena, Opera del Duomo 175, fol. 53r].
5. He receives 12 florins for a panel of the Virgin in the Church of San Giovanni Fuorcivitas in Pistoia (5 November 1332) [Zdekauer, "Opere d'arte senese nella chiesa di San Giovanni Fuorcivitas di Pistoia," *BSSP,* VIII, 1901, 177].[58]
6. Is paid 12 soldi for painting nineteen escutcheons on the books of the captain of the people and for painting the "legnio de la fiera" (27 May 1348) [ASS, Biccherna 223, fol. 143r].

Guido di Ghezzo (★—see also Guido di Ghezzo Juniore)
1. Has property valued at 285 lire, 6 soldi, and 8 denari (c. 1318) [ASS, Estimo 131, fol. 245r].[59]
2. Living in San Donato, he protests to Petra, widow of the painter Cosone, over a shop she has rented him in San Cristoforo (3 March 1328) [Borghesi and Banchi, *Nuovi documenti,* 12–13].
3. He cedes to Matteo Rosselli, painter of Florence, a credit that he has against Paolo di Andrea, painter of Siena (8 June 1333) [Borghesi and Banchi, *Nuovi documenti,* 19–20].
4. Borghesi and Banchi (*Nuovi documenti,* 20) summarize a series of documents relating to this painter from the hospital of Sant'Onofrio, dated 1327, 1328, 1330, 1332, 1334, and 1340. None deals with pictures.
5. Biccherna records 18 lire, 12 soldi, and 4 denari owing to Guido di Ghezzo, Nicchola dipentore, Andrea di Vanni, and Meo di Guido "camicciaio" (July–December 1339) [ASS, Biccherna 406, fol. 19v].

---

58. Zdekauer assumes this is Guido Cinatti.   59. See Appendix II.

Guido di Nerio
1. Living in San Donato, he receives £50 as the dowry of his future wife, Beccha di Tano (24 May–8 July 1318) [ASS, Gabella dei contratti 40, fol. 11r, and Bacci, *Dipinti inediti,* 144–45].
2. Matriculates in the Florentine Painters' Guild (1327) [Bacci, *Dipinti inediti,* 145–46].
3. Witnesses a will (27 March 1346?) [Contratti/Sapienza: Siena, BC, MS A.III.1, fol. 502v].

Guido Tinacci
1. [Ghuido tinacci] Is paid 3 soldi for "due tefanie [chests or boxes] che chonprano per la chasa" (16 April 1344) [ASS, Spedale 851, fol. 31v].

Guidone di Graziano (★)
1. Living in San Donato, he sells property to the Ospedale della Misericordia (1292) [Benvoglienti: Siena, BC, MS C.IV.17, fol. 236r: citing Denunzie dei contratti 321, 1292, fol. 868r].

Guidone di Jacopo
1. Living in the *popolo* of San Antonio (1342–43) [Milanesi: Siena, BC, MS P.III.50, fol. 591r: citing Denunzie dei contratti, 1342–43, fol. 84v].

Guidoni (★ under Guido di Graziano)
1. Is paid 3 lire and 5 soldi for painting the standard of San Martino "et in maniera sive Barattariorum" (16 November 1278) [ASS, Biccherna 73, fol. 47v].
2. Is paid 10 soldi for painting the books of the *camarlengo* and the *provveditori* (July 1286) [ASS, Biccherna 93, fol. 196r].[60]
3. Is paid 6 soldi for painting the books of the *camarlengo* and the *provveditori* (end of January 1288) [ASS, Biccherna 96, fol. 47v].
4. Is paid 10 soldi for painting the books of the *camarlengho* and the *provveditori* (18 January 1289) [ASS, Biccherna 99, fol. 43r].[61]
5. Is paid 10 soldi for painting the books of the *camarlengo* and the *provveditori* (September 1290) [ASS, Biccherna 103, fol. 69r].
6. Is paid £10 for painting the Virgin Mary in the palace of the commune (2 August 1295) [ASS, Biccherna 112, fol. 97r].
7. Is paid £15 for the image of the Blessed Virgin Mary in the palace of the commune (27 August 1295) [ASS, Biccherna 112, fol. 101v].
8. Is paid £10 for painting a *Maestà* in the palace of the commune (28 October 1295) [ASS, Biccherna 112, fol. 121v].
9. Is paid 6 lire and 10 soldi for Saints Peter and Paul and for 102 gold letters before the image of the Virgin (15 November 1295) [ASS, Biccherna 112, fol. 124v.].[62]
10. Is paid £1 for fifty coats of arms on the books of the podestà (30 June 1319) [ASS, Biccherna 137, fol. 118r].[63]

60. This notice is repeated in Biccherna 94, fol. 172r.
61. Notice repeated in Biccherna 100, fol. 36r.
62. The structure of these payments, through August to November, clearly suggests fresco is involved. Particularly the late addition of Saints Peter and Paul and the 102 gold letters (an inscription) could only have been integrated with the image of the Virgin if the painter was working in fresco. For the entire project, Guidoni received a total of 36 lire and 10 soldi.
63. This and the following notices likely refer to a second "Guidoni."

11. Is paid 12 soldi for painting thirty-two books of the captain of the people with his arms (30 June 1319) [ASS, Biccherna 137, fol. 120r].
12. Is paid 10 soldi for twenty-five books with arms of the former captain of the people (23 October 1319) [ASS, Biccherna 139, fol. 122r].
13. Is paid 10 soldi for painting the arms of the captain (4 May 1321) [ASS, Biccherna 140, fol. 168r].
14. Is paid 14 soldi and 4 denari for forty-three escutcheons on the books of the podestà (26 June 1321) [ASS, Biccherna 140, fol. 185r].
15. Is paid 1 lira, 7 soldi, and 8 denari for painting chests (22 September 1321) [ASS, Biccherna 143, fol. 64r].
16. [Guidoni] Is paid 7 soldi for 21 escutcheons on books of the captain of the people (12 October 1321) [ASS, Biccherna 143, fol. 68v].
17. Is paid 12 soldi for painting book covers (10 February 1345) [ASS, Biccherna 216, fol. 100v].

Guiduccio di Mino
1. Witness to legal transaction regarding dowry of the future wife of the painter Masarello di Gilio (30 May 1303) [Borghesi and Banchi, *Nuovi documenti*, 6–8].

Jachomo di Frate Mino (★)
1. As "dipignitore dela nostra chapella," he receives 26 florins and 39 soldi (19 January–17 August 1355) [ASS, Spedale 515, fol. 20r].
2. "Iacomo di frate Mino" enrolled in the Painters' Guild (1356) [Milanesi, *Documenti*, I, 27].
3. Listed as "Jacobus fratris Mini" in the "Libro delle Capitudini delle Arti" (1363?) [Milanesi, *Documenti*, I, 50].

Jacobo
1. Is paid 5 lire, 8 soldi, and 9 denari for painting in the palace of the commune that was the palace of the lord Nigi (5 April 1294) [ASS, Biccherna 110, fol. 125v].

Jacobuccio
1. Is paid 1 soldo for a "cappello lampidia" in the palace of the commune before the *Maestà* of the Virgin Mary (14 April 1291) [ASS, Biccherna 105, fol. 84r].[64]

Jacomino
1. Documented (5 May 1356) [Benvoglienti: Siena, BC, MS C.v.7, fol. 268v: citing "Notizie di vari contratti della Sapienza"].

Jacomo di Bindo (★ under Jacomo di Bindiccio d'Arrigo)
1. Is paid 1 lira, 3 soldi, and 4 denari for painting forty coats of arms on the books of the podestà (30 December 1329) [ASS, Biccherna 163, fol. 50r].
2. Is paid 10 soldi for painting fifteen books of the "sindacho" (30 December 1329) [ASS, Biccherna 163, fol. 50r].
3. In parish of San Donato (no date) [Milanesi, *Documenti*, I, 34].
4. Registered in the Painters' Guild (1356) [Milanesi, *Documenti*, I, 34].
5. Listed in the "Libro delle Capitudini delle Arti" (1363?) [Milanesi, *Documenti*, I, 50].

---

64. Also recorded in Biccherna 104, fol. 80. I suspect that this is the kind of shade we see covering a lamp before the panel of the Virgin in the *Verification of the Stigmata* in the *Saint Francis Legend*, Assisi.

Jacomo di Cino
1. Living in S. Pietro a Ovile and married to Giovanna di Donato (1352) [Milanesi, *Documenti*, I, 31].
2. Is paid 1 lira and 10 soldi for three coats of arms of the commune on a palace acquired by the commune (31 December 1352) [ASS, Biccherna 230, fol. 134r].
3. A "Iacomo di Cino Arrighi" is registered in the Painters' Guild (1356) [Milanesi, *Documenti*, I, 31].
4. [Jachomo di Cino] Named as one of the castellans of Paganico (6 August 1361) [ASS, Biccherna 241, fol. 70r].
5. Is paid 20 soldi by the cathedral for painting the wall "dietro a le due tauole di duomo che si mutaro" (March 1362) [Milanesi, *Documenti*, I, 31].
6. Listed in the "Libro delle Capitudini delle Arti" (1363?) [Milanesi, *Documenti*, I, 50].[65]

Jacomo di Piero
1. Registered in the Painters' Guild (1356) [Milanesi, *Documenti*, I, 38].

Jacomuccio (★)
1. Living in San Donato a lato dei Montanini, he pays 10 soldi in relation to the *dazio* of 1292 (8 October 1292) [ASS, Biccherna 108, fol. 126r].
2. Is paid 11 lire and 8 soldi in connection with painting two *palii* given to the king and queen of Sicily (20 March 1294) [ASS, Biccherna 110, fol. 121v].

Lando
1. [Landus] Buried in San Domenico (12 May 1357) [Laurent, *I necrologi*, 82].

Lando[66]
1. Is paid 12 soldi for painting four coats of arms on property belonging to the duomo (June 1358) [Siena, Opera del Duomo 184, fol. 74v].

Lando di Dominico
1. As "Landus Dominici" listed in the "Libro delle Capitudini delle Arti" (1363?) [Milanesi, *Documenti*, I, 51].

Lando di Stefano (★ under Lando di Stefano di Bindo)
1. Registered in the Painters' Guild (1356) [Milanesi, *Documenti*, I, 37].

Lando di Vinuccio (★)
1. [Landus Vinuccij] Living in the *popolo* of San Salvatore, he receives £100 as the dowry of his future wife, Barthalomea (3 November 1344?) [Milanesi: Siena, BC, MS P.III.50, fol. 224r: citing Denunzie dei contratti 1342–44, fol. 239r].

Lappo di Cenni
1. Is paid 1 lira and 6 soldi for painting two banners of the "vicariati" (April 1311) [Spogli: Siena, BC, MS A.VII.15, fol. 223v: citing B. 103, fol. 122r].

Lorenzo di Vanni
1. Registered in the Painters' Guild (1356) [Milanesi, *Documenti*, I, 35].

---

65. Milanesi also publishes later notices.
66. The date of this notice makes it clear that this is a second painter named Lando.

Lorino
1. Is paid 12 soldi as salary for painting the rooms of the captain of the people(?) (9 June 1295) [ASS, Biccherna 111, fol. 124v].

Lucas Tonis
1. Listed in the "Libro delle Capitudini delle Arti" (1363?) [Milanesi, *Documenti,* I, 49].

Lucha[67]
1. Described as "nostro allevato dipintore" and paid 5 soldi for an ounce of indigo bought to mark houses (13 March 1344) [ASS, Spedale 851, fol. 21r].
2. Is paid 5 soldi for making a sign for a mill at "monterone" that belonged to the hospital, and for materials (26 May 1344) [ASS, Spedale 851, fol. 42v].
3. With Cristofano di Stefano, he is paid for providing the Opera del Duomo with ultramarine and other colors for the restoration of the *Madonna* on the facade of the cathedral (September 1358) [Siena, Opera del Duomo 185, fol. 45v].[68]
4. He and Cristofano are paid a salary of 7 florins for fifteen days' work on restoring the *Madonna* on the facade of the cathedral (September 1358) [Siena, Opera del Duomo 185, fol. 46r].[69]

Lutinus Piovani
1. Listed in the "Libro delle Capitudini delle Arti" (1363?) [Milanesi, *Documenti,* I, 49].

Magino di Midule
1. In a list compiled by Milanesi of artists in the "Libro de' Giurati alla Mercanzia" (1326) [Milanesi: Siena, BC, MS P.III.46, fol. 428v].

Martino di Ser Vanni
1. In a list compiled by Milanesi of artists in the "Libro de' Giurati alla Mercanzia" (1326) [Milanesi: Siena, BC, MS P.III.46, fol. 428r].

Masarello di Gilio[70] (★ under Morsello di Cilio and Francesco di Mino detto Massarello Pittore)
1. [Massaruccio] Is paid 8 soldi for painting the book of the Gabella (1290) [Borghesi and Banchi, *Nuovi documenti,* 8].
2. [Massarello] Is paid 5 soldi for painting fifteen books of the captain of the people (7 November 1295) [ASS, Biccherna 112, fol. 123r].
3. [masserello] Is paid 4 soldi and 6 denari for painting arms of the captain of the people in twenty-seven books (26 October 1296) [ASS, Biccherna 113, fol. 208r].
4. [Massarello] Is paid 4 soldi and 6 denari for painting thirty-six books of the commune with the arms of the captain of the people (26 October 1298) [Borghesi and Banchi, *Nuovi documenti,* 8].
5. [Masarello quondam Gilii] His future wife, "Palmeria filia Micchellis," gives him, as her

---

67. This is unlikely to be Fra Luca, who on 5 October 1321 received £13 for a panel with the Crucifixion and our Lady for the altar of the palace of the podestà (Biccherna 142, fol. 128). Fra Luca is nowhere described as a painter.

68. This notice and the next, Fehm (*Luca di Tommè,* 195) assumes to be references to Luca di Tommè.

69. See "Cristofano di Stefano" above.

70. Note that only two items below have the full form of the painter's name, but in this case I have combined those notices with others that refer simply to Masarello. The latter name is unusual enough that the connection seems warranted.

dowry, a house in San Donato valued at £140 (30 May 1303) [Borghesi and Banchi, *Nuovi documenti*, 6–8].

6. [massarello] Is paid £7 for a painted cross for the altar of the Nove (26 April 1306) [ASS, Biccherna 118, fol. 227v].[71]

7. [Masarello] Is paid, along with his "companions," 43 lire and 14 soldi for painting and "zendadi" of the baldachins presented to King Robert the Wise of Naples and his queen (31 October 1310) [ASS, Biccherna 124, fol. 231v].

8. [Masarello] Is paid 2 lire and 10 soldi for painting the "penonj de vichariati" (20 December 1310) [ASS, Biccherna 124, fol. 269r].

9. [Massarello] Is paid £3 for two panels to record the expenses from the "rubbaria fatta per i Nobil di Sticciano" for the Palazzo Pubblico (December 1311) [Spogli: Siena, BC, MS A.III.15, fol. 235v: citing B. 104, fol. 107v].[72]

10. In an account of a larger sum for baldachins given to the Prince of Taranto in 1315 and for the "paglio" for the feast of the Virgin, he is paid 22 lire and 10 soldi (28 November 1315) [ASS, Biccherna 377, fol. 115r]. See also "Tavena" below.

11. [Massarellus Gilij] Has house in Sant'Egidio a lato dei Rustichelli valued at 153 lire, 6 soldi, and 8 denari (c.1318) [ASS, Estimo 137, fol. 87r].

12. [Massarello] Is paid 10 soldi for serving on a commission of the commune (30 May 1320) [Borghesi and Banchi, *Nuovi documenti*, 8].

13. [massarello] Among those paid for providing decorations for the visit of the duke of Calabria, his wife, and his son, in July of 1326 [ASS, Biccherna 390, fol. 2v].

14. [Massarello] Masarello the painter(?), resident in Sant'Egidio, declares himself debtor to Bindoccio (19 March 1337) [Borghesi and Banchi, *Nuovi documenti*, 8].

15. Buried in San Domenico (10 February 1340) [Laurent, *I necrologi*, 54].

Matteo

1. [Maetheus] Buried in San Domenico (7 June 1363), [Laurent, *I necrologi*, 94].

Matteo di Meo (★)

1. [Matheus Mei] Listed in the "Libro delle Capitudini delle Arti" (1363?) [Milanesi, *Documenti*, I, 50].

Matteo di Mino (★)

1. Living in the *popolo* of Sant'Antonio, he rents a house from the Misericordia (1355) [Milanesi: Siena, BC, MS P.III.50, fol. 209r: citing "Protoc. di s. Mino di Feo, Carte della Misericordia, fol. 131r"].

Meo di Piero (★)

1. Registered in the Painters' Guild (1356) [Milanesi, *Documenti*, I, 36].

Meuccio di Bernardino

1. [Meuccio Bernardini] Pays 4 soldi in a *dazio* (December 1311) [Milanesi: Siena, BC, MS P.III.49, fols. 448r–448v: citing only "Libro del Dazio"].

71. Notice repeated in Biccherna 119, fol. 233v.
72. An unusual task. The painter is paid for "due Tavole, nelle quale erano scritti le spese fatte del Comune per cagione della rubbaria fatta per i Nobili di Sticciano, una del quali tavole fu posta nel Consiglio della Campana, e l'altra nel Concistoro."

2. Living in the *lira* of San Viglio di fuori, he pays 3 lire and 8 soldi for a *dazio* (3 March 1312) [Bacci, *Fonti e commenti,* 104].

Minatello (★ under Minuccio di Filippuccio)
1. Is paid 8 soldi for twenty-eight coats of arms on the books of the captain of the people (20 April 1328) [ASS, Biccherna 157, fol. 32r].
2. Is paid £15 for six months' salary for guarding "la selva de lagho" (27 September 1329) [ASS, Biccherna 159, fol. 33v].[73]

Mino (★ under Ser Mino di Simone)
1. Is paid £19 as salary, and as part of a total of £22, for painting the Virgin and other saints in the palace of the commune (12 August 1289) [ASS, Biccherna 101, fol. 74v].
2. Record of a debt of 15 soldi and 6 denari that Mino owes the Curia del Placito, to be paid on 21 October 1294 [ASS, Curia del Placito 397, fol. 14r].[74]
3. Is paid 20 soldi for painting books (9 August 1295) [ASS, Biccherna 112, fol. 107v].
4. Is paid 20 soldi for painting the books of the prison officials (9 September 1295) [ASS, Biccherna 112, fol. 107v].
5. Is paid £5 for completing a painting of Saint Christopher in the "Palazo del Consiglio" (1302) [Milanesi: Siena, BC, MS P.III.52, fol. 70r].
6. Is paid 2 soldi by the commune (16 November 1314) [ASS, Biccherna 128, fol. 93v].

Mino di Graziano
1. Charged 9 soldi as tax on grain brought from Monteriggione(?) (1290) [Milanesi: Siena, BC, MS P.III.51, fol. 230r: citing Denunzie dei contratti 1290, Libro 1, fol. 53v].[75]
2. Participates in a sale of a house (1292–98) [Milanesi: Siena, BC, MS P.III.51, fol. 228v: citing Denunzie dei contratti, 1292–98, fol. 67v].
3. He, along with Mino Prete and Sabatino di Ramo, is brought before the judge of the Terzo di Camollia regarding rent owed to the Misericordia for a shop they have (4 December 1310) [Borghesi and Banchi, *Nuovi documenti,* 8–10].
4. He owns property in San Donato, in the "contrada di Camporeggi" (12 June 1312) [Carli: Siena, BC, MS C.VII.20, separate sheet after fol. 147r].
5. Mentioned in the book of the *presta* of 1321[76] [Milanesi: Siena, BC, MS P.III.50, fol. 527r: citing "Libro della Presta del 1321," fols. 111r and 116v].

Mino di Voglia (★)
1. [Minus vollie] Recorded as holding jointly with his brother property urban and rural evaluated at 288 lire, 6 soldi, and 8 denari (c. 1319) [ASS, Estimo 131, fol. 242r]. See Appendix II.

---

73. One imagines that Minatello's career as a painter was not entirely successful. The Sienese commune directly controlled not only the forest known as Selva del Lago but also the forest at Montefalcone and others in the valley of the Merse. Both guardians (*forestarii*) and a judge (*judex silve*) dealt with the forests. See Redon, "L'ermo, la città e la foresta."

74. It would seem the debt was paid early, for on fol. 16r of Curia del Placito 397, under the date of 7 September 1294, Mino pays 15 soldi and 6 denari.

75. Perhaps this is grain brought to Siena from rural property belonging to the painter.

76. For the role of the forced loans, *preste*, in Sienese finance, see Bowsky, *Finance,* 166–88.

2. Is paid 12 soldi and 8 denari for painting thirty-eight coats of arms in the book of the podestà (31 December 1331) [ASS, Biccherna 171 fol. 93r].

Mino Prete
1. He and Sabatino di Ramo and Mino di Graziano are brought before the judge of the Terzo di Camollia regarding rent for a workshop they have from the Misericordia (4 December 1310) [Borghesi and Banchi, *Nuovi documenti*, 8–10].

Minuccio[77] (★ under Minuccio di Filipuccio and Minuccia di Mino di Filippuccio)
1. Is paid 8 soldi for twenty coats of arms on the books of the former captain of the people (29 April 1333) [ASS, Biccherna 176, fol. 62v].
2. Is paid 16 soldi "for his salary" for forty-four books painted with the arms of the podestà (26 June 1333)[78] [ASS, Biccherna 176, fol. 97r].

Minuccio di Filippuccio[79] (★)
1. Is paid 12 denari for painting arms of the podestà in a cupboard in the office of the Biccherna (17 February 1295) [ASS, Biccherna 111, fol. 92r].
2. [minuccio filippi] Is paid £5 for painting false witnesses in the palace of the commune (12 November 1298) [ASS, Biccherna 114, fol. 192v].
3. Mino and Memmo di Filippuccio own a house, valued at 333 lire, 6 soldi, and 8 denari, in the parish of San Donato (c. 1318) [ASS, Estimo 131, fol. 49r]. See Appendix II.

Misarello
1. Is paid £3 for painting a panel, on which are written the names of the banished and the criminal, in the house of the captain of war (24 October 1343) [ASS, Biccherna 213, fol. 117r].[80]

Monaldo di Palmerio
1. Has property in San Donato a lato dei Montanini and in San Giovanni worth 89 lire, 6 soldi, and 8 denari (1320) [ASS, Estimo 131, fol. 304r].[81]

Muccio di Nerio (★ under Meuzio Neri)
1. He and his brother, Ugolino di Nerio, have property in Siena and at Sovignano (c.1318) [ASS, Estimo 131, fols. 154v–155r, 333]. See Appendix II.
2. Living in San Donato, he buys land in Sovignano (25 August–20 September 1319) [Bacci, *Dipinti inediti*, 146–47].
3. [Minuccio di Nerio] He is deceased (*popolo* of San Donato a lato dei Montanini) (3 September 1342) [Bacci, *Dipinti inediti*, 148–49].

Nanni di Franciescho
1. Registered in the Painters' Guild (1356) [Milanesi, *Documenti*, I, 36].

---

77. Bacci (*Dipinti inediti*, 147–48) takes the two notices concerning Minuccio to be references to Muccio di Nerio.

78. This payment is noteworthy because it specifies that the sum is for salary. Most other, similar items give us no indication whether the payment includes cost of materials.

79. This is likely Mino di Filippuccio, brother of Memmo di Filippuccio, as indicted by the third notice below.

80. This cannot be a reference to Masarello, since he died in 1340.

81. See Appendix II.

Nanni di Mino
1. [nanni di maestro Mino Pittore] Acts as legal representative (28 April 1358) [Contratti/Sapienza: Siena, BC, MS A.III.1, fol. 234r].

Nello di Betto (★)
1. Alive in 1352 [Milanesi: Siena, BC, MS P.III.49, fol. 532v: citing Denunzie dei contratti 1352, fol. 86r].
2. Registered in the Painters' Guild (1356) [Milanesi, *Documenti*, I, 34].
3. In the *popolo* of Sant'Antonio (1357?), he married Caterina di Giacomo in January 1357 [Milanesi, *Documenti*, I, 34].
4. Worked with Lippo Vanni to decorate the new Sala del Consiglio in the Palazzo Pubblico (1359) [Milanesi, *Documenti*, I, 34].

Neri di Franciescho di Neri
1. Registered in the Painters' Guild (1356) [Milanesi, *Documenti*, I, 38].

Nerino di Jacomo
1. Registered in the Painters' Guild (1356) [Milanesi, *Documenti*, I, 38].

Nerio di Muccio
1. Is buried in San Domencio (31 May 1340) [Laurent, *I necrologi*, 56].[82]

Nerio di Ugolino
1. Living in San Donato, he buys land "and other things" at a price of £130 (12 June–7 July 1311) [Bacci, *Dipinti inediti*, 142].[83]
2. Involved in loan of 30 florins (1 March 1325) [Bacci, *Dipinti inediti*, 149–50].[84]

Nicchola
1. [Niccholla] Mentioned in the book of the *presta* of 1321 [Milanesi: Siena, BC, MS P.III.50, fol. 527r: citing fol. 115v in that book].
2. Mentioned as part of a group that is owed 18 lire, 12 soldi, and 4 denari by the commune (July–December 1339) [ASS, Biccherna 406, fol. 19v].

Niccholino
1. Is paid 4 soldi and 3 denari for painting twelve books with the arms of the former captain of the people (28 April 1310) [ASS, Biccherna 123, fol. 234r].

Niccholuccio (★ under Niccoluccio di Massarello)
1. [Niccoluccio] Documented in 1289 [Benvoglienti: Siena. BC, MS C.IV.6, fol. 5r: citing Entrata B. 84, fol. 7r].[85]
2. [nicchuluccio] Along with "Vitaluccio," he is paid for painting fifty books with the arms of the podestà (25 June 1311) [ASS, Biccherna 125, fol. 157r].
3. Is paid 13 soldi and 4 denari for forty coats of arms on the books of the notaries of malefactors and of the "sindacho" (31 December 1328) [ASS, Biccherna 159, fol. 71v].

---

82. In Bacci, *Dipinti inediti*, 149.

83. Bacci assumes this is Ugolino's father. He also prints (149–50) the notice of 1 March 1325 below, regarding Nerio di Ugolino, suggesting that this must be Ugolino's son, since the elder Nerio di Ugolino was deceased by 1318.

84. This notice does not identify Nerio di Ugolino as a painter.

85. Very likely a painter distinct from that of the following notices.

4. Mention of his wife, Monna Buona (2 January 1338) [ASS, Biccherna 404, fol. 7r].

Niccholuccio di Balzanello
1. Is paid 18 soldi and 8 denari for painting twenty-eight books of the captain of the people at the rate of 8 denari each (19 October 1316) [ASS, Biccherna 132, fol. 124r].

Niccholuccio di Masarello (★)
1. Among the painters paid for providing decorations for the visit of the duke of Calabria, his wife, and his son (July 1326) [ASS, Biccherna 390, fol. 2v].
2. Is paid 17 soldi for thirteen coats of arms on the books of the podestà and the "sindacho" (30 June 1329) [ASS, Biccherna 161, fol. 3v].
3. [Niccoluoro Massarellj] Is paid 15 soldi for painting the books of the podestà (18 June 1331) [ASS, Biccherna 168, fol. 193v].

Niccola di Mino
1. [nichola mini] Is paid £14 for painting twenty-five "penoni de' vichariati" (12 December 1310) [ASS, Biccherna 124, fol. 263r].
2. Recorded as having property, held jointly with his brother Vannuccio, in the city valued at £350 (c. 1318) [ASS, Estimo 131, fol. 286r].[86] See Appendix II.
3. In a list of artists compiled by Milanesi from the "Libro de' Giurati alla Mercanzia" (1326) [Milanesi: Siena, BC, MS P.III.46, fol. 428v].
4. [nicholella di mino] Among those painters providing decorations for the visit of the duke of Calabria, his wife, and his son (July 1326) [ASS, Biccherna 390, fol. 2v].[87]
5. Is paid 5 soldi and 6 denari for painting, among other things, "due bossoli"[88] (30 April 1333) [ASS, Biccherna 177, fol. 64v].

Niccolò di maestro Vannuccio
1. Registered in the Painters' Guild (1356) [Milanesi, *Documenti*, I, 34].

Niccolò di Segna (★)
1. Rents a workshop in San Donato, "contrada di Camporegio," from the Misericordia for two years, 29 September 1331 to 29 September 1333, for 8 florins (4 November 1331) [Bacci, *Fonti e commenti*, 44].

Niccolò di Ser Sozzo (★ under Niccolò di Ser Sozzo Tegliacci)
1. Listed in the "Libro delle Capitudini delle Arti" (1363?) [Milanesi, *Documenti*, I, 50].[89]
2. Buried in San Domenico (15 June 1363) [Laurent, *I necrologi*, 95].

---

86. A later addition to Estimo 131, on fol. 311, indicates that Vannuccio di Mino had acquired a modest dwelling in San Donato, valued at 118 lire, 6 soldi, and 8 denari. The addition notes that the change has been noted in the book of the lords of the Terzo di Camollia, where "Ceccho Puccii" had been. Perhaps, then, this dwelling originally belonged to the artist cited above, Cecco di Puccio.

87. Although this artist is called Nicholella di Mino, I place this item here because in the list of painters in this document he is next to "vanuccio di mino," the brother of Niccola di Mino.

88. Ballot boxes.

89. Milanesi believed that Niccolò came from the Tegliacci family, and therefore lists (*Documenti*, I, 50 n. 2) various posts in government supposedly held by the painter. The formulation of the name, in such notices, is unclear from Milanesi's remarks.

Niccolò di Vanni
1. Recorded as living on 5 May 1356 [Benvoglienti: Siena, BC, MS C.v.7, fol. 268r: citing Contratti/Sapienza].

Nicholello (★)
1. Makes part payment on a fine of 11 lire and 8 soldi imposed by the commune (18 September 1332). On 16 January 1333 he paid 5 lire and 12 soldi and the rest on 4 May 1333 [ASS, Biccherna 398, fol. 37r].[90]
2. Is paid 6 soldi and 8 denari for sixteen coats of arms on the books of the captain of the people (29 October 1332) [ASS, Biccherna 174, fol. 47r].
3. Is paid 1 lira, 1 soldo, and 4 denari for sixty-four coats of arms in the books of the podestà, captain of the people, and other officials (31 December 1338) [ASS, Biccherna 198, fol. 63v].[91]

Nuccio di Neruccio (★)
1. Registered in the Painters' Guild (1356) [Milanesi, *Documenti*, I, 36].

Nutino di Piovano (★)
1. In parish of Sant'Egidio (1347?) [Milanesi, *Documenti*, I, 49].
2. Resident in Sant'Egidio, he receives dowry from his wife, "Iacoba filia olim benini" (2 December 1349) [Milanesi: Siena, BC, MS P.III.50, fol. 588r: citing Denunzie dei contratti, 1349, fol. 154v].

Orlando di Domenico
1. Is paid 6 lire and 8 soldi by the Opera del Duomo (14 August 1350) [Siena, Opera del Duomo 180, fol. 55r].

Paganello di Biagio di Bernarduccio
1. Alive in 1350 (12 April 1350) [Benvoglienti: Siena, BC, MS C.v.7, fol. 267r: citing "contratti della Sapienza"].

Pagno Compagni
1. Living in the "Livra de la Porta all'Archo," Terzo di Città (1311) [Bacci, *Fonti e commenti*, 100].

Paolo
1. Is paid 14 soldi and 7 denari for twenty-eight coats of arms in the books of the former captain of the people (30 October 1327) [ASS, Biccherna 155, fol. 34v].

Paolo di Andrea (★)
1. In a list compiled by Milanesi from the "Libro de' Giurati alla Mercanzia" (1326) [Milanesi: Siena, BC, MS P.III.46, fol. 428v].
2. He has a debt to Guido di Ghezzo that the latter cedes to Matteo Rosselli, painter of Florence (8 June 1333) [Borghesi and Banchi, *Nuovi documenti*, 19–20].[92]

---

90. This is a Memoriale volume, officially for July to December 1332, but the nature of the Memoriale volumes is such that the payments of January and May could have been added later.

91. Also recorded in Biccherna 199, fol. 17v.

92. This may indicate that Paolo was working in Florence at this time.

Paolo di Giovanni
1. Registered in the Painters' Guild (1356) [Milanesi, *Documenti*, I, 38].

Paolo di Neri (★)
1. In parish of San Quirico (no date) [Milanesi, *Documenti*, I, 30].
2. Married Margherita di Ambrogio Salvi (5 July 1343) [Milanesi, *Documenti*, I, 30]. As a dowry, Margherita brought the painter half a house in the *popolo* of Sant'Andrea, valued at £80, and cash of £170 [Milanesi: Siena, BC, MS P.III.50, fol. 590v: citing Denunzie dei contratti, 1342–43].
3. Is paid 16 lire and 12 soldi for painting the portico at the convent of Lecceto (June 1343) [Milanesi, *Documenti*, I, 30].
4. Has debt of 2 florins to the Ospedale di Santa Maria della Scala that he satisfies with painting the arch to the *pellegrinaio* (1349) [ASS, Spedale 514, fol. 203v].
5. Registered in the Painters' Guild (1356) [Milanesi, *Documenti*, I, 30].
6. Listed in the "Libro delle Capitudini delle Arti" (1363?) [Milanesi, *Documenti*, I, 50].
7. Painting the vaults in Siena cathedral (1365) [Lusini, *Il duomo*, I, 251 and 314–15 n. 16].
8. Restores the Madonna and angels in the cathedral that are splashed with wax (1366) [Milanesi, *Documenti*, I, 31].

Paolo di Viva
1. Registered in the Painters' Guild (1356) [Milanesi, *Documenti*, I, 35].

Pasquino di Cenne
1. Forms a company, in Florence, with other artists to work together on "coverte da vantaggio relevate con gesso e dipinte" (25 September 1330) [Borghesi and Banchi, *Nuovi documenti*, 14–16].
2. Along with Vanni Cinuzzi, he provides an estimate of the value of equipment and merchandise in a Florentine workshop shared by Tommè di Vanni of Siena and Francesco di Cialli of Florence (17 December 1341) [Milanesi, *Nuovi documenti*, 37].

Petro
1. Is paid 9 soldi and 4 denari for twenty-eight coats of arms of the captain of the people on his books (30 April 1324) [ASS, Biccherna 149, fol. 134v].
2. Is paid 11 soldi for twenty-two coats of arms painted on twenty-two books of the former captain of the people (6 November 1329) [ASS, Biccherna 163, fol. 39v].
3. Is paid 1 soldi and 6 denari for painting a "fama" on the book of condemnations (30 June 1330) [ASS, Biccherna 165, fol. 49v].
4. Is paid 9 soldi for twenty-seven coats of arms on the books of the former captain of the people (24 October 1330) [ASS, Biccherna 167, fol. 48r].
5. Is paid £2 for painting the new door of the cathedral (August 1333) [Siena, Opera del Duomo 174, fol. 26r].
6. Is paid 8 soldi and 4 denari for twenty-six coats of arms of the former captain of the people (18 November 1337) [ASS, Biccherna 190, fol. 29v].
7. His mother is buried at San Domenico (27 August 1343) [Laurent, *I necrologi*, 66].

Petro di Pietro
1. Is paid 9 soldi for twenty-seven coats of arms on the books of the captain of the people (4 May 1331) [ASS, Biccherna 168, fol. 182r].

2. Is paid 6 soldi and 8 denari for painting twenty books of the captain of the people (14 December 1331) [ASS, Biccherna 171, fol. 81r].
3. Is paid 8 soldi and 8 denari for painting the books of the captain of the people (15 November 1336) [ASS, Biccherna 186, fol. 37r].
4. Is paid 8 soldi and 4 denari for twenty-six coats of arms on the books of the former captain of the people (18 November 1337) [ASS, Biccherna 190, fol. 29v].
5. Is paid 13 soldi and 8 denari for forty-one coats of arms on the books of the former podestà (3 January 1338) [ASS, Biccherna 191, fol. 85r].[93]
6. [petro pierj] He is paid 14 soldi and 4 denari for forty-three coats of arms on the books of the podestà (30 June 1338) [ASS, Biccherna 191, fol. 132r].[94]

Petruccio Dietisalvi (★ under Petruccio di Dietisalvi Petroni)
1. Is paid 35 soldi for painting a panel with the arms of Rinaldo of Spoleto, the former podestà (1293) [Benvoglienti: Siena, BC, MS C.IV.6, fol. 6r: citing B. 94, fol. 199r].
2. Is paid 15 soldi for painting the covers of a book listing prisoners (5 March 1302) [ASS, Biccherna 116, fol. 281v].
3. Is paid 1 lira, 6 soldi, and 8 denari for sixty-four coats of arms on the book of malefactors and on those of the notaries of the podestà (27 June 1302) [ASS, Biccherna 116, fol. 357v].
4. Is paid 1 soldo and 8 denari for four coats of arms on four books (28 June 1302) [ASS, Biccherna 116, fol. 358v].
5. Is paid 5 soldi for painting eleven coats of arms on the books of the captain of the people (5 November 1302) [ASS, Biccherna 117, fol. 325r].
6. Is paid 1 lira, 7 soldi, and 6 denari for sixty coats of arms of the podestà on the books of his notaries (31 December 1302) [ASS, Biccherna 117, fol. 360v].
7. His sons living in the parish of Vallepiatta di sotto, Terzo di Città (21 May–1 December 1311) [Bacci, *Fonti e commenti*, 97].

Petruccio di Lorenzo
1. Is paid 1 lira and 10 soldi for part of the painting "in tabula Dominorum Novem" (25 February 1306) [Bacci, *Dipinti inediti*, 75].[95]

Petrus Tavene
1. See "Guccio" above, no. 3.
2. Buried in San Domenico (19 September 1339) [Laurent, *I necrologi*, 53].

Piero di Bacharello
1. First in parish of San Pellegrino, and then in Sant'Egidio (no date) [Milanesi, *Documenti*, I, 36].
2. Registered in the Painters' Guild (1356) [Milanesi, *Documenti*, I, 36].
3. Married Pia di Gucciarello (24 March 1359) [Milanesi, *Documenti*, I, 36].[96]
4. [Piero di Banchello] Wrote his will (1363) [Faluschi: Siena, BC, MS E.V.14, fol. 69r: citing Testamenti I, 1363, fol. 72v].

---

93. Also in Biccherna 194, fol. 2r.
94. Also in Biccherna 194, fol. 49r.
95. Bacci, probably correctly, regarded this document as referring to Pietro Lorenzetti.
96. Pietro's wife died in December of 1377 and was buried in San Domencio (Laurent, *I necrologi*, 122).

Piero di Donato
1. Registered in the Painters' Guild (1356) [Milanesi, *Documenti*, I, 38].[97]

Piero di Gerfalco
1. Listed in the "Libro delle Capitudini delle Arti" (1363?) [Milanesi, *Documenti*, I, 50].

Pietro di Ser Dota (★)
1. In *popolo* of San Cristofano (1348?) [Milanesi, *Documenti*, I, 30].
2. Married Margherita, daughter of Tino di Camaino (24 February 1348) [Milanesi, *Documenti*, I, 30].[98]
3. In his will, Vannes di Pietro leaves Pietro di Ser Dota "omnes et singulas tabulettas pictas vel non pictas quas dictus Vannes habet sub pignore a dicto Petro," and "totum aczurrum quem dictus Vannes habet in domo suo habitationis vel alibi in quocumque loco" (12 July–16 November 1348) [Bacci, *Fonti e commenti*, 172–73].[99]
4. He paid the Confraternity of the Virgin, located in the Ospedale della Scala, 46 florins as part payment on a "possessione" it had inherited from Ambrogio Lorenzetti and that he was buying (1350) [Wainwright, "The Will of Ambrogio Lorenzetti," 544].
5. Registered in the Painters' Guild (1356) [Milanesi, *Documenti*, I, 30].
6. Is paid 30 soldi by the cathedral for washing and cleaning the panels of "santo Sano" and "santo Bartolomeio" (March 1360) [Milanesi, *Documenti*, I, 30; Bacci, *Fonti e commenti*, 172].
7. [Petrus ser Dote] Named in the "Libro delle Capitudini delle Arti" (1363?) [Milanesi, *Documenti*, I, 50].

Pietro di Vannuccio
1. Living in Sant'Egidio, he and Romano di Mino rent a workshop in the *popolo* of San Pellegrino from the Misericordia (10 April 1355) [Milanesi: Siena, BC, MS P.III.50, fol. 209r: citing Carte della Misericordia, fol. 101r].

Puccio
1. Painted the high altarpiece for the cathedral in Massa Marittima (1316) [Milanesi: Siena, BC, MS P.III.52, fol. 64r: citing "Tomo 11° a carte 436. Carte della Dep. di Massa"].[100]

Rinforzato (★)
1. Is paid 50 soldi for painting in the room of the podestà in the palace of the podestà (14 April 1294) [ASS, Biccherna 110, fol. 125r].

---

97. Not the son of Donato Martini. His sons are mentioned in Simone Martini's will and are listed as Giovanni, Barnaba, and Simone.

98. By 1377, he had a second wife.

99. This is an unusual and therefore particularly interesting document. It would seem that Pietro had given Vanni panels, painted and unpainted, as a pledge, presumably against a debt he owed. Now, on 12 July 1348, in the very midst of the first outbreak of the bubonic plague, Vanni forgives the debt and returns the panels to Pietro. The fact that Vanni is also willing to Pietro all the blue pigment (likely ultramarine blue) that he, Vanni, has in his possession may reflect another part of the pledge Pietro had made or indicate that Vanni dealt in pigments or was a fellow painter. I know, however, no documentation that would justify the last interpretation.

100. The reference is to the altarpiece (now cut down) that is a version of Duccio's *Maestà* for Siena cathedral. Whether Milanesi meant "Duccio" rather than "Puccio," we do not know.

Romano
1. Is paid £4 for restoring two angels on the altar and for painting "ei scrittura due ceppi che stanno in duomo per acattare" (August 1355) [Siena, Opera del Duomo 181, fol. 43v].
2. Is paid for "refreshing" two angels on the altar of the cathedral, likely for the *Maestà* (April 1356) [Siena, Opera del Duomo 181, fol. 80v].
3. Is paid 7 lire and 10 soldi for painting containers for wax to be presented on the feast of the Assumption (August 1357) [Siena, Opera del Duomo 184, fol. 30r].

Romano di Mino (★)
1. Living in San Donato, he receives a dowry from his future wife, Andrea di Cecco di Martino, of £80 (November 1336) [Milanesi: Siena, BC, MS P.III.51, fol. 224v: citing Denunzie dei contratti 1336, fol. 1v].
2. Married Andrea di Cecco di Martino (1336) [Milanesi, *Documenti*, I, 50].[101]
3. Rented a workshop in San Pellegrino, along with Pietro di Vannuccio, from the Misericordia (10 April 1355) [Milanesi: Siena, BC, MS P.III.50, fol. 209r: citing Carte della Misericordia, fol. 101r].
4. Sold painted panel for 80 florins (£252) to "Antonio Karoli de gorenna" (22 February 1349) [Milanesi, *Documenti*, I, 50].
5. Listed in the "Libro delle Capitudini delle Arti" (1363?) [Milanesi, *Documenti*, I, 50].

Sabatino[102]
1. His widow has a house in Sant'Egidio worth 73 lire, 6 soldi, and 8 denari (c. 1318) [ASS, Estimo 136, fol. 219r].
2. His widow is buried in San Domencio; Sabatino is deceased (13 September 1340) [Laurent, *I necrologi*, 62].

Sabatino di Ramo (★)
1. He and Mino Prete, resident in the *popolo* of Sant'Egidio, and Mino di Graziano, resident in the *popolo* of San Donato, are brought before the judge of the Terzo di Camollia over payment of rent for a workshop that they hold from the Misericordia (4 December 1310) [Borghesi and Banchi, *Nuovi documenti*, 8–10].[103]

Sandro di Masarello
1. Living in Sant'Egidio, he brings a dowry to the marriage with his future wife, Neruccia di Neri, of £54 (19 July 1304) [Contratti/Sapienza: Siena, BC, MS A.VII.1, fol. 320v: citing no. 2056].

Santino
1. Is paid 13 soldi for twenty-six coats of arms in the books of the captain of the people (29 October 1333) [ASS, Biccherna 177, fol. 159r].
2. Is paid 14 soldi and 4 denari for forty-three books painted with the arms of the podestà (31 December 1335) [ASS, Biccherna 183, fol. 83r].

---

101. Here is a situation common to several cases in Milanesi. In *Documenti*, he simply refers to the marriage without citing a document; in his notes, he cites contracts involving dowries and has a specific reference.

102. Likely Sabatino di Ramo.

103. It seems likely this is the same painter called simply Sabatino as above. The name is not common.

3. Is paid 7 soldi and 8 denari for painting books of the notaries of the captain of the people (4 May 1336) [ASS, Biccherna 184, fol. 165r].
4. Is paid 13 soldi for thirty-nine coats of arms on books (30 June 1336) [ASS, Biccherna 184, fol. 186r].

Santino di Angelo[104] (★)
1. [Santino del maestro angnolino] Is paid 8 soldi for painting two panels for the book "dele ricolto de chassari" (31 December 1335) [ASS, Biccherna 183, fol. 73v].
2. Is paid 12 soldi and 6 denari for thirty coats of arms of the captain of the people for the Biccherna (1 May 1338) [ASS, Biccherna 191, fol. 115r].[105]

Simone di Giovanni
1. Registered in the Painters' Guild (1356) [Milanesi, *Documenti*, I, 38].

Talumuccio
1. Is paid £1 for painting books of the captain of the people and of the podestà (29 December 1315) [ASS, Biccherna 130, fol. 110r].

Tavena[106]
1. [taverna] Is paid 5 soldi for fifteen coats of arms in the books of the former captain of the people (7 May 1311) [ASS, Biccherna 125, fol. 131v].
2. In larger payment for baldachins for the 1315 visit of Filippo, prince of Taranto, and for the "paglio" for the feast of the Virgin, he is paid 20 lire and 12 soldi (28 November 1315) [ASS, Biccherna 377, fol. 115r].[107]

Tavena d'Andrea (★)
1. Living in San Donato a lato dei Montanini, he has property there and elsewhere valued at roughly £962 (c. 1318) [ASS, Estimo 131, fols. 159r–162v]. See Appendix II.

Thome
1. His wife is buried in San Domenico (28 February 1363) [Laurent, *I necrologi*, 89].

Tommaso d'Andrea (★)
1. Named in the Denunzie dei contratti (1356) [Milanesi: Siena, BC, MS P. III.49, fol. 172v].

Tommaso di Niccholuccio
1. Registered in the Painters' Guild (1356) [Milanesi, *Documenti*, I, 35].

Tommè di Vanni
1. Shares a workshop, in Florence, with Francesco di Cialli of Florence (17 December 1341) [Milanesi, *Nuovi documenti*, 37].

Tuccio di Betto (★)
1. [tucio di botto] Is paid 10 soldi for coats of arms for the books of the former podestà (3 January 1340) [ASS, Biccherna 206, fol. 2r].

---

104. Once more I separate out these items where a full name is given, although it is highly likely this is the same painter as mentioned in the preceding items.

105. The same payment is recorded in Bicherna 194, fol. 32r.

106. Likely Tavena d'Andrea.

107. See the similar item under "Masarello" above.

2. Named in a document involving the Ospedale della Scala (1342) [Milanesi: Siena, BC, MS P.III.53, fol. 368v].[108]
3. [Tuccius berti tuccii] Living in the parish of Sant'Antonio, he sells (land?) (27 February 1343) [Milanesi: Siena, BC, MS P.III.50, fol. 590r: citing Denunzie dei contratti 1342/43, fol. 2v].

Tura Comini
1. Is paid 14 soldi for forty-two coats of arms on a book of the malefactors and the books of the notaries of the "vicario vecchio" (4 February 1327) [ASS, Biccherna 154, fol. 9r].

Vanni di Bindo (★)
1. In a list compiled by Milanesi for the artists in the "Libro de' Guirati alla Mercanzia," he is described as "Vanni Bindi detto piastra dipegnitore" (1326) [Milanesi: Siena, BC, MS P.III.46, fol. 428v].[109]

Vanni di Bono (★)
1. Pays 5 soldi as a fine for unspecified offence (1298) [Benvoglienti: Siena, BC, MS C.IV.6, fol. 7r: citing B. 98, fol.9r].

Vanni di Dietisalvi
1. Living in San Donato, in the contrada di Chiaravalle (26 April 1331) [Benvoglienti: Siena, BC, MS C.V.7, fol. 274r: citing Contratti/Sapienza].

Vannuccio di Mino (★)
1. With his brother Niccola, he owns a house in the Terzo di Camollia, "populo Mansionis Templi," worth £350 (1323) [ASS, Estimo 131, fol. 286r]. See Appendix II.
2. He owns a house next to the Misericordia in San Donato valued at 118 lire, 6 soldi, and 8 denari (1323?) [ASS, Estimo 131, fol. 311r]. See Appendix II.
3. [vanucio di mino] Among those paid for decorations for the visit of the duke of Calabria, his wife, and his son (July 1326) [ASS, Biccherna 390, fol. 2v].
4. Is paid 9 soldi for twenty-two coats of arms for the books of the former captain of the people (29 April 1346) [ASS, Biccherna 219, fol. 134r].

Vicienti di Vanni (★)
1. Living the parish of Sant'Antonio, he is mentioned in relation to a fine of 40 soldi and to his paying off that obligation (28 February–6 June 1347) [ASS, Biccherna 408, fols. 30v, 92r].

Vigoroso (★ under Vigoroso di Claudio)
1. Is paid 9 soldi for painting the books of the *camarlengo* and the *provveditori* (January 1292) [ASS, Biccherna 107, fol. 144r].
2. Is paid 10 soldi for painting the books of the *camarlengo* and the *provveditori* (23 July 1292) [ASS, Biccherna 108, fol. 136v.].
3. [vighoroso] Is paid 10 soldi for painting the books of the officials of the podestà with his arms (31 December 1293) [ASS, Biccherna 109, fol. 171r].

Vitaluccio
1. Is paid 16 soldi for forty-eight coats of arms of the podestà (28 June 1309) [ASS, Biccherna 122, fol. 200r].

108. The nature of the transaction is unclear.
109. A painter identifed as "Piastra pictor condam Bindi de Senis" is documented as living in Pisa in 1305. See "The Sienese Abroad" in Chapter IV.

274 APPENDIX III

2. Is paid 16 soldi and 8 denari, along with "nicchuluccio," for painting fifty books with arms of the podestà (25 June 1311) [ASS, Biccherna 125, fol. 157r].
3. Is paid 14 soldi, along with "guido cini," for twenty-one coats of arms on the books of the captain of the people (28 October 1314) [ASS, Biccherna 128, fol. 82r].
4. Is paid 13 soldi for twenty-three coats of arms of the captain of the people on his books (26 April 1315) [ASS, Biccherna 129, fol. 85v].
5. Is paid 16 soldi and 8 denari for fifty coats of arms of the podestà on his books (15 June 1317) [ASS, Biccherna 133, fol. 138v].
6. Is paid 10 soldi and 6 denari for twenty-six coats of arms of the captain of the people on his books (22 October 1317) [ASS, Biccherna 134, fol. 105r].
7. Is paid 10 soldi for thirty coats of arms of the captain of the people (30 October 1318) [ASS, Biccherna 136, fol. 94v].

Vitaluccio di Rosso[110] (★)
1. [vitaluccio Russi] Is paid 19 soldi and 7 denari for fifty-nine coats of arms of the podestà (30 June 1310) [ASS, Biccherna 123, fol. 275r].
2. Is paid 18 soldi and 9 denari for painting the books of the podestà (29 December 1310) [ASS, Biccherna 124, fol. 274v].
3. Is paid 9 soldi for painting twenty-three books of the captain of the people with his arms (24 October 1315) [ASS, Biccherna 130, fol. 86r].
4. Is paid 1 lira, 1 soldo, and 3 denari for coats of arms in the books of the podestà (28 June 1316) [ASS, Biccherna 131, fol. 97r].
5. Is paid, along with "his companion," 1 lira, 2 soldi, and 6 denari for fifty-four books of the podestà (30 December 1316) [ASS, Biccherna 132, fol. 140v].
6. Is paid 11 soldi and 8 denari for twenty-eight books painted for the captain of the people (28 April 1317) [ASS, Biccherna 133, fol. 125r].
7. [Vitaluccio Russi] Is paid 13 soldi and 4 denari for forty coats of arms in the books of the podestà (20 December 1317) [ASS, Biccherna 134, fol. 119v].

---

110. Personally, I have no doubt that this is the same painter paid in the preceding notices, but since the following payments are ones in which the full name is given, I prefer to err on the side of caution and separate the two groups.

APPENDIX IV: A SAMPLING OF PAYMENTS FOR DECORATING BOOK COVERS UNDER THE NINE

One of the recurring commissions offered painters by the Nove was the decoration of book covers for the records of various offices and officials of the regime. The most important series comprises covers for the Latin versions of the current accounts (Entrata/Uscita) of the office of the Biccherna, the state treasury, organized according to two semesters: January to June and July to December. From 1250 to 1302, we have only Latin versions of the accounts, but from the latter year onward, accounts in both Latin and the vernacular survive. From the Trecento, a series of working accounts known as *Memoriale* also survives. Frequently the covers were acquired at the beginning of each semester for the accounts of the previous semester, but there are instances where payment was made at the end of a semester or, at that time, money was set aside for the future acquisition of a decorated cover.

Over time, the term "Biccherna cover" has been extended to include painted book covers of various sorts, but in the following I use the term to designate the volumes belonging to the treasury, to the books of the four *provveditori* and the treasurer. Other items are described as in the relevant document.

Payment notices, in the accounts of the Biccherna, do not always name the painter employed. I have included such items only when they relate to the covers of the Entrata/Uscita, the Biccherna cover proper. The Entrata/Uscita covers that survive from the regime of the Nove generally display an image of the treasurer and the coats of arms of the four *provveditori*.[1] The evidence presented below suggests that the covers of the Entrata/Uscita had a special place in the minor commissions of the commune.

The commune, through the treasury, also paid for the decoration of other types of books, principally those of the officials and/or notaries of the podestà and the captain of the people. From the descriptions of documents cited below and the small sums involved, we know that these commissions were for marking such books with the coat of arms of the captain or the podestà, thus providing officials of the commune with a comparatively easy means of identification. The office of the General Gabella, responsible for administering a wide variety of taxes on items of consumption and business transactions, also commissioned painted covers for their books; indeed, the most elaborate covers produced under the Nine come from the Gabella.[2] Payments for these works must have been direct, that is, internal to Gabella accounting, for, with one possible exception cited below, they do not appear in the Biccherna accounts.

1. For qualifications to this statement, see below.
2. These are illustrated in Borgia et al., *Le Biccherne*, 88–89, 96–97.

The following material, though seemingly of minor importance, is revealing. Here, as in the commissions for far more important works, we note a tendency for the same painter to be given repeated commissions, something we have already noted above in the case of Guido Cinatti.[3] Vitaluccio di Rosso appears quite frequently in payments over the years 1309 to 1318 and then is succeeded by Guido Cinatti. A "Petro" or "Petro di Petro" appears intermittently between 1326 and 1338. Santino di Angelo is named in documents of 1333, 1335, 1336, and 1338. If the payments to a certain Giovanni all refer to the same painter, then he received fairly regular work between 1339 and 1345. In the early years of his career, Bartolommeo Bulgarini painted the Entrata/Uscita cover three times (1338, 1341, and 1342). One commission (23 July 1337) to Francesco di Vannuccio also falls at the beginning of that painter's career.

The case of Bulgarini is worthy of special note, for it is one of the few trecento instances where a major painter took on such tasks. In the late Dugento, Duccio seems to have taken on this type of work: in 1279, 1285, 1292, 1294, and 1295. If the "Insegnia" of the notices below was Segna di Bonaventura, then the latter executed decorations of the type in 1306, 1307, 1309, 1311, and 1322; but here we already deal with a painter of second rank. I do not think it mere happenstance that the names of the Lorenzetti brothers, Simone Martini, or even Lippo Memmi are missing from the trecento notices.[4] By the early fourteenth century, these tasks seem to have devolved upon the minor "minor masters." And it may well be that painters whose careers thrived had a good reason for not taking on such work, especially the production of escutcheons on books of the captain of the people or of the podestà. In June of 1302, Petruccio Dietisalvi was paid for painting sixty-four escutcheons at the rate of 5 denari each. In April of 1306, Ghezzo was paid 4 denari for each of thirteen escutcheons; in May 1311, Tavena's painted coats of arms earned him 4 denari apiece.[5] Vitaluccio's remuneration for fifty escutcheons painted in 1317 was 4 denari each. But in May of 1321 Guido was paid only 2.3 denari for each coat of arms; in June of 1324 he received 2.7 denari apiece; and in January of 1325 Guido Cinatti received only 3 denari for each coat of arms. There are instances where payments moved further upward: in November of 1310, each escutcheon brought Cecco di Puccio 6 denari; in 1316 Niccholuccio di Balzanello received 8 denari apiece; in November of 1329 and December of 1330, painters were paid at the rate of 6 denari per escutcheon. But these payments are extraordinary. Converting the figures into payments per escutcheon from notices of April 1327, January 1328, December 1331, June 1336, January and June of 1338, June 1340, and June 1346, we find the rate of payment continued to be 4 denari, the same rate as that of 1306.

The rate of payment for the cover the Entrata/Uscita, the Biccherna proper, is more complicated. From the 1290s we seem to have several payments for decorating those covers at the rate of 10 soldi apiece. In June of 1306 Segna received £1 for the cover of two books of the Entrata/Uscita.[6] The commune paid the same sum for the same task in June 1307, December 1310, and

---

3. See pages 73–76. I shall not deal, in what follows, with the Guido/Guidoni/Guido di Cino/Guido Cinatti problem, since we cannot be sure if these items, at least in part, refer to the same Guido.

4. Although some have attributed a surviving Gabella cover of 1344 to Ambrogio Lorenzetti, I find the attribution unconvincing. See Borgia et al., *Le Biccherne,* 96–97.

5. This rate of payment may have been set as early as 1299. In June of that year Guido was paid for decorating fifty-four books with the arms of the podestà. If we assume that each book had a single escutcheon, he received 4 denari apiece.

6. The reference to two books here, as elsewhere, likely refers to the book of the Entrata (income) and the book of the Uscita (expenditures) that were bound together and given covers. In fact, Biccherna 118, the Latin version of accounts for

June 1311. This is also the rate of payment documented in December of 1302, December 1307, December 1314, December 1315, June 1325, June and December 1328, June 1329, June and December 1330, and December 1334. In October of 1321 Guido Cinatti received 1 lira and 10 soldi, but less in April of 1324. Some 1 lira and 10 soldi was paid to the unnamed painter of the Entrata/Uscita cover in December 1337 and in June and December 1343. Although Bartolommeo Bulgarini received £2 for his efforts in June of 1338, he was paid only 1 lira and 10 soldi in December of 1341 and June of 1342. In June of 1346 an unnamed painter received 1 lira and 10 soldi.

I have said that matter of the Entrata/Uscita covers is complicated because the surviving works vary in content. The cover for January–June 1294 has four coats of arms and an inscription, but no image of the treasurer; the same is true for the cover of July–December 1304, while that of January–June 1310 carries an image of the treasurer but no coats of arms. The covers from July–December 1314, January–June 1320, January–June 1321, July–December 1324, July–December 1329, January–June 1331, July–December 1339, and January–June 1340 all carry the combination of arms of the *provveditori* and an image of the treasurer. The cover of July–December 1343 has the same combination but adds two other figures, likely the scribes of the Biccherna; one scribe accompanies the treasurer on the cover of January–June 1348. Two figures are also depicted on the cover for the January–June 1353 volume, but the covers of January–June 1346 and January–June 1350 return to representing only the treasurer and the arms of the *provveditori*.[7]

The records of payment for these and other book covers are fascinating, particularly in the context of the erosion of the Sienese lira by inflation. When the Nove took power in 1287, the Florentine gold florin was worth about 36 Sienese soldi, or 1 lira and 16 soldi. By 1355, it took 70 Sienese soldi, or 3 lira and 10 soldi, to buy a florin. In other words, between 1287 and 1355 the value of the lira of account decreased by about 50 percent. While there are differences in the pictorial content of the Entrata/Uscita covers (and these should be kept in mind, for they may well have influenced the sum paid by the commune), payments for those works suggest some attempt by the commune to compensate painters for inflation. When, in June of 1306, Segna received £1 for his Biccherna cover, the exchange rate was 53 soldi and 8 denari (2 lire, 13 soldi, and 8 denari) to the florin. By December of 1337, when the remuneration seems to have settled at 1 lira and 10 soldi, the florin was worth 63 soldi and 3 denari (or 3 lire and 3 soldi). Thus, the painter of that year was paid more than simple inflation required.

The payments for escutcheons on book covers tell a very different story. With payment generally remaining 4 denari apiece over several decades, the minor "minor masters" would seem to have suffered badly, to have been increasingly pressed by economic circumstances in terms of real income.

We do not have adequate documentation for commissions regarding any other repeated small task to allow further generalizations about the financial circumstances of the minor "minor masters." Thus the evidence discussed above and documented below is of importance.

January to June 1306, contains the Entrata and Uscita bound together. This was standard practice and is the reason that the notices generally speak of "books" when only one painted cover is involved.

7. For these works, see Borgia et al., *Le Biccherne*.

THE NOTICES[8]

1287 January, Duccio is paid 10 soldi for painting the books of the Four [ASS, Biccherna 95, fol. 96r].[9]

1288 At the end of January, Guidoni receives 6 soldi for the books of the treasurer and of the four *provveditori* [ASS, Biccherna 96, fol. 47v].[10]

—— 2 October, Dietisalvi receives 9 soldi for the Biccherna cover [ASS, Biccherna 97, fol. 101r].[11]

1289 18 January, Guidoni receives 10 soldi for painting the books of the treasurer and four *provveditori* [ASS, Biccherna 99, fol. 43r].[12]

—— November(?), Ghuccio receives 10 soldi for painting two books of the treasurer and the Four [ASS, Biccherna 101, fol. 132r].[13]

1290 September, Guidoni receives 10 soldi for the Biccherna cover [ASS, Biccherna, 103, fol. 69r].[14]

1291 27 January, Duccio is paid 10 soldi for painting the emblem of the books of the treasurer and the Four [ASS, Biccherna 104, fol. 64v].[15]

—— 6 August, Duccio is paid 10 soldi for painting the books of the treasurer and the Four [ASS, Biccherna 106, fol. 121v].[16]

1292 mid-January, Vigoroso receives 9 soldi for painting the books of the treasurer and the four *provveditori* [ASS, Biccherna, 107, fol. 144r].[17]

—— 23 July, Vigoroso receives 10 soldi for the books of the treasurer and the four *provveditori* [ASS, Biccherna 108, fol. 136v].[18]

1293 31 December, Vigoroso receives 10 soldi for painting the books of the officials of the podestà with his arms [ASS, Biccherna 109, fol. 171r].

1294 2 March, Duccio is paid 10 soldi for

---

8. Although I have tried to be systematic in my reading of the Biccherna accounts, I do not want to claim that the following documentary notices are absolutely complete. It is easy to miss items. But I do feel confident that these notices represent a very high percentage of such payments.

9. Presumably for the semester July–December 1286. Duccio had received 10 soldi for the same task in July 1279 (Biccherna 75, fol. 42v) and on 8 October 1285 (Biccherna 91, fol. 389v). Personally, I have no doubt that this and other payments of similar phrasing refer to the cover for the Entrata/Uscita.

In many of the Biccherna volumes, we encounter different numberings of the folios that have accumulated over the centuries. Here, and in the following notices, the folio numbers given are those of the most recent numbering.

10. Presumably for the semester July–December 1288.

11. The same notice appears in Biccherna 98, fol. 96v. For earlier references to book covers and the painter, see Appendix III.

12. The same item appears in Biccherna 100, fol. 36.

13. Biccherna 101 is for July–December 1289. The payment is therefore likely for the cover to January–June 1289. The reference to "two books" is almost certainly a reference to the Entrata and Uscita volumes for the period, bound together. The phrasing occurs in other items below.

14. Presumably the cover for the volume of January–June 1290.

15. Presumably for the cover of July–December 1290. Both White and Stubblebine misdate this entry to 1292. The same payment is found in Biccherna 105, fol. 68v.

16. Likely for January–June 1291.

17. Presumably the cover for July–December 1291.

18. Presumably for January–June 1292.

painting the books of the treasurer and the Four [ASS, Biccherna 110, fol. 116v].[19]

1295 31 January, 10 soldi paid to an unnamed painter for the covers of the treasurer and the Four [ASS, Biccherna 111, fol. 86r].[20]

—— 9 September, Mino receives 20 soldi for painting book covers [ASS, Biccherna 112, fol. 107v].

—— 19 October, Duccio receives 10 soldi for painting the books of the treasurer and the Four [ASS, Biccherna 112, fol. 116r].[21]

—— 7 November, Massarello receives 5 soldi for painting fifteen books of the captain of the people [ASS, Biccherna 112, fol. 123r].

1296 26 October, Massarello receives 4 soldi and 6 denari for painting twenty-seven books of the commune with the arms of the captain of the people [ASS, Biccherna 113, fol. 208r].

1298 29 December, Segna is paid for painting four books with the insignia and arms of the podestà, Ugolino de Correggia [ASS, Biccherna 114, fol. 213r].

1299 June, Guido receives 18 soldi for painting fifty-four books of the notaries of the malefactors with the arms of the current podestà [ASS, Biccherna 115, fol. 3v].

1302 5 March, Petruccio Dietisalvi receives 15 soldi for painting a book wherein is written the name of prisoners ("incarcierati") and other tasks [ASS, Biccherna, 116, fol. 281v].

—— 27 June, Petruccio Dietisalvi receives 1 lira, 6 soldi, and 8 denari for painting coats of arms on the books of malefactors and on books of notaries of the podestà, at the rate of 5 denari apiece [ASS, Biccherna 116, fol. 357v].

—— 28 June, Petruccio Dietisalvi receives 1 soldo and 8 denari for painting four coats of arms on four books (one on each) of the *esecutori*[22] [ASS, Biccherna 116, fol. 358v].

—— 5 November, Petruccio Dietisalvi receives 5 soldi for painting eleven coats of arms of the captain of the people on his books [ASS, Biccherna 117, fol. 325r].

—— 31 December, Petruccio Dietisalvi is paid 1 lira, 7 soldi, and 6 denari for painting sixty escutcheons of the podestà on the books of his notaries [ASS, Biccherna 117, fol. 360v].

—— 31 December, £1 is set aside of the painting of the covers of the Entrata/Uscita [ASS, Biccherna 117, fol. 388r].[23]

1306 27 April, Ghezzo receives 4 soldi and 4 denari for painting thirteen coats of arms of the captain of the people on the books of his notaries, at the rate of 4 denari each [ASS, Biccherna 119, fol. 237r].

—— 30 June, Segna is paid £2 for painting two books of the Entrata/Uscita of the treasurer and the Four [ASS, Biccherna 118, fol. 150r].[24]

1307 20 April, Insegnia receives 4 soldi and 8 denari for fourteen escutcheons with arms of the captain at the rate of 4 denari apiece [ASS, Biccherna, 120, fol. 321r].[25]

---

19. This is an odd date (in March) for such a payment. Some have associated this payment with an Entrata/Uscita now in Berlin (Borgia et al., *Le Biccherne*, 66–67). That cover, however, is for the period January–June 1294. It seems more likely this is a payment for the cover of July–December 1293.

20. Preumably for July–December 1294.

21. Presumably for January–June 1296. Was Duccio making a habit of being late in fulfilling these commissions?

22. The reference here is likely to the executors of the Gabella.

23. Presumably for July–December 1302.

24. Presumably for January–June 1306. See note 7 above.

25. Some documentary notices, this among them, that actually refer to "Insegnia" have been interpreted as referring to Segna di Bonaventura.

—— 21 June, Insegnia is paid £1 for painting sixty escutcheons of the arms of the podestà on the books of his officials [ASS, Biccherna 120, fol. 371v].[26]

—— 20 November, Baldinuccio di Dino receives 9 soldi for painting nineteen arms of the captain of the people, presumably on book covers, at the rate of 6 denari each [ASS, Biccherna, 121, fol. 323r].

—— 30 December, Cientti(?) di Mino receives 19 soldi for painting fifty coats of arms on the books of the podestà, at the rate of 4 denari apiece [ASS, Biccherna 121, fol. 353v].

—— 30 December, an unnamed painter is paid £1 for painting the books of the treasurer and the Four [ASS, Biccherna 121, fol. 380v].[27]

1309 5 May, Insegnia receives 3 soldi for twelve escutcheons in the books of the captain of the people [ASS, Biccherna 122, fol. 169r].

—— 28 June, Vitaluccio receives 16 soldi for painting forty-eight coats of arms of the podestà, presumably on books, at the rate of 4 denari each [ASS, Biccherna 122, fol. 200r].

—— 30 June, Insegnia receives £1 for painting the cover of the books of the treasurer and the Four of the Biccherna, the Entrata/Uscita [ASS, Biccherna 122, fol. 227r].[28]

1310 28 April, Niccholino receives 4 soldi and 3 denari for painting twelve books with the arms of the former captain of the people [ASS, Biccherna 123, fol. 234r].

—— 30 June, Vitaluccio di Rosso receives 19 soldi and 7 denari for painting fifty-nine coats of arms of the podestà, presumably on books, at the rate to 4 denari each [ASS, Biccherna, 123, fol. 275r].

—— 13 November, "Ciecho" di Puccio receives 8 soldi for painting fourteen coats of arms of the former captain of the people on his books [ASS, Biccherna 124, fol. 243r].

—— 29 December, Vitaluccio di Rosso receives 18 soldi and 9 denari for painting the books of the podestà [ASS, Biccherna 124, fol. 274v].

—— 31 December, "Ciecho" di Puccio receives £1 for painting the Biccherna cover [ASS, Biccherna 124, fol. 301v].[29]

1311 7 May, Tavena receives 5 soldi for painting fifteen coats of arms on the books of the former captain of the people, at a rate of 4 denari each [ASS, Biccherna 125, fol. 131v].

—— June, Segna is paid £1 for painting the books of the treasurer and the Four [ASS, Biccherna 125, fol. 171v].[30]

—— 25 June, Vitaluccio and Nichuluccio receive 16 soldi and 8 denari for painting fifty books with the arms of the podestà [ASS, Biccherna 125, fol. 157r].

1314 28 October, Vitaluccio and Guido di Cino receive 14 soldi for painting twenty-one coats of arms on books of the captain of the people, at the rate of 8 denari apiece [ASS, Biccherna 128, fol. 82r].

—— 31 December, £1 paid for painting of the Entrata/Uscita; no painter named [ASS, Biccherna 128, fol. 128v].[31]

1315 26 April, Vitaluccio receives 13 soldi for painting twenty-three books with arms of the captain of the people [ASS, Biccherna 129, fol. 85v].

While this is highly probable, I retain the actual name in this and other payments. This notice is previously unpublished.

26. Previously unpublished.
27. Presumably for July–December 1307.
28. Presumably for January–June 1309.
29. Presumably for July–December 1310.
30. Likely for January–June 1311.
31. Presumably the cover for July–December 1314.

—— 24 October, Vitaluccio di Rosso receives 9 soldi for painting twenty-three books of the captain of the people [ASS, Biccherna 130, fol. 86r].

—— 29 December, Talumuccio receives £1 for painting twenty-four books of the captain of the people and of the podestà [ASS, Biccherna 130, fol. 110r].

—— 31 December, £1 paid for the painting in the Entrata/Uscita; no artist named [ASS, Biccherna 130, fol. 126v].[32]

1316 28 June, Vitaluccio di Rosso receives 1 lira, 1 soldo, and 3 denari for painting arms of the podestà on his books [ASS, Biccherna 131, fol. 97r].

—— 19 October, Niccholuccio di Balzanello receives 18 soldi and 8 denari for painting twenty-eight books of the captain of the people with his arms, at the rate of 8 denari each [ASS, Biccherna 132, fol. 124r].

—— 30 December, Vitaluccio di Rosso and his companion receive 1 lira, 2 soldi, and 6 denari for painting fifty-four books of the podestà, at the rate of 5 denari a book [ASS, Biccherna 132, fol. 140v].

1317 28 April, Vitaluccio di Rosso receives 11 soldi and 8 denari for painting twenty-eight books of the captain of the people at the rate of 5 denari each [ASS, Biccherna 133, fol. 135r].

—— 15 June, Vitaluccio receives 16 soldi and 8 denari for painting fifty coats of arms of the podestà on his books, at the rate of 4 denari each [ASS, Biccherna 133, fol. 138v].

—— 22 October, Vitaluccio receives 10 soldi and 6 denari for painting twenty-six escutcheons of the captain of the people on his books [ASS, Biccherna 134, fol. 105r].

—— 20 December, Vitaluccio di Rosso receives 13 soldi and 4 denari for painting forty coats of arms on the books of the podestà [ASS, Biccherna 134, fol. 119v].

1318 30 October, Vitaluccio receives 10 soldi for painting thirty escutcheons of the captain of the people, presumably on his books [ASS, Biccherna 136, fol. 94v].

1319 23 October, Guido is paid 10 soldi for twenty-five coats of arms on the books of the former captain of the people [ASS, Biccherna 138, fol. 116r].

—— 5 December, Guido Cinatti receives 16 soldi for painting forty-eight escutcheons on the books of "conte benedetto" [ASS, Biccherna 138, fol. 125v].

1321 4 May, Guido receives 10 soldi for fifty-one escutcheons for the "court" of the captain of the people [ASS, Biccherna 141, fol. 189v].[33]

—— 12 October, Guido receives 7 soldi for painting twenty-one escutcheons on the books of the captain of the people [ASS, Biccherna 142, fol. 128v].[34]

—— 26 October, Guido Cinatti receives 1 lira and 10 soldi for painting the books of the Entrata/Uscita [ASS, Biccherna 142, fol. 132v].[35]

—— 14 December, Guido di Cinatto is paid 18 soldi for painting forty-eight coats of arms on the books of the podestà and for painting three "bossoli" [ASS, Biccherna 142, fol. 147v].

1322 11 January, Guido Cinatti is paid 8 soldi and 9 denari for painting thirty-five coats of arms on the book of "francischo" [ASS, Biccherna 144, fol. 89r].

---

32. Likely the cover for July–December 1315.

33. The sum and the number of escutcheons suggest the item deals with book covers.

34. This item is also in Biccherna 143, fol. 68v.

35. Likely for January–June 1321. This item is also in Biccherna 143, fol. 72v. The cover for January–June 1321 still exists. See Borgia et al., *Le Biccherne*, 80–81.

—— 27 May, Segna receives 12 soldi for painting the treasurer's books for the last six months [ASS, Biccherna 144, fol. 119v].[36]

—— 29 October, Guido di Cinatto is paid 3 lire and 16 soldi for a variety of tasks, including sixty-seven escutcheons on the books of the "conte di fondi" and for painting the book of the former treasurer [ASS, Biccherna 145, fol. 119v].

1323 31 October, Guido is paid 2 lire and 8 soldi for escutcheons on various books [ASS, Biccherna 148, fol. 118r].

1324 9 January, Guido receives 14 soldi for forty-three escutcheons on the books of the podestà [ASS, Biccherna 149, fol. 109r].

—— 2 April, Guido di Cinatti receives 1 lira and 4 soldi for various tasks, including painting the "book of our predecessors" and repairing another [ASS, Biccherna 149, fol. 127r].[37]

—— 30 April, Petro receives 9 soldi and 4 denari for painting twenty-eight arms on the books of the captain of the people [ASS, Biccherna 149, fol. 134v].

—— 30 June, Guido di Cinatti receives 14 soldi for painting sixty-two coats of arms on the books of the podestà [ASS, Biccherna 149, fol. 170r].

1325 5 January, Guido di Cinatto is paid 10 soldi and 3 denari for painting forty-one escutcheons with the arms of the former podestà on his books [ASS, Biccherna 150, fol. 2v].

—— 2 May, Guido di Cinatto receives 8 soldi and 4 denari for painting twenty-five coats of arms on the books of the captain of the people [ASS, Biccherna 150, fol. 45r].

—— 30 June, £1 to an unnamed painter for painting the cover of the Entrata/Uscita [ASS, Biccherna 150, fol. 82v].[38]

1327 4 February, Tura di Comino receives 14 soldi for painting forty-two coats of arms on the book of malefactors and of the notaries of the "vicario vecchio" [ASS, Biccherna 154, fol. 9r].

—— 21 April, Bartolomeo di Vanni receives 8 soldi and 9 denari for painting twenty-one coats of arms on twenty-one books of the captain of the people [ASS, Biccherna 154, fol. 24r].

—— 30 October, Paolo is paid 14 soldi and 7 denari for twenty-eight escutcheons painted on the books of the former captain of the people [ASS, Biccherna 155, fol. 34v].

—— 28 November, Guido Cinatti receives 16 soldi for painting the "book of our predecessors" [ASS, Biccherna 155, fol. 42v].[39]

1328 20 January, Andrea receives 14 soldi for painting forty-two escutcheons on the books of the "vichario vecchio" [ASS, Biccherna 157, fol. 5v].

—— 20 April, Minatello receives 8 soldi for painting twenty-four arms on the books of the captain of the people [ASS, Biccherna 157, fol. 32r].

—— 30 June, Guido receives £1 for painting the cover of the Entrata/Uscita [ASS, Biccherna 157, fol. 72v].[40]

—— 6 July, Francesco is paid 15 soldi and 4 denari for painting forty-six coats of arms on the books of the "vichario vecchio" [ASS, Biccherna 159, fol. 2v].

36. It is this kind of record that inspires caution when a notice regards the treasury but does not specifically refer to the Entrata/Uscita volumes. The sum involved here was, by 1322, low for the payment of a Biccherna cover.

37. Since the payment also includes remuneration for painting four pairs of candle standards, the total sum seems low if the "book of our predecessors" is a reference to the Entrata/Uscita.

38. Presumably for January–June 1325.

39. Almost certainly for January–June 1327.

40. Presumably the cover for January–June 1328.

—— 15 November, Guido receives 7 soldi for twenty-one coats of arms on the books of the captain of the people [ASS, Biccherna 159, fol. 56r].

—— 31 December, Niccholuccio is paid 13 soldi and 4 denari for painting forty coats of arms of the books of the notaries of malefactors and of the "sindaco" [ASS, Biccherna 159, fol. 71v].

—— 31 December, an unnamed painter is paid £1 for the cover of the Entrata/Uscita [ASS, Biccherna 159, fol. 84v].[41]

1329 30 June, Niccholuccio di Massarello receives 17 soldi for painting thirteen coats of arms on the books of the podestà and of the "sindacho" [ASS, Biccherna 161, fol. 3v].

—— 30 June, an unnamed artist receives £1 for painting a book of uncertain type [ASS, Biccherna 161, fol. 16r].[42]

—— 6 November, Petro receives 11 soldi for painting twenty-two coats of arms on twenty-two books of the former captain of the people [ASS, Biccherna 163, fol. 39v].

—— 30 December, Jacomo di Bindo receives 10 soldi for painting twenty-five books of the "sindacho" [ASS, Biccherna 163, fol. 50r].

—— 30 December, Jacomo di Bindo receives 1 lira, 3 soldi, and 4 denari for painting forty coats of arms on the books of the podestà [ASS, Biccherna 163, fol. 50r].

1330 29 April, Minuccio receives 8 soldi for painting twenty coats of arms on the books of the former captain of the people [ASS, Biccherna 167, fol. 62v].

—— 26 June, Minuccio receives 16 soldi for painting arms of the podestà on forty-four of his books [ASS, Biccherna 167, fol. 97r].

—— 30 June, Petro receives 1 soldo and 6 denari for painting on a book of condemnations [ASS, Biccherna 165, fol. 49v].

—— 30 June, Guido Cinatti receives £1 for painting "our parchment book," presumably the Entrata/Uscita [ASS, Biccherna 165, fol. 114v].[43]

—— 24 October, Petro receives 9 soldi for twenty-seven arms painted on the books of the former captain of the people [ASS, Biccherna 167, fol. 48r].

—— 31 December, Guido Cinatti is paid 18 soldi and 6 denari for thirty-seven escutcheons painted on the books of the podestà [ASS, Biccherna 167, fol. 76r].

—— 31 December, £1 paid for the painting of the Entrata/Uscita; no painter named [ASS, Biccherna 167, fol. 86v].[44]

1331 4 May, Petro di Pietro receives 9 soldi for painting twenty-seven coats of arms on the books of the captain of the people [ASS, Biccherna 168, fol. 182r].

—— 18 June, Niccoluccio di Massarello receives 15 soldi for painting arms on books of the podestà [ASS, Biccherna 168, fol. 193v].

—— 14 December, Petro di Pietro is paid 6 soldi and 8 denari for painting twenty books of the captain of the people [ASS, Biccherna 171, fol. 81r].

—— 31 December, Mino di Voglia is paid 12 soldi and 8 denari for painting thirty-eight coats of arms on the books of the podestà [ASS, Biccherna 171, fol. 93r].

—— 31 December, Guido is paid £1 for the cover of the Entrata/Uscita for July–December 1331 [ASS, Biccherna 171, fol. 111v].

1332 29 October, Nicholella receives 6 soldi and 8 denari for painting sixteen escutcheons on all the books of the captain

---

41. Presumably for the cover of July–December 1328.
42. Likely the cover for January–June 1329.
43. Presumably for January–June 1330.
44. Likely for July–December 1330.

of the people [ASS, Biccherna 174, fol. 47r].

1333 29 October, Santino receives 13 soldi for painting twenty-six escutcheons on the books of the captain of the people [ASS, Biccherna 177, fol. 159r].

1334 15 November, Guido receives 10 soldi for painting coats of arms on the books of the captain of the people [ASS, Biccherna 181, fol. 43r].

—— 30 December, £1 spent for the cover of the Entrata/Uscita [ASS, Biccherna 181, fol. 69v].[45]

1335 30 October, Francesco is paid 8 soldi for painting the books of the former captain of the people [ASS, Biccherna 183, fol. 44r].

—— 31 December, Santino di Angelo receives 8 soldi for painting two covers for the "livro dele ricolto de chassari" that Niccholo of the treasury had made [ASS, Biccherna 183, fol. 73v].

—— 31 December, Santino is paid 14 soldi and 4 denari for painting forty-three coats of arms of the podestà on forty-three books [ASS, Biccherna 183, fol. 83r].

—— 31 December, the treasury spends £2 for the panels and the painting thereof for the Biccherna [ASS, Biccherna 183, fol. 83v].

1336 4 May, Santino is paid 7 soldi and 8 denari for painting the books of the notaries of the captain of the people [ASS, Biccherna 184, fol. 165r].

—— 30 June, Santino receives 13 soldi for painting thirty-nine escutcheons on the books of the former captain of the people(?), at a rate of 4 denari each [ASS, Biccherna 184, fol. 186r].

—— 15 November, Petro di Pietro is paid 8 soldi and 8 denari for painting the books of the captain of the people [ASS, Biccherna 186, fol. 37r].

1337 12 July, Guido receives 4 soldi for painting a book cover [ASS, Biccherna 190, fol. 4r].

—— 23 July, Francesco di Vannuccio receives 10 soldi for forty coats of arms painted on the books of the officials of the former podestà [ASS, Biccherna 190, fol. 6r].

—— 18 November, Petro is paid for painting twenty-six escutcheons of the arms of the former captain of the people [ASS, Biccherna 190, fol. 29v].[46]

—— 31 December, 1 lira and 10 soldi are paid to the unnamed painter of the Biccherna cover [ASS, Biccherna 190, fol. 54r].[47]

1338 3 January, Petro di Pietro receives 13 soldi and 8 denari for painting forty-one escutcheons of the arms of the former podestà on his books [ASS, Biccherna 191, fol. 85r].[48]

—— 1 May, Santino di Angelo receives 12 soldi and 6 denari for painting thirty escutcheons of the arms of the captain of the people for the Biccherna [ASS, Biccherna 191, fol. 115r].[49]

—— 30 June, Petro di Pietro is paid 14 soldi and 4 denari for forty-three escutcheons of the arms of the podestà on his books [ASS, Biccherna 191, fol. 132r].[50]

—— 30 June, Bartolommeo Bulgarini receives £2 for painting the parchment book [ASS, Biccherna 194, fol. 62v].[51]

---

45. Likely for July–December 1334.
46. Although this item contains no reference to books, the task, the sum, and the phrasing of the entry suggest that this item relates to the repeated commissions cited above and below.
47. Likely for July–December 1337.
48. The same item appears in Biccherna 194, fol. 2.
49. The same item appears in Biccherna 194, fol. 32, where books are specifically mentioned.
50. The same item appears in Biccherna 194, fol. 49.
51. This is almost certainly the Entrata/Uscita, since, under the same date, Biccherna 191 (fol. 145v) records 40 soldi (£2) set aside for the task. Presumably for the cover of January–June 1338.

—— 31 December, Nicholello is paid 1 lira, 1 soldo, and 4 denari for sixty-four escutcheons on the books of the podestà, of the captain of the people, and of other officials [ASS, Biccherna 198, fol. 63v].[52]

1339 26 May, Giovanni receives 8 soldi for painting the books of the former captain of the people [ASS, Biccherna 201, fol. 65v].

—— 25 June, Giovanni receives 11 soldi for painting [the books] of the podestà and his court [ASS, Biccherna 201, fol. 79v].

—— 5 November, Giovanni is paid for painting books of the notaries of the captain of the people with his arms [ASS, Biccherna 202, fol. 121r].

1340 3 January, Tuccio di Betto receives 10 soldi for coats of arms for the books of the former podestà [ASS, Biccherna 206, fol. 2r].

—— 28 April, Giovanni di Sera receives 9 soldi for twenty-seven coats of arms on the books of the captain of the people [ASS, Biccherna 206, fol. 38v].

—— 30 June, Giovanni is paid 14 soldi and 4 denari for forty-three escutcheons on the books of the notaries "del maleficio" [ASS, Biccherna 206, fol. 64r].

1341 26 April, Giovanni receives 13 soldi for thirty-nine escutcheons on the books of the captain of the people [ASS, Biccherna 207, fol. 123v].

—— 30 June, Giovanni is paid 12 soldi and 4 denari for thirty-seven coats of arms on the books of the podestà [ASS, Biccherna 207, fol. 148r].

—— 3 November, Giovanni di Sera is paid 9 soldi for twenty-seven escutcheons on the books of the former captain of the people [ASS, Biccherna 209, fol. 130r].

—— 12 December, Giovanni di Sera is paid 13 soldi for thirty-nine coats of arms on the books of the podestà [ASS, Biccherna 209, fol. 139v].

—— 31 December, Bartolommeo Bulgarini receives 1 lira and 10 soldi for painting the book of the Entrata/Uscita of that semester [ASS, Biccherna 209, fol. 166r].[53]

1342 23 April, Giovanni receives 14 soldi for painting the arms of the captain of the people on his books [ASS, Biccherna 210, fol. 151v].

—— 27 June, Giovanni di Sera receives 14 soldi for thirty-five coats of arms on the books "of the officials" [ASS, Biccherna 210, fol. 185r].

—— 30 June, Bartolommeo Bulgarini receives 1 lira and 10 soldi for painting the Entrata/Uscita volume for the January-to-June semester [ASS, Biccherna 210, fol. 199v].

1343 30 April, Giovanni di Sera is paid 10 soldi for painting twenty-five books of the captain of the people [ASS, Biccherna 212, fol. 173r].

—— 21 June, Giovanni di Sera is paid 13 soldi and 9 denari for thirty-three coats of arms on the books of the podestà [ASS, Biccherna 212, fol. 199v].

—— 30 June, the treasury pays 1 lira and 10 soldi for the painting of the Biccherna cover; no artist named [ASS, Biccherna 212, fol. 239r].[54]

—— 1 October, Giovanni is paid 15 soldi for escutcheons on books of the commune in the treasury [ASS, Biccherna 213, fol. 111v].

—— 31 December, the treasury pays 1 lira and 10 soldi for the Biccherna cover; no painter named [ASS, Biccherna 213, fol. 160r].[55]

52. The same item appears in Biccherna 199, fol. 17v.
53. Presumably for July–December 1341.
54. Likely the cover for January–June 1343.
55. Presumably for July–December 1343. This cover still exists. See Borgia et al., *Le Bicchern*e, 94–95.

1345 25 June, Giovanni is paid 14 soldi for painting the books of the podestà [ASS, Biccherna 216, fol. 159r].

—— 30 June, Giovanni di Sera receives 15 soldi for painting the "libri casseros" [ASS, Biccherna 216, fol. 174r].

—— 26 October, Giovanni di Sera is paid 13 soldi and 6 denari for twenty-six escutcheons on the books of the captain of the people and the captain of war [ASS, Biccherna 217, fol. 122v].

—— 31 December, Giovanni di Sera is paid 15 soldi and 9 denari for forty-two coats of arms on the books of the lord Guidoni(?) de Montone [ASS, Biccherna 217, fol. 141v].

1346 29 April, Vannuccio di Mino is paid 9 soldi for painting twenty-two escutcheons on the books of the former captain of the people [ASS, Biccherna 219, fol. 134r].

—— 30 June, Guido Cinatti receives 14 soldi and 8 denari for forty-four escutcheons on the books of the podestà [ASS, Biccherna 219, fol. 151v].

—— 30 June, the treasury pays 1 lira and 10 soldi for painting of the Biccherna cover; no artist named [ASS, Biccherna 219, fol. 168r].[56]

1347 23 October, Giovanni di Sera receives 7 soldi for twenty-nine coats of arms on the books of the captain of the people [ASS, Biccherna 221, fol. 129v].

1347 28 December, Guido di Cinatto receives 18 soldi and 10 denari for various tasks, including forty-eight escutcheons of the arms of the podestà on the books of the notaries of malefactors [ASS, Biccherna 221, fol. 146v].

1348 27 May, Guido di Cino is paid 12 soldi for painting nineteen books of the captain of the people and for painting the "legnio de la fiera" [ASS, Biccherna 223, fol. 143r].[57]

1350 23 April, unnamed painter receives 1 lira and 11 soldi for painting the book(s) of "branche di nicholo e conpagni" [ASS, Biccherna 410, fol. 8r].

1352 27 February, Blasio is paid 18 soldi and 4 denari for twenty-three escutcheons on the books of malefactors [ASS, Biccherna 229, fol. 96r].

---

56. Presumably for January–June 1346. This cover still exists. See Borgia et al., *Le Biccherne,* 100–101.

57. In 1346, Guido Cinatti was paid for painting "lo stile che tiene la banderia de la fiera." This 1348 payment may be for the same task.

SELECTED BIBLIOGRAPHY

PRIMARY SOURCES

(A) From the Archivio di Stato di Siena

Since it may assist other scholars, I list all the Entrata/Uscita and Memoriale volumes that I have read in a systematic fashion. I have sampled or consulted other archival sources in the Archivio di Stato only in connection with specific projects or problems and cite them in the relevant footnotes.

Entrata/Uscita Volumes

 88 Entrata/Uscita, January–June 1285
 90 Entrata/Uscita, July–December 1285
 91 Entrata/Uscita, July–December 1285
 92 Entrata/Uscita, January–June 1286
 93 Entrata/Uscita, July–December 1286
 95 Entrata/Uscita, January–June 1287
 96 Entrata/Uscita, January–June 1288
 97 Entrata/Uscita, July–December 1288
 98 Entrata/Uscita, July–December 1288
 99 Entrata/Uscita, January–June 1289
100 Entrata/Uscita, January–June 1289
101 Entrata/Uscita, July–December 1289
102 Entrata/Uscita, July–December 1289
103 Entrata/Uscita, July–December 1290
104 Entrata/Uscita, January–June 1291
105 Entrata/Uscita, January–June 1291
106 Entrata/Uscita, July–December 1291
107 Entrata/Uscita, January–June 1292
108 Entrata/Uscita, July–December 1292
109 Entrata/Uscita, July–December 1293
110 Entrata/Uscita, January–June 1294
111 Entrata/Uscita, January–June 1295
112 Entrata/Uscita, July–December 1295
113 Entrata/Uscita, July–December 1296
114 Entrata/Uscita, July–December 1298
115 Entrata/Uscita, January–June 1299
116 Entrata/Uscita, January–June 1302
117 Entrata/Uscita, July–December 1302
119 Entrata/Uscita, January–June 1306
120 Entrata/Uscita, January–June 1307
121 Entrata/Uscita, July–December 1307
122 Entrata/Uscita, January–June 1309
123 Entrata/Uscita, January–June 1310
124 Entrata/Uscita, July–December 1310
125 Entrata/Uscita, January–June 1311
126 Entrata/Uscita, January–June 1313
128 Entrata/Uscita, July–December 1314
129 Entrata/Uscita, January–June 1315
130 Entrata/Uscita, July–December 1315
131 Entrata/Uscita, January–June 1316
132 Entrata/Uscita, July–December 1316
133 Entrata/Uscita, January–June 1317
134 Entrata/Uscita, July–December 1317
135 Entrata/Uscita, July–December 1318
136 Entrata/Uscita, July–December 1318
137 Entrata/Uscita, January–June 1319
138 Entrata/Uscita, July–December 1319
139 Entrata/Uscita, July–December 1319
140 Entrata/Uscita, January–June 1321
141 Entrata/Uscita, January–June 1321
142 Entrata/Uscita, July–December 1321
143 Entrata/Uscita, July–December 1321
144 Entrata/Uscita, January–June 1322
145 Entrata/Uscita, July–December 1322
146 Entrata/Uscita, January–June 1323
148 Entrata/Uscita, July–December 1323

149 Entrata/Uscita, January–June 1324
150 Uscita, January–June 1325
152 Entrata/Uscita, January–June 1327
154 Uscita, January–June 1327
155 Uscita, July–December 1327
157 Uscita, January–June 1328
159 Uscita, July–December 1328
161 Uscita, June 1329
163 Uscita, July–December 1329
165 Uscita, January–June 1330
167 Uscita, July–December 1330
168 Entrata/Uscita, January–June 1331
171 Uscita, July–December 1331
174 Uscita, July–December 1332
176 Uscita, January–June 1333
177 Entrata/Uscita, July–December 1333
181 Uscita, July–December 1334
183 Uscita, July–December 1335
184 Entrata/Uscita, January–June 1336
186 Uscita, July–December 1336
189 Uscita, July–December 1337
190 Uscita, July–December 1337
191 Entrata/Uscita, January–June 1338
194 Uscita, January–June 1338
198 Uscita, July–December 1338
199 Uscita, November–December 1338
201 Uscita, January–June 1339
202 Entrata/Uscita, July–December 1339
206 Uscita, January–June 1340
207 Entrata/Uscita, January–June 1341
209 Entrata/Uscita, July–December 1341
210 Entrata/Uscita, January–June 1342
212 Entrata/Uscita, January–June 1343
213 Entrata/Uscita, July–December 1343
214 Entrata, January–June 1344
215 Entrata/Uscita, July–December 1344
216 Entrata/Uscita, January–June 1345
217 Entrata/Uscita, July–December 1345
219 Entrata/Uscita, January–June 1346
221 Entrata/Uscita, July–December 1347
223 Entrata/Uscita, January–June 1348
224 Entrata/Uscita, January–June 1349
225 Entrata/Uscita, July–December 1349
226 Entrata/Uscita, January–June 1350
227 Entrata/Uscita, January–June 1351
228 Entrata/Uscita, July–December 1351
229 Entrata/Uscita, January–June 1352
230 Entrata/Uscita, July–December 1350
233 Uscita, January–June 1354
234 Entrata/Uscita, June–December 1354
235 Entrata/Uscita, July–December 1355
236 Entrata/Uscita, January–June 1357
237 Entrata/Uscita, July–December 1357
238 Entrata/Uscita, January–June 1358
239 Uscita, January–June 1359
240 Entrata/Uscita, January–June 1360
241 Entrata/Uscita, July–December 1361
242 Entrata/Uscita, July–December 1362
243 Entrata/Uscita, January–June 1363

Memoriale Volumes

373 Memoriale, January–June 1314
374 Memoriale, July–December 1314
375 Memoriale, July–December 1314
376 Memoriale, January–June 1315
377 Memoriale, July–December 1315
378 Memoriale, July–December 1316
379 Memoriale, January–June 1317
380 Memoriale, January–June 1319
381 Memoriale, July–December 1319
382 Memoriale, July–December 1321
383 Memoriale, January–June 1322
384 Memoriale, July–December 1322
385 Memoriale, January–June 1323
386 Memoriale, July–December 1323
387 Memoriale, January–June 1325
388 Memoriale, July–December 1325
389 Memoriale, January–June 1326
390 Memoriale, July–December 1326
391 Memoriale, January–June 1327
392 Memoriale, July–December 1327
393 Memoriale, January–June 1328
394 Memoriale, January–June 1329
395 Memoriale, July–December 1329
396 Memoriale, January–June 1330
397 Memoriale, July–December 1331
398 Memoriale, July–December 1332
399 Memoriale, January–June 1333
400 Memoriale, January–June 1334
401 Memoriale, July–December 1336
402 Memoriale, January–June 1337
403 Memoriale, July–December 1337
404 Memoriale, January–June 1338
405 Memoriale, July–December 1338
406 Memoriale, July–December 1339
407 Memoriale, July–December 1341
408 Memoriale, January–June 1347
409 Memoriale, July–December 1348
410 Memoriale, January–June 1350
411 Memoriale, January–June 1352
412 Memoriale, January–June 1352
413 Memoriale, January–June 1353
414 Memoriale, January–June 1354
415 Memoriale, January–July 1356

(B) From the Archivio dell'Opera del Duomo di Siena

171 (old 327)	Entrata/Uscita, January–June 1320	182 (old 335)	Entrata/Uscita, July 1356–June 1357
173 (old 328)	Uscita, January–June 1326	184 (old 337)	Entrata/Uscita, July 1357–June 1358
174 (old 329/2)	Entrata/Uscita, July 1329–January 1330	185 (old 338)	Entrata/Uscita, July 1358–June 1359
175 (old 319)	Entrata/Uscita, 1334	186 (old 339)	Entrata/Uscita, July 1359–June 1360
176 (old 329/3)	Entrata/Uscita, 1 July–31 December 1335	187 (old 340)	Entrata/Uscita, July 1359–May 1360
178 (old 331)	Entrata/Uscita, July–December 1339 and January–June 1340	188 (old 341)	Entrata/Uscita, July 1360–July 1361
179 (old 332)	Entrata/Uscita, July 1344–June 1345	189 (old 342)	Entrata/Uscita, July 1361–June 1362
180 (old 333)	Entrata/Uscita, July 1350–June 1351	190 (old 343)	Entrata/Uscita, July 1362–July 1363
181 (old 334)	Entrata/Uscita, July 1355–June 1356	198 (old 351)	Entrata/Uscita, 13 September 1371–30 September 1372
		491 (old 329)	Debitori/Creditori, 1 July 1329–24 July 1330

UNPUBLISHED SECONDARY SOURCES

Siena's Biblioteca Comunale and Archivio di Stato di Siena house rich collections of secondary sources in manuscript form: the work of local scholars and antiquarians of the seventeenth, eighteenth, and nineteenth centuries. Few of the works listed below have been cited in modern literature on Siena, its history, and its art. The reader—and future researcher—should know that of the following works I have read all of the sections that relate to Siena c. 1260–c.1360.

Benvoglienti, Uberto. (1668–1733). *Diario cronologico delle cose di Siena*. Siena, BC, MS A.IV.14.

———. *Memorie istoriche dal 1286 al 1479*. Siena, BC, MS A.IV.13.

———. *Miscellanee*. Siena, BC, MSS C.IV.1–C.IV.28 inclusive, and C.V.1–C.V.28 inclusive. (The vast majority of these volumes contain nothing related to painting in the period 1260–1363. Particularly relevant volumes are C.IV.6, C.IV.12, and C.V.16.)

Bichi, Galgano (1663–1727). *Miscellanea di copie di cose e materie diverse alla città di Siena . . . formato per commissione del illustrissimo signori abate Galgano de Bichi (1725)*. ASS, MS D.88.

———. *Spogli di notizie dai libri dell'archivio della Bicchema del comune di Siena* (early eighteenth century). 4 vols. Siena, BC, MSS A.VII.15–A.VII.18.

Buondemonte, F. M. *Mescolanze diverse*. Siena, BC, MS A.IX.10.

Carapelli, A. M. *Cronotaxis S. Domenico in Campo Regio in Siena*. In G. Bichi, *Miscellanea*, ASS, MS D.88.

———. *Memorie di San Domencio in Campo Regio*. 2 vols. Siena, BC, MSS B.VII.8 and B.VII.9.

———. *Notizie del Duomo di Siena e di Pisa, con altri ragguagli ec*. Siena, BC, MS B.VII.12.

———. *Notizie delle chiese, e cose riguardevoli di Siena* (c. 1720). Siena, BC, MS B.VII.10.

Carli, G. C. *Notizie di belle arti*. Siena, BC, MS C.VII.20.

———. *Selva di notizie, e riflessioni per la storia di pittori, scultori, e architetti senesi*. Siena, BC, MS L.V.16. (This is, almost completely, repetition of material in F. Montebuoni, Siena, BC, MS L.V.14, with small errors in transcription.)

Cittadini, C. *Notazioni varie ai libri di Bicchema* (1722). ASS, MS D.2.

———. *Spogli dei libri della Bicchema*. Siena, BC, MSS A.V.20 and A.V.22.

De Angelis, L. *Miscellanee* (eighteenth and nineteenth centuries). Siena, BC, MSS A.VIII.5–A.VIII.7 inclusive.

Donati, G. *Spogli di libri de' Consiglio della Campana Esistente nell'Archivio delle Reformagioni di Siena: Fatto da me Giulio Donati d'ordine dell'illustrissimo signore abbate Domini de Conti Bichi—L'anno 1726: Parte terza da luglio 1317 a tutto giugno 1334*. ASS, MS C.5.

Faluschi, G. *Chiese Senesi*. Siena, BC, MSS E.IV.16 and E.IV.17.

———. *Spedale di S. M. della Scala Raccolta di documenti dell'archivio dello spedale, e d'altri archivi relativi allo spedale stesso* (1821). Siena, BC, MS E.V.14.

———. *Spogli d'archivi*. Siena, BC, MSS E.VI.18–E.VI.19.

Gandellini, F. G. *Memorie*. Siena, BC, MS L.V.15.

Indice delle Deliberazioni del Consiglio Generale. Vol. I: 1248–1346, Vol. II: 1347–1574. ASS, MSS C.1–C.2.

Macchi, G. *Diario I, diario II*. Siena, BC, MSS A.XI.22 and A.XI.23.

———. *Memorie (notizie di tutte le chiese che sono nella città di Siena)* (early eighteenth century). ASS, MSS D.107–D.112 inclusive.

———. *Notizie relative all'Ospedale di S. M. della Scala e di Altri* (early eighteenth century). ASS, MSS D.113, D.113/2.

Milanesi, Gaetano. (1813–95). *Miscellanee*. Siena, BC, MSS P.III.30–P.III.53 inclusive. (These volumes contain material that Milanesi published, as well as unpublished notices.)

Montebuoni, F. *Notizie de' pittori sanesi* (eighteenth century). Siena, BC, MS L.v.14.

Notizie di alcuni pittori senesi (eighteenth century). Siena, BC, MS C.III.16.

Pecci, G. A. (1693–1768). *Miscellanea*. Siena, BC, MS A.III.11.

———. *Raccolta universale di tutte l'iscrizioni, arme, e altri monumenti, di antichi, come moderni, e esitenti in diversi luoghi della città di Siena fino a questo presente anno 1730.* ASS, MSS D.4 (Terzo di Città, 1730), D.5 (Terzo di San Martino, 1730), and D.6 (Terzo di Camollia, 1731).

Piccolomini, G. *Siena illustre per antichità*. Siena, BC, MS C.II.23. (Latest date in text is 1637. Piccolomini died in 1649.)

Sestigiani, A. *Spogli delle pergamene dell'archivio della Casa della Sapienza di Siena 1195–1695. Copia*. Siena, BC, MS A.VII.1.

Spinelli, B. *Notizie storiche e documenti di alcune chiese della città di Siena* (nineteenth century). Siena, BC, MSS A.VIII.49–A.III.55 inclusive.

Spogli delle deliberazioni del Concistoro e del Consiglio del Popolo . . . 1/1/1338 (st. com. 1339–4/1387 (eighteenth century). Vol. I. Siena, BC, MS A.VII.23.

Spogli di contratti da vari archivi di Siena (1226–1568). Siena, BC, MS A.v.29.

Spogli di notizie dai libri dell'Archivio della Biccherna. Vol. I: 1230–1312, Vol. II: 1315–68. Siena, BC, MSS A.VII.15 and A.VII.16.

Squarci, E. *Correzioni al diario sanese di Gerolomo Gigli spettanti alle belle arti (1723–56)*. Siena, BC, MS C.v.3. (This is actually contained within a volume of *Miscellanee* by Uberto Benvoglienti. Annotations by Squarci are also found in Siena, BC, MS L.v.16. See G. G. Carli.)

———. *Correzioni alla relazione delle cose più notabili della città di Siena descritta dal Cav. Gio. Ant. Pecci. in Siena 1752*. Siena, BC, MS C.v.3, fols. 324–31. (This is in a volume of Benvoglienti's *Miscellanee*.)

Tizio, Sigismondo. *Historiarum senensium*. Siena, BC, MSS B.III.6–B.III.15. (This is a good eighteenth-century copy of the original now in the Vatican. Tizio died in 1528. Siena, BC, MSS B.III.16–B.III.25 inclusive are volumes of indexes to Tizio's work. Another index is provided by Uberto Benvoglienti, Siena, BC, MS C.v.1.)

PUBLISHED LITERATURE

Abulafia, D. *Frederick II: A Medieval Emperor*. London, 1988.

Antal, F. *Florentine Painting and Its Social Background: The Bourgeois Republic Before Cosimo de' Medici's Advent to Power: XIV and Early XV Centuries*. London, 1947.

Ascheri, M., et al. *L'Università di Siena: 720 anni di storia*. Milan, 1991.

Bacci, Pèleo. "Commentarii dell'arte senese III: Notizie su Duccio, i figli, il nipote e i bisnipoti, pittori." *BSSP*, n.s., III, 1932, 233–48.

———. *Dipinti inediti e sconosciuti di Pietro Lorenzetti, Bernardo Daddi, etc.* Siena, 1939.

———. "L'elenco delle pitture, sculture, e architetture di Siena compilato nel 1625–26 da Mons. Fabio Chigi poi Alessandro VII." *BSSP*, n.s., X, 1939, 1–57.

———. *Fonti e commenti per la storia dell'arte senese*. Siena, 1944.

Bacon, Roger. *The Opus Majus of Roger Bacon*. Trans. R.B. Burke. 2 vols. New York, 1962.

Bagnoli, A., and L. Bellosi, eds. *Simone Martini e "chompagni."* Exhibition catalogue. Florence, 1985.

Baird, J., G. Baglivi, and J. Kane, trans. *The Chronicle of Salimbene de Adam*. Binghampton, N.Y., 1986.

Balestracci, Duccio. "Li 'lavorati non cognosciuti': Il salariato in una città medievale (Siena 1340–1344)." *BSSP*, LXXXII–LXXXIII, 1975–76, 67–157.

Balestracci, Duccio, and Gabriella Piccinni. *Siena nel trecento: Assetto urbano e strutture edilizie*. Florence, 1977.

Banchi, L. *Capitoli della Compagnia dei Disciplinati di Siena de' secoli XIII, XIV, e XV*. Siena, 1866.

Banchi, L., and F.-L. Polidori, eds. *Statuti senese scritti in volgare ne' secoli XIII e XIV*. 3 vols. Bologna, 1863, 1871, 1877.

Barber, M. *The Trial of the Templars*. Cambridge, 1978.

Barcellona, F. S. "Un martire locale: Ansano." *BSSP*, XCVII, 1990, 10–33.

Bargagli-Petrucci, F. *Le fonti di Siena e i loro acquedotti*. 2 vols. Siena, Florence, and Rome, 1903–6.

Battistini, M. "Andrea e Fino da Siena, pittori del sec. XIV dipingono a Volterra." *BSSP*, XXVII, 1920, 107.

Baxandall, M. *Painting and Experience in Fifteenth Century Italy*. Oxford, 1972.

Beatson, E. H., N. E. Muller, and J. Steinhoff. "The St. Victor Altarpiece in Siena Cathedral: A Reconstruction." *Art Bulletin*, LXVIII, 1986, 610–31.

Bellosi, L., ed. *Simone Martini: Atti del convegno.* Florence, 1988.

Belting, Hans. *Das Bild und sein Publikum im Mittelaltar.* Berlin, 1981.

———. "The 'Byzantine' Madonnas: New Facts About Their Italian Origin and Some Observations on Duccio." *Studies in the History of Art* (National Gallery of Art, Washington, D.C.), XII, 1982, 7–22.

———. *Likeness and Presence: A History of Images Before the Era of Art.* Trans. E. Jephcott. Chicago, 1994.

Berenson, B. *Drawings of the Florentine Painters.* 3 vols. Chicago, 1938.

Blume, D. *Wandmalerei als Ordenspropaganda: Bildprogramme in Chorbereich franziskanischer Konvente Italiens bis zur Mitte des 14. Jahrhunderts.* Worms, 1983.

Boase, T. S. R. *Boniface VIII.* London, 1933.

Bomford, D., et al. *Art in the Making: Italian Painting Before 1400.* London, 1989.

Bonaini, F. *Cronaca del convento di Santa Caterina dell'ordine dei predicatori in Pisa.* Florence, 1845.

Borghesi, S., and L. Banchi. *Nuovi documenti per la storia dell'arte senese.* Siena, 1898.

Borgia, L., et al. *Le Biccherne.* Rome, 1984.

Borsook, E. *Gli affreschi di Montesiepi.* Florence, 1968.

———. "Effects of Technical Developments on the History of Italian Mural Painting of the Fourteenth and Fifteenth Centuries." In *La pittura nel XIV e XV secolo: Il contributo dell'analisi tecnica alla storia dell'arte,* ed. H.W. van Os and J.R.J. van Asperen de Boer, Atti del XXIV Congresso Internazionale di Storia dell'Arte, III, 161–69. Bologna, 1983.

———. *The Mural Painters of Tuscany.* 2d ed. London, 1980.

Bortolotti, L. *La città nella storia d'Italia: Siena.* Rome, 1982.

Boskovits, M. "Sul trittico di Simone Martini e di Lippo Memmi." *Arte cristiana,* LXXIV, 1986, 69–78.

Bowsky, William M. "The Anatomy of Rebellion in Fourteenth-Century Siena: From Commune to Signory." In *Violence and Civil Disorder in Italian Cities, 1200–1500,* ed. L. Martines. Berkeley and Los Angeles, 1972, 229–72.

———. "The *Buon Governo* of Siena (1287–1355): A Medieval Italian Oligarchy." *Speculum,* XXXVII, 1962, 368–81.

———. *The Finance of the Commune of Siena, 1287–1355.* Oxford, 1970.

———. "The Impact of the Black Death upon Sienese Government and Society." *Speculum,* XXXIX, 1964, 1–34.

———. *A Medieval Italian Commune: Siena Under the Nine, 1287–1355.* Berkeley and Los Angeles, 1981.

Brandi, C. "Il restauro della Madonna di Coppo di Marcovaldo nella chiesa dei Servi di Siena." *Bollettino d'arte,* XXVI, 1950, 160–70.

———. "Ricomposizione e restauro della pala del Carmine di Pietro Lorenzetti." *Bollettino d'arte,* XXXIII, 1948, 68–77.

———. "Una sinopia di Simone Martini." *Arte antica e moderna,* XIII–XVI, 1961, 17–20.

Brandi, C., et al. *Palazzo Pubblico di Siena: Vicende costruttiva e decorazione.* Milan, 1983.

Brandi, C., et al. *Il restauro della "Maestà" di Duccio.* Rome, 1959.

Braun, Joseph. *Der christliche Altar in seiner geschichtlichen Entwicklung.* 2 vols. Munich, 1924–28.

Brentano, R. *Rome Before Avignon: A Social History of Thirteenth-Century Rome.* New York, 1974.

Buonsignori, V. *Storia della Repubblica di Siena.* Siena, 1856 (reprint: Bologna, 1976).

Burckhardt, T. *Siena, città della Vergine.* Milan, 1978.

Caggese, R. "La Repubblica di Siena e il suo contado nel secolo XIII." *BSSP,* XIII, 1906, 3–120.

Cairola, A., and E. Carli. *Il Palazzo Pubblico di Siena.* Rome, 1963.

Camille, M. *The Gothic Idol: Ideology and Image-Making in Medieval Art.* Cambridge, 1989.

Cannon, J. "The Creation, Meaning, and Audience of the Early Sienese Polyptych: Evidence from the Friars." In *Italian Altarpieces, 1250–1550: Function and Design,* ed. E. Borsook and F. Superbi Gioffredi, 42–80. Oxford, 1994.

———. "Pietro Lorenzetti and the History of the Carmelite Order." *Journal of the Warburg and Courtauld Institutes,* L, 1987, 18–28.

———. "Simone Martini, the Dominicans, and the Early Sienese Polyptych." *Journal of the Warburg and Courtauld Institutes,* XLV, 1982, 69–93.

Cardini, F., et al. *Banchieri e mercanti di Siena.* Rome, 1987.

Carli, E. *Il Duomo di Siena.* Genoa, 1979.

———. *Mani d'Angelo per Simone.* Siena, 1973.

———. "Relazione sul restauro della Madonna di Guido da Siena del 1221." *Bollettino d'arte,* XXXVI, 1951, 248–60.

Carniani, A. *I Salimbeni, quasi una signoria.* Siena, 1995.

Castelnuovo, E., ed. *Ambrogio Lorenzetti: Il buon governo.* Milan, 1995.

Catoni, Giuliano. "Gli oblati della Misericordia: Poveri e benefattori a Siena nella prima metà del trecento." In *La società del bisogno,* by G. Pinto, 1–17. Florence, 1989.

Cennini, Cennino d'Andrea. *Cennino d'Andrea Cennini: The Craftsman's Handbook: The Italian "Il Libro dell'Arte."* Trans. D. V. Thompson Jr. New Haven, 1933 (reprint: New York, 1960).

Cherubini, Giovanni. *Signori, contadini, borghesi: Ricerche sulla società italiana del basso medioevo.* Florence, 1974.

Cherubini, Giovanni, et al. "La proprietà fondiaria in alcune zone del territorio senese all'inizio del trecento." *Rivista di storia dell'agricoltura,* XIV, 1974, 2–176.

Christiansen, K. "Simone Martini's Altar-Piece for the Commune of Siena." *Burlington Magazine,* CXXXVI, 1994, 148–60.

Ciampoli, D., and T. Szabó. *Viabilità e legislazione di uno state cittadino del dugento: Lo Statuto dei Viari di Siena.* Siena, 1992.

Ciccuto, M. *Figure di Petrarca: Giotto, Simone Martini, Franco bolognese.* Naples, 1991.

Cioni, E. *Scultura e smalto nell'oreficeria senese dei secoli XIII e XIV.* Florence, 1998.

Cipolla, C. M. *Clocks and Culture, 1300–1700.* New York, 1977.

———. *Guns, Sails, and Empires.* New York, 1965.

———. *Storia economica dell'Europa pre-industriale.* Bologna, 1974.

———. "Studi di storia della moneta." *Università di Pavia: Studi nelle scienze giuridiche e sociali pubblicati dall'istituto di esercitazione presso la facoltà di giurisprudènza,* XXIX, 1948, 31–239.

Cirigliano, M., trans. *Guido Cavalcanti: The Complete Poems.* New York, 1992.

Cohn, N. *Europe's Inner Demons: An Enquiry Inspired by the Great Witch-Hunt.* London, 1975.

Cohn, Samuel K., Jr. *The Cult of Remembrance and the Black Death: Six Renaissance Cities in Central Italy.* London and Baltimore, 1992.

———. *Death and Property in Siena, 1205–1800: Strategies for the Afterlife.* Baltimore and London, 1988.

Consilino, F. E. "Un martire 'romano': Crescenzio." *BSSP,* XCVII, 1990, 34–48.

Cormack, R. *Writing in Gold: Byzantine Society and Its Icons.* New ed. New York, 1996.

Cosenza, M. E., ed. *Petrarch: The Revolution of Cola di Rienzo.* 3d ed. New York, 1966.

Cousins, E., trans. *Bonaventure: The Soul's Journey into God: The Tree of Life, the Life of St. Francis.* New York, 1978.

Crawford, O. G. S., ed. *Ethiopian Itineraries Circa 1400–1524.* Cambridge, 1958.

D'Alatri, M. *Eretici e inquisitori in Italia.* 2 vols. Rome, 1986.

Dale, S. "Ambrogio Lorenzetti's *Maestà* at Massa Marittima." *Source,* VIII, no. 2, 1989, 6–11.

Dal Poggetto, P. *Ugolino di Vieri: Gli smalti di Orvieto.* Forma e Colore 9. Florence, 1965.

Dante. *Dante: The Banquet.* Trans. C. Ryan. Saratoga, Calif., 1989.

Davis, C. T. *Dante and the Idea of Rome.* Oxford, 1957.

Dawson, C., ed. *The Mongol Mission: Narratives and Letters of the Franciscan Missionaries in Mongolia and China in the Thirteenth and Fourteenth Centuries.* New York, 1955.

De Benedictis, C. *La pittura senese 1330–1370.* Florence, 1979.

———. "Simone Martini a San Gimignano e una postilla per il possibile Donato." In *Simone Martini: Atti del convegno,* ed. L. Bellosi, 187–91. Florence, 1988.

———. "Sull'attività orvietana di Simone Martini e del suo seguito." *Antichità viva,* XV, no. 6, 1976, 3–11.

Degenhart, B. "Das Marienwunder von Avignon: Simone Martini's Miniaturen für Kardinal Stefaneschi und Petrarca." *Pantheon,* XXXIII, 1975, 191–203.

Degenhart, B., and A. Schmitt. *Corpus der italienischen Zeichnungen 1300–1450.* Berlin, 1968.

Degrassi, D. *L'economia artigiana nell'Italia medievale.* Rome, 1996.

Delcorno, C. *Giordano da Pisa e l'antica predicazione volgare.* Florence, 1975.

———, ed. *Giordano da Pisa: Quaresimale fiorentino 1305–1306.* Florence, 1974.

della Valle, Guglielmo. *Lettere sanesi sopra le belle arti.* Vol. I: Venice, 1782; Vol. II: Rome, 1785; Vol. III: Rome, 1786.

De Luca, G., ed. *Prosatori minori del trecento.* I, *Scrittore di religione.* Milan and Naples, 1954.

Derbes, Anne. *Painting the Passion in Late Medieval Italy: Narrative Painting, Franciscan Ideologies, and the Levant.* Cambridge and New York, 1996.

Deuchler, F. *Duccio.* Milan, 1984.

de Voragine, Jacobus. *Jacobus de Voragine: The Golden Legend: Readings on the Saints.* Trans. W.G. Ryan. 2 vols. Princeton, 1993.

Donati, F. "Il palazzo del comune di Siena: Notizie storiche." *BSSP,* XI, 1904, 311–54.

———. "Provvisioni della repubblica sopra i matrimoni." *Miscellanea storica senese,* I, 1893, 167–68.

Douglas, L. *Storia della Repubblica di Siena.* Siena, 1926 (reprint: Rome, 1969).

Durandus, G. *The Symbolism of Churches and Church Ornaments: A Translation of the First Book of the Rationale Divinorum Officiorum Written by William Durandus.* Trans. J. M. Neale and B. Webb. 3d ed. London, 1906.

Eco, U. *Art and Beauty in the Middle Ages.* Trans. H. Bredin. New Haven and London, 1986.

Edbury, P. W. *The Kingdom of Cyprus and the Crusades, 1191–1374.* Cambridge, 1991.

Edgerton, S. *The Renaissance Rediscovery of Linear Perspective.* New York, 1975.

Eisenberg, M. "The First Altarpiece for the 'Cappella de' Signori' of the Palazzo Pubblico in Siena: '. . . tales figure sunt adeo pulcre. . . .'" *Burlington Magazine,* CXXIII, 1981, 134–48.

Enaud, F. "Un apport français à l'histoire de l'art: La découverte des 'Sinopie' de Simone Martini à Avignon." In *Atti del II Congresso Internazionale del Restauro,* 800–810. Venice, 1964.

———. "Les fresques de Simone Martini à Avignon." *Les monuments historiques de la France,* III, 1963, 115–80.

English, Edward. *Enterprise and Liability in Sienese Banking, 1230–1350.* Cambridge, Mass., 1988.

Epstein, S. R. *Alle origini della fattoria toscana: L'ospedale dello Scala di Siena e le sue terre (meta '200–meta '400).* Florence, 1986.

Falletti-Fossati, Carlo. *Costumi senesi nella seconda metà del secolo XIV.* Siena, 1881 (reprint: Bologna, 1980).

Farulli, G. *Notizie istoriche dell'antica e nobile città di Siena.* Lucca, 1722 (reprint: Sala Bolognese, 1975).

Fehm, S. *Luca di Tommè.* Carbondale and Edwardsville, Ill., 1986.

———. "A Pair of Panels by the Master of Città di Castello and a Reconstruction of Their Original Altarpiece." *Yale University Art Gallery Bulletin,* XXXI, no. 2, 1967, 16–27.

Feldges, U. *Landschaft als topographisches Porträt: Der Wiederbeginn der europäischen Landschaftsmalerei in Siena.* Bern, 1980.

Feldges-Henning, U. "Zu Thema und Datierung von Simone Martini's Fresko 'Guido Riccio da Fogliano.'" *Mitteilungen des Kunsthistorischen Institutes in Florenz,* XVII, 1973, 273–76.

Fiumi, E. "Fioritura e decadenza dell'economia fiorentina." *Archivio storico italiano,* CXV, 1957, 385–439; CXVI, 1958, 443–510; CXVII, 1959, 427–502.

Franchi, F. C., and G. Cascarella. "Le Grance dello Spedale di Santa Maria della Scala nel contado senese." *BSSP,* XCII, 1985, 66–92.

Franchina, L., ed. *Piazza del Campo: Evoluzione di una immagine, documenti, vicende ricostruzioni.* Siena, 1983.

Francis, H. S. "An Altarpiece by Ugolino da Siena." *Bulletin of the Cleveland Museum of Art,* XLVIII, 1961, 194–205.

Frederick, K. "A Program of Altarpieces for the Siena Cathedral." *Rutgers Art Review,* IV, 1983, 18–35.

Fredericksen, B. "Documents for the Servite Origin of Simone Martini's Orvieto Polyptych." *Burlington Magazine,* CXXVIII, 1986, 592–97.

Freedberg, D. *The Power of Images.* London and Chicago, 1989.

Freuler, G. *Biagio di Goro Ghezzi a Paganico.* Florence, 1986.

Friedman, D. *Florentine New Towns: Urban Design in the Late Middle Ages.* Cambridge, Mass., and London, 1988.

Frinta, M. "The Decoration of the Gilded Surface in Panel Painting Around 1300." In *Europäische Kunst um 1300: Akten des XXV Internationalen Kongresses für Kunstgeschichte, Vienna, 1983,* 69–75. Vienna, 1986.

———. "An Investigation of the Punched Decoration of Medieval Italian and Non-Italian Panel Paintings." *Art Bulletin,* XLVII, 1965, 261–65.

———. "On the Punched Decoration in Medieval Panel Painting and Manscript Illumination." In *Conservation and Restoration of Pictorial Art,* ed. N. Brommelle and P. Smith, 54–60. London, 1976.

———. "Raised Gilded Adornment of the Cypriot Icons and the Occurrence of the Technique in the West." *Gesta,* XX, no. 2, 1981, 333–47.

Gallavotti Cavallero, D. *Lo Spedale di Santa Maria della Scala in Siena: Vicenda di una committenza artistica.* Pisa, 1985.

Gardner, Julian. "Altars, Altarpieces, and Art History: Legislation and Usage." In *Italian Altarpieces, 1250–1550: Function and Design,* ed. E. Borsook and F. Superbi Gioffredi, 5–40. Oxford, 1994.

———. "Backs and Fronts: Settings and Structures." In *La pittura nel XIV e XV secolo: Il contributo dell'analisi tecnica alla storia dell'arte,* ed. H. W. van Os and J.R.J. van Asperen de Boer, Atti del XXIV Congresso Internazionale di Storia dell'Arte, III, 297–322. Bologna, 1983.

———. "Boniface VIII as a Patron of Sculpture." In *Roma anno 1300,* ed. A.M. Romanini, 513–27. Rome, 1983.

———. "The Cappellone di San Nicola at Tolentino: Some Functions of a Fourteenth-Century Fresco Cycle." In *Italian Church Decoration of the Middle Ages and Early Renaissance,* ed. W. Tronzo, 101–17. Bologna, 1989.

———. "The Cult of a Fourteenth-Century Saint: The Iconography of St. Louis of Toulouse." In *I francescani nel trecento,* Atti del XIV Convegno della Società Internazionale di Studi Francescani, 167–93. Perugia, 1988.

———. "The Decoration of the Baroncelli Chapel in Santa Croce." *Zeitschrift für Kunstgeschichte,* XXXIV, 1971, 89–114.

———. "Saint Louis of Toulouse, Robert of Anjou, and Simone Martini." *Zeitschrift für Kunstgeschichte,* XXXIX, 1976, 12–33.

———. "Some Franciscan Altars of the 13th and 14th Centuries." In *The Vanishing Past: Studies of Medieval Art, Liturgy, and Metrology Presented to Christopher Hohler,* ed. A. Borg and A. Martindale, 29–38. Oxford, 1981.

———. "The Stefaneschi Altarpiece: A Reconsideration." *Journal of the Warburg and Courtauld Institutes,* XXXVII, 1974, 57–103.

———. *The Tomb and the Tiara: Curial Tomb Sculpture in Rome and Avignon in the Later Middle Ages.* Oxford, 1992.

Gardner von Teuffel, C. "The Buttressed Altarpiece: A Forgotten Aspect of Tuscan Fourteenth-Century Altarpiece Design." *Jahrbuch der Berliner Museen,* XXI, 1979, 22–65.

———. "Masaccio and the Pisa Altarpiece: A New Approach." *Jahrbuch der Berliner Museen,* XIX, 1977, 23–68.

Gewirth, A., trans. *Marsilius of Padua: The Defender of Peace: The Defensor Pacis.* New York, 1957.

Giannarelli, E. "Savino, Bartolomeo e l'alternanza dei patroni." *BSSP*, xcvii, 1990, 64–83.

Gibbs, R. *Tomaso da Modena: Painting in Emilia and March of Treviso, 1340–80*. Cambridge, 1989.

Gigli, G. *Diario senese*. 2d ed. 3 vols. Siena, 1854 (originally published in 1723).

Gilbert, C. E. "Cecco d'Ascoli e la pittura di Giotto." In *Poets Seeing Artists' Work*, 33–48. Florence, 1991.

———. "Some Special Images for Carmelites, Circa 1330–1430." In *Christianity and the Renaissance*, ed. T. Verdon and J. Henderson, 161–207. Syracuse, N.Y., 1990.

Goldthwaite, R. *The Building of Renaissance Florence: An Economic and Social History*. London and Baltimore, 1980.

Gombrich, E. H. *Art and Illusion: A Study in the Psychology of Pictorial Representation*. Princeton, 1960.

Gordon, D. "Simone Martini's Altar-Piece for Sant' Agostino, San Gimignano." *Burlington Magazine*, cxxxiii, 1991, 771.

Gordon, D., and A. Reeve. "Three Newly-Acquired Panels from the Altarpiece for Santa Croce by Ugolino di Nerio." *National Gallery Technical Bulletin*, viii, 1984, 36–52.

Grant, E. "The Condemnation of 1277, God's Absolute Power, and Physical Thought in the Late Middle Ages." *Viator*, x, **?**, 211–44 (reprinted in E. Grant, *Studies in Medieval Science and Natural Philosophy*, London, 1981).

———. *The Foundations of Modern Science in the Middle Ages*. Cambridge, 1996.

Guerrini, A. "Intorno al politico di Pietro Lorenzetti per la Pieve di Arezzo." *Rivista d'arte*, xxxii, 1988, 3–29.

Guidoni, E. *Il Campo di Siena*. Rome, 1971.

Habig, M. "Marignoli and the Decline of Medieval Missions in China." *Franciscan Studies*, xxvi, 1945, 21–36.

———, ed. *St. Francis of Assisi, Writings and Early Biographies: English Omnibus of Sources for the Life of St. Francis*. 4th ed. Chicago, 1983.

Hager, H. *Die Anfänge des italienischen Altarbildes: Untersuchungen zur Entstehungsgeschichte des toskanischen Hochaltarretabels*. Munich, 1962.

Haines, M. *The Sacrestia delle Messe of the Florentine Cathedral*. Florence, 1983.

Heywood, W. *The "Ensamples" of Fra Filippo: A Study of Medieval Siena*. Siena, 1901.

Hills, P. *The Light of Early Italian Painting*. London and New Haven, 1987.

Hoeniger, Cathleen. "The Painting Technique of Simone Martini." Ph.D. dissertation, Princeton University, 1989.

———. *The Renovation of Paintings in Tuscany, 1250–1500*. Cambridge, 1995.

Holmes, George. *Florence, Rome, and the Origins of the Renaissance*. Oxford, 1986.

Hook, J. *Siena: A City and Its History*. London, 1979.

Housley, N. *The Italian Crusades: The Papal Angevin Alliance and the Crusades Against Christian Lay Powers, 1254–1343*. Oxford, 1982.

Hughes, S., and E. Hughes., trans. *Jacopone da Todi: The Lauds*. New York, 1982.

Humfrey, P., and M. Kemp, eds. *The Altarpiece in the Renaissance*. Cambridge, 1988.

Iorio, D. A. *The Aristotelians of Renaissance Italy*. Lewiston, Queenston, and Lampeter, 1991.

"Kalendarium Ecclesiae Metropolitanae Senensis." In *Chronache Senesi*, A. Lisini and F. Iacometti, n.s., xv, pt. vi, 3–38. See Lisini.

Kanter, L. "Ugolino di Nerio: Saint Anne and the Virgin." *Annual Bulletin of the National Gallery of Canada*, v, 1981–82, 9–28.

Kantorowicz, E. H. *Kaiser Friedrich der Zweite*. Berlin, 1928 (trans. E. O. Lorimer, London, 1931: *Frederick the Second*).

———. *The King's Two Bodies: A Study in Medieval Political Theology*. Princeton, 1957.

Keller, H. "Die Bauplastik der Sieneser Doms: Studien zu Giovanni Pisano und seiner künstlerischen Nachfolge." *Kunstgeschichtliches Jahrbuch der Bibliotheca Hertziana*, i, 1937, 138–220.

Kieckhefer, R. *Unquiet Souls: Fourteenth-Century Saints and Their Religious Milieu*. Chicago and London, 1984.

Klesse, B. *Seidenstoffe in der italienischen Malerei des 14. Jahrhunderts*. Bern, 1967.

Kosegarten, A. Middeldorf. *Sienesische Bildhauer am Duomo Vecchio: Studien zur Skulptur in Siena 1250–1330*. Munich, 1984.

Kretzmann, N., A. Kenny, and J. Pinborg, eds. *The Cambridge History of Later Medieval Philosophy*. Cambridge, 1982.

Kupfer, Marcia. "The Lost Wheel Map of Ambrogio Lorenzetti." *Art Bulletin*, lxxviii, 1996, 286–310.

Ladis, A. "Immortal Queen and Mortal Bride: The Marian Imagery of Ambrogio Lorenzetti's Cycle at Montesiepi." *Gazette des beaux-arts*, cxix, 1992, 189–200.

———. *Taddeo Gaddi: Critical Reappraisal and Catalogue Raisonné*. Columbia, Mo., and London, 1982.

Ladis, A., and C. Wood., eds. *The Craft of Art: Originality and Industry in the Italian Renaissance and Baroque Workshop*. Athens, Ga., 1995.

Lambert, M. D. *Franciscan Poverty: The Doctrine of the Absolute Poverty of Christ and the Apostles in the Franciscan Order, 1210–1323*. London, 1961.

Land, Norman. "Giotto as an Ugly Genius: A Study in Self-Portrayal." *Explorations in Renaissance Culture*, xxiii, 1997, 23–26.

———. *The Viewer as Poet*. University Park, Pa., 1994.

Larner, J. *Culture and Society in Italy, 1290–1420*. London, 1971.

Laurent, M. H., ed. *I necrologi di San Domenico in Camporegio*. Florence, 1937.

Lee, R. *Ut Pictura Poesis: The Humanist Theory of Painting*. New York, 1967.

Lee, S. E., and Wai-Kam Ho. *Chinese Art Under the Mongols: The Yüan Dynasty (1279–1368)*. Exhibition catalogue. Cleveland, 1968.

Lerner, R., and M. Mahdi, eds. *Medieval Political Philosophy: A Sourcebook*. Ithaca, N.Y., 1963.

Lindberg, D. C., "Lines of Influence in Thirteenth-Century Optics." *Speculum*, XLVI, 1971, 66–83.

———. *Roger Bacon's Philosophy of Nature: A Critical Edition, with English Translation, Introduction, and Notes, of De Multiplicatione Specierum and De Speculis Comburentibus*. Oxford, 1983.

———. *Theories of Vision from Al-Kindi to Kepler*. Chicago, 1976.

———, ed. *Science in the Middle Ages*. Chicago and London, 1978.

Lisini, A. "Elenco dei pittori vissuti nel secolo XIII e XIV." *La Diana*, II, 1927, 295–306.

———, ed. *Il costituto del comune di Siena volgarizzato nel MCCCIX–MCCCX*. 2 vols. Siena, 1903.

Lisini, A., and F. Iacometti, eds. *Cronache Senesi*. In *Rerum Italicarum Scriptores*, n.s., XV, pt. VI, Bologna, 1931–37.

Lopez, R. S. "China Silk in Europe in the Yuan Period." *American Oriental Society Journal*, LXXII, 1952, 72–76.

Loyrette, H. "Une source pour la reconstruction du polyptyche d'Ugolino da Siena à Santa Croce." *Paragone*, CCCXLIII, 1978, 15–23.

"Ls." "Il prezzo della carta da scrivere nei secoli XIII e XIV." *Miscellanea storica senese*, V, 1898, 57–59.

Lunt, W. E. *Papal Revenues in the Middle Ages*. 2 vols. New York, 1934.

Lupi, C. "L'arte senese a Pisa." *BSSP*, XI, 1904, 379–80.

Lusini, V. *La Basilica di S. Maria dei Servi*. Siena, 1908.

———. *Il Duomo di Siena*. 2 vols. Siena, 1911–39.

Madaule, J. *The Albigensian Crusade: An Historical Essay*. New York, 1967.

Maginnis, Hayden B. J. "Ambrogio Lorenzetti's *Presentation in the Temple*." *Studi di storia dell'arte*, II, 1991, 33–50.

———. "Assisi Revisited: Notes on Recent Observations." *Burlington Magazine*, CXVII, 1975, 511–17.

———. "Boccaccio: A Poet Making Pictures." *Source*, XV, no. 2, 1996, 1–17.

———. "Cast Shadow in the Passion Cycle at San Francesco, Assisi: A Note." *Gazette des beaux-arts*, LXXVII, 1971, 63–64.

———. "Chiarimenti documentari: Simone Martini, I Memmi e Ambrogio Lorenzetti." *Rivista d'arte*, XLI, 1989, 3–23.

———. "The Craftsman's Genius: Painters, Patrons, and Drawings in Trecento Siena." In *The Craft of Art: Originality and Industry in the Italian Renaissance and Baroque Workshop*, ed. A. Ladis and C. Wood, 25–47. Athens, Ga., 1995.

———. "The 'Guidoriccio' Controversy: Notes and Observations." *RACAR*, XV, 1988, 137–44.

———. "The Lost Facade Frescoes from Siena's Ospedale di S. Maria della Scala." *Zeitschrift für Kunstgeschichte*, LI, 1988, 180–94.

———. *Painting in the Age of Giotto: A Historical Reevaluation*. University Park, Pa., 1997.

———. "The Passion Cycle in the Lower Church of San Francesco, Assisi: The Technical Evidence." *Zeitschrift für Kunstgeschichte*, XXXIX, 1976, 193–208.

———. "Pietro Lorenzetti: A Chronology." *Art Bulletin*, LXVI, 1984, 183–210.

———. "Pietro Lorenzetti's Carmelite Madonna: A Reconstruction." *Pantheon*, XXXIII, 1975, 10–16.

———. "The So-called Dijon Master." *Zeitschrift für Kunstgeschichte*, XLII, 1980, 121–38.

———. "Tabernacle 35." *Source*, XII, no. 4, 1993, 1–4.

———. "The Thyssen Bornemisza Ugolino." *Apollo*, CXVIII, 1983, 16–21.

Malavolti, O. *Dell'historia di Siena*. 3 vols. in 1. Venice, 1599 (reprint: Bologna, 1968).

Manetti, R., and G. Savino. "I libri dei Disciplinati di Santa Maria della Scala di Siena." *BSSP*, XCVII, 1990, 122–92.

Manni, D. M., and A. M. Biscioni. *Prediche del b. F. Giordano da Rivalto*. Florence, 1739.

Manzoni, L. *Statuti e matricole dell'Arte dei Pittori delle città di Firenze, Perugia, Siena*. Rome, 1904.

Marrara, D. "I magnati e il governo del comune di Siena dallo statuto del 1274 alla fine del XIV secolo." In *Studi per Enrico Fiumi*, 239ff. Pisa, 1979.

Martindale, A. *Simone Martini: Complete Edition*. Oxford, 1988.

Martini, G. "Siena da Montaperti alla caduta dei Nove (1260–1355)." *BSSP*, LXVIII, 1961, 75–128.

Mazzi, C. "Descrizione della festa in Siena per la cavalleria di Francesco Bandinelli nel 1326." *BSSP*, XVIII, 1911, 324–58.

———. "Il vescovo Donodeus Malavolti e l'Ospizio di S. Marta in Siena." *BSSP*, XIX, 1912, 200–248; XX, 1913, 65–114.

Meersemann, G. C. *Ordo Fraternitatis: Confraternite e pietà dei laici nel medioevo*. 3 vols. Rome, 1977.

Meiss, Millard. "Bartolommeo Bulgari, altrimenti detto 'Ugolino Lorenzetti.'" *Rivista d'arte*, XVIII, 1936, 113–36.

———. *Giotto and Assisi*. New York, 1960.

———. *Painting in Florence and Siena After the Black Death*. Princeton, 1951.

———. "Reflections of Assisi: A Tabernacle and the Cesi

Master." In *Scritti di storia dell'arte in onore di Mario Salmi*, II, 75–111. Rome, 1962.

———. "Ugolino Lorenzetti." *Art Bulletin*, XIII, 1931, 376–97.

Milanesi, Gaetano. *Documenti per la storia dell'arte senese*. 3 vols. Siena, 1854.

———. *Nuovi documenti per la storia dell'arte toscana*. Florence, 1901.

Misciatelli, P. *Mistici senesi*. 3d ed. Siena, 1913.

Mollat, G. *The Popes at Avignon, 1305–1378*. London, 1963.

Monti, G. M. *Le confraternite medievali dell'alta e media Italia*. 2 vols. Venice, 1927.

Moorman, John R. H. *The History of the Franciscan Order from Its Origin to the Year 1517*. Oxford, 1968.

Morandi, U. *Il castellare dei Malavolti a Siena*. Rome, 1969.

Moscadelli, Stefano. *L'Archivio dell'Opera della Metropolitana di Siena, inventario*. Munich, 1995.

Mucciarelli, R. *I Tolomei: Banchieri di Siena*. Siena, 1995.

Muller, Norman. "Reflections in a Mirror: Ambrogio Lorenzetti's Depiction of the Trinity." *Art Bulletin*, LXI, 1979, 101–2.

———. "Reflections on Ugolino di Nerio's Santa Croce Polyptych." *Zeitschrift für Kunstgeschichte*, LVII, 1994, 45–74.

———. "Three Methods of Modelling the Virgin's Mantle in Early Italian Painting." *Journal of the American Institute for Conservation*, XVII, 1978, 10–18.

Musa, M., trans. *Dante: La Vita Nuova*. Bloomington, Ind., 1962.

Muzzi, O., R. Stopani, and T. Szabo. *La Valdelsa, la Via Francigena e gli itnerari per Roma e Compostella*. Poggibonsi and San Gimignano, 1988.

Nardi, P. "I borghi di San Donato e di S. Pietro a Ovile: 'Populi,' contrade e compagnie d'armi nella società senesi dei secoli XI–XIII." *BSSP*, LXXIII–LXIV, 1966–68, 7–59.

Nicholl, D., and C. Hardie, trans. and eds. *Dante: Monarchy and Three Political Letters*. New York, 1954.

Nims, M., trans. *Poetria Nova of Geoffrey of Vinsauf*. Toronto, 1967.

Norman, D. "The Commission for the Frescoes of Montesiepi." *Zeitschrift für Kunstgeschichte*, LVI, 1993, 289–300.

Odier, J. Bignani. "Le testament du Cardinal Richard Petroni, 13 janvier 1314." *Papers of the British School at Rome*, XXIV, 1956, 142–57.

Oertel, R. "Wandmalerei und Zeichnung in Italien: Die Anfänge der Entwurfszeichnung und ihre monumentalen Vorstufen." *Mitteilungen des Kunsthistorischen Institutes in Florenz*, V, 1940, 217–314.

Olschki, L. *Guillaume Boucher: French Artist at the Court of the Khans*. Florence, 1946.

Origo, I. *The Merchant of Prato, Marco Datini*. London, 1957.

Ortalli, G. *La pittura infamante*. Rome, 1979.

Panofsky, E. *Renaissance and Renascences in Western Art*. Stockholm, 1960.

Parronchi, A. *Studi su la dolce prospettiva*. Milan, 1964.

Patrucco, M. F. "Un Santo 'Milanesi': S. Vittore." *BSSP*, XCVII, 1990, 49–63.

Pazzagli, P. R. *The Criminal Ban of the Sienese Commune, 1225–1310*. Milan, 1979.

Pecci, G. A. *Storia del vescovado della città di Siena*. Lucca, 1748.

Pecham, John. *John Pecham and the Science of Optics: Perspectiva Communis*. Ed. and trans. D. C. Lindberg. Madison, Wis., 1970.

Pennington, H. *Pope and Bishops: The Papal Monarchy in the Twelfth and Thirteenth Centuries*. Philadelphia, 1984.

Pesciolini, G. V. "I bagni di Petriolo nel medievo." *La Diana*, VI, 1932, 110–35.

Petrarca, Francesco. *Prose*. Ed. G. Martellotti et al. Milan and Naples, 1955.

———. *Rerum familiarium libri I–VIII*. Trans. A. S. Bernardo. New York, 1975.

Piccolomini, P. *La vita e l'opera di Sigismondo Tizio, 1458–1528*. Rome, 1903.

Pinto, G. *La società del bisogno*. Florence, 1989.

———. *I Tolomei, banchieri di Siena: La parabola di un casato nell XIII e XIV secolo*. Siena, 1995.

Polzer, J. "A Contribution to the Early Chronology of Lippo Memmi." In *La pittura nel XIV e XV secolo: Il contributo dell'analisi tecnica alla storia dell'arte*, ed. H.W. van Os and J.R.J. van Asperen de Boer, Atti del XXIV Congresso Internazionale di Storia dell'Arte, III, 237–52. Bologna, 1983.

———. "The Technical Evidence and the Origin and Meaning of Simone Martini's 'Guidoriccio' Fresco in Siena." *RACAR*, XIV, nos. 1–2, 1987, 16–51.

Previtali, G. "Introduzione ai problemi della bottega di Simone Martini." In *Simone Martini: Atti del convegno*, ed. L. Bellosi, 151–66. Florence, 1988.

Previtali, G., et al. *Il gotico a Siena: Miniature pitture oreficerie oggetti d'arte*. Florence, 1982.

Procacci, U. *Sinopie e affreschi*. Milan, 1961.

Prunai, G. "I capitoli della Compagnia di S. Domenico in Campo Regio." *BSSP*, XLVII, 1940, 117–56.

———. "Lo studio senese dalle origini alla migratio bolognese sec. XIII—1321." *BSSP*, 3d ser., VIII, 1949, 53–79; IX, 1950, 3–54.

Ragusa, I., and R. B. Green, trans. and eds. *Meditations on the Life of Christ: An Illustrated Manuscript of the Fourteenth Century*. Princeton, 1961.

Redon, O. "L'eremo, la città e la foresta." In *Lecceto e gli eremi agostiniani in terra di Siena*, 9–43. Milan, 1990.

———. *L'espace d'une cité: Sienne et le pays siennois (XIIIe–XIVe siècles)*. Rome, 1994.

Romagnoli, Ettore. *Biografia cronologica de' bellartisti senesi* (c. 1832). 13 vols. Florence, 1976.

Romanini, A. M., ed. *Roma anno 1300*. Rome, 1983.

Rosen, David. "The Invention of Eyeglasses." *Journal of the History of Medicine and Allied Sciences,* XI, 1956, 13–46, 183–218.

Rowlands, J. "The Date of Simone Martini's Arrival in Avignon." *Burlington Magazine,* CVII, 1962, 25–26.

Rowley, George. *Ambrogio Lorenzetti*. 2 vols. Princeton, 1958.

Rubin, P. L. *Giorgio Vasari: Art and History*. London, 1995.

Runciman, S. *A History of the Crusades*. 3 vols. Cambridge, 1954.

———. *The Sicilian Vespers: A History of the Mediterranean World in the Later Thirteenth Century*. Cambridge, 1960.

Sacchetti, Francesco. *Il trecentonovelle*. Ed. V. Marucucci. Rome, 1996.

Salvini, R. *Giotto (bibliografia)*. Rome, 1938.

Santi, F. *Galleria Nazionale dell'Umbria: Dipinti, sculture e oggetti d'arte di età romanica e gotica*. Rome, 1989.

Sapengo, N. *Storia letteraria d'Italia: Il trecento*. Milan, 1942.

Satkowski, J. *Duccio di Buoninsegna: The Documents and Early Sources*. Ed. Hayden B. J. Maginnis. Athens, Ga., 2000.

Saunders, J. J. *The History of the Mongol Conquests*. London, 1971.

Sayers, J. *Innocent III: Leader of Europe, 1198–1216*. London and New York, 1994.

Scheller, R. W. *Exemplum: Model-Book Drawings and the Practice of Artistic Transmission in the Middle Ages (ca. 900–ca. 1450)*. Amsterdam, 1995.

Schmidt, V. "Artistic Imagination Versus Religious Function: Ambrogio Lorenzetti's Annunciation at Montesiepi." In *Power of Imagery: Essays on Tome, Italy, and Imagination,* ed. P. van Kessel, 133–48, 290–96. Sant' Oreste, 1993.

Seidel, M. *Ambrogio Lorenzetti cronista nunziale*. Turin, 1993.

———. "Il beato Agostino Novello e quattro suoi miracoli." In *Simone Martini e "chompagni,"* exhibition catalogue, 56–72. Florence, 1985.

———. "*Castrum pingatur in palatio,* 1: Richerche storiche e iconografiche sui castelli dipinti in Palazzo Pubblico di Siena." *Prospectiva,* XXVIII, 1982, 17–41.

———. "Condizionamenti iconografico e scelta semantica: Simone Martini e la tavola del beato Agostino Novello." In *Simone Martini: Atti del convegno,* ed. L. Bellosi, 75–80. Florence, 1988.

———. "Die Fresken des Ambrogio Lorenzetti in S. Agostino." *Mitteilungen des Kunsthistorischen Institutes in Florenz,* XXII, 1978, 185–252.

———. "Ikonographie und Historiographie, 'Conversatio Angelorum in Silvis': Eremiten-Bilder von Simone Martini und Pietro Lorenzetti." *Städel Jahrbuch,* n.s., X, 1985, 77–142.

———. "Wiedergefundene Fragmente eines Hauptwerks von Ambrogio Lorenzetti." *Pantheon,* XXVI, 1978, 119–27.

Senigaglia, Q. "Lo Statuto dell'Arte della Mercanzia senese." *BSSP,* XIV, 1907, 211–48.

Setton, K. *The Papacy and the Levant, 1204–1571*. 4 vols. Philadelphia, 1976–84.

———, ed. *A History of the Crusades*. 3 vols. London, 1969.

Shannon, A. C. *The Popes and Heresy in the Thirteenth Century*. Villanova, Pa., 1949.

Shearman, J. "A Note on the Early History of Cartoons." *Master Drawings,* XXX, no. 1, 1992, 5–8.

Skaug, Erling S. *Punch Marks from Giotto to Fra Angelico: Attribution, Chronology, and Workshop Relationships in Tuscan Panel Painting, with Particular Consideration to Florence, c. 1330–1430*. 2 vols. Oslo, 1994.

———. "Punch-Marks—What Are They Worth? Problems of Tuscan Workshop Interrelationships in the Mid–Fourteenth Century: The Ovile Master and Giovanni di Milano." In *La pittura nel XIV e XV secolo: Il contributo dell'analisi tecnica alla storia dell'arte,* ed. H. W. van Os and J.R.J. van Asperen de Boer, Atti del XXIV Congresso Internazionale di Storia dell'Arte, III, 253–82. Bologna, 1983.

Smalley, B. *The Study of the Bible in the Middle Ages*. 3d ed. Oxford, 1983.

Southard, E. C. *The Frescoes in Siena's Palazzo Pubblico, 1289–1539: A Study in Imagery and Relations to Other Communal Palaces in Tuscany* (Ph.D. dissertation, Indiana University, 1978). New York, 1979.

———. "Simone Martini's Lost *Marcus Regulus:* A Document Rediscovered and a Subject Clarified." *Zeitschrift für Kunstgeschichte,* XLII, 1979, 217–19.

Spuler, B. *History of the Mongols Based on Eastern and Western Accounts of the Thirteenth and Fourteenth Centuries*. Berkeley and Los Angeles, 1972.

Starn, R., and L. Partridge. *Arts of Power: Three Halls of State in Italy, 1300–1600*. Berkeley and Los Angeles, 1992.

Steenberghen, F. van. *Aristotle in the West*. Louvain, 1970.

———. *Thomas Aquinas and Radical Aristotelianism*. Washington, D.C., 1980.

Stopani, R. *La Via Francigena in Toscana*. Florence, 1984.

Stubblebine, James. "Duccio and His Collaborators on the Cathedral *Maestà*." *Art Bulletin,* LV, 1973, 185–204.

———. *Duccio di Buoninsegna and His School*. 2 vols. Princeton, 1979.

———. *Guido da Siena*. Princeton, 1964.

Sumption, J. *The Albigensian Crusade*. London, 1978.

Tachau, K. *Vision and Certitude in the Age of Ockham: Optics, Epistemology, and the Foundation of Semantics*. Leiden, 1988.

Tatarkiewicz, W. *History of Aesthetics*. 3 vols. The Hague, 1970–74.

Thorndike, L. *A History of Magic and Experimental Science.* Vol. II: New York, 1929; vol. III: New York, 1934.

Tierney, B. *The Origins of Papal Infallibility, 1150–1350: A Study on the Concepts of Infallibility, Sovereignty, and Tradition in the Middle Ages.* Leiden, 1972.

Tillmann, H. *Pope Innocent III.* Amsterdam, New York, and Oxford, 1980.

Tintori, L. " 'Golden Tin' in Sienese Murals of the Early Trecento." *Burlington Magazine,* CXXIV, 1982, 94–95.

———. "Segnalazioni sul costante progresso tecnico nelle pitture murali di Simone Martini." In *Tecnica e stile: Esempi di pittura murali del Rinascimento italiano,* ed. E. Borsook and F. Superbi Gioffredi, 11–16. Florence, 1986.

Tintori, L., and Millard Meiss. "Additional Observations on Italian Mural Technique." *Art Bulletin,* XLVI, 1964, 377–80.

———. *The Painting of "The Life of St. Francis" in Assisi.* New York, 1962.

Toker, F. "Gothic Architecture by Remote Control: An Illustrated Building Contract of 1340." *Art Bulletin,* LXVII, 1985, 67–95.

Tommasi, Giugurta. *Dell'historie di Siena.* 2 vols. in 1. Venice, 1625–26 (reprint: Bologna, 1973).

Torriti, P. *La Pinacoteca Nazionale di Siena: I dipinti dal XII al XV secolo.* Genoa, 1977.

Trachtenberg, Marvin. *Dominion of the Eye: Urbanism, Art, and Power in Early Modern Florence.* Cambridge, 1997.

Trexler, R. "Florentine Religious Experience: The Sacred Image." *Studies in the Renaissance,* XIX, 1973, 7–40.

Trombelli, G. C., ed. *Ordo officiorum ecclesiae Senensis.* Bologna, 1766.

Tronzo, W. "Between Icon and Monumental Decoration of a Church: Notes on Duccio's *Maestà* and the Definition of the Altarpiece." In *Icon,* ed. G. Vikan, 36–47. Washington, D.C., 1988.

———, ed. *Italian Church Decoration of the Middle Ages and Early Renaissance.* Bologna, 1989.

Ullmann, W. *Medieval Papalism: The Political Theories of the Medieval Canonists.* London, 1949.

Urso, G. D. *Beato Ambrogio Sansedoni, 1220–1287.* Siena, 1986.

van der Ploeg, K. *Art, Architecture, and Liturgy: Siena Cathedral in the Middle Ages.* Groningen, 1993.

van Os, H. W. *Sienese Altarpieces, 1215–1460: Form, Content, Function.* 2 vols. Groningen, 1984–90.

Varanini, G., ed., *Cantari religiosi senesi del trecento.* Bari, 1965.

Vauchez, A. "La commune de Sienne, les ordres mendiants et le culte des saints: Histoire et enseignements d'une crise, novembre 1328–avril 1329." *Mélanges de l'école française de Rome: Moyen Âge—temps modernes,* LXXXIX, 1977, 757–67.

Vaughan, R., trans. and ed. *Chronicles of Matthew Paris: Monastic Life in the Thirteenth Century.* Gloucester and New York, 1984.

Vescovini, G. F. *Studi sulla prospettiva medievale.* Turin, 1965.

von Schlosser, J., ed. *Lorenzo Ghibertis Denkwürdigkeiten (I Commentarii).* Berlin, 1912

Vikan, G., ed. *Icon.* Washington, 1988.

Wackernagel, M. *The World of the Florentine Renaissance Artist: Projects and Patrons, Workshop and the Art Market.* Trans. A. Luchs. Princeton, 1981.

Wainwright, V. "The Will of Ambrogio Lorenzetti." *Burlington Magazine,* CXVII, 1975, 543–44.

Waley, Daniel. *The Italian City-Republics.* 3d ed. Harlow, Essex, 1988.

———. *The Papal State in the Thirteenth Century.* London, 1961.

———. *Siena and the Sienese in the Thirteenth Century.* Cambridge, 1991.

Watt, J. A. *The Theory of Papal Monarchy in the Thirteenth Century: The Contributions of the Canonists.* New York, 1965.

White, John. *The Birth and Rebirth of Pictorial Space.* 3d ed. Cambridge, Mass., 1987.

———. "Carpentry and Design in Duccio's Workshop." *Journal of the Warburg and Courtauld Institutes,* XXXVI, 1970, 92–105.

———. *Duccio: Tuscan Art and the Medieval Workshop.* London, 1979.

———. "Measurement, Design, and Carpentry in Duccio's Maestà." *Art Bulletin,* LV, 1973, 332–66, 547–69.

Wood, F. *Did Marco Polo Go to China?* London, 1995.

Yule, Sir Henry. *Cathay and the Way Thither.* 4 vols. London, 1913–16 (reprint: Wiesbaden, 1967).

Zanardi, Bruno. *Il cantiere di Giotto: Le storie di San Francesco ad Assisi.* Milan, 1996.

Zdekauer, L. *Il mercante senese nel dugento.* Siena, 1925.

———. "Opere d'arte senese nella chiesa di San Giovanni Fuorcivitas di Pistoia." *BSSP,* VIII, 1901, 176–77.

———. "Le spese di selciatura e di riparazione della via di Malcucinato (1334)." *BSSP,* III, 1896, 402–5.

———. "Statuti criminali del foro ecclesiastico di Siena (sec. XIII–XIV)." *BSSP,* VII, 1900, 231–64.

———. *La vita privata dei senesi nel dugento.* Siena, 1896 (reprint: Bologna, 1964).

———. *La vita pubblica dei senesi nel dugento.* Siena, 1897 (reprint: Bologna, 1967).

———, ed. *Il constituto del comune di Siena dell'anno 1262.* Milan, 1897.

Zeri, F. "Pietro Lorenzetti: Quattro panelli della pala del 1329 al Carmine." *Arte illustrata,* LVIII, 1974, 146–56.

INDEX: GENERAL

This index contains the names of Sienese artists. When an artist is not Sienese, his place of origin is signaled.

Acre, 20
Acta Sanctorum, 166
Agarazzi, Filippo, Fra, 167, 169
Agnola di Donato (daughter of Donato Martini), 58
Agnolo (painter), 225
Agnolo (Angelo) di Nalduccio (painter), 226, 243
Agnolo di Tura, chronicle, 10, 50, 50 n. 21, 63 n. 93, 125 n. 21, 127 n. 32, 129, 136–37
Agostino, Fra, 31 n. 51
Agostino di Giovanni, 69–70
Agostino Novello, Beato, 25–26, 31, 31 n. 50, 34, 69, **Color Plates 7–8, Figs. 14, 63**
Agostini, Domenico, 144 n. 131
Aiuti, Bonaventura, 132
Alberti, Leon Battista, 182
Albizzeschi, family, 51
Aldobrandeschi, family, 26
Alexander III, Pope (1159–81), 4, 138 n. 102
Alexander VII, Pope (1655–67), 66 n. 116
Alhazen, 176, 182–83; *De aspectibus* (*Perspectiva*), 176
Altomonte, Museo di S. Maria della Consolazione: Simone Martini, *Saint Ladislas of Hungary*, 109, 115
Ambrogio di Duccio (painter, likely the son of Duccio di Buoninsegna), 46, 49 n. 13, 142, 144 n. 131, 228, 243
Ambrogio "dipentore in champoreggi" (painter), 243
Andelo (painter), 243
Andrea (painter), 131, 243, 282
Andrea da Siena, 156
Andrea di Bonaiuto (painter, Florentine), 52

Andrea di Cecco di Martino (wife of Romano di Mino), 47, 271
Andrea di Franciescho (painter), 243
Andrea di Guido (painter), 243
Andrea di Turino (painter), 243
Andrea Pisano (sculptor, Pisan), 110, **Fig. 73**
Andreino (painter), 244
Andrernus (painter), 244
Angelo di Conociuto (painter), 244, 254
Angevins of Naples, 4, 19, 66, 66 n. 135, 68, 82, 148, 155
Angnolino di Gintile (painter), 244
Ansano, San, 31, 35, 35 n. 73, 36 n. 78, 37, 69
Ansedonia, 124, 124 n. 13
Antal, Frederick, *Florentine Painting and Its Social Background*, 11
Antonio (painter), 244
Antonio Dietisalvi (painter), 244
Antonio di Giovanni (painter), 53 n. 34, 244
Arcidosso, 124
Arezzo, 10, 12, 35–36, 55, 155
  Museo Statale di Arte Medievale e Moderna: replica of the San Bernardino *Madonna*, 152, **Fig. 9**
  Santa Maria della Pieve: Pietro Lorenzetti, Arezzo polyptych, 62, 70–72, 98 n. 44, 102 n. 63, 105, 107, 130, 153, 171, **Color Plates 13–14**
Aristotle, xx, 2–3, 174, 177, 185, 188
  Libri naturales, 3, 188
Arnold of Villanova, 163
Arras, synod of, 162
Arnolfo di Cambio (sculptor/architect, Florentine), 184
Asciano, San Francesco: Simone Martini follower, *Madonna and Child Enthroned*, 154

Assisi, 1, 11, San Francesco
  Lower Church, 14: followers of Giotto, Infancy Cycle, 108, 113; Pietro Lorenzetti, Passion Cycle, 88, 94 n. 35, 95, 108, 113 n. 89, 153, 178, 189, **Figs. 39–44**; Simone Martini, Chapel of Saint Martin, 26, 95, 115–16, 176, 181, **Figs. 47–50, 78**
  Upper Church: Roman School, *Saint Francis Legend*, 91 n. 24, 115, 118, 180, 187
Averroës, 2, 176
Avignon, 2, 5, 14, 51, 58 n. 60, 77, 91–92, 155, 198, 251

Bacci, P. 241
Bacon, Roger, 163, 174, 176–77, 179–81, 179 n. 79, 183 n. 99, 188
Balduccio di Dino (painter), 244, 280
Bandinelli, family, 160 n. 233
Barna Bertini (painter), 244
Barnaba di Donato (son of Donato Martini), 58
Baroncelli, Gherardo, drawing for a chapel of, in Santa Croce, Florence, 114
Baroncelli, Tano, drawing for a chapel of, in Santa Croce, Florence, 114
Barthalomea (wife of Lando di Vanuccio), 260
Bartholomew, Master, 165, 169
Bartolo di Fredi (painter), 60, 60 n. 82, 89, 226
Bartolomeo, Saint, 36, 36 n. 77
Bartolomeo di Mino, Fra, 31 n. 51
Bartolomeo di Vanni (painter), 244, 282
Bartolommeo da Siena, Fra, 20
Bataxe (painter), 245
Beccha di Tano (wife of Guido di Nerio), 258
Belting, H., 165, 168

Benciarini, Gura, 129
Benvoglienti, U., 124, 242
Berenson, B., 112
Berlin, Staatliche Museen Preussischer Kulturbesitz: Gemäldegalerie: Sienese Straus Master, *Annunciation*, 109, **Fig. 91**; Ugolino di Nerio, 131; *Saints Paul and John the Baptist*, **Fig. 13**
Bernone di Monforte, 131, 243
Betti, Andrea, Fra, 127
Biagio di Goro (painter), 76, 226, 245
Biagio di Masarello, 47, 227
Bibbiano Giulieschi, 55
Bindi, Piastra (painter), 156
Bindo (painter), 49 n. 12, 228, 245
Bindo, Messer (notary), 146, 196
Bindo, Paolo (carpenter?), 141
Bindo, Ser ("scrittore"), 113 n. 90, 126, 126 n. 31
Bindo di Cecco (painter), 245
Bindo di Dietisalvi (painter), 246
Bindotto di Cecco, 134 n. 78
Birmingham, Barber Institute of Fine Art: Simone Martini, *Saint John the Evangelist*, 109, **Fig. 70**
Blasio (painter), 246, 286
Blasius Marinelli (painter), 246
Blaxius (painter), 246
Boccaccio, 6, 10, 45, 80 n. 199; *Amorosa visione*, 175; *Decameron*, 80 n. 199, 186
Bologna, 39; university of, 25
Bonaccorso (painter), 143, 246
Bonaccorso di Pace (painter), 61, 80 n. 198, 151 n. 182, 226, 246, 246 n. 21
Bonaventura(?) (painter), 247
Bonaventura di Viva de' Mocali, 56
Bonaventure, Saint, 122, 168, 187; *Legenda maior* (of Saint Francis), 187; *Soul's Journey into God*, 122; *Tree of Life*, 187
Bonfigli, Coltino (*operaio*), 127, 159–60
Boniface VIII, Pope (1294–1303), 1, 38, 163–64; statue of, 184
Bonsignori, family, 20–21, 21 n. 17, 28
Borgo San Sepolcro, cathedral: close to Niccolò di Segna, *Resurrection* polyptych, 106–7, **Fig. 61**
Boston, Museum of Fine Arts: Duccio workshop, triptych, 109, 148
Bowsky, W., 23, 231
Brandino di Ser Cieio (painter), 198, 247
Braun, Joseph, 168
bricks, 70, 173
Bridget of Sweden, Saint, 168
Brunelleschi F. (sculptor and architect, Florentine), 182
Bulgarini, family, 78; Bulgarino di Simone, 78; Gheri di Simone, 78, 89 n. 19; Simone di Bulgarino, 78 n. 194; Simone di Gheri Bulgarini, 132 n. 62
Bulgarini, Bartolommeo (painter), 14, 28, 76, 78–80 n. 194, 89 n. 19, 91–92, 132 n. 62, 139, 144, 154, 171, 191, 198, 276, 284–85
Buona, Monna (wife of Niccholuccio), 266
Buonconvento, 55–56
Byzantium, 121, 174

Cambridge (Mass.), Harvard University, Fogg Art Museum: Simone Martini, *Crucified Christ*, 109, **Fig. 68**; Bartolommeo Bulgarini, *Nativity*, 139, **Fig. 27**
Campuglia, Bono (*operaio*), 127, 127 n. 34, 131, 133, 158, 250, 252, 252 n. 43
Carlo of Calabria, Duke, 66, 68, 68 n. 135, 133, 244, 262, 266
cartoons, 188 n. 114
Casciano Alta (Pisa), San Niccolò: Lippo Memmi, polyptych, 154
Castel del Piano, 124
Castelnuovo Berardenga, *badia*, 12
Castiglion Fiorentino, Collegiata di San Giuliano, 12; Segna di Bonaventura, *Madonna and Child Enthroned with Saints and Angels*, 153, **Fig. 13**
Caterina di Donato Martini (daughter of Donato Martini, wife of Giovanni di Sera), 47, 58, 60, 255, 255 n. 51
Catherine of Siena, Saint, 44, 122, 168
Cavalcanti, Guido, 175
Cecchino (painter), 128, 247
Cecco (painter), 247
Cecco d'Ascoli, 163–64; *Commentary on the Sphere*, 163–64
Cecco di Goro (painter), 247
Cecco di Martino (painter), 226, 247
Cecco di Puccio (painter), 59, 227, 247, 266 n. 86, 280
Cecco di Tuccio (?) (painter), 247
Cecco di Vanni (painter), 229, 247
Cechus de Bozoli (painter), 247
Celano, Thomas, 167
Cennini, Cennino d'Andrea (painter, Florentine), 80, 80 n. 199, 92, 96, 96 nn. 38–39, 97 n. 43, 100 n. 53, 109, 146 n. 152, 178
Cerchi, Umiliana, Beata, 165–66, 175
Chantilly, Musée Condé, F.R.I.1: drawing after frescoes in the Lower Church of San Francesco, Assisi, 113, 113 n. 89
Charles I, King of Naples, 4, 19
Chele di Vanni (painter), 248

Chello (carpenter), 131, 247
Cherubini, G., 55
Chiavelli, Biagio (*operaio*), 159
China, 98
Christofano del Maestro Bindoccio (painter), 248, 253
Cicerchia, Giovanna di Mino (wife of Pietro Lorenzetti), 55, 79; Mino, 79; Niccolò di Mino, 70, 79 n. 195
Ciecco, 131
Ciecho de la grammatica, Maestro, 141
clocks, 6
Cientti di Mino (painter), 248, 280
Cimabue, Giovanni (painter, Florentine), 9
Cinatti, Guido (painter), 59, 73–75, 194, 197, **Fig. 23**
Ciono di Franco, 171
Clement IV, Pope (1265–68), 5, 177
Clement V, Pope (1305–14), 5
Clement VI, Pope (1342–52), 77
Cleveland, Cleveland Museum of Art: Ugolino di Nerio, polyptych, 105, **Fig. 57**
Cola di Fuccio (miniaturist), 145, 145 n. 138, 151, 187 n. 111, 229, 245, 245 n. 17, 248
Cola di Tino di Camaino, 47, 55, 79
Colle Val d'Elsa, 22, 149, 149 n. 166, 152, 154; San Francesco (ex), 152, 154
Collecchi, 60
Colombini, Giovanni, Beato, 35
Conradin, 4
contracts, 11, 62–63, 114
Copenhagen, Statens Museum for Kunst: Master of Palazzo Venezia, *Saints Corona and Vittorio*, 139, **Figs. 28–29**
Coppo di Marcovaldo (painter, Florentine), 85
Cortona, 11; Museo Diocesano: Pietro Lorenzetti, cut-away crucifix, 153; crucifix, 153, **Fig. 102**; *Madonna and Child Enthroned*, 153
Cosone (painter), 248, 257
Cosone di Cello (painter), 226, 248
Crescenzio, San, 35–36, 36 nn. 75, 77–78
Crete, 169
Crevole, Santa Cecilia, 149 n. 166
Cristofano (painter), 144 n. 131, 248
Cristofano di Cosa (painter), 248
Cristofano di Cosone (painter), 249
Cristofano di Muccio (painter), 60, 231, 249
Cristofano di Stefano (painter), 249, 261
Cristofano di Tura (painter), 249
Curia del Placito, 22, 263
Cyprus, 169

Daddi, Bernardo (painter, Florentine), 149, 169
Dante, 6, 10, 45, 81; *Convivio*, 81, 178–79; *De monarchia*, 81; *Divine Comedy*, 175, 178, 186; *Vita nuova*, 116, 186
Datini, Marco, 119 n. 1
Dei, Andrea, 50
Derbes, A., 176
Dietavive, Ser Bindo (miniaturist), 49 n. 13, 228, 246
Dietisalvi (painter), 77, 125, 226, 249, 278
Domenicho di Buonachorso (painter), 250
Domenico d'Agostino, 113 n. 94
Domenico di Bartolo (painter), 64 n. 99, 144
Domenico Orlandi (painter), 47, 131
Donato (painter), 250
Duccio (carpenter), 140
Duccio di Buoninsegna (painter), 1, 4, 5–6, 12–14, 45–46, 47 n. 3, 49, 49 n. 14, 50, 50 nn. 20–21, 53–54, 59–60, 62–63, 63 nn. 88–89, 92–93, 64, 66, 70–71, 76–77, 88, 88 n. 14, 95, 95 n. 36, 96–97, 99–100, 102–5, 109, 115, 125, 138, 148–49, 152–53, 155, 157, 178, 181, 185 n. 105, 189, 191, 193, 195, 197, 225–26, 228, 278–79, 278 nn. 9, 15, 279 n. 21, **Color Plates 1–2, 10–11, Figs. 10–11, 15–16, 52–53, 56, 64, 80, 86**
Duccio di Donato (goldsmith), 68, 127
Durandus, William, 81, 162

Emilia d'Elci, 38, 150
English, E., 21
eyeglasses, 7, 110–11, 186

Faluschi, G., 146
Fazio di Dietisalvi (painter), 47, 77, 226, 251
Fede di Nalduccio (painter), 60, 91 n. 25, 134 n. 78, 227, 245, 251, 251 n. 34
Feuccio (carpenter?), 141
Fides (painter), 251 n. 37
Filippo, Prince of Taranto, 66, 272
Filippo Vannis (painter), 251
Fina Jacomi (painter), 252
financial crisis, bankers, 21
Fino da Siena (painter), 156
Fioretti, 166
Florence, 6–7, 9, 11–12, 16, 39, 102, miraculous images of, 165–66
  Accademia: Circle of the San Bernardino Master, *Madonna and Child Enthroned*, 90, 115, **Fig. 79**

Arte dei Medici e Speziali, 86, 153, 195
Arte della Mercanzia, 89 n. 17
Bargello, 124
Biblioteca Nazionale: MS B.R.55, Geoffrey of Monmouth, *Historiae Regnum Brittaniae*, 112
Bue, *popolo*, 52
Fortezza di Basso: Ambrogio Lorenzetti, the Vico l'Abate *Madonna* (1319), 153, **Fig. 103**
Galleria degli Uffizi: Duccio di Buoninsegna, the Rucellai *Madonna*, 12, 62, 62 n. 87, 71, 97, 99–100, 102, 106, 152, 155, 195, **Figs. 10–11**; Ambrogio Lorenzetti, *Madonna and Child with Saints Nicholas and Proculus*, 153, 178–79, 189, **Fig. 104**; *Presentation of Christ in the Temple* (the San Crescenzio altarpiece), 66, 72–73, 73 n. 158, 100, 108, 108 n. 72, 139, 141, 156, 179, 182, **Figs. 21–22**; *Scenes from the Life of Saint Nicholas of Bari*, 153, 178–79, 189, **Figs. 105–8**; Giotto, the Ognissanti *Madonna*, 106; Taddeo Gaddi, *Madonna and Child Enthroned* (1355), 103 n. 64; the Saint Nicholas Master, the Badia polyptych, 106, **Fig. 58**; Pietro Lorenzetti, *Madonna and Child Enthroned* (1340), 66, 100, 107, 154, **Fig. 54**; Simone Martini and Lippo Memmi, *Annunciation* (the San Ansano altarpiece) (1333), 70 n. 154, 71–73, 98–99, 102, 115, 139–40, 157–58, 178, **Color Plate 9, Figs. 17–20**
Museo dell'Opera del Duomo: Arnolfo di Cambio, *Boniface VIII*, 184
Museo Horne: Pietro Lorenzetti, *Saint Catherine of Alexandria*, 103, **Fig. 55**
Hospital of the Scala: Ambrogio Lorenzetti, *Annunciate* (lost), 147
Orsanmichele, 165, 169
Sant'Agostino, chapter house: Ambrogio Lorenzetti, decorations (lost), 153
Sant'Ambrogio (parish), 52
Santissima Annunziata (church), 122, 165–66, 169
Santa Croce, 13, 52; Ugolino di Nerio, polyptych, 100, 105–6, 154, **Fig. 13**
  Bardi Chapel, 13; Ugolino di Nerio, altarpiece, 154
  Bardi di Vernio Chapel: Bartolommeo Bulgarini, polyptych, 78, 154
  Baroncelli Chapel: Giotto and workshop, Baroncelli *Coronation of the Virgin*, 106; Taddeo Gaddi, Scenes from the Life of the Virgin (frescoes), 112; Sienese, drawing for the chapel, 114
  Peruzzi Chapel, 180
San Giovanni, *quartiere*, 53
San Lorenzo (church), 53
San Lorenzo (parish), 52, 52 n. 31
Santa Maria del Fiore (cathedral), 80, 137
  campanile, 113 n. 94; Andrea Pisano, *Painting*, 110, **Fig. 73**
  facade, 184
Santa Maria del Fiore (parish), 52
Santa Maria Novella (church), 12, 53, 62, 106, 110, 166
  Ugolino di Nerio, high altarpiece (lost), 154
  Confraternity of the Laudesi, 62, 155, 171
  Strozzi Chapel, Orcagna, Strozzi altarpiece (1357), 142
Santa Maria Novella (parish), 52, 52 n. 31
San Michele Visdomini (church), 53
San Michele Visdomini (parish), 52, 52 n. 31
San Pier Maggiore (parish), 52
San Procolo: Ambrogio Lorenzetti, *Virgin and Child with Saints Nicholas and Proculus*, 153, **Fig. 104**; Scenes from the Life of Saint Nicholas of Bari, 153, **Figs. 105–8**
Via de' Pucci, 53
Via del Giglio, 53
Via Gori, 53
Fourth Lateran Council (1215), 4
Francesco (painter), 143, 252, 282
Francesco da Carrara, 171
Francesco di Cialli (painter, Florentine), 89 n. 17, 268, 272
Francesco di Nerio (painter), 57–58, 57 n. 58, 228, 252
Francesco di Piero (painter), 252
Francesco di Segna (painter), 60, 252
Francesco di Simone (painter), 227, 252
Francesco del Tonghio, 136 n. 91
Francesco di Vannuccio (painter), 252–53, 253 n. 44, 284
Franciescho di Mano (painter), 253
Franciescho di Vanni (painter), 227, 253
Franciescho di Vanni, "detto Chiancianese" (painter) 85, 353
Francio (painter), 253
Francis of Assisi, Saint, 1–2, 5–6, 122, 166–67, 174
Frederick Barbarossa, Holy Roman Emperor, 18
Frederick II of Hohenstaufen, Holy Roman Emperor, 4
fresco technique, 94–95

Gabriello di Mino, 80
Gaddi, Agnolo (painter, Florentine), 52
Gaddi, Taddeo (painter, Florentine), 52, 103 n. 64, 112, 171, 186 n. 106
Galen, 176
Galgano di Duccio (painter), 46–47, 60, 226, 253
Galgano di maestro Minuccio (Gano di maestro Minnuccio?) (painter), 253
Gallerani, family, 20–21, 28, 51
Gallerani, Andrea, Beato, 33–34, 40, 84 n. 1, 93, 151–52, 170
Gallerani, Bernardo, Bishop, 152
Gano del maestro Minnuccio (Galgano di maestro Minnuccio?) (painter), 143
Gano di Orlando (painter), 225, 253
Gardner von Teuffel, C., 141
Gentile da Montefiore, Cardinal, 176
Geoffry of Vinsauf, *Poetria nova*, 180 n. 87
Gerard of Wales, 165
Gervase of Tilbury, 165
Gherardo da Parma, 25
Ghezi, Nuto, 139 n. 94
Ghezzo (painter), 253, 276, 279
Ghezzo bendaio (painter), 254
Ghezzo Buonfigliuoli detto Bitatto (painter), 254
Ghiberti, Lorenzo (sculptor, Florentine), 9, 13, 108, 132, 136 n. 96, 147, 198
Ghuccio (painter), 278
Giacommuccio, 225,
Giacomo di Pietro, 227
Giacomuccio di Conociuto (painter), 254
Gilio, 47, 77
Giordano da Pisa, Fra, 76 n. 182, 110, 131 n. 55, 166, 185–86
Giorgio di Duccio (painter), 47, 254
Giotto di Bondone (painter, Florentine), 9–10, 52, 80–82, 95, 113 n. 94, 115 n. 99, 171, 174, 180
Giotto di Buondone (Sienese), 160 n. 233
Giovacchino Senese, Beato, 31, 31 n. 50
Giovanna (wife of Donato Martini), 251
Giovanna di Donato (wife of Jacomo di Cino), 260
Giovanni (painter), 254, 276, 285–86
Giovanni da Milano (painter, Milanese/Florentine), 52, 118
Giovanni del Biondo (painter, Florentine), 52
Giovanni d'Agostino, 114
Giovanni di Benedetto (painter), 254

Giovanni di Donato (son of Donato Martini), 58
Giovanni di Goro (carpenter), 139 n. 104
Giovanni di Guido (miniaturist), 254
Giovanni di Guido (*operaio* of the commune), 265 n. 55
Giovanni di Paolo (painter), 198, 227, 255
Giovanni da Pisa, 85
Giovanni di Sera (painter), 47, 60, 75, 255, 255 n. 52, 285–86
Giovanni di Vitalera (painter), 256
Giovanni Pisano, 17, 113 n. 91, 184
Giovannino di Neri, 74
Giuncarico, 124
Giunta Pisano (painter, Pisan), 12
Giusaffa di Filippo (painter), 256
Glarentsa, 20
Gombrich, E., 189
Gratian, *Decretum*, 5
Gregory I, Pope (590–604), 162–63, 168
Gregory VII, Pope (1075–85), 4
Gregory IX, Pope (1227–41), 5, 20, 163
Grosseteste, Robert, 163, 177
Grosseto, 12; Museo Diocesano: "Guidesque" *Last Judgment*, 152
Guarnieri di Graziano (painter), 225
Guccio (painter), 256
Guccio di Mannaia (goldsmith), 68, 151
Guido (painter), 65, 75, 77, 89, 125, 127 n. 38, 133–34, 143, 241, 256–57, 279, 281–84 (more than one painter)
Guido Cinatti (painter), 241, 257, 276–77, 281–83, 286, **Fig. 23**
Guido da Siena (painter), 12, 90, 98, 115, 149, 152, **Figs. 7, 32**
Guido di Cenni (painter), 257
Guido di Cino (painter), 75 n. 178, 89 n. 20, 156, 227, 257, 280, 286
Guido di Ghezzo (painter), 59, 156, 225, 228, 233, 238, 257, 267
Guido di Graziano (painter), 225, (Guidone di Graziano), 258
Guido di Nerio (painter), 56, 86, 226, 231, 258
Guido Tinacci (painter), 258
Guidone di Jacopo (painter), 227, 258
Guidoni (painter), 125, 130, 133, 258–59, 278
Guidono (carpenter), 140
Guidoriccio da Fogliano, 66, 69, 244, 246, 255,
Guiduccio di Mino (painter), 258

halo design, 99
heresy, 30
Hippolytus, Fra, 165 n. 18

Hohenstaufen, family, 22
Honorius III, Pope (1216–27), 163
Honorius IV, Pope (1285–87), 20
Horace, 82
Hugues de St. Cher, Cardinal, 110

Iacoba filia olim benini (wife of Nutino di Piovano), 267
images, ex-voto, 166, 170
Impruneta, 165
Innocent III, Pope (1198–1216), 1, 4–5, 19, 154 n. 189, 165
Innocent IV, Pope (1243–54), 5, 20
Innocent V, Pope (1353–62), 5
Insegnia (painter), 279–80
Iohanna magistri Buondi (wife of Galgano di Duccio), 253

Jacobo (painter), 259
Jacobuccio (painter), 259
Jacobuone, 125
Jacobus de Voragine, *Golden Legend*, 188
Jacomino (painter), 259
Jacomo, 227
Jacomo de' Silevana, Count, 146, 196
Jacomo di Bindo (painter), 226, 259, 283
Jacomo di Cino (painter), 76, 143 n. 128, 227, 260
Jacomo di Frate Mino (Jacopo di Mino?), 259
Jacomo di Piero (painter), 260
Jacomuccio (painter), 225, 260
Jacopo di Cione (painter, Florentine), 52
Jacopo di Mino (Jacomo di Frate Mino?) (painter), 145
Jacopo di Mino del Pelliciaio (painter), 171, *Coronation of Saint Catherine of Alexandria*, **Fig. 99**
Jacopo di Vanni Ugolini, 69
Jacopone da Todi, Fra, 186
John XXII, Pope (1316–36), 5, 39, 164
John Duns Scotus, xx
John of Genoa, *Catholicon*, 162
Justinian, Emperor, *Corpus juris civilis*, 5, 43, 82, 176, 186 n. 108

Ladis, A., 112
Lando (painter), 260
Lando di Domenico (painter), 260
Lando di Pietro (architect), 69, 113 n. 90, 245
Lando di Stefano (painter), 91 n. 25, 260
Lando di Vinuccio (painter), 60, 228, 260
Lapa (wife of Antonio Dietisalvi), 244
Lecceto, 167

Leonardo da Vinci, 9
Letter of the Three Patriarchs, 169
Liber Sextus (decretals), 35
Lini, Segna (*operaio*): (Sengia Lini), 73 n. 158; (Segna di Lino) 158; (Segnia lini) 160 n. 233
Lisini, A., 53, 53 n. 35, 54
Liverpool, Walker Art Gallery: Simone Martini, *Holy Family*, 109, **Fig. 69**
Lolo (*zendadaio*), 133
London, National Gallery: Duccio, *Healing of a Man Born Blind*, 181, **Fig. 15**; Duccio, the London Triptych, 109; Pietro Lorenzetti, *Saint Sabinus Before the Governor*, 141 n. 112
Lorenzetti, Ambrogio (painter), 13–14, 25, 29, 39, 45, 47–48, 48 n. 8, 49, 54–55, 64–66, 69, 72–73, 77–79, 86, 92, 95, 97, 99–100, 108, 115–16, 129–31, 136 n. 96, 139, 141–42, 144, 144 n. 131, 145–46, 149–50, 153, 156, 158–60, 178, 181–83, 189, 191–96, 198, **Color Plates 5–6, 15, Figs. 21–22, 62, 81, 89–90, 103–8**
Lorenzetti, Pietro (painter), 10, 13–14, 36, 39, 47–49, 55, 55 n. 44, 62, 62 n. 87, 64, 66, 70–72, 77–78, 79 n. 196, 88, 94 n. 35, 95, 96 n. 40, 97, 98 n. 44, 99–100, 105–7, 115–16, 130, 139–42, 146, 148–50, 153–55, 171, 182, 189, 192–93, 198, **Color Plates 13–14, Figs. 30, 39–46, 54–55, 59–60, 82, 102**
Lorenzo di Vanni (painter), 260
Lorino (painter), 261
Louis IX, Saint, 4, 20
Lotti, Berto, 145 n. 137, 156
Luca di Tommè (painter), 92, 136 n. 95, **Fig. 35**
Lutinus Piovani (painter), 261

Macchi, G., 32, 146–47
Macerato, baths of, 24, 89, 132–33, 250
Maffei, Domenico, 250
Magdalena di Cecco di Nuccio (wife of Bonaccorso di Pace), 246
Magine di Midule (painter), 261
Maitani, Lorenzo (architect/sculptor), 171
Malavolti, family, 21, 28, 34, 38, 51, 51 n. 23
Malavolti, Donodeus, Bishop of Siena, 38, 38 n. 85, 39, 39 n. 87, 104, 150, 196
Malavolti, Rinaldo, Bishop of Siena, 38, 136 n. 91, 196
Malavolti, Niccolò, 38
Mandylion of Edessa, 169
Manucci, Bindo, 127 n. 37

Margherita di Ambrogio Salvi (wife of Paolo di Neri), 268
Margherita di Tino di Camaino (wife of Pietro di Ser Dota), 47
Mariscotti, Ser Jacopo di Gilberti (*operaio*), 60
Martin of Tours, Saint, 116
Martindale, A., 58
Martino di Ser Vanni (painter), 261
Martino di Tino di Camaino, 47, 55, 79
Marsilius of Padua, 3, 183, 185, *Defensor pacis*, 3, 185
Martini, Donato (painter), 47, 51 n. 28, 58, 61, 77, 89, 132 n. 62, 133, 133 n. 73, 191, 226, 229, 251, 255
Martini, Simone (carpenter), 241
Martini, Simone (painter), 10, 13–14, 25, 39, 46, 48, 51, 51 n. 28, 54–55, 57–58, 60, 64–66, 70, 70 n. 154, 71–73, 73 n. 158, 77–82, 90 n. 93, 91–92, 94–95, 95 n. 36, 98–99, 99 n. 49, 102–3, 108, 111, 115–16, 122, 124–29, 129 n. 50, 130, 132, 133 n. 73, 136 n. 96, 138–40, 145–46, 148–49, 153–56, 159, 174, 176, 178, 181, 191–92, 195, 197–98, 226–27, 229, 231, 241, 276, **Color Plates 3–4, 12, 16, Figs. 14, 17–20, 36–38, 47–50, 63, 68–70, 78**
Masaccio (painter, Florentine), 182
Masarello (painter), 66, 125 n. 23, 133, 279
Masarello di Gilio (painter), 47, 53, 59–60, 225, 227, 259, 261–62, 261 n. 70, 264 n. 80
Massa Marittima, 115; Ambrogio Lorenzetti, *Maestà*, 153; Duomo, 270; Ducciesque *Maestà*, 115, **Fig. 80**
Master of the Loeser Madonna (painter), 92, 148, 151, **Fig. 95**
Master of Palazzo Venezia (painter), 78, 91–92, 139, 145, **Figs. 28, 29, 93**
Matteo (painter), 262
Matteo di Mino (painter), 227, 262
Matthew Paris, 164–65
Mauvoison, Robert, Archbishop of Aix, 164
Meditations on the Life of Christ, 175, 189–90
Meiss, M., 112, 115, 115 n. 99, 117, 121–22
Meliore da Toscana (painter, Tuscan), 104
Memmo di Filippuccio (painter), 47, 53, 57, 57 nn. 54–55, 57, 225, 227, 231, 233, 264
Memmi, Federigo (painter), 47, 51 n. 28, 57, 91–92, 131, 145, 145 n. 137, 159, 251

Memmi, Giovanna (wife of Simone Martini), 47, 57–58
Memmi, Lippo (painter), 47, 57–58, 64, 72, 73, 80, 91–92, 95, 102, 131, 139–40, 145, 145 n. 137, 148, 150, 150 n. 168, 154, 159, 191, 197, 276, **Color Plate 9, Figs. 17–20, 95, 98, 100**
Menghi, Ristoro di Giunta, 28
Meo (carpenter), 151 n. 182
Meo da Siena (painter), 105
Meo di Cecco, 143 n. 128
Meo di Guido da Siena, 153, 156
Meo di Mino (carpenter), 131; (as Meo Mini), 243
Meo di Piero (painter), 262
Meuccio, 133
Meuccio di Bernardino (painter), 228, 262
Michael VIII, Byzantine Emperor, 20
Michael Scotus, *Liber introductorius*, 163
Milanesi, G., 53, 85, 241–42
Miniatello (painter), 75–76, 263, 263 n. 73, 282
Mino (painter), 125, 263, 263 n. 74, 279
Mino di Filippuccio (painter), 47, 57, 225, 231, 233, 264; (as Minuccio di Filippuccio?), 134, 264
Mino di Graziano (painter), 89, 225, 263–64, 271
Mino di Voglia (painter), 59, 226, 233, 238, 263, 283
Mino Prete (painter), 89, 89 n. 16, 227, 264, 271
Minuccio (locksmith), 143
Minuccio (painter), 264, 264 n. 77, 283
Minuccio di Mino, 56
Misarello (painter), 264, 264 n. 80
Moccolelli, Chele (*operaio*), 126, 126 n. 25, 157–58, 198 n. 2
Monsindoli, 57, 251
Montamiata, San Salvatore, 26
Monaldo di Palmerio (painter), 59, 226, 239
Montanini, family, 51
Montanini, Biagio, 145, 196
Montaperti, battle of, 22, 170, 198
Montemassi, 124
Monteriggione, 263
Monte Oliveto, 34
Monteano, 60
Montecatini, battle of, 148, 155
Montecchio: Ducciesque *Madonna*, 115, **Fig. 84**
Montecirota, 17
Montefalcone, 101
Montesiepi, Chapel of San Galgano: Ambrogio Lorenzetti, frescoes, 153
Montalcino, 248

Montieri, 17
Muccio (carpenter?), 141
Muccio di Nerio (painter), 56, 226, 231, 234–35
Muller, N., 156

Naddo, 74
Nanni di Franciescho (painter), 264
Nanni di Mino (painter), 265
Naples, 13; Museo di Capodimonte: Simone Martini, *Saint Louis of Toulouse*, 98, 181, 195, **Color Plate 16**
Nardo di Cione (painter, Florentine), 52, 171
narrative painting, 189
Nello di Betto (painter), 227, 265
Nelli, Pietro (painter, Florentine), 52
Neri detto Bustorcio del quondam Bandini da Sticciano, 146
Neri di Franciescho di Neri (painter), 265
Nerino di Jacomo (painter), 265
Nerio di Muccio (painter), 56 n. 49, 231, 265
Nerio di Ugolino (painter), 56, 225, 231, 231 n. 6, 241, 265, 265 nn. 83–84
Neruccia di Neri (wife of Sandro di Masarello), 60, 271
New York, Frick Collection: Duccio di Buoninsegna, *Temptation on the Mountain*, 1, 8, 178, 181, 191–92, **Color Plates 1–2**
Metropolitan Museum: Orbit of Ugolino di Nerio, triptych, 109, **Fig. 67**
Pierpont Morgan Library: I.1.B, Florentine drawing after frescoes in the Lower Church of San Francesco, Assisi, 113, 113 n. 89; Circle of Bernardo Daddi, *Martyrdom of Saint Miniato*, 112
Nicchola (painter), 265
Niccholino (painter), 265, 280
Niccholuccio (painter), 89 n. 20, 265, 274, 283
Niccholuccio di Balzanello (painter), 266, 276, 281
Niccholuccio di Masarello (painter), 47, 266, 283
Niccola di Mino (painter), 59, 133, 226, 228, 239, 266
Niccolò di Cecco del Mercia, 113 n. 94
Niccolò di maestro Vannuccio (painter), 266
Niccolò di Segna (painter), 78 n. 194, 89, 89 n. 19, 191–93, 197, 226, 252 n. 41, 266; related to, **Fig. 61**
Niccolò di Ser Sozzo (painter), 14, 79, 92, 198, 266, 266 n. 89, **Fig. 35**

Niccolò di Tommaso (painter, Florentine), 52
Niccolò di Vanni, 267
Nicholas III, Pope (1277–80), 20
Nicholas IV, Pope (1288–92), 20
Nicholas, Saint, 31
Nicholas of Rouen, Cardinal, 110
Nichollelo (painter), 267, 283, 285
Nicodemus, 166
Nuccio (painter), 131, 247
Nuccio di Neruccio (painter), 267
Nuta di Palamede (wife of Franesco di Segna), 252
Nuti, Niccola, 171
Nutino di Piovano (painter) (as Nutino Piovani), 227, 267

Oertel, R., 112
Opicino de Canistris, *Liber de Laudibus civitatis Ticinensis*, 48 n. 10
Orcagna (painter, Florentine), 55, 142, 171
optics, 176–83, 183 nn. 98–99
Orlando di Domenico (painter), 47
Orvieto, 11, 155
Duomo: Ugolino di Vieri, *Reliquary of the Host*, 111 n. 79
Opera del Duomo: drawings for a pulpit in the cathedral, 114; drawings for the facade of the cathedral, 113, 113 n. 92, **Fig. 74**
Ottawa, National Gallery of Canada: Ugolino di Nerio, *Saint Anne and the Virgin*, 147, 153, **Fig. 94**
Oxford, Ashmolean Museum: Sienese Straus Master, *Lamentation*, 109, **Fig. 72**; Sienese Straus Master?, *Madonna and Child*, 109, **Fig. 65**

Pace di Bonaccorso (son of Bonaccorso di Pace), 246
Pacino di Bonaguida (painter, Florentine), 187
Padua, Arena Chapel, Giotto, frescoes, 95, 115 n. 99
Paganico, 26, 76, 260
Pagno di Compagno (painter), 228
Palmiera filia Micchelis (wife of Masarello di Gilio), 261–62
Pannocchieschi, family, 26
Paolo (carpenter), 140
Paolo (painter), 267, 282
Paolo di Andrea (painter), 257, 267, 267 n. 93
Paolo di Giovanni (painter), 268
Paolo di Neri (painter), 60, 143, 145–46, 228, 268
Paolo di Tingo de' Pilestri, 66, 72, 100, 148
Paolo di Viva (painter), 268
papal banking, 19–21, 20 nn. 9–10

Papal States, 5, 19
Paparoni, family, 39 n. 86
paper, 6, 116 n. 102, 117
Paris
Bibliothèque Nationale: MS lat. 5931, Cardinal Jacopo Stefaneschi, *De Miraculo Mariae*, 116
Louvre Museum, Taddeo Gaddi (attributed to), drawing, *Presentation of the Virgin*, 112
Pasadena, Norton Simon Museum: Pietro Lorenzetti, *Saints Elisha and John the Baptist*, 150
Pasquino di Cenne (painter), 86, 89, 89 n. 17, 156, 268
Patrizi, Francesco, Beato, 35
Patrizi, Patrizio di Francesco, 35
patroni, 118
Pavia, 17
Pecham, John, 177, 178 nn. 76–77, 179; *Perspectiva communis*, 177, 183, 183 n. 99
Persia, 98
perspective, mathematical, 182–83
Perugia, 11, 39, 155
Galleria Nazionale di Umbria: Shop of Duccio, *Madonna and Child*, 154; Meo da Siena, altarpiece, 105; Vigoroso da Siena, altarpiece (1280), 104, 152
San Domenico, 154
Santa Maria di Montelabate, 153
Peter Mallus, 165
Petra (widow of Cosone), 257
Petra (wife of Giovanni di Paolo), 255
Petrarch, 6–7, 10, 45–46, 46 n. 1, 81–82, 110, 116, 155, 171, 186; *Letter to Posterity*, 110; *Virgil Frontispiece*, 55; Petrarch's *Madonna* by Giotto, 171; will, 171
Petriolo, baths of, 24, 89, 132–33; loggia, 158 n. 215, 250, 252
Petro (painter), 268, 276, 282–84
Petro di Pietro (painter), 75, 142 n. 115, 225, 268–69, 276, 283–84
Petroni, family, 151, 197, 248
Petroni, Bindo, 38
Petroni, Catelino, 38
Petroni, Riccardo, Cardinal, 38, 38 n. 85, 68, 136, 150, 196
Petruccio Dietisalvi (painter), 269, 276, 279
Petruccio di Lorenzo (painter), 269
Philip the Fair, King of France, 164
Pia di Gucciarello (wife of Piero di Bacharello), 269
Piccolomini, family, 19, 21, 51 n. 23
Piccolomini, Ambrogio di Nino, 35
Pier Pettinaio, Beato, 31, 34, 69
Piero di Bacharello (painter), 227–28, 269, 269 n. 96

Piero di Donato (painter), 270
Piero di Gerfalco (painter), 270
Pietro di Ser Dota (painter), 47, 47 n. 5, 55, 143 n. 124, 227, 270, 270 n. 98
Pietro di Vannuccio (painter), 227, 270–71
Pietro of Anjou, Prince, 66, 148, 155
Pisa, 10, 12, 17, 106, 155–56
   Hospital of Santa Chiara: Piastra Bindi, altarpiece, 156
   Museo Nazionale di San Matteo: Simone Martini, polyptych (1319), 91, 98, 105, **Color Plate 12, Figs. 36–38**
   Santa Caterina, 91, 110; Master of the Glorification of Saint Thomas Aquinas, *Glorification of Saint Thomas Aquinas*, 154
Pistoia, 10, 66
   Ospedale del Ceppo, 76
   San Giovanni Fuorcivitas, 170–71; Guido di Cino, *Madonna*, 75 n. 178, 156, 257
plague, bubonic (1348), 15, 23–24, 26, 34, 37, 53, 191
Plato, 176
Pontignano, Certosa, 38
portolan charts, 6, 183
Previtali, G., 151
Princeton, Princeton University: Guido da Siena(?), *Annunciation*, 90, 115, **Fig. 33**; Shop of Ugolino di Nerio, *Madonna and Child*, 115, **Fig. 85**
progress, historical, 186
Ptolemy, 179 n. 78
Puccio, 270, 270 n. 100
Puccio di Simone (painter, Florentine), 52

Ranierio da Siena, Fra, 20
Ricco da Camerino, 166
Ricci, Bindo (carpenter), 141
Rinaldo of Spoleto, 269
Rinforzato (painter), 125 n. 24, 270
Robert the Wise, king of Naples, 66, 68, 82, 98, 155, 262
Roccastrada, 60
Romagnoli, E., *Biografia cronologica de' bellartisti senesi*, 242
Romano (painter), 271
Romano di Mino (painter), 47, 47 n. 5, 60, 143, 143 n. 124, 226–27, 270–71
Rome, Old Saint Peter's, 138
   Saint Paul's-outside-the-walls, 138
Roriczer, Matthias, 102
Rosselli, Matteo (painter, Florentine), 257, 267
Rossi, family, 248

Rubin, P., 80
Rustichetti, family, 51

Sabatino (painter), 59, 271
Sabatino di Ramo (painter), 89, 89 n. 16, 226, 263–64, 271
Sacchetti, Franco, 10, 45, 86 n. 7, 110, 119 n. 1, 166
Salimbeni, family, 20–21, 28, 35 n. 72, 51, 51 n. 23
Salvucci, Francesca (niece of Simone Martini), 58
Salvucci, Giovanna (niece to Simone Martini), 58
San Ansano a Dofana, 35
San Bernardino Master (painter), 90, 97
San Gimignano, Palazzo Comunale: "Guidesque" *Madonna*, 152; Lippo Memmi, *Maestà*, 148, 154–55, **Fig. 95**
   Collegiata: following of Simone Martini, New Testament Cycle, 91, 154
   Sant'Agostino, 152
San Leonardo a Lago, 34, 101
Sandro di Masarello (painter), 47, 60, 226, 271
Sansedoni, Ambrogio, Beato, 30, 30 n. 46, 31, 34–35, 42, 74,
Sansedoni, Goro, 114
Santino (painter), 271, 284
Santino di Angelo (painter), 272, 276, 284
Sant'Angelo in Monte (Siena), 77
Santiago di Compostella, 17
Saracini, family, 51 n. 23
Sassetta (painter), 198
Sassoforte, 124
Savino, San, 35–36, 36, 74, 36 nn. 74, 78
Scabello del fu Chiavellino, 184, n. 101
Segna (painter), 279–80, 282
Segna di Bonaventura (painter), 13, 47, 53–54, 54 n. 42, 77, 115 n. 101, 125–27, 150, 150 n. 168, 158, 191, 193, 197, 227, 252 n. 41, 276–77, **Figs. 12, 97**
Selva del Lago, 101, 263
Serenus, Bishop of Marseilles, 162
sgraffito, 98–99, 103, 103 n. 64
Shearman, J., 117–18
Shroud of Turin, 169
Simone di Donato (son of Donato Martini), 58
Simone di Giovanni (painter), 272
Skaug, E., 52
Solafico, Angeliero, 19
Stopani, R., 17 n. 2
Sodoma (painter), 124 n. 13
Southard, E., 126
Sovignano, 56–57, 233

Spini, Alessandro, Fra, 110
Squarcilupi, family, 21
Stefaneschi, Jacopo, Cardinal, 116, 155
Szabo, T., 17 n. 2

Taddeo di Bartolo (painter), 53 n. 34, 129
Talamone, 26, 173, 181, plan, 181, **Fig. 5**
Talumuccio (painter), 272, 281
Tarlati, Guido, Bishop of Arezzo, 62, 171
Taurello (notary), 38
Tavena (painter), 66, 272, 272 n. 106, 276, 280
Tavena d'Andrea (painter), 59, 59 nn. 74–75, 226, 233, 235–38, 272
Tavinia (widow of Duccio di Buoninsegna), 59
technology and painters, 111 n. 80
Templars, 164
time, 63 n. 89
Toma di Jacomuccio di Guido (wife of Fede di Nalduccio), 251, 251 n. 34
Thomas Aquinas, Saint, 3, 31, 168, 168 n. 24, 169, 174–75, 177 n. 71
Thome (painter), 272
Tino di Camaino (sculptor), 44–48, 55, 79
Tizio, Sigismondo, 32, 124 n. 13, 136 nn. 91–93, 150, 155
Toker, F., 114, 114 nn. 97–98
Tolomei, family, 20, 20 n. 11, 21, 21 n. 17, 28, 34, 35 n. 72, 38, 39 n. 86, 40, 51, 51 n. 23, 143 n. 122, 145–47, 155, 196
Tolomei, Bernardo, Beato, 34–35
Tolomei, Blasius quondam domini Tolomei, 38
Tolomei, Giovanni di Tese, 28, 40, 143 n. 122, 145–47, 196
Tolomei, Nello di Mino, 155
Tolomei, Pestaglio di Tavena, 38
Tomaso da Modena (painter, Modenese), 110
Tommasi, Giugurta, 136 n. 93
Tommaso di Andrea (painter), 272
Tommaso di Niccholuccio (painter), 272
Tommaso del Mazza, 52
Tommè di Vanni da Siena (painter), 89 n. 17, 268, 272
Tomuccio quondam Dini, Ser, 60
Tondino di Guerino (goldsmith), 127
Tonne di Giovanni, 171
Trachtenberg, M., 184
Tressa, 12; river, 50; fountain, 158
Treviso, San Nicolò (convent), Tomaso da Modena, *Dominicans*, 110
Tuccio di Betto (painter), 227, 272–73, 285

Tura Comini (painter), 273, 282
Tura Giovanni (carpenter?), 141

Ughi, Mino di Cino, 28, 80, 159, 159 n. 227
Ugolino di Nerio (painter), 13, 47, 51 n. 26, 55–56, 100, 102, 105–6, 115, 147, 153–54, 156, 191, 226, 231, 231 n. 3, 234–35, 241, 252 n. 39, **Figs. 13, 57, 67, 83, 85, 94**
Ugolino di Vieri (goldsmith), 111 n. 79
Urban IV, Pope (1260–64), 4, 20
urbanism and the arts, xx, 9–10

valley of the Merse, 101
Vanni, Andrea (painter), 89, 226, 257
Vanni, Lippo (painter), 14, 131, 145, 145 n. 138, 151, 265, **Fig. 101**
Vanni Cinuzzi, 89 n. 17
Vanni di Bindo (painter), 273, 273 n. 109
Vanni di Bono (painter), 273
Vanni di Cione, 171
Vanni di Dietisalvi (painter), 226, 273
Vannuccio di Mino (painter), 59, 226, 228, 239, 266, 266 nn. 86–87, 273, 286
Vasari, Giorgio, 9–10, 12–13, 46
Vatican, Cappella Magna, 118
Venice, 19
 Crystal Workers' Guild, 111
Ventura, Guido, 136 n. 94
Vercelli, 17
Verio di Ugolino, 229
Veronica, Saint, 165
Veronica, relic, 165
Via Francigena, 17, 17 n. 2, 18, 22, 49, 132, 154, 172–73
Viciento di Vanni (painter), 227, 273
Vico d'Arbia, 58 n. 62
Vienna, Albertina: Inv. 4, drawing after frescoes in the Lower Church of San Francesco, Assisi, 113, 113 n. 89
Vieri del fu Cola di Oliviero Barote, 20 n. 13
Vigoroso (painter), 104, 225, 273, 278
Villani, Filippo, 10; *De origine civitatis Florentiae et euisdem famosis civibus*, 80
Villani, Giovanni, 10, 165–66, 172 n. 45
Vita da Cortona, Fra, 165
Vitaluccio (painter), 265, 273–74, 280–81
Vitaluccio di Rosso (painter), 75, 77, 89, 274, 276, 280–81
Viterbo, 177
Vittorio, San, 35–36, 36 nn. 76–78
Volterra, 156

War of the Sicilian Vespers, 5
weather, 109
White, J., 102, 180
William of Auvergne, Bishop of Paris (1228–49), 164
William of Moerbeke, 2, 177, 177 n. 71
William Ockham, xx
Williamstown (Mass.), The Sterling and Francine Clark Art Institute: Shop of Ugolino di Nerio, polyptych, 115, **Fig. 83**
Witelo, 177, 183 n. 99; *Perspectiva*, 177

Zanardi, B. 118

INDEX: SIENA

age of majority, 92 n. 31

baldachins. See *palio/palii*
bequests, pious, 37–38, 37 n. 80
Biblioteca Comunale, 242
   MS F.VI.11, 163
   MS I.V.8, *Libro di Collatione de' Santi Padri*, 151
   MS I.VI.9, *La Passione e la Resurrezione di Gesù* (attributed to Niccolò Cicerchia), *Laudi*, Jacopone da Todi, 79 n. 195, 151
Biccherna covers, 70, 73–76, 132 n. 65, 134, 275–86, **Figs. 23, 91–92**
bricks, 70

Camollia, 18
Campo, 17–18, 24, 48, 48 n. 10, 49, 69, 172
Camporegio, 140
candles. *See* wax
Castel Montone, 18
Castelvecchio, 17–18, 193
cathedral, 1, 8, 17, 29, 35, 39, 43, 48, 48 n. 10, 69, 90, 107, 196
   altar/chapel of Saint Bartholomew, 135
   altar/chapel of Saint Catherine of Alexandria, 136
   altar/chapel of Saint John, 136
   altar/chapel of Saint Michael Archangel, 136
   altar/chapel of Saint Paul, 136
   altar/chapel of San Ansano, 140 n. 110. *See also* Florence, Galleria degli Uffizi, Simone Martini and Lippo Memmi, *Annunciation*
   altar/chapel of San Crescenzio. *See* Florence, Galleria degli Uffizi, Ambrogio Lorenzetti, *Presentation of Christ in the Temple*
   altar/chapel of San Jacopo Interciso: Ambrogio "dipentore in chamoreggi," gilded candlesticks, 243

   altar/chapel of San Savino. *See* Museo dell'Opera del Duomo, Pietro Lorenzetti, *Birth of the Virgin*
   altar/chapel of San Vittorio. *See* Cambridge (Mass.), Harvard University, Fogg Museum, Bartolommeo Bulgarini, *Nativity*, and Copenhagen, Statens Museum for Kunst, Master of Palazzo Venezia, *Saints Corona and Vittorio*
   altars in 1215 (list), 135
   banners, 29, 143 n. 128
   baptistery, 137
   campanile, 113–14 n. 94, 137, **Fig. 76**
   chapel of Pope Alexander VII: "Guidesque" *Madonna del Voto*, 90, 137 n. 99
   cleaning of altarpieces, 143 n. 124
   crypt, 95
   cupola, 137–38
   dedication, 138 n. 102
   door, painted, Petro, 142, 142 n. 115, 268
   Duomo Nuovo, 18, 113–14 n. 94, 172
   exterior, *Saint* (sculpted), 115, **Fig. 51**
   facade, 137, 143–44, **Fig. 3**; *Standing Madonna and Child* (sculpture), 143–44, 144 n. 131, 249, 261, 268
   high altar, 137–38 n. 99
      angels/candlesticks, polychrome sculpture, Ambrogio di Duccio, 243; Ambrogio Lorenzetti, 142, 159; Romano di Mino, 271
      candles, 142–43
      lamp, 143 n. 122
   interior, **Fig. 4**
   inventory of 1389, 136
   Ordo officiorum ecclesiae Senensis, 135
   patron saints, feasts of, 135 n. 89
   Porta del Perdono, 135–36
   roof, 137 n. 99

   tomb of Cardinal Riccardo Petroni, 114 n. 94, 136
civic Christianity, 6, 29–30, 44, 196
charitable institutions
   Misericordia, 28, 33, 33 n. 62, 34, 38–40, 51–52, 78, 84 n. 1, 89, 89 n. 19, 132, 184 n. 101, 192, 245, 251, 258, 262, 264, 266, 270, 271, 273
   Ospedale di Monna Agnese, 41
   Ospedale di San Lazzaro, 42
   Ospedale di Sant'Andrea, 51
   Ospedale di Santa Croce, 33
   Ospedale di Santa Maria della Scala, 7, 17–18, 27–28, 28 n. 40, 29–30, 32, 32 n. 58, 33, 33 n. 61, 35, 38–40, 40 n. 88, 41, 46, 49 n. 13, 55, 57, 58 n. 58, 67, 74, 77–79, 84 n. 1, 92, 93 n. 33, 94, 120, 122, 133–34, 136 n. 92, 144–48, 157, 159, 184 n. 101, 191, 195, 244, 246–48, 251, 251 n. 34, 254, 259, 261, 268, 273
      altar of Saint John the Baptist, 146
      altars, endowed, 145–46
      Cappella del Manto, 146
      chapel, high altar, 146; altarpiece, **Fig. 56**
      chapel of Giovanni di Tese Tolomei, 145
      chapel of Saint Luke, 147
      chapel of Saints Joachim and Anna, 147
      chapel of the relics, 146
      commemoration of the deceased, 147 n. 156
      facade, frescoes (lost): Anonymous, *Assumption of the Virgin*; Pietro Lorenzetti, *Birth of the Virgin*; Ambrogio Lorenzetti, *Presentation of the Virgin in the Temple*; Simone Martini, *Marriage of the Virgin* and *Return of the Virgin to the house of her Parents*, 108, 146–47, 157

granges of, 148
panel pictures: Bartolommeo Bulgarini, 144, **Figs. 24–26**; Master of Palazzo Venezia, *Mystic Marriage of Saint Catherine*, 144–45, **Fig. 93**
pellegrinaio, Domenico di Bartolo, *Distribution of Alms*; Paolo di Neri, arch leading to, lost decoration, 146, 268
pellegrinaio nuovo, 145
rectors, 28, 28 n. 40, 80, 143 n. 122, 145–47, 159, 160 n. 230, 196
statute, 34
Ospedale di Santa Marta, 39, 150
Ospedale di Sant'Onofrio, 257
Società degli Esecutori delle Pie Disposizioni, Lippo Vanni, reliquary, 151, **Fig. 101**
churches and convents
Abbazia di San Donato, 22, 66 n. 116, 95
Sant'Agnese, 39
Sant'Agostino, 42, 42 n. 97, 150; Ambrogio Lorenzetti, *Maestà*, 151
Sant'Antonio in Fontebranda (destroyed), Jacopo di Mino Pelliciaio, *Coronation of Saint Catherine of Alexandria* (1362), 150, **Fig. 99**
San Biagio, 150
Santa Chiara, 38
San Cristoforo, 21, 34, 129, 129 n. 46
Santa Croce, 41
San Desiderio, 26
San Domenico, 19, 30–31, 33, 33 n. 64, 42 n. 97, 49 n. 13, 51, 58 n. 60, 74, 90, 231, 246, 251, 253 n. 47, 255, 255 n. 51, 260, 262, 265–66, 268, 271–72
Guido da Siena, *Madonna*, 90, 115, 149, 185, **Fig. 32**
Lippo Memmi, *Madonna and Child with Saints Peter and Paul*, 150, **Fig. 100**
Master of the Loeser Madonna, *Madonna and Child with Saint John the Baptist and a Donor*, 148, 151, **Fig. 96**
San Donato (destroyed), 51 n. 25, 231, 233
Sant'Egidio, 34, 39, 150
San Francesco, 22, 31, 54 n. 42, 115
Ambrogio Lorenzetti, *Franciscan Martyrdom*, 151; *Ordination of Saint Louis of Toulouse*, 115, **Fig. 81**; cloister frescoes, 108, 151, 189–97; Pietro Lorenzetti, *Crucifixion*, 95, **Figs. 45–46**
San Giusto, Ducciesque crucifix, 150
Lorenzetti following, polyptych, 150
San Luca, 93–94, 94 n. 33, 150
Santa Maria dei Servi, 42
Coppo di Marcovaldo, *Madonna del Bordone* (1261), 85, 185
Lippo Memmi, *Madonna and Child*, 150, **Fig. 98**
Segna di Bonaventura, *Madonna and Child*, 150, **Fig. 97**
Santa Maria della Misericordia, 93, 93 n. 33
San Niccolò, 32, 150
San Pellegrino, 22
Master of Città di Castello, *Madonna and Child Enthroned*, 150
Simone Martini Following, *Beato Andrea Gallerani*, 152
San Pietro a Ovile, 22
San Pietro alle Scale, Ambrogio Lorenzetti, polyptych, 150
San Pietro in Banchi (destroyed), 149
Santa Petronilla, 30
Ambrogio Lorenzetti and workshop, *Four Saints*, 150
Santo Spirito, 42
San Vigilio, 22
coinage, xix, 17, 41, 138
communal forests, 101, 101 n. 58
Compagnia del Cappelletto, 136 n. 95
condottieri, 67
confraternities, 12, 29, 32–34, 39, 44–45, 52, 79 n. 195, 149, 151, 186, 187 n. 111
constitution, 18, 27, 27 n. 35, 29–30, 37, 43, 65 n. 100, 67, 71, 77 n. 186, 84 n. 1, 92 n. 31, 113 n. 91, 116, 123, 123 n. 8, 132, 134–36, 142, 143 n. 122, 171–73, 175, 245

disease, 26
dowries, 40, 45, 60–61, 246, 249, 251, 251 n. 34, 252–53, 255, 258–62, 267–68, 271

episcopal palace, 137

famine, 26
fountains, 24, 48 n. 10, 69–70, 70 n. 149, 157–60
Fonte Becci, 67
Fonte Branda, 42 n. 97, 51, 157–60
Fonte Gaia, 24
Fonte Nuovo, 77, 158, 250

gates, 196
Porta Busetto, 58 n. 58
Porta di Camollia, 33, 48, 69, 131–32, 171
Porta Laterina, 48
Porta Pispini, 48
Porta Peruzzini, 248
Porta Romana, 48, 132: Simone Martini(?), *Coronation of the Virgin*
Porta Salaia, 132, 132 n. 65
Porta San Viene, 132
guilds
Arte degli Orafi, 87, 87 n. 10, 88 n. 2, 90 n. 23, 92, 192
Arte del Fuoco, 26, 43, 43 n. 100
Arte de' Carnaioli, 41–42, 87, 87 n. 11
Arte de' Chiavari, 36 n. 78, 42, 87, 97 n. 11
Arte de' Cuoiai e Calzolai, 36 n. 78, 42, 87, 87 n. 11
Arte de' Giudici e Notai, 41
Arte de' Pittori, 36 n. 78, 43, 46, 53, 53 n. 35, 84–94, 139 n. 103, 145, 146 n. 145, 162–63, 194, 197
membership in 1356, 85 n. 4; statute, 199–224:
account books, 205 (XIII)
assemblies, 201 (I), 202 (IV), 203 (V), 209 (XXIV), 215 (XXXIX), 217–18 (XLVI, XLVIII), 220 (L), 221–22 (LV)
candles, 201 (I), 209 (XXVII), 218 (XLVII), 220 (L), 220 n. 10, 222 (LVI)
cloth dyers, 222–23 (LVII)
decorum, 207 (XVIII)
disputes, 207 (XIX)
dues, 205 (XIII)
election of officers, 202–3 (IV)
emendations, 208–9 (XIV)
estimates, work, 217 (XLIV)
feast of Saint Luke, 210 (I), 218 (XLVII), 219–20 (L), at the church of Saint Luke, 210 (I), at Santa Maria della Misericordia, 219 (XLIX), at the church of the Ospedale della Scala, 211–21 (LV)
feast of the Beato Andrea Gallerani, 219 (XLIX)
foreign painters, 204–5 (X, XI), 220 (LII), 221 (LIII)
funerals, 202 (III)
holy days, 202 (II), 204 (X), 212–14 (XXXV, XXXVI)
materials, 205–6 (XIV)
Merchants' Guild, 202 (II), 204 (X), 212 (XXXVI), 223 (LVII, LVIII, LIX), 224 (XL)
messenger, 203 (VII)
Misericordia, 219 (XLIX), 219–20 (V)
oath of fealty, 211 (XXXII)
ostricism, 215 (XL)
rector, *passim*
reputation, 216 (XLIII)
signs for taverns, 221 (LIV)

Treasurer, 202 (IV), 205 (XIII), 206 (XV), 208 (XXI), 210 (XXIX), 211 (IV), 214 (XXXVII), 217 (XLV), 218 (XLVIII), 221 (LIV), 223–24 (LX)
watchmen, secret, 204 (X)
Arte della Lana, 36 n. 78, 42, 42 n. 97, 43, 87 n. 11, 134, 157
Arte della Mercanzia, xix, 28, 36 n. 78, 41, 42 n. 92, 43–44, 87, 87 n. 11, 134, 139 n. 105, 243–44, 249, 252, 256–57, 261, 266–67

justice, 26

literacy, 184 n. 101

Museo dell'Opera del Duomo, 12
 drawing for the baptistery facade, 113, **Fig. 75**
 drawing for a new campanile, 113, 113 n. 94, **Fig. 76**
 Duccio di Buoninsegna, *Maestà*, 1, 8, 63, 63 n. 93, 66, 70, 88, 88 n. 14, 96, 99, 100, 101 n. 56, 102, 105, 115, 138, 143 n. 127, 185 n. 105, 189, **Color Plates 1–2, 10–11, Figs. 15–16**
 Lorenzetti, Pietro, *Birth of the Virgin* (1342), 36, 66, 72, 100, 107–8, 116, 139–41, 141 n. 112, 182, **Fig. 30**
 Madonna degli occhi grossi, 137 n. 99
 Reliquary of the Head of San Galgano, 111 n. 79

Opera del Duomo, 24, 29, 41, 61, 63 n. 88, 70, 72, 120, 136 n. 93, 138, 157
 Lorenzetti, Pietro, "storie," 142, 142 n. 114

palaces
 Palazzo di Sugio Iuncte degli Arzocchi, 125 n. 17
 Palazzo Pubblico, 8, 13, 17–18, 22, 24–25, 29, 43, 65, 69–70, 78, 93 n. 33, 101, 122–23, 172, 196, **Fig. 2**
  Chapel, 128; Duccio di Donato, chalice, 127; drape of gold, 127; Gospel book, 127; Masarello, painted cross, 262; missal, 127, 127 n. 34, 158; silver lamps, 127; Simone Martini, altarpiece, 127, 127 n. 39, crucifix, 127, two wooden angels, 127, pedestal for a crucifix, 127
  Chapel, sacristy, 127; fire in, 127 n. 33
  Concistoro, Segna di Bonaventura restores a *Madonna* "before the Concistoro," 126, 158; Simone Martini, *Marco Regolo*, 65, 65 n. 105, 129
  dormitory, new, 158
  facade, 129, **Fig. 2**
  loggia (destroyed), 126, 126 n. 28; Simone Martini, 126
  loggia, third floor, Ambrogio Lorenzetti, *Madonna and Child Enthroned*, 131, **Fig. 90**
  Palazzo del Podestà, altar, 127, 171; *camera* of the Podestà, 126, n. 25
  prisons, 129, 129 n. 49, 245
  Sala della Biccherna, Guido Cinatti, 75; Lippo Vanni, *Coronation of the Virgin*, 131; a *Madonna*, 128, 128 n. 40; Segna di Bonaventura, a painted panel, 125; Simone Martini, *Saint Christopher*, 65, 129
  Sala del Consiglio, Bartolo di Fredi, lost decoration (1361), 131; Giovanni di Benedetto and Lippo, lost decoration (1361), 254; Nello di Betto and Lippo Vanni, lost decoration (1359), 265
  Sala del Mappamondo, Ambrogio Lorenzetti, *Mappamondo* (lost), 131, 160, 183; Anonymous, "the story of the Conte d'Elci" (lost), 123–24; Anonymous, *A Subject Town*, 124 n. 11, **Figs. 87–88**; Simone Martini, *Arcidosso and Castel del Piano*, 65, 129, *Maestà*, 64, 70, 94–95, 95 n. 36, 108, 122, 124, 130, 138, 153, 158, 185, **Color Plates 3–4**, *Montemassi and Sassoforte*, 65, 129
  Sala dei Pilastri, 126
  Sala della Pace, 25; Ambrogio Lorenzetti, 64, 66, 69, 100, 108, 130, 141, 158, 178–79, 192, **Color Plates 5–6**
  Torre del Mangia, 24, 129, 160, **Fig. 2**; Lippo and Federigo Memmi, aborted project, 92, 131, 159–60, 251
  Uffizio delle Gabelle, Ambrogio Lorenzetti, *Annunciation* (1344), 128, **Fig. 89**; Lippo Memmi, *San Ansano*, 65 n. 129
  Unknown location: Anonymous, *Madonna with Saints Peter and Andrew*, 128, 128 n. 41; Anonymous, *Madonna with San Ansano and San Galgano*, 128; Cecchino, *Annunciate* (lost), 128; Guido, twelve figures of false witnesses and forgers of coin (lost), 65
 palio/palii, 65–66, 68, 133, 260, 262

parishes (*popoli*)
 Magione del Tempio, 59, 228, 232–33, 235, 273
 San Cristoforo, 49, 227–28, 248, 255, 257, 270
 San Donato, 40, 49, 49 n. 11, 50–51, 54, 56, 56 n. 48, 57, 93, 96 n. 38, 192–93, 225–26, 231–32, 245, 247–48, 251, 253, 256–59, 262–63, 265–66, 271
 San Giorgio, 57–58 n. 58, 72, 228, 252
 San Martino, 229, 247
 San Maurizio, 140
 San Pellegrino, 228, 269–71
 San Pietro a Ovile, 49, 49 n. 11, 51, 54, 140, 227, 251, 260
 San Pietro in Castelvecchio, 49–50, 52, 54, 228
 San Quirico in Castelvecchio, 49, 49 n. 12, 52, 228, 243, 245–46, 253, 268
 San Salvatore, 228, 260
 San Vigilio di fuore, 263
 Sant'Andrea, 60, 268
 Sant'Antonio, 49, 227, 258, 262, 273
 Sant'Egidio, 49, 50, 54, 59, 96 n. 38, 192–93, 226–27, 247, 251–52, 267, 269–71

Pinacoteca Nazionale, 50
 Duccio di Buoninsegna, *Madonna of the Franciscans*, no. 20, 109, **Fig. 64**; polyptych, no. 28, 104, 115, **Figs. 52–53**; polyptych, no. 47, 105, 115, 144–45, 147, **Fig. 56**
 Ducciesque, crucifix, no. 21, 150
 Guido da Siena, dossal, no. 7, 104, 115, 149, 152, **Fig. 7**
 "Guidesque," dossal, no. 6, 104, 115, 149, **Fig. 6**; reliquary shutters (legend of the Beato Andrea Gallerani), no. 5, 152
 Jacopo di Mino, *Coronation of Saint Catherine of Alexandria*, no. 145, 150, **Fig. 99**
 Lorenzetti, Ambrogio, *Annunciation* (1344), no. 88, 128, 182, **Fig. 89**; the small *Maestà*, no. 65, **Color Plate 15**; Ambrogio and workshop, *Saints*, nos. 77, 77a, 77b, 77c, 150; following of, crucifix, no. 598, 150; polyptych, no. 50, 150
 Lorenzetti, Pietro, Carmelite altarpiece, 106, 115, **Figs. 59–60**; *Madonna* from Castiglione d'Orcia (on deposit), 96 n. 40
 Luca di Tommè and Niccolò di Ser Sozzo, polyptych, no. 51, 92, **Fig. 35**

Martini, Simone, *Beato Agostino Novello*, on deposit, **Color Plates 7–8, Figs. 14, 63**
Martini, Simone, following of, four saints, nos. 85, 86, 93, 94, 150
Master of Città di Castello, *Madonna and Child Enthroned*, no. 18, 150
Master of Palazzo Venezia, *Mystic Marriage of Saint Catherine of Alexandria*, no. 108, 144–45, **Fig. 93**
Master of Saint Peter, Saint Peter altarpiece, no. 15, 90–91, 115, 149, **Fig. 34**
Master of San Bernardino, San Bernardino *Madonna*, no. 16, 90, 97, 149, **Fig. 8**
Master of Tabernacle 35, triptych, no. 35, 109, 148, **Fig. 66**
Memmi, Lippo, *Saint Francis* and *Saint Louis of Toulouse*, nos. 48–49, 154
pittura infamante, 134
police, 26, 67
population, 23
public officials, 27

religious thought, 44
religious orders
    Augustinians, 101
    Carmelites, 30, 32, 41, 64, 72, 106, 135
    Dominicans, 2, 12, 22, 30–31, 38, 41–42 n. 97, 51, 150
    Franciscans, 11–12, 38, 41, 186
    Servites, 30, 38, 41–42, 42 n. 94, 71–72, 85, 135, 150
    Umiliati, 39 n. 80, 41, 47, 57, 150

seal of the commune, 31, 126 n. 30
Seminario Arcivescovile, Segna di Bonaventura, *Madonna and Child*, 115 n. 101
streets
    Banchi di sopra, 50
    Costa Larga, 172
    Costarella dei Barbieri, 69
    Camporegio, Via del, 50
    Malborghetto, Via di, 101
    Malcucinato, Via, 69, 129
    Montanini, Via dei, 50–51
    Paradiso, Via del, 50
    Pittori, Via dei, 50
    Rossi, Via dei, 50
    Sapienza, Via della, 50
    Stalloreggi, Via, 50
    Thommaso Pendola, Via, 50
studium generale, 22, 25

Table of Possessions, 28–29, 51 n. 25, 55, 59, 67–68, 158, 160 n. 233, 231–40
taxation districts (*lire*)
    Abbazia di San Donato di sotto, 160 n. 233
    Magione del Tempio, 59
    Manetti, dei, 254
    Porta all'Archo, 367
    San Cristoforo a lato alla Chiesa, 51, n. 27
    San Cristoforo a lato dei Tolomei, 51 n. 27
    San Donato a lato alla Chiesa, 193
    San Donato a lato dei Montanini, 51 n. 25, 59, 75, 158, 193, 233–40, 260, 263–64, 266, 272–73
    San Donato di sotto, 51 n. 25
    Sant'Egidio a lato dei Malavolti, 49
    Sant'Egidio a lato dei Rustichelli, 262
    Stalloreggi di dentro, 50, 50 n. 21, 54, 59
    Stalloreggi di fuori (Laterino), 50, 50 n. 21, 59,
    Vallepiatta di sotto, 269
Terzo di Camollia, 18–19, 49, 77, 89, 229, 248, 263
Terzo di Città, 19, 49, 52, 57, 77, 193, 229, 233, 247, 254
Terzo di San Martino, 18–19, 253
trade and banking, 19–21

urbanism, 171–73, 196

vescovado, 39 n. 86, 172

wax, 29, 29 n. 43, 31, 31 n. 50, 33, 42, 42 n. 95, 69, 69 n. 143, 75, 84 n. 2, 93, 142, 142 nn. 118–19, 143, 143 n. 128, 245, 246, 248, 250, 252, images, 164, votives, 166, 170
wills, 37–39, 48, 48 n. 8
working year (for painters), 87, 87–88 n. 11

COLOR PLATES

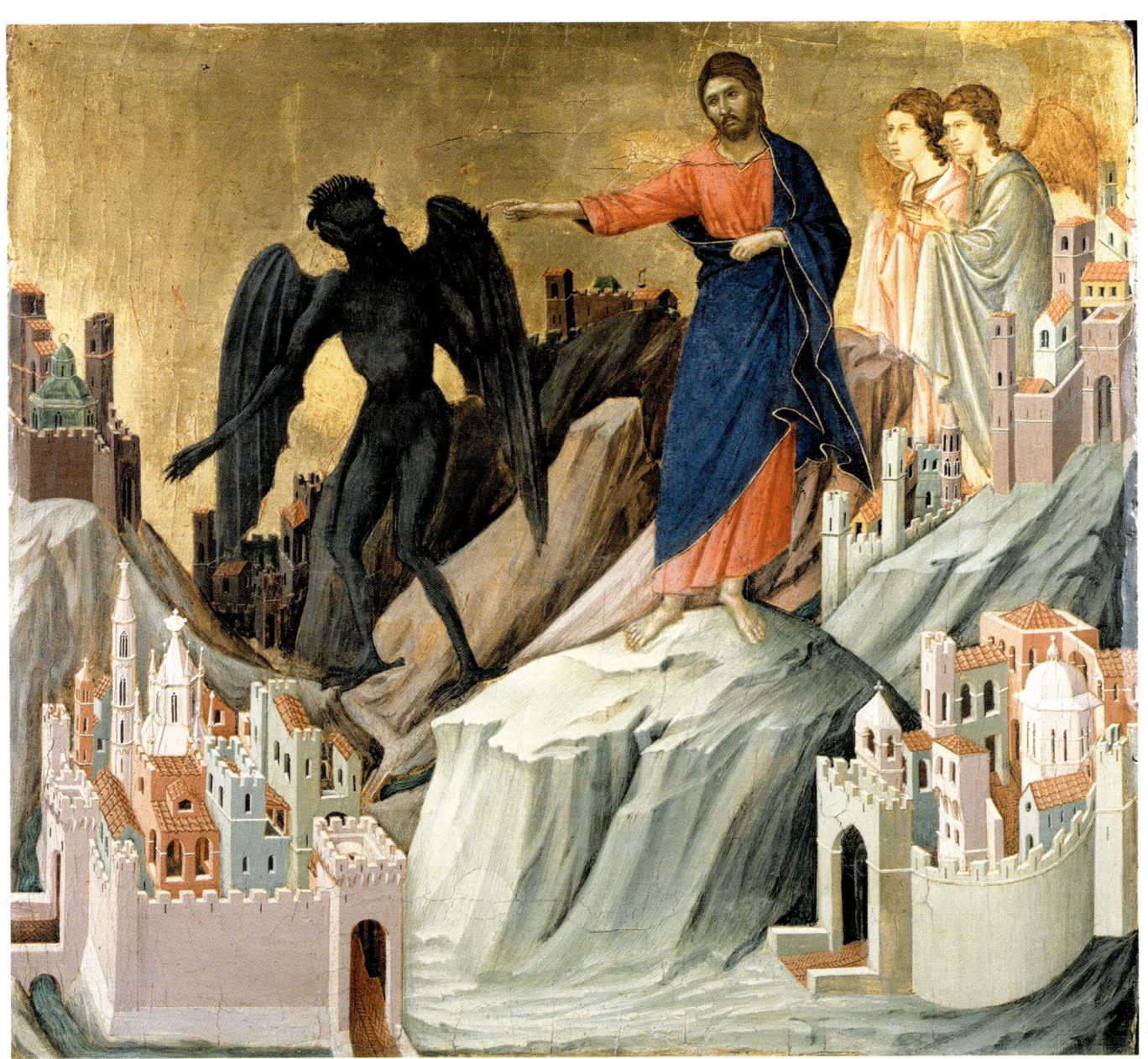

Color Plate 1. Duccio di Buoninsegna, *Temptation on the Mountain*. New York, Frick Collection.

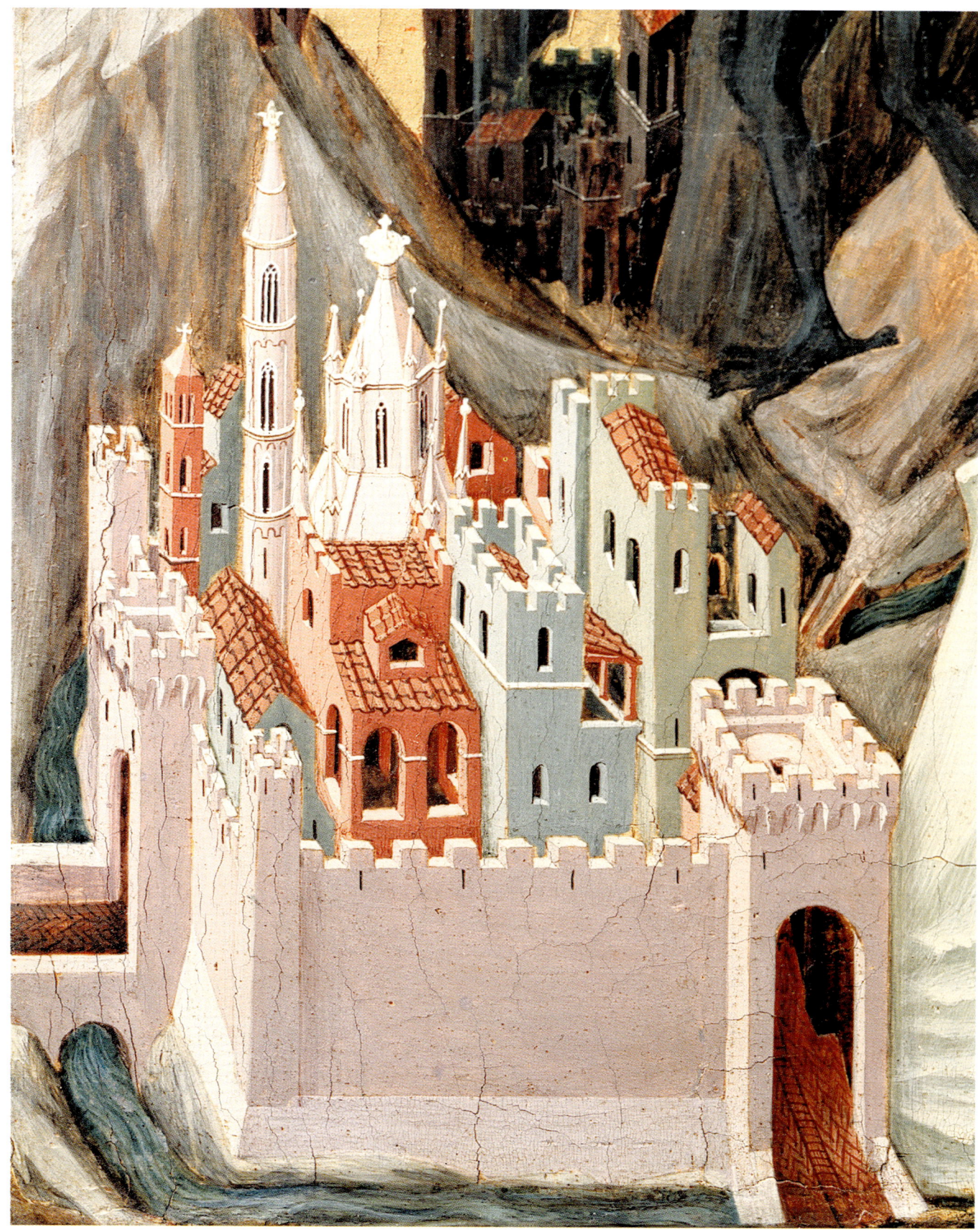

Color Plate 2. Duccio di Buoninsegna, *Temptation on the Mountain,* detail. New York, Frick Collection.

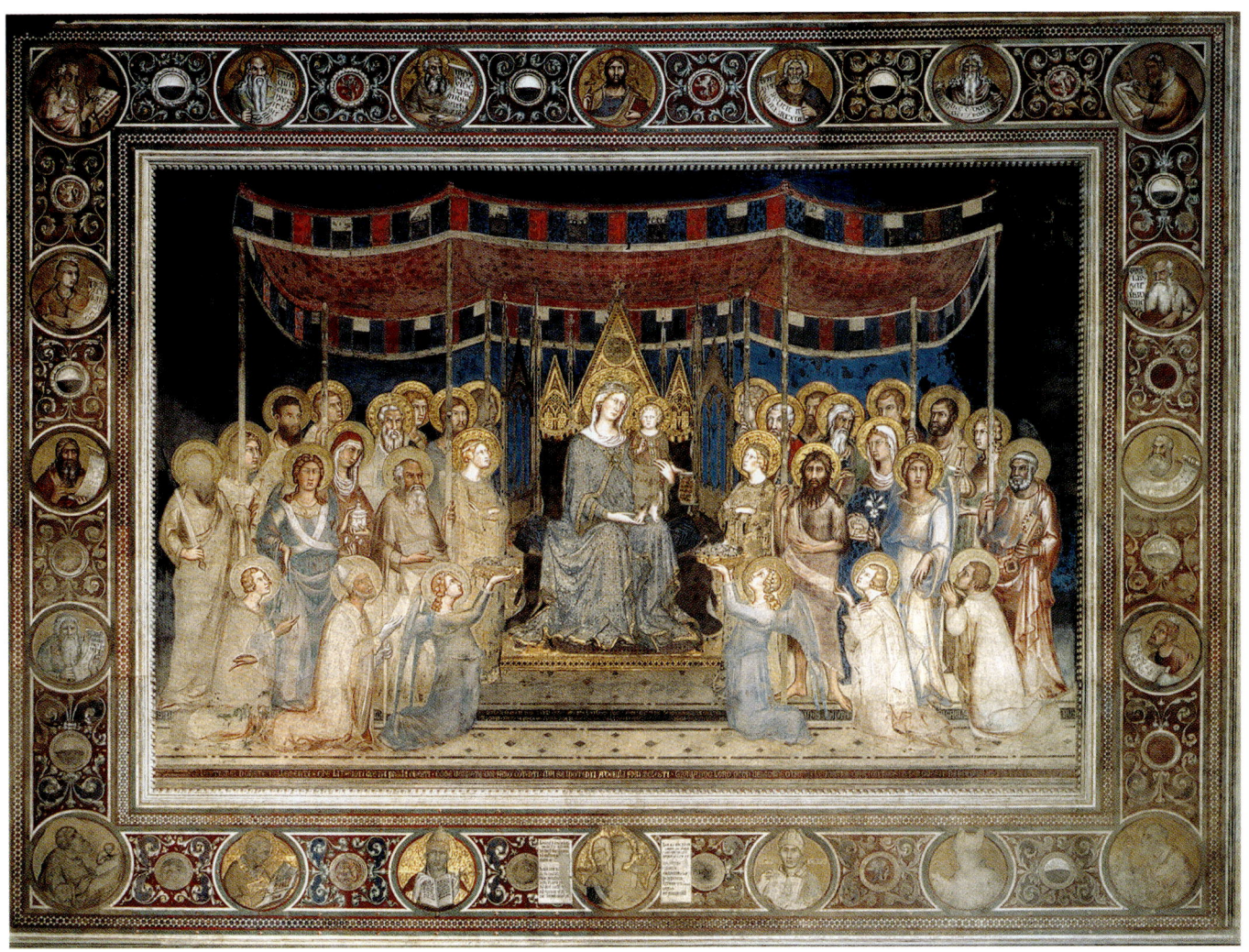

Color Plate 3. Simone Martini, *Maestà*. Siena, Palazzo Pubblico.

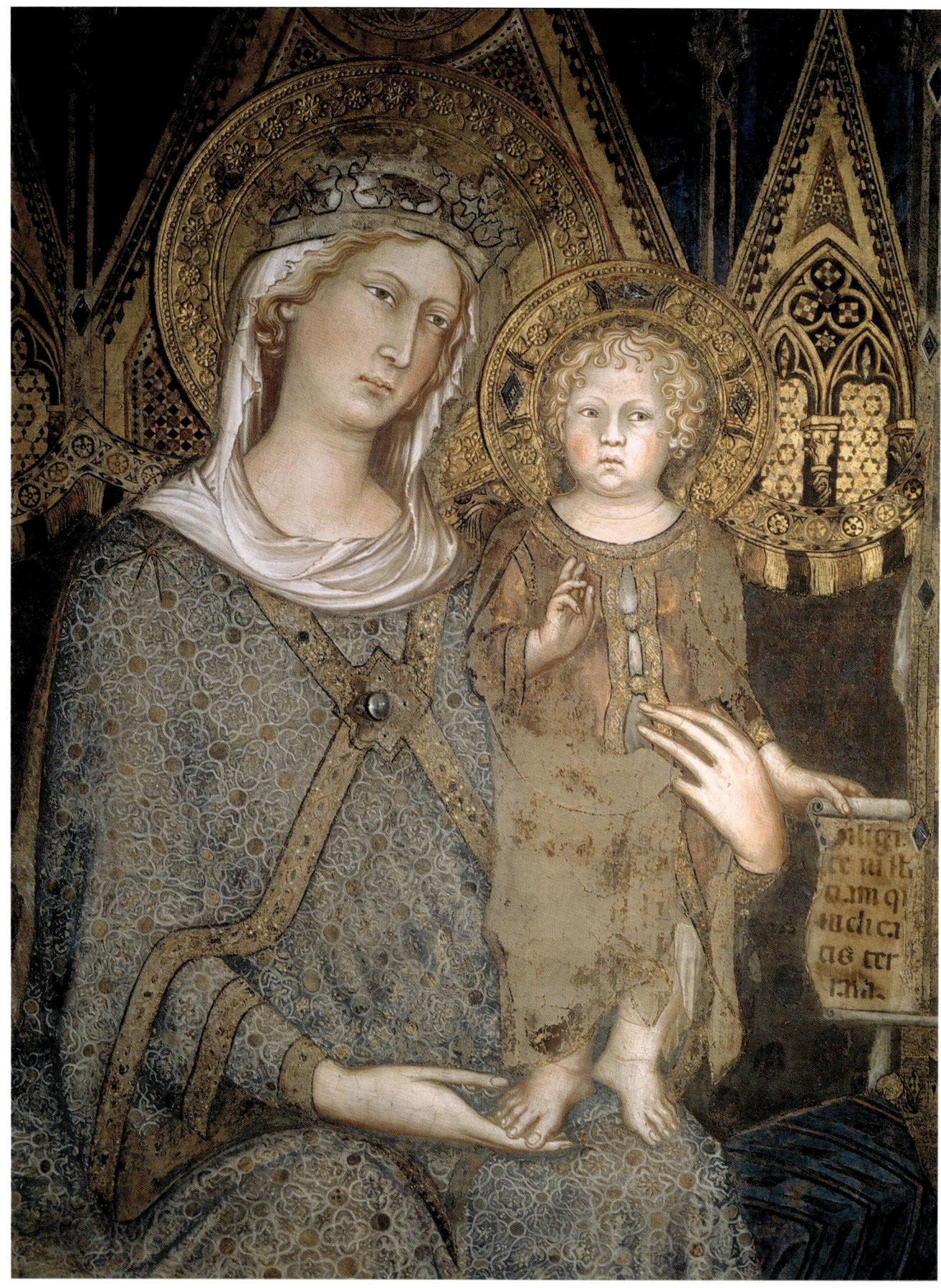

Color Plate 4. Simone Martini, *Maestà*, detail. Siena, Palazzo Pubblico.

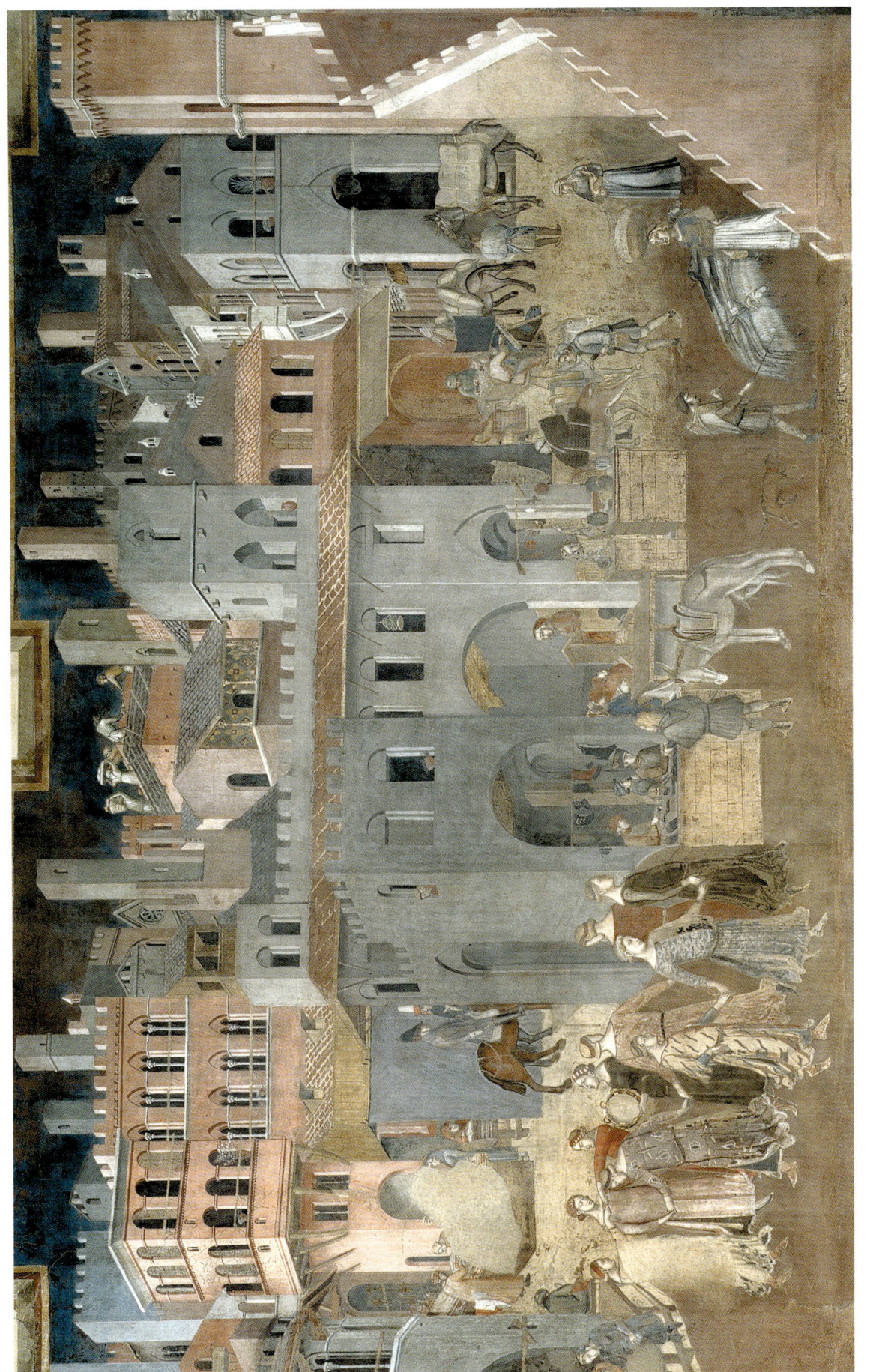

Color Plate 5. Ambrogio Lorenzetti, *The Effects of Good Government*, detail: the city. Siena, Palazzo Pubblico.

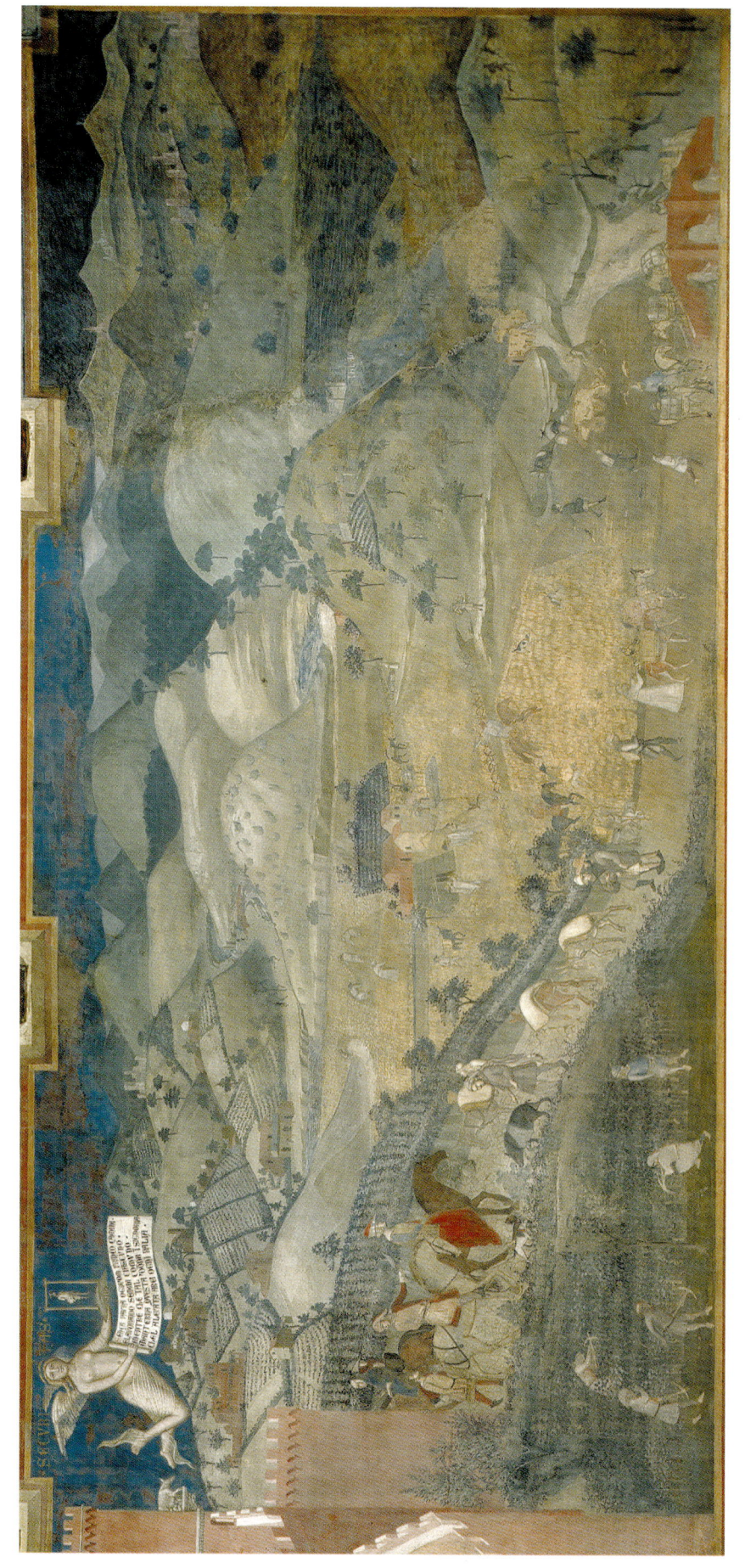

Color Plate 6. Ambrogio Lorenzetti, *The Effects of Good Government*, detail: the countryside. Siena, Palazzo Pubblico.

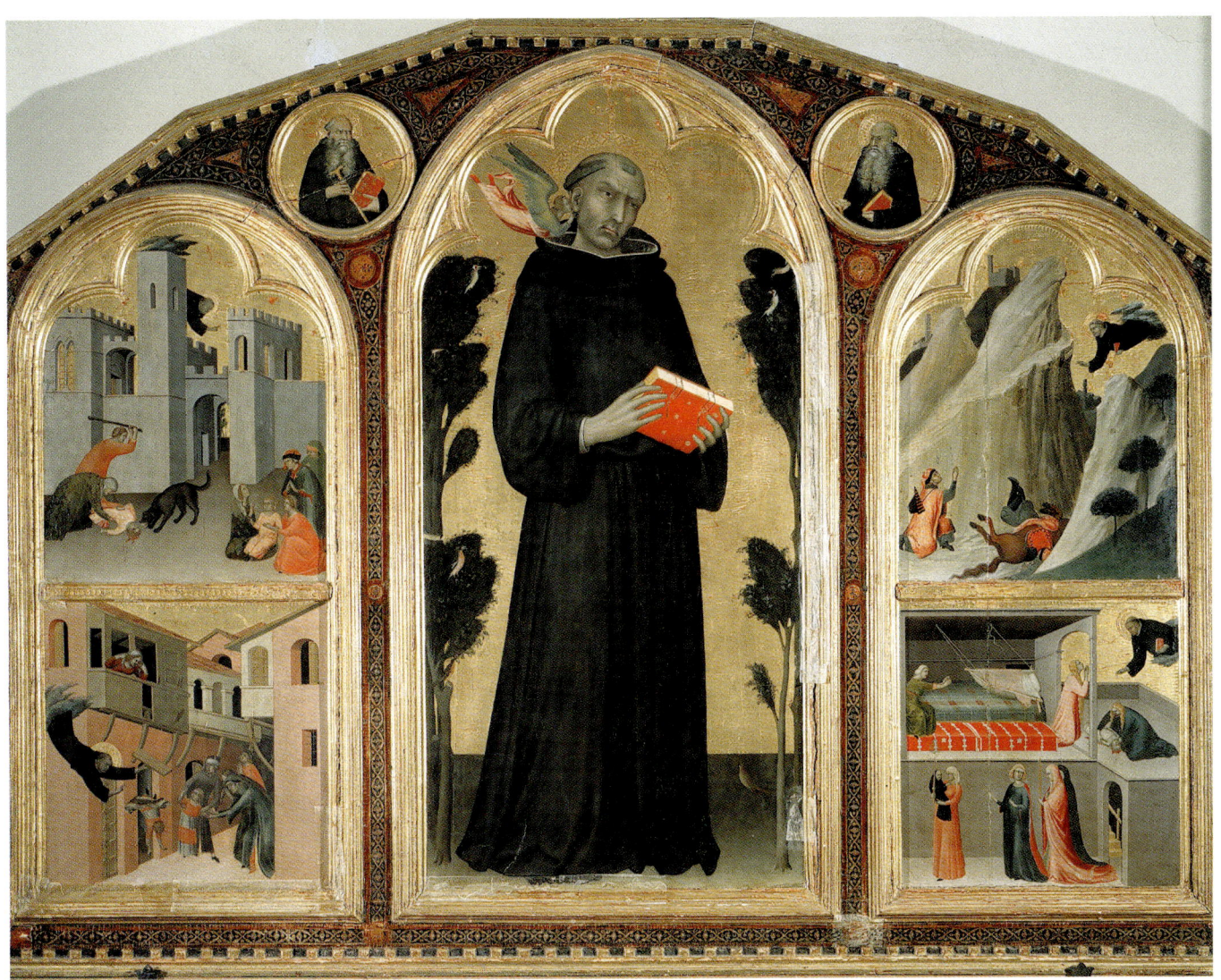

Color Plate 7. Simone Martini, *Beato Agostino Novello*. Siena, Pinacoteca Nazionale.

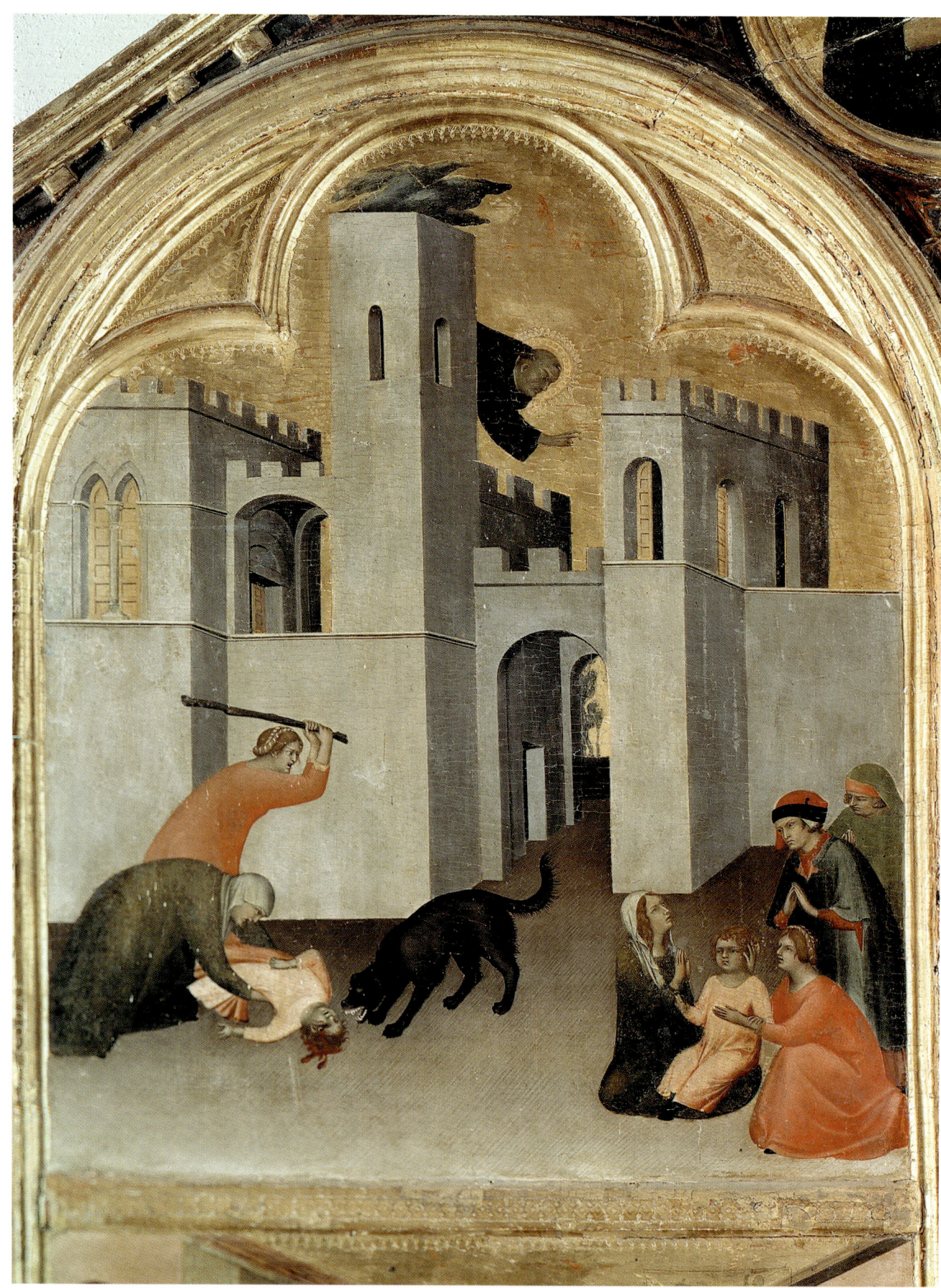

Color Plate 8. Simone Martini, *Beato Agostino Novello,* detail. Siena, Pinacoteca Nazionale.

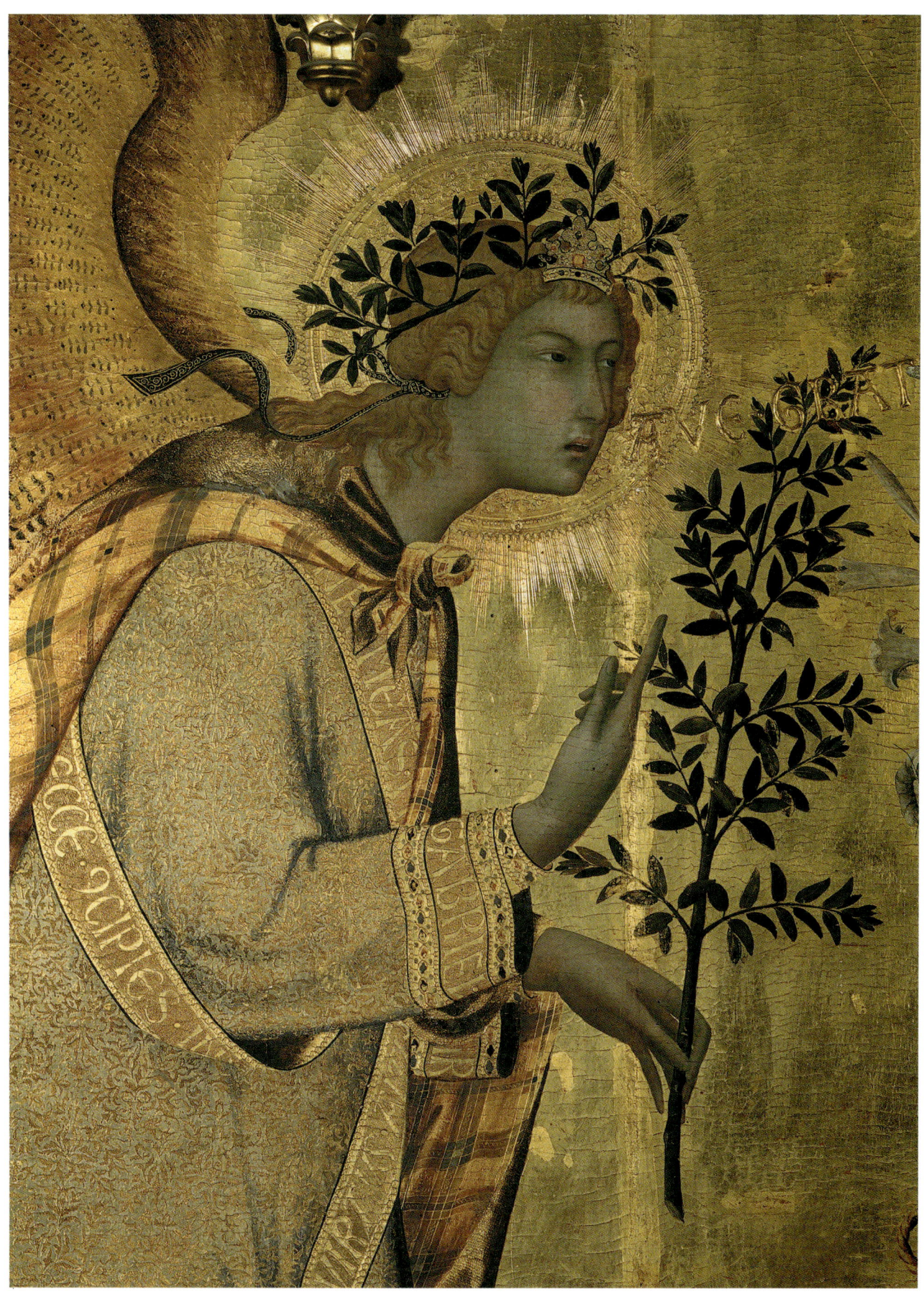

Color Plate 9. Simone Martini and Lippo Memmi, *Annunciation,* detail: the archangel Gabriel. Florence, Galleria degli Uffizi.

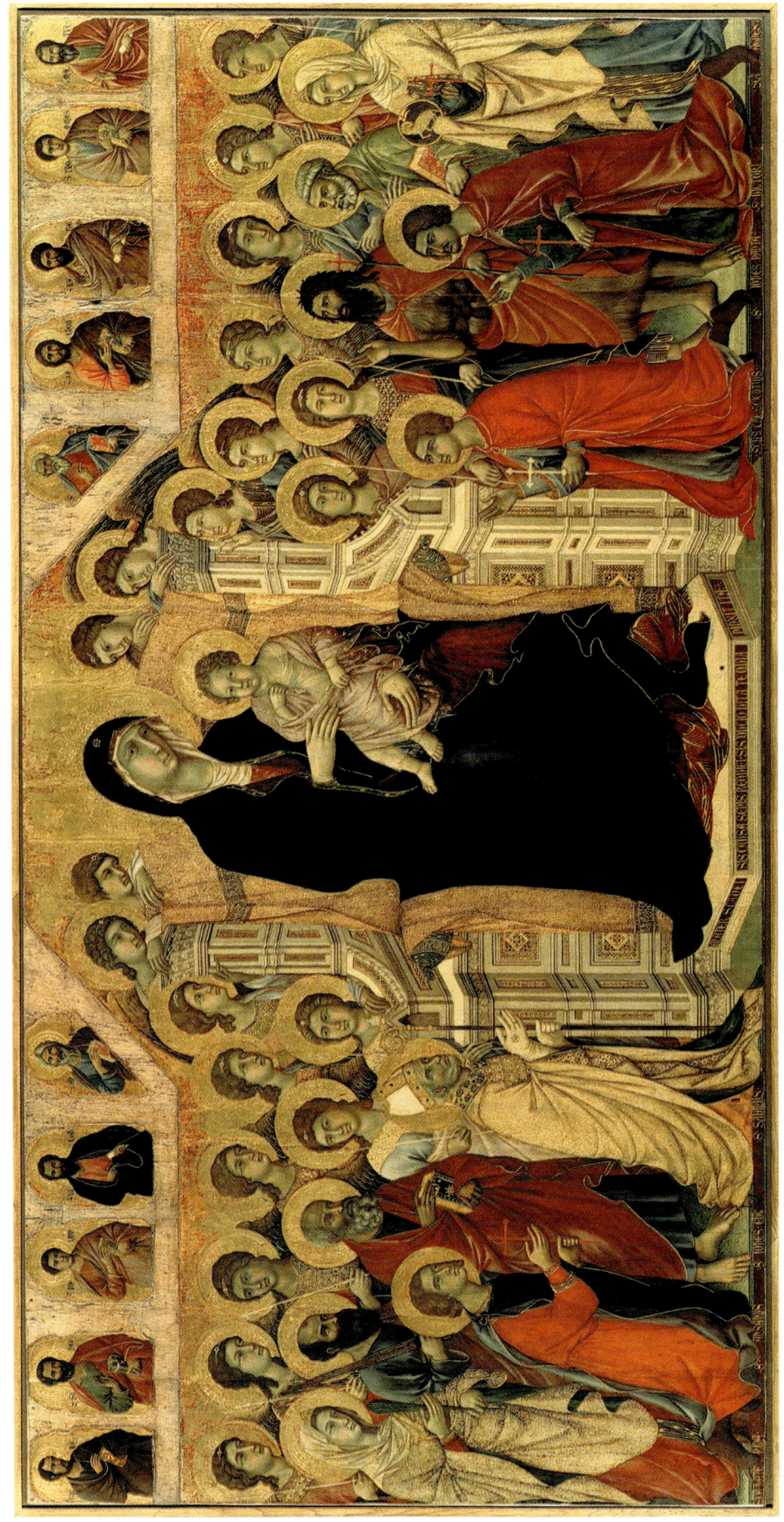

Color Plate 10. Duccio di Buoninsegna, *Maestà*, front. Siena, Museo dell'Opera del Duomo.

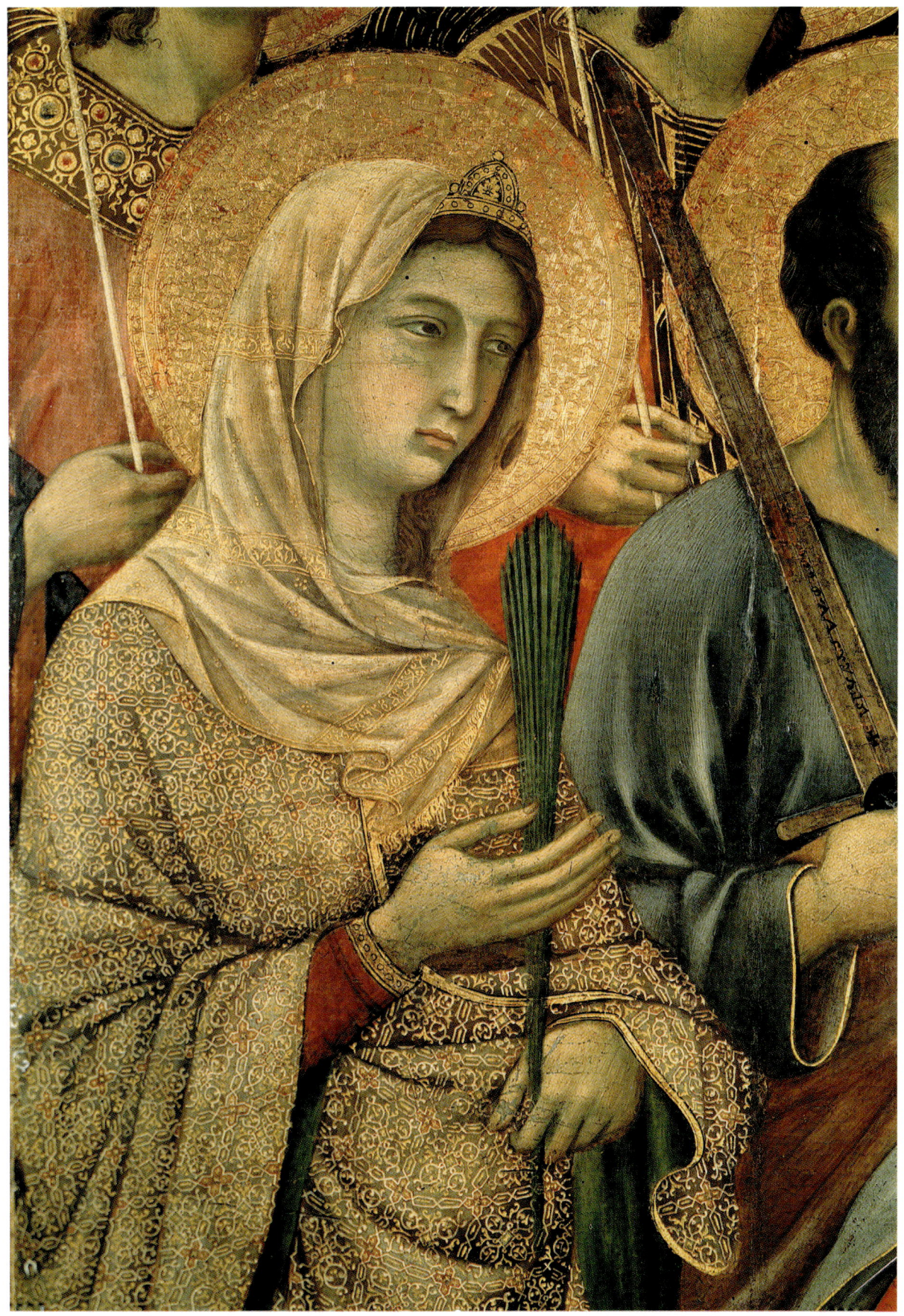

Color Plate 11. Duccio di Buoninsegna, *Maestà,* front, detail: Saint Catherine of Alexandria. Siena, Museo dell'Opera del Duomo.

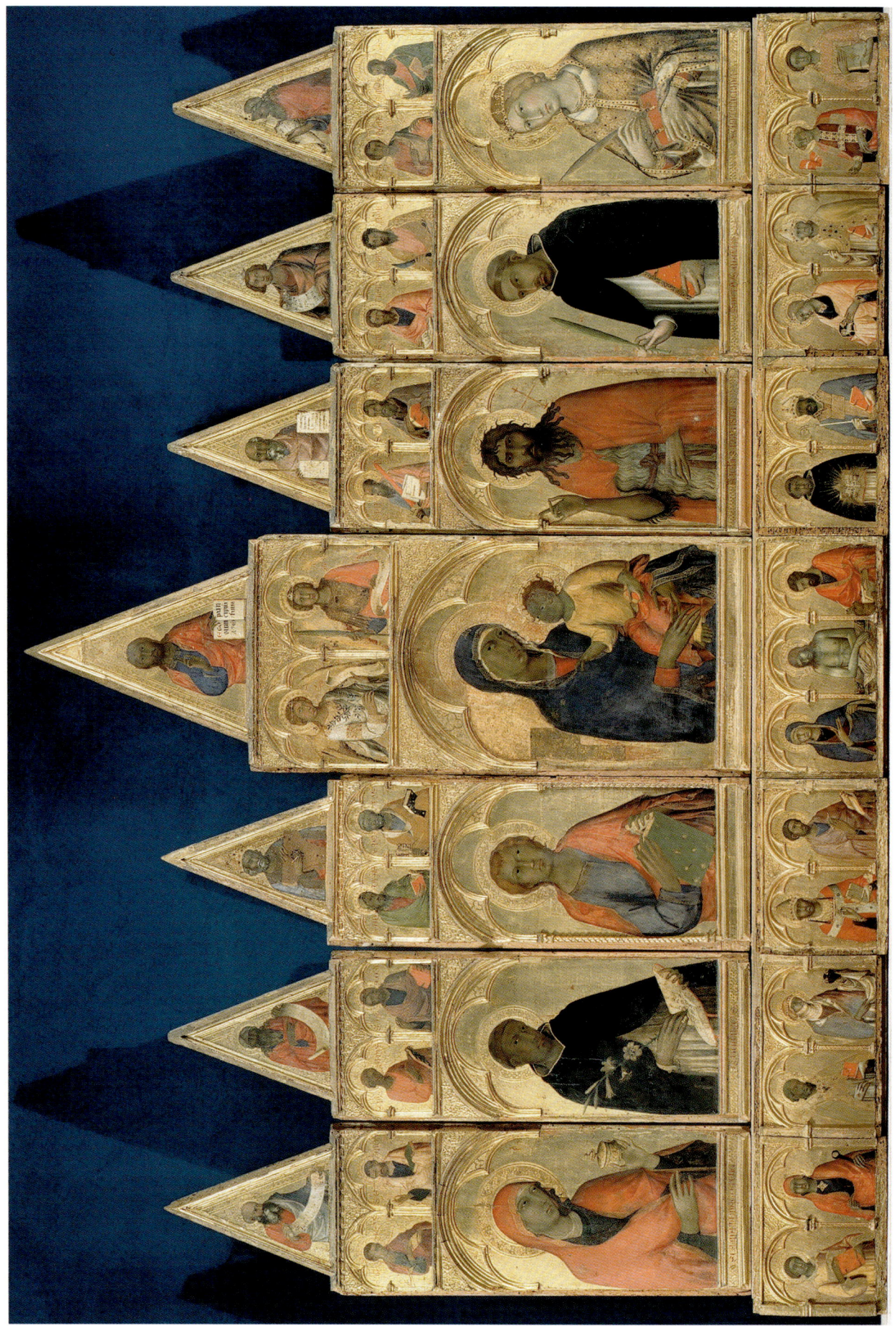

Color Plate 12. Simone Martini, the Pisa altarpiece. Pisa, Museo Nazionale di San Matteo.

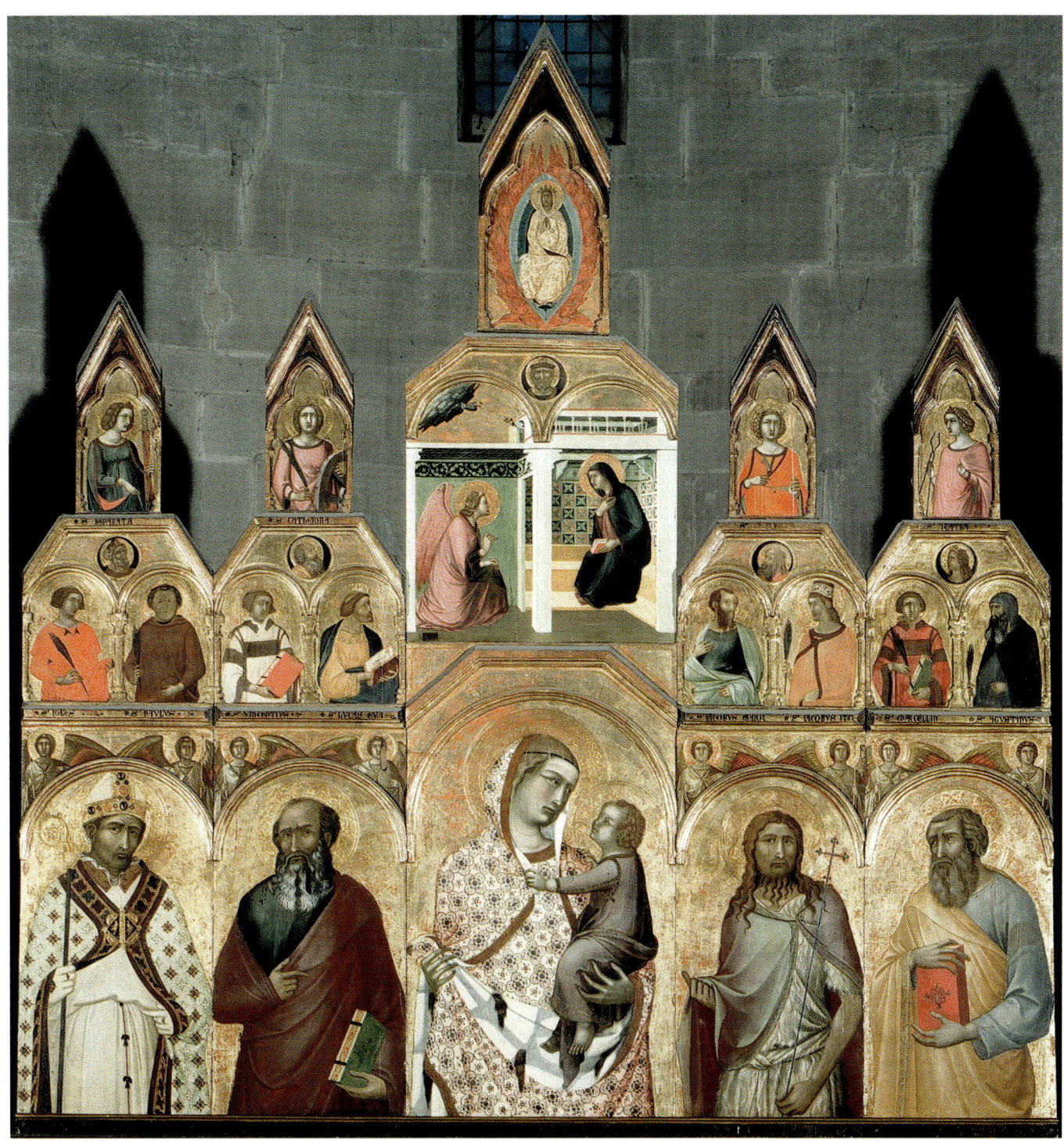

Color Plate 13. Pietro Lorenzetti, the Arezzo polyptych. Arezzo, Santa Maria della Pieve.

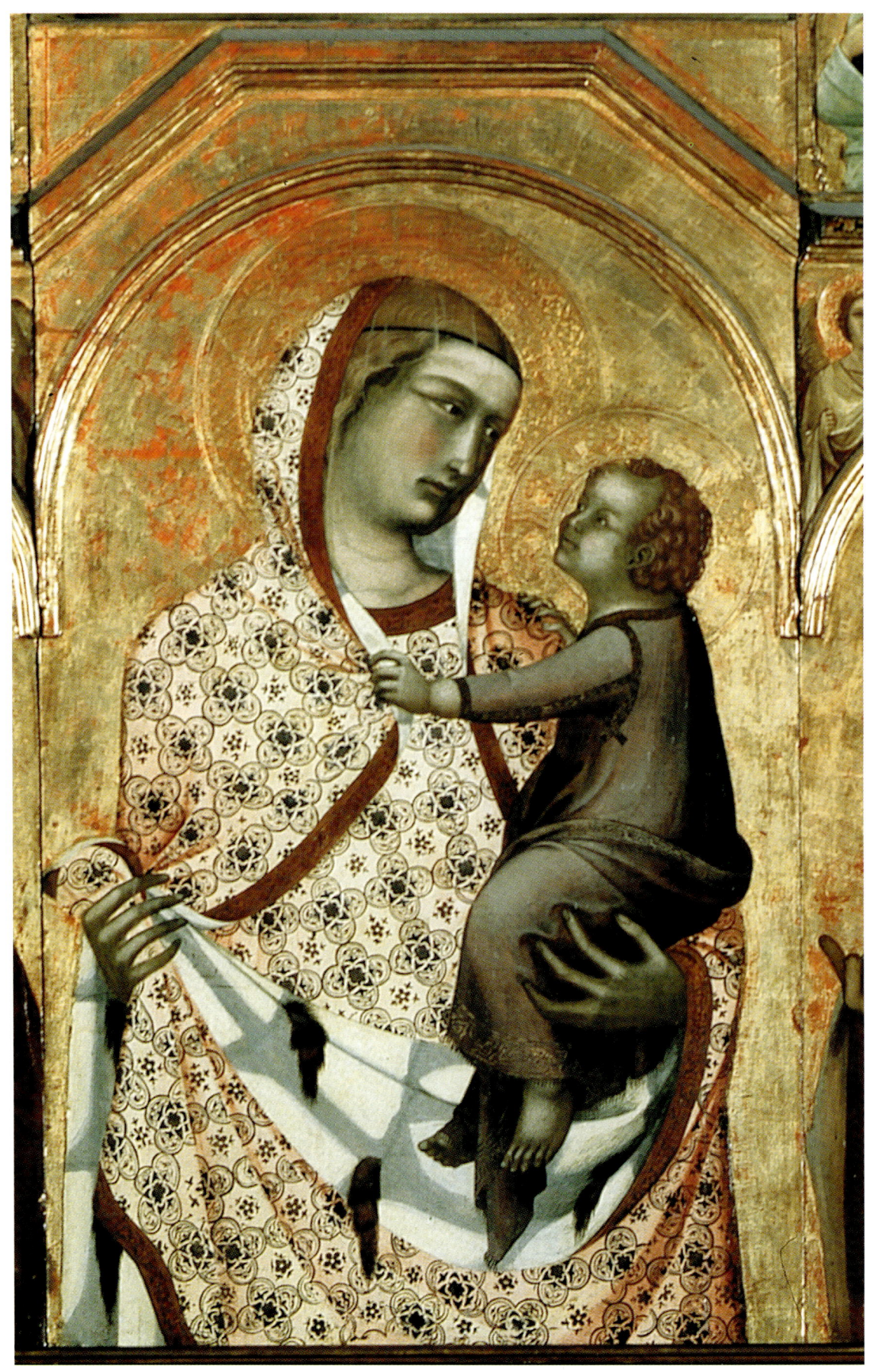

Color Plate 14. Pietro Lorenzetti, the Arezzo polyptych, detail. Arezzo, Santa Maria della Pieve.

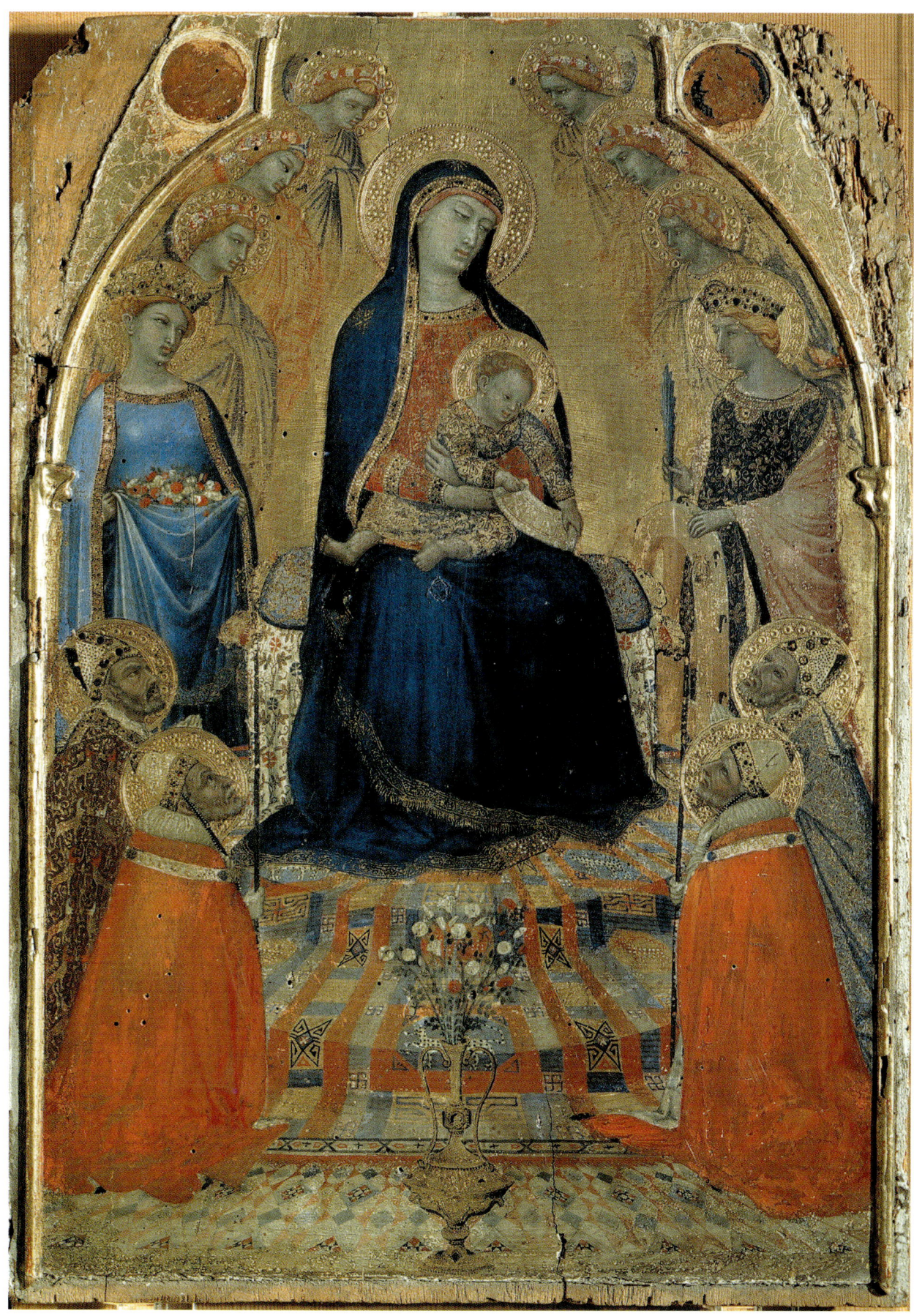

Color Plate 15. Ambrogio Lorenzetti, *Maestà*. Siena, Pinacoteca Nazionale.

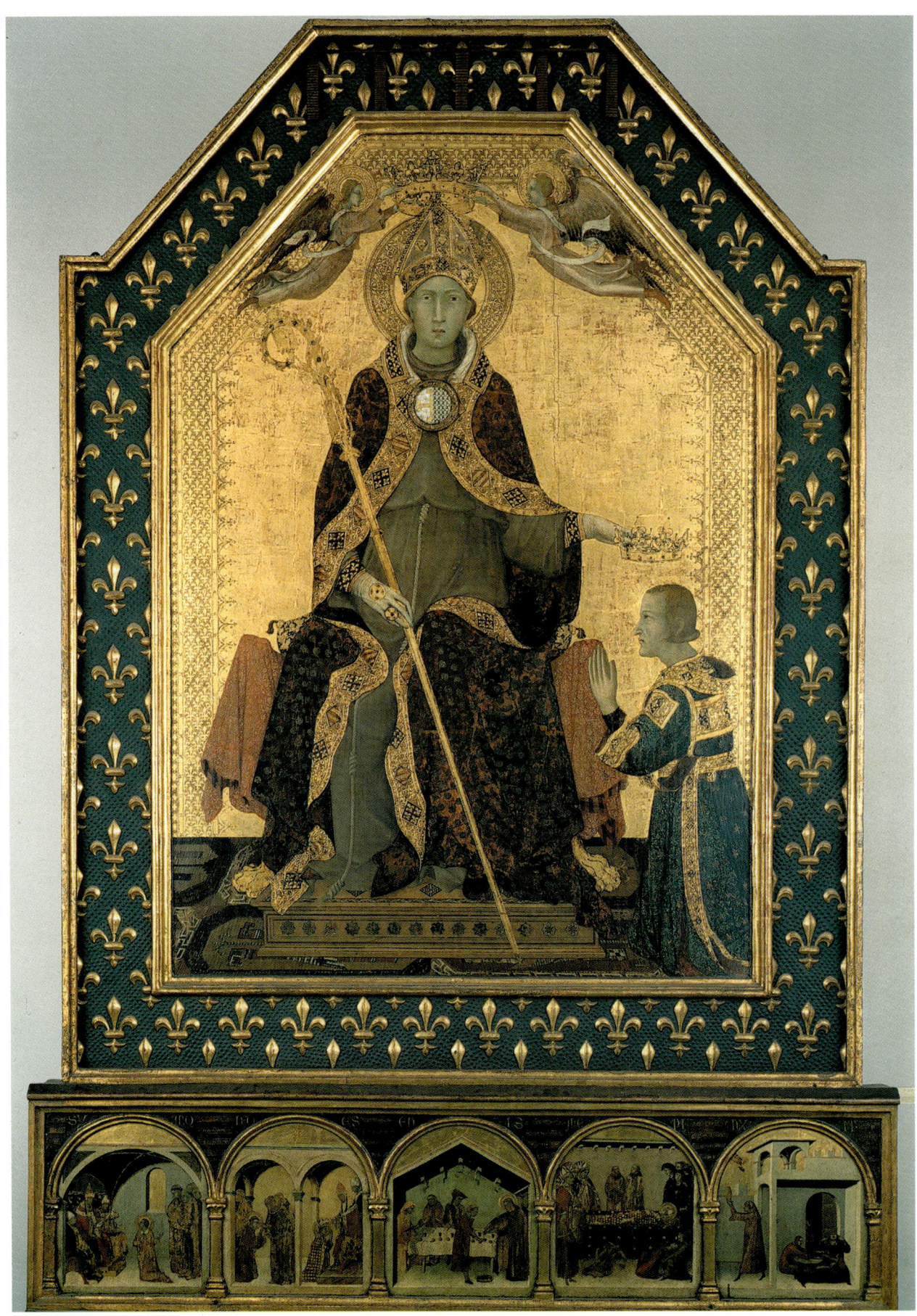

Color Plate 16. Simone Martini, *Saint Louis of Toulouse*. Naples, Museo di Capodimonte.

FIGURES

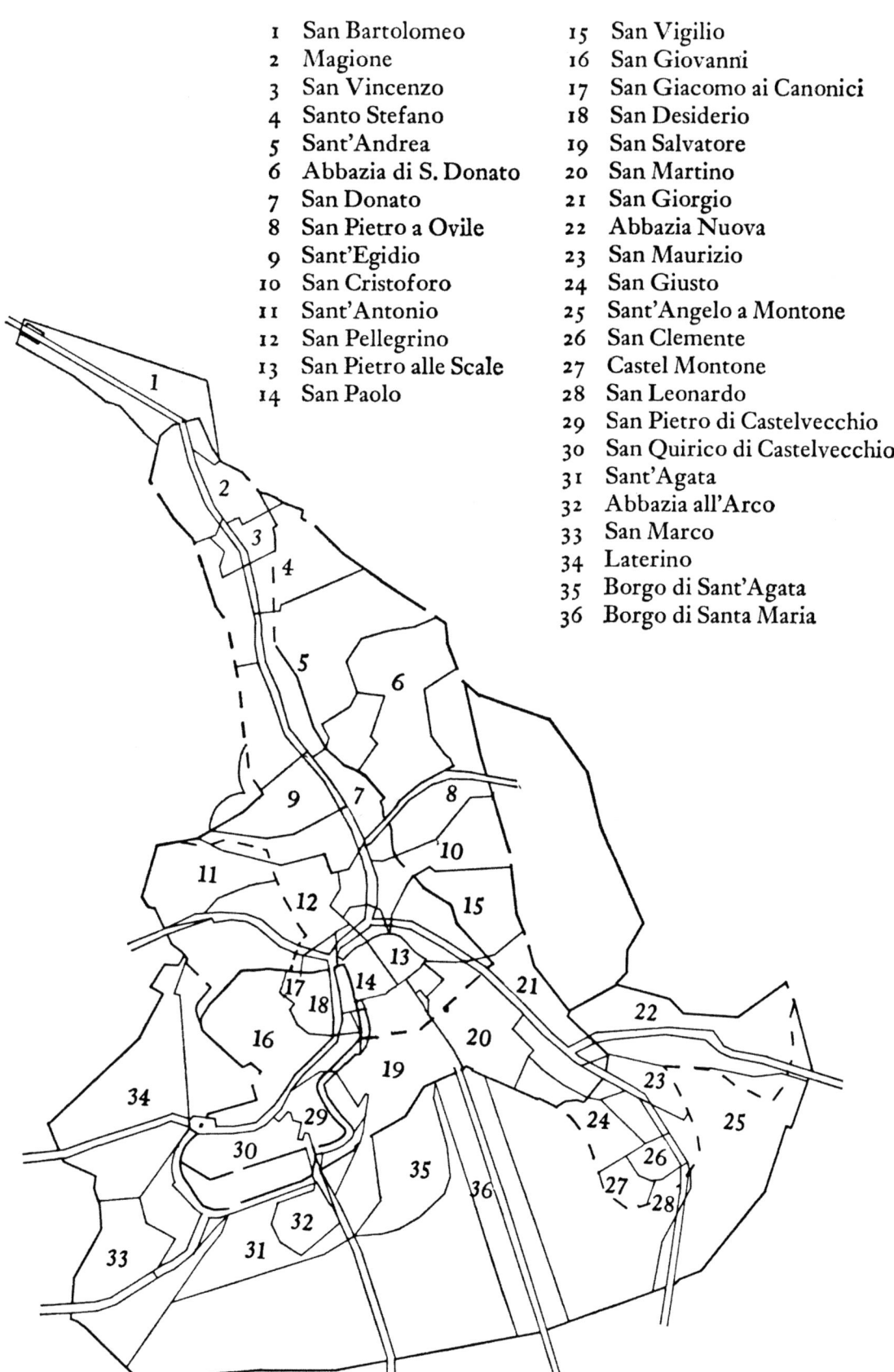

Fig. 1 Map of Siena's parishes.

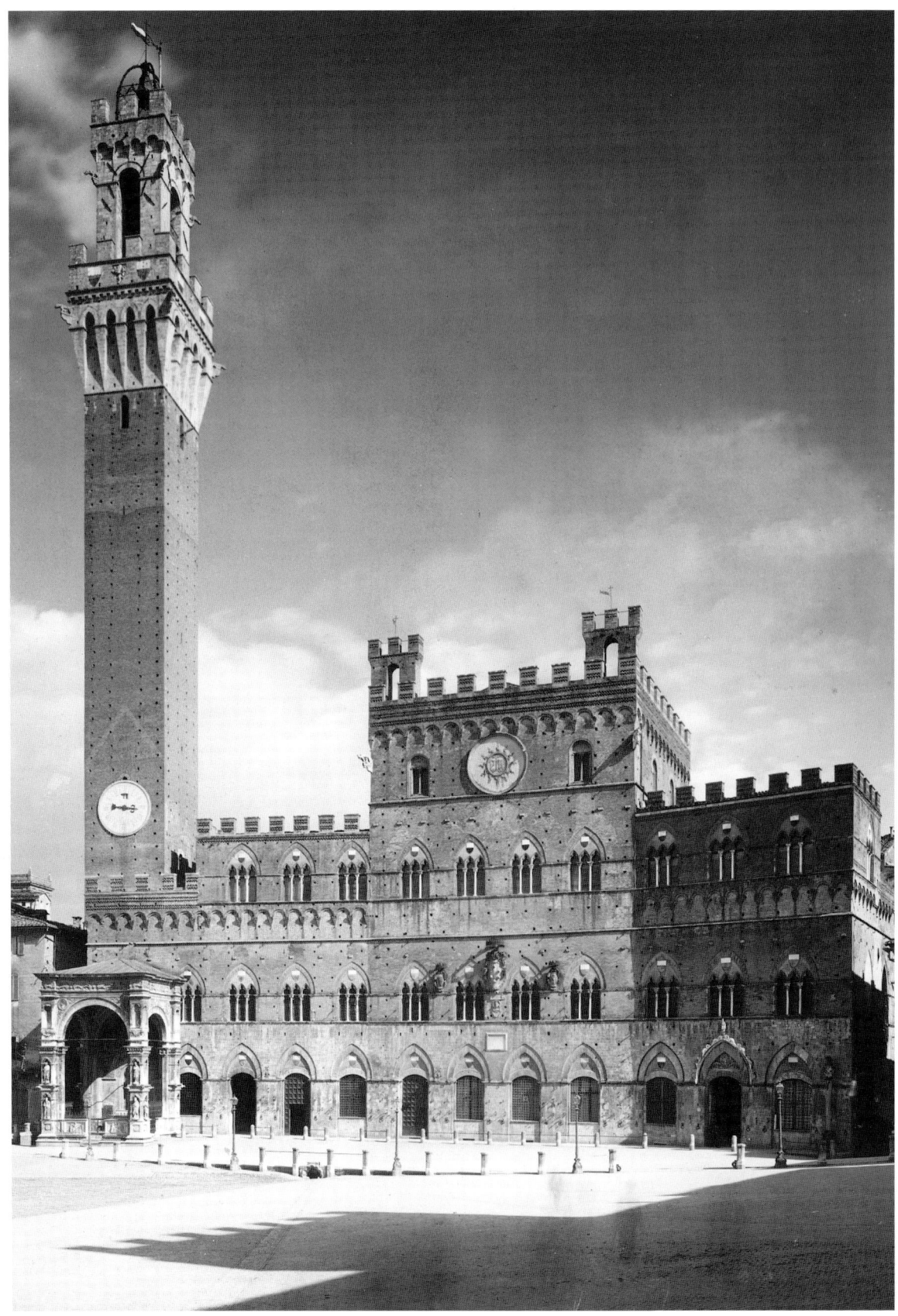

Fig. 2 The Palazzo Pubblico, Siena.

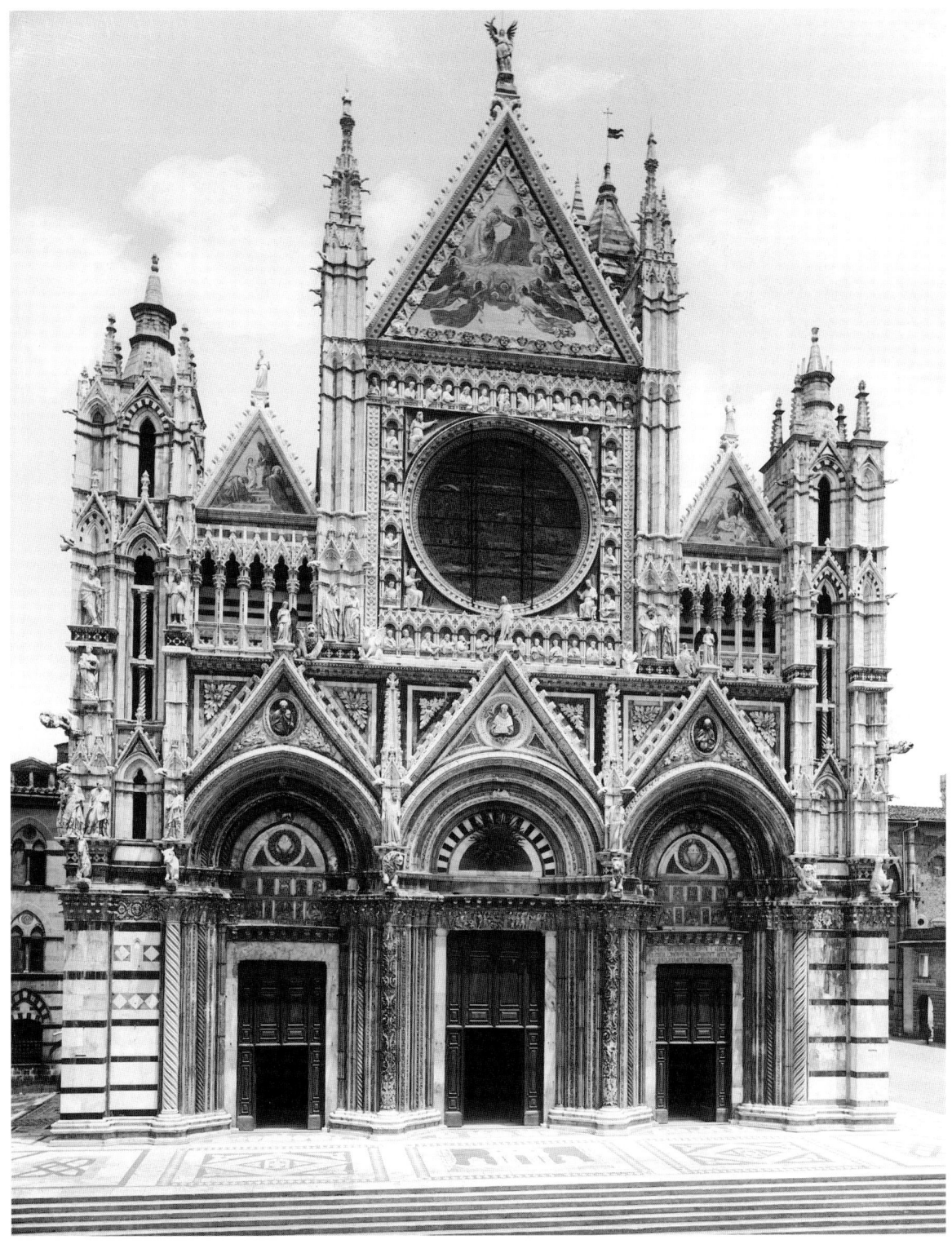

Fig. 3 Siena cathedral, facade.

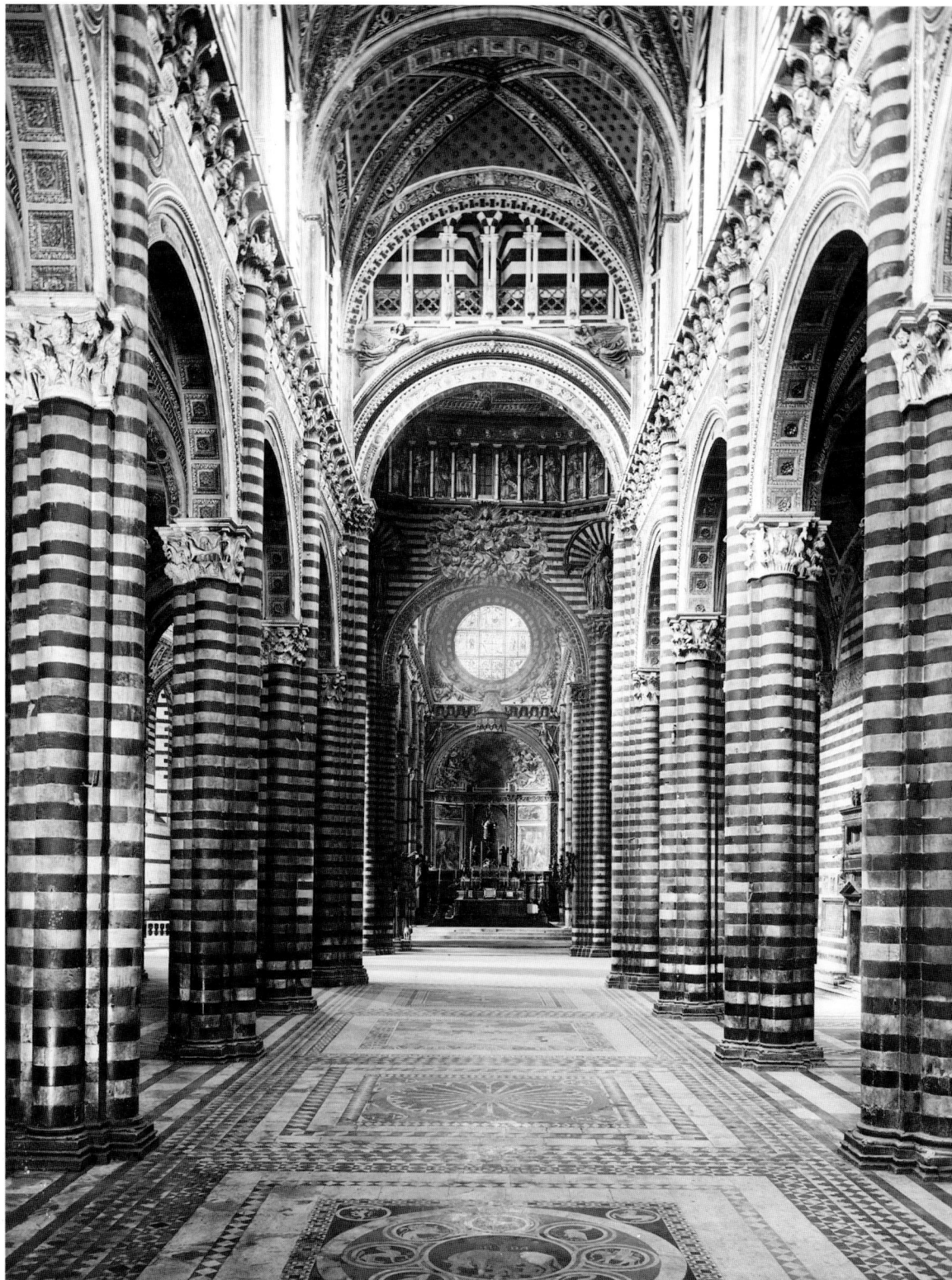

Fig. 4 Siena cathedral, interior.

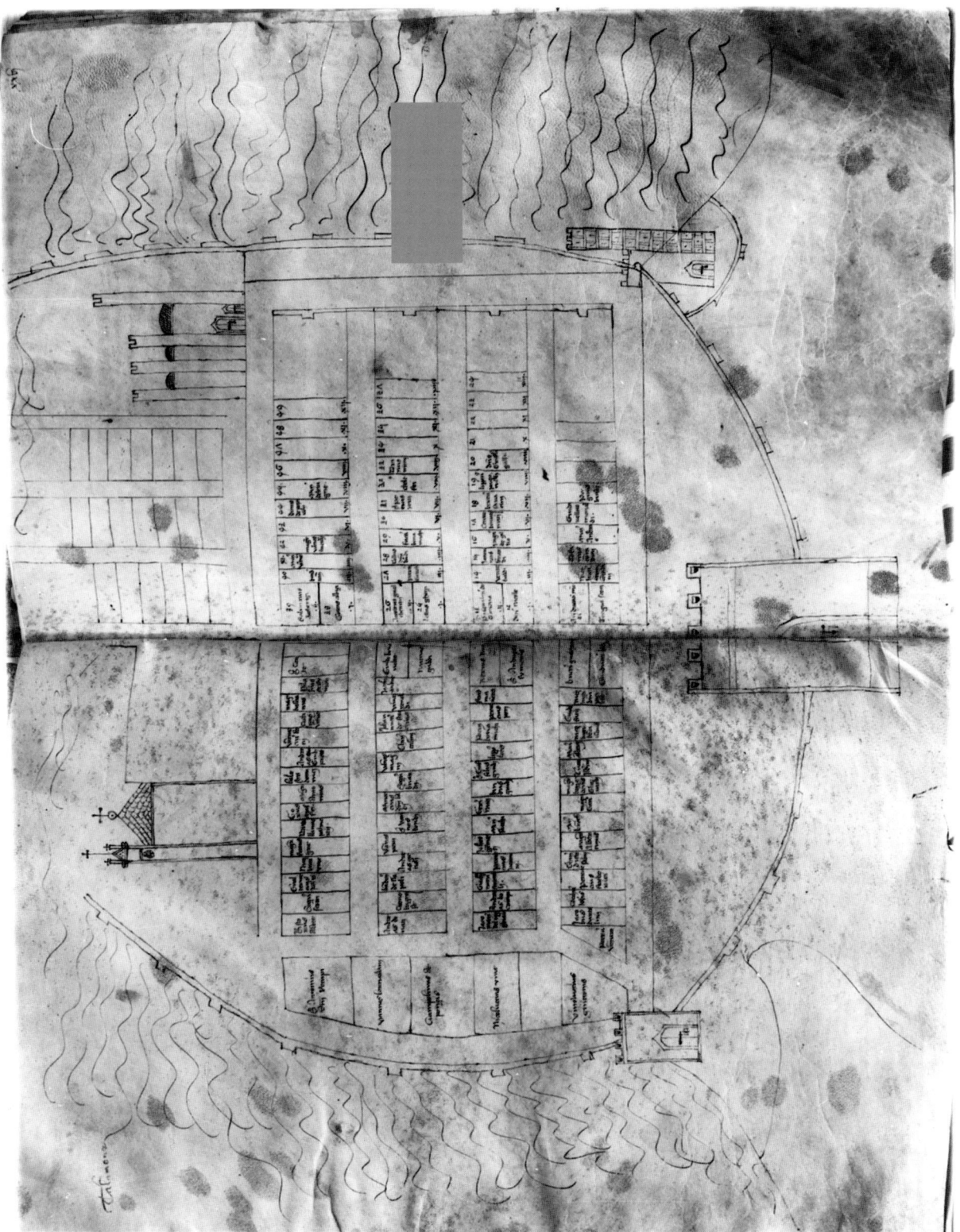

Fig. 5 Plan of Talamone (1306). Siena, Archivio di Stato di Siena.

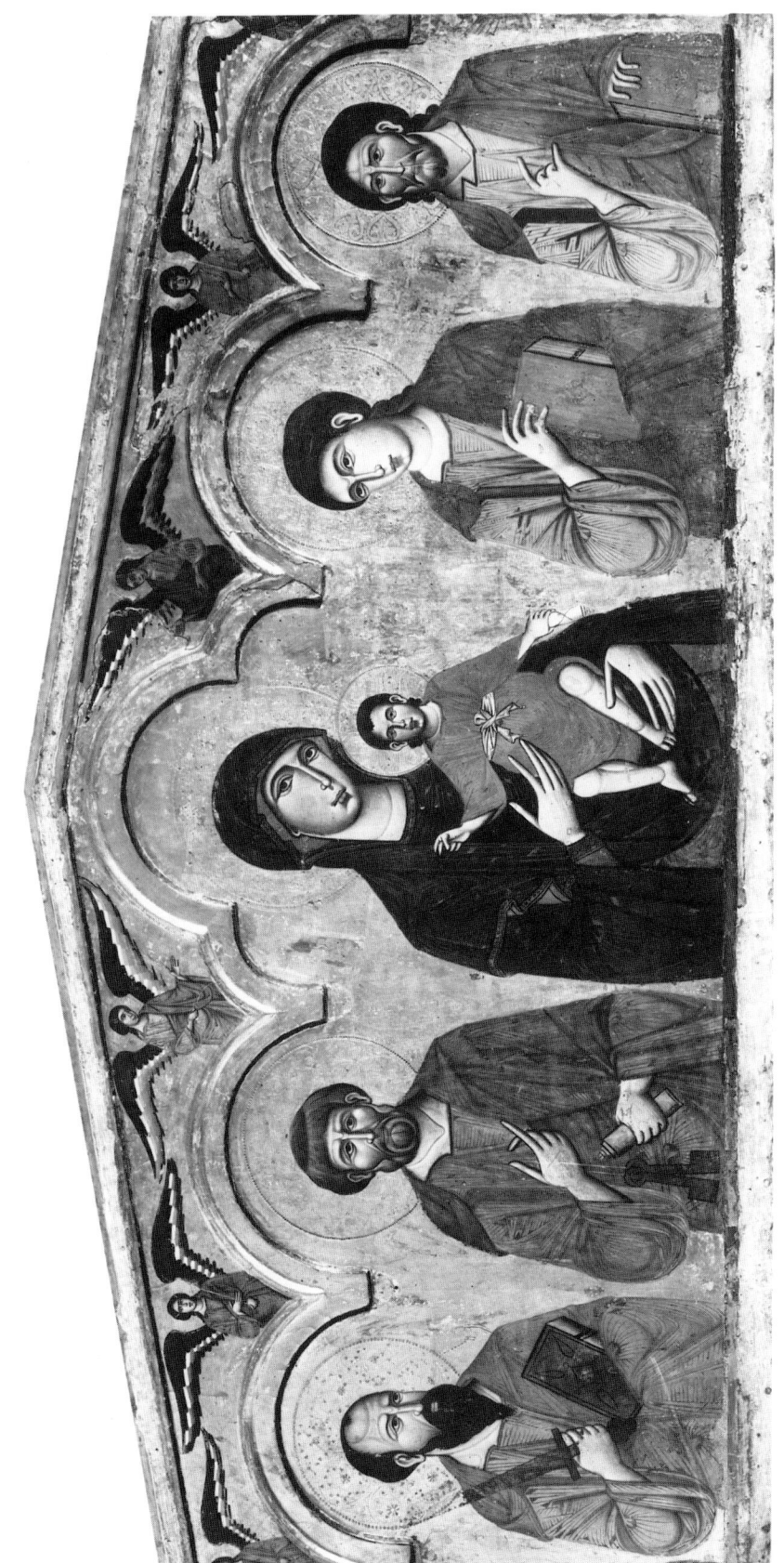

Fig. 6 Dossal no. 6. Siena, Pinacoteca Nazionale.

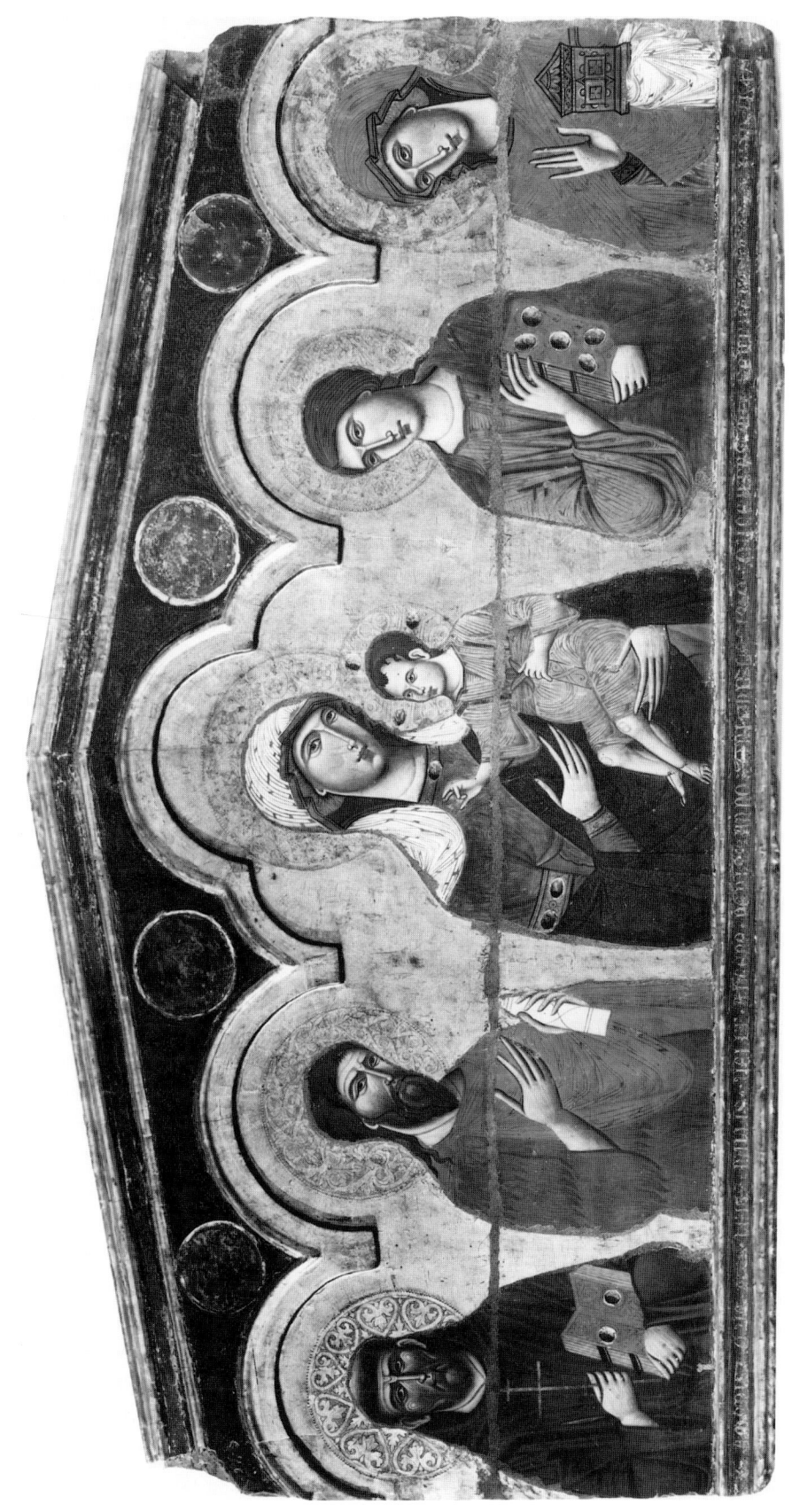

Fig. 7 Dossal no. 7. Siena, Pinacoteca Nazionale.

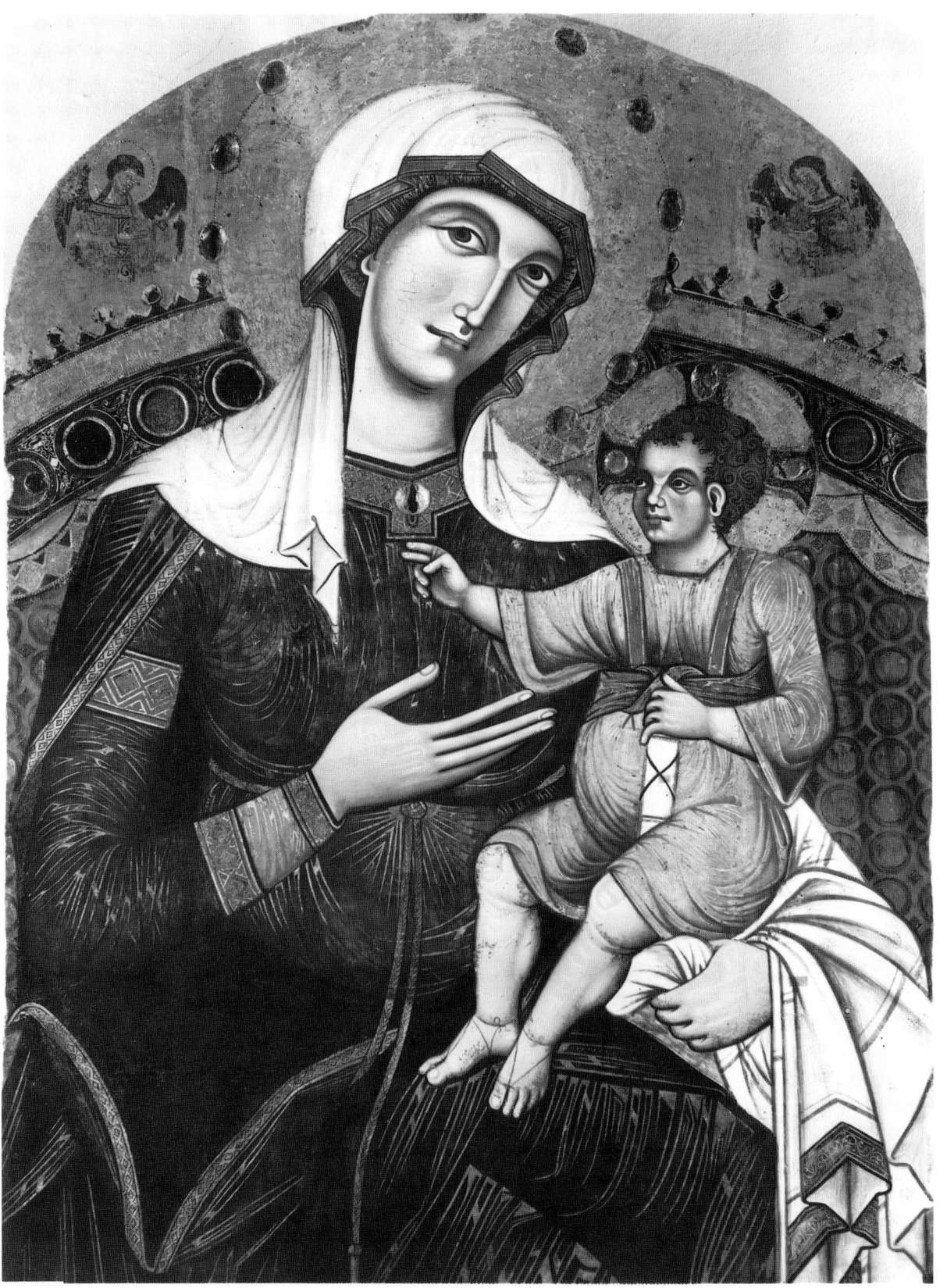

Fig. 8 San Bernardino Master, San Bernardino *Madonna*. Siena, Pinacoteca Nazionale.

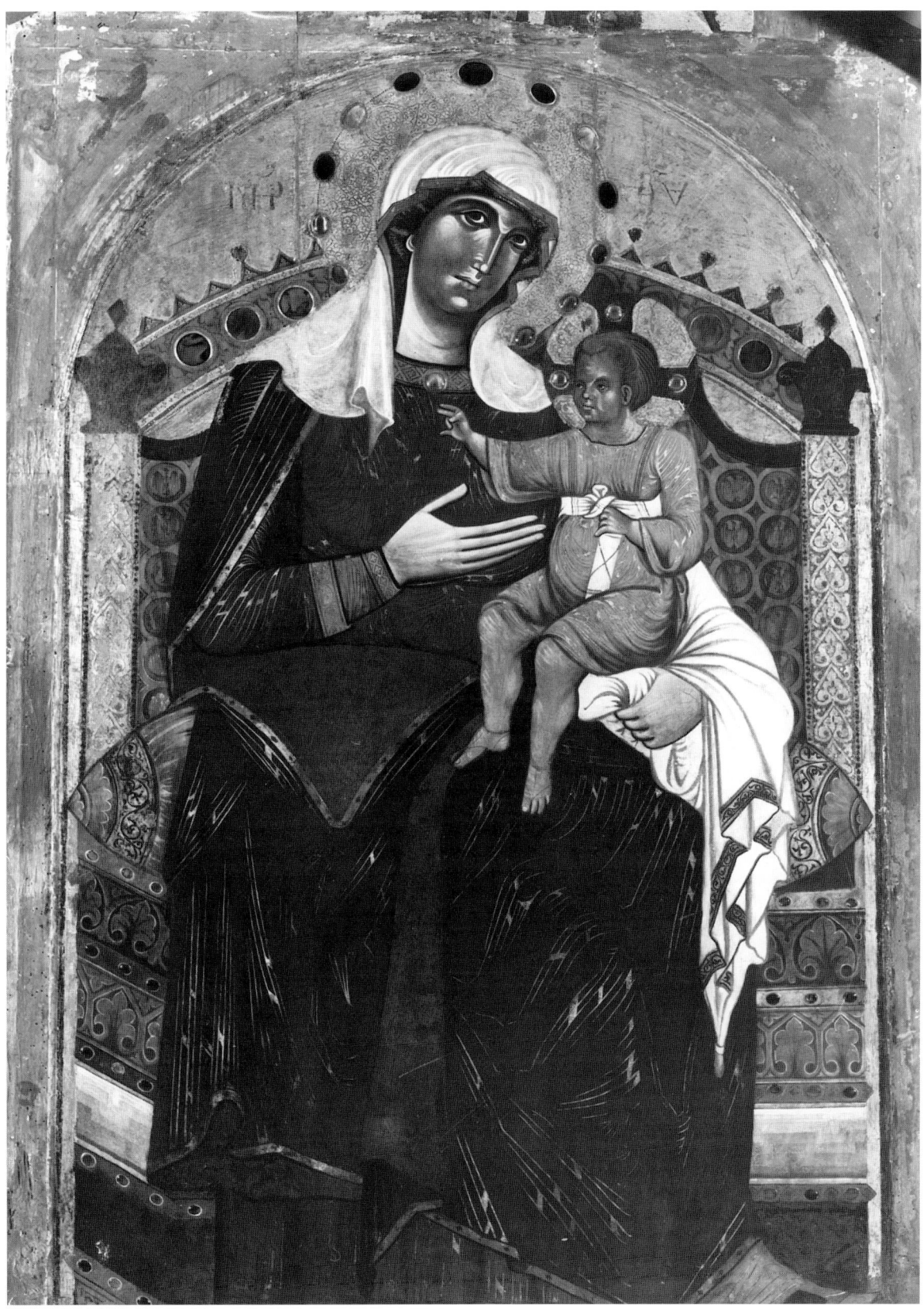
Fig. 9 Replica of the San Bernardino *Madonna*. Arezzo, Museo Statale di Arte Medievale e Moderna.

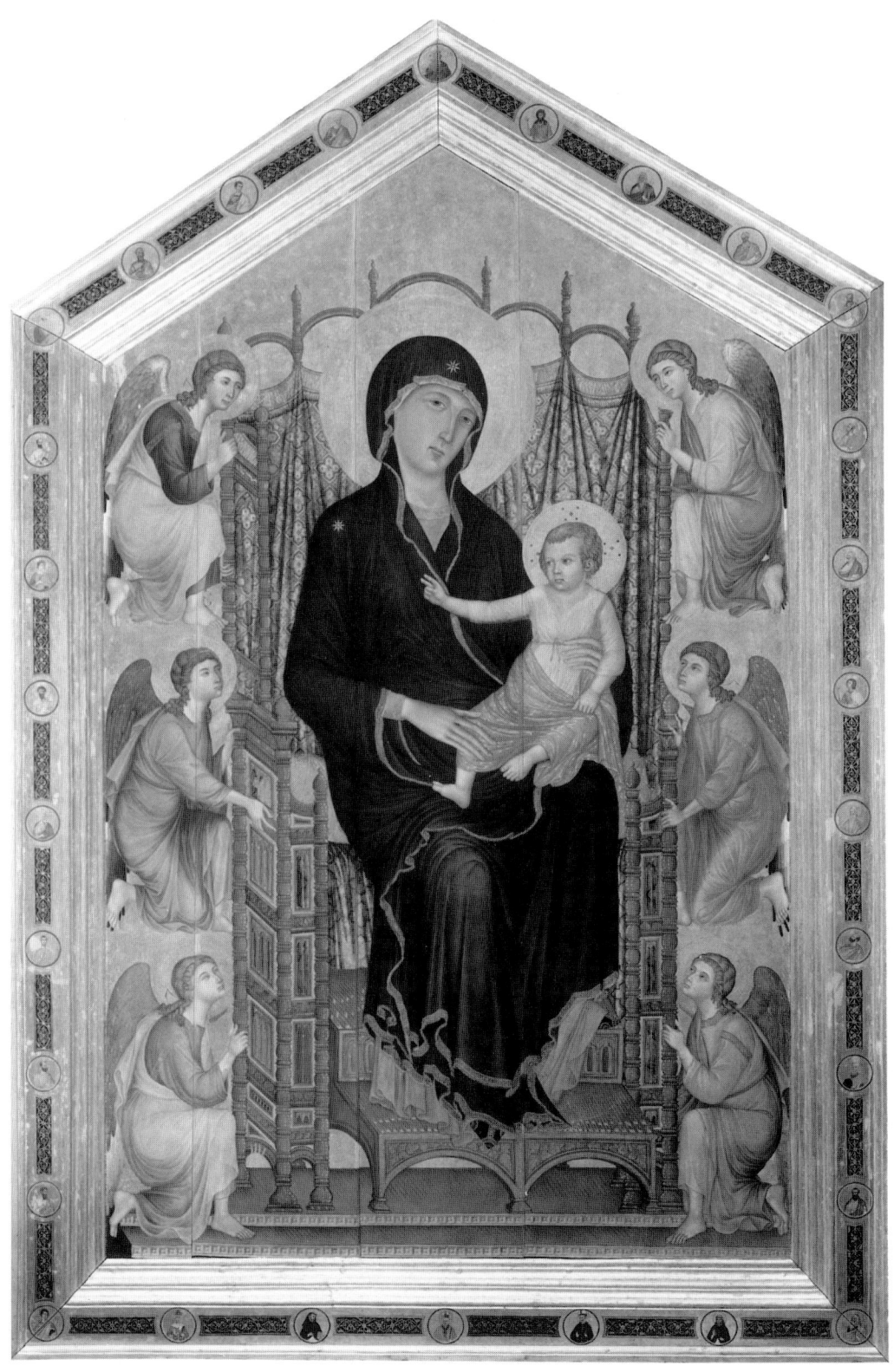

Fig. 10 Duccio di Buoninsegna, Rucellai *Madonna*. Florence, Galleria degli Uffizi.

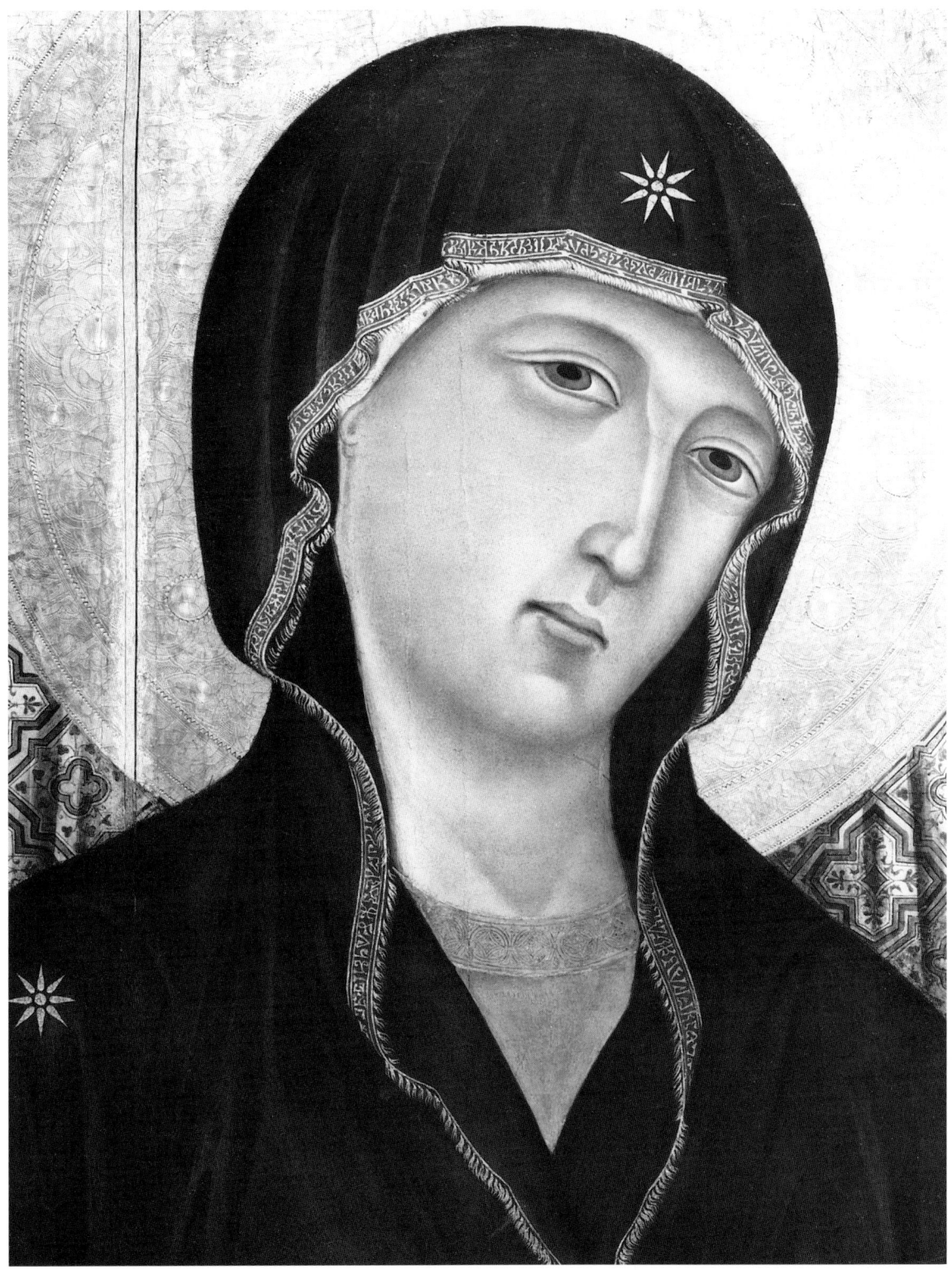

Fig. 11 Duccio di Buoninsegna, Rucellai *Madonna,* detail. Florence, Galleria degli Uffizi.

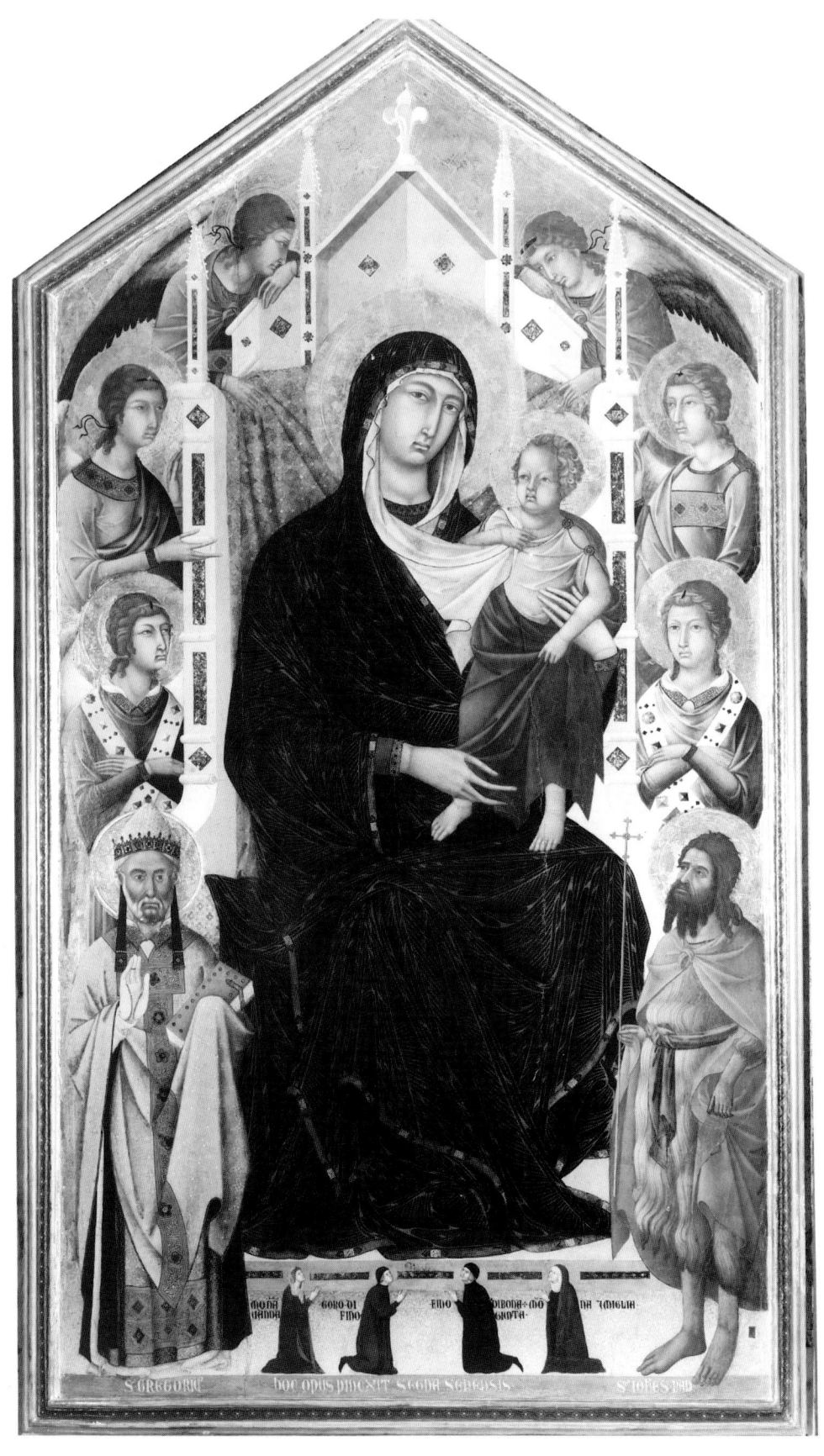

Fig. 12 Segna di Bonaventura, *Madonna*. Castiglion Fiorentino, Collegiata di San Giuliano.

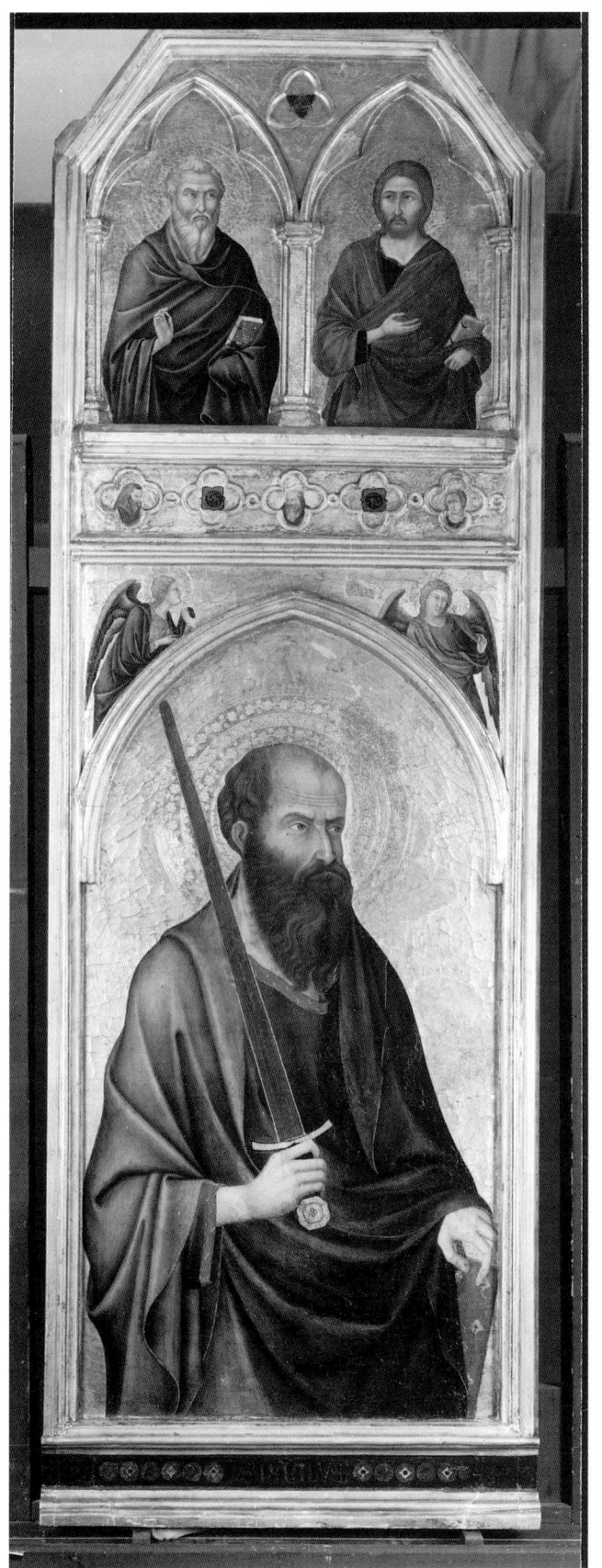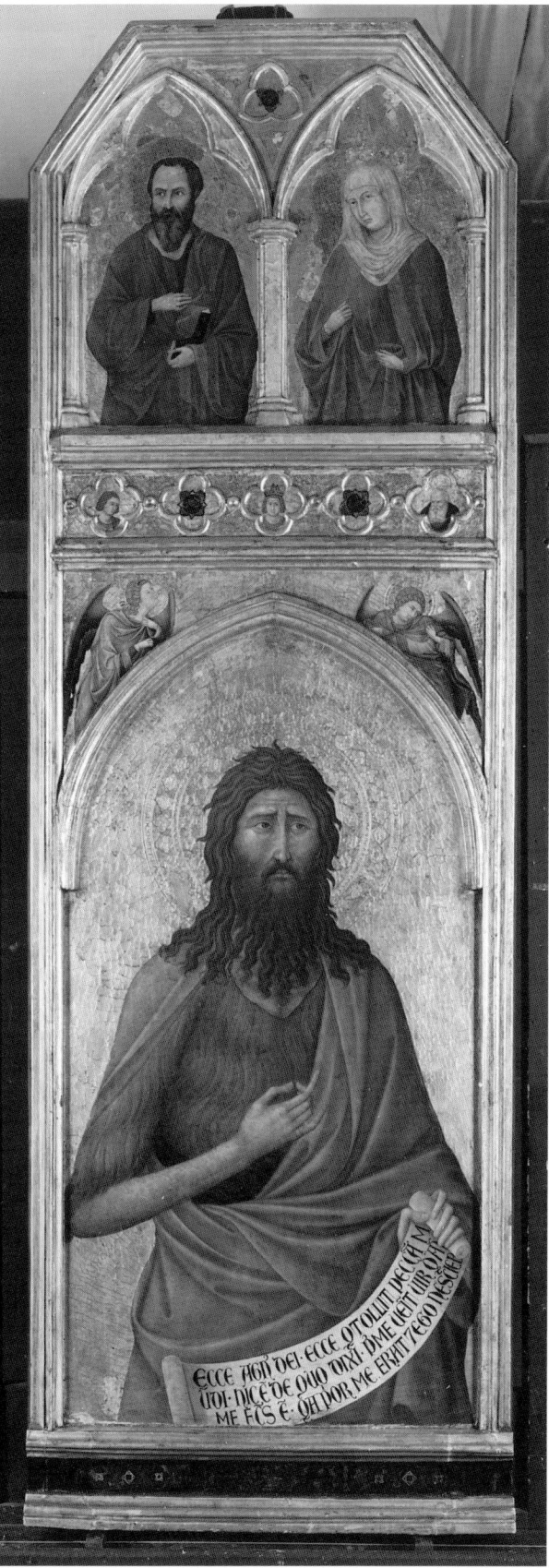

Fig. 13 Ugolino di Nerio, Saints Paul and John the Baptist (from the Santa Croce altarpiece). Berlin, Staatliche Museen Preußischer Kulturbesitz, Gemäldegalerie.

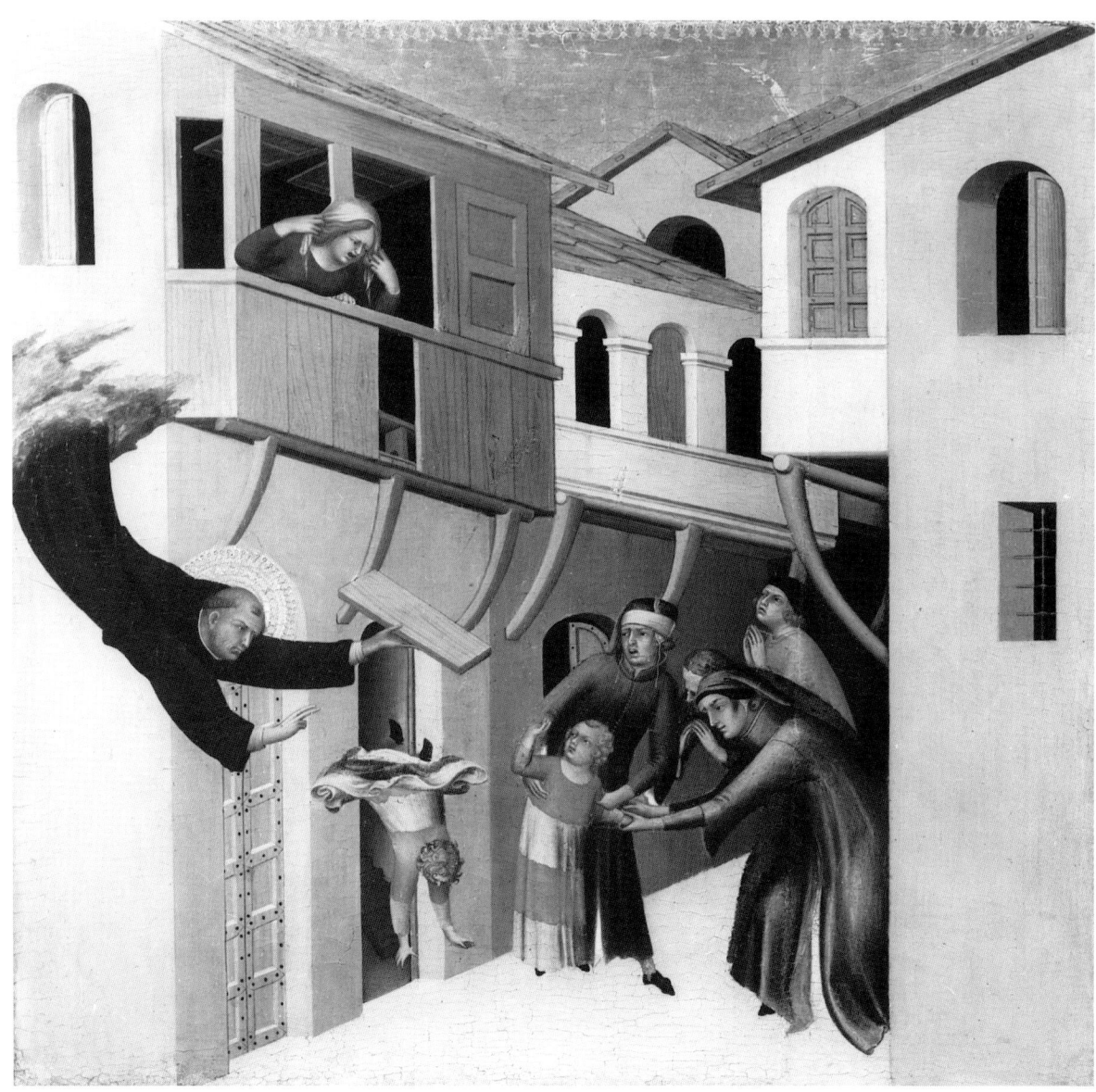

Fig. 14 Simone Martini, *Beato Agostino Novello,* detail. Siena, Pinacoteca Nazionale.

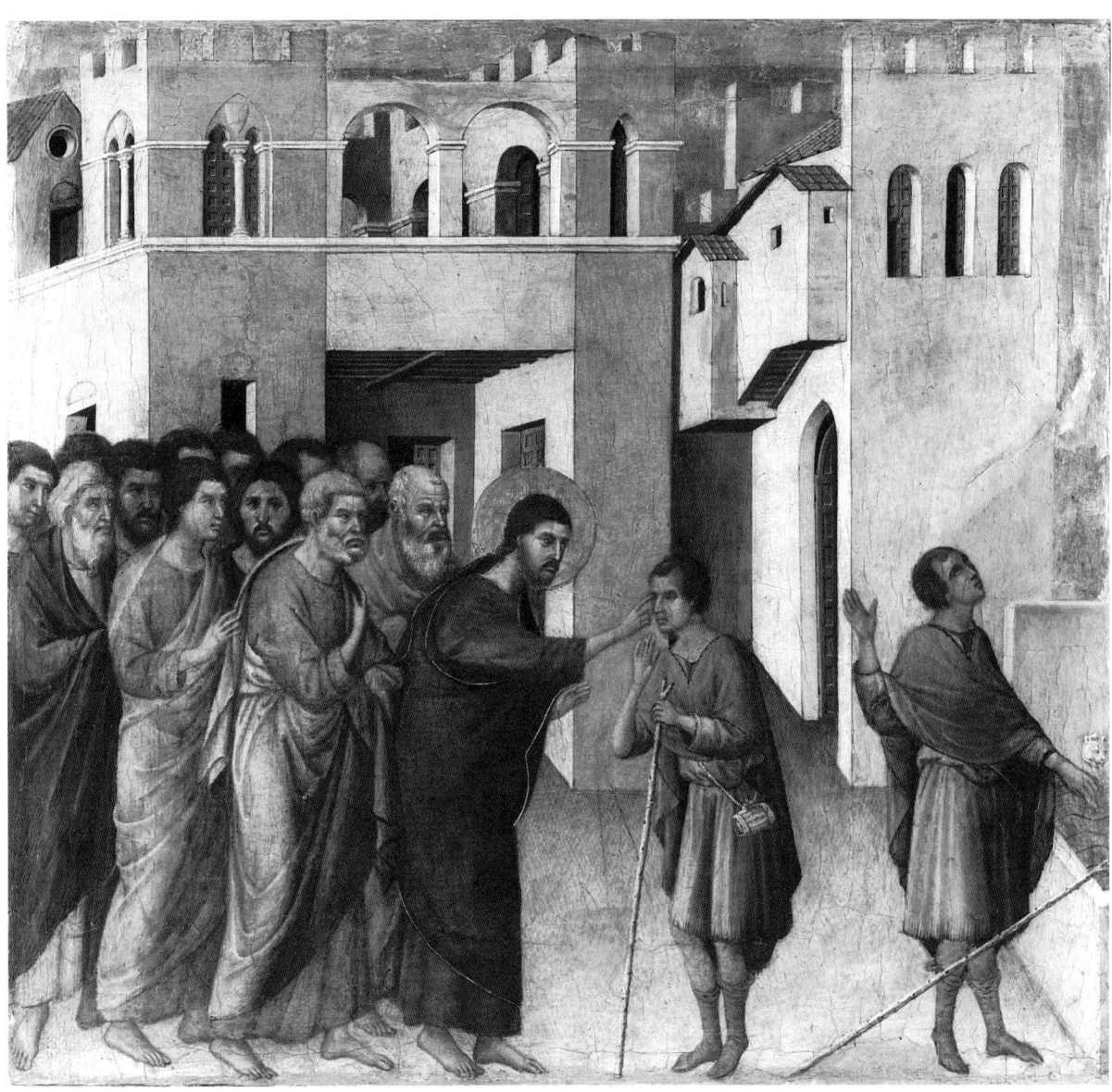

Fig. 15 Duccio di Buoninsegna, *Healing of a Man Born Blind* (detail from the *Maestà*). London, National Gallery.

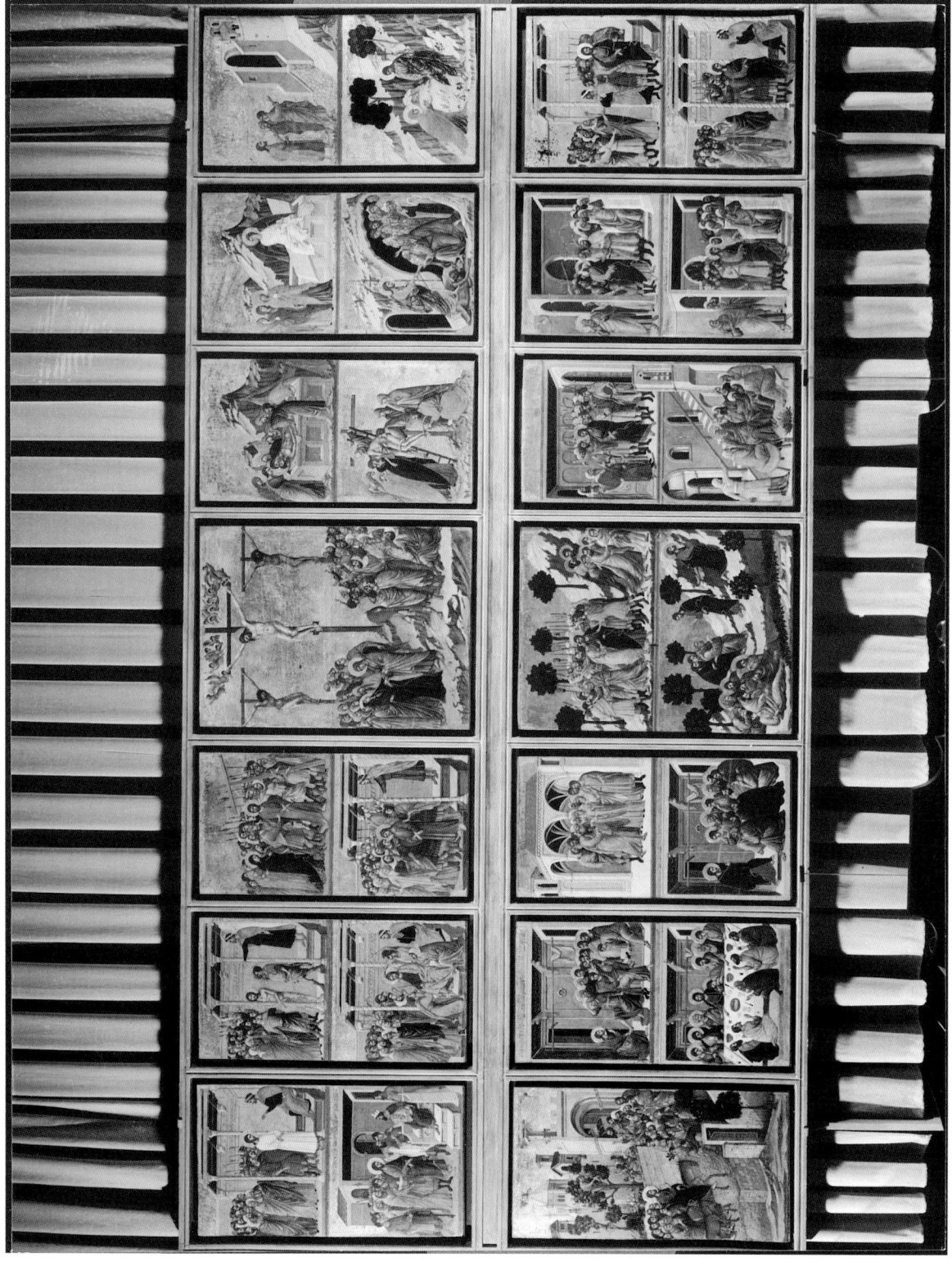

Fig. 16 Duccio di Buoninsegna, back of the *Maestà*. Siena, Museo dell'Opera del Duomo.

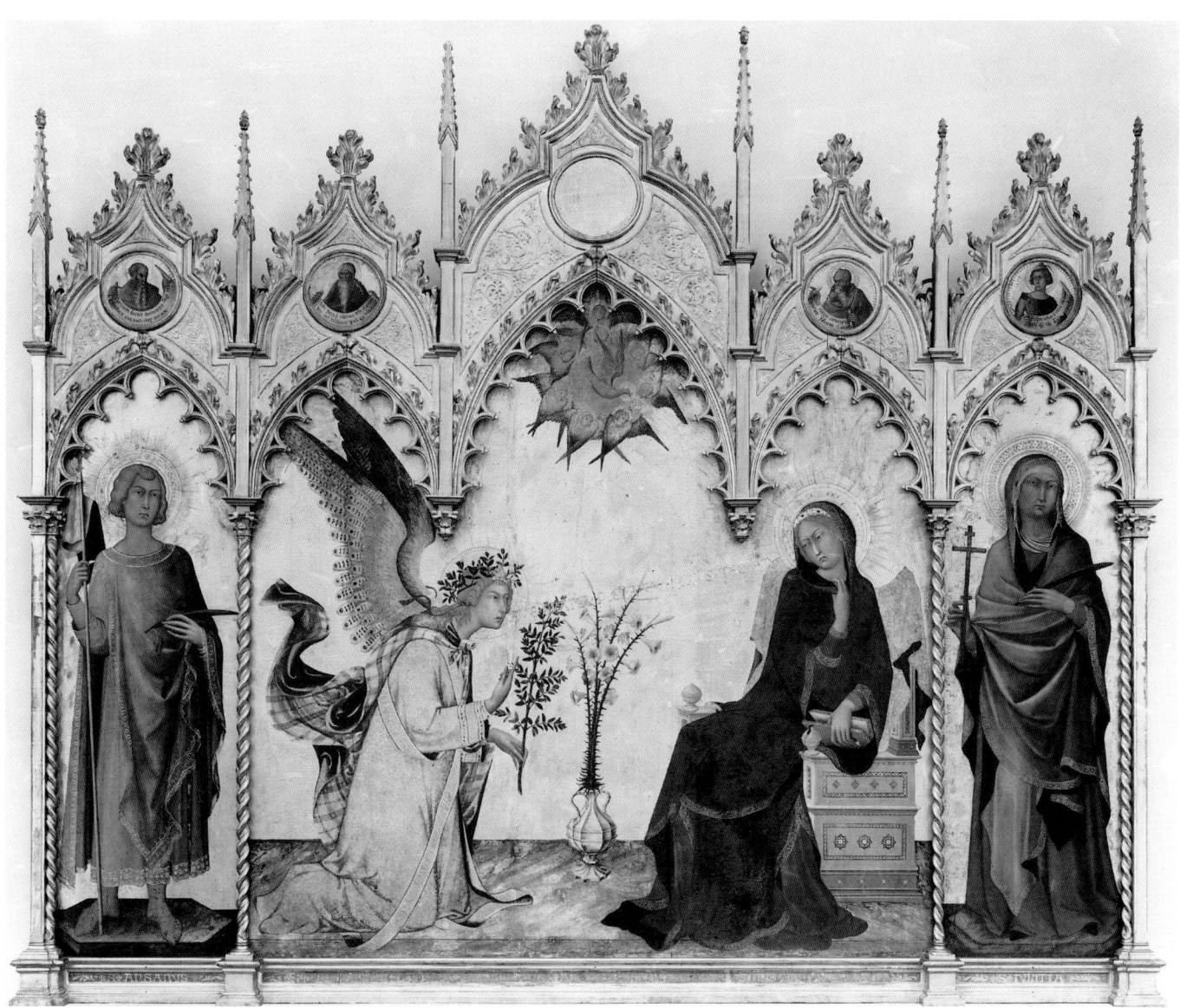

Fig. 17 Simone Martini and Lippo Memmi, *Annunciation* (1333). Florence, Galleria degli Uffizi.

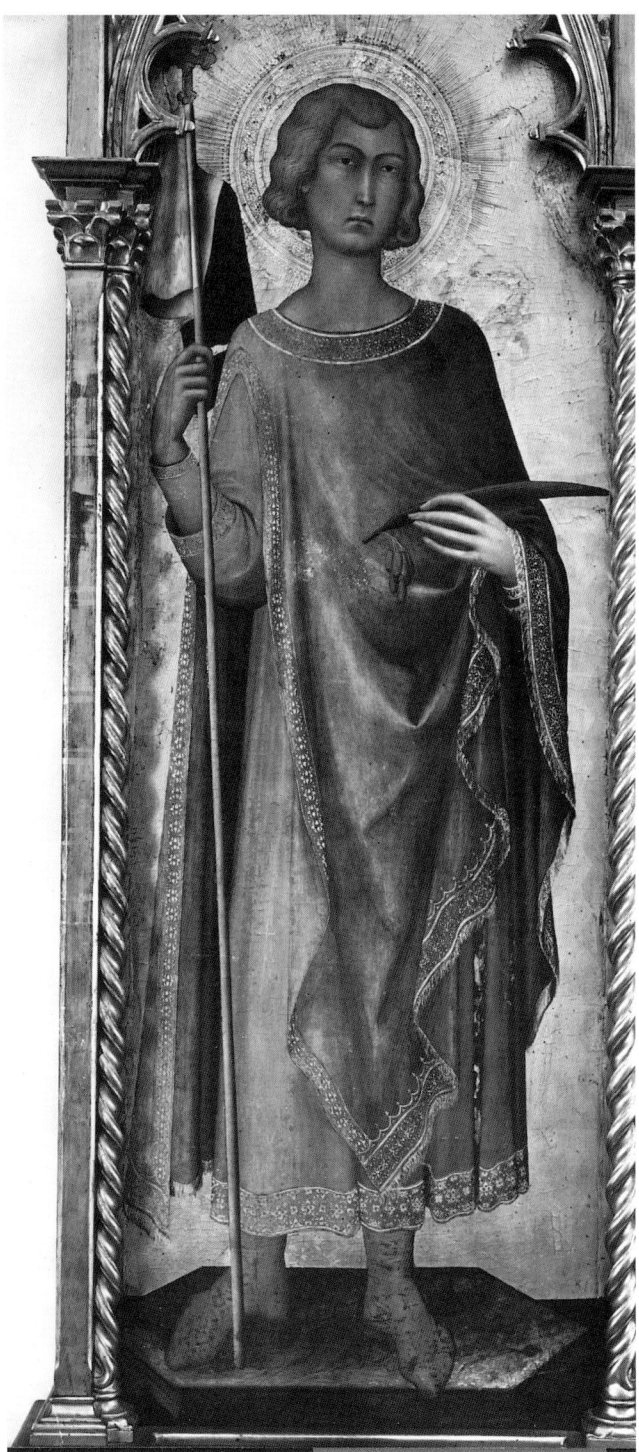

Fig. 18 Simone Martini and Lippo Memmi, *Annunciation*, detail: San Ansano. Florence, Galleria degli Uffizi.

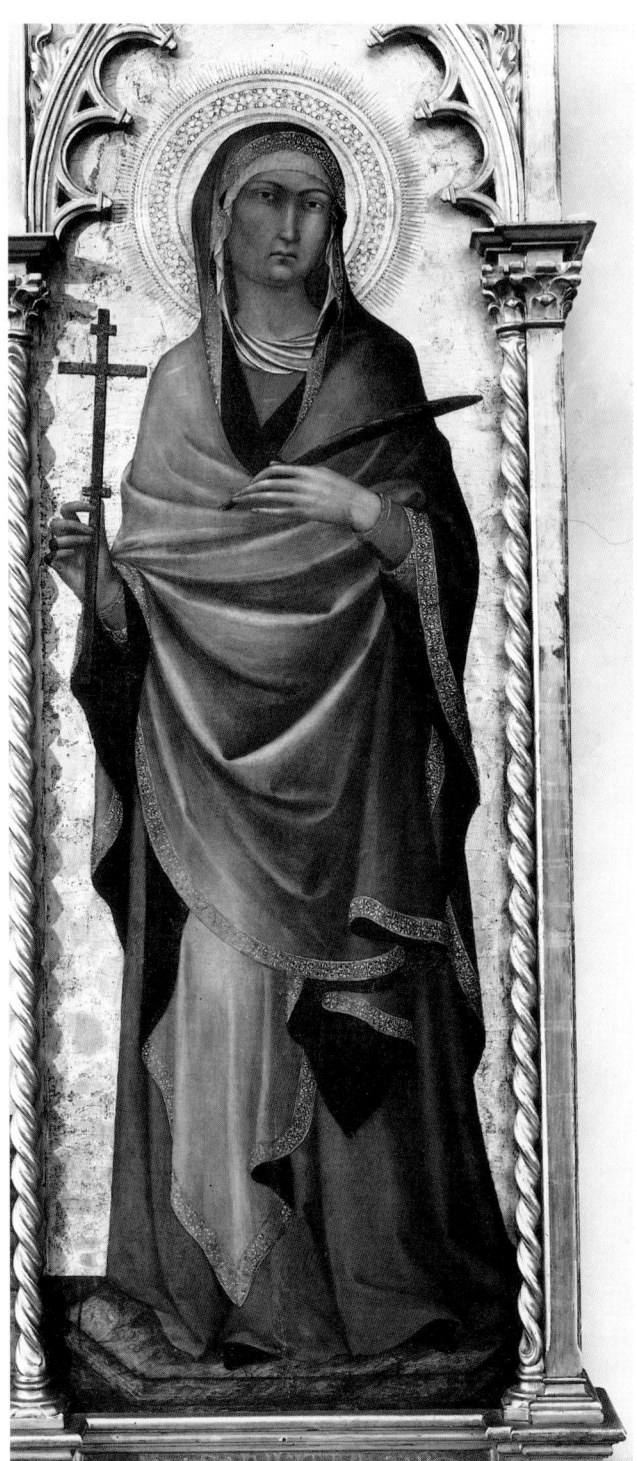

Fig. 19 Simone Martini and Lippo Memmi, *Annunciation*, detail: Santa Massima. Florence, Galleria degli Uffizi.

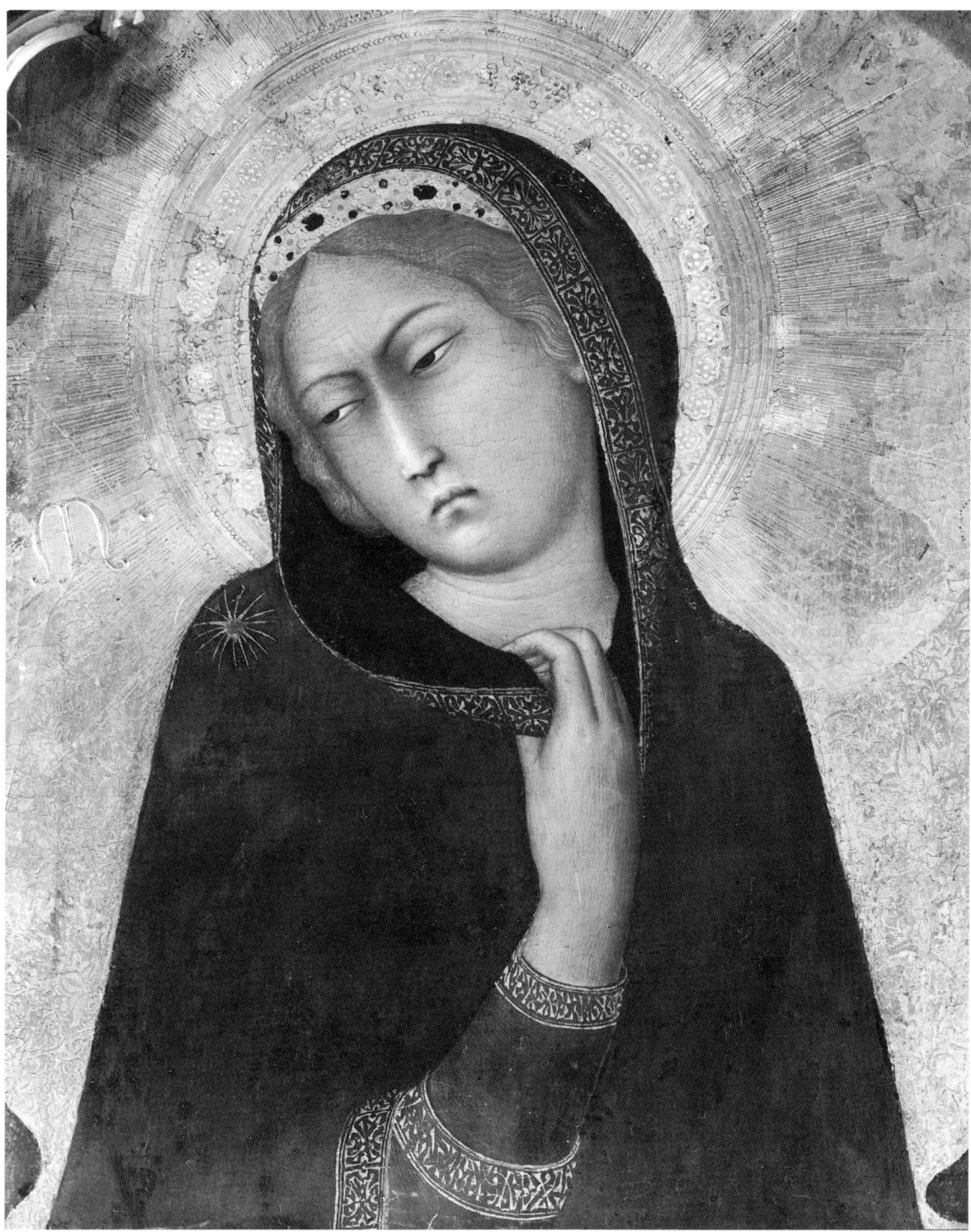

Fig. 20 Simone Martini and Lippo Memmi, *Annunciation,* detail: head of the Virgin. Florence, Galleria degli Uffizi.

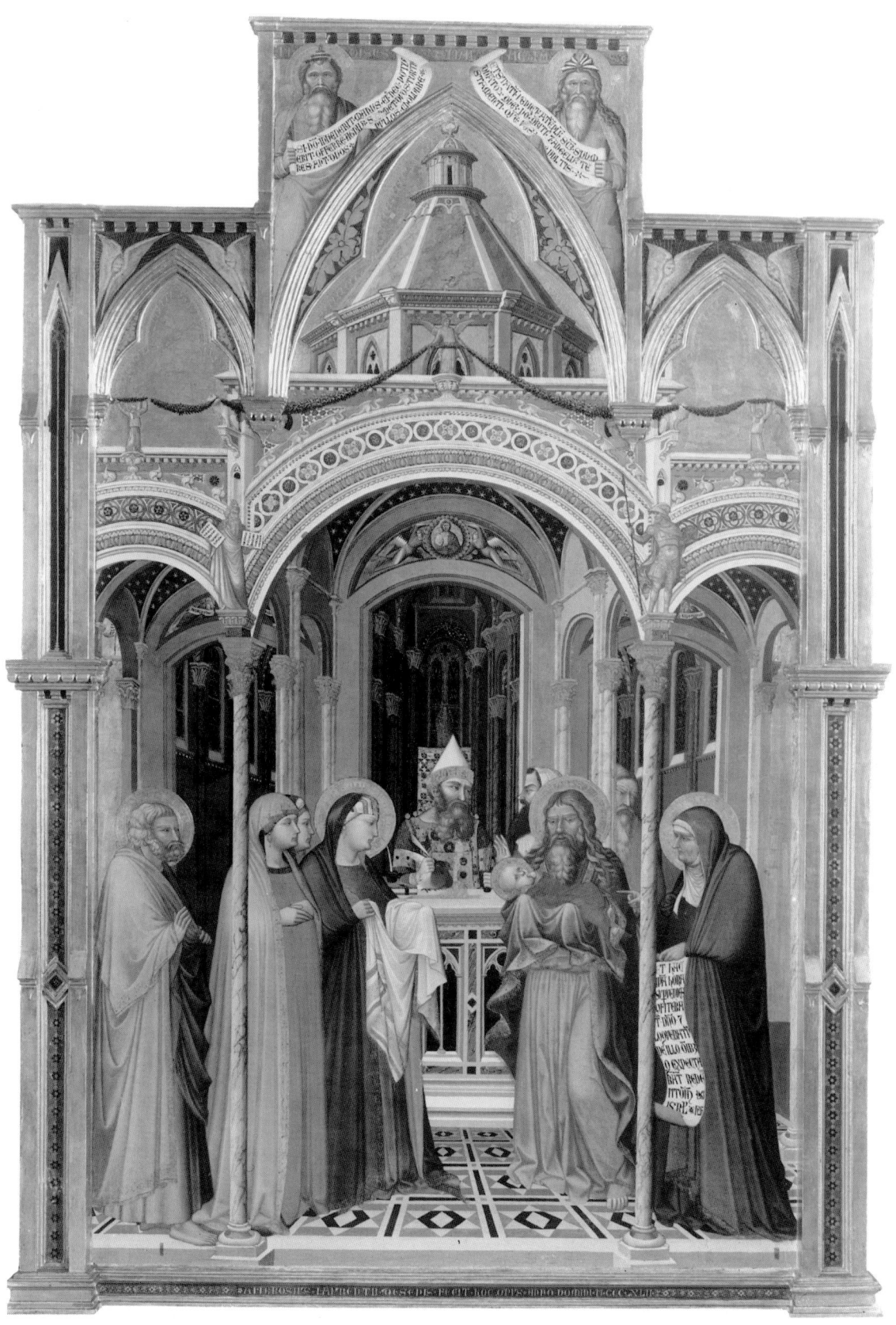

Fig. 21 Ambrogio Lorenzetti, *Presentation in the Temple*. Florence, Galleria degli Uffizi.

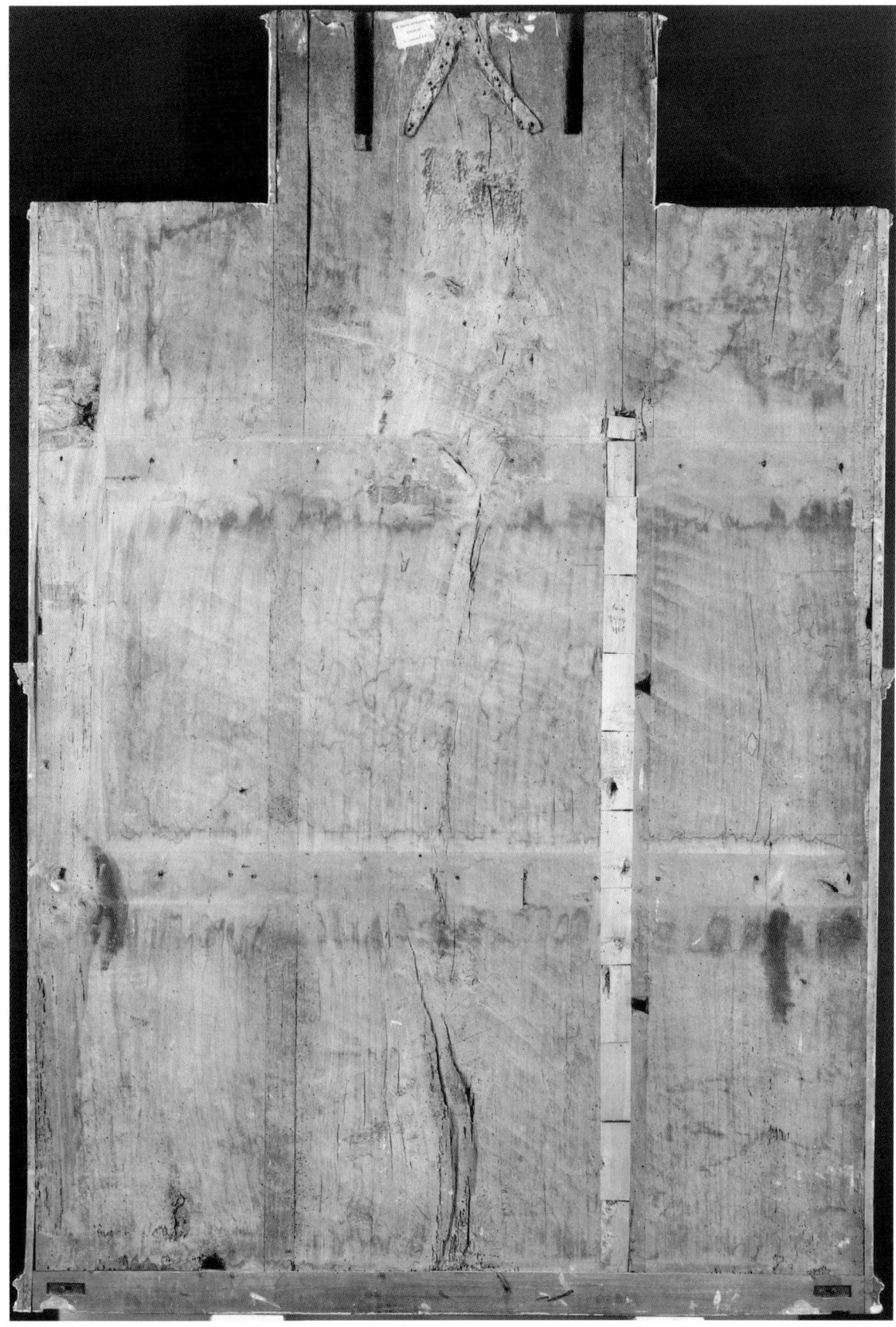

Fig. 22 Ambrogio Lorenzetti, *Presentation in the Temple,* back of the panel. Florence, Galleria degli Uffizi.

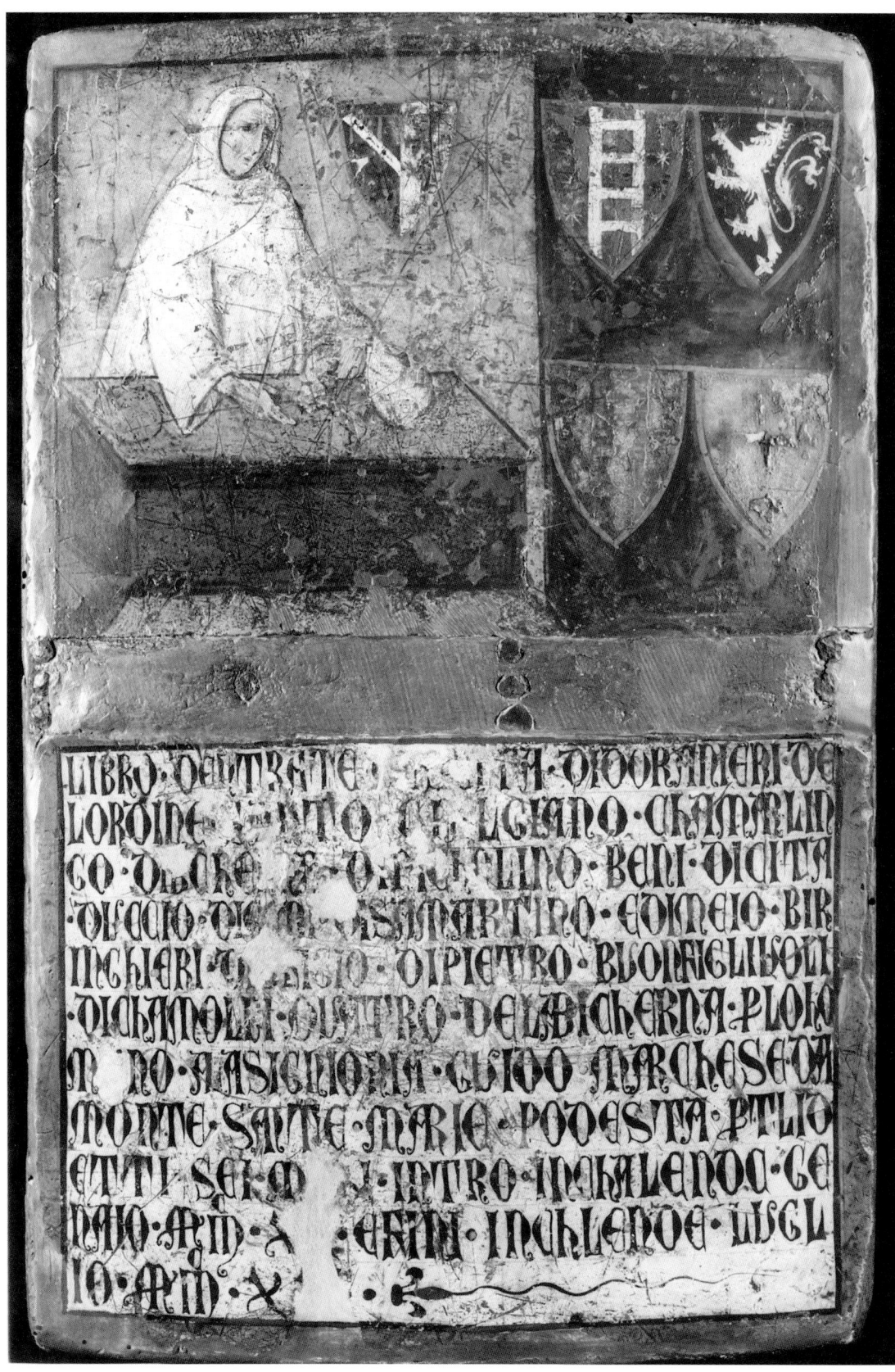

Fig. 23 Guido Cinatti, Biccherna cover. Siena, Archivio di Stato di Siena.

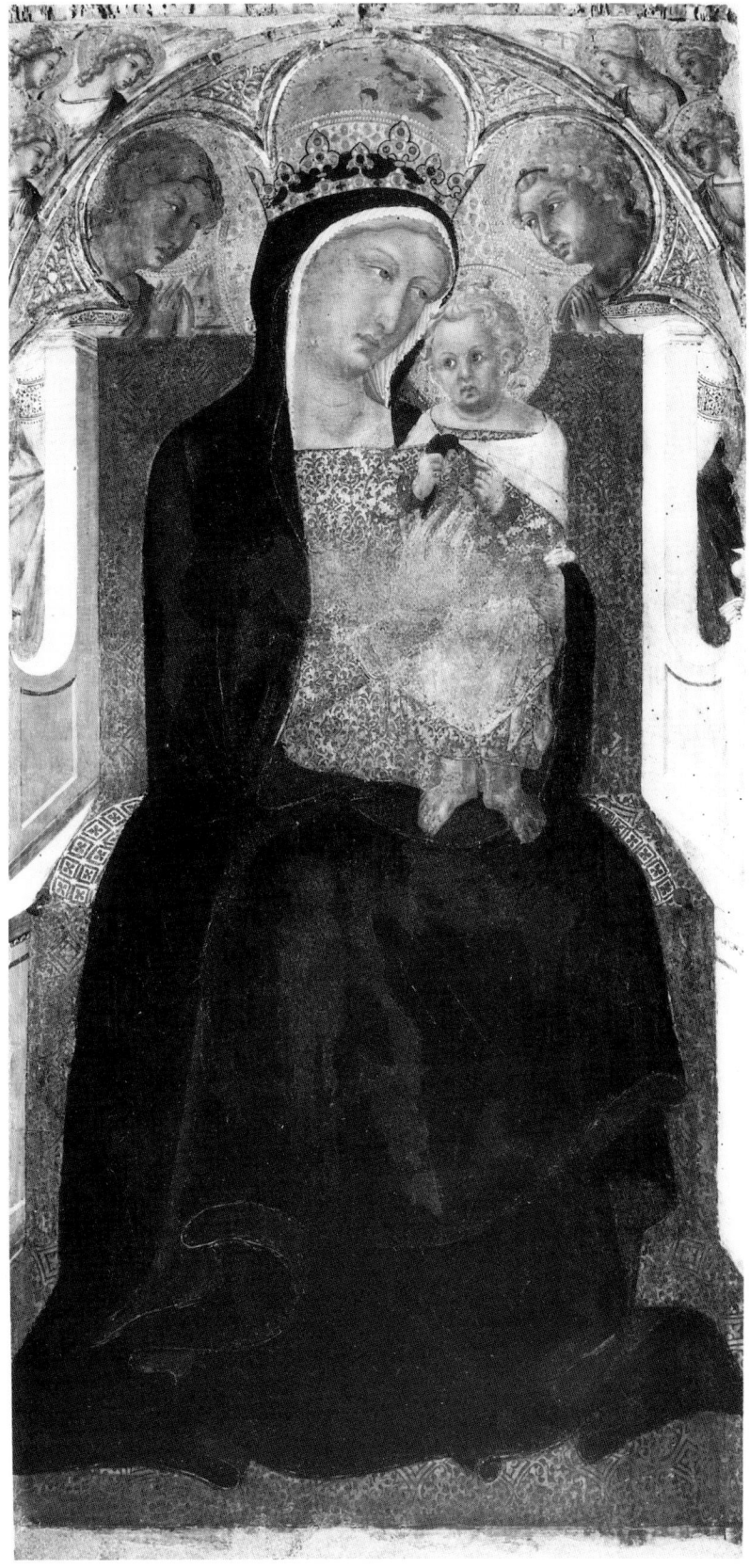

Fig. 24 Bartolommeo Bulgarini, *Madonna and Child Enthroned*. Siena, Pinacoteca Nazionale.

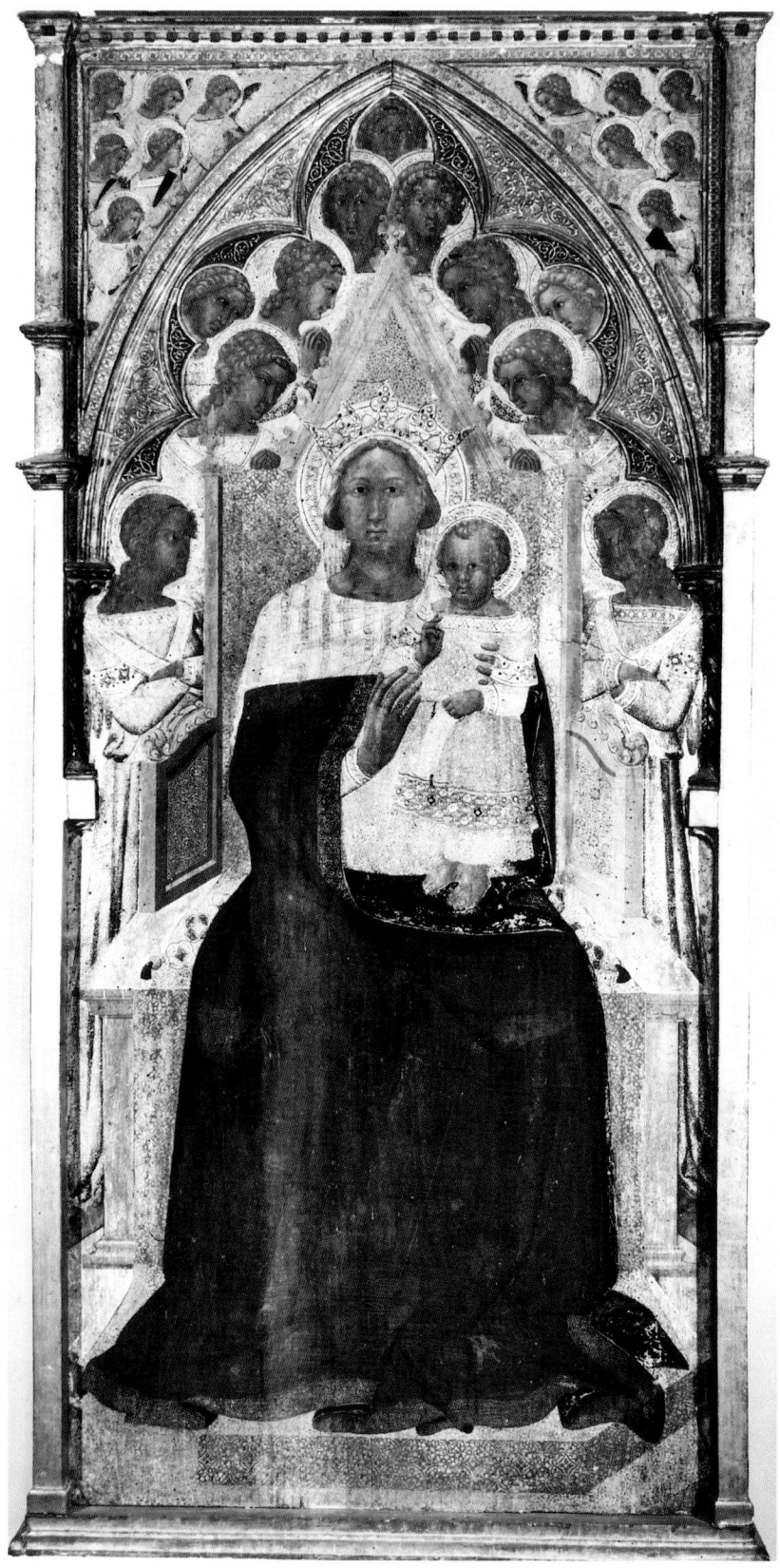

Fig. 25 Bartolommeo Bulgarini, *Madonna and Child Enthroned*. Siena, Pinacoteca Nazionale.

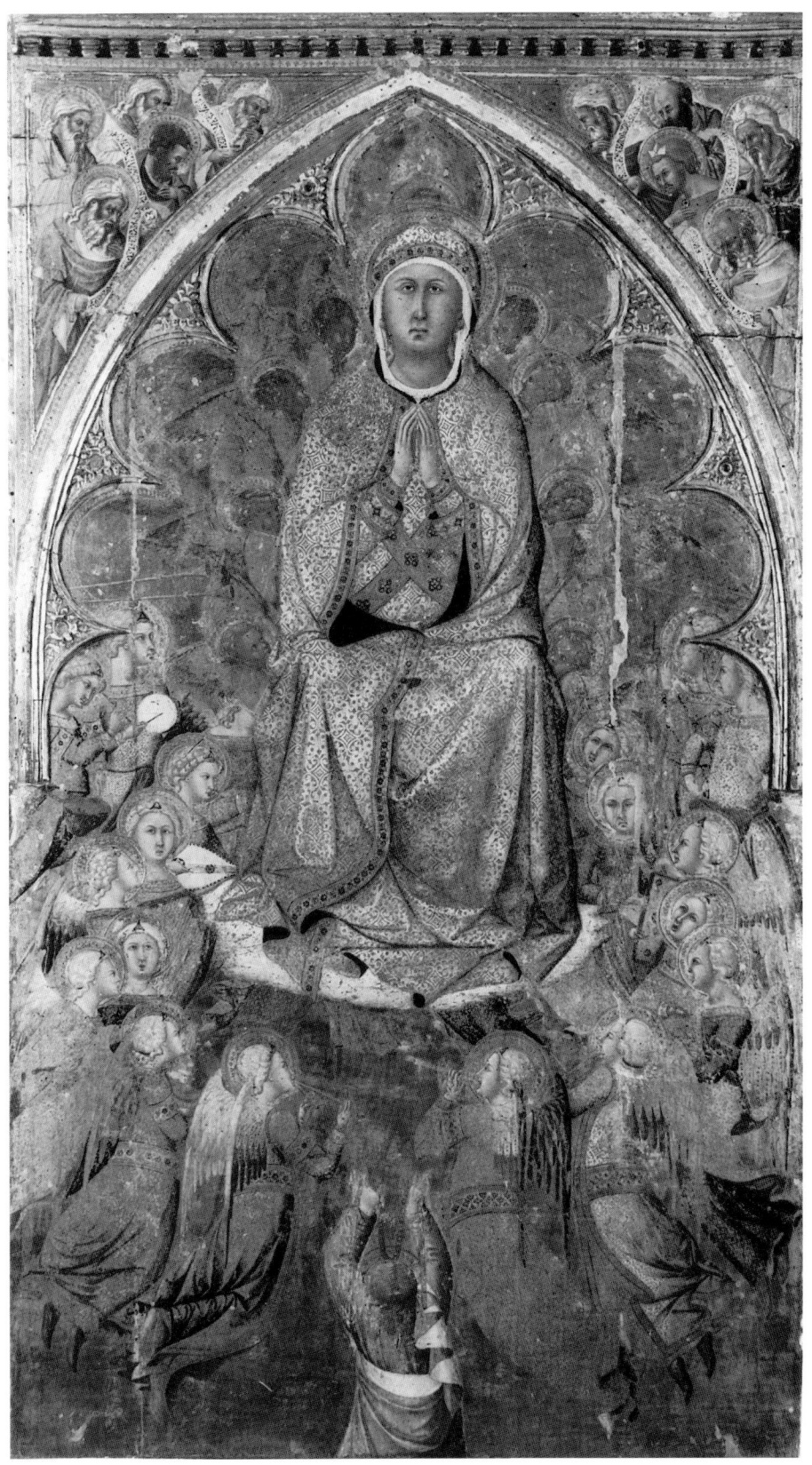

Fig. 26 Bartolommeo Bulgarini, *Assumption of the Virgin*. Siena, Pinacoteca Nazionale.

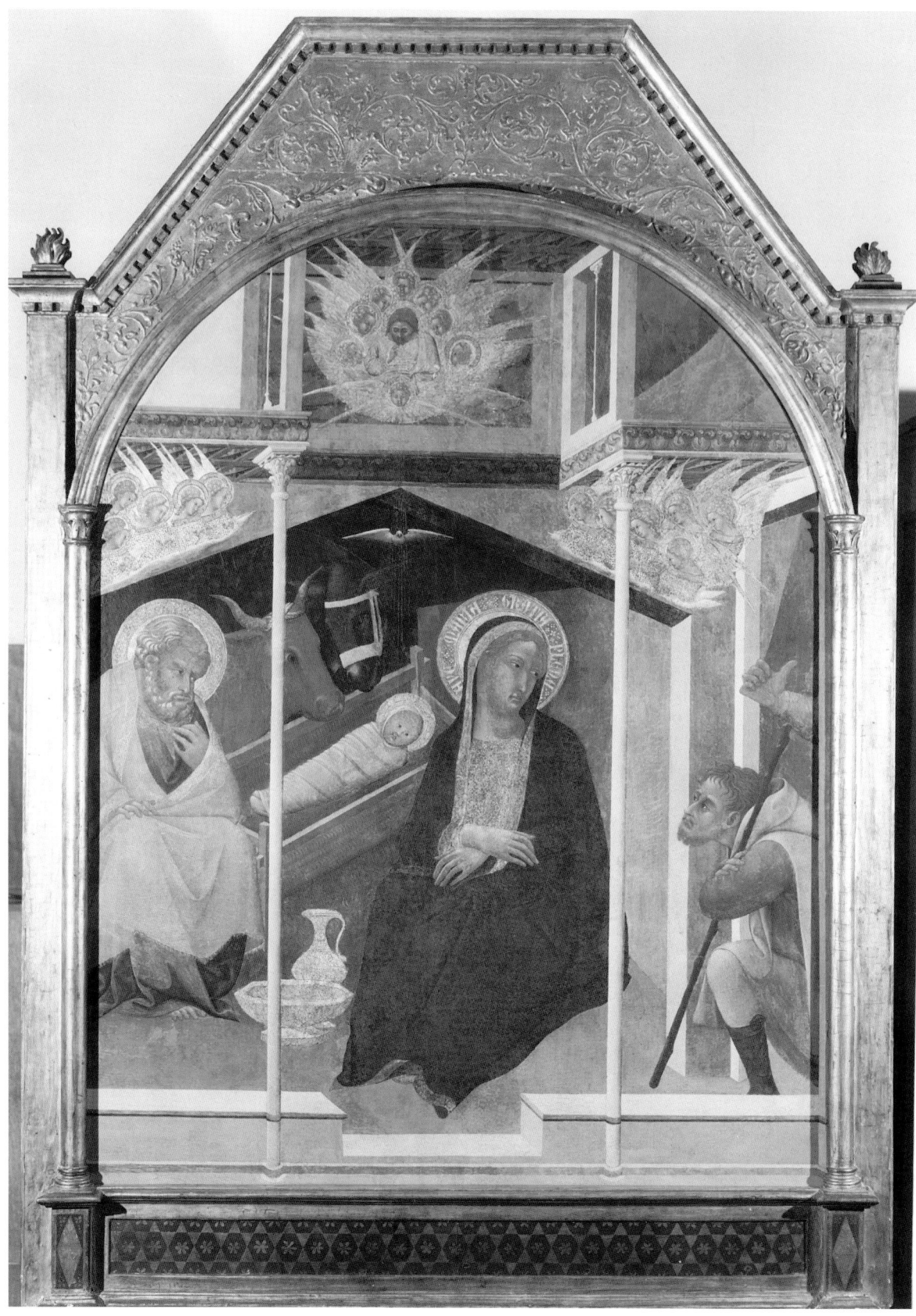

Fig. 27 Bartolommeo Bulgarini, *Nativity*. Cambridge, Mass., Fogg Art Museum.

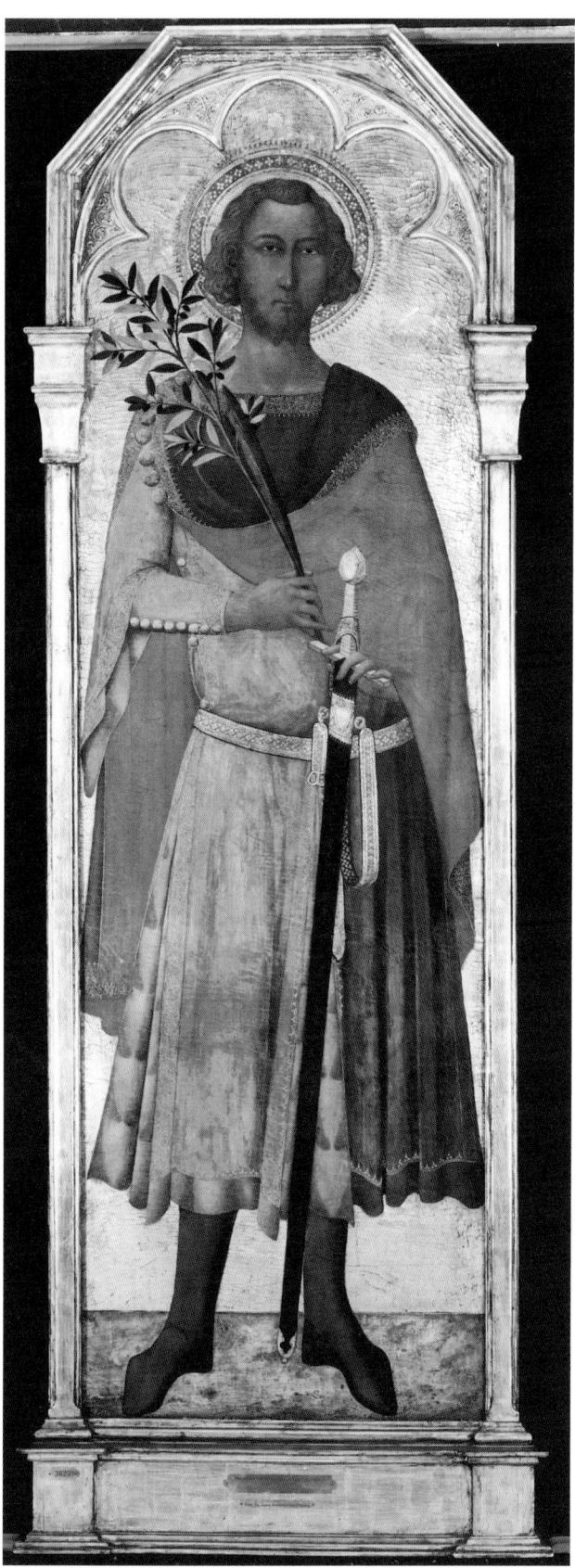 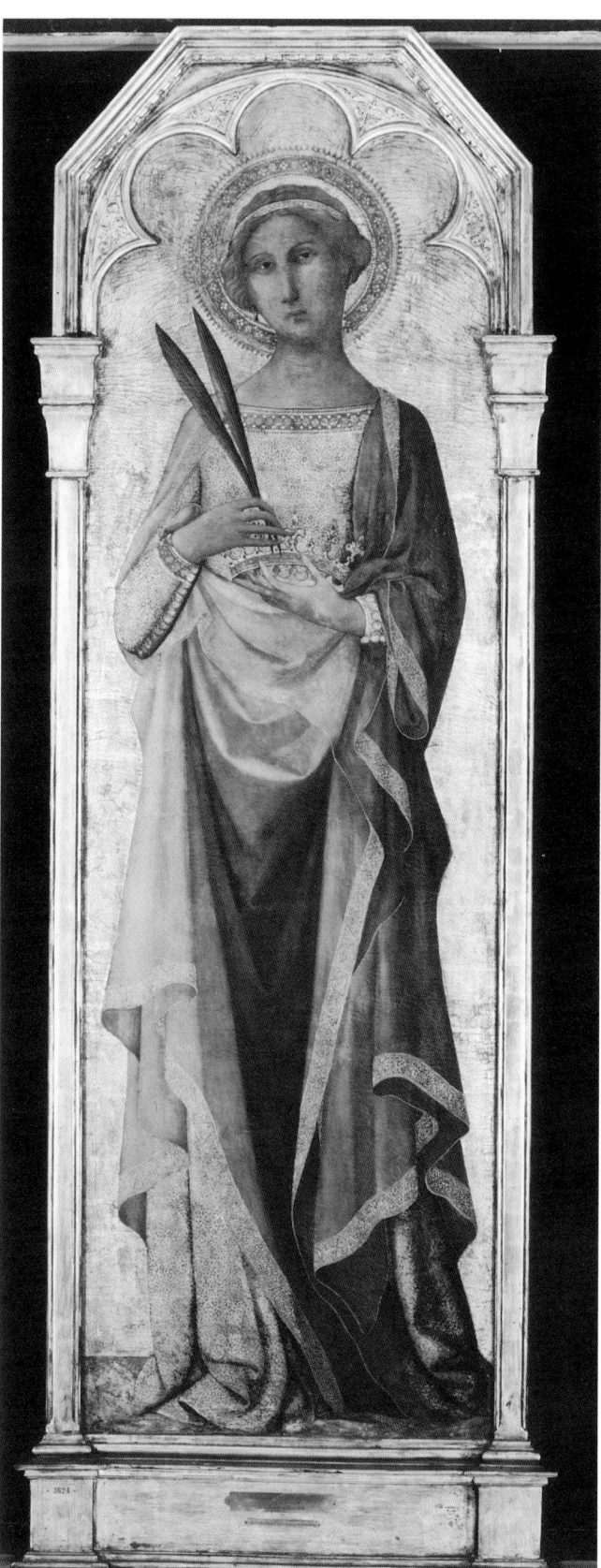

Fig. 28 Master of Palazzo Venezia, *San Vittorio*. Copenhagen, Statens Museum for Kunst.

Fig. 29 Master of Palazzo Venezia, *Santa Corona*. Copenhagen, Statens Museum for Kunst.

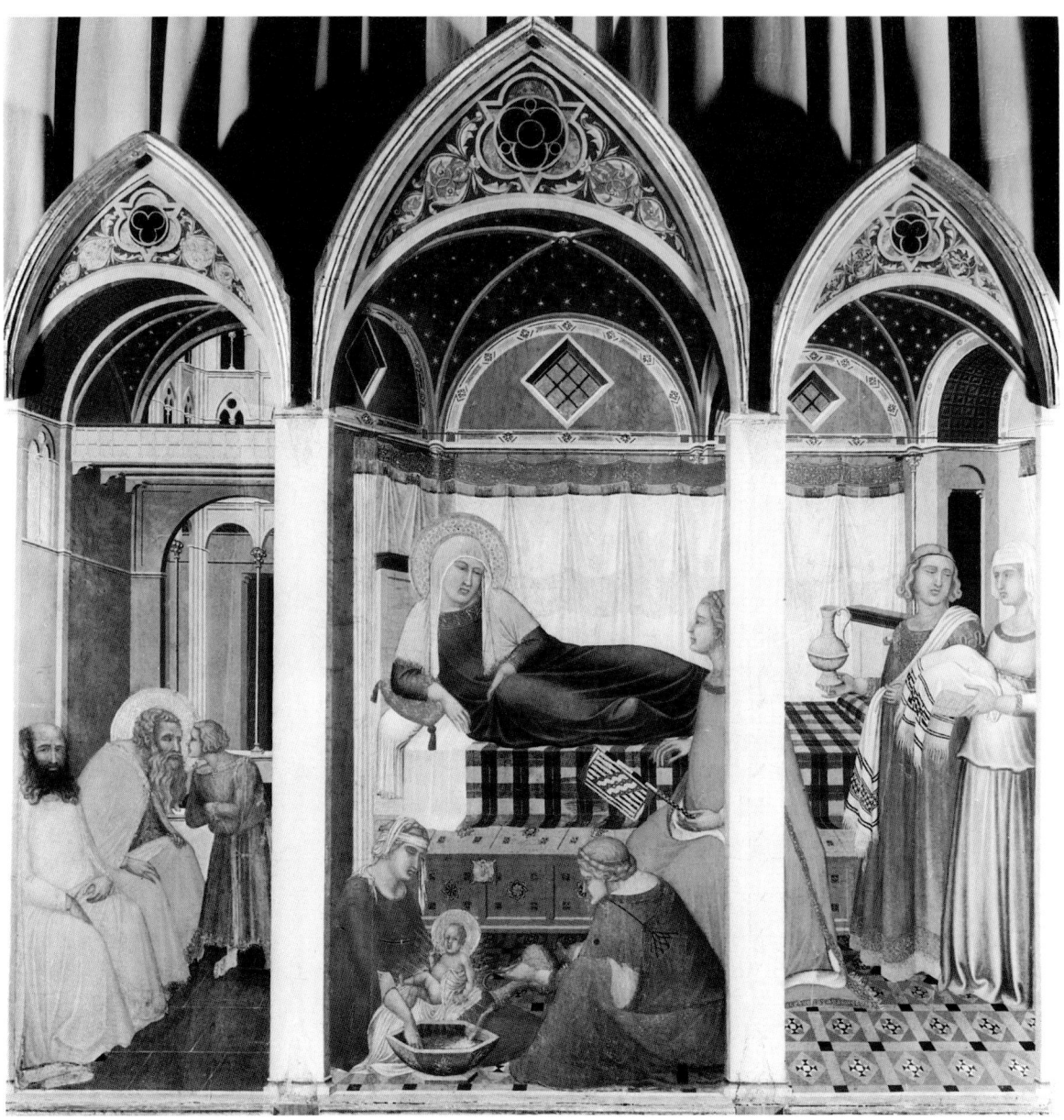

Fig. 30 Pietro Lorenzetti, *Birth of the Virgin*. Siena, Museo dell'Opera del Duomo.

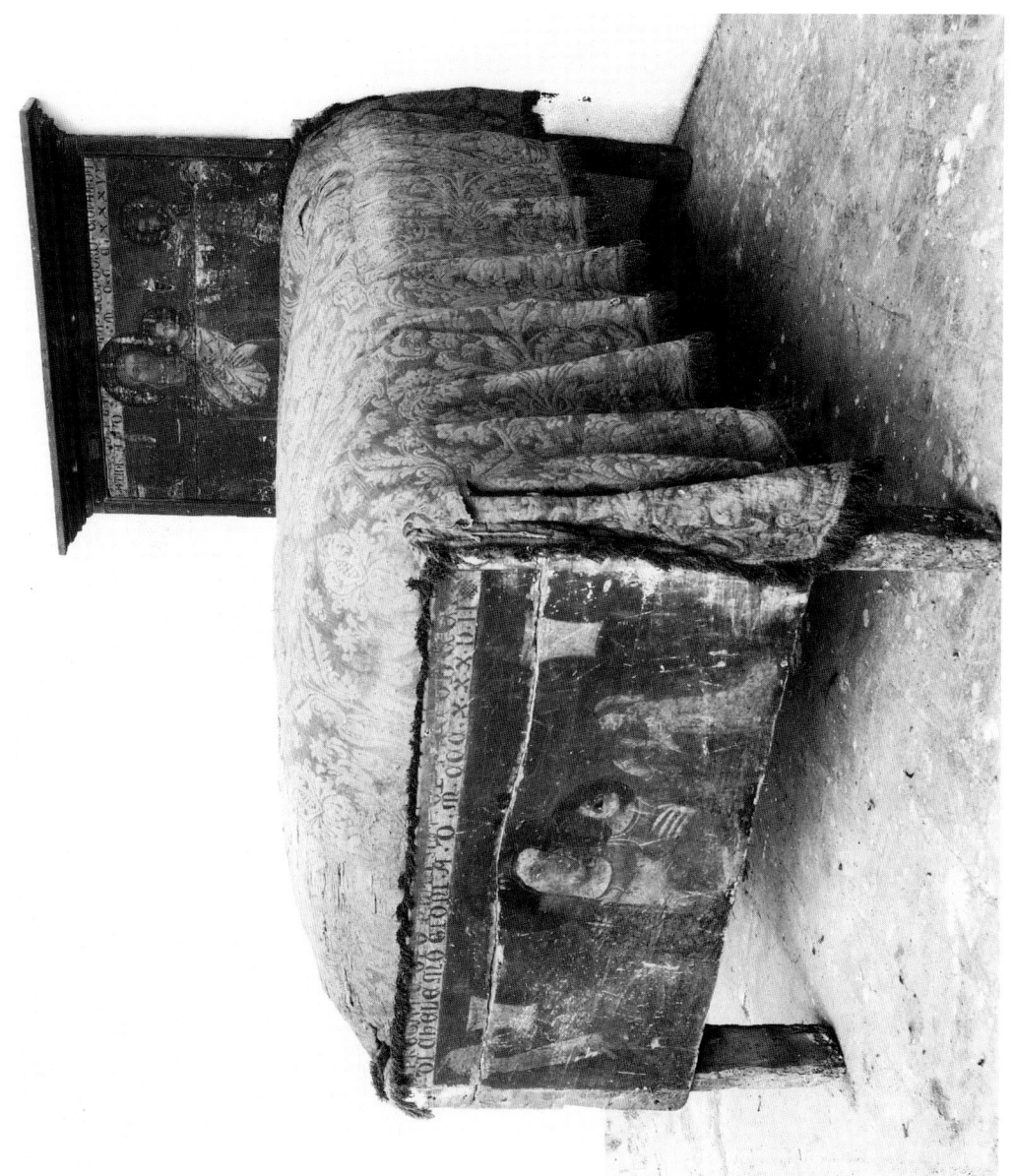

Fig. 31 Painted bed (1337). Pistoia, Ospedale del Ceppo.

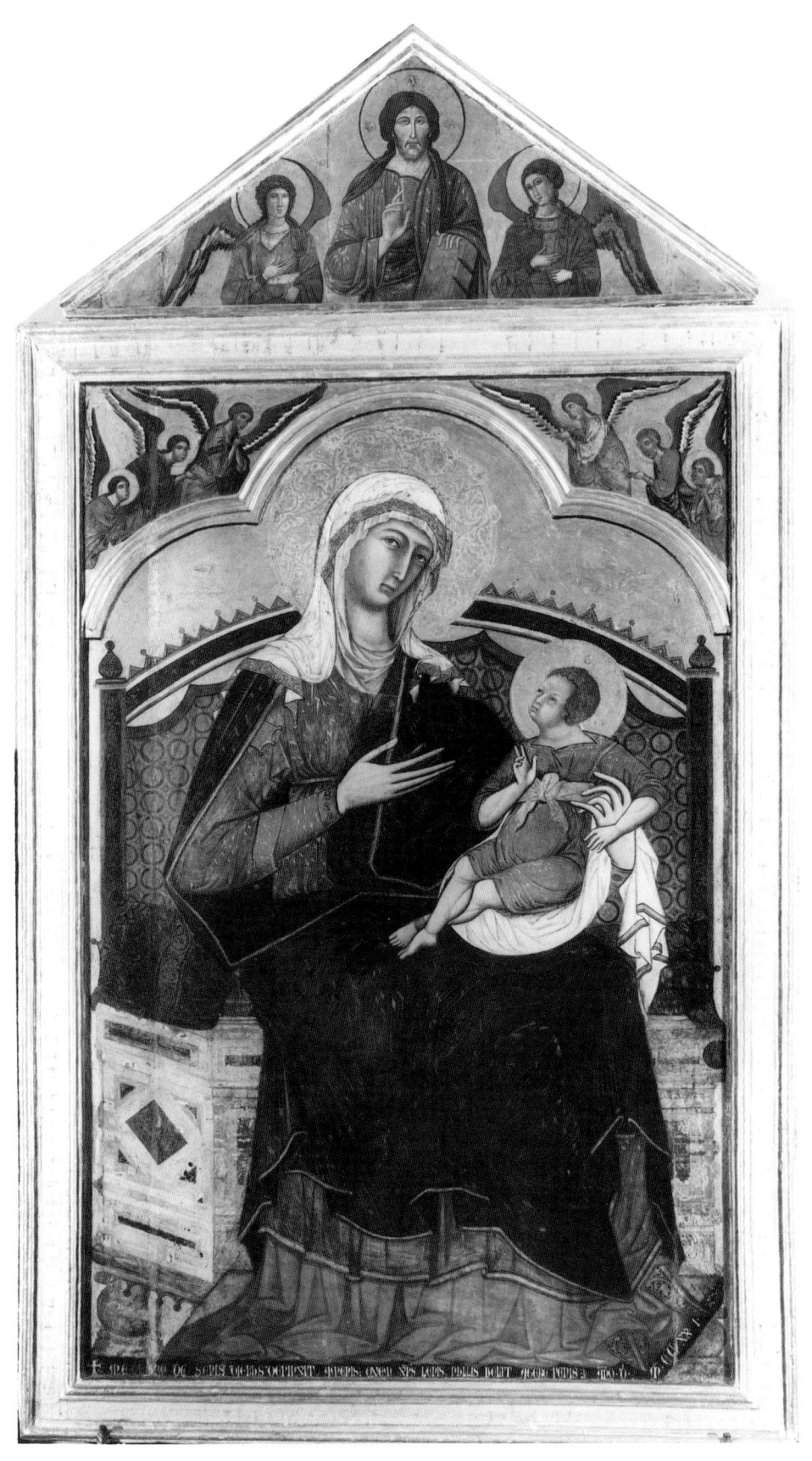

Fig. 32 Guido da Siena, San Domenico *Madonna*. Siena, San Domenico.

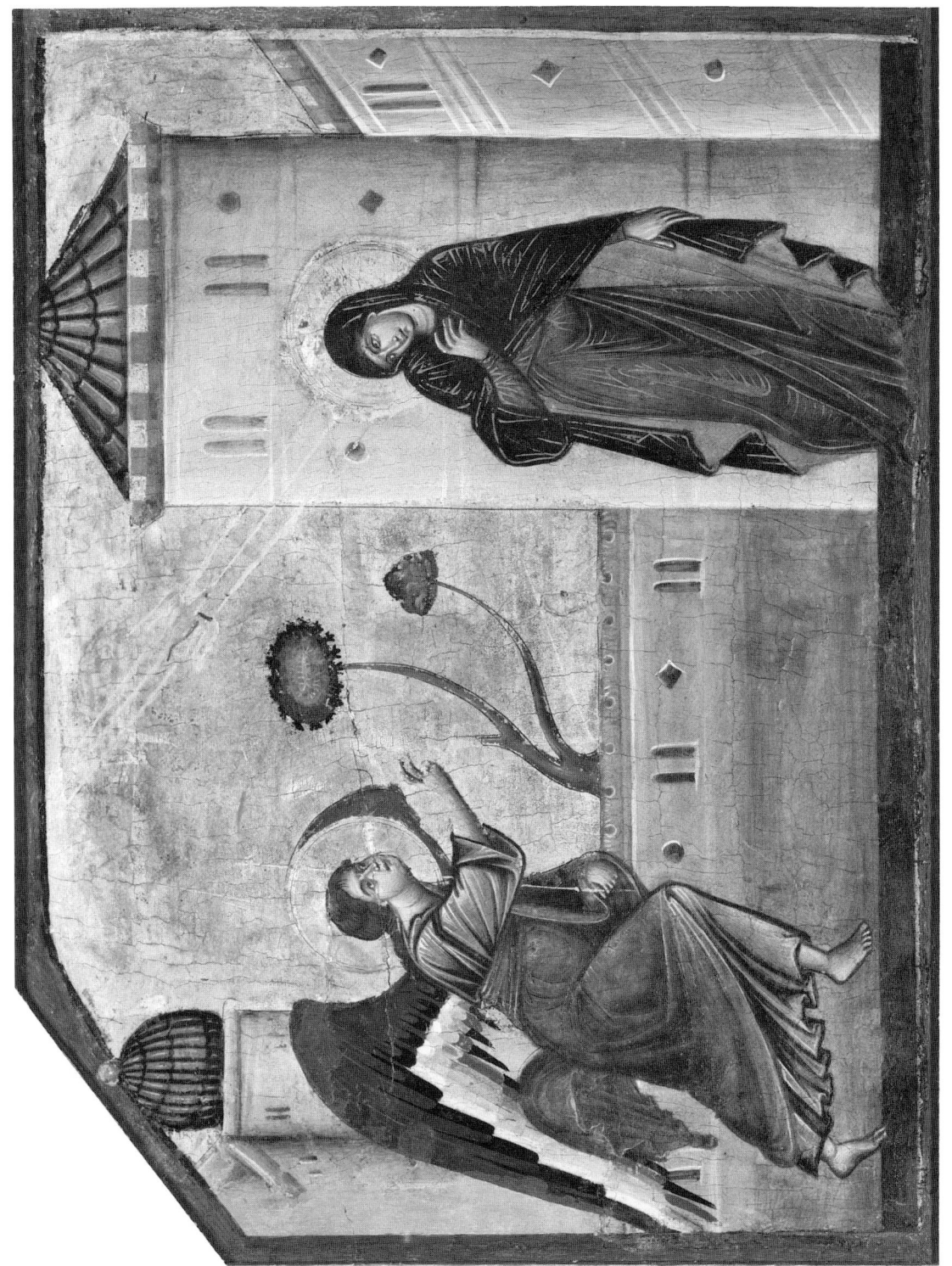

Fig. 33 Guido da Siena (?), *Annunciation*. Princeton, Art Museum.

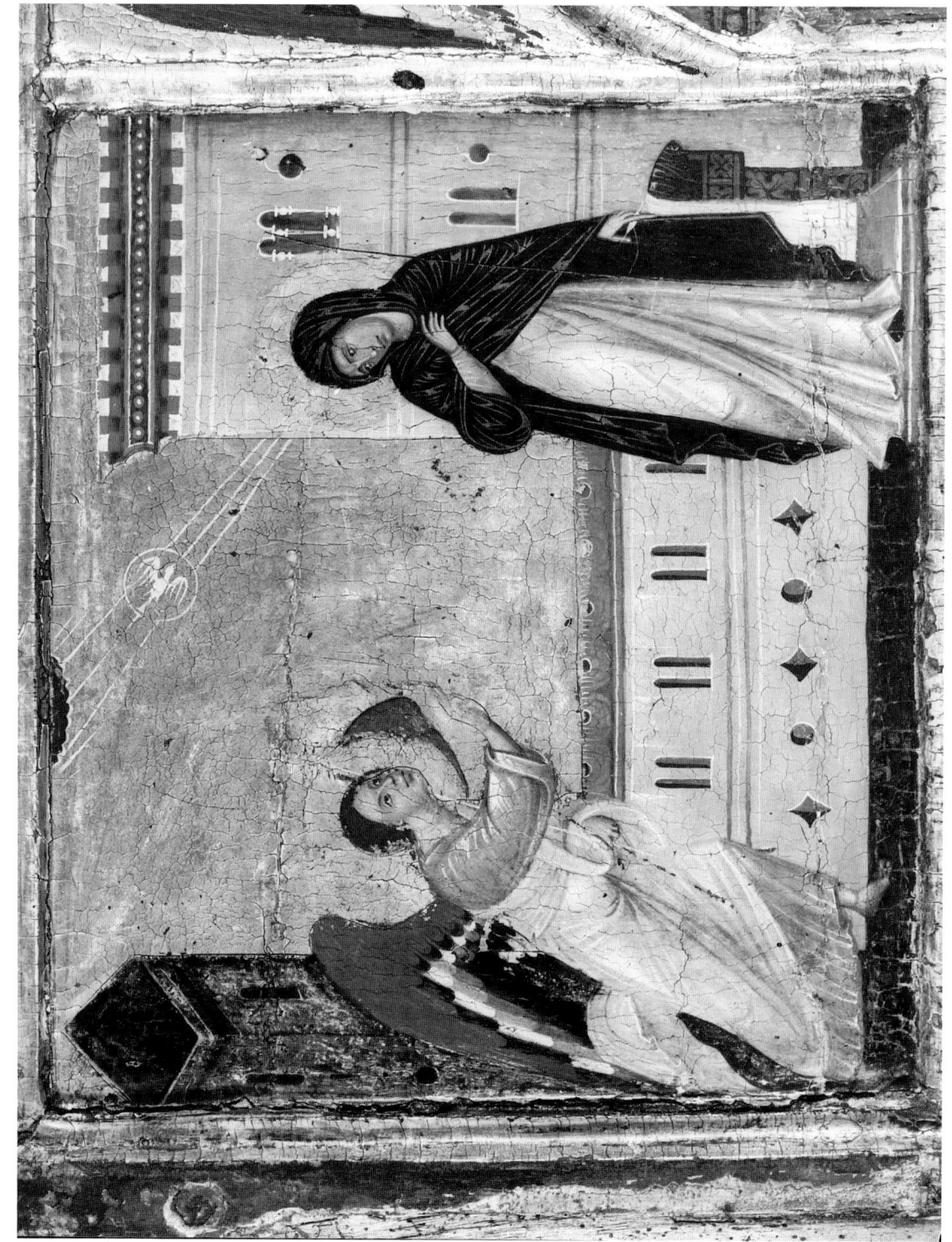

Fig. 34 Saint Peter Master, *Annunciation*, detail of the Saint Peter altarpiece. Siena, Pinacoteca Nazionale.

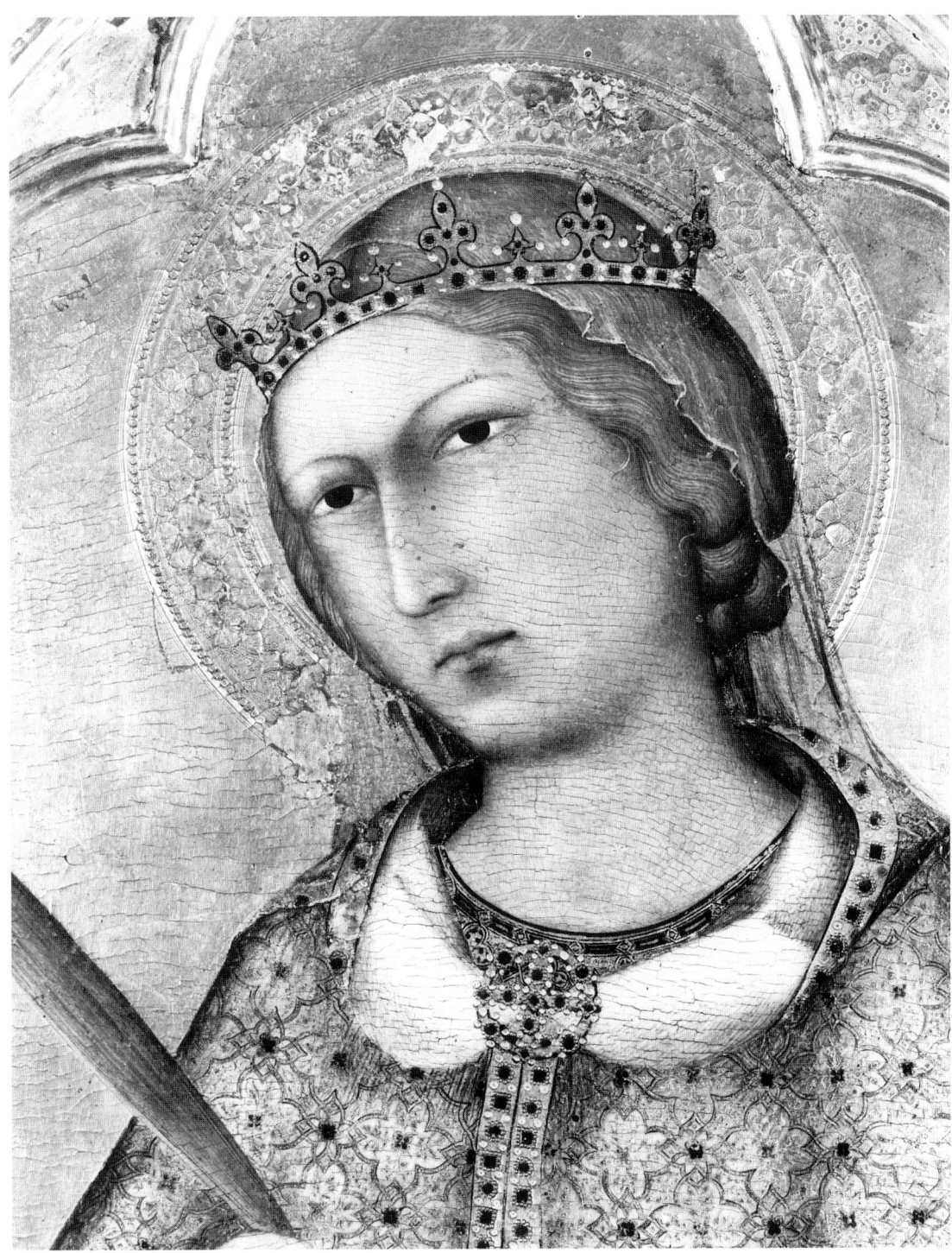

Fig. 35 Simone Martini, the Pisa altarpiece, detail: head of Saint Catherine. Pisa, Museo di San Matteo.

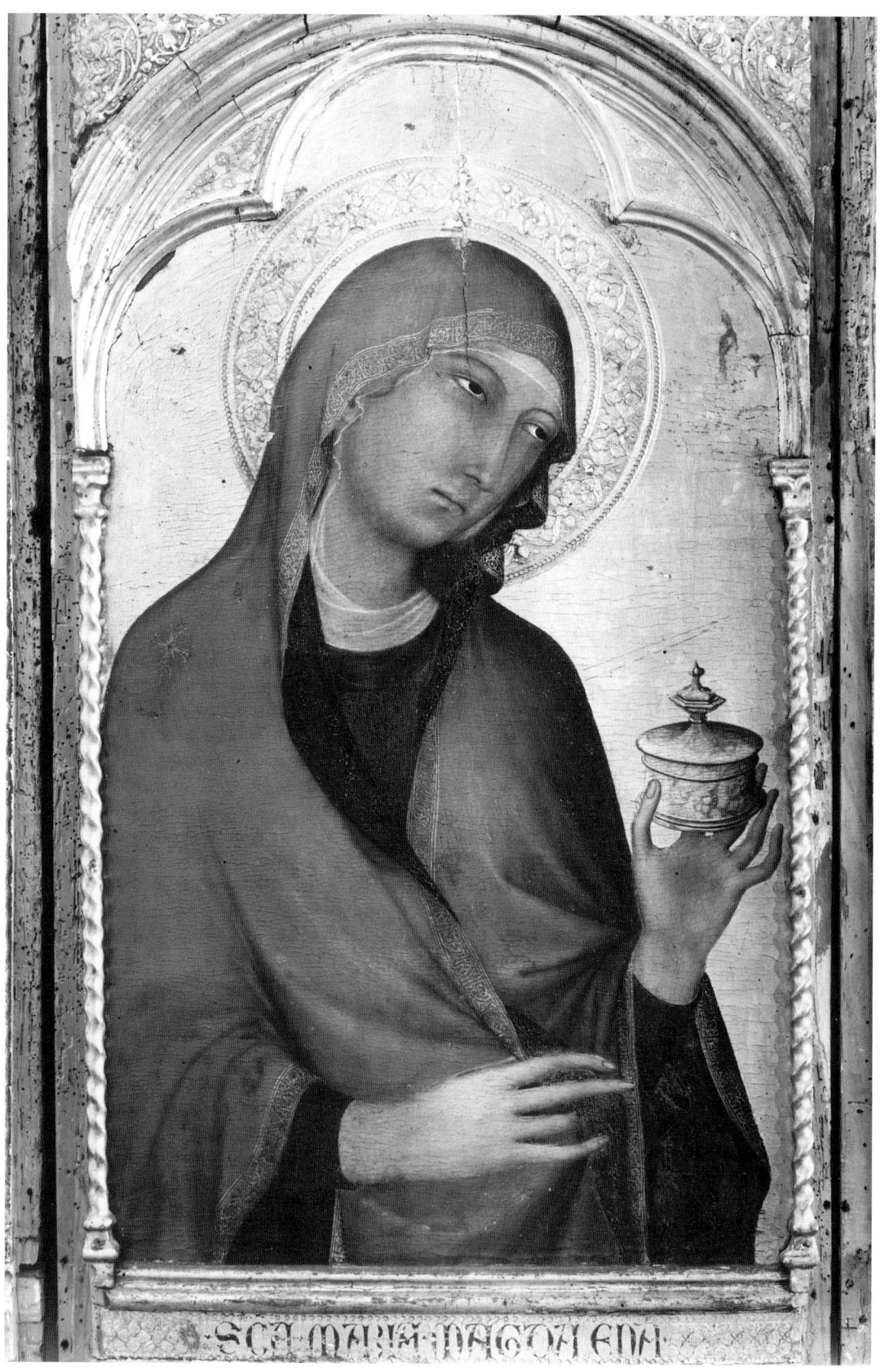

Fig. 36 Simone Martini, the Pisa altarpiece, detail: Saint Mary Magdalen. Pisa, Museo di San Matteo.

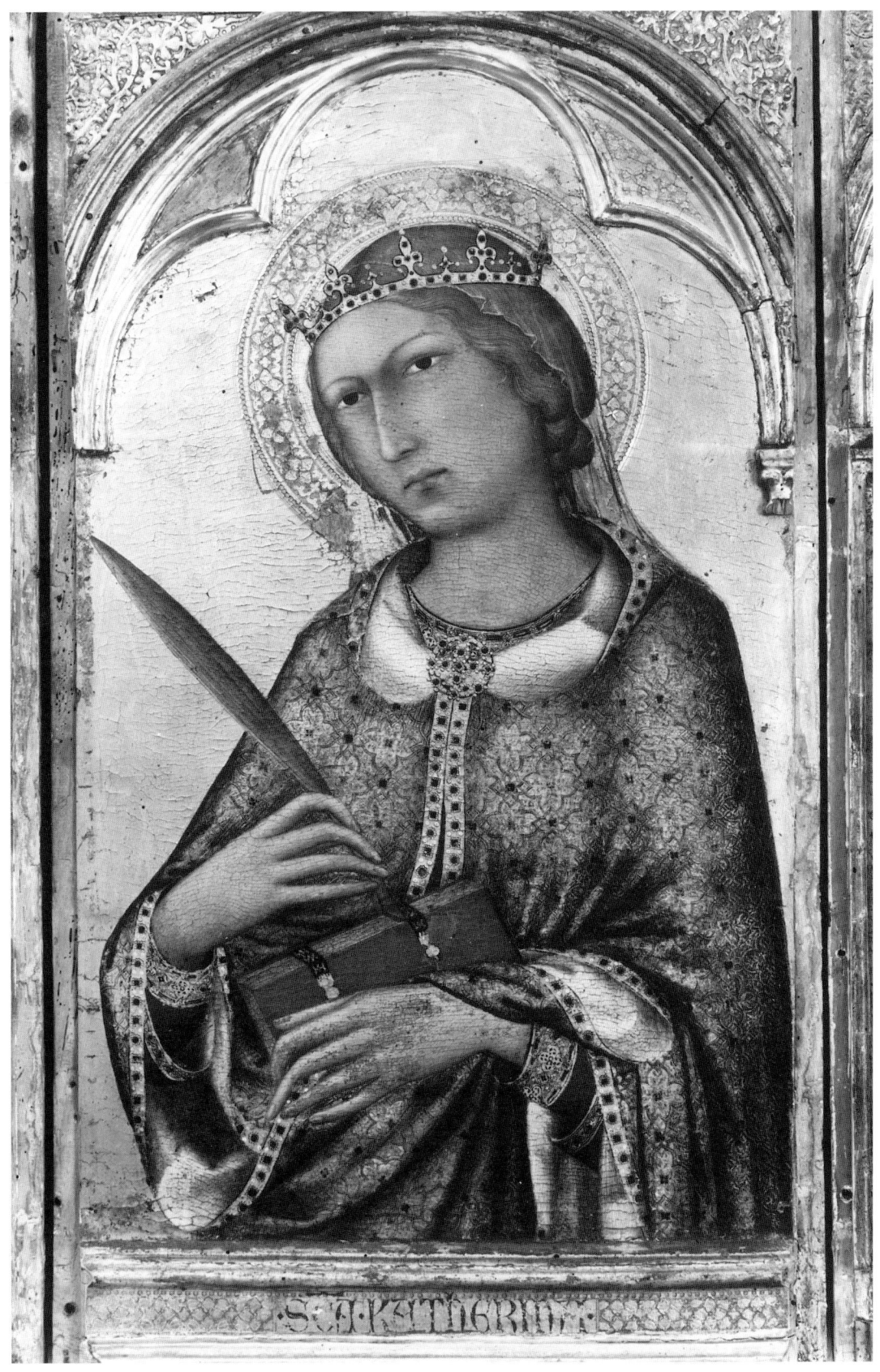

Fig. 37 Simone Martini, the Pisa altarpiece, detail: Saint Catherine of Alexandria. Pisa, Museo di San Matteo.

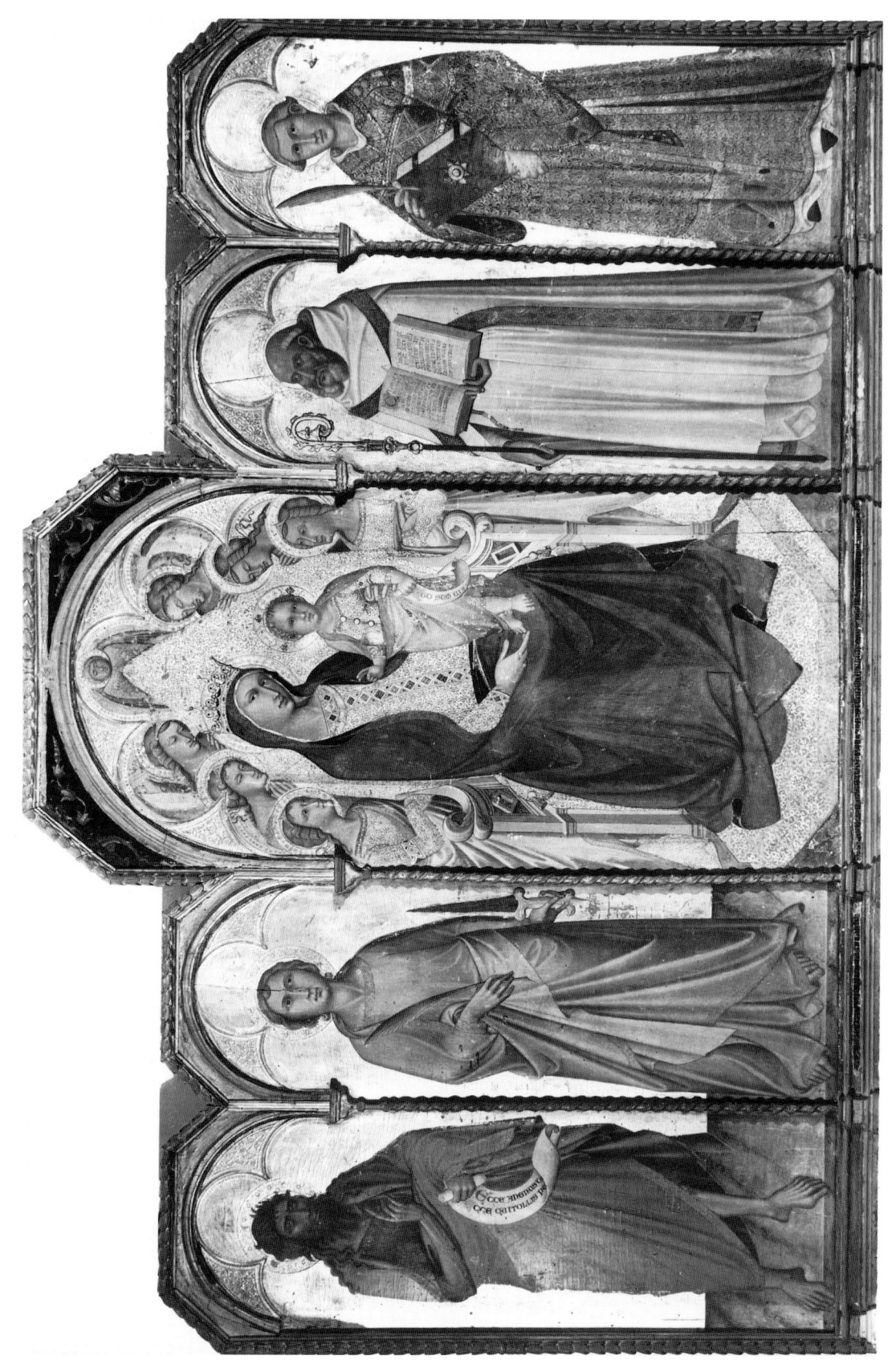

Fig. 38 Luca di Tommè and Niccolò di Ser Sozzo, polyptych (1362). Siena, Pinacoteca Nazionale.

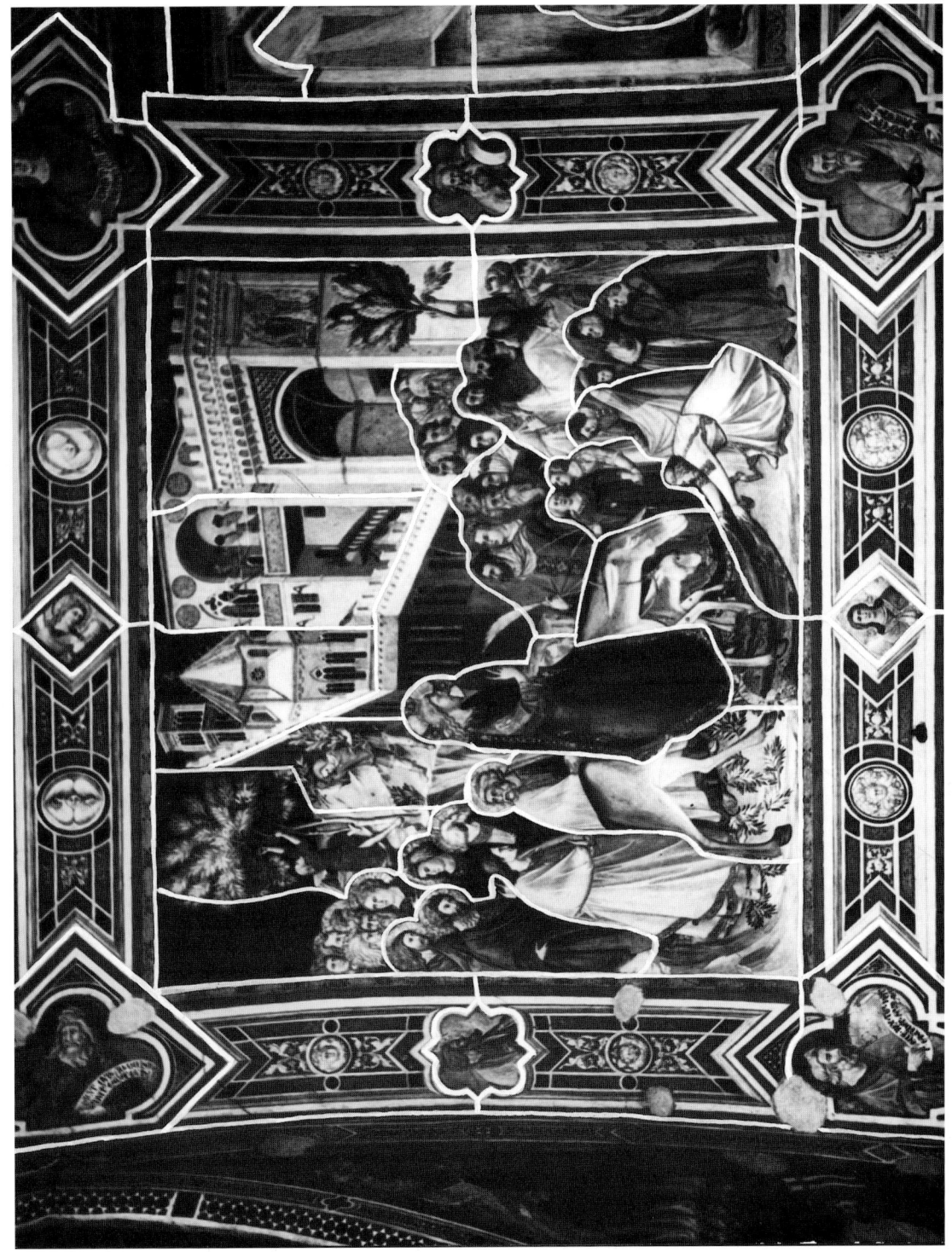

Fig. 39 Pietro Lorenzetti, diagram of the *giornate* for the *Entry into Jerusalem*. Assisi, San Francesco, Lower Church.

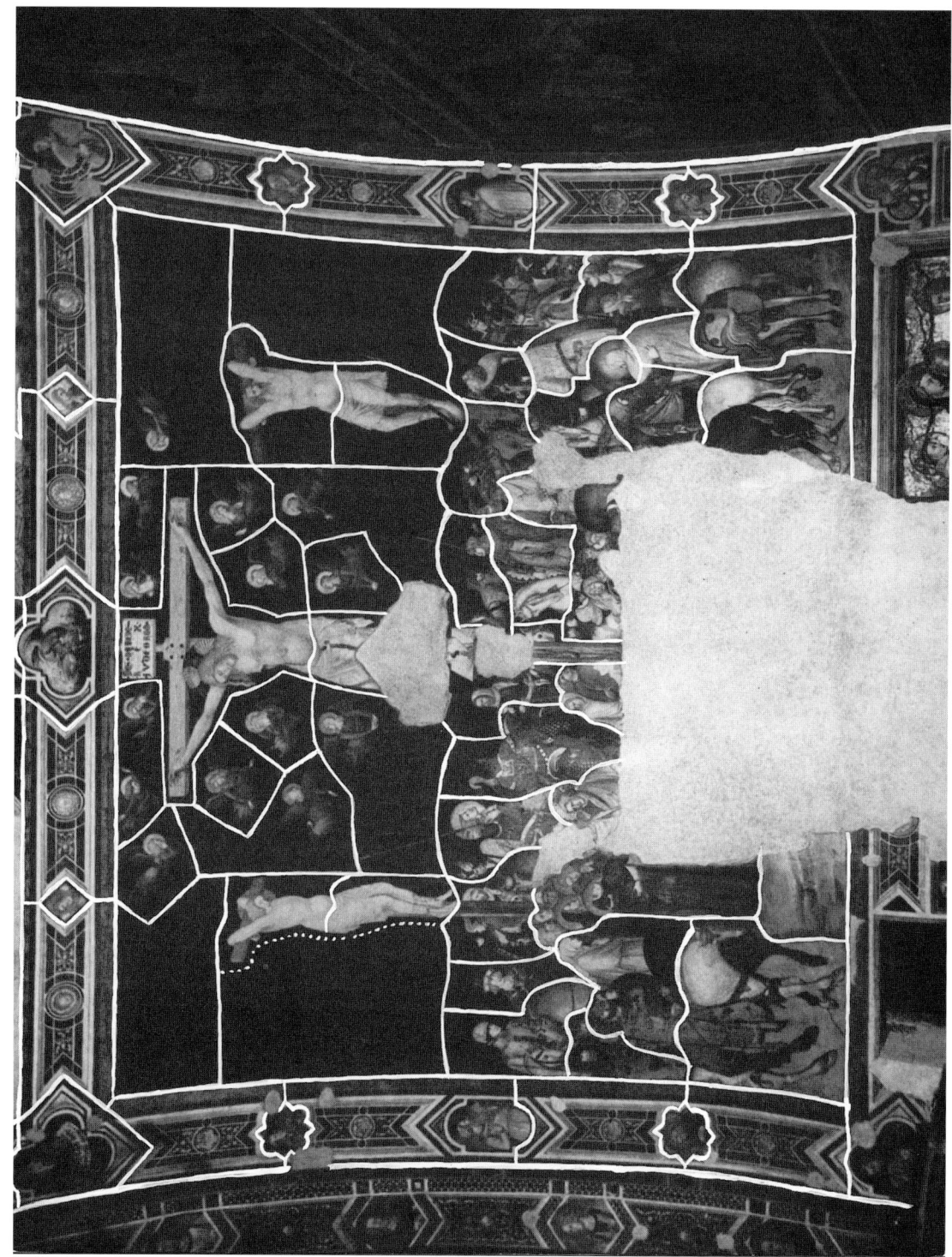

Fig. 40 Pietro Lorenzetti, diagram of the giornate for the *Crucifixion*. Assisi, San Francesco, Lower Church.

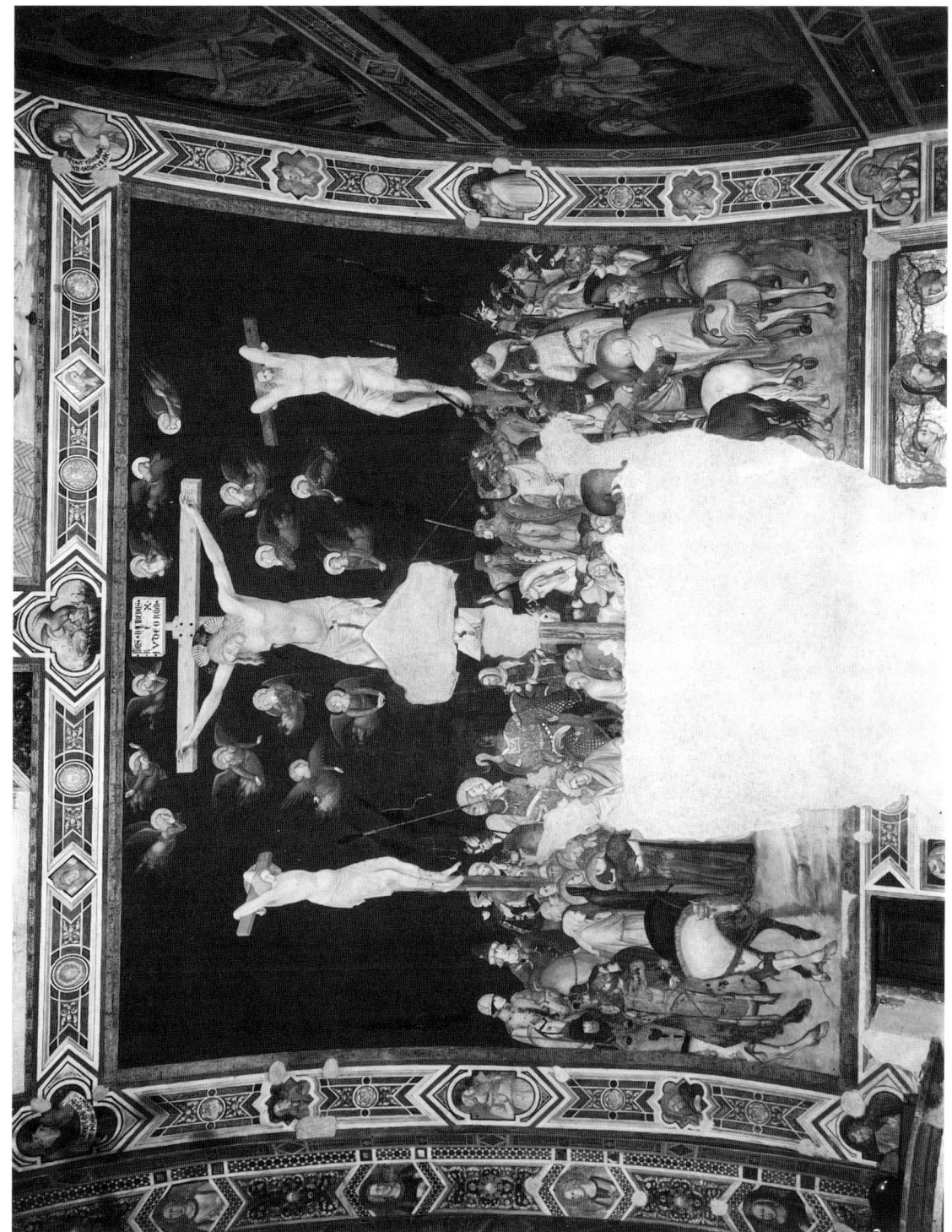

Fig. 41 Pietro Lorenzetti, *Crucifixion*. Assisi, San Francesco, Lower Church.

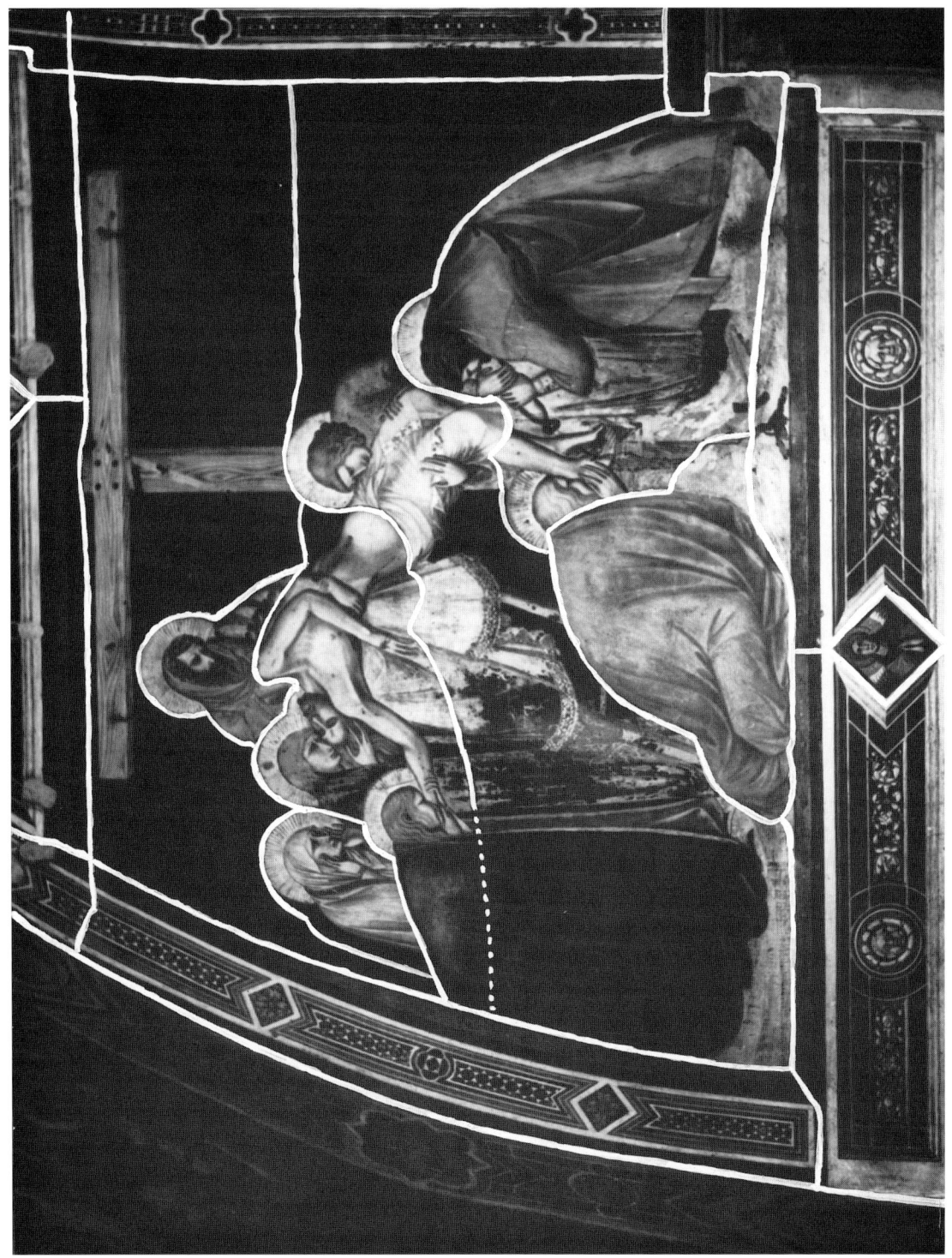

Fig. 42 Pietro Lorenzetti, diagram of the *giornate* for the *Deposition*. Assisi, San Francesco, Lower Church.

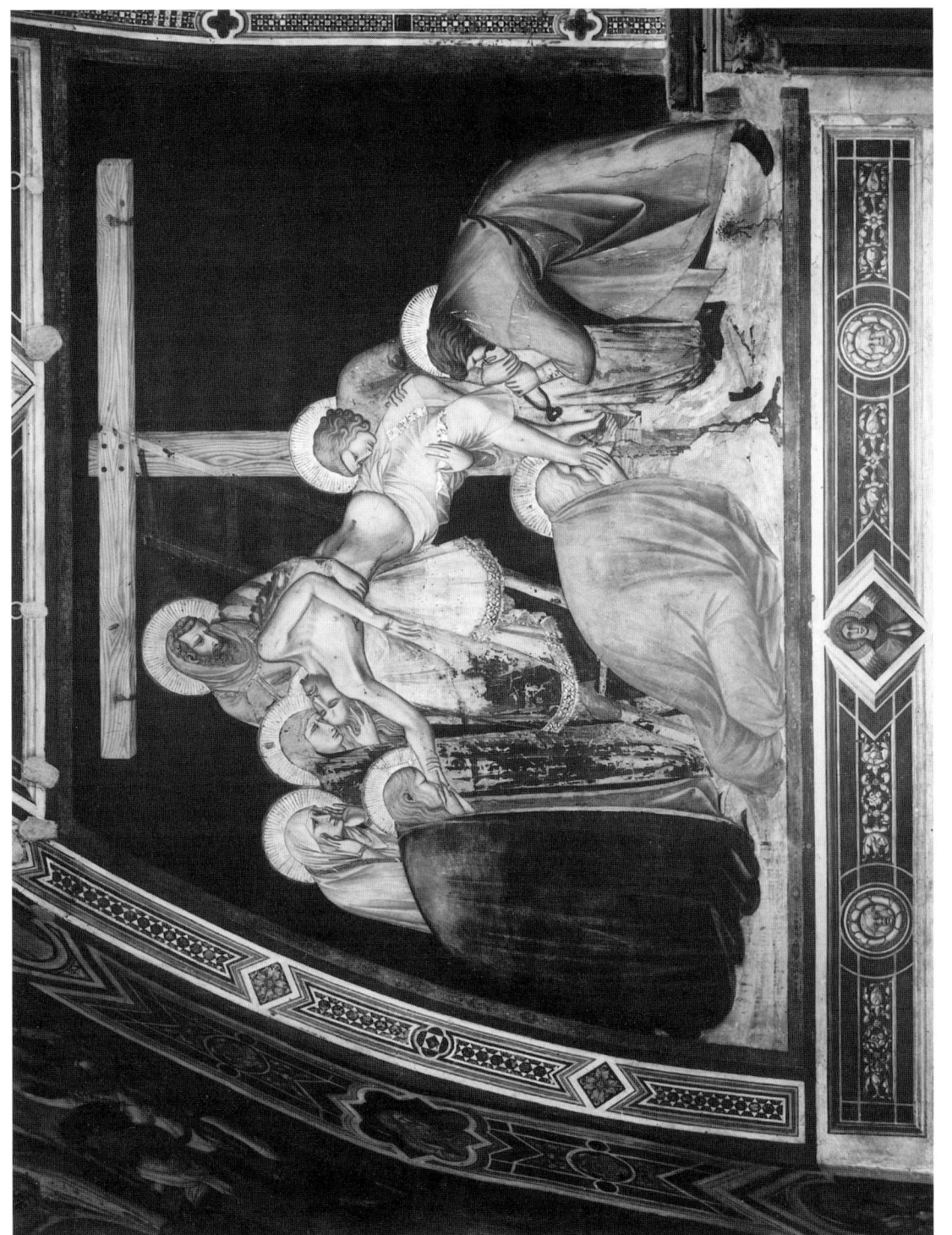

Fig. 43 Pietro Lorenzetti, *Deposition*. Assisi, San Francesco, Lower Church.

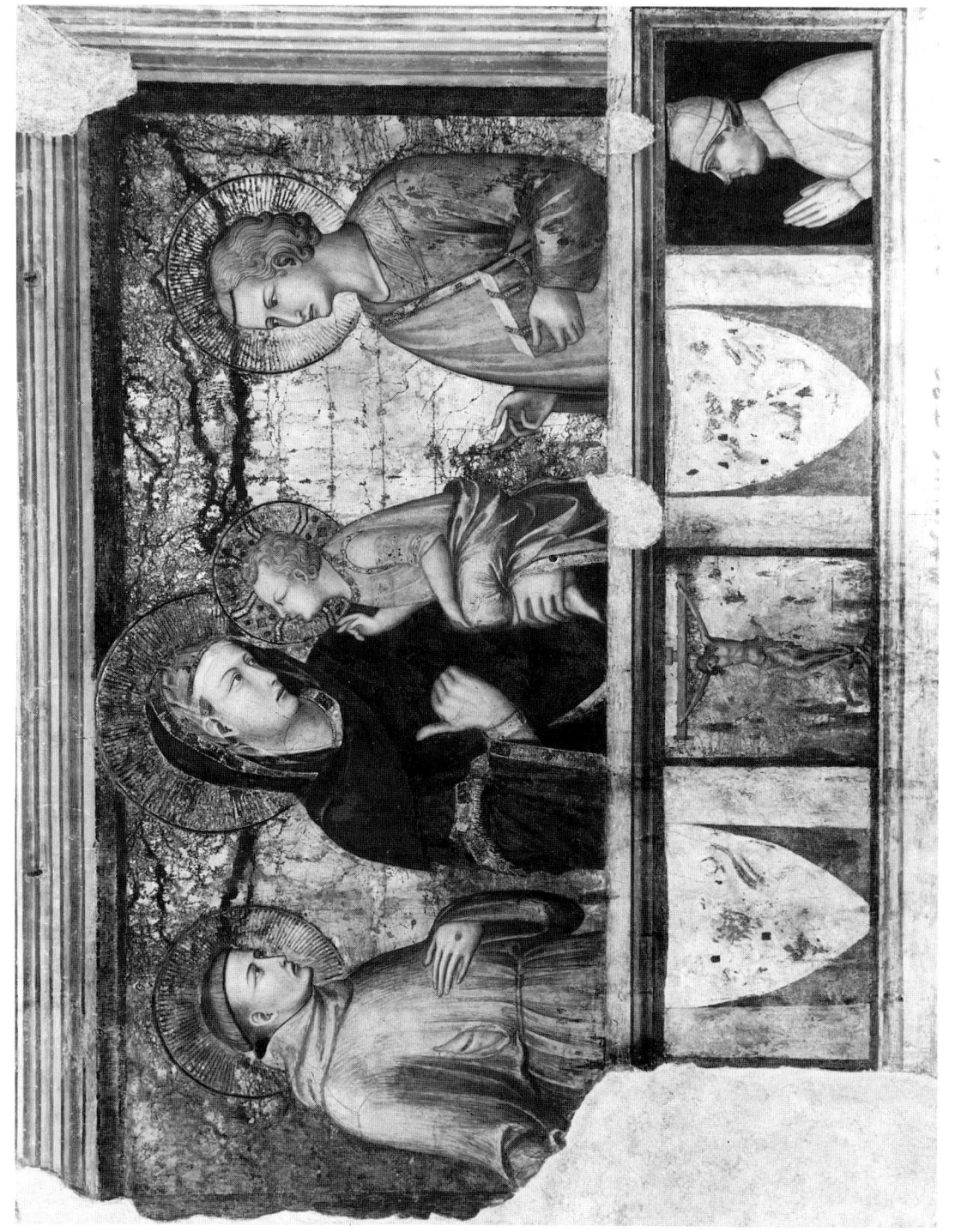

Fig. 44 Pietro Lorenzetti, fictive altarpiece. Assisi, San Francesco, Lower Church.

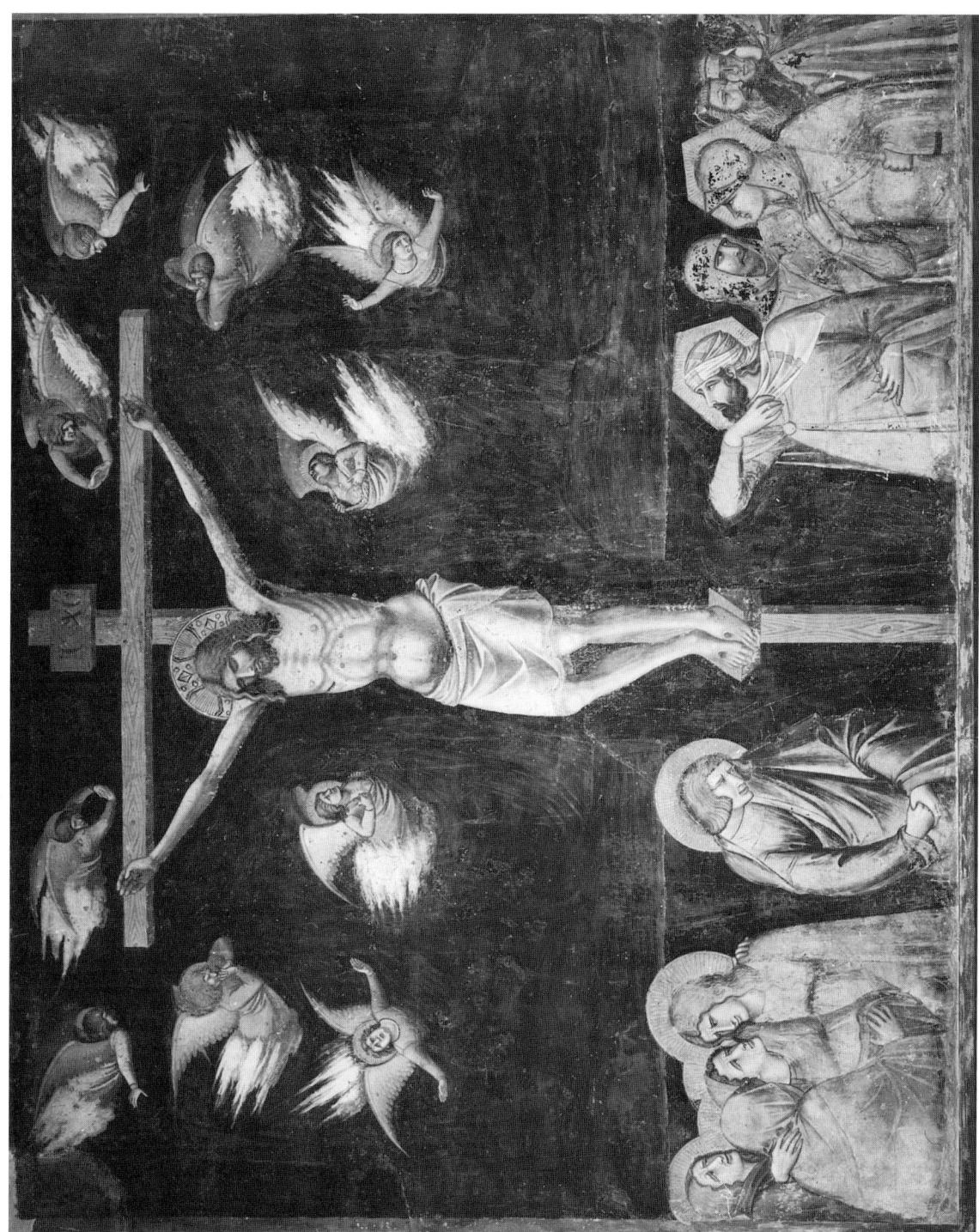

Fig. 45 Pietro Lorenzetti, *Crucifixion*. Siena, San Francesco.

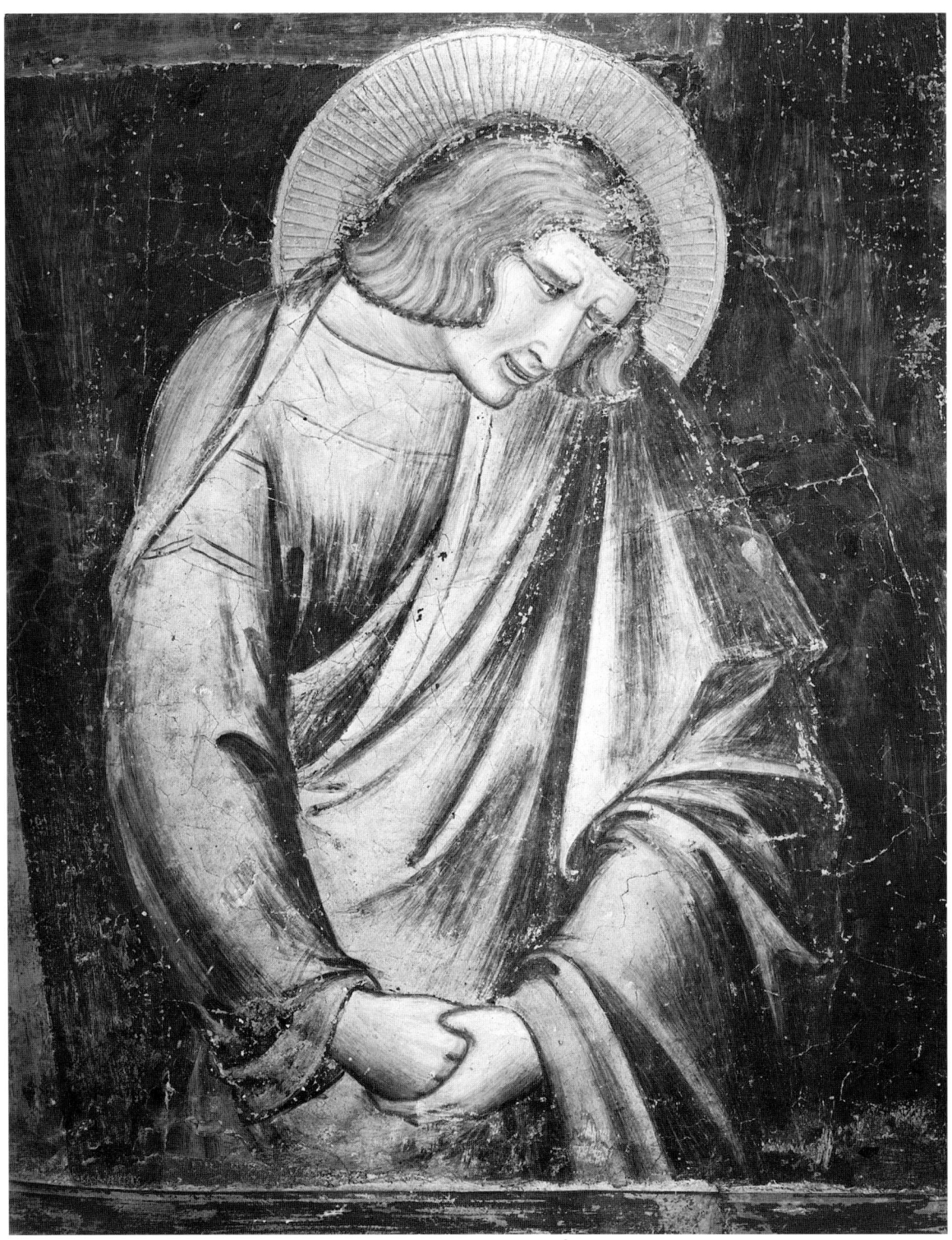

Fig. 46 Pietro Lorenzetti, *Crucifixion,* detail: Saint John the Evangelist. Siena, San Francesco.

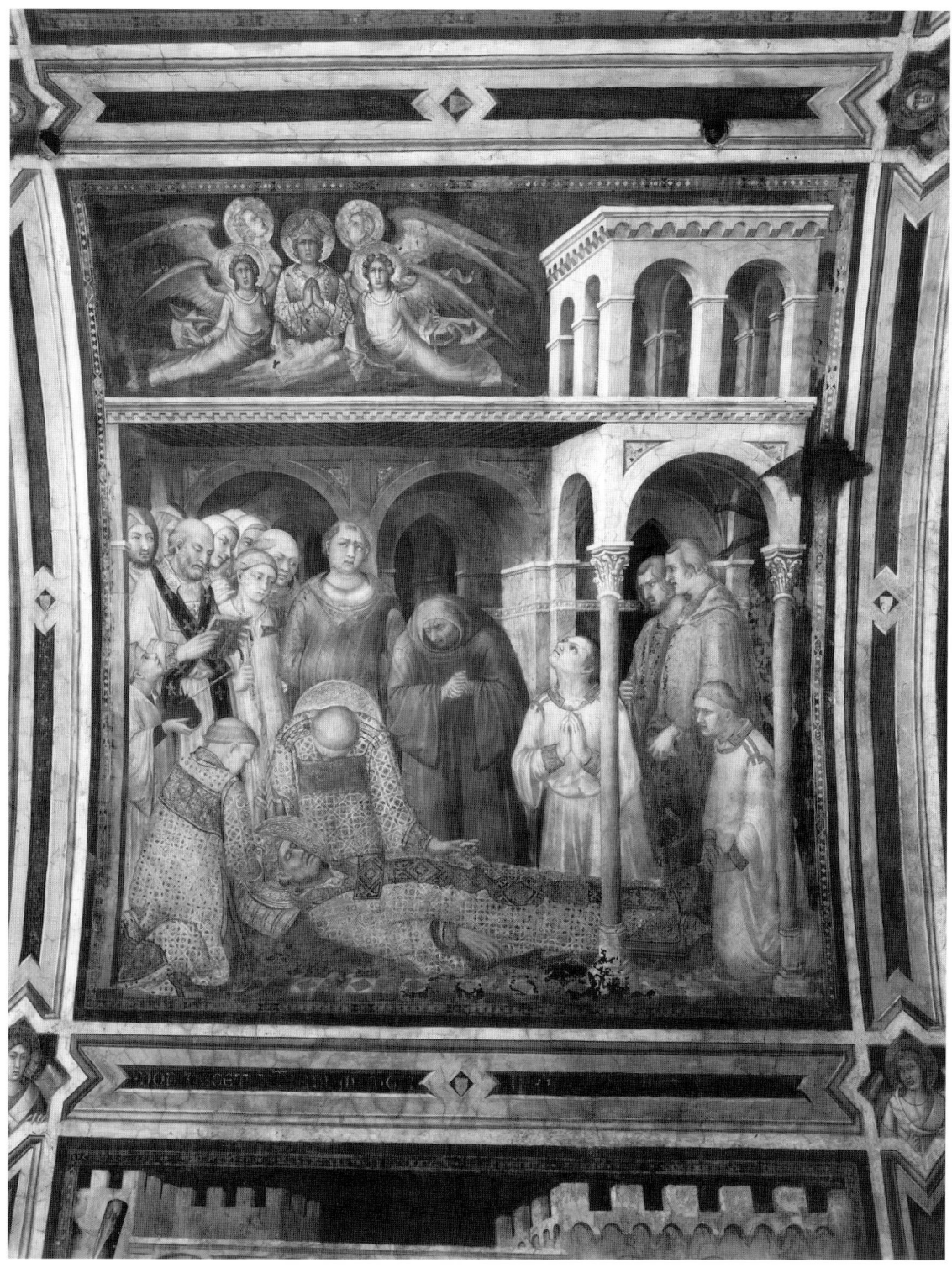

Fig. 47 Simone Martini, *Death of Saint Martin*. Assisi, San Francesco, Lower Church.

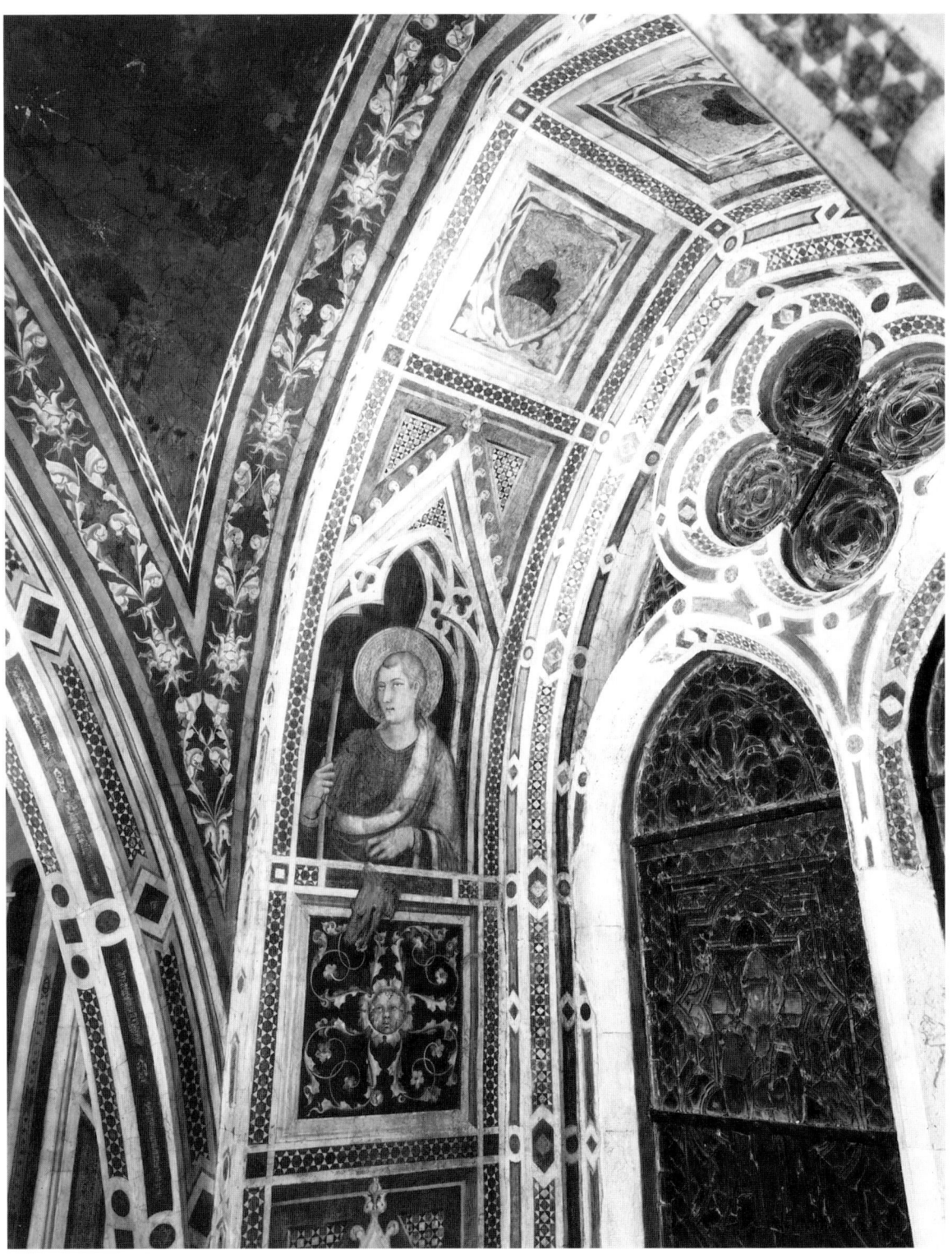

Fig. 48 Simone Martini, saint in the window embrasure. Assisi, San Francesco, Lower Church.

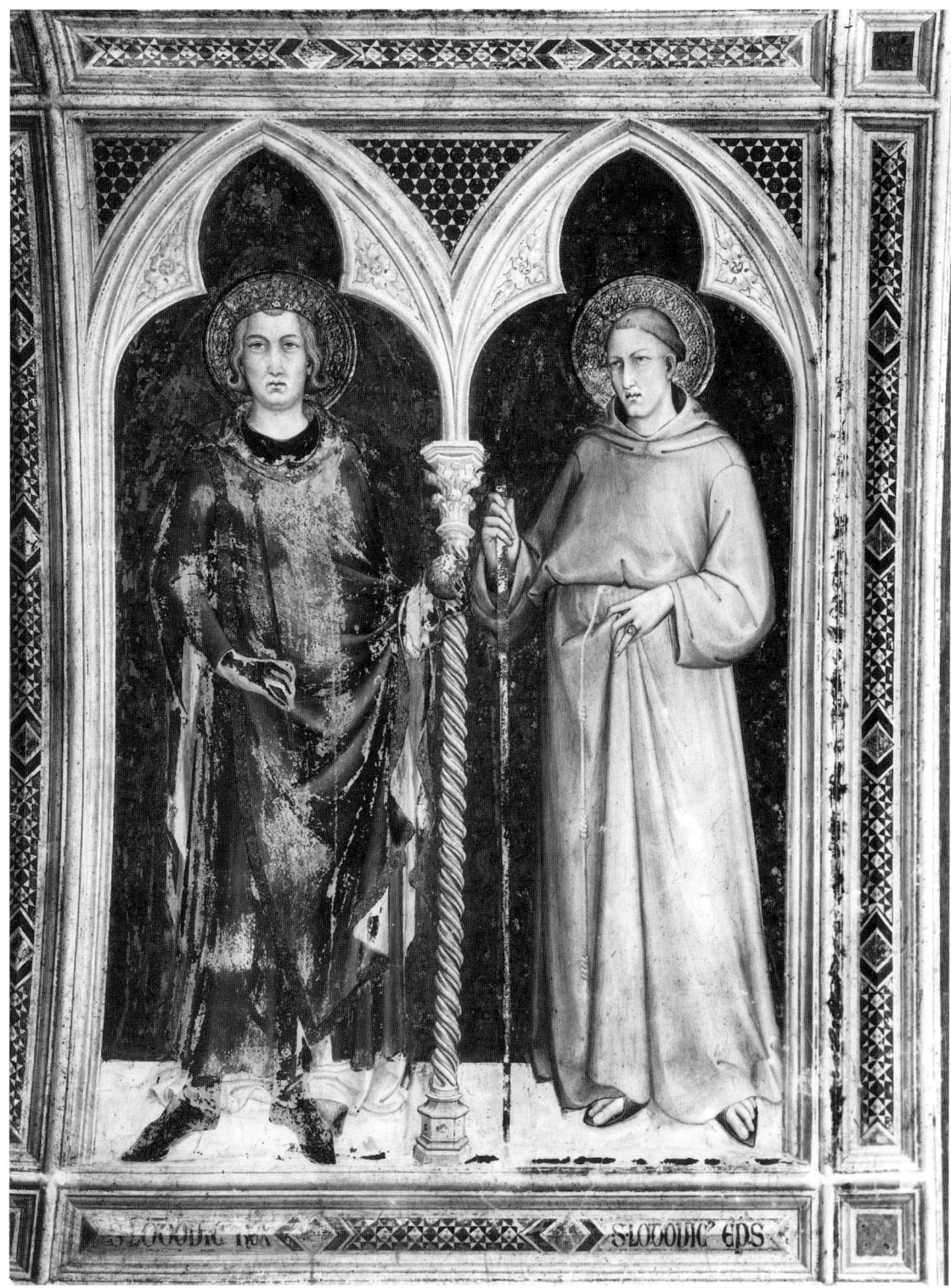

Fig. 49 Simone Martini, *Saints Louis IX of France and Louis of Toulouse*. Assisi, San Francesco, Lower Church.

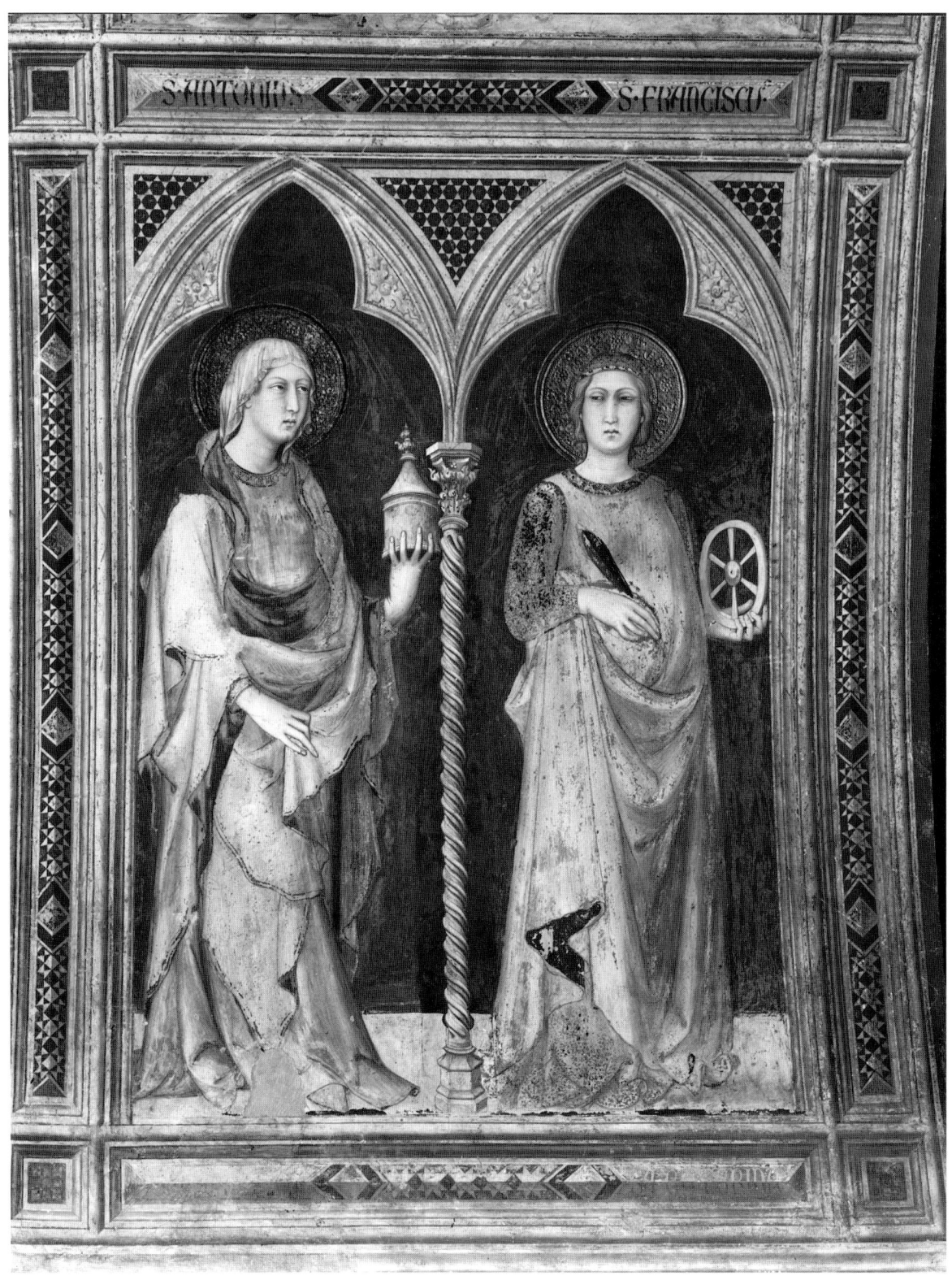

Fig. 50 Simone Martini, *Saints Mary Magdalen and Catherine of Alexandria*. Assisi, San Francesco, Lower Church.

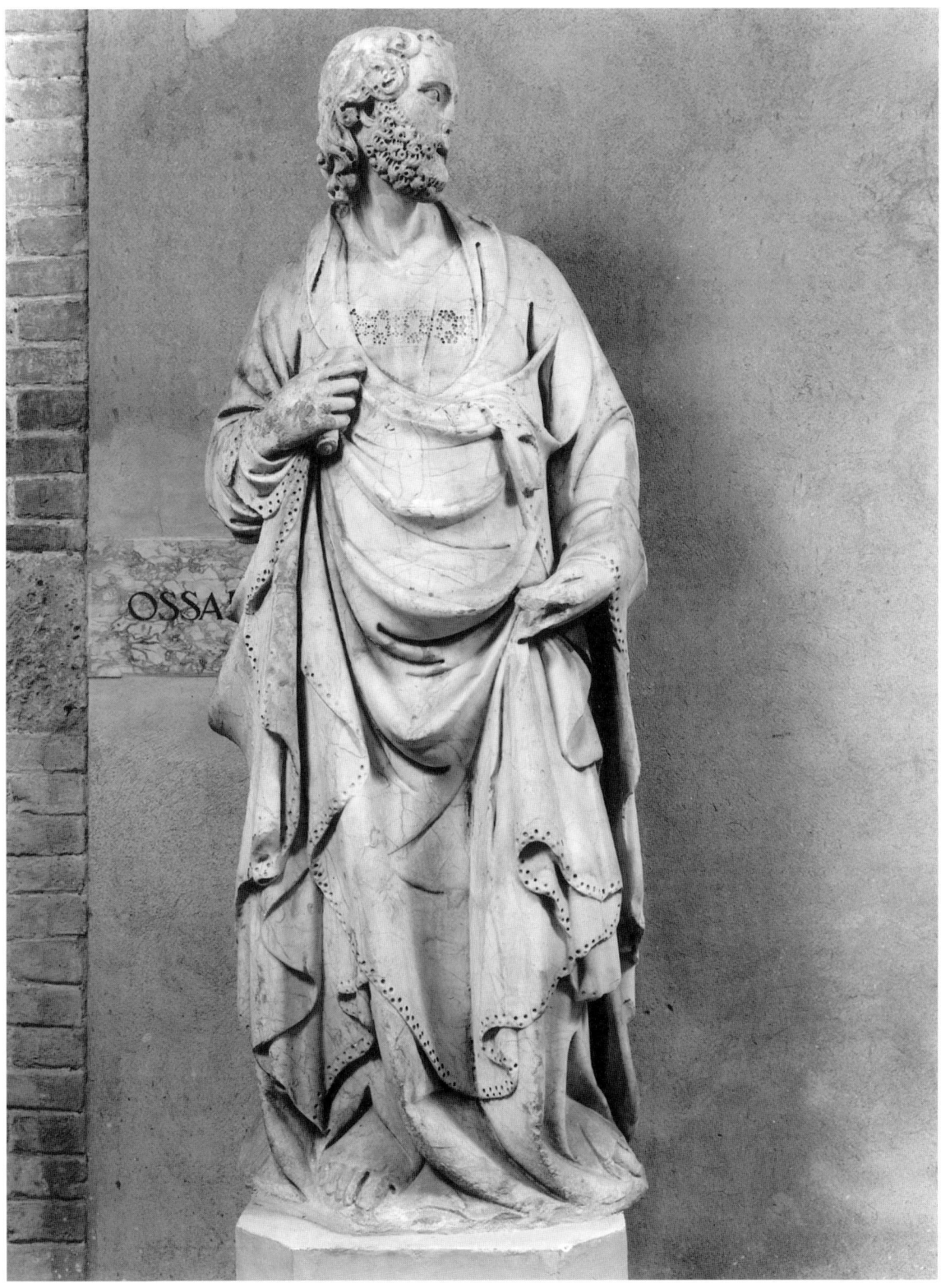

Fig. 51 Saint, from the roof of Siena cathedral. Siena, Museo dell'Opera del Duomo.

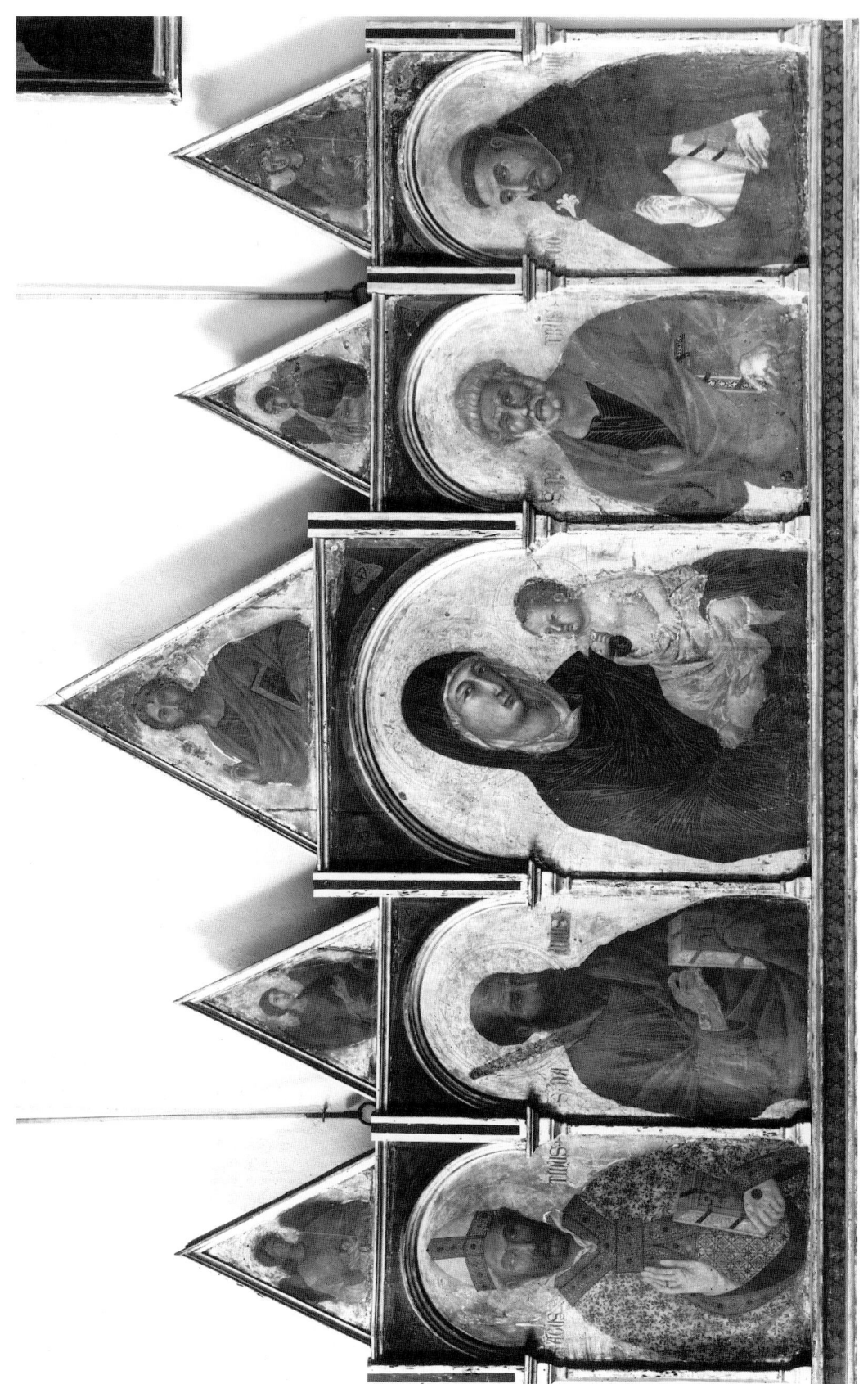

Fig. 52 Duccio di Buoninsegna, Polyptych no. 28. Siena, Pinacoteca Nazionale.

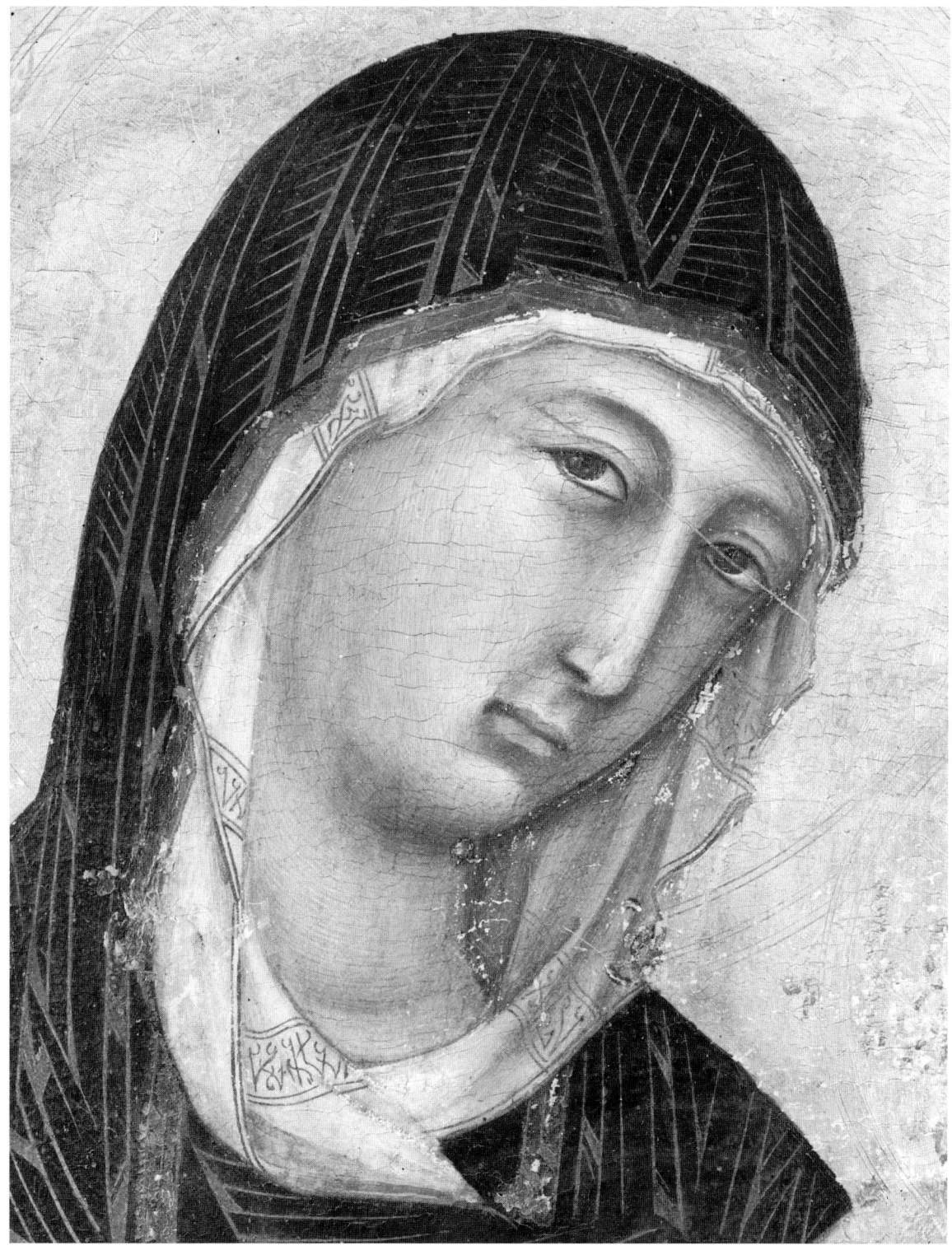

Fig. 53 Duccio di Buoninsegna, Polyptych no. 28, detail: head of the Virgin. Siena, Pinacoteca Nazionale.

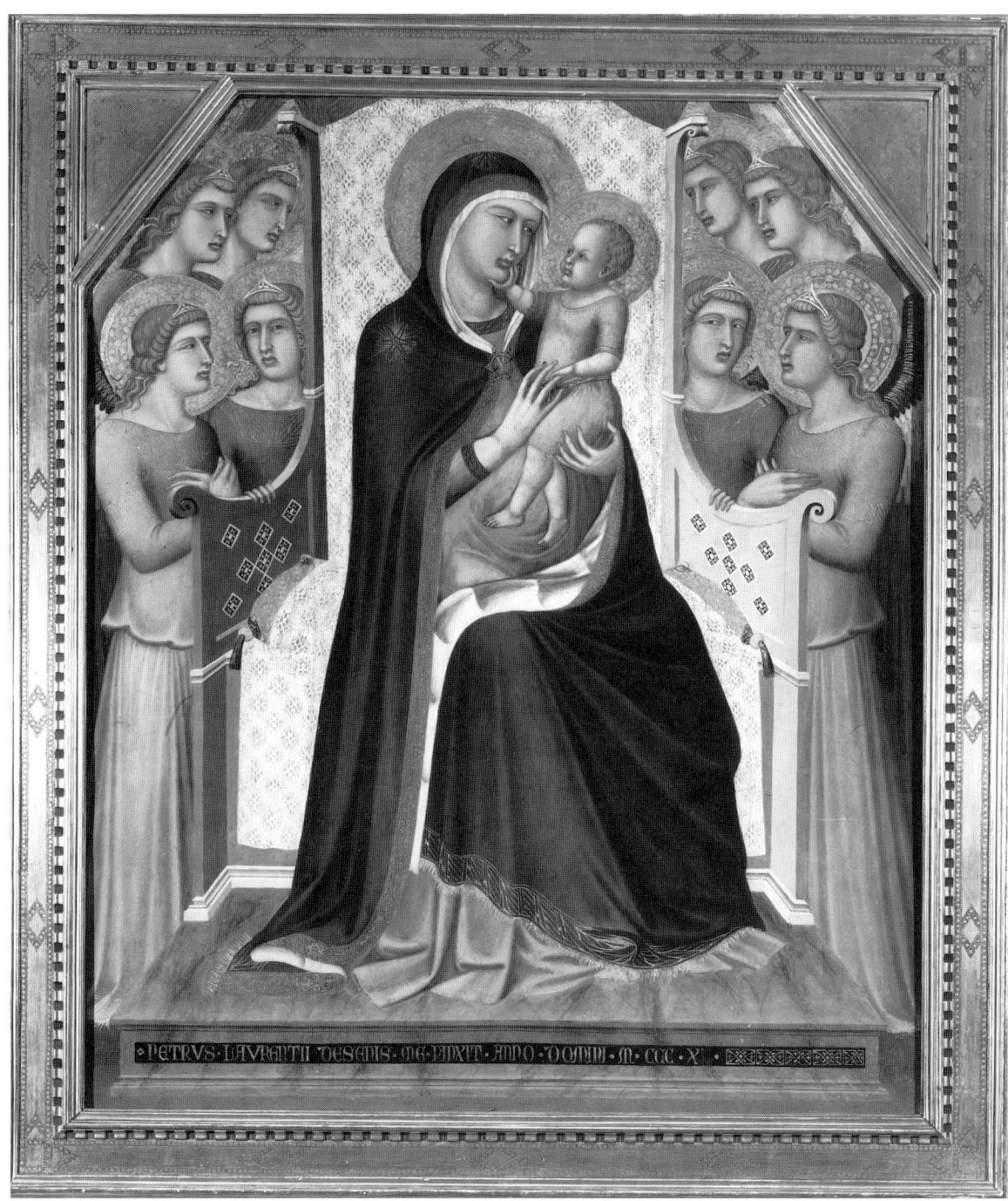

Fig. 54 Pietro Lorenzetti, *Enthroned Madonna and Child* (1340). Florence, Galleria degli Uffizi.

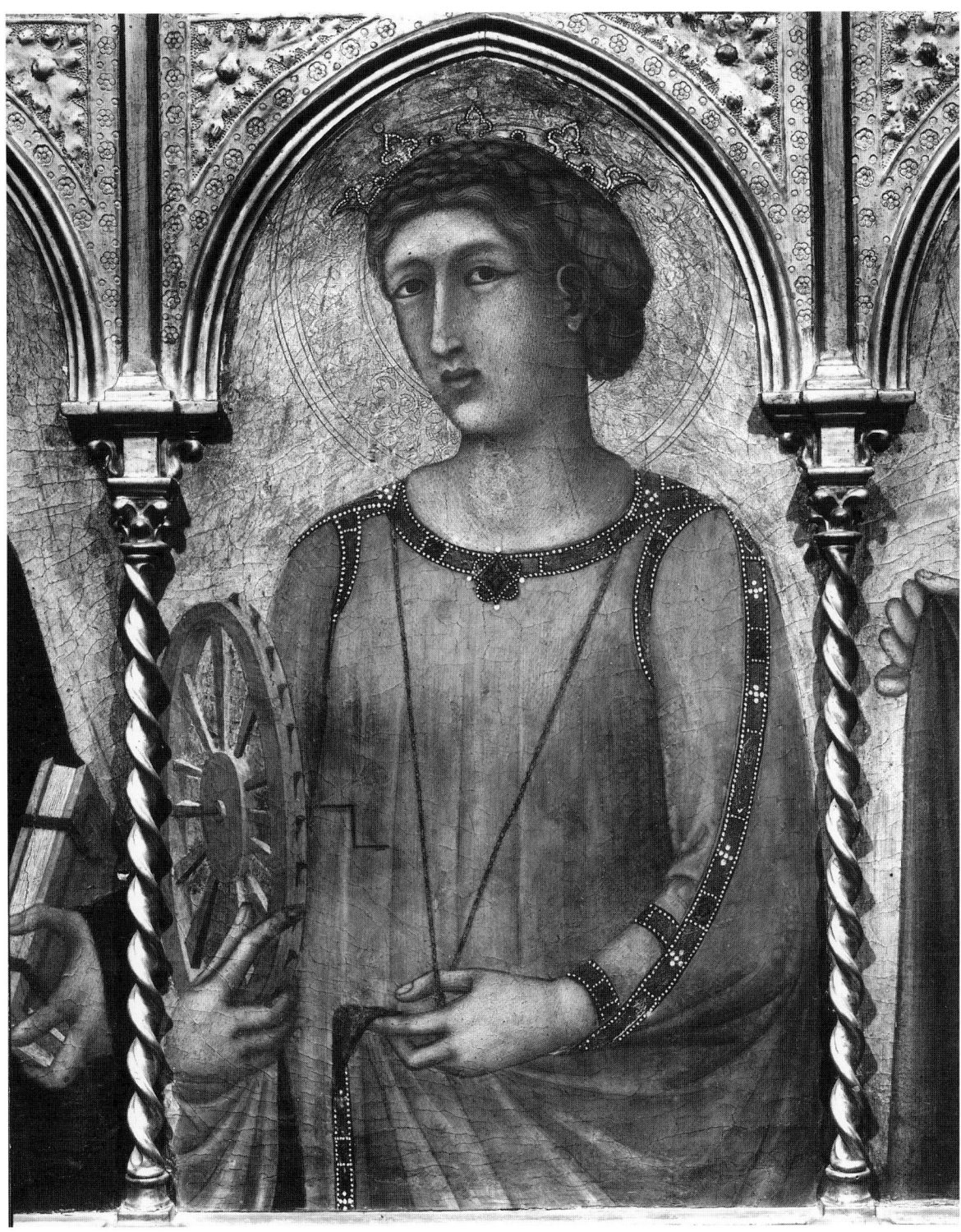

Fig. 55 Pietro Lorenzetti, *Saint Catherine of Alexandria*. Florence, Museo Horne.

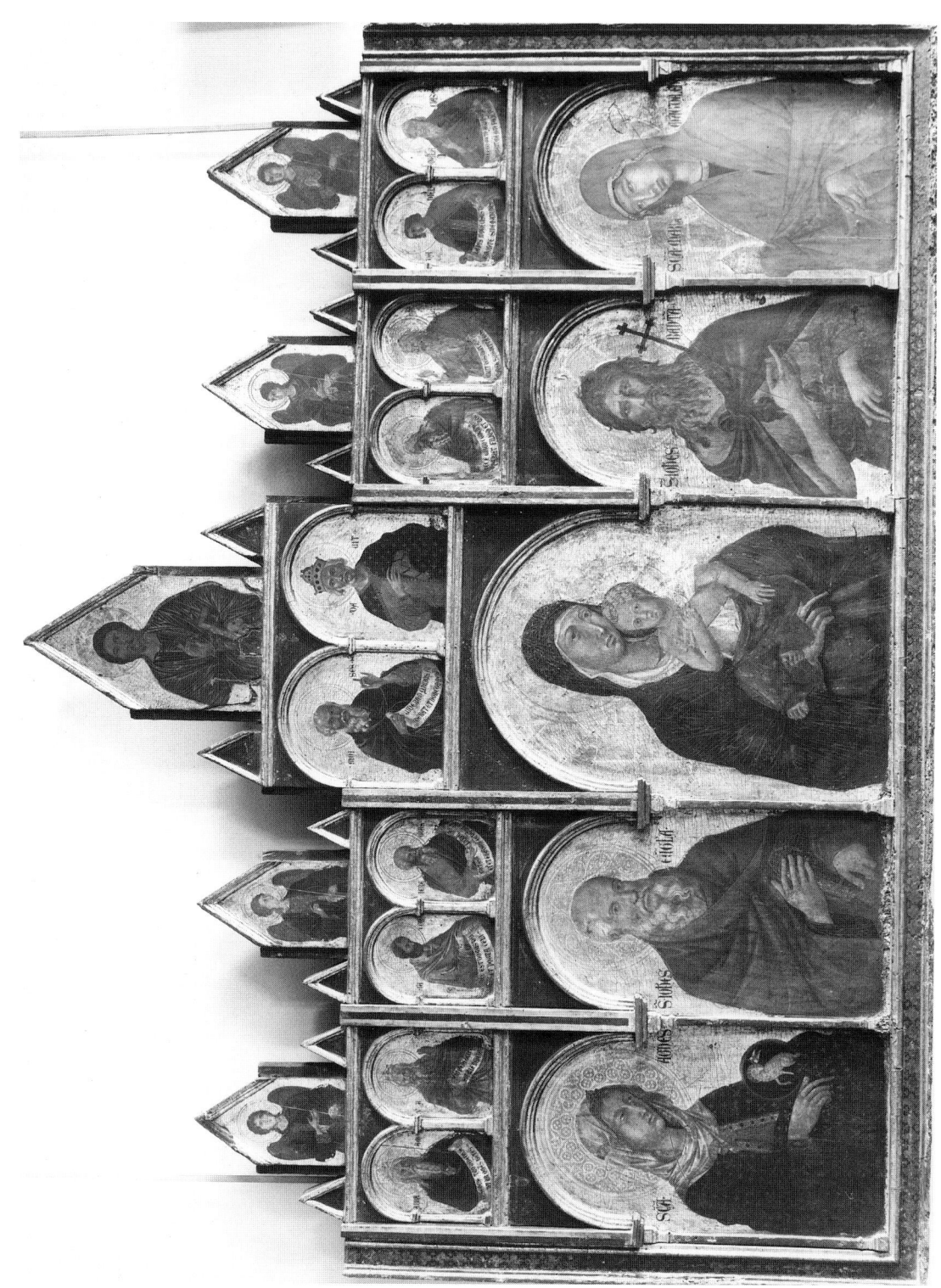

Fig. 56 Duccio di Buoninsegna, Polyptych no. 47. Siena, Pinacoteca Nazionale.

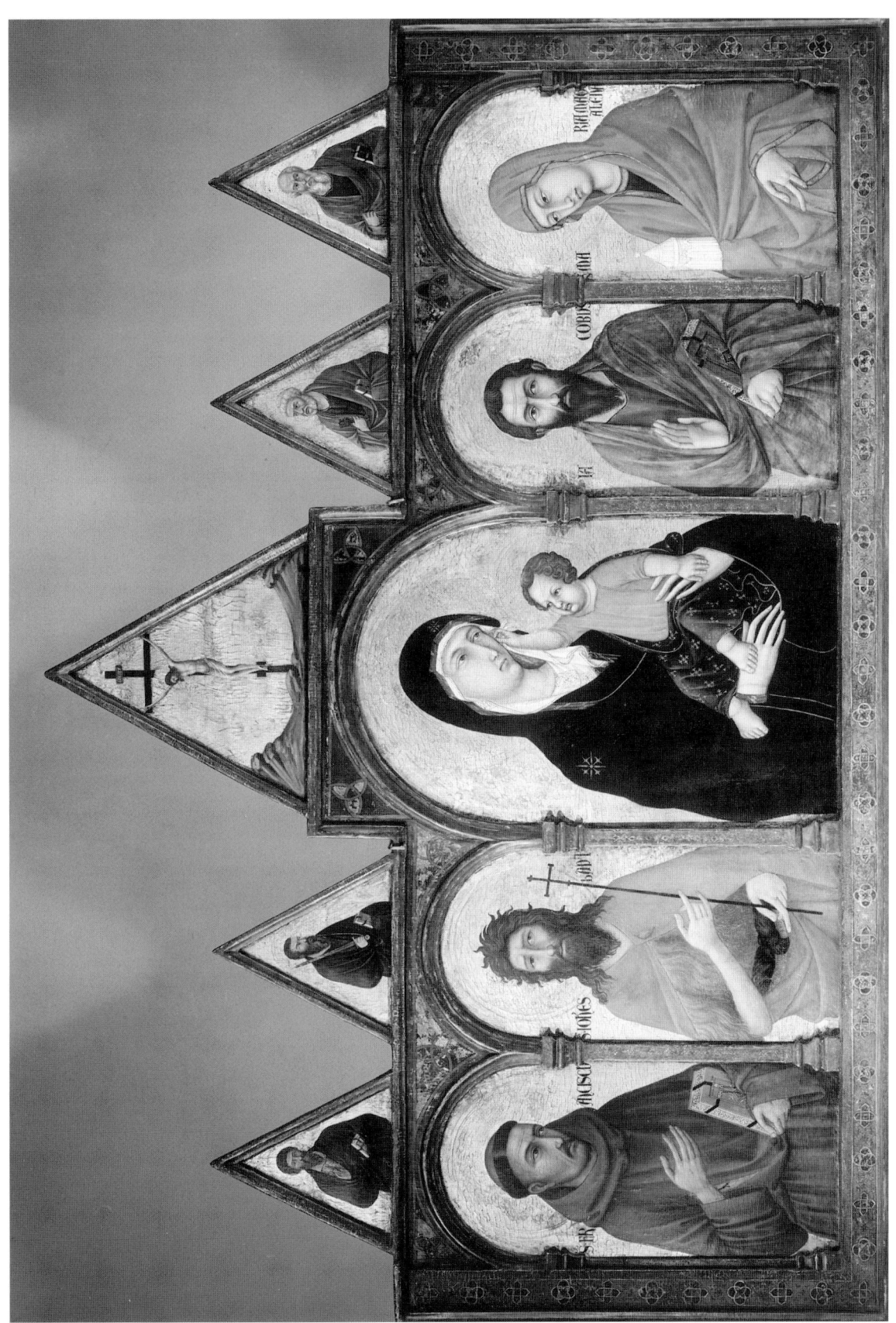

Fig. 57 Ugolino di Nerio, polyptych. Cleveland, Cleveland Museum of Art.

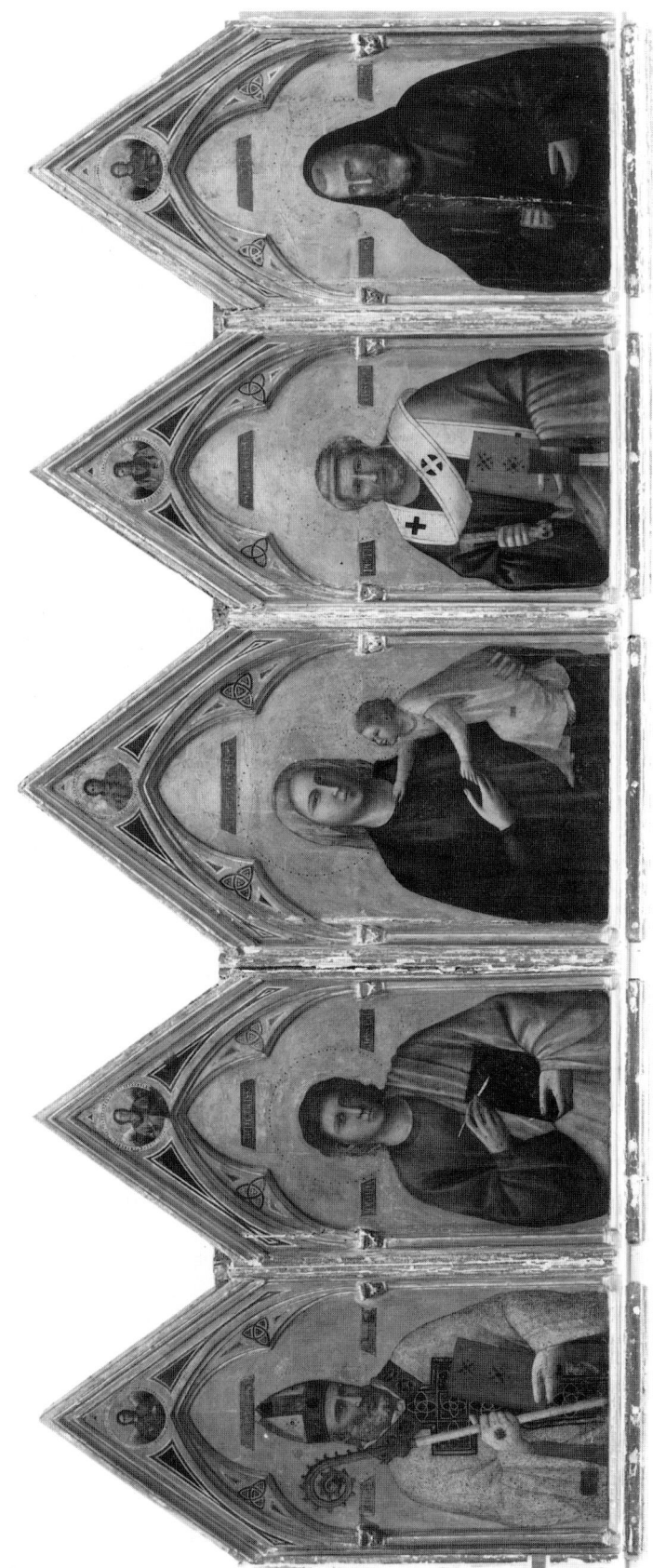

Fig. 58 Saint Nicholas Master, the Badia polyptych. Florence, Galleria degli Uffizi.

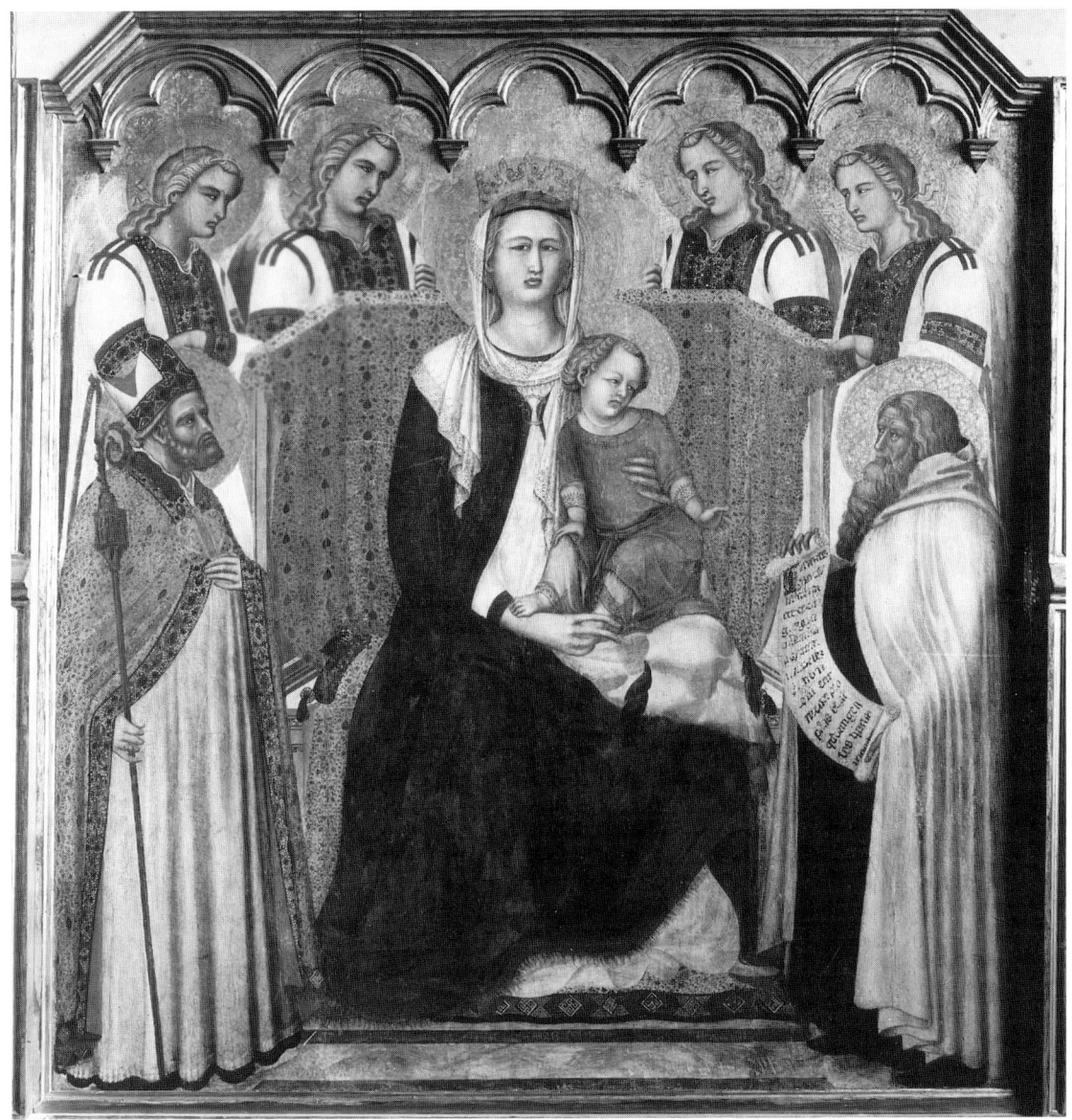

Fig. 59 Pietro Lorenzetti, the Carmelite polyptych, detail: central panel. Siena, Pinacoteca Nazionale.

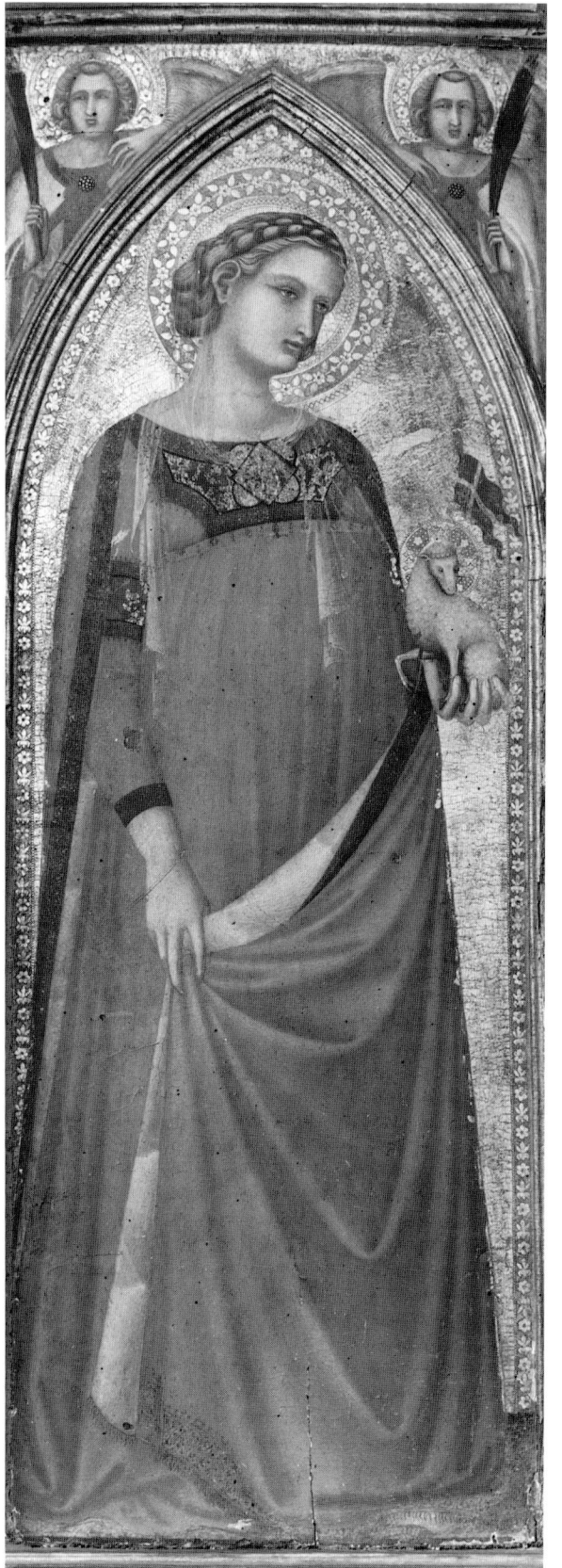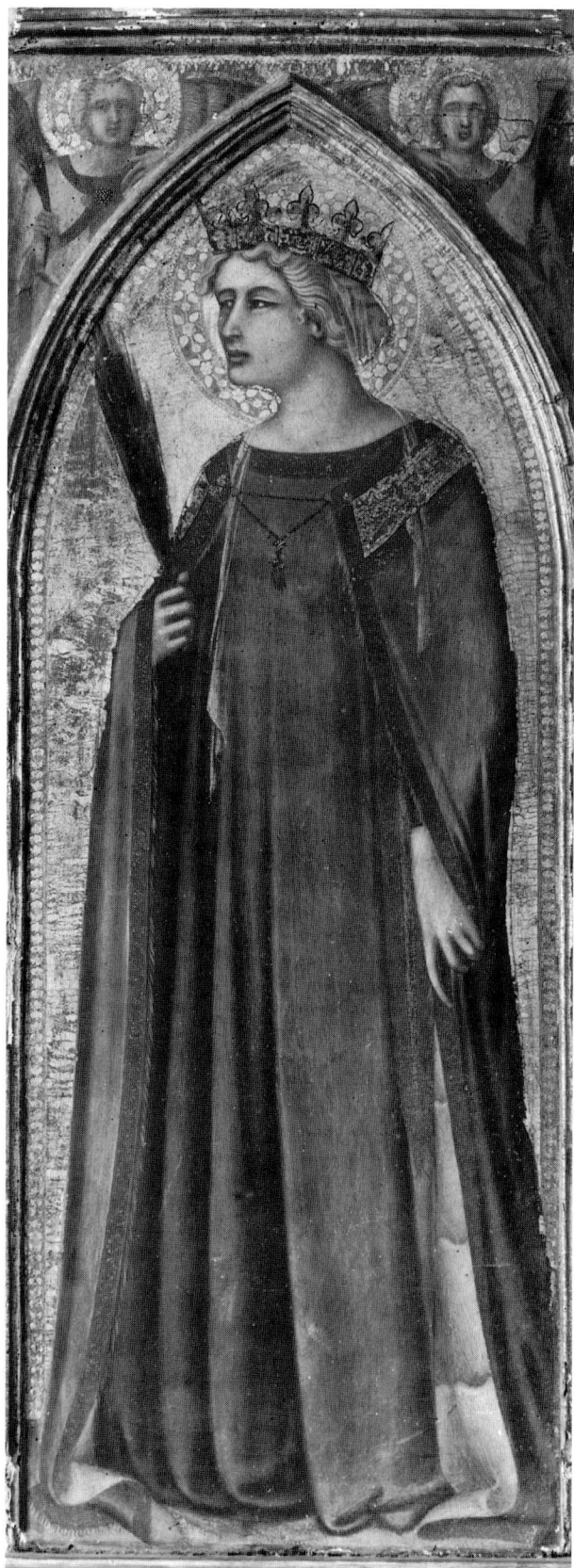

Fig. 60 Pietro Lorenzetti, the Carmelite polyptych, detail: *Saints Agnes and Catherine of Alexandria*. Siena, Pinacoteca Nazionale.

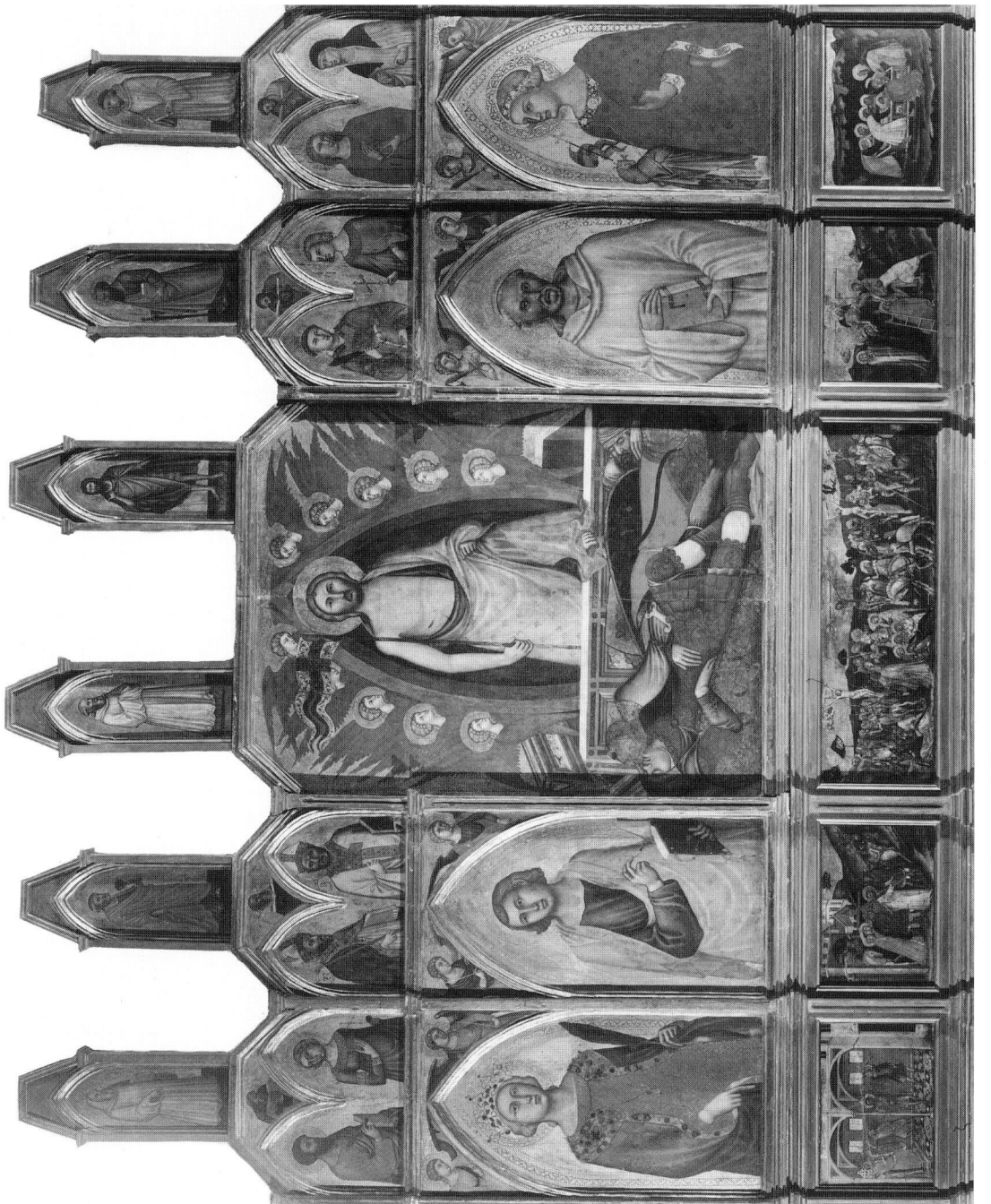

Fig. 61 Related to Niccolò di Segna, *Resurrection* polyptych. Borgo San Sepolcro, Pinacoteca Comunale.

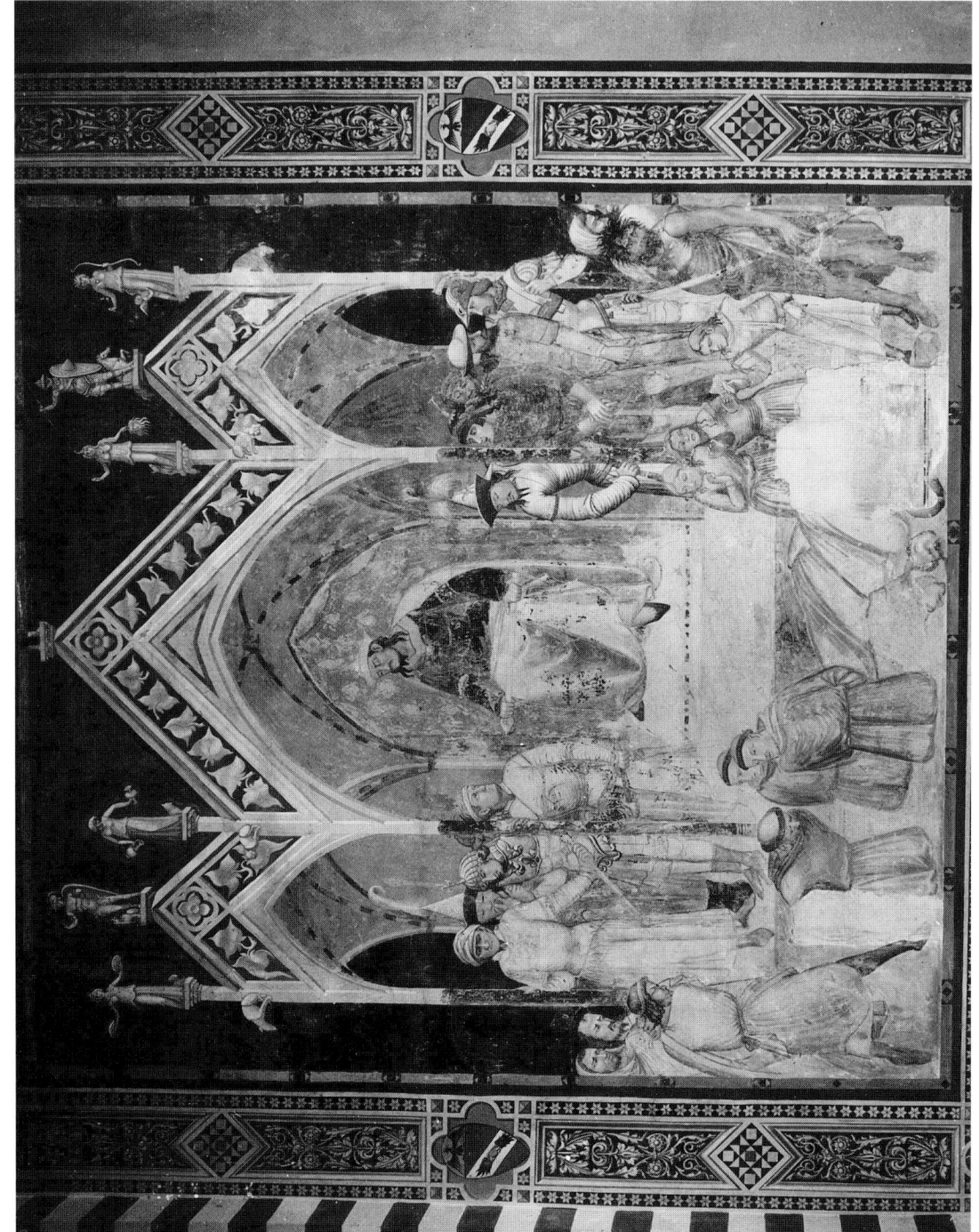

Fig. 62 Ambrogio Lorenzetti, *Franciscan Martyrdom*. Siena, San Francesco.

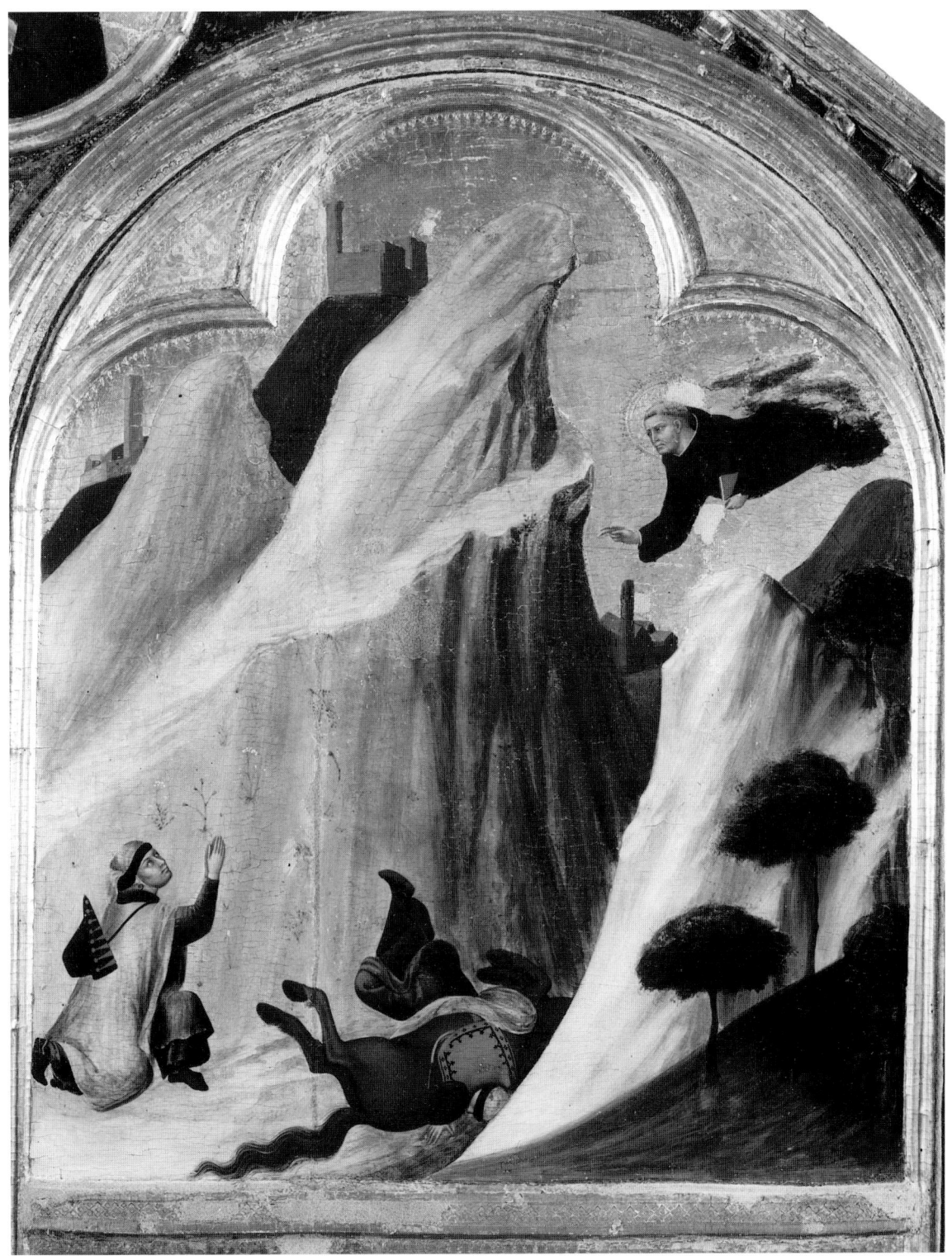

Fig. 63 Simone Martini, *Beato Agostino Novello,* detail. Siena, Pinacoteca Nazionale.

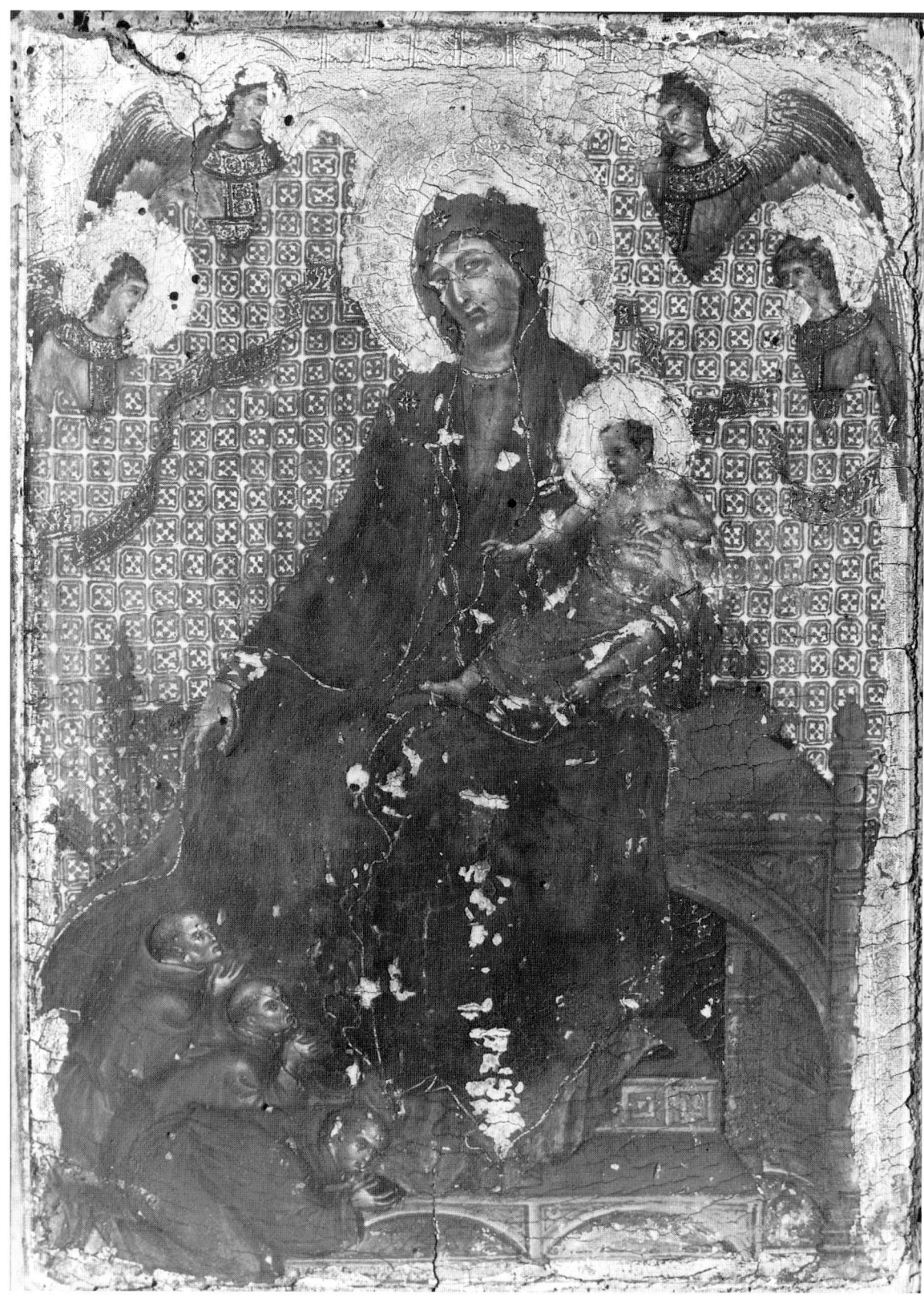

Fig. 64 Duccio di Buoninsegna, *Madonna of the Franciscans*. Siena, Pinacoteca Nazionale.

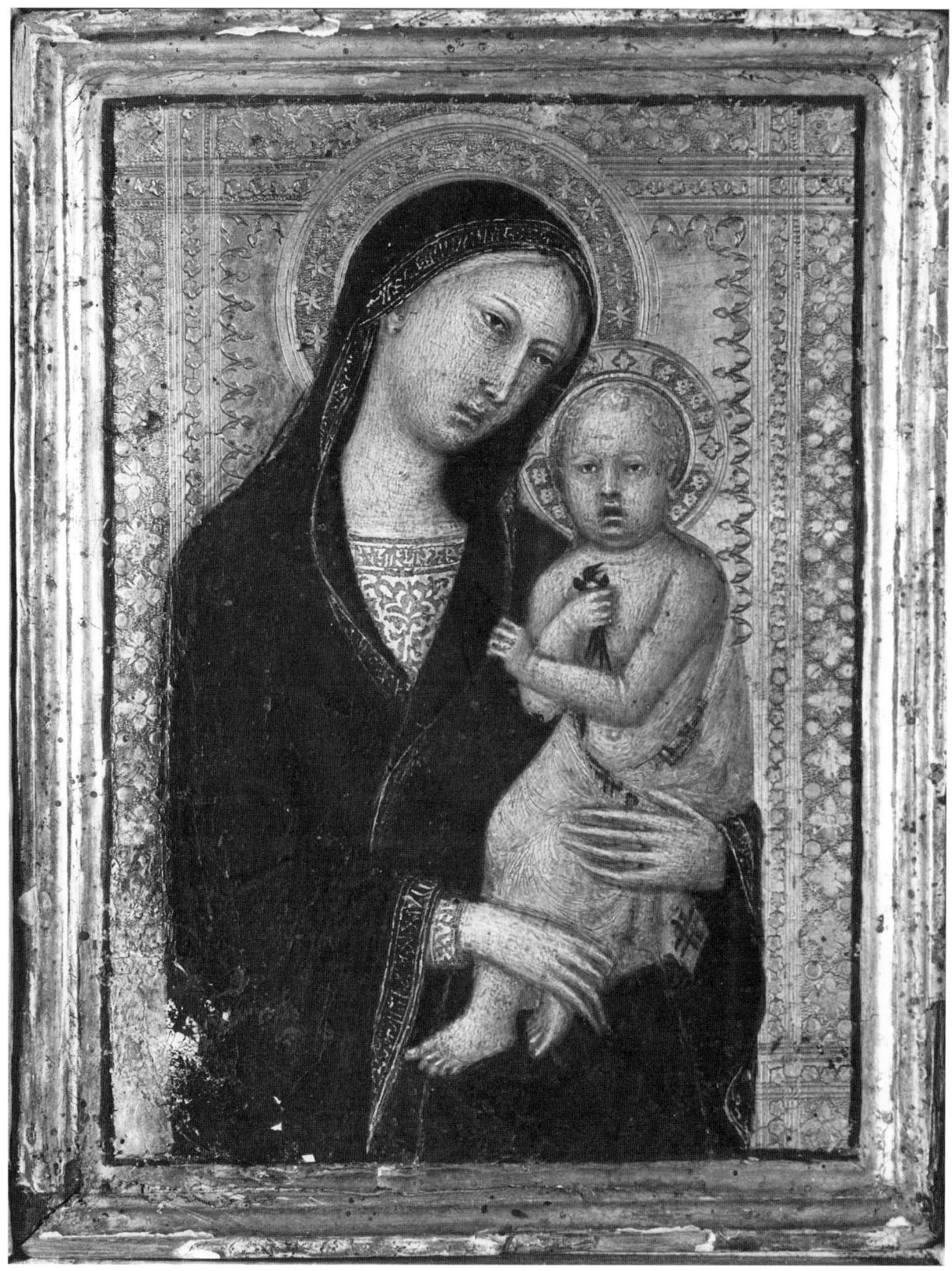

Fig. 65 The Sienese Straus Master (?), *Madonna and Child*. Oxford, Ashmolean Museum.

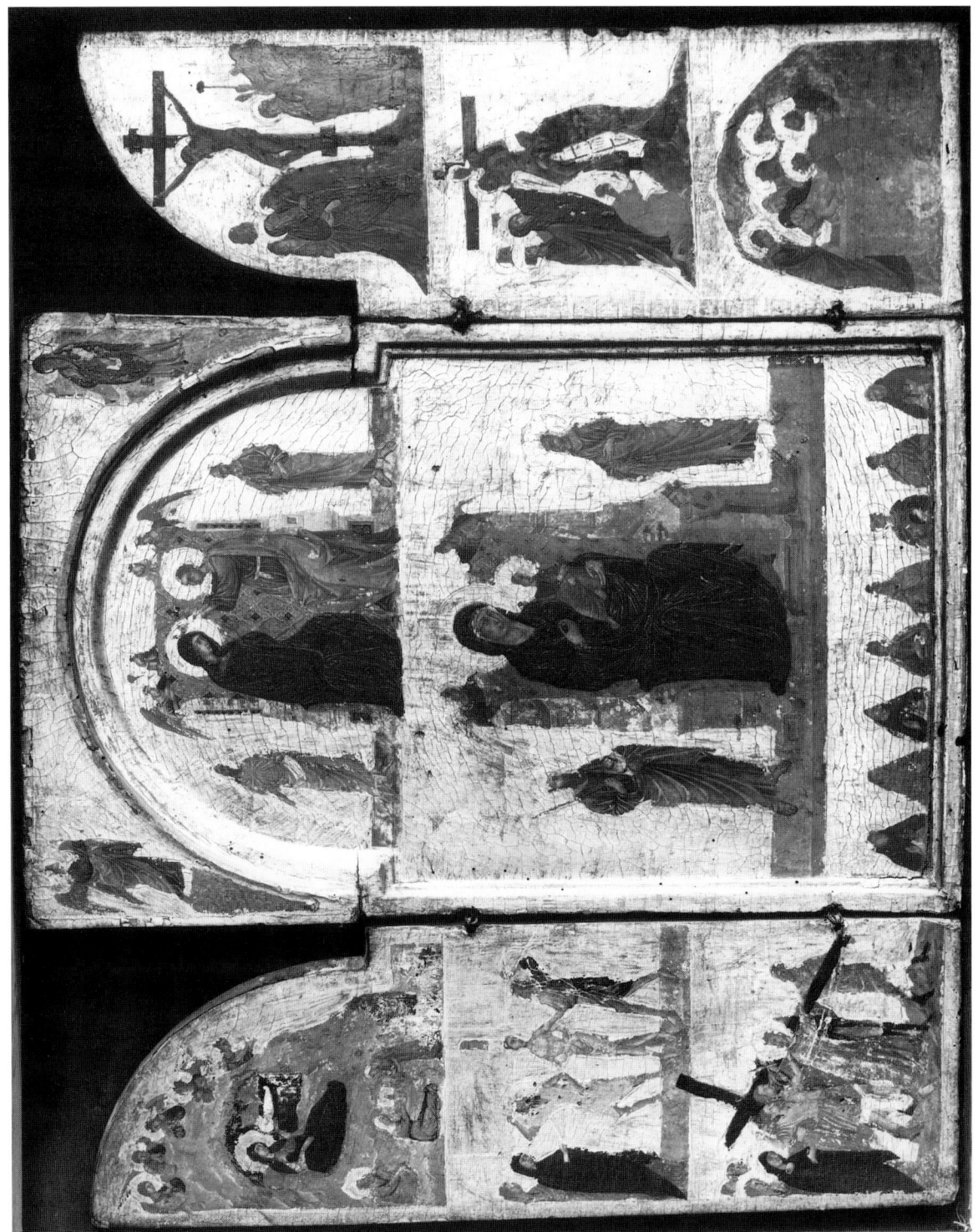

Fig. 66 Master of Tabernacle 35, Tabernacle 35. Siena, Pinacoteca Nazionale.

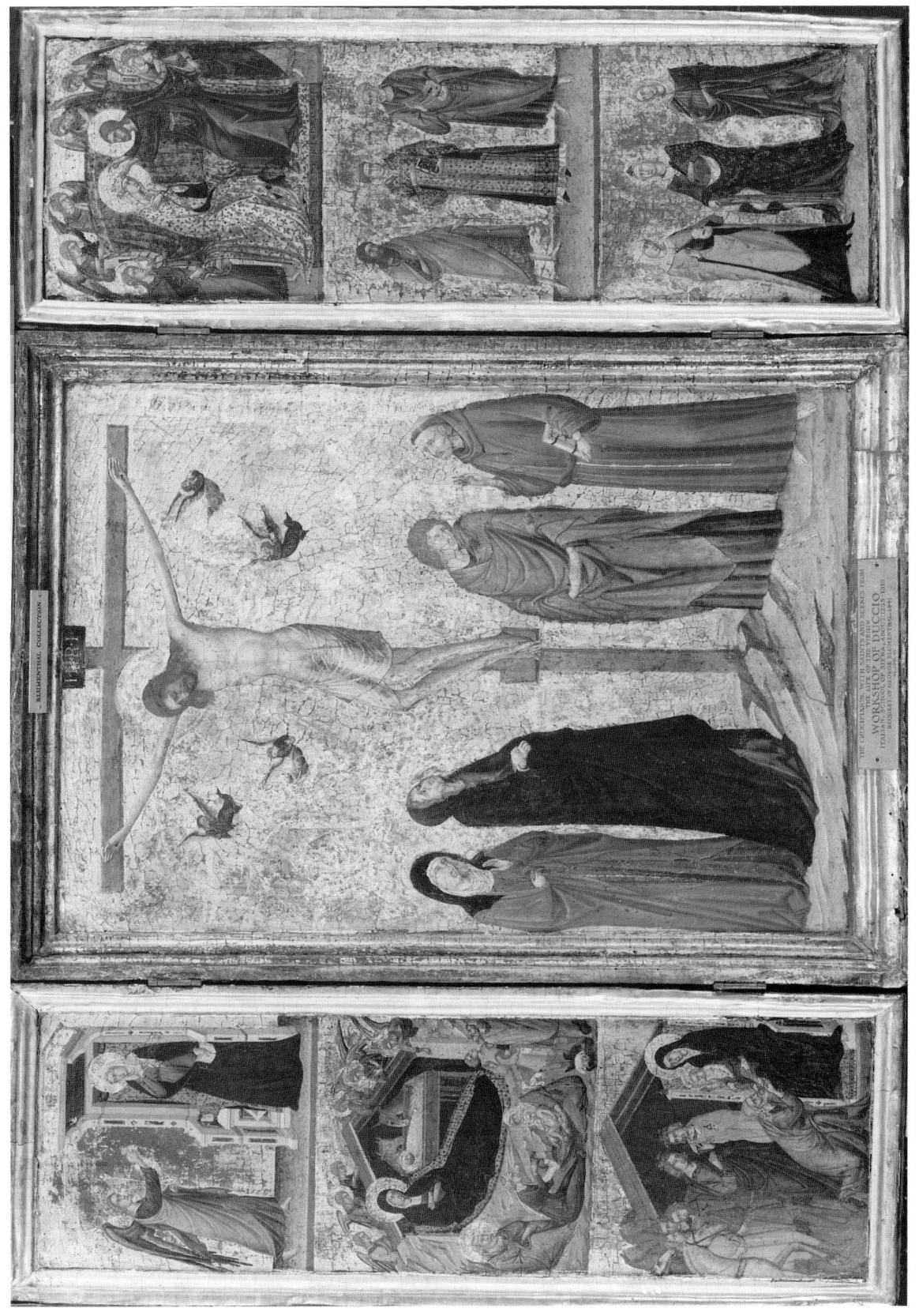

Fig. 67 Orbit of Ugolino di Nerio, triptych. New York, Metropolitan Museum.

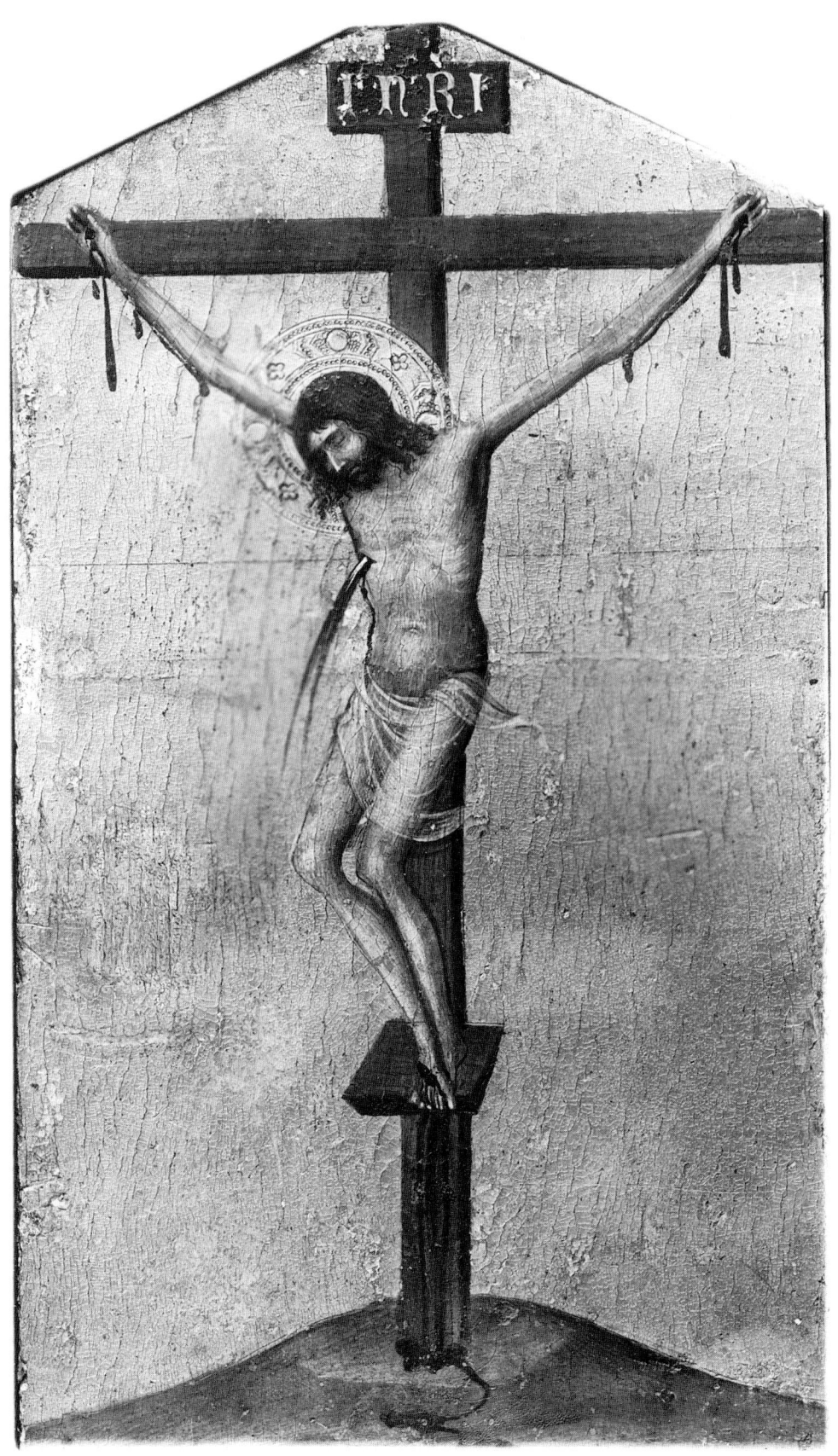

Fig. 68 Simone Martini, *Crucified Christ*. Cambridge, Mass., Fogg Art Museum.

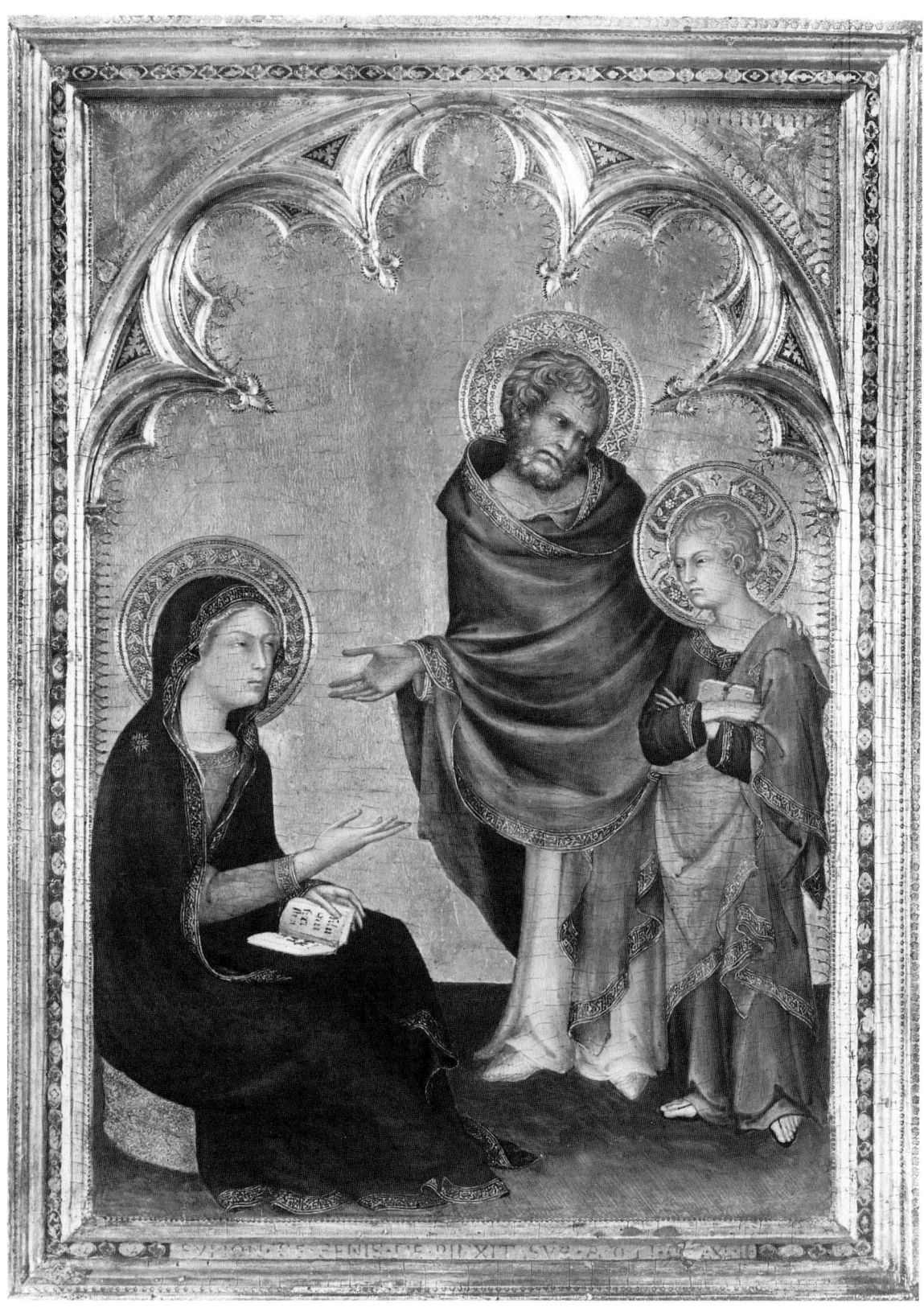

Fig. 69 Simone Martini, *Holy Family* (1342). Liverpool, Walker Art Gallery.

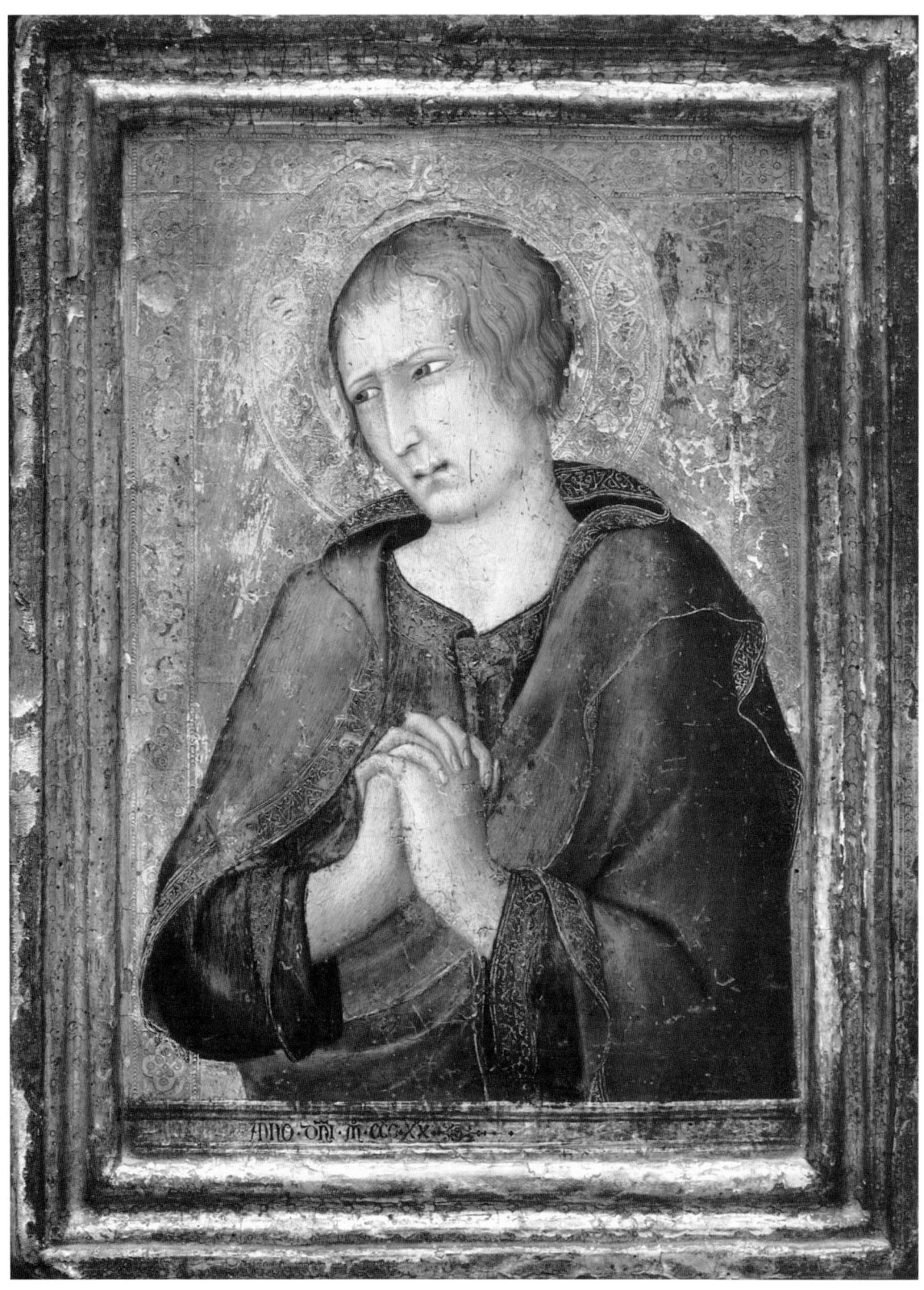

Fig. 70 Simone Martini, *Saint John the Evangelist*. Birmingham, Barber Institute of Fine Art.

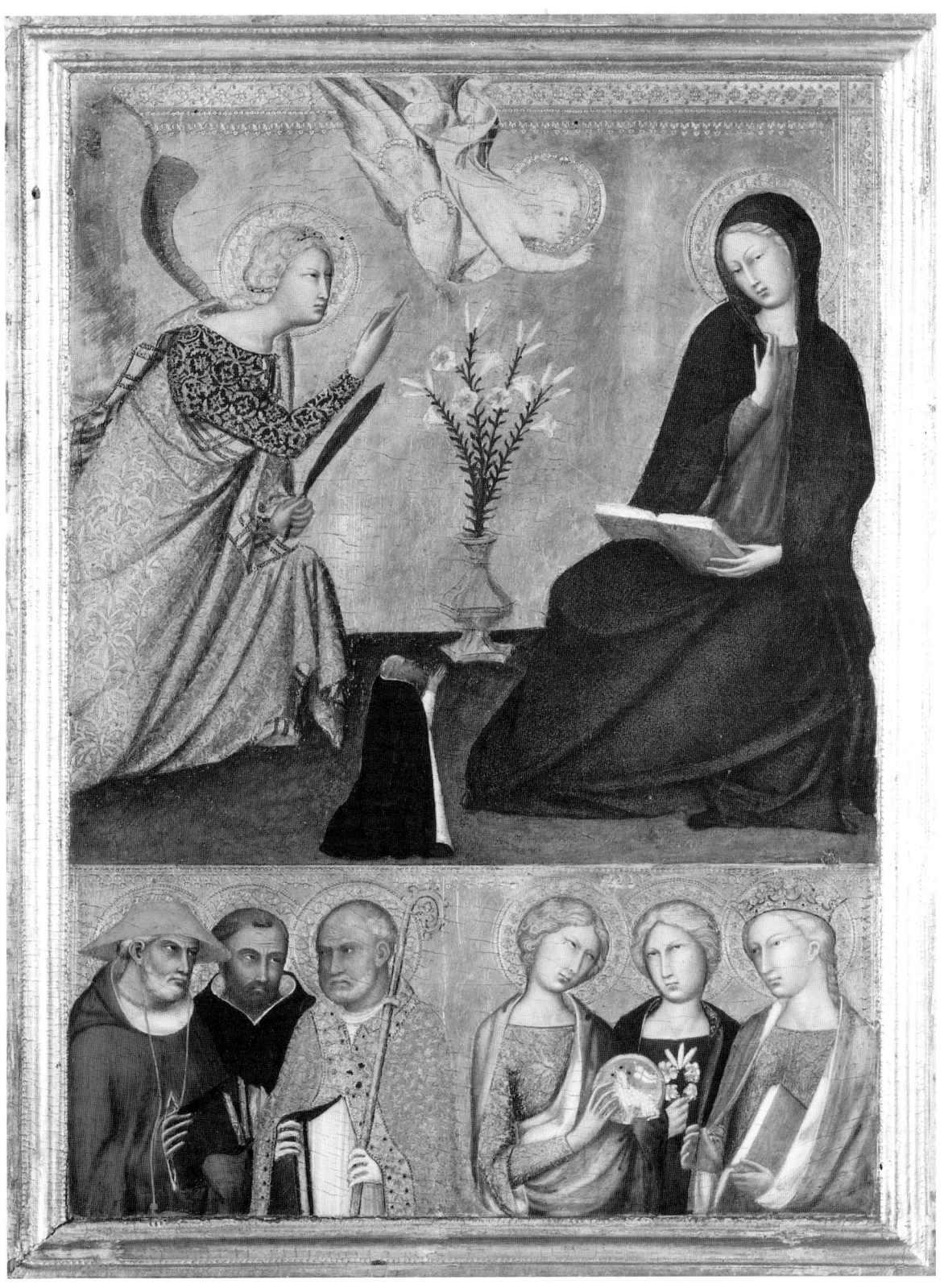

Fig. 71 The Sienese Straus Master, *Annunciation*. Berlin, Staatliche Museen Preußischer Kulturbesitz, Gemäldegalerie.

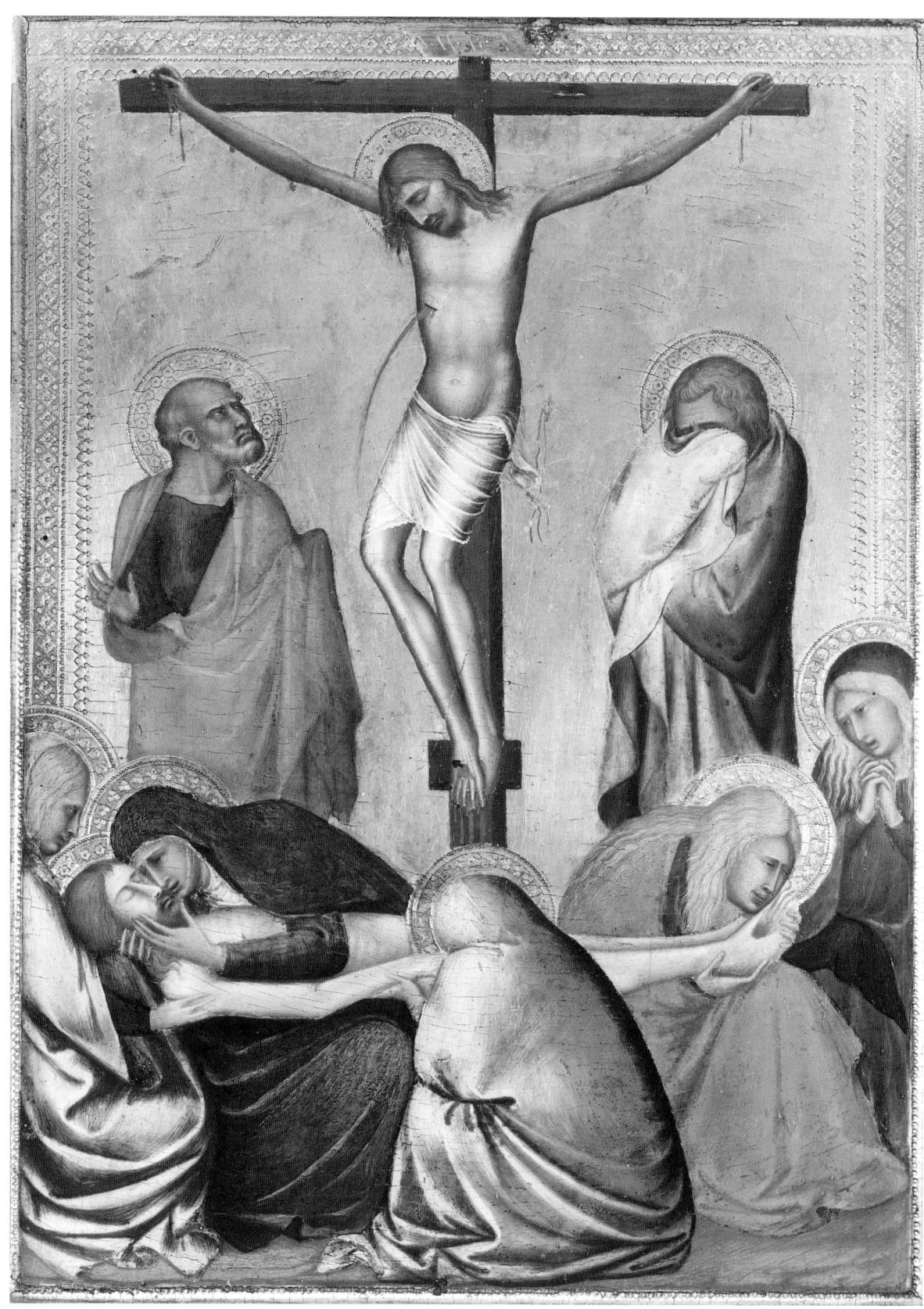

Fig. 72 The Sienese Straus Master, *Lamentation*. Oxford, Ashmolean Museum.

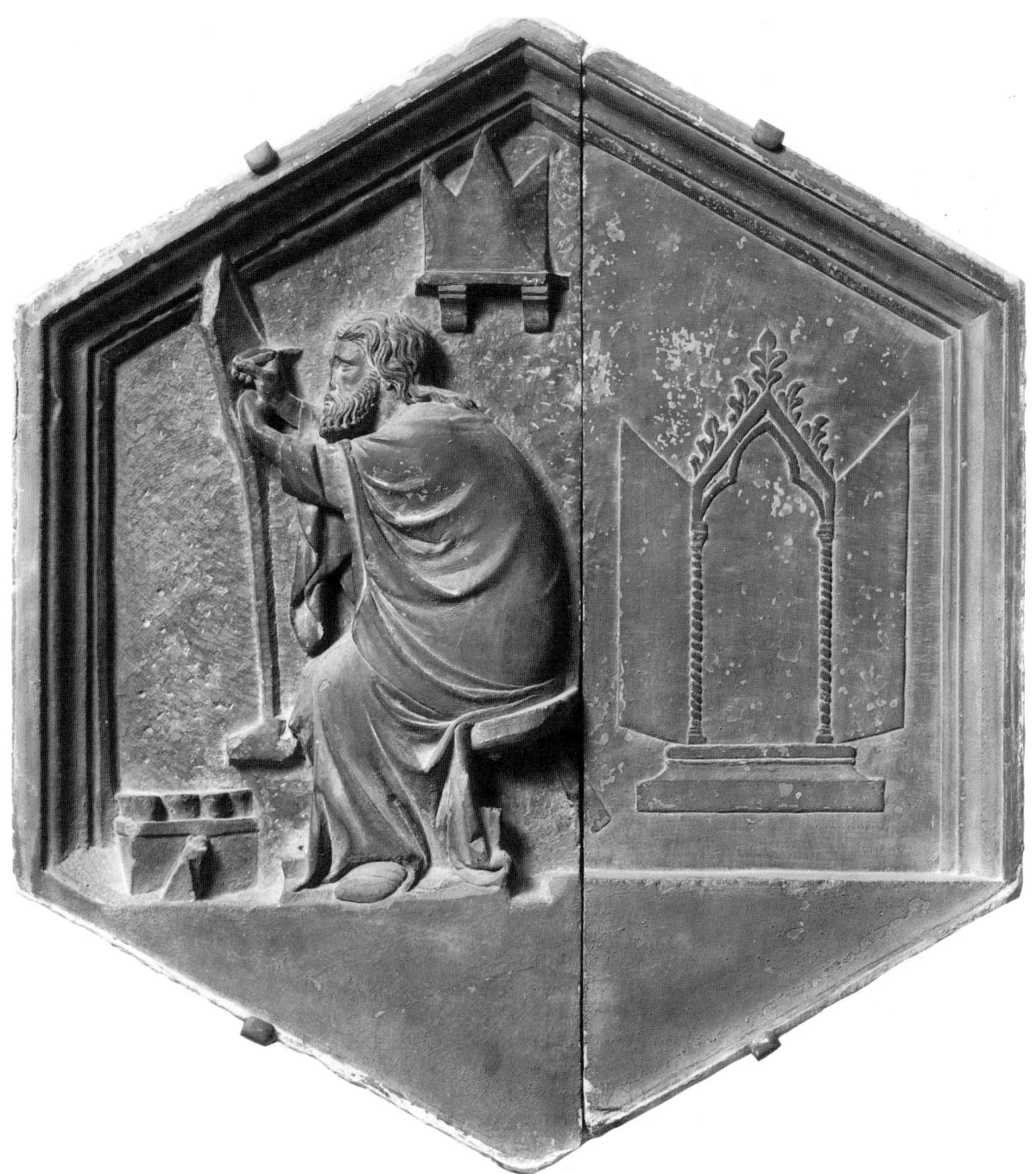

Fig. 73 Andrea Pisano, *Painting*. Florence, cathedral, campanile.

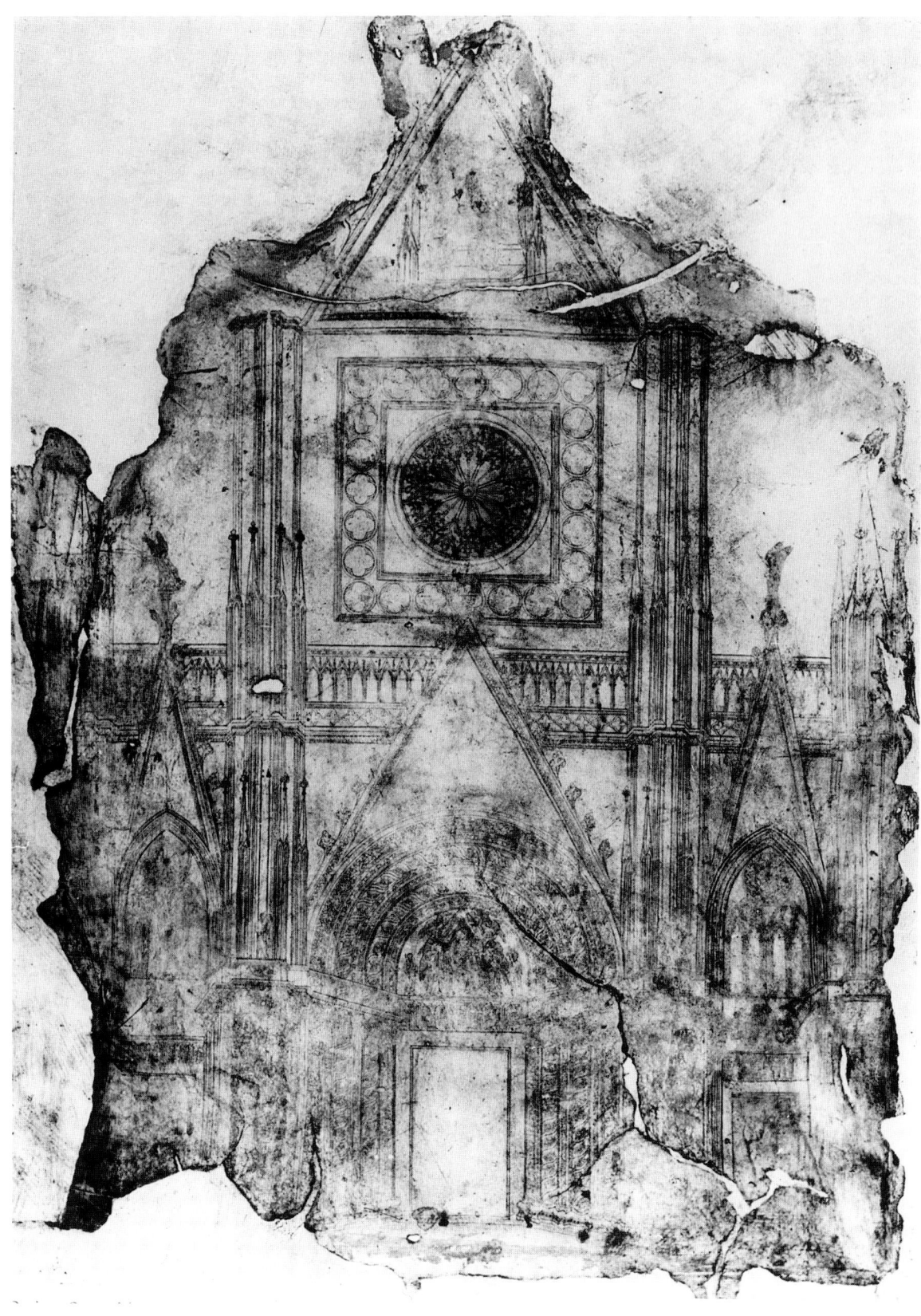

Fig. 74 Drawing for the facade of Orvieto cathedral. Orvieto, Opera del Duomo.

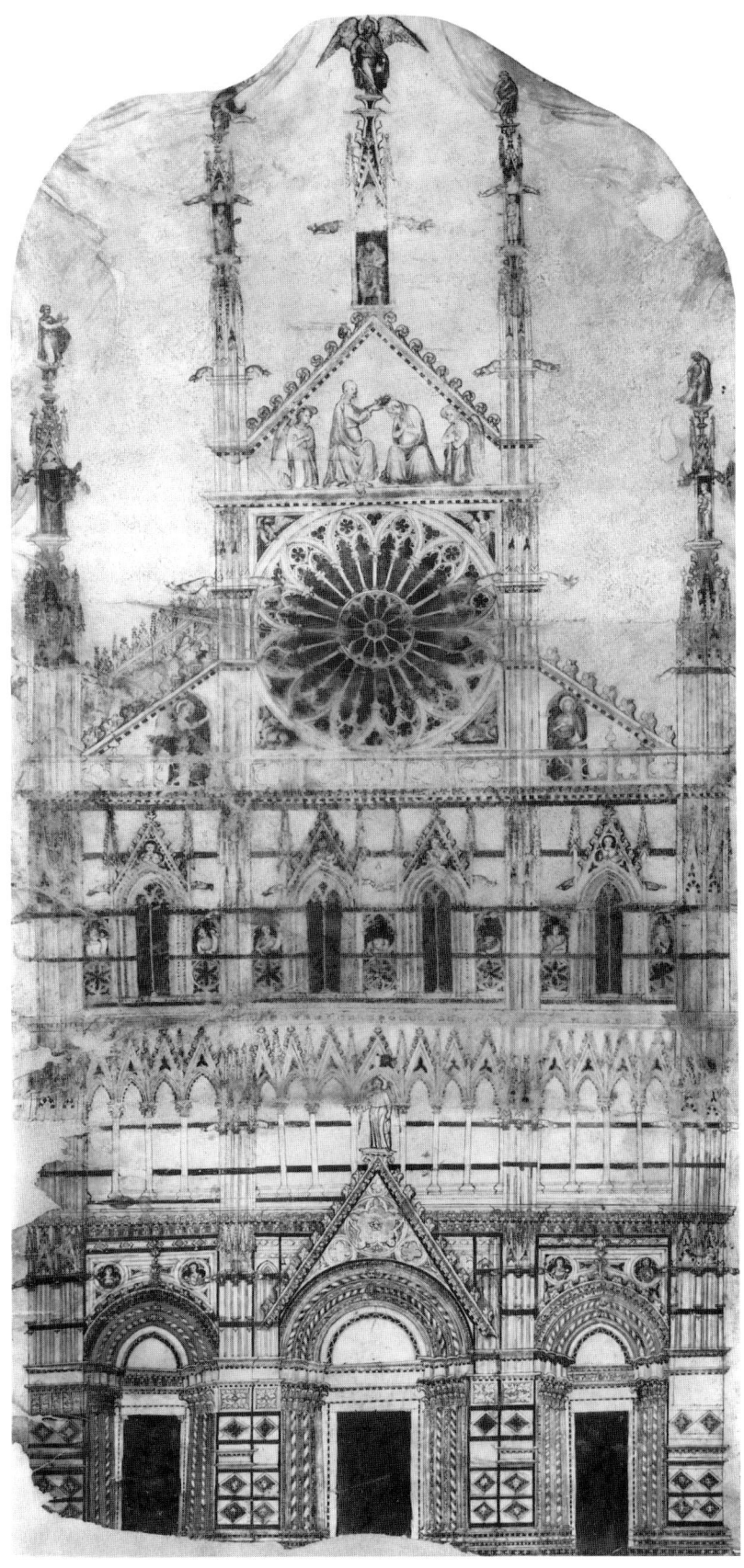

Fig. 75 Drawing for the facade of the Siena baptistery. Siena, Museo dell'Opera del Duomo.

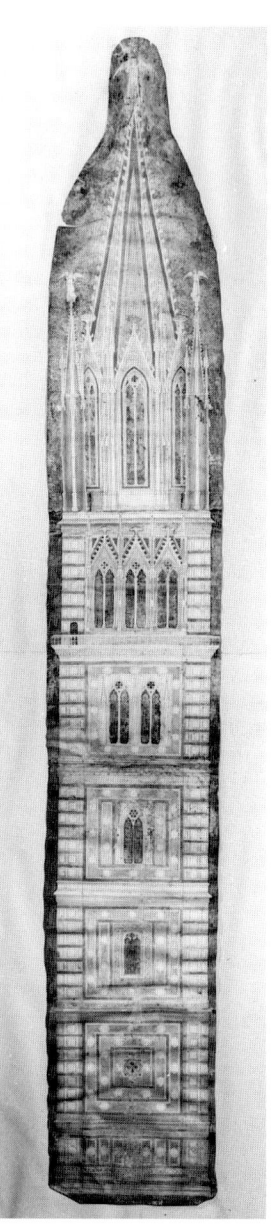
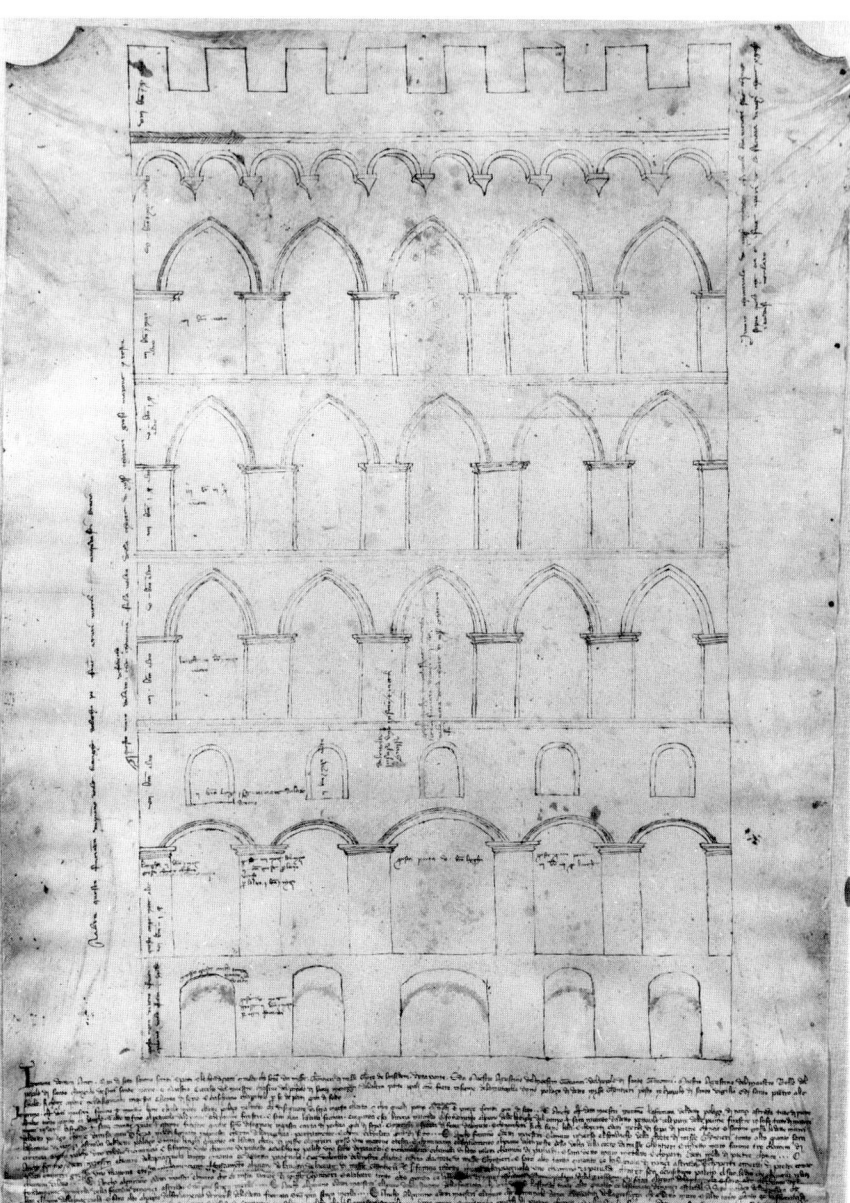

Fig. 76 Drawing for a new campanile. Siena, Museo dell'Opera del Duomo.

Fig. 77 Drawing for the facade of the Palazzo Sansedoni, Siena. Monte dei Paschi, Siena.

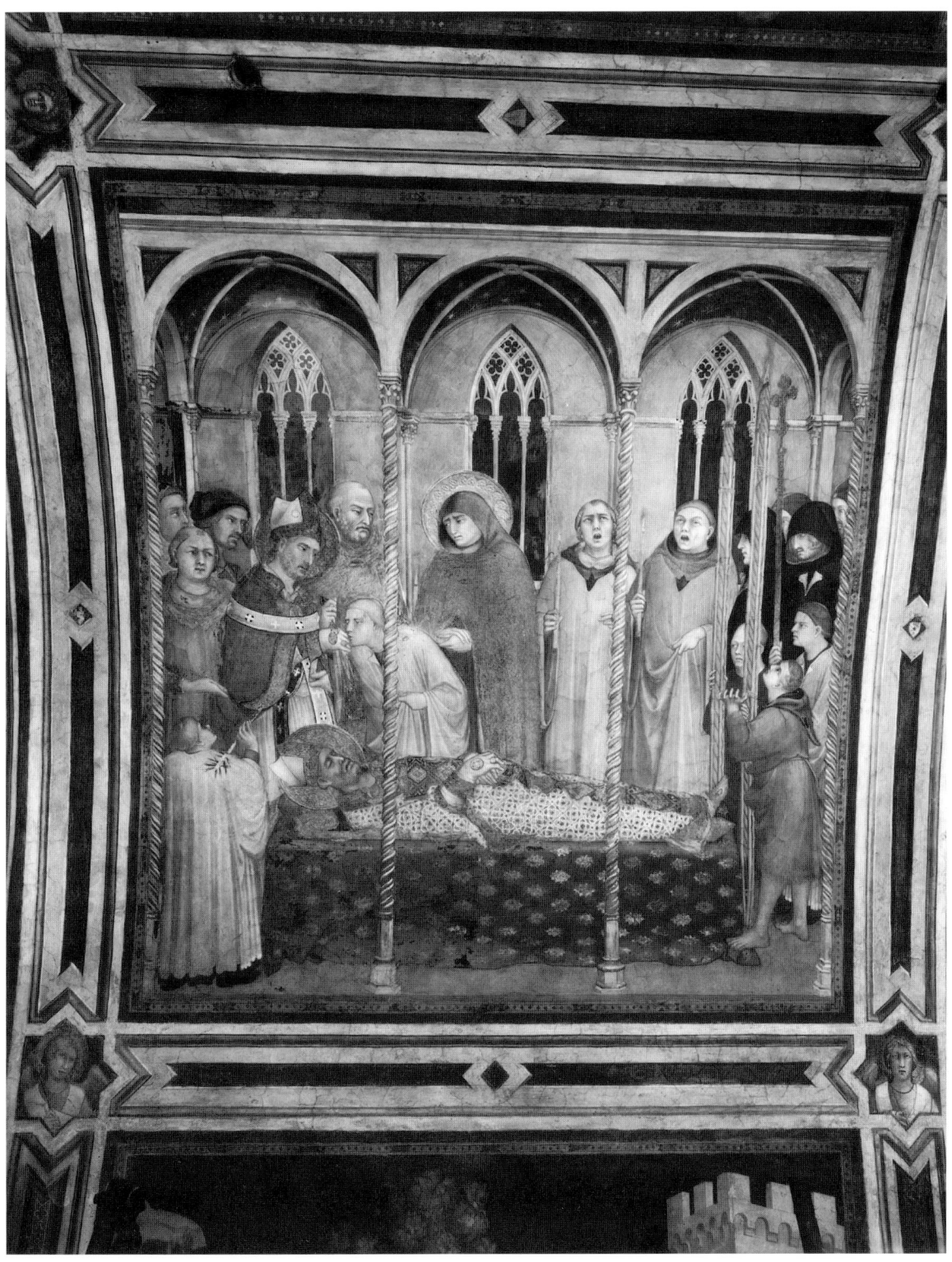

Fig. 78 Simone Martini, *Obsequies for Saint Martin*. Assisi, San Francesco, Lower Church.

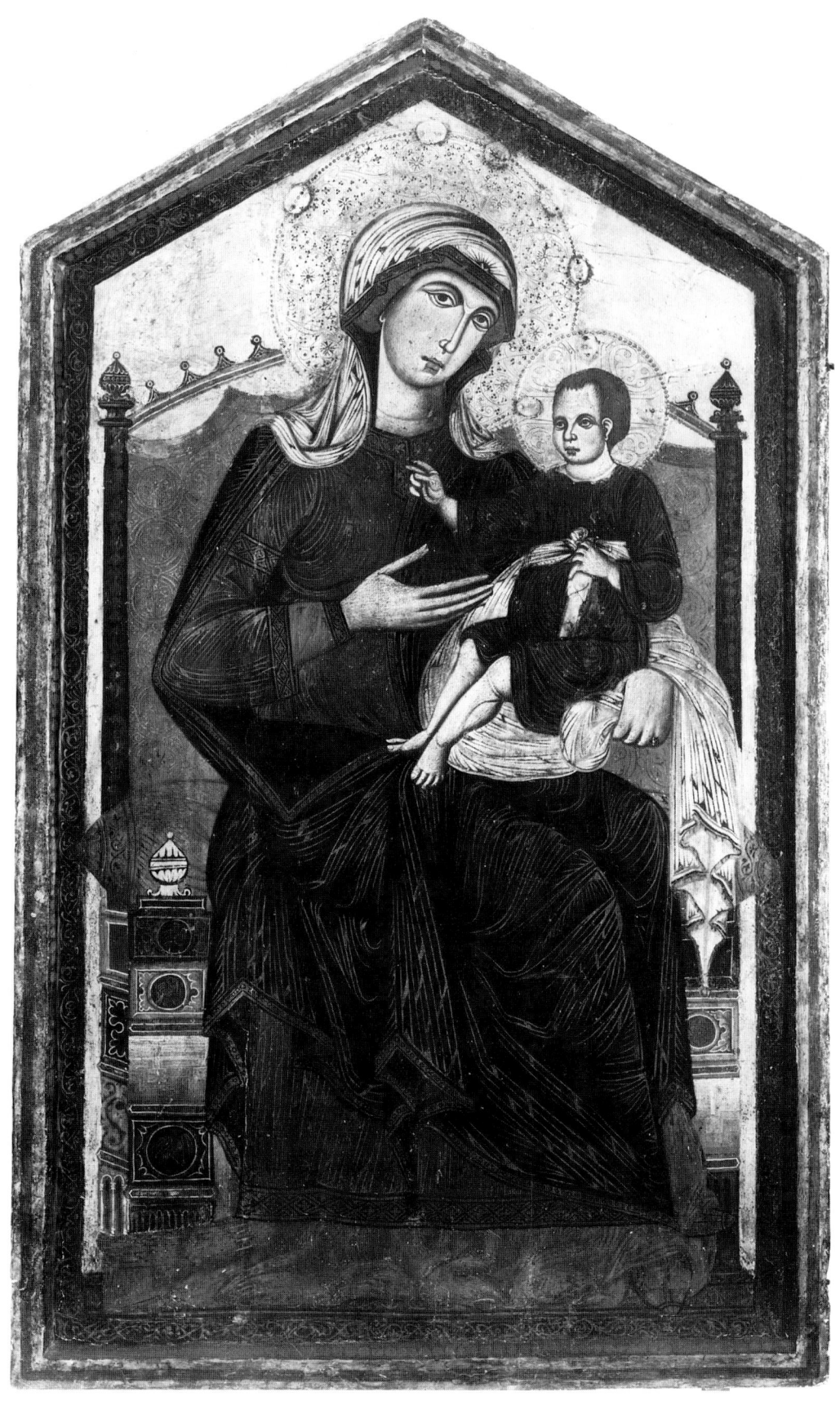

Fig. 79 Circle of the San Bernardino Master, *Madonna and Child Enthroned*. Florence, Accademia.

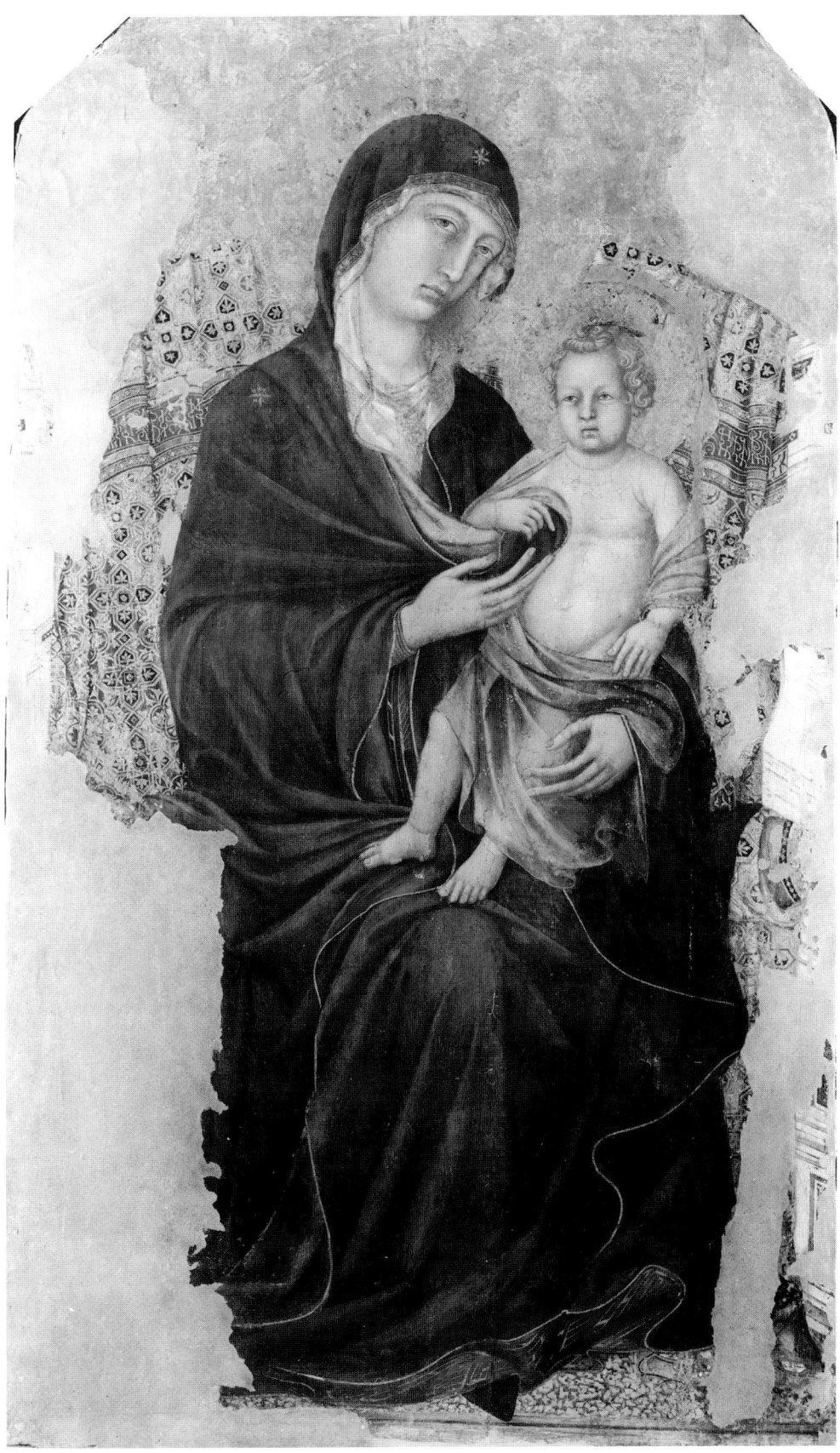

Fig. 80 Orbit of Duccio, *Maestà*. Massa Marittima, cathedral.

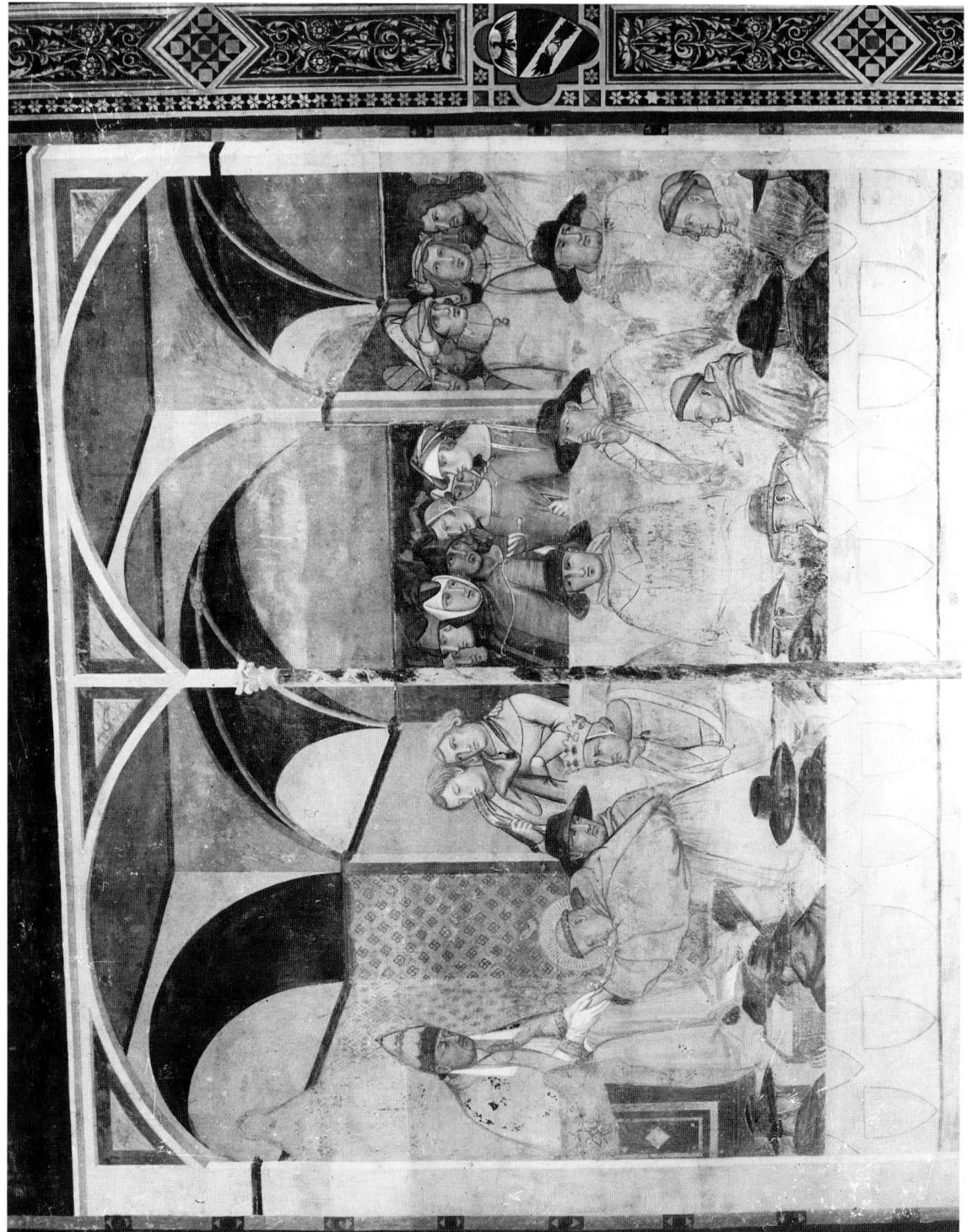

Fig. 81 Ambrogio Lorenzetti, *Ordination of Saint Louis of Toulouse*. Siena, San Francesco.

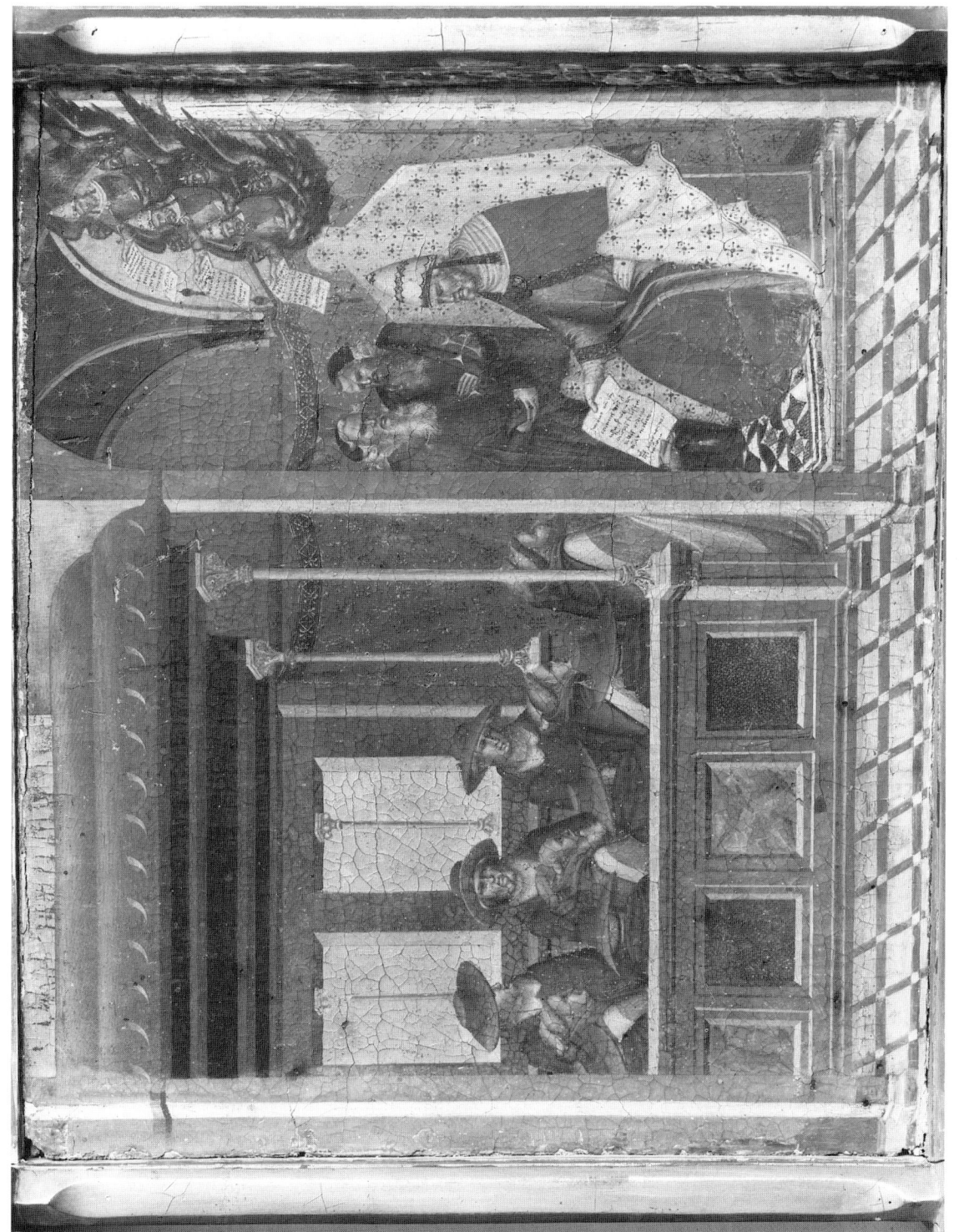

Fig. 82 Pietro Lorenzetti, predella scene from the Carmelite altarpiece. Siena, Pinacoteca Nazionale.

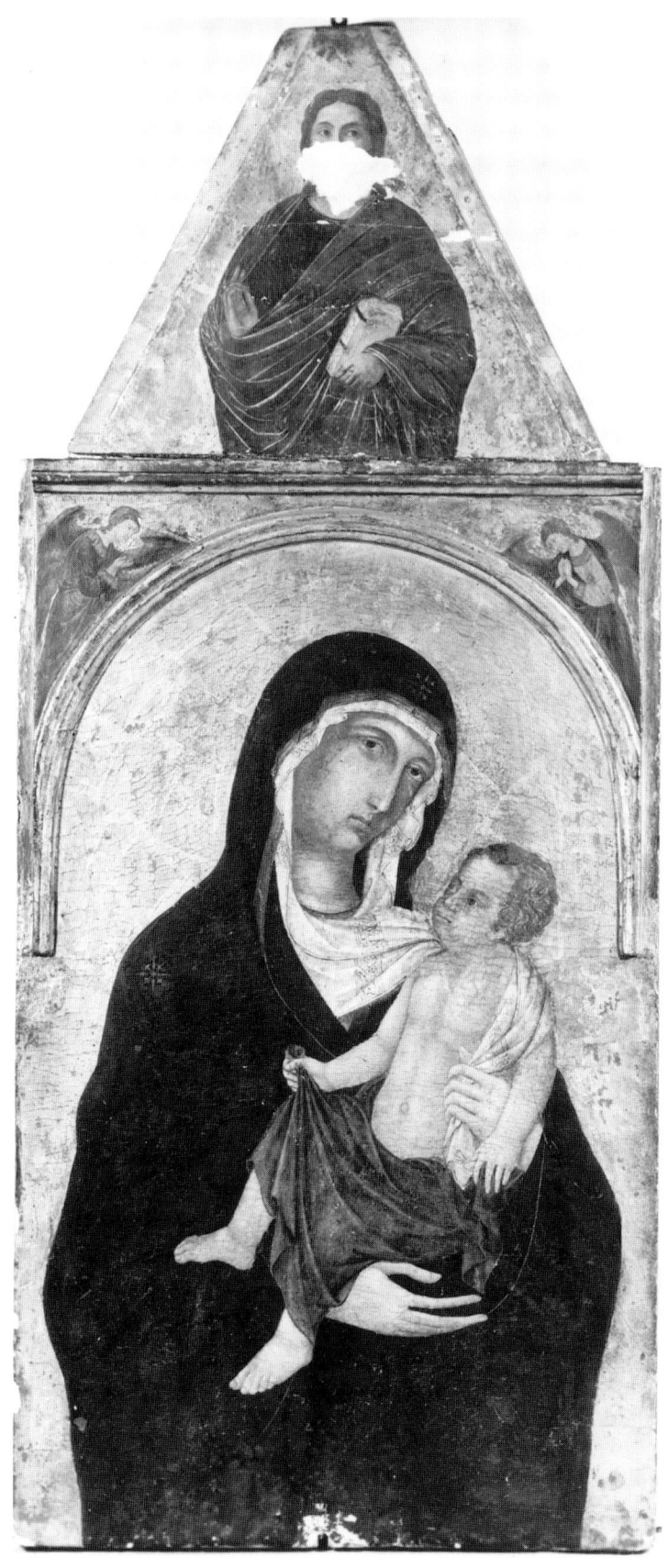

Fig. 83 Shop of Ugolino di Nerio, polyptych, detail: Madonna. Williamstown, Mass., Sterling and Francine Clark Art Institute.

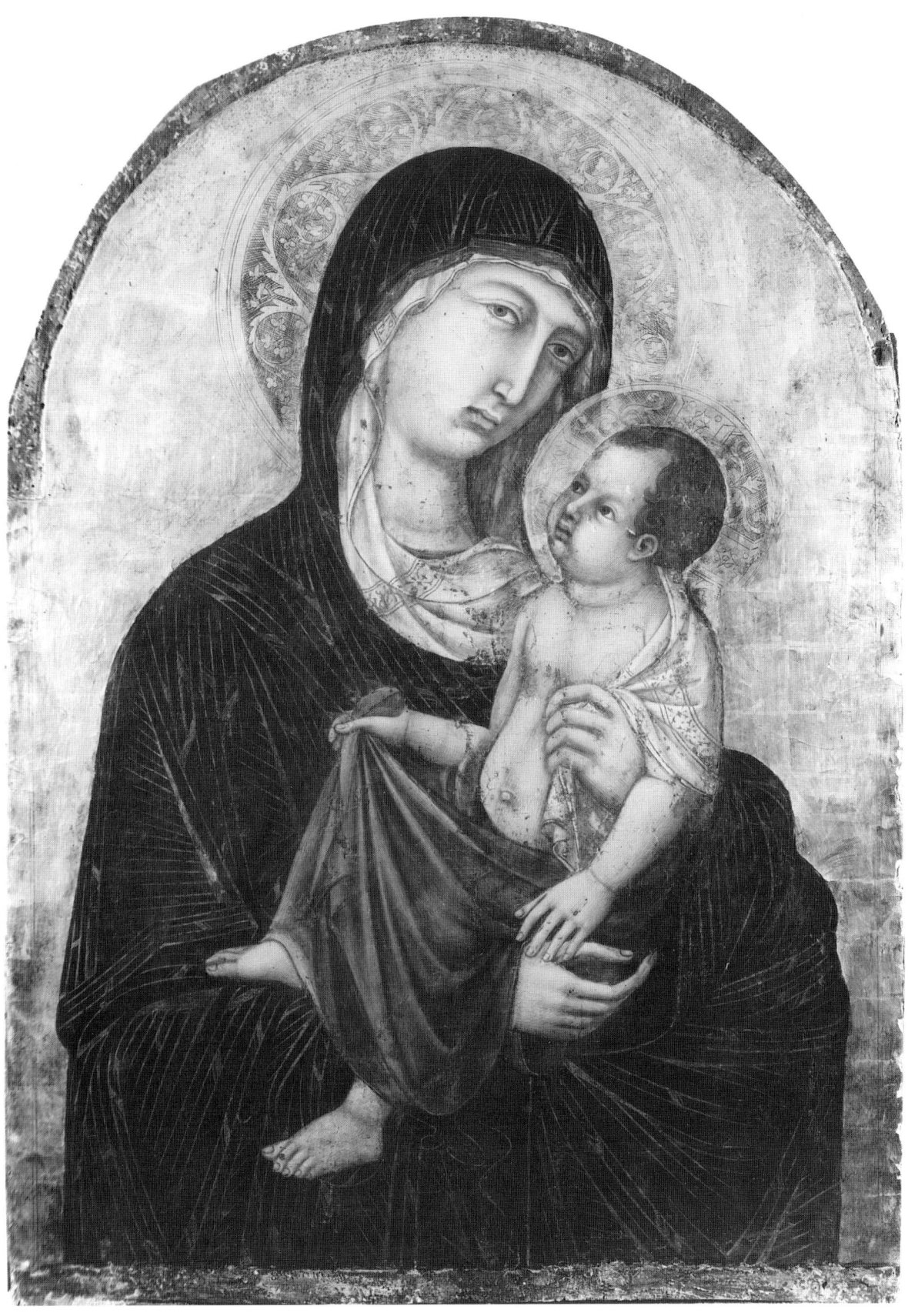

Fig. 84 Follower of Duccio, *Madonna and Child*. Montecchio, Chiesa della Compagnia della Madonna della Grotta.

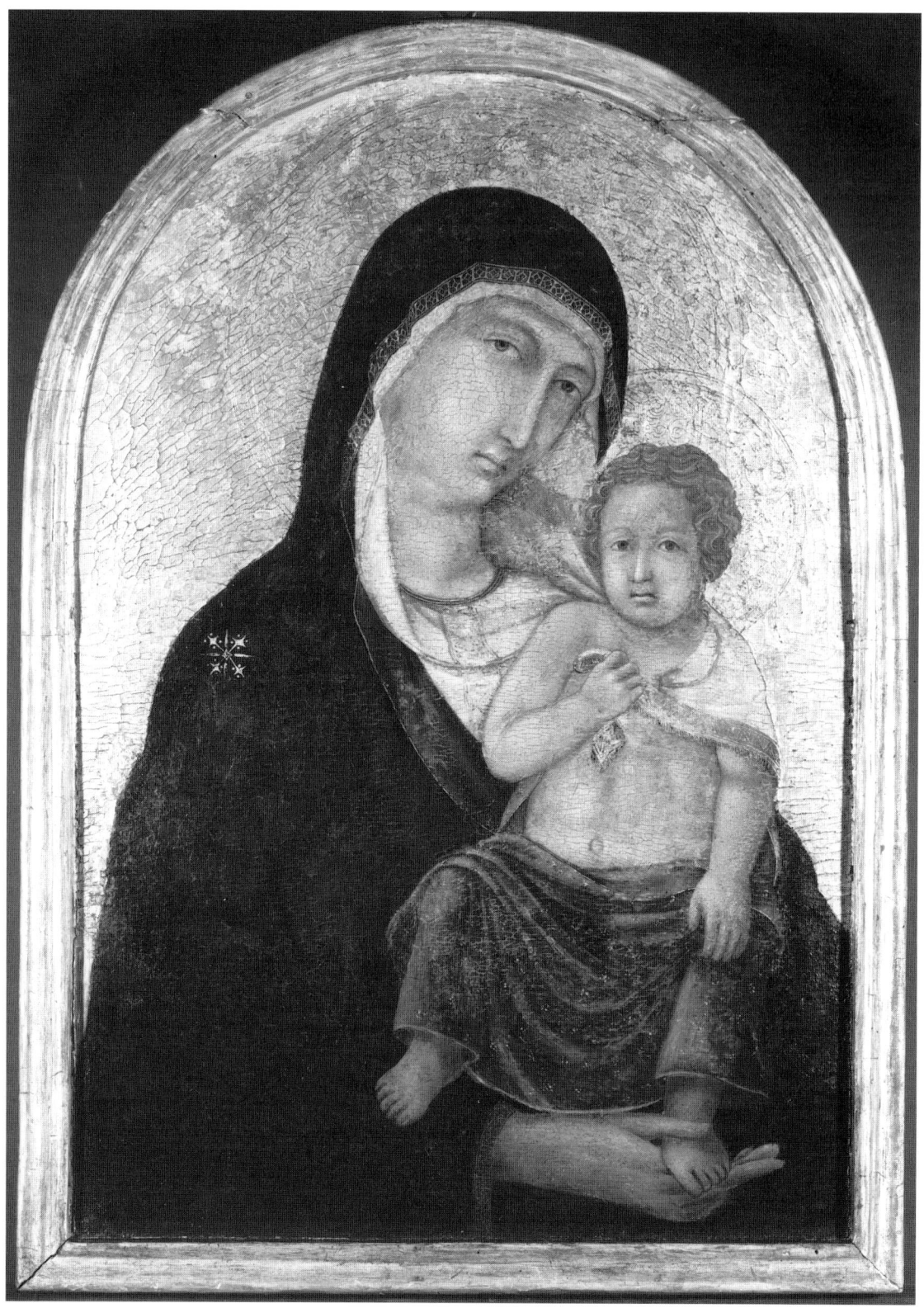

Fig. 85 Shop of Ugolino di Nerio, *Madonna and Child*. Princeton, Art Museum.

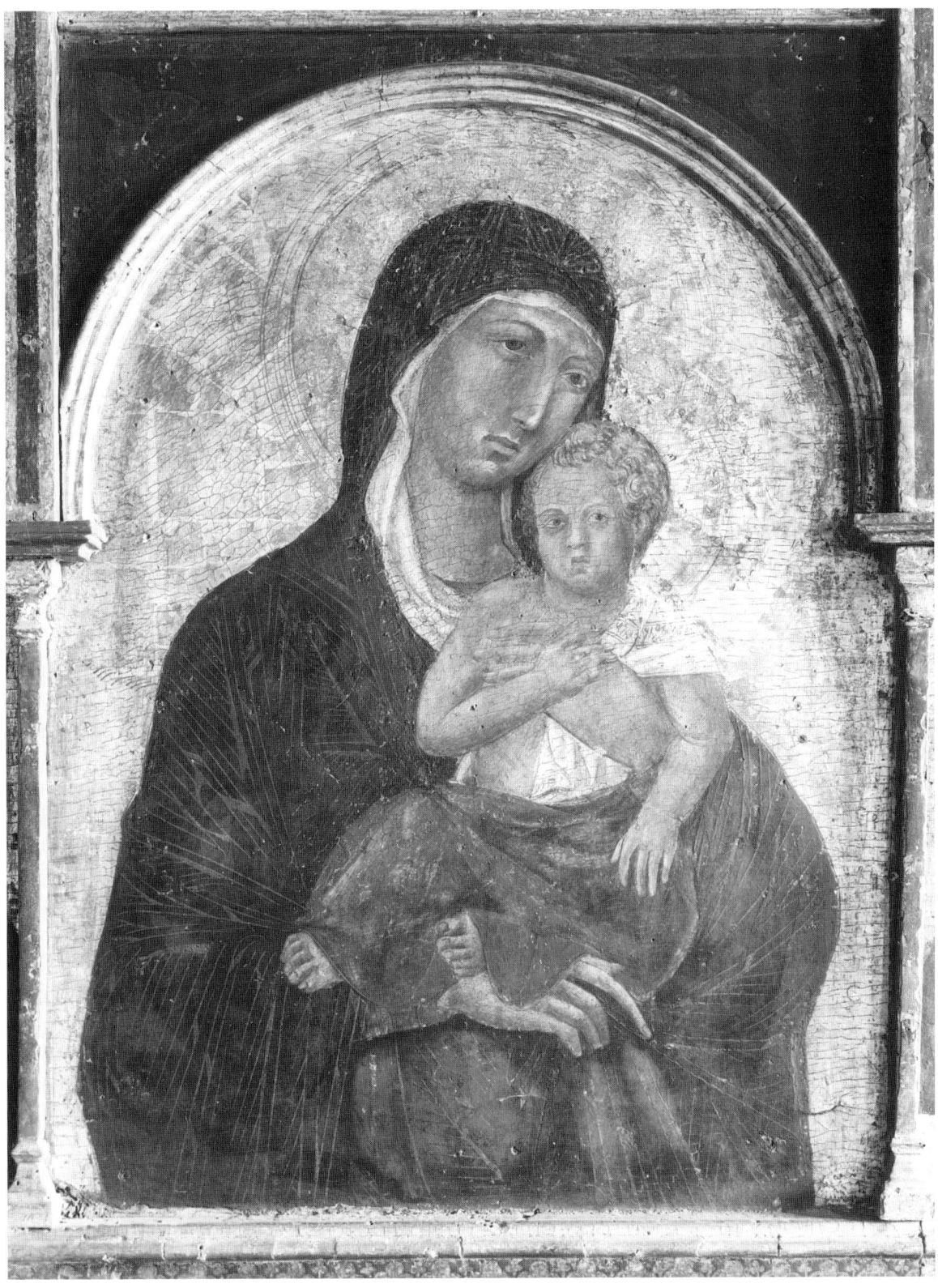

Fig. 86 Duccio di Buoninsegna, Polyptych no. 47, detail: Madonna. Siena, Pinacoteca Nazionale.

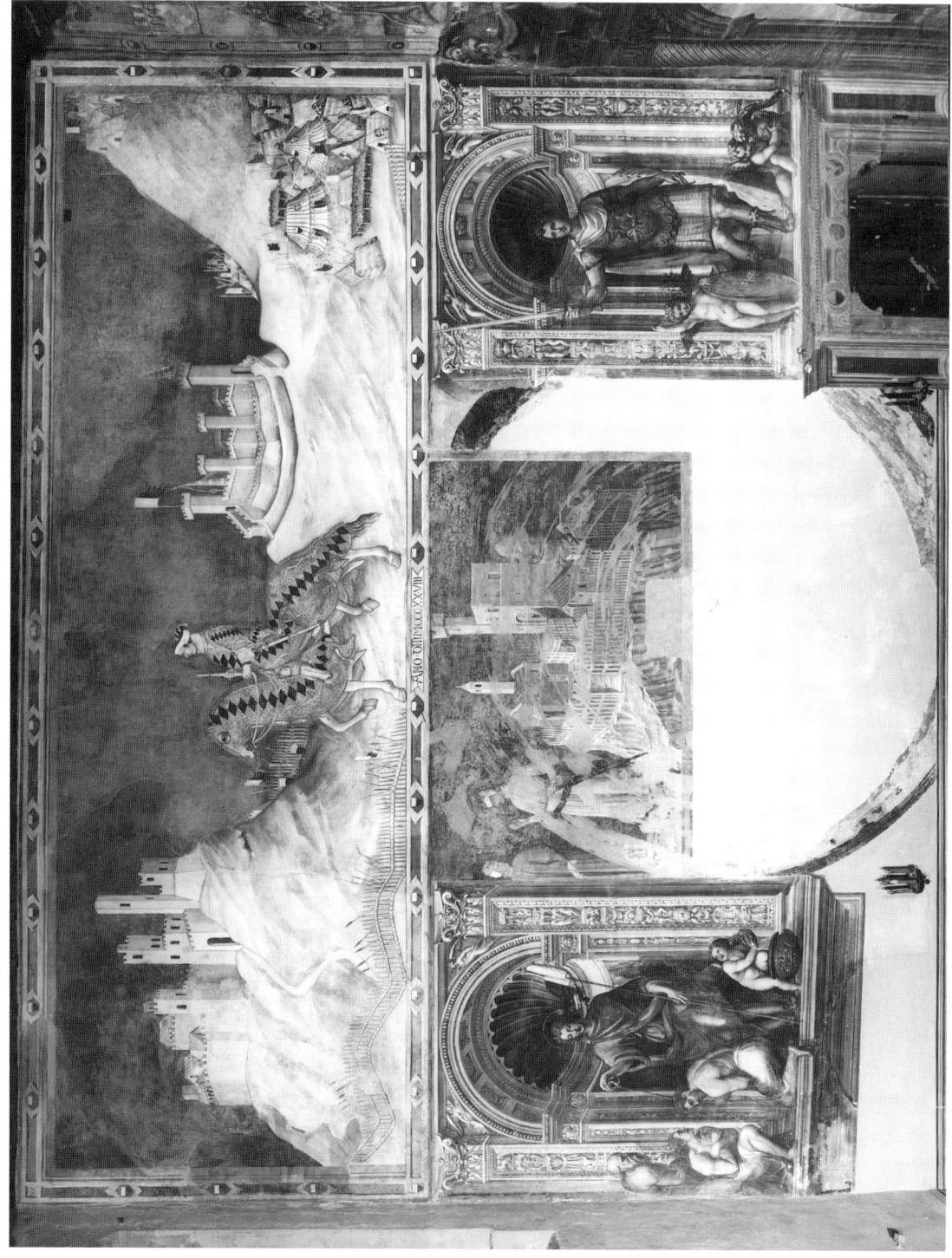

Fig. 87 Northeast wall. Sala del Mappamondo, Palazzo Pubblico, Siena.

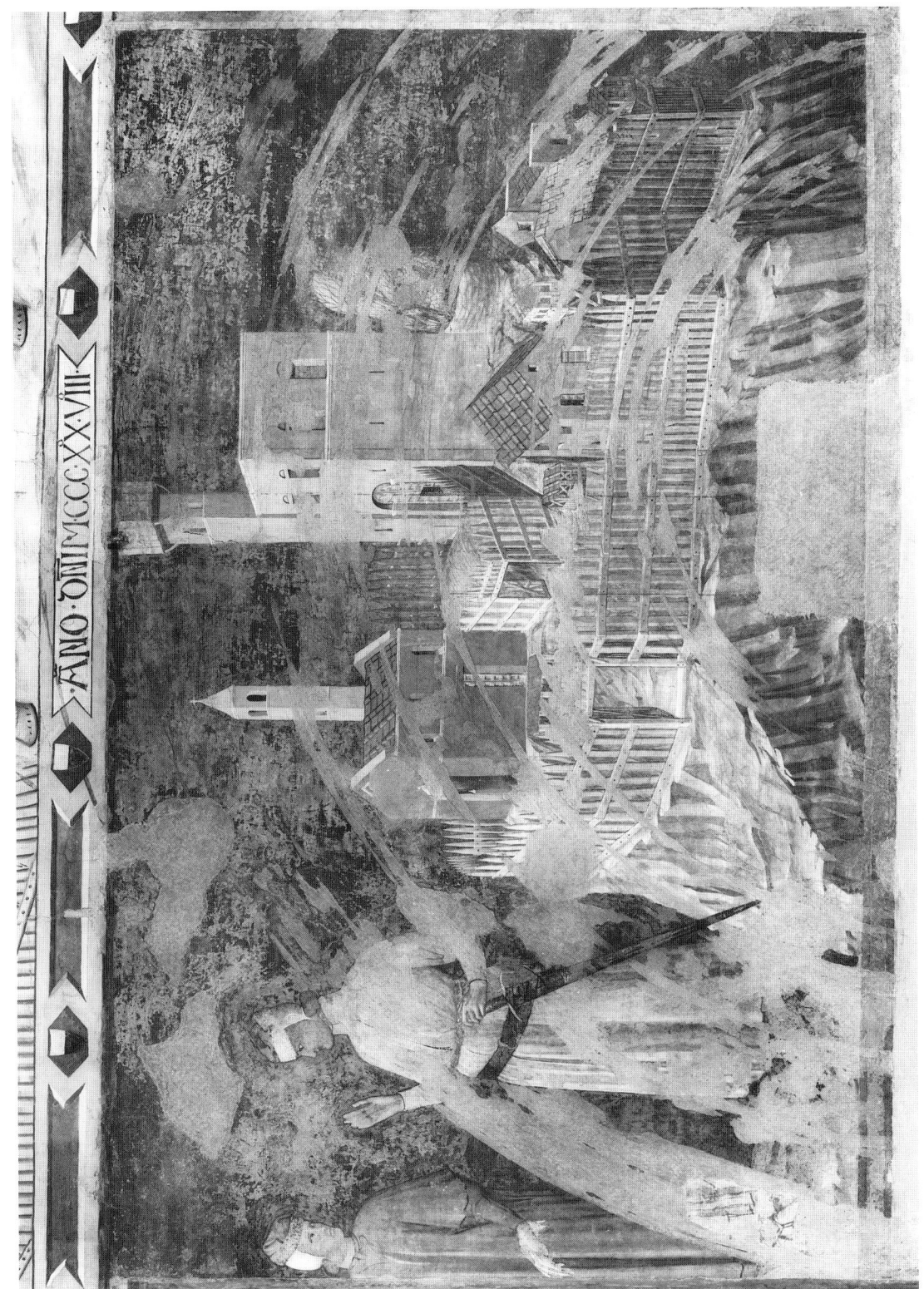

Fig. 88 *A Subject Town*. Sala del Mappamondo, Palazzo Pubblico, Siena.

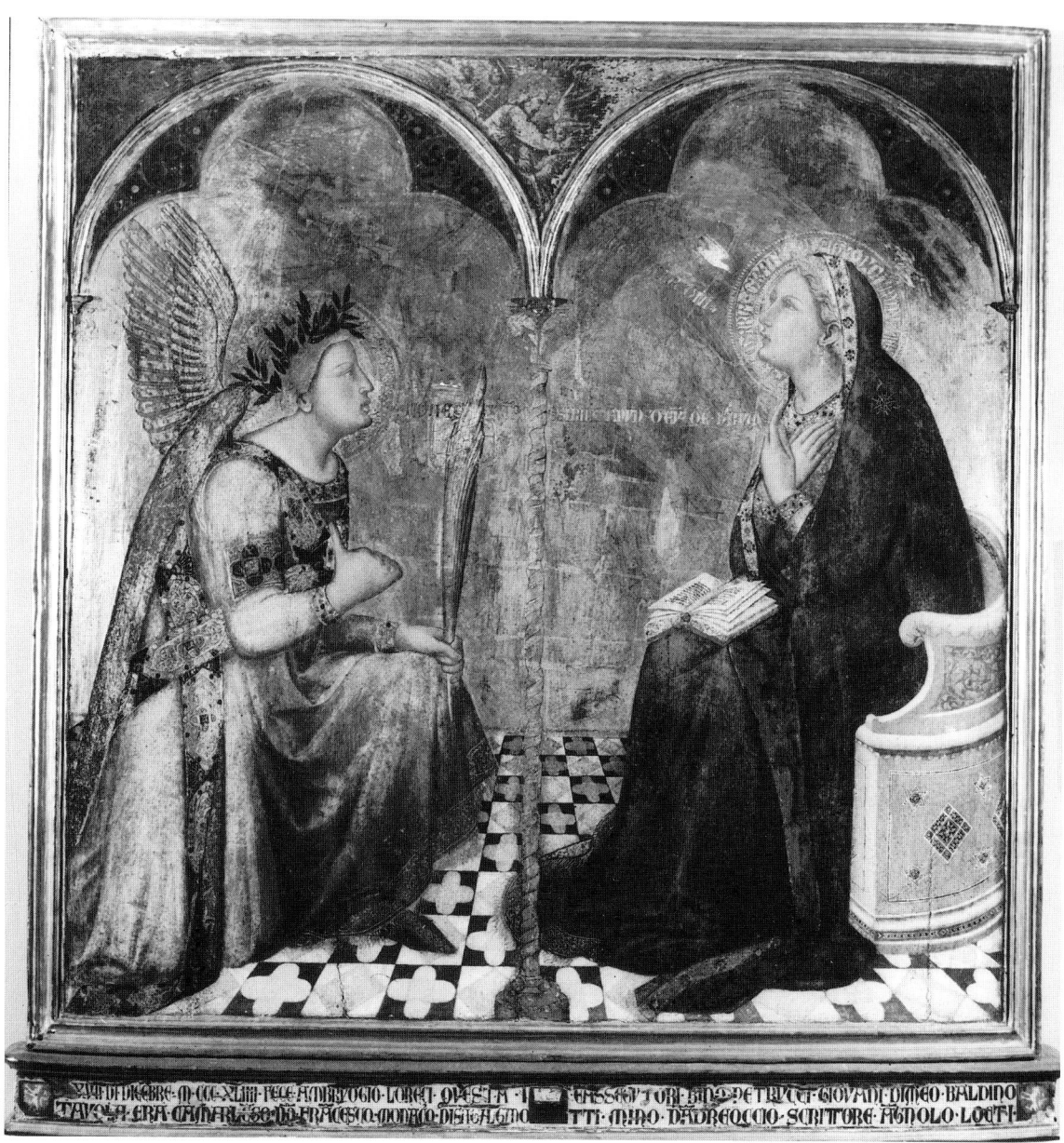

Fig. 89 Ambrogio Lorenzetti, *Annunciation* (1344). Siena, Pinacoteca Nazionale.

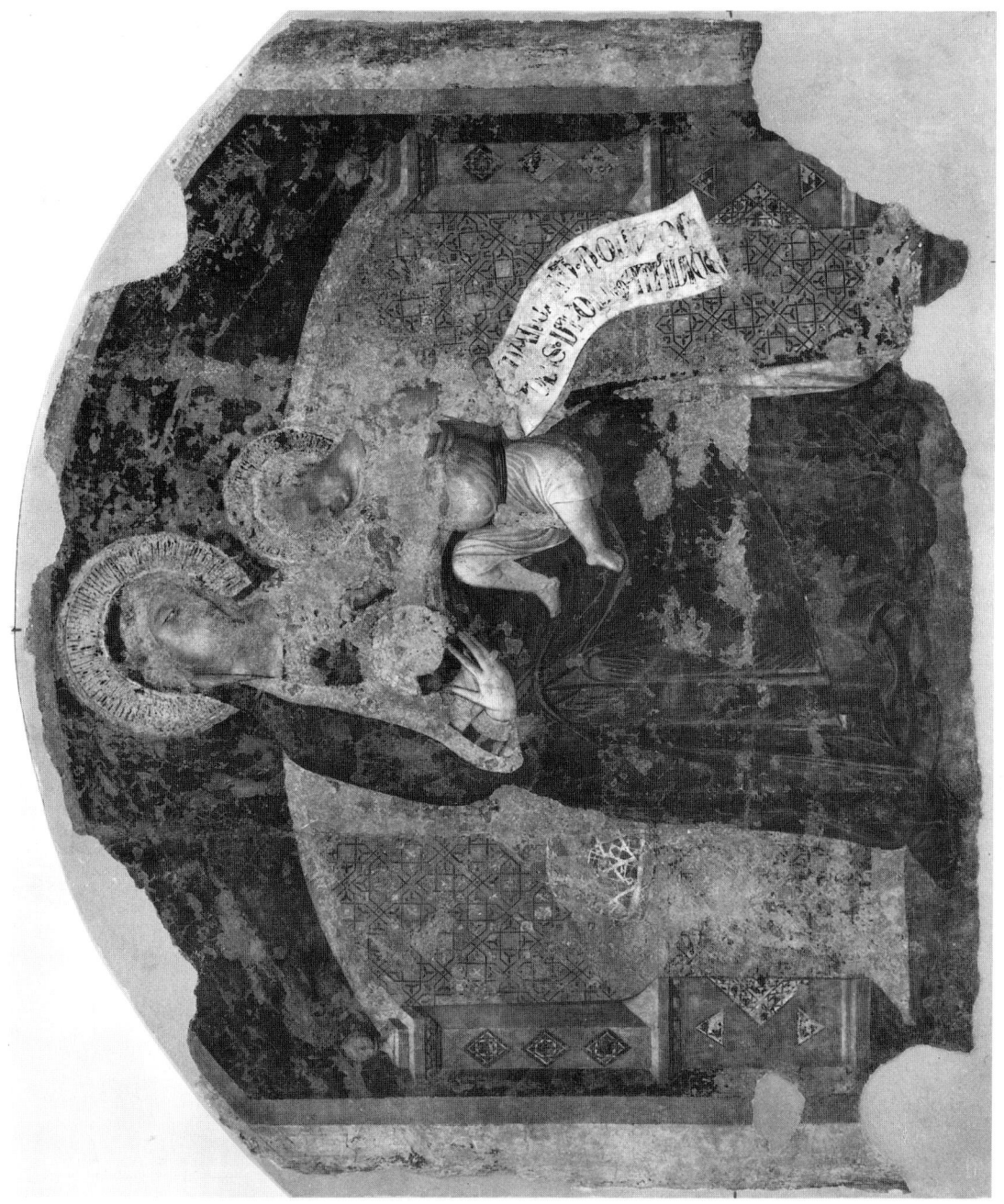

Fig. 90 Ambrogio Lorenzetti, *Madonna and Child Enthroned*. Siena, Palazzo Pubblico.

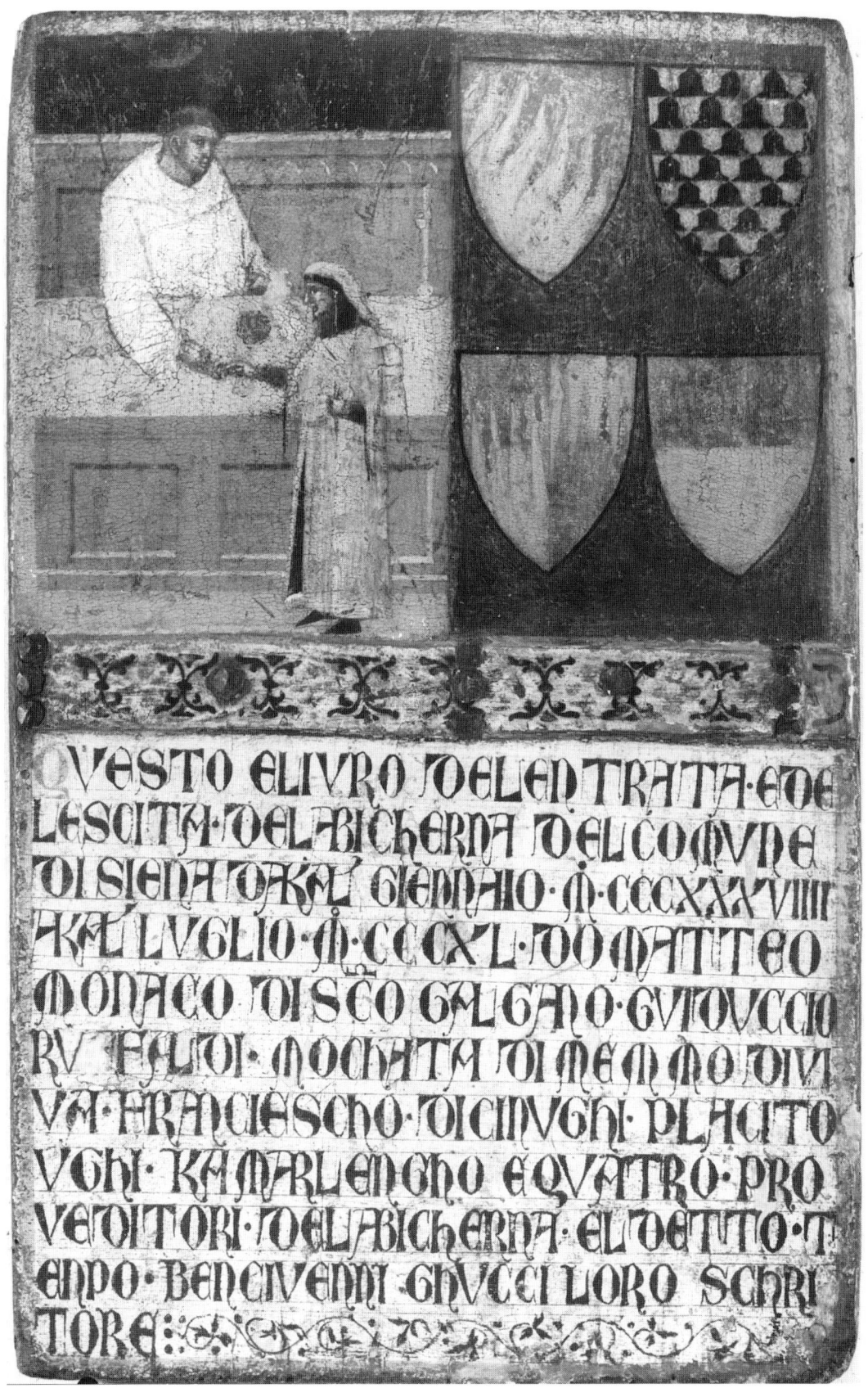

Fig. 91 Biccherna cover for the January–June 1340. Archivio di Stato di Siena, Siena.

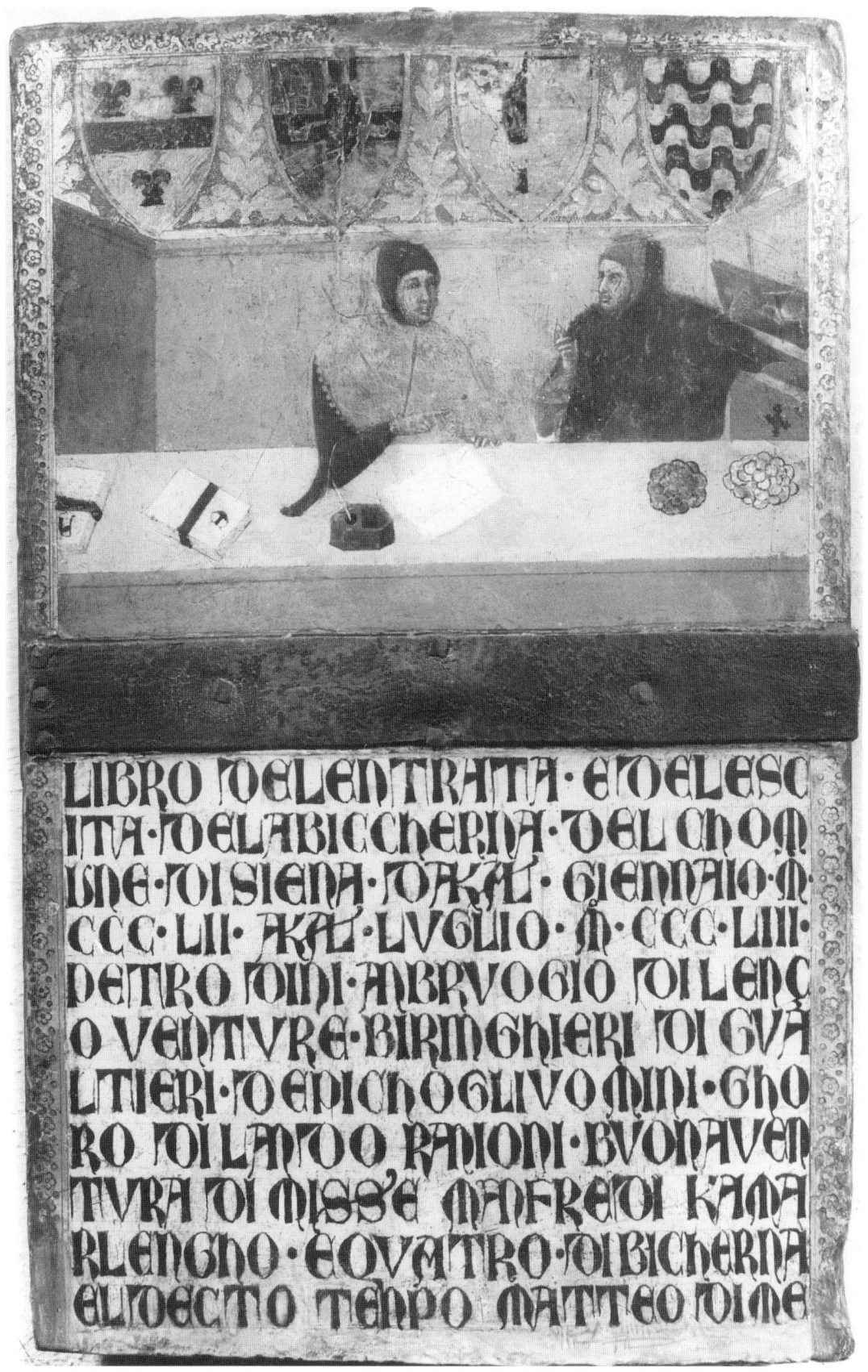

Fig. 92 Biccherna cover for January–June 1353. Archivio di Stato di Siena, Siena.

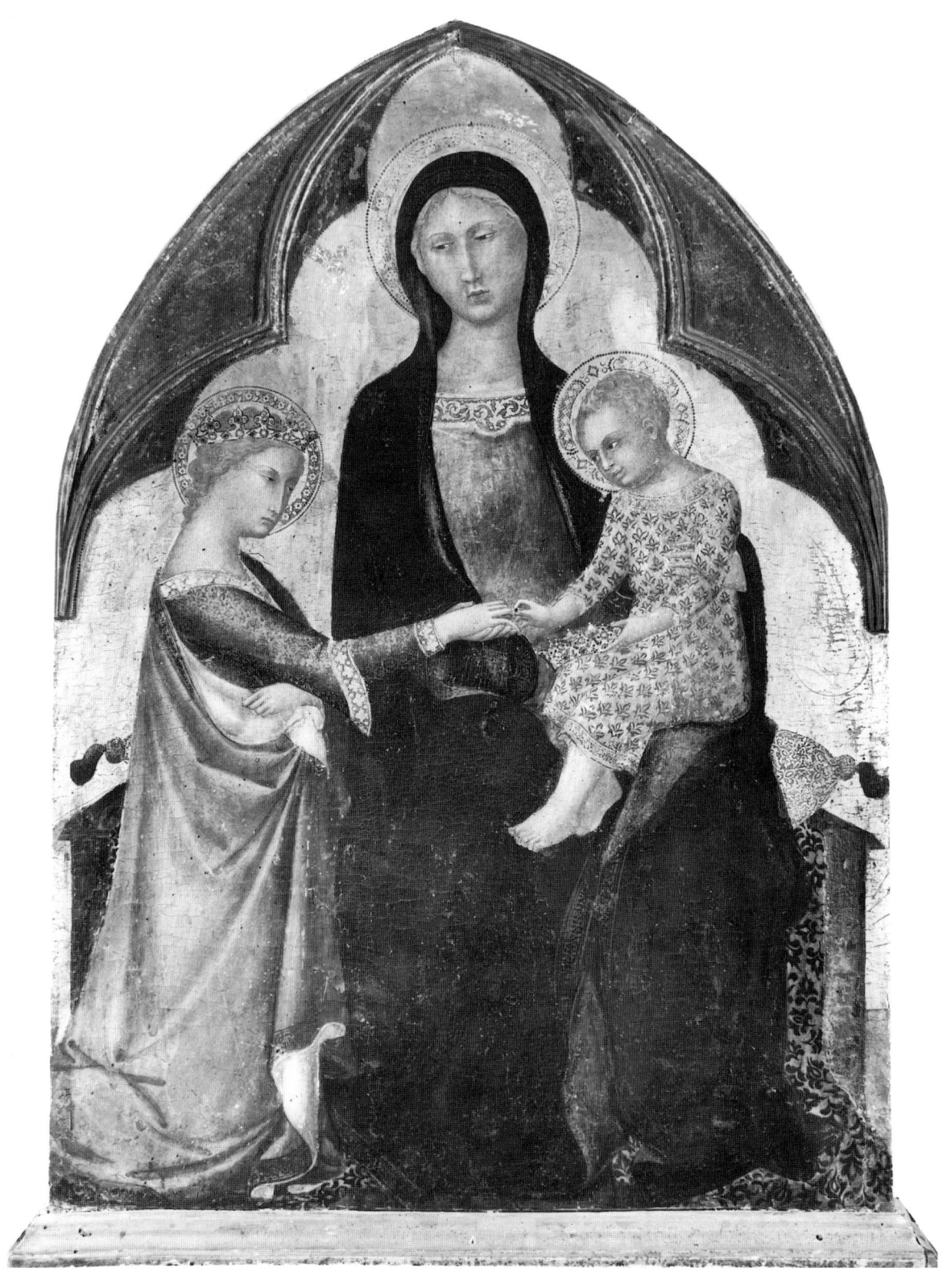

Fig. 93 Master of Palazzo Venezia, *Mystic Marriage of Saint Catherine*. Siena, Pinacoteca Nazionale.

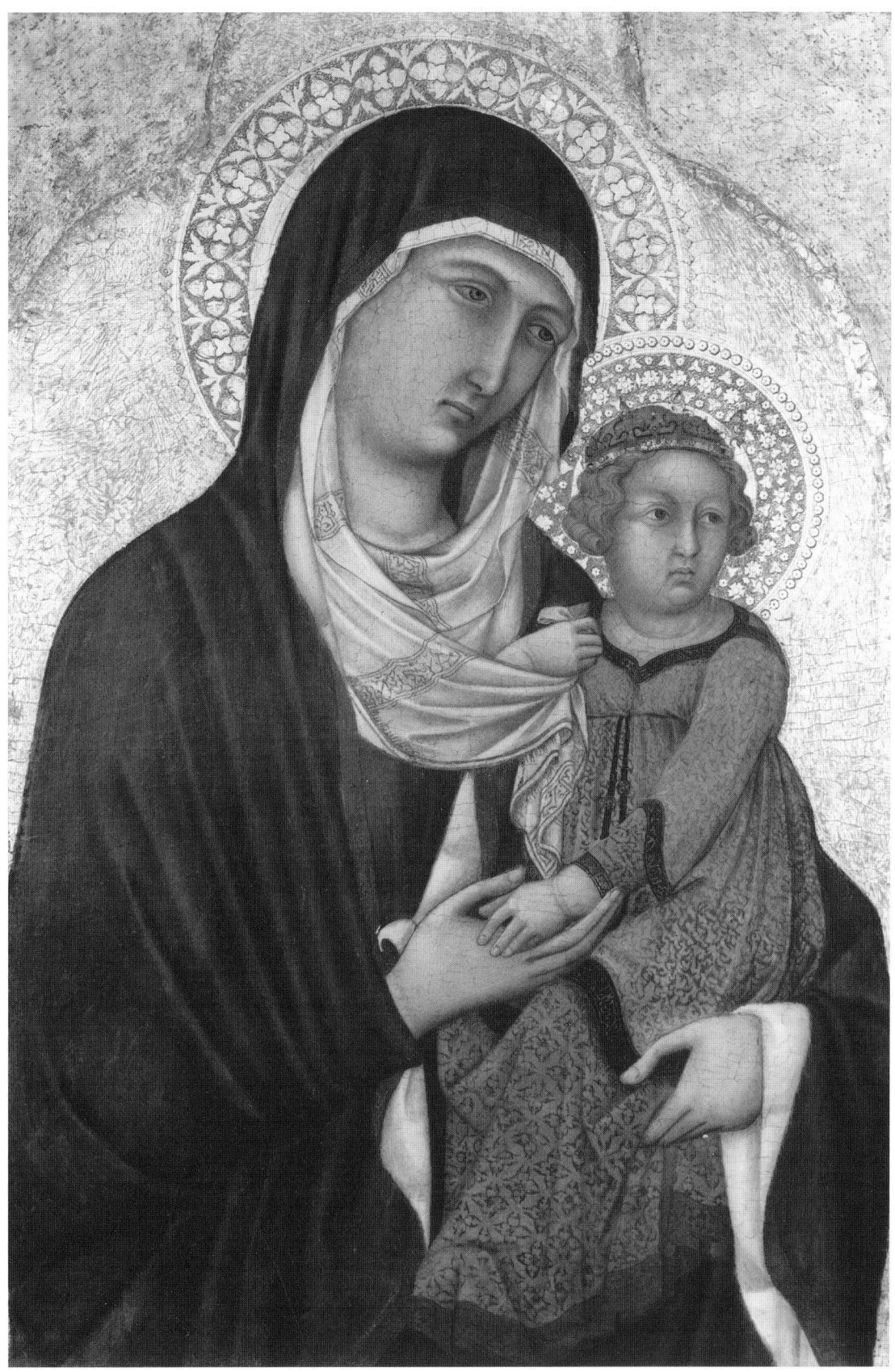

Fig. 94 Ugolino di Nerio, *Saint Anne and the Virgin*. Ottawa, National Gallery of Canada.

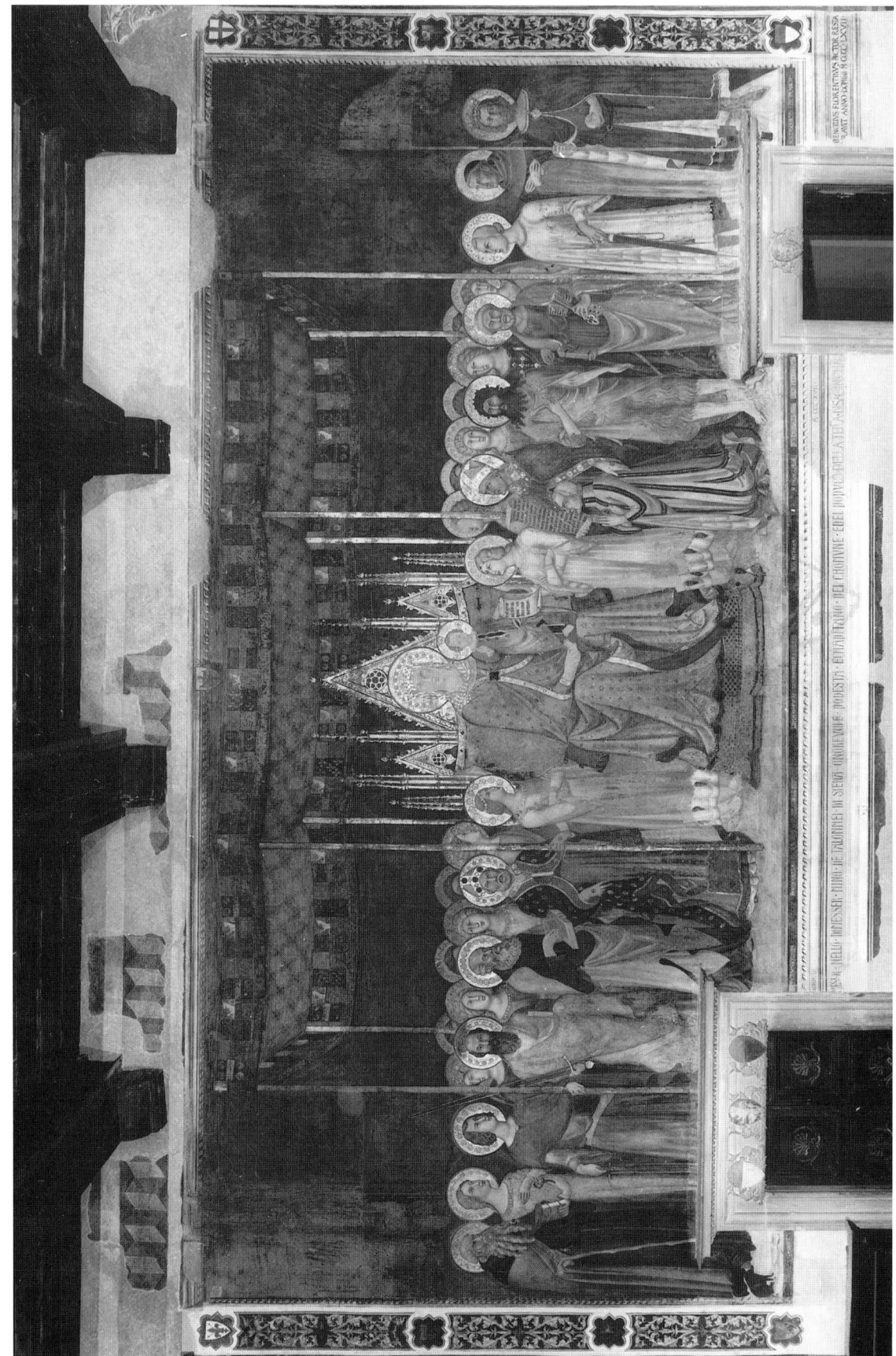

Fig. 95 Lippo Memmi, *Maestà*. San Gimignano, Palazzo Comunale.

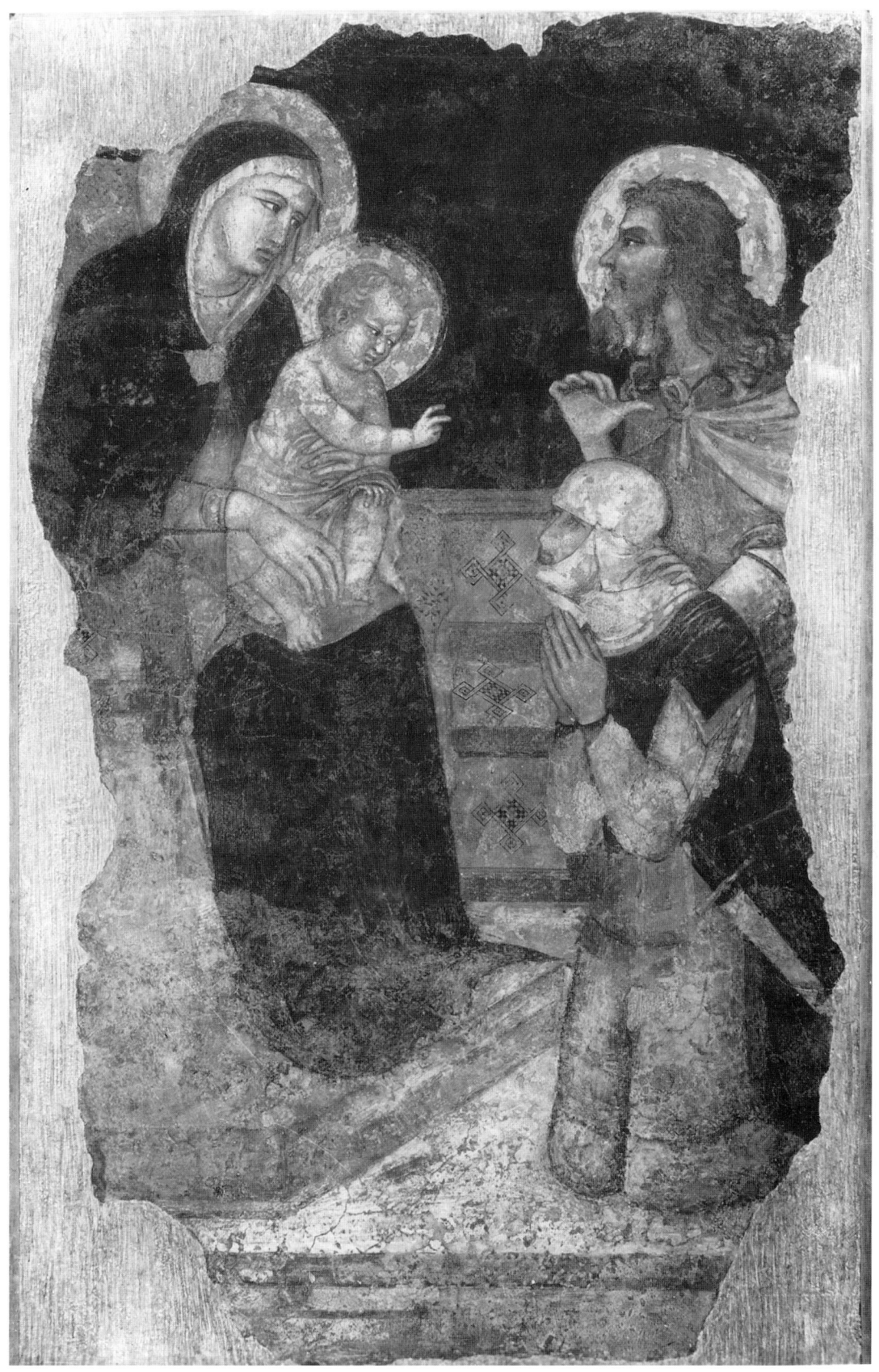

Fig. 96 Master of the Loeser Madonna, *Virgin and Child with Saint John the Baptist and Donor*. Siena, San Domenico.

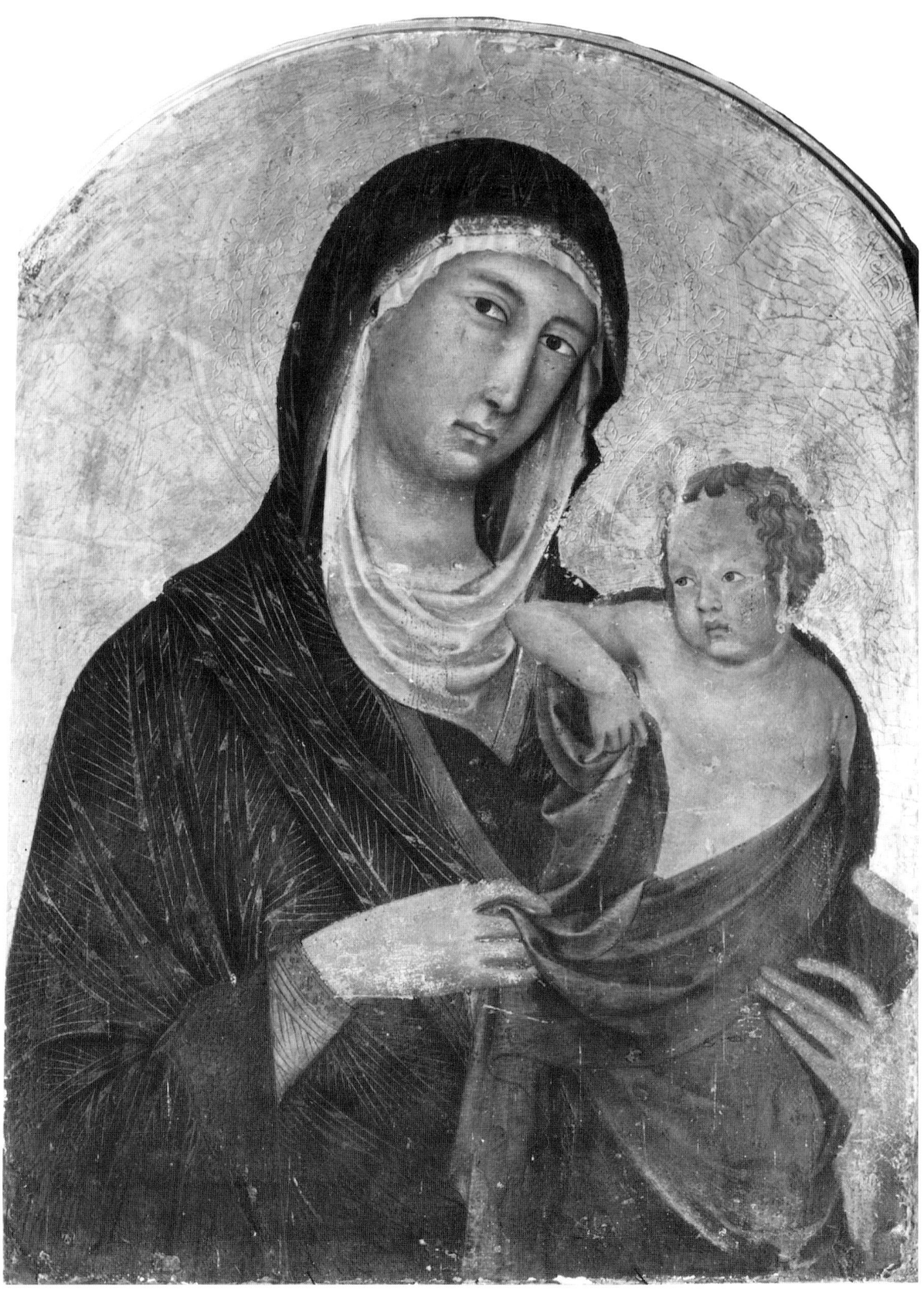

Fig. 97 Segna di Bonaventura, *Madonna and Child*. Siena, Santa Maria dei Servi.

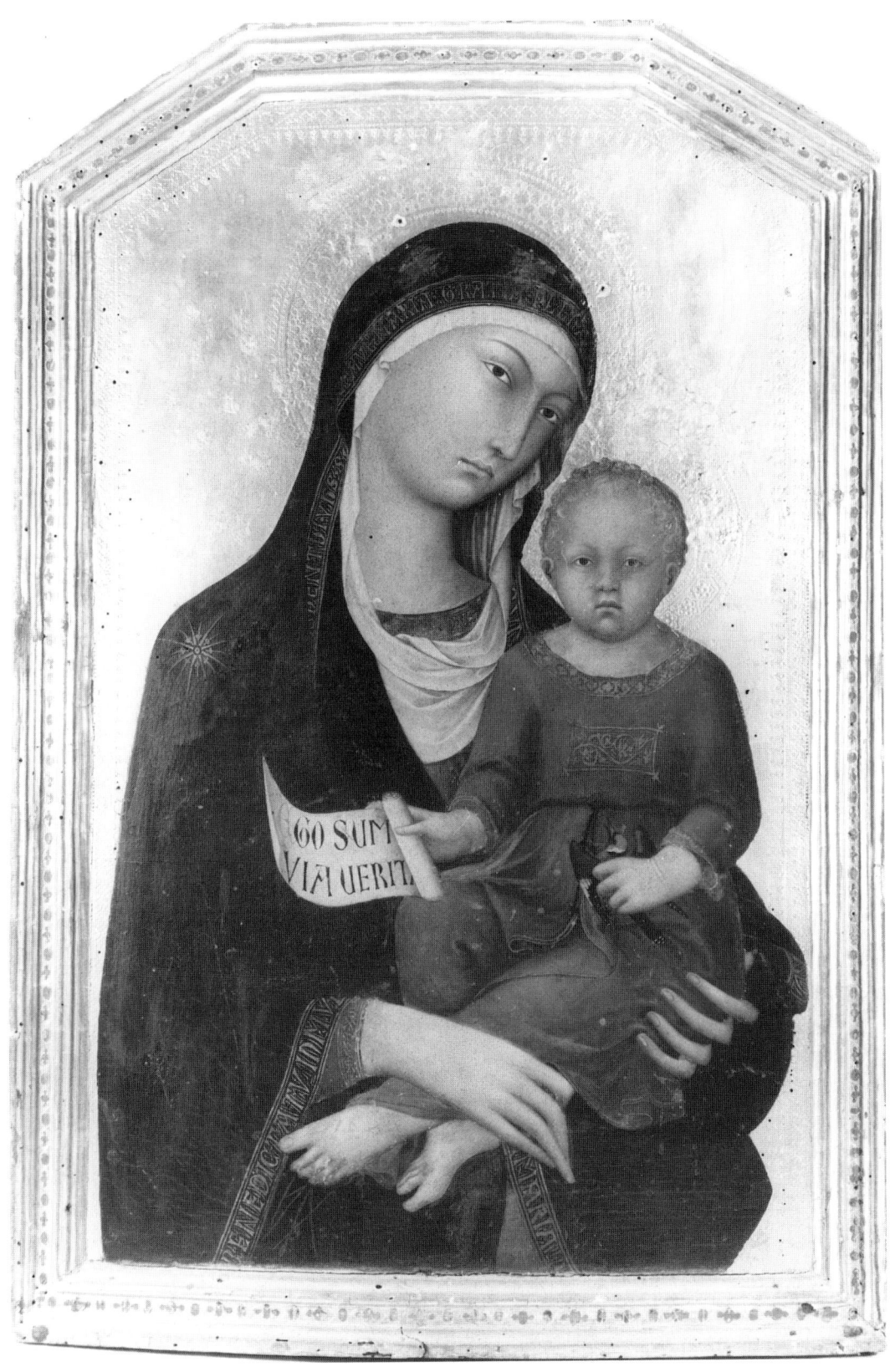

Fig. 98 Lippo Memmi, *Madonna and Child*. Siena, Santa Maria dei Servi.

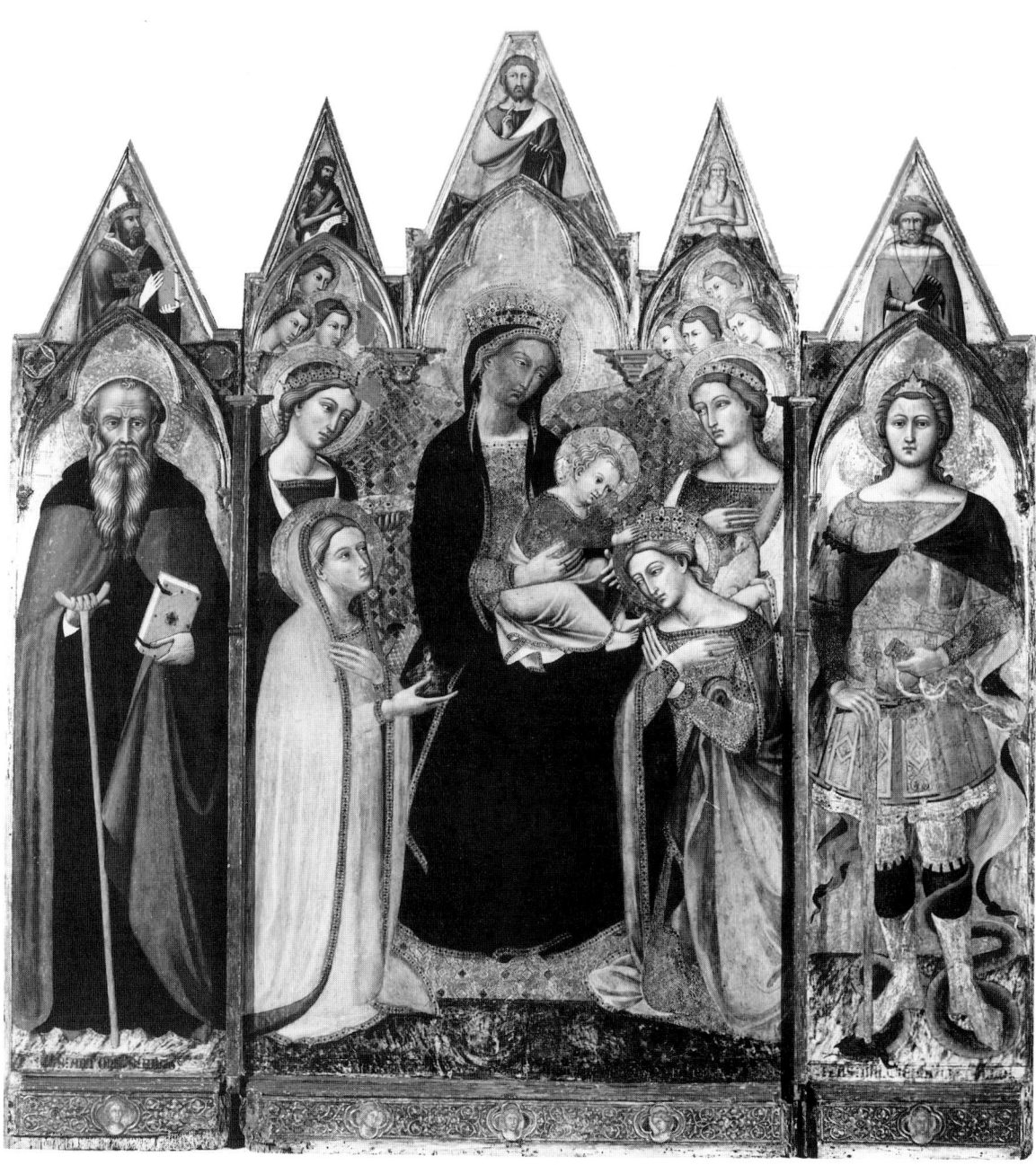

Fig. 99 Jacopo di Mino, *Coronation of Saint Catherine*. Siena, Pinacoteca Nazionale.

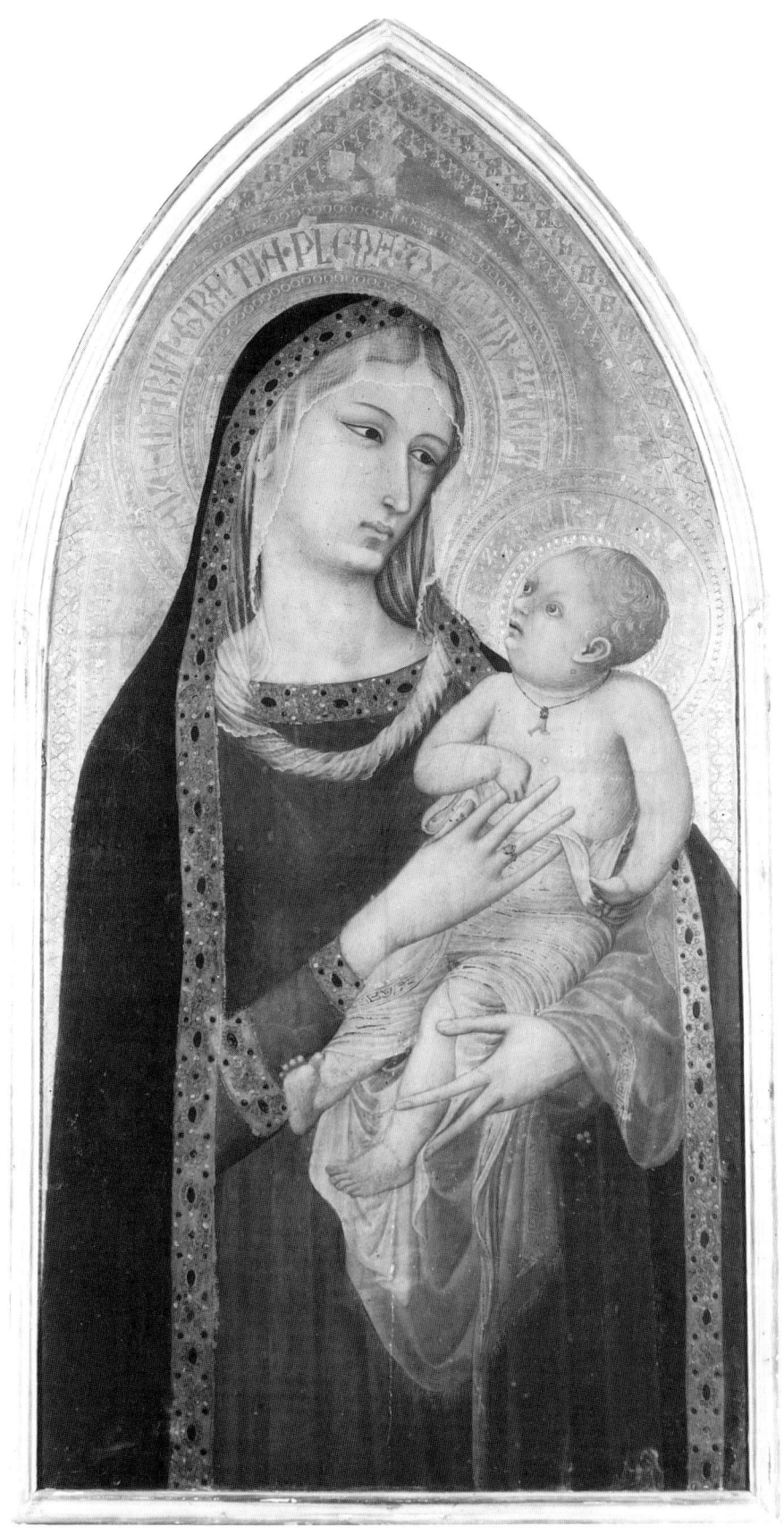

Fig. 104 Ambrogio Lorenzetti, *Madonna*. Florence, Galleria degli Uffizi.

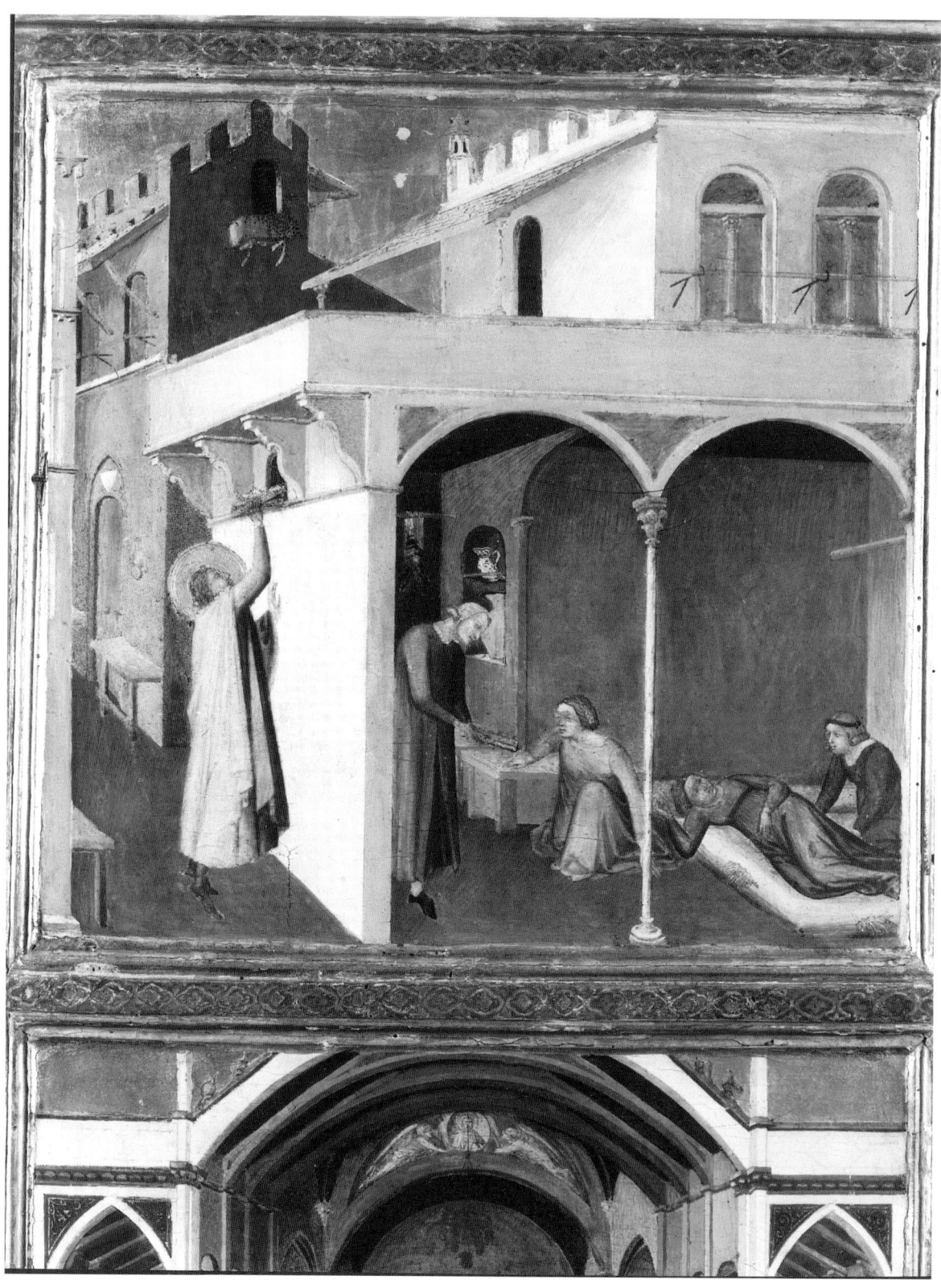

Fig. 105 Ambrogio Lorenzetti, *Stories of Saint Nicholas of Bari*, detail: Saint Nicholas gives gold to a destitute family. Florence, Galleria degli Uffizi.

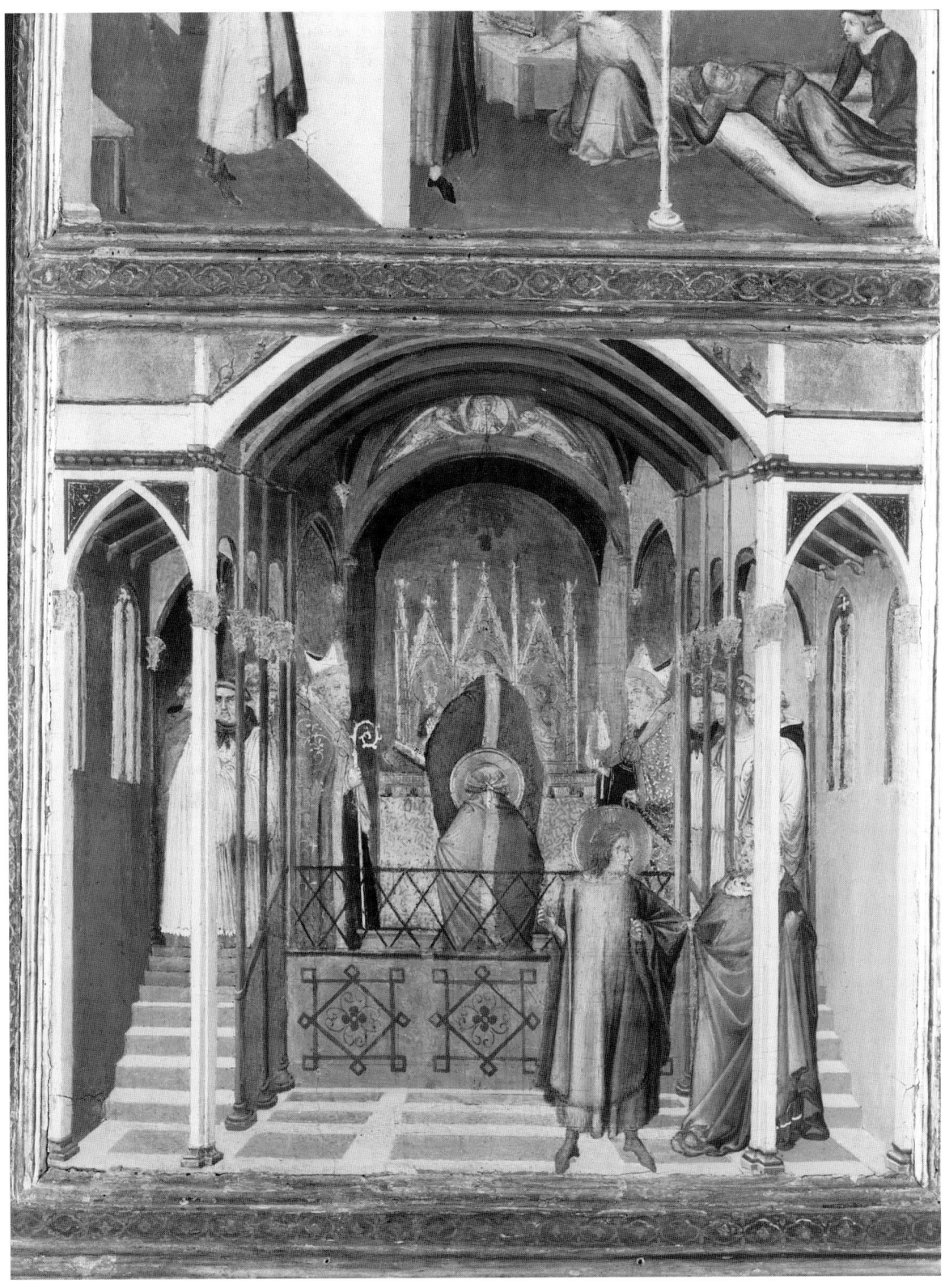

Fig. 106 Ambrogio Lorenzetti, *Stories of Saint Nicholas of Bari,* detail: consecration of Saint Nicholas. Florence, Galleria degli Uffizi.

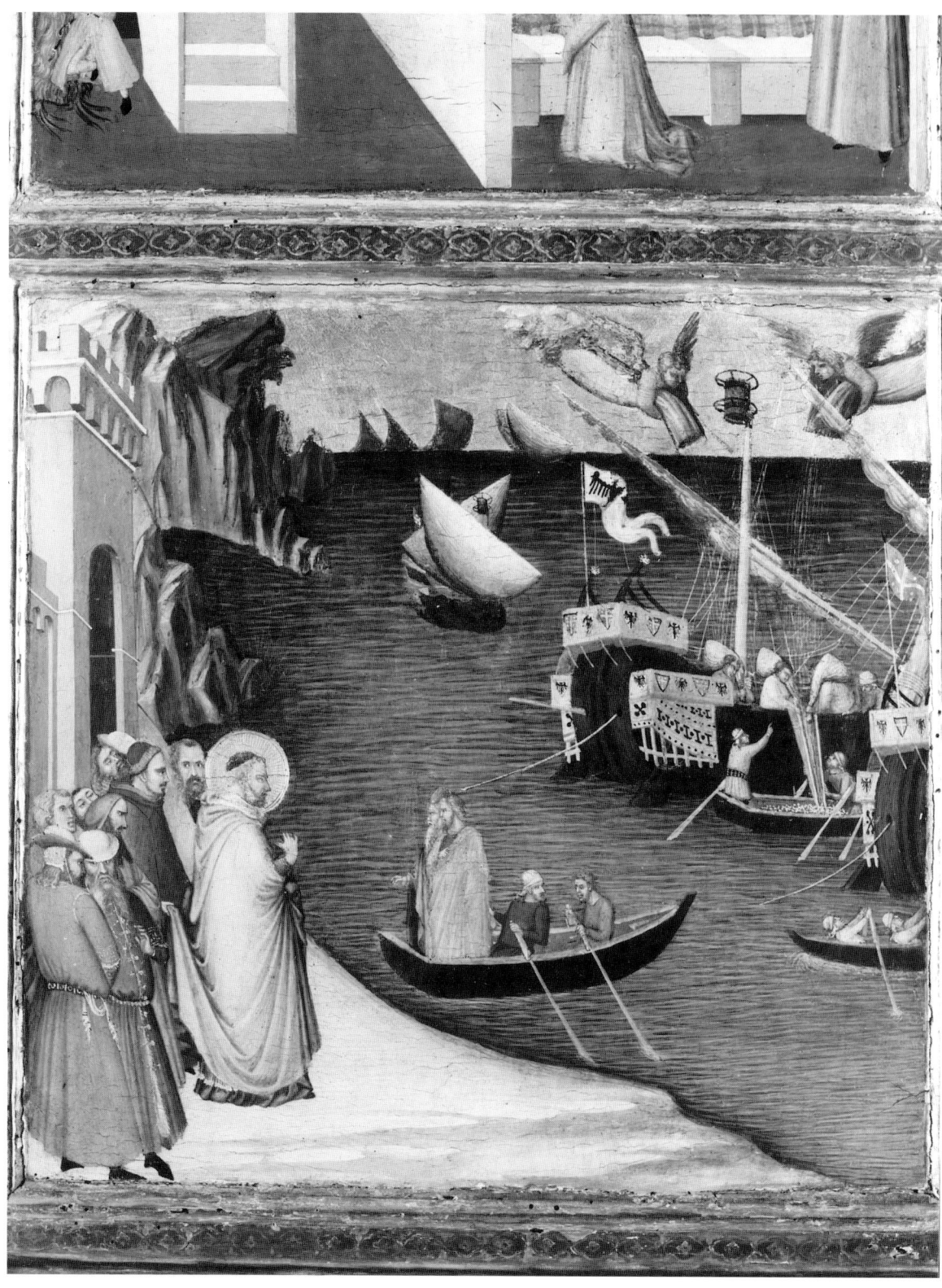

Fig. 107 Ambrogio Lorenzetti, *Stories of Saint Nicholas of Bari*, detail: Saint Nicholas and the miraculous provision of grain. Florence, Galleria degli Uffizi.

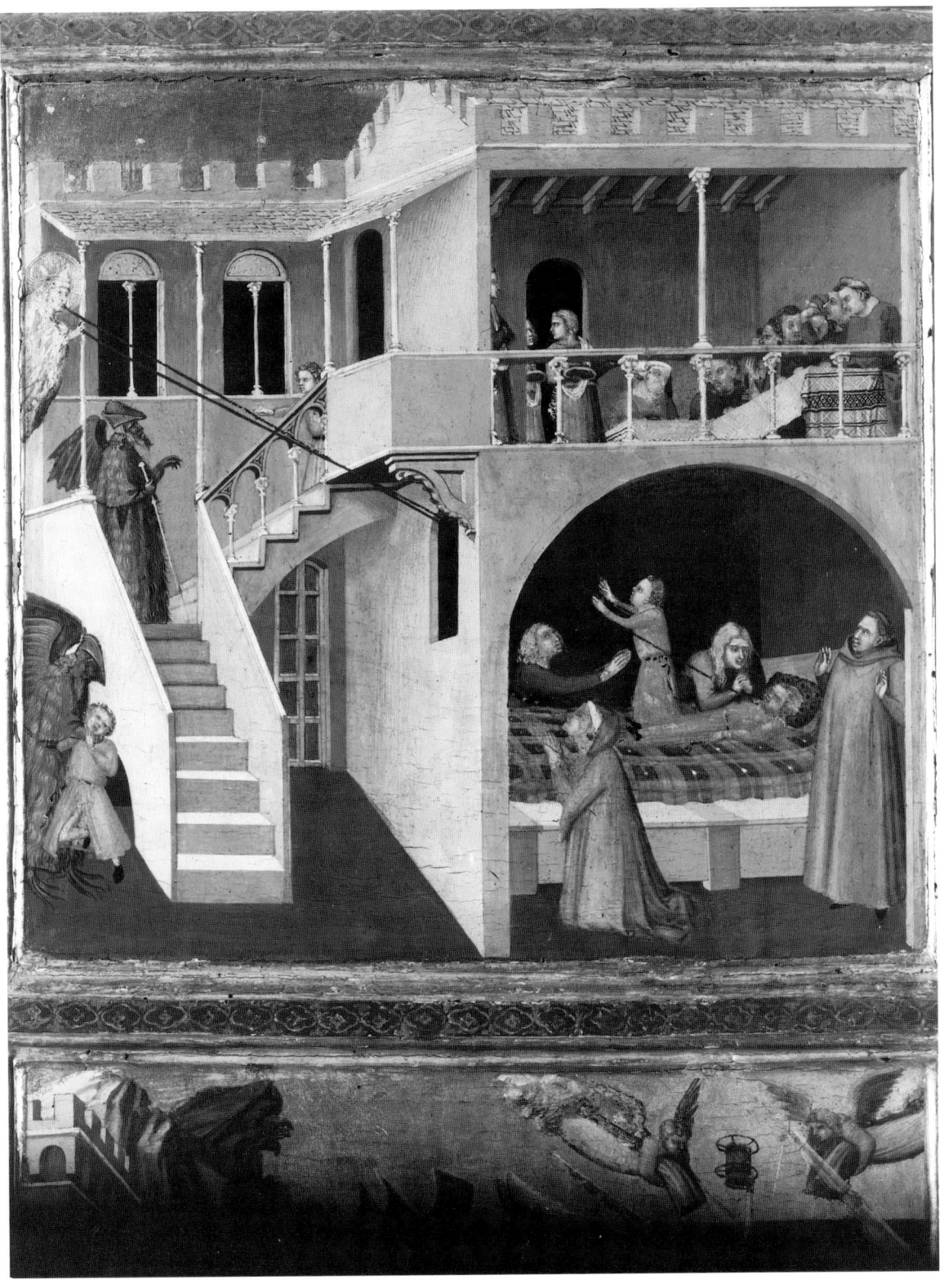

Fig. 108 Ambrogio Lorenzetti, *Stories of Saint Nicholas of Bari*, detail: Saint Nicholas raises the son of a merchant. Florence, Galleria degli Uffizi.